SEVENTY YEARS

The Coole Edition
General Editors
T. R. Henn, C.B.E., Litt.D.
Colin Smythe, M.A.

Lady Gregory: a photograph taken at the time of her wedding.

SEVENTY YEARS:
BEING THE AUTOBIOGRAPHY OF
LADY GREGORY

edited and with a foreword by
Colin Smythe

COLIN SMYTHE LIMITED
GERRARDS CROSS
1973

First published in 1973 by Colin Smythe Ltd., Gerrards Cross,
Buckinghamshire as the thirteenth volume of the Coole Edition
of Lady Gregory's works.

ISBN 0 900675 896

Produced in Great Britain
Printed by Billing & Sons Ltd.
Guildford, Surrey

FOREWORD

THE DISCOVERY last Autumn of the final version of Lady
Gregory's autobiography (even though early versions exist in
the Berg Collection of The New York Public Library) was
an event of major importance in the field of Anglo-Irish
Literature. Indeed, it must be a rare occurrence in any field
of studies that a complete major work turns up forty years
after the author's death.

Lady Gregory had started on the autobiography a few
months after the publication (in December 1913) of *Our Irish
Theatre: A Chapter of Autobiography*: the earliest material
is dated 29 July 1914 and even the final version has passages
that indicate this early date (see p.266). However, Lady
Gregory only got down to writing it in earnest after the end
of the First World War and worked on it for the next four
years, reading each chapter to W. B. Yeats on its completion
for his comments. Each version was pruned and tightened
up, and in the final version initials replaced many names to
save embarrassment or danger, as she was working on the
book during a very unsettled period politically and she even
changed her sister's initials from A.W. to A.P. in the chapter
on the Rising. *Seventy Years* was put into its final shape by
April, 1923, but it is far from clear what happened to it over
the next few years. There is no indication as to when it was
finally completed and typed: it may have been shown to
John Murray, but if it was, then it was not accepted. The
references in the Journals are few, so one can only suppose
that after it was finished it was put aside. Occasionally Lady
Gregory would bring it out as when she wrote: "Yesterday,
on 14th February, 1924, I got out *Seventy Years* to arrange
some articles from it. But when it comes to the point I
dislike the idea so strongly of having just the gossip, the
'folk-lore' printed without the redeeming part of my life,
and without what I think will make a fine book, the later
history of the country, that I will put it away again; though
if money is necessary before the year is out I must face it."

The autobiography was a form of investment, only to be
realised as a last resort. On 30 October, 1927 she wrote in
her Journals: "I shrink from my Memoir [the autobio-

graphy] appearing during my lifetime, if I can get on without it, keeping the children's home."

According to W. B. Yeats's recollections, it was 1923 or 1924 that Lady Gregory told him that she proposed to put Constant Huntington of G. P. Putnam's Sons[1] in some position equivalent to that of literary executor. A little later she became anxious lest her diaries, which dealt partly with the Black-and-Tan period in Ireland, might be mutilated as a result of possible pro-British prejudice. She therefore asked Yeats to take over this position, but it was understood that the publisher would still be Putnams.

In 1928 Yeats became seriously ill and rather than burden him down with further work Lady Gregory told him that she was going to give Huntington complete control in her Will. Yeats recovered however, and about fifteen months before her death Lady Gregory again made Yeats the final arbiter. A few months later, according to a letter from Yeats to Lady Gregory's solicitors, Whitney Moore & Keller, dated 1 October 1932, Yeats began to stay almost permanently at Coole.

Early in 1931, Yeats prevailed on her to send the autobiography to Huntington, who after reading it, wrote to Lady Gregory that he thought it required condensation and returned the typescript to her. By this time he had also received the unedited Journals.

Lady Gregory started cutting her book down in size, but never got further than the first chapters, and although she added notes here and there throughout the work, she found she was no longer fit enough to do the work required on it. Yeats wanted her to make sure it was published during her lifetime, but Lady Gregory was undecided, and as she had never published anything which she felt to lack form or was dissatisfied with, she decided to leave the editing to somebody else.

Yeats went to London in March 1932, taking the typescript with him to discuss it with Huntington and also to get him to draw up a contract for it. They discussed the matter of an editor, Huntington suggesting first Ethel Colbourn Mayne and then T. Sturge Moore. As the latter was an old friend of both Lady Gregory and himself, Yeats accepted this suggestion. Over the next month, the agreement saw a

---

[1] Putnams had published nearly all Lady Gregory's plays, *Our Irish Theatre,* and *Visions and Beliefs in the West of Ireland.*

number of changes, but the final version was ready for Yeats to take back to Coole when he returned there on 27th April. It was not signed until the 10th May, less than a fortnight before Lady Gregory's death early on 23 May, and gave Putnams an exclusive licence "to edit abridge arrange make selections from and print and publish said collection, (the autobiographical material, diaries and letters) in whole or in part in book serial and translation form". Too late Yeats realised that this gave Putnams full control over the diaries (which had been sent to Putnams the previous year) as well as the autobiography. However he realised that Huntington would act upon Lady Gregory's desire as expressed in the codicil to her Will dated 20 October, 1931 in which she stated: "I wish the final decision as to arrangement and arrangement of any of the material left unarranged to be made by my friend of so many years W. B. Yeats whose verdict would be final", and Huntington did in fact do so.

Huntington sent the typescript of *Seventy Years* to Sturge Moore at the end of June 1932, telling him that he was disappointed with it. It hardly dealt at all with the Irish Literary Revival with which Lady Gregory's name was primarily associated: there was too much about Sir William Gregory, his friends and other matters which would have had little interest for the readers of the time. Huntington therefore suggested an abridgement, stating that he was very doubtful of the wisdom of attempting publication of the complete work during the then depressed conditions. He hoped that Sturge Moore would agree with him, and return the typescript so that he could set about looking for an editor for the diaries, about which he was much more excited: as an editor T.S.M. was not suitable for the purely Irish items. However, contrary to the publisher's expectation, Sturge Moore was impressed with the autobiography and particularly liked the early portion. As he wrote to Yeats on the 6th July: "Accounts of childhood and youth are almost always interesting and I found Lady Gregory's extremely so. I also think that she has probably given a proportion to her life which might appeal to a wider public than that which is interested in the Irish Literary Movement."

Huntington had suggested that the second half of the autobiography should be fused with the diaries, but on this Sturge Moore would give no opinion. He was, however, sure that the first half was as important as the second, but in his letter to Yeats of 9 September, 1932 he said that Huntington "rejected totally all idea of publishing Lady Gregory's memoirs [the autobiography] at all as they stand as he felt sure that under present conditions such a book could not possibly pay. I then suggested that at least an account of her life up to her meeting with you might be extracted from the memoirs as an introduction to the extracts from her diaries which you had then written to me you thought of making yourself with Lennox Robinson. He expressed himself delighted with this idea and the reasons which I gave him for thinking that some knowledge of Lady Gregory's previous life and upbringing could not fail to enhance the effect of your book."* The typescript was then returned to Putnams, who left T.S.M. with the impression that they would be immediately sending it on to Yeats. They did not do so. In late September Yeats discussed the matter with Lady Gregory's solicitors, who felt, as a result of this interview that he "had no personal interest in the matter, that he was embarrassed if anything at the position in which he found himself with regard to the matter and that his only concern was to see that whatever might be done would be in accordance with Lady Gregory's wishes and would be to the advantage of her grand-children whom she intended to benefit from her Writings."

Yeats told the solicitors that he would be seeing Huntington in October before going on his lecture tour to the U.S.A. Whatever decision was made then, the papers remained in the hands of Putnams for the next ten years. Then in 1943 they thought the time had come to do a selection from the *Journals,* which were to be edited by Lennox Robinson. However, he did not see the typescript of *Seventy Years,* for as soon as the project was mooted, Mrs. Gough asked Putnams for its immediate return to her because she had also heard that Lady Gregory's autobiography was going to be used as source material for a biography of Lady Gregory, possibly written by Lennox Robinson. Robinson was in fact to write one about ten years later, commissioned by the Abbey Theatre, but it was so poor that it was never published.[2] When the other Directors of the Abbey suggested that it

* Reproduced by kind permission of Miss Riette Sturge Moore and Mr. D. Sturge Moore.

[2] The typescript was eventually sold by Putnams to the Berg Collection of The New York Public Library.

should be radically revised, he replied he could not and would not do so. There the matter rested until his death.

Curiously, the biography contains an extract from her early memoirs which is not in the autobiography, so he must have had access to some papers.

This extract deals with the funeral of Sir William. The special train bringing his body from Dublin arrived early. Evidently neither Lady Gregory nor Robert were present. She desired no pageantry. Sir William "had always disliked the idea of decking the dead with flowers and I had told near friends of this. But just at the last three wreaths came that I know would have pleased him. One was from a poor London parish, one from a Ceylon native and the third from the Greek community in England, in gratitude for his help to their country many years ago. These went with him to Coole where his people laid him beside his mother who had devoted her life to him, and his father who had died in their service in the Famine years."

II

In September 1907 Robert married Margaret Graham Parry and though much of the early years of their marriage was spent in Paris, their three children, Richard, Anne and Catherine were born and brought up at Coole.[3]

Even before Robert's death, Margaret was telling her friends of the unsatisfactory arrangement that, although Coole became Robert's when he attained his majority in 1902, he did not like to put his mother out of her home.[4] The situation was that Sir William Gregory's Will stated Lady Gregory had "so far as the rules of law will permit . . . the option of residing rent free at Coole Park, Galway during her life". She had a life interest in the contents of the house, but the leasehold house in London (3 St. George's Place) and almost everything in it was left to her absolutely. As the estate was settled under an indenture dated 4 November, 1841 made by William's father, the Will does not leave it to Robert, but only the income from it. The indenture was broken when it became no longer workable.

[3] See *Me and Nu : Childhood at Coole,* by Anne Gregory (Colin Smythe, 1970).
[4] See *Lord Dunsany : A Biography,* by Mark Amory (Collins, 1972) p.73.

Lady Gregory had acted as guardian of Coole during
Robert's minority, maintaining the estate (and particularly
its famous woods) so as to hand it intact to him. On his death
she continued the same work, always hoping that she would
be able to convince Margaret that Coole should eventually
revert to Richard as the next male heir, but as Coole had
passed direct to Margaret under Robert's Will, she was
understandably more concerned with the financial aspects
of keeping the estate going; and this divergence of opinion
inevitably brought about friction.

In the 1920s, when there were further land troubles before
and after the setting up of the Irish Free State, rates and
costs continued to rise while incomes remained static or
decreased. Lady Gregory had an income of £800 p.a. settled
on her by Sir William's Will as well as whatever came in
from her writing. It was not enough, and in 1928 Margaret
sold the estate to the Irish Land Commission, and Lady
Gregory, who by now was resigned to leaving Coole when
it was sold, was able to stay on as a tenant for the rest of her
life. In the same year Margaret married Captain Guy Gough
of Lough Cutra Castle.

In spite of her understandable resentment that as Robert's
wife she was never really the lady of the house in his
home, and in spite of their disagreement over the future of
Coole, about which she was often very bitter, Margaret
always admired her mother-in-law, and indeed still wrote
about her in the most glowing terms thirty years after Lady
Gregory's death.

III

As far as can be ascertained, the typescript of *Seventy
Years* is in the form Lady Gregory regarded as final. Early
versions of the Contents page indicate a further chapter,
"Letters 1914-1918", but this seems to have been merged
with "Some Letters". Mrs. Gough seems to have objected to
parts of the autobiography, though her reasons for so doing
are not clear, and she held the typescript until 1972. However, it is probable that for the last fifteen years or so she
forgot she even had it and certainly did not tell her children
of its existence; and it was discovered quite by accident.

The typescript required very little editing except for
general typing errors. It was obviously not typed by Lady

Gregory and in a few places there are gaps in sentences
which it is impossible to fill. Often these gaps had been left
by Lady Gregory herself as she was uncertain of the name of
the place or person.

The present text follows as closely as possible what are
believed to have been Lady Gregory's wishes. Where typing
errors and omissions exist these have been corrected, and
missing words inserted, as it is certain Lady Gregory would
have noticed typing mistakes herself had she checked the
typescripts for these. Poems, when they appear in letters,
have not been touched, but when they appear as quotations
they have been compared with the published version and
corrected when necessary.

Author's notes are marked by * † etc., whereas notes
inserted by the editor are shown thus [1], [2], [3], etc. On occasion
Lady Gregory referred to people in the text by their initials:
a list of these appears on p.561, together with the names of
the people they refer to. On occasion, Lady Gregory deliber-
ately obscured the names of the people she was writing about,
as A.Z., or Mrs. O., Mr. P. and Mr. Q., for example. With a
few exceptions, these have been left as they are, in deference
to the author's wishes. When somebody is merely referred to
by his or her surname, the full name will be found in the
Index. Square brackets are used to indicate sections of the
text which have been deleted by Lady Gregory in the course
of her own revision, but which the general editors considered
it was important to keep in for the sake of completeness.

COLIN SMYTHE.

CONTENTS

	Foreword by Colin Smythe . . .	v
	Illustrations	xv
	Acknowledgements	xvi
I	The First Decades	1
II	Marriage	21
III	Education in Politics: Egypt . . .	33
IV	Folklore in Politics: Mr. Gladstone and Ireland	56
V	Among the Poor	80
VI	London Table Talk	96
VII	Athenaeum Friends:	
	(i) A. W. Kinglake . . .	126
VIII	(ii) Sir Frederic Burton . .	139
IX	(iii) Sir Henry Layard . .	152
X	(iv) Henry James . . .	181
XI	(v) Sir Alfred Lyall . . .	186
XII	(vi) Robert Browning . .	198
XIII	Letters to and from Wilfrid Blunt . .	203
XIV	The Twelve Years Ended . . .	262
XV	The Autobiography	264
XVI	Schools and Holidays	281
XVII	London Again	289
XVIII	Mr. Gregory's Letter-Box . . .	300
XIX	The Changing Ireland	306
XX	New Threads in the Pattern . . .	329

XXI	The Boer War and the Theatre	352
XXII	Work and Play at Coole	376
XXIII	The Epics	390
XXIV	Seven Years, 1903-1910	411
XXV	Roosevelt	453
XXVI	Some Letters	467
XXVII	Folk-lore of the War	509
XXVIII	The Rising	532
XXIX	My Grief	550
	List of initials	561
	List of Lady Gregory's publications	563
	Index	567

A portrait of Lady Gregory by Augustus John, in the possession of Mrs. R. Kennedy, by whose permission and that of Romilly John it is reproduced here. Under it Lady Gregory wrote, "the swift, unflinching terrible judgement of the young!"

A photograph taken in 1913 in Sir Hugh Lane's home, Lindsey House, with Rembrandt's Lady with Gloves, now in the National Gallery of Ireland, behind her. Courtesy of the Mansell Collection.

ILLUSTRATIONS

	facing page
Lady Gregory at the time of her wedding	*frontis*
A portrait of Lady Gregory by Augustus John	xiv
A photograph taken c.1913 at Lindsey House	xv
Dudley Persse	16
Frances Persse	16
Sir William, Lady Gregory and Robert at Coole	16
Roxborough House	17
Coole House	17
Sir William Gregory c.1882	32
Lady Gregory's fans	33
Arabi Bey	128
Wilfrid Scawen Blunt	129
A. W. Kinglake	144
Sir Frederic Burton	145
Sir Henry Layard	192
Lady Layard	192
Henry James	193
Sir Alfred Lyall	208
Robert Browning	209
Theodore Roosevelt	464
Robert Gregory as a child	465
Robert Gregory in flying kit	465
Margaret and Richard Gregory c.1911	465
Catherine, Anne and Richard Gregory	485
A bronze of W. B. Yeats	480
W. B. Yeats and George Moore	481
Bernard Shaw	481
G. W. Russell, (A.E.)	481
J. M. Synge	481

ACKNOWLEDGEMENTS

Thanks are due to the following: to Mr. Diarmuid Russell for permission to quote letters and poems by A.E.; the Syndics of the Fitzwilliam Museum, Cambridge, for permission to quote the letters of W. S. Blunt, the Society of Authors as the literary representative of the Estate of John Masefield for permission to quote extracts from his letters; to Michael and Anne Yeats for permission to quote from the poems and letters of W. B. Yeats and from the letters of J. B. Yeats the elder; to the trustees u/w/o Clara Clemens Samossoud for permission to quote from letters of Mark Twain (S. L. Clemens); to Major Richard Gregory for permission to use many of the photographs which appear in this book.

I

THE FIRST DECADES

IF THE CHILDREN at Coole should ever read this account of
their grandmother as a child, although they might easily
enough think of her learning lessons (for that is what she is
doing to this day), they would find it very hard to think of
her as of their own age, lightfooted, running along that
hillside of Slieve Echtge they can see a glimpse of from the
upper windows of the house. So I think it will be best to
tell this part of her life just as if she were one of the children
of fancy they read about in their story books.

At the midnight hour between the fourteenth and
fifteenth of March 1852, the planet Jupiter, so astrologers
say, being in mid heaven, a little girl was born at Roxborough
that is in Connacht. She was the fifth daughter of her
mother, and there were two stepdaughters also in the house.
And although her mother had four sons of her own, besides
a stepson, [this birth made the numbers even, and] she
liked boys better than girls and wished for more sons than
daughters, and so was sorry this was not a boy. Yet when,
according to the old nurse's story, this little-welcomed girl
had nearly gone out with but a breath of the world's air,
being laid aside and forgotten for a while in the quilt of
covering when the mother said that she would have been
sorry for such a loss, because the other children would have
been disappointed at not having a new baby to play with.
And anyway she was the last girl in the family; there came
four brothers after that. And so with eight boys to their
five daughters, their mother had to be satisfied.

When the christening day came and the big china bowl*
was carried to the church and back again, to be used instead
of the white basin there that was not without some cracks,
the youngest daughter of the house was weighted with a
many syllabled "Isabella Augusta", borrowed from a never
to be seen godmother, a Miss Brown of Bath.

The reason of this little girl's story being told, now written
by her later self, is that her passing out of sight is in the

---

*Famille rose, sold at the auction of H. Persse, Woodville, Rox', 1922.

course of nature not far off, and she knows that according to
the fashion of the time, there is a trade in such things as
the life history of anyone whose name has gone far enough
or has been held in enough repute to bring as many buyers
as will pay for the making of the book. And her name has
come to be thus known, chiefly she thinks through her
having written eleven short plays, and in a lesser degree
through some longer ones; and by her translations and
arrangement of many of the old stories and legends of
Ireland, and even through other writings that are to her
mind of less value, not having in them a record of the old
vanished world, but of the visible world of today, and in
this lower place she thinks this book now to be written will
of necessity stand. And yet, if written it must be, she will
herself take the burden and not expect another to do well
what she thinks can not be done supremely well, or put the
task on some friend dear to her, or leave it to some indifferent
scribe. And indeed it is not as herself but as another that
she must write of that early self, so far away does it seem to
her now, though standing clearer in the memory than the
self maybe, some score or more years later, when the outline
grows confused by the tangled interests and associations
that have caught it into their nest. And if she does not always
put down her own errors and mistakes it is not because she
does not know and is not sorry for them. And she thanks
God that she has been able to work so long, and above all
that anything she has done that is worth the doing has been
in Ireland and through Ireland, and for Ireland's sake.

For it was her happy fortune to have been cradled there,
never indeed leaving the county of Galway that was her
birthplace, save for crossing the border into Clare now and
again, when the heather was in bloom on the Munster side
as well as on the Connacht side of a dividing stream, until
taken on a visit to Dublin in that fifteenth year that is
between childhood and girlhood, purple hilltops there also
calling from the untrodden land. And she was happy in
being in the care of old Mary Sheridan, the seventh of her
nurselings in the house.

It was but yesterday, November 1921, she told her little
grand-daughters, when they read in their history book of the
war with Napoleon, how that old nurse had been as a child
in a theatre where all the people had of a sudden stood up
and shouted because news had come of the landing of the
French at Killala—"she told me she remembered it, and

that happened a hundred and twenty-three years ago".
"And does that make you one-hundred and twenty-three
years old grandmamma?" they asked. They themselves, or
the elder[1], may have some faint recollection of the rising of
1916, but they will not either of them forget the shots so
often heard last winter, fired by the passing Black-and-
Tans on their devastating round, even less the ambush last
May when their mother was the sole survivor of a carful
of five!

Mary Sheridan had lived also in the family of Hamilton
Rowan the rebel, and would tell of his escape in a boat
and his uneasiness lest the boatmen should recognise him,
for there was a reward upon his head; and how they had
indeed recognised him, but had told him that he was safe
with them whatever might be the offered reward. She told
also when once she had come with her children to the
room where he was breakfasting, a sudden anger had seized
him as he read the newspaper, and he had flung a knife
that slashed the face of a portrait of Lord Norbury, the
Judge, that hung upon the wall. And once on the hall door
steps the little girl had wondered to see her, that proud old
nurse that seldom so condescended, in eager converse with
a white-haired woman, a wandering beggar, and listening,
learned that woman also had a memory of that rising and
that landing of the French.

Sometimes, not very often, nurse Sheridan would be
persuaded by the half dozen younger children to "tell a
story". And it would not be of the people of today, but of
horses wearing silver bells, [that must be stuffed with wool
before the captive Princess could escape from the witch
who held her;] or of a wolf that swallowed whole and alive
the goat's six little kids, [but falling asleep after the meal
was cut open by a wise seventh hidden in the clock case,
and who while the six leaped away safe and sound put
stones in their places, so that going to drink, the weight
overbalanced the wolf, and he fell into the river and was
drowned;] or of the Hairy Girl who became beautiful when
that enchantment had been broken and who lived in a castle
guarded by cats, one, the most terrible, bearing the name
Maol-Wall; so that one at least of the hearers remembers
being afraid to cross the dusky passage from the boys' to the
girls' nursery, while trembling from the thought of those
monsters, beyond nature terrible.

[1] Richard was the eldest, followed by Anne and Catherine.

That was up at the top of the house under the sloping roof of what was said to have been the first house slated in the county. Downstairs, the stories worth listening to, that made their lodging in the mind, had come from the Eastern world, the wonderful histories of the flood and the Tower of Babel, and David and the Giant, and Jonah who was swallowed by the Great Fish. For the Bible was read through and through at family prayers from year's end to year's end, and what better food for the imagination could be given? A chapter of the Old Testament in the morning, at evening prayer a chapter of the New; how happy when near the last cover of the book came the vision of precious stones in the New Jerusalem, and of the Tree of Life that bore twelve manner of fruit.

These teachings were perhaps to be of more lasting worth to one young pupil than the schoolroom tasks from Mangnall's *Questions*[2] and Abbot's *Astronomy* and Pinnock's *Greece* and *Little Arthur's History of England,* or any set by what appears in memory's panorama as a procession of amiable incompetent governesses. A little French was learned, and many scales and exercises on the piano made music seem for many a day a hard enemy. At reading the little girl was slow, and she blushed as she stumbled through her verses at a Bible Class held for a while by a Wesleyan Minister. Memory became a more efficiently trained servant through the accident of a long poem, written but rejected for the Newdigate prize at Oxford, having found its way to a bookstall, where her brothers' tutor bought it. And that his couple of pence might not run all to waste, he gave this *Destruction of Nineveh,* telling of God's vengeance long delayed and fiery wrath descending low with arm uplifted high to his boy pupils' little sister to learn by heart. For it is likely those many pages of blank verse may have been of more use in strengthening her memory than would have been a poem on some more winning subject and holding sweeter sounds. The Mother, "The Mistress", as she was called by all, children as well as servants, [as it seems,] did not consider book learning as of any great benefit to girls; for sometimes a new governess asking for new lesson books would be told to wait until the girls could answer all of

---

[2] Mangnall, Richmal, *Historical & Miscellaneous Questions* (1812). *Pinnock's improved edition of Dr. Goldsmith's History of Greece,* London (many editions). *Little Arthur's History of England* by Maria Graham, London, 1835 (under the initials C.M.)

Mangnall's questions, and of course they never could. Religion and courtesy, and holding themselves straight, these were to her mind the three things needful. French perhaps also, for her grandmother had been a Huguenot. She was less indulgent to the girls than to the boys, and for all the large expenditure and the plenty, even luxury, in food, she would not willingly allow a fire to be lighted in the schoolroom until the dahlias had been cut down by the frost. She set an example in courtesy, having fine manners inherited perhaps from that French ancestress Frances Algoin, whose little book—*Frances Algoin her Book—1st January 1724/5* —is on the table where these lines are written; and so taught by example as well as precept. In her long life she was never seen to appear impatient with the dullness or ill-manners of a guest, and she would always defend the absent against the criticisms of her flock. It was but the other day that some acquaintance was told by a French tutor whose wandering spirit had led him in his early life to Roxborough to teach the younger boys for a while, how when he arrived at night, a frightened stranger, after a nine miles drive along a dreary road, a tall lady in black velvet and diamonds had come to the open hall door and welcomed him to Ireland with a friendliness he had remembered through half a hundred years. He may not remember that she gave thought to his soul's welfare also, and although he had declared himself a Protestant, was one day overheard giving him instruction in his own language, on the errors of Rome, translating from the open book of *Revelations* the words "Babylon est tombée, tombée, tombée".

It was during the long evenings in the drawing-room that the little girl's love of reading began. All the family and many of the household, but not the old nurse or other Catholic servants, gathered there for family prayers. After they were over, a silver urn was brought in and the Mistress made tea at a table at the end of the room, where tutor and governess and children might sit for a while. There was no conversation during the evening in which all might join. The Master's* wheeled chair was beside the fire. The Mistress had her place near; the elder brothers when at home, and the elder sisters had their easy chairs; the younger boys escaped to a more lively part of the house. There was

*Old Dudley Persse of Roxborough had been paralysed from the waist down from an early age, though this never interfered with his duties—or his pleasures.

silence except when the musical sister played on the piano,
or the Mistress read extracts with approval from the leading
articles of *The Times*. The two youngest daughters occupied
two high-backed chairs on the fireless side of the round
table in the middle of the room. One, intelligent beyond
her years and sociable, would listen to any scraps of talk
and sometimes even herself look at a newspaper. The
youngest, very shy and quiet except when with the younger
boys, would open one or other of the few books that lay on
the table, arranged like the spokes of a wheel, the lamp in
the centre its hub. The book best remembered is *Lalla
Rookh,* for although its text was forbidden as "not fit for
little girls", each engraved illustration had some lines of
the poem under it, and the broken context gave it mystery:

> Ah turn not from me that dear face!
> Am I not thine, thine own loved bride,
> The one, the chosen one whose place
> In life or death is by thy side!

What romance in those lines, with the picture of the
plague-stricken lover and the pale turbaned girl bending
over him, did not this awaken! And there was one page
dreaded yet opened in spite of trembling, the unveiled face
of the hideous Prophet of Khorassan. There were two or
three *Books of Beauty* also, [the fairest of these beauties to
the childish mind a lovely Irish-born Princess of Capua,
whose sorrowful eyes seem to mourn ceaselessly for her
native land]. And when no one was looking a page would
be opened, a frontispiece showing "The Marchioness of
Londonderry and her child", and two little cheeks would
glow with pride and shyness because the elder sisters had
been heard to say that the child in the picture was "like
Augusta"; and this was the only flattery she had to bring
to mind in those early days, in that overflowing plain-
speaking household. But when there were dinner parties,
and these not only at the great winter shooting parties but
in summer time, there was a greater evening joy to be found.
For then the centre table was covered with a cloth of velvet
pile, and a few carefully kept books in handsome bindings
were brought out and laid upon it, chief among them a
large volume of English ballads, a never failing treasury of
delight. And of these the one most stirring was *Chevy Chase,*
not only from its own simplicity and high matter and the
unforgettable dauntlessness of him who seemed its greatest
hero—

For Witherington my heart is woe,
I write in doleful dumps,
For when his legs were hewn away
He fought upon his stumps.

But because this Persse household claimed descent from these Persses of the ballad; a Duke of Northumberland had been a guest at Roxborough; another part of the property in the county bore the Border name of Newcastle; while over the hills in a fold of Slieve Echtge, where wild deer ran in the woods, the Irish names of yet another Daroda, Dairebrian, Druim-da-rod had been long overlaid with the less lovely yet still romantic name of Chevy Chase*. That ballad book, and some poems of Wordsworth's on shining paper, with gilded edges, and the *Books of Beauty*, and a Shakespeare in small print, in red morocco [(but the time had not come for opening that)] were taken away by the elder sister when she married, yet were not quite out of reach, for they adorned another drawing-room table on a neighbouring estate, Castle Taylor, but some five or six miles to the north west.

The eldest brother was but seldom at home. He had been wounded in the Crimean War; there was a tradition, it could hardly be a recollection, of his eldest sister having fainted in the manner that belonged to that generation, when the news came, and fallen from a little beadworked stool in the drawing-room that used to hurt the bare elbows of the child that sometimes knelt at it for family prayers. He was brave; his name is given in Kinglake's story of the storming of the Alma, and there was a coloured print at Roxborough representing him, (or so it was said, and it was a good likeness) with words that justified a tradition that he had killed in that battle seven Russians. He himself was but a tradition in those early days, for some quarrel or coolness with his father had kept him away. Then there was a reconciliation and he came back for a while. He was very quiet in manner, very kind, very handsome, with fair hair and beard and blue eyes. One of the young step-brothers was learning music, and one evening when he played among his little tunes, "Partant pour la Syrie", the soldier came across the room very much moved and put a sovereign into his hand. He had so often heard that air

*Only apparently to the Roxborough people.

that was composed by Louis Napoleon's mother, Queen
Hortense, played in those Crimean Camps.

As for gaieties, there were not any for the children
especially, and so not ever having been known were never
missed; it was delight sufficient to act as audience at an
occasional servants' ball, or at the great dance in the barn
that followed and crowned each year's sheep-shearing.
McDonough, the piper, whose father had learned strange
tunes among the Sidhe, who had so bewitched the pipes
that "they would play of themselves when thrown up into
the rafters," would sit with a colleague high on a corn bin;
his name has now passed into folk lore as one who had but
to "squeeze the pipes" at that festival to bring golden
sovereigns rattling into his plate on the barn floor. And
even the days of the shearing were a long delight, the
chasing with long crooks of the sheep, the packing of the
immense sacks of wool, the taste of the shearers' oaten bread.
In the winter the great days were those when the house was
filled with county friends, owners of neighbouring estates,
for the three days shooting at home, and [it might be] a
fourth at Chevy Chase. The children of the house would
trot after the procession of guests and keepers and beaters
from the covers by the river through Eserkelly and Cahir-
linny to Moneen Pollah, and even across Castleboy to
Kynadife, [though the Echtge hillsides were too steep for
the little limbs,] and would nibble at the sandwiches carried
out and eaten standing according to the hardy custom of
those days. And so a lasting picture remains of the Master
taking aim and never missing from his tall white horse
Ehren Breitstein, (a name turned by the stable keepers to
Iron Brightside) and the straight shooting of the county
lords, Clonbrock like the fowler in the Arabian tale, finding
the loss of one eye no impediment to his skill; his son
Gerald, blue-eyed, with golden curls and Grecian features,
the very type and model of a young man's beauty. Dunkellin,
stout, brown-haired, with humorous prominent eyes, eyes
so short-sighted that he had walked into the enemy's lines
in the Crimea believing them to be British lines—"the
Russian officers were very kind," he wrote to W. H. Gregory
(his fellow M.P. for the county), "even offering to lend me
money, I could not help thinking how many a Galway
landlord would have been glad to exchange places with me."
He was looked on with wondering interest by at least one
of those following children. For she had heard one of the

grown-up people quote some lines concerning him, from a paper that had in itself a mysterious sound, *The Owl*: "Where can the heir of Clanricarde be? Eating, or hunting with a double T?"

And another had said, "That means ratting", and so she having never heard of the Parliamentary term for a change of mind or conscience, [or (outside the Bible) of the cave of Adullam*] gazed astonished at a man who in her imagination turned at some times from this fine aristocratic covert shooting to that stable occupation of killing rats. And with a yet greater amazement did she witness the skill with which his father, the ancient and ghostlike Marquis of Clanricarde, was used to turn aside during a lull in the beaters' noisy cries to blow his nose with his fingers. It was told that he had so much admired one of the daughters of the house of an older generation [(one who would tell of a holiday from lessons given her on the day the bells rang for the victory of Waterloo)] as to leave the Portumna bonfires for his coming of age and drive the twenty miles across the county to finish the great day in her company. But he married a Canning's daughter, and she a Lord Clanmorris, after whose death she turned to religion, and was only kept back, as we were told, from joining the Plymouth Brethren by a fear that her favourite velvet would be brought into the common possession of goods. But the friendship between the old Marquis and her brother, Dudley Persse, was not broken. Charles Lever tells of their hunting together and that Clanricarde once seeing his companion disappear over a wall that had hidden a steep drop called out, "What's on the other side, Dudley?" and the answer came from below, "I am, thank God". Clear in memory also are the feasts of the four evenings, all the countryside coming in turn to dinner; the children watching from some nook the procession of guests walk arm in arm across the hall; listening to the buzz of conversation that would rise into a sudden loudness each time the door was opened for service [(a puzzling repetition as it seemed of a phrase above the hubbub "that's just what I was going to

---

*"Although he (Dunkellin) joined the so-called 'Cave of Adullam' and by his successful motion . . . against a rental franchise overthrew the Government of which he had been previously a supporter, he was still a staunch Liberal", *Autobiography* of Sir W. Gregory (2nd edition, 1894, pp. 141-142). For the original Cave of Adullam see I *Samuel* Ch22 : 1.

say")]; the artfully arranged dishes left down on the hall tables for a few moments as they were carried out, perhaps not Mrs. Glasse's Desert Island of cake with gravel walks of shot comfits, yet a tempting prey to little pilferers, a jelly nest containing eggs of blanc-mange, a tower of spun sugar, its head hidden in clouds of thickened cream. Then the procession of ladies alone; after that the buzz of voices continuing, rising even louder in the one room, while those in the other grew fainter and more languid until the coming of the men. Sometimes, not often, there was a little music; once a daughter of the family doctor had the courage to send next day a messenger for a roll of songs brought by her, but, humiliation, not asked for.

Religion was taught by the Mistress. The children were questioned after morning prayers on the Old Testament chapter that had been read. They stood round the dining-room fire, and were sometimes told they must not come nearer to it than the edge of the hearthrug, but this law can not have been severely enforced, for one child at least can remember the smooth touch of the marble of the chimney piece jamb against which she used to lean, longing to grow to the level of its shelf; and at length, on tiptoe and triumphant, being able to see in the mirror above it her forehead at least and eyes. In the evening they were sometimes examined from a card beginning: "What sin have I this day committed in thought, word and deed?" But that was soon given up, perhaps because they were more prone to remind each other of the faults to be confessed than to tell out of their own; and this sometimes led to a scuffle, and most often on the Sunday evening after the idleness of the day. For if they were told, "This is Sunday Sabbath Day; That is why we must not play," the boys would whisper, "This is Sunday Sabbath night; That is why we'll have a fight." The theology was very definite, and although repeated rumours and then authoritative state-ments of geologists at last forced the Mistress to give up the six days creation of the world in favour of six periods, she refused other concessions. And a certain summer evening is remembered, [most likely a Sunday evening, for she would then try to turn the conversation to more or less biblical subjects] when the children coming in to dessert found her reproving with some heat a guest, a young Mr. Browne, a cousin of Lord O[2]. [They did not hear him say anything at

2 Probably Baron Oranmore & Browne.

all, but it must have been] for saying that possibly only a part and not the whole of the world had been drowned in Noah's time. Later, when he had been called out into the quiet air by the sons of the house, she continued her argument, saying she had but lately read in some sermon book that to give up belief in any one fact given in the Bible was the same thing as to reject the Bible altogether. And the Master murmured in sympathy, "And I thought he seemed a quiet sort of young chap". But he was never invited to visit the house again.

It was a pleasant walk to the friendly little Killinane Church across wide Castleboy, the estate won through long lawsuits*, with its river and trees and sloping lawns. Neighbours from two or three houses came there, and there was a customary chatting at the door after service, (though the children were in agreement with an early saying of the elder brother, "I hate the nasty how d'ye do's". In yet remembered days a troop of village girls used to come and sing in the choir, Catholics some of them, but tempted by the drive in an open carriage provided by Lord Guillamore's son, old Archdeacon O'Grady, not as it seems aiming at their conversion, but at their support of the scanty Protestant voices in the hymns. But with his death they ceased to come. He was the last incumbent before Disestablishment struck out Church livings as a provision for younger brothers. [The son of a Lord Guillamore he was liberal and kindly; proud of showing the figs that ripened on his garden walls and the red-blossomed rhododendrons, rare in that limestone soil, growing indeed in peat, for which rumour said he had dug pits to a depth of eighteen feet. The clerk was the Kilchriest schoolmaster, Mr. Bateman, a Wesleyan, very severe with the cane. When now and again his pastor came on a visit a Wesleyan service would be held in the schoolroom, and perhaps through courtesy the "Church of England" congregation as it then was, would attend. He led the singing in church until with the new Archdeacon, Burkett, a harmonium was provided. A blanket was also provided to keep it from damp during the week, but one cold winter day the old sexton, Murphy, carried it away to cover his own limbs and it never came back, and the notes of the

*From another Persse who was ruined by the long struggle against the richer and more powerful elder branch, but whose descendant Ed. Martin Persse in 1931 married the only daughter of the last [word illegible] owner.

harmonium grew very hoarse. Old Murphy used, as the sermon was about to begin, to bring in an armful of sticks gathered under the trees and put them in the stove, poking the fire till it crackled. There were large square pews, well cushioned, with high hassocks on which a child could stand and watch pheasants and rabbits picking or nibbling on the grass-grown graves. An elder brother, whose training at the Bar had given him respect for law and order, told the old sexton on a visit home that the tall nettles in the churchyard were unseemly and should be done away with. But he was indignant and cried out "and what would the Master say if I was to cut them before the young pheasants are reared?"]

The children were sometimes taken to Sunday School at Kilchriest and they were allowed to go out of doors on Sunday but not to play or work in the garden or put a hand to any occupation; but this was not much to grumble at, with all the wide demesne around them, and the river with its wild fowl, and its reeds.

The "Monday books," as the children used to call them, were all hidden away on the Saturday night, and in their places would be found Mrs. Sherwood's *Stories on the Church Catechism,* which had its attractive chapters, and her *Henry Milner* which was dull, and *Ministering Children* which laid in at least one little reader the foundations of philanthropy. And if, when that lasting delight *The Fairchild Family* was read aloud, she blushed under the meaning looks of the others when the misdeeds of that villain of the piece, "Miss Augusta" Noble, were held up to odium, she loved (as do at this day her grandchildren) Master Henry's fall into the tub of pig's wash, and the greediness of Mr. Crosbie, and all the consequences of hunting the farmer's pig in the lane. The elders were not so well off; there were some sermons for them, and *Doing and Suffering,* the story of an invalid girl who had died, and a *Life* of Hedley Vicars, [a stepdaughter, Maria, had been given one Christmas the *Life* of Dr. Kitto, but a few weeks later the Mistress took up a new book, an unusual intruder, and asked where it had come from, and in the silence Arabella, a little pitcher always ready of speech, said, "Maria got it in exchange for the *Life* of Dr. Kitto". And it is hard to say which was in deeper disgrace, Maria with the authorities or Arabella with the elder sisters.]

Sometimes in the evening a story would be read to them

from a Sunday magazine or religious paper[3], [but they came to know the form of these and would prophesy, when the good poor boy was taken into the merchant's office, that he would marry the merchant's daughter in the end].

Dr. Cumming's prophecies were now and then brought to the drawing room to eke out the Sunday Books, but they were usually kept in the Mistress's dressing room. He had proved in them by various calculations that the Emperor Louis Napoleon was the beast of the Revelations, [the Roman letters of his name coming through some calculations to] the mystic number 666. He was to begin the war that would only end with Armageddon, and the end of the world was very near. [Those who accepted these interpretations would find signs of this approaching end in "Wars and Rumours of Wars" as they looked through the newspapers, though this was in the peaceful times, after the Crimean and the American Civil War.] But after France's pre-destined Emperor had rushed to his own Armageddon against Prussia, the Mistress became less confident, although she would still refuse to buy some new dress or spend money on such things as furniture because the end of the world might soon be here and turn all to dust.

It was not only that tale of the landing of the French at Killala that led the youngest daughter of the house to her country's history. She would often finger the lichen-grown letters cut on a stone of the bridge near the avenue gates "Erected by William Persse Colonel of the Roxborough Volunteers in the year 1782 in memory of Ireland's Emancipation from foreign Jurisdiction"; when those Volunteers had gained for at least a while the freedom of the Irish Parliament to make its own laws. So it came about that she would bring out the sixpences, earned if memory held good, by repeating on the Sunday evenings Bible verses learned during the week; and standing on tiptoe at the counter of the little Loughrea book-shop would purchase one by one the paper covered collections of national ballads, *The Harp of Tara, The Irish Song Book,* and the like. It was perhaps because of the old bookseller calling attention to this by saying in his shop one day, "I look to Miss Augusta to buy all my Fenian books," that led to a birthday present of *The Spirit of the Nation,* a shilling copy, bound in green

---

[3] In the revised version this sentence was joined by "and" to the beginning of the new paragraph.

cloth, from the sister next in age to her, with Dr. Johnson's
sarcasm written in it "Patriotism is the last refuge of a
Scoundrel". It is not likely that the idea of her having any
thoughts of sympathies different from their own had ever
entered the mind of any of the elders of the house.

Childhood had thus slipped away, and it was perhaps some
fifteen years after that midnight arrival in the world when
religion in that Evangelical form in which it had always
been set before the child, drove all other thoughts from the
mind of the growing child. The theology taught had been
that of the hymn "There is a dreadful hell, With everlasting
pains", "Where sinners must with devils dwell in darkness,
fire and chains". To escape it even if you had been absolutely
sinless would be impossible, and were it possible there would
still be the guilt of Adam's disobedience, for which as one
of his descendants, you were responsible; there was no
escape except being washed in the Blood of the Lamb, and
that could not be unless you were converted, unless you
believed while still in this earthly life; there was no place
for repentance, no Purgatory. It was before Disestablishment,
and the difficult Athanasian Creed was still given out two
or three times in the year by the Archdeacon "which faith
except everyone keep whole and undefiled, without doubt
he shall perish everlastingly". And to this others besides the
Clerk would give a whole hearted "Amen".

So it was no wonder that she was troubled. Was she a
believer? Lacking it, what must she do to be saved? What
was the wall between her and heaven; the closed door
between her and Christ? She would break it open by
prayer; she would earn its unclosing by a blameless day. But
belief, like Queen Vashti, was shy and would not come to
order, and before the day was over a moment's forgetfulness
of this high task would seem a crime, and prayer itself a
vanity. The matter must be fought out alone, it is not in a
large and critical family that such a secret of the heart could
be made common property. The restlessness of the mind
increased. Then of a sudden one morning in the cottage on
Lough Corrib her father had taken as a fishing lodge, she
rose up from her bed at peace with God. All doubts and all
fears had gone, she was one of His children, His angels
were her friends. The ballads, and poems and patriotic
songs had become as ashes; His word, the Bible was her
only book. She need no longer strive to do His will, it was
her delight to do it. She was a little ashamed of this ecstasy,

a little shy, unwilling to have it known. [Yet it came to be accepted, without words, little by little, that she was not as it were quite in the same world as the others, that it was by a different table of values that she lived. "I am not like Augusta who grew into religion from her childhood," one married sister wrote, long after to another, Adelaide Lane.] She was very happy.

For what might have been a long time the Bible and religious books, the only ones of which there were a plenty in the house, satisfied her. Then she began to discriminate. George Herbert's poems, given to a brother as a school prize, stayed more comfortably in the mind than the hymns of doctrine held to in the first fervour, as did the monk's vision of the jewel decked city, the sardius and amethyst of the New Jerusalem. The sermon books gave way to à Kempis's *Imitation of Christ*. As to novels, she had been taught to consider them food unfit for the use of Christ's flock; and indeed the daughters of the house were forbidden to read even the Waverleys until they attained the age of eighteen. And for this she was afterwards grateful, for coming later they never won her heart and all her romantic sympathies were kept for Ireland.

Although the books that had lain on the table at stated times, the *Ballads* and the yet unopened Shakespeare, had been taken away, the centre table was not quite unfurnished. Each Christmas a box of books would arrive to be chosen from, children's books chiefly, and religious ones, the *Sunday at Home,* the *Leisure Hour.* But from one of these boxes an elder sister, Gertrude, saying frankly she did not care for reading but would choose the biggest, took and laid on the drawing-room table the two volumes of Chambers' *Encyclopaedia of English Literature.*

That was to the younger sister the breaking of a new day, the discovering of a new world. She looked forward to those evening hours when she could read those volumes, first straight through, then over and over, a page here and there, till some of the poems given were known almost off by heart. The Bible had its appointed hours but was no longer everything, it may be its own beauty of words and imagination had spoiled her for common books; or she had become aware that there was other beauty and other poetry that might come near it, and had learned to know under what names this might be found. She knew now what to ask for at Christmas or from a brother in good humour, for the

boys had more money in their pockets than the girls, given
for the shooting of mischievous pests, and they were glad
to give the sister who was their companion and favourite a
share in this now and again, and would let her make her
own choice. In this way there came into her possession by
degrees Scott's poems, and Tennyson's (the Pre-Raphaelite
edition), and even the excitement of each new volume of
his as it came out, Scott, Burns, Montaigne, Matthew Arnold's
essays, and Clough and Hood and Keats; and above and
beyond all, most enduring of joys, Malory's *Morte D'Arthur*.

Yet the distinctly religious life lasted through all her
early girlhood, although it leaned perhaps more by degrees
to the practical, the philanthropic, than to the spiritual
side, for she gave up a good deal of her time to works of
charity, taking the poorest village on the estate, Illerton
at the foot of Slieve Echtge, as her especial care; going day
after day the couple of miles on foot with food and comforts,
saving her pocket money for such purposes, she visited the
sick and clothed the children, and tended the dying. These
visits of charity sometimes brought her under suspicion of
wishing to turn those she succoured from the Catholic faith,
for that was the fashion of the day among those zealous
Protestants, who were possessed with the same assurance
held by zealous Catholics, that their own faith was the only
one that had its correspondence fixed with Heaven, that
travelled the path to that door. The eldest stepdaughter
had given her energy to this cause of leading those who
were astray to that path, and the children had one day been
awed by hearing the account of an actual hand to hand
struggle between her and the parish priest, each holding on
to one arm of a disputed child. She had married and gone
to England, and perhaps lost there some illusions as to the
infallibility of Protestant piety, for there is memory of a
letter read at the breakfast table, telling of a negro cook
she and her husband had found praying on the English
sands for a good master, and so had engaged him and then
of a later letter of disappointment that he had turned out
to be a rogue. Then the eldest daughter at home had taken
up the same work, holding her own, it is said, in written
arguments with the priests. She believed it was her duty,
her mission, to turn the people to the written word of God
in the Bible free from the interpretation of their church,
and in this belief she was never shaken to her life's end,
but continued her work with a gallant heart, though her

Above: Lady Gregory's parents. Dudley and Frances Persse. Below: a photograph taken outside the entrance of Coole House, c.1887. On the left Robert and Lady Gregory, and far right, Sir William Gregory.

Above: Roxborough House, the Persse home, about seven miles north east of Coole. Below: Coole Park, the entrance front.

youngest sister carries in her memory a word said to her
with some emotion: "I sometimes think how happy you
are not to feel called to this business as I do. It is a heavy
task". For as if by some imperceptible change the daughters
of the family, after her, showed little or no interest in that
side of the religious life. And as to the youngest; she did
not "feel called to this business" of controversy, but was for
a time held in suspicion especially by a priest who believed
that in her work of visiting and helping the poor in his
flock she must have some hidden aim. But he found and
confessed later that this was not so; and she was told that
in later days he was sad at having shown a discourtesy to
one who had now been joined in marriage with a man who
had been so good a member for the County, so trusted by
Catholics, so liberal and so kind.

There was no formal "coming out" at ball or races for
this youngest of the Miss Persses. There were not many
gaieties near at hand, and she had no mind for such amusements, from no actual belief perhaps that such frivolity was
wrong, although religion as she had learned it did not lend
its countenance to such, but rather because of the saving
of money for the poor. Hunting might have been a temptation, had it not been forbidden to girls at Roxborough, for
the impulse towards the gay exercise of youth took her riding
with the brothers she had been used to follow at their other
sports, over many stone walls across country, sometimes
with an occasional pack of harriers, and once, only once,
with the foxhounds, when a triumphant run ended on the
very lawn of Roxborough in full sight of her astonished
father. It may be she would have been more tempted by
dress and society had she nursed any expectation of being
admired. But the Mistress, disappointed in a birthday prayer
that she might grow not only in wisdom but in stature,
made her aware, and this was true enough, that she was not
to think herself the equal of her sisters, all tall, handsome,
and one at least beautiful. Yet going to stay at cousin's
houses she gained more confidence, especially in finding
that her hands which because of winter chilblains she had
grown up in a habit of hiding whenever a table made it
possible were now, that disfigurement being outgrown, even
admired.

Guests in the meanwhile with a respect for letters were
not quite unknown, one of these having leave to borrow
from the Galway College Library, and bringing a yet greater

joy by some poems written out in a manuscript book, some
at least of these, never as it happens since met with, keeping
still their place in the reader's memory as,

> With reverend tread,
> And uncovered head,
> Pass by the dome gate,
> Where buried lie,
> The men of July,
> And the dog howls desolate.

And once a wild undergraduate of Trinity College
brought on a visit by a wild son of the house, would drift,
coming back at evening from sports or races, to the youngest
sister's side, and would talk of what she cared for, and enter
into the enthusiasms that then possessed her. For she had but
lately, having attained the freedom of her eighteenth year,
bought a Shakespeare, green, the Globe edition, rebound
later when some pages were all but worn away. And finding
all new to her, even the very stories of the plays, she felt
the joys of an explorer; and leaving no page unread learned
even the sonnets at her dressing-table, repeating them aloud
on the mountain side. In those evenings she would be full
of the day's discoveries, and where could she have found
better sympathy than in one who, for all his wild ways,
was Dowden's favourite pupil and the first man in literature
of his year? Alas that the caution of elders interrupted that
companionship, those delightful conversations in which one
or the other of the great poets or writers was ever a third.
There was an abrupt banishment, a sudden silence. It was
not until years had passed that she came to know that he had
written to her, and that the letter had been opened by the
authorities, the Church itself being represented by the
Archdeacon of the time. But as she was told, the broken
seal had but disclosed a friendly note giving the authorship
of a once discussed quotation. Her heart had not been
wounded nor had her hand trembled at the parting, and
if she has now and again blushed at the recollection, it is
with shame for herself and yet more for Dowden's favourite
pupil, that the line whose authorship they could not
recognise was "Among the faithless faithful only he".
But the study of the great dramatist went on unabated,
and if her acquaintance with his splendid sentences was of
necessity less than long intimacy had given her with those of
another Book, it was the German translations of Shakespeare

and of the Bible that were from familiarity her best text
books when she set out to teach herself the German language.

Then while in her early twenties there came a sudden
change, and being given the charge of an elder brother[4]
whose health had failed, she left the large household, the
comradeship of the boys, the great plenty, the fireside comfort, the winter shooting parties, the wide demesne, the
hillsides where she had often started the wild deer as she
climbed to look at the shadowy mountain tops of Connemara
beyond the shining Atlantic Bay, for a quiet hotel on the
Riviera, monotonous walks beside the invalid's chair, or
drives on the dusty roads; the companionship of one that
she had never intimately known, so much was he her elder,
and whose turn for satire had increased the shy tremors of
her early days. And as she saw it, Cannes was not France,
it had no history, no national life, no language but a patois,
few inhabitants save an organized English society, seeking
health, or the mild gaieties of the seventies.

But with the springtime in each of these three (four?)
years there came what made up for all, a few weeks of Italy;
the journey through olive groves to the palaces of Genoa,
or across the yet untunnelled Alps to Lombardy, to the
Lakes, to Tuscany. And having begun to learn its language,
and to know a little of the grammar, with the audacity of
the young she began to read Dante, at first with the help
of a French translation, and then, making her own, she
wrote it out to the very end of the Purgatorio and the triple
stars. And the beautiful sound of the language was added
to the other unbounded joys of those blossoming Italian
Aprils, the freedom of cities, the glory of the arts, the
triumphant beauty of Dante's Florence above all.

There had not been much of the education of sorrows
in the home at Roxborough. No heavy grief had come until,
after those foreign winters had begun, the death of the dear
Cornish sister Gertrude, and soon after that the death of old
Mary Sheridan. Then in the autumn of 1878 a younger
brother fell ill with pleurisy; it was before the day of
trained nurses, and his younger sister was with him night
and day. One day at lunch-time going to the dining-room for
something needed for him she heard one of those at the
table say that during the night the cry of the banshee had
been heard; and although looking on such tales as idle,

4 Richard Persse.

anxiety about her brother made her feel a sudden dread. In the evening he was still very ill, and towards midnight he had fallen asleep, when she heard voices and a stir in the house and going to the staircase saw a group of the servants, and [asked them not to make any noise.] one among them came up the stairs to her and said, "the Master is dead".

To those of his children still living under the roof, it seemed as if all had been shattered around them. Roxborough had been such a hive of life, with its stables full of horses, its kennels full of sporting dogs, Gordon setters, retrievers, greyhounds—the deerhound had been long done away with; the sawmill with its carpenters and engineers and turners; the gamekeepers and trappers; the long array of labourers coming each morning to their work; the garden so well tilled, so full, at this September time, of grapes and melons and peaches and apples, inexhaustible fruit. Must they leave it all? Where should they go? For the eldest son, the stepbrother, was now lord of all and was impatient to take possession.

*   *   *

The Mistress took a house in Dublin to be a home for herself and those of her children who might need it. The immediate change meant less to the youngest daughter than to the others, for she went for the third time with the invalid to the South of France.

II

MARRIAGE

IN THE THIRD winter abroad a visitor to Cannes came sometimes and talked with me and read to me from little
manuscript books into which from time to time he had
copied prose or poetry he cared for. And on our way back
to Ireland that spring we stayed for a few days in London
at 3 St. George's Place as guests of Sir William Gregory.

My husband's *Autobiography* has told the story of his
life and I will but quote from some chapters written by his
old friend, the Hon. Frank Lawley, in his *Racing Life of
Lord George Bentinck* (1892). Mr. Lawley tells that he was
brought up in the society of Dublin Castle, in the house of
his grandfather, the Rt. Hon. William Gregory, then
Under-Secretary, of whom it was said, from his great
influence and experience that "Gregory was the dry nurse
of young English Statesmen".

"In 1842 young Mr. William Gregory was invited to stand
for Dublin in opposition to Lord Morpeth who was vigorously supported by O'Connell. It would have been difficult
for a young man, not yet twenty-five, to encounter a more
formidable opponent. The seat for Dublin was of no slight
importance, and the Whigs were extremely anxious to wrest
it from the Tories. On the nomination day O'Connell, then
Lord Mayor of Dublin, was so pleased with the plucky way
in which his youthful antagonist had stood up to him that
he exclaimed 'Young man, may I shake you by the hand?
Your speech has so gratified me that if you will but whisper
REPEAL, only *whisper* it mind you, Daniel O'Connell will
be the first man at the polling booth to vote for you
tomorrow.' The mystic word was not whispered, or uttered,
but from that time O'Connell and Gregory were always the
best of friends. Sir William was returned by a triumphant
majority."

He says also, "Few men have ever lived whose experience
was more diversified; he was a man of ready sympathy to
whom *quicquid agunt homines* was full of interest. He had
known everybody who was anybody, for even as a Harrow
lad he was intimate with illustrious Harrovians like Sir

Robert Peel, Lord Palmerston, Lord Aberdeen, and Sir James Graham. He knew the Turf and all its intricacies as well as Scott's William of Deloraine knew the passes and fords of the Scottish Border. Although not more than twenty-two years old when accompanied by the Earl of Winchelsea and other undergraduates he rode on a series of hacks strewn along the road, from Christ Church to Epsom and back to see his first Derby, he was at once admitted to the best society in the United Kingdom and soon became a prominent pillar of the English Turf. He was on the most intimate terms of friendship with Lord George Bentinck, the noble owner of Crucifix, Miss Elis and Gafer . . . I have long regretted that he could never be prevailed upon to write a history of the 'Sport of Kings'. He was the only man of my acquaintance possessed of the literary ability and also of the keen insight into character requisite to enable him to draw correct pen portraits of heroes of the Turf who are to the present generation mere *homines umbrae* . . .

"During the last thirty years of his life, however, politics, literature and art engaged his attention to such a degree that . . . he had no time or inclination for composing a work *de longue haleine* on the pursuits of his youth.

"Fortunately for himself, Sir William Gregory's active connection with the Turf as an owner of racehorses ceased for ever in the spring of 1855. Under all circumstances and all conditions he never ceased to be an industrious worker, and his Catholic taste for the classics, for literature of all kinds and for art in particular, was well known to his many friends. The dissolution of 1857 gave him an opportunity of returning to Parliament as Liberal member for his native county of Galway . . . Upon domestic subjects, especially upon those connected with Ireland, with the British Museum, the National Gallery and matters of art and taste he was a frequent speaker. He was appointed a Trustee of the National Gallery by Mr. Disraeli, and sworn as a member of the Privy Council for Ireland in 1871 under Gladstone's first administration . . . In 1872 he was appointed Governor of Ceylon. At last 'the hour and the man had both come' . . . It has often been remarked that the best Colonial Governors come from Ireland; and of those who have served her Majesty within my recollection, none was ever more successful than Sir William Gregory."

I had first seen him [(though he always declared he had seen me as a child and had said to my mother "that is the prettiest of all your daughters")] at a cricket match at Roxborough. There was a long table in the dining-room where guests were being given lunch, and I came in and went from chair to chair seeing that their wants were supplied. Sir William came late, was brought in and put in almost the only place left empty, it was at the head of the table. I, as I came to him, a stranger, for he had but just returned from his five years' government of Ceylon, felt a little shy, most likely I blushed as was then my habit. I think I must have been looking rather nice, for later when someone told my still unmarried sister that I, who have made so good a marriage, lived so quietly and had dressed so simply, she answered that on the day that had such an influence on my fate I had worn a Paris dress [(bought at the Bon Marché on my way home)] and a Mrs. Heath hat. I kept the hat for many years, a black and white straw with bunches of corn ears and poppies. Anyhow, Sir William greeted me with all his great charm of manner, and I sat next him for a while, glad of an opportunity of talking about Ceylon, as one of my brothers thought of going there. After lunch also we walked and talked for a good deal of the afternoon. (It is but the other day I read in Sir Horace Rumbold's *Recollections of a Diplomatist* that they had made a journey together with him and that "the hours pass quickly in Gregory's company".)

[A little later we were at dinner one evening, when a message came from a neighbour's house with a note asking if I would come over and stay the night "to meet two agreeable men, Edward O'Brien and William Gregory". The summer evening was still bright and a brother offered to drive over and I had a pleasant evening there. It was not until long afterwards that our hostess—his cousin—explained that sudden invitation. It was just before dinner that he had spoken of me in a way that made her certain he liked me; and she had sent her messenger at once.]

Very soon after that he wrote to ask me, with my elder brother Richard, to dine and sleep at Coole. He took us for a drive, my first through the woods I was to know so well and that Yeats has made known to so many as "The Seven Woods":

> Shan-walla where a willow-bordered pond
> Gathers the wild duck from the winter dawn;
> Shady Kyle-dortha; sunnier Kyle-na-no,

> Where many hundred squirrels are as happy
> As though they had been hidden by green boughs
> Where old age cannot find them; Pairc-na-lee,
> Where hazel and ash and privet blind the paths;
> Dim Pairc-na-carraig, where the wild bees fling
> Their sudden fragrances on the green air;
> Dim Pairc-na-tarav, where enchanted eyes
> Have seen immortal, mild, proud shadows walk;
> Dim Inchy wood, that hides badger and fox
> And marten-cat, and borders that old wood
> Wise Biddy Early called the wicked wood;
> Seven odours, seven murmurs, seven woods . . .

The lake that touched on woodlands is often in his poems also, and its wild swans that come and go.

We drove also to the pool where the river rises and dips again under rocks, beside which Colman, the Saint, who has left his name and his blessing on so many wells of healing, was born.

The plain white house has little changed through the years. It was not the first time that I had seen it, for one day in my childhood I had been taken there, in old Mrs. Gregory's time. We had walked in the garden, where she showed us a mulberry tree covered with fruit—and did not offer us any. When I came here the summer after my marriage I thought "Now I shall be able to taste mulberries". But alas! the tree was dying, and had no fruit. I have planted others over and over again and some failed and one at least is flourishing now, but has not yet begun to bear. But the memory of that disappointment, those untasted berries, has made me always careful to give children, rich or poor, some little pleasant thing to eat or take away whenever they come, so that my poor little great-niece, Vera Shawe Taylor, said once as I took her to rummage in the store room, "It is always Christmas in this house".

[And I remember that an old barrister, my brother's friend, a lover of literature and art, who had helped me in those years of nursing, giving me books, Pope's *Iliad* and *Odyssey,* with the Flaxman illustrations; and Milton's *Prose,* and above all Jarvis's translation of *Don Quixote,* had once driven to Coole, at that time empty, and coming back spoke of it as a house showing a fine intellectual tradition, of the library with its rich collection of books, and had said with what seemed a flight of fantasy, "That is the only house I have seen in the county that would make a right setting for you".]

There had always been a certain distinction about Coole[1], [and about its owner when representing the county in Parliament or when there were echoes of his doings in London or Ceylon. And his mother spent her winters abroad, in the South of France, not then so common a harbour as it became; there were occasional guests, some of high rank, and she openly said there were very few neighbours she could associate with. My mother she was kind enough to make an exception, and the Shawe Taylors and the Goughs. Her early and brilliant married life at the Under Secretary's Lodge in the Phoenix Park and the distinction of her son were the excuse for this. But my sister at Castle Taylor, and I, and Lady Layard and I, used sometimes to say to one another, "How is it that our predecessors managed to give themselves airs, and we have never managed to do so?"]

[My brother, asked after our return from that visit how we had got on, had said rather discontentedly, that our host had "talked more to Augusta than to me". He had showed us his Ceylon treasures, and had given me a pearl ring. That did not mean much, for he was ever a giver of presents— a quoter of "les petits cadeaux entretiennent l'amitié"—and my mother, never quite sure he had not married me as a compliment to her, used to show us, and gave me later, an embroidered Maltese shawl he had once brought her from the Mediterranean.]

[I think it must have been about this time that (as he told me afterwards) he had, in making his will, directed I should be given my choice of any six books from the Coole Library. I have often wondered what they would have been. Johnson's *Dictionary*, that fine edition, would probably then, as it would certainly now, have been one of them, I have so often used it since I have been here. And Evelyn's *Silva* perhaps, and Lord Berners' *Froissart*. There are more valuable books than these, but I was not mercenary at that time.]

Yet Roxborough with its romance of river and hillsides came for a long time first in my imagination. It was not until my child's birth that I began really to care for Coole, looking before as well as after. And that love has grown

[1]In her revision, Lady Gregory deleted three paragraphs and joined this sentence to the paragraph beginning "Yet Roxborough with its romance of river", etc.

through the long years of widowed life, when the woods especially became my occupation and delight. [Only yesterday, 23 October 1918, the little grandchildren Anne and Catherine, walked with me in these woods through the afternoon, or rather ran and hid and rushed out again so happily through the autumn coloured larch and the shining silvers and the nut thickets, and I saw that these would be a romantic memory to them hereafter. It was for my son I was yet planting there a year ago.]

After that visit [and that pearl ring,] I did not seem to meet Sir William often; I think only at Cannes and during that week in London. And on his last day at Cannes he had called three times to see me, and three times the porter, Henri, had told him I was out, as porters do. I had got to like him very much. He cared for the things I cared for, he could teach me and help me so much. But although at that time I cannot say the thought of marriage did not occur to me—I lived in too large and irreverent a family for that detachment of mind—yet it did not fit into the life that seemed planned out for me. The winter after my father's death I seemed more bound than ever to the invalid. The doctors told me when we went abroad that he was losing ground, and it was possible he would not even live to arrive at Cannes. But he lived to come back to the next summer to Roxborough.* It was there that he weakened, and one night when I was alone with him he died.

My half-brother, Dudley, who had succeeded, then needed my care and Algernon, that brother[2] who had taken over the management of the estate, had gone through a hard and anxious time and was glad of my help. We planned to keep the herdsmen when going with sheep and cattle to Ballinasloe Fair from the public houses, and sent a cricket tent to be pitched outside the town with arrangements for cooking and a store of food. It served the purpose well, and I hoped to get a manager and send our "temperance tent" to other fairs and assemblies. Then we found our labourers were paying very high prices for food at the Kilchriest shops, and we[3] got supplies of tea and sugar, flour, and bacon and

*Wrong dates? 1880—It should be 1879 autumn [obscure, as faintly pencilled on previous page].

[2] The beginning of this sentence replaced "Yet another brother, the eldest, Dudley, needed my care. I was tied as before."

[3] "We" replaced "with Algernon's help, I".

opened a shop at the Steward's Lodge on Friday afternoons when their wages were paid. It was a great boon. The wives came to buy their goods and were astonished to find how far their money went, and how good were the purchases. Miss Samuella, the Archdeacon's sister, took me to task and said I was injuring the respectable Protestant shopkeepers of Kilchriest. But when I asked here where she got her own supplies, she confessed from Dublin; so I felt she had no right to object. [I hoped to get in other goods by degrees.]

Once, during this time, my mother had a visit from Sir William in Dublin, and he spoke to her with some indignation of the life I was kept to, a life of self-sacrifice he thought it. I did not feel it so. My heart was in Roxborough, the fields, the hills, the villages. I still found opportunity in the mornings and on our drives to see and help some of the poor people. The Gort doctor had told Sir William of meeting me at that time at the bedside of a dying boy, whom I had to visit every day because he would only take nourishment from my hand. I had to look after the housekeeping also, for there were still some of the old servants who were used to the old wasteful times, the lavish killing of beasts, the masses of meat for all in the house and yard and stables, the beer barrels, the large household, and all this had to be changed and brought within bounds.

About Christmas time Algernon went for a two days' shoot at Coole where he found I think Gerald Dillon, Lord Crofton, John Blakeney and one of the Grevilles, Lord Warwick's brother. He came back pleased with the good woodcock shoot, and the good dinners and the pleasant company. He brought with him a book Sir William had given him for me to read. He was half sarcastic. I don't think he, or the others, yet believed that I could really enjoy reading. A little time afterwards, Sir William came to lunch one day to say goodbye, as he was going abroad for the rest of the winter. He looked ill and was, I thought, depressed, and when he said goodbye I felt sad and lonely. [I used to say to myself that when one is sad one should try to make things happier for someone else, and so when I went for my usual drive with Dudley I stopped at the Kilchriest Dispensary—it was the day on which the doctor from Loughrea attended—and gave or promised help to some of the patients. Then I settled down to my usual life. I was reading in the evenings *The Stones of Venice,* which I had unexpectedly found in the Castle Taylor bookshelves, though it seemed without much prospect of ever seeing Venice itself.]

One morning soon afterwards, when I opened the postbag before morning prayers, which I read as had been the habit, to a dwindled household, there was a letter for me, from Sir William, and chancing to turn it over, I saw it was sealed, which was unusual. The servants were waiting and I read the chapter and the prayer. Then I opened the letter. It was written from London, and in it he asked me to marry him.

I felt extraordinarily happy and serene, happy in the thought of being with him, of serving him, of learning from him. And I was happy also in the thought of not leaving the country, the neighbourhood that I loved, for it was but a drive of seven miles to Coole, in the next barony, the next parish.

Then came a difficulty. I had said in my answer to him I could not leave Roxborough until there was someone to take my place there. I could not walk out of the door leaving the two brothers who needed me. But a very simple solution was found. An uncle's widow and her daughter were looking for a new home. It was a benefit to them to go for a while to Roxborough.

All my family were pleased, some of them astonished; feeling perhaps as an old neighbour did, saying to Algernon after church at Killinane, "How did that little thing get the big man?". The boys were pleased to think of all the shootings that would run together; Castle Taylor, adjoining the Roxborough property; Coole woods but separated by a fence from the Shawe-Taylor's woods of Garrylands. One of them hoped that the last unmarried sister would marry Edward Martyn of Tillyra, because then they could shoot the whole countryside without a break. (She did marry in the county afterwards and have her shooting parties, [afterwards] but they were at Moyne Park to the north of the county and not marching with the home boundaries.) And old Rick Burke, the steward, who had given me fourpenny bits at the Customs Gap at Eserkelly Fair in my childhood, took off his hat with a great sweep whenever he met me. But Dudley was sad. He had become used to my care. And I saw tears in Algernon's eyes one day when a tenant coming to the office on business and saying, "So you're going to join with the Gregorys," said also, "What at all will you do? You will never get so good a helper."

According to our wish we were not given wedding presents [there had been several marriages in the county just then, and I think all our friends were pleased] but my elder brother [however,] gave me a phaeton which is still in existence. It was quite smart in its beginning when we chose it in London, but as little round tubs came into fashion it seemed from year to year to grow longer and longer and went out of fashion. It was very useful later in my lonely life. I drove in it every year to Galway with Robert in his holidays to stay the night with my mother who had moved there. And, drawn by the pony, Shamrock, I went many a time to Chevy in the mountains or to Duras by the sea, to visit old Count de Basterot; and once across the mountains and through two unbridged rivers to see the place where Biddy Early, the witch doctor, had made her prophecies and cures.

So an announcement in *The Times* (1880) said: —
"On the 4th March, by special licence, at St. Matthias Church, Dublin, the Rt. Hon. Sir William Gregory of Coole Park, Co. Galway, and 3 St. George's Place, Hyde Park Corner, to Augusta, daughter of the late Dudley Persse, Esq., D.L., of Roxborough, Co. Galway."

I wore a grey hat and grey travelling dress and [I had been so long in mourning for my father and for Richard, I did not like to change to colours. But I have always been rather sorry I did not, however quiet the wedding, wear white, with wreath and veil. I feel it was a break of tradition, something missed out of my life; or perhaps, I should like to remember myself in bride's attire. I did not feel like that at the time. Indeed, I had lived so simple and so self-forgetting a life for so long I gave little thought to clothes.] that wedding dress is seen in a photograph taken at Constantinople, with a little black bonnet my husband liked very much; a bonnet such as is never seen in these days, except on a charwoman in an omnibus. For years afterwards, whenever I looked at that photograph, the strings, like my phaeton, seemed to have grown longer. For strings went first, shorter and shorter, until by a gradual transition akin to the casting of claws by a crab, the bonnet became a toque.

We stayed but a short while in London, some of my own part of it under the dressmakers, for there had been but little opportunity before my marriage for these, and there was hospitality before us in the cities we were about to visit, Rome and Athens and Constantinople. And there was the Queen's drawing-room to be attended, and I am glad this was not put off.

It happened one night, long after, that I was alone in a box at a New York Theatre, and my mind, entangled in some business of the day, had strayed between Act and Act. And when the curtain went up again, it seemed to me as if some thirty years had melted away, for I saw before me the Throne Room at Buckingham Palace, as I had first seen it, and the fine ladies with trains and veils, wearing plumes of feathers as I had worn them, curtseying or bending to kiss the Queen's hand as I as a bride had kissed it. And there in the background stood a figure as I had seen it, dominating as it seemed all the rest, a diamond star glittering from his black velvet; an unforgettable Eastern face. And there came back the memory of a momentary disappointment when my husband, having to hurry away to meet some members of the Arundel Society who wished to consult him about some lately uncovered frescoes at Rome, had been sorry he could not wait to make me known to Disraeli; for although never his follower in politics there had always been friendliness between them, even at one time intimacy, and no doubt, according to his habit, he would have greeted his friend's bride with some finely phrased compliment. And it happened there never was opportunity again that year, and in the next year he died. And this disappointment, long forgotten, came back with sudden sharpness in that sudden sight of Mr. Arless on the stage.

Rome, Athens, Constantinople, a wonderful wedding journey. In Rome the pictures and statues and churches were too many and too confusing for a short visit. I was rather bewildered by it all. There are too many ages huddling on one another in Rome—"the exhaustless scattered fragmentary city" as it is called by Goethe.

[The other day and since I wrote those last words, I met the daughter of one who had been an attaché at the Embassy at Rome. His name brought back to me of a sudden my arrival there, my confusion and bewilderment in sightseeing. It happened that he had come to Rome for the first time on the same day as I. He, like me, was being asked "Have you seen St. Peter's" or told he must see the Vatican Galleries or the Capital or it might be the frescoes at the Baths of Caracalla. Our ignorance brought about sympathy we found it comforting to confess it to each other, and to talk of the trivial things of the day.]

My first real dinner party was a sudden entering into society after my quiet years. Sir Augustus Paget coming out from church on our first Sunday asked us to dine at the Embassy to meet the Crown Princess of Prussia, Princess Royal of England.

I wrote, "it was a small dinner at a round table, the guests were the Duc de Ripaldo, the Duchess Massimo, Gay Paget very lovely, two or three of the Embassy people, and the Princess Royal of England, Crown Princess of Prussia". I did not feel shy, I liked the flowers and the lighted rooms. I was dressed in white satin and old lace, a dress made to represent the one I should have worn on March 4th, and Lady Paget and the Duchess were also in white and in that matter I felt at ease, [though I had not then put into words my axiom as to dress, that it should be such as to make one feel at ease in whatever company you are in. The Princess wore a black barège or some such material, almost high. She was a striking figure at the reception afterwards with her dark intellectual face and royal air, receiving the Roman ladies with their fine dresses and jewels. I don't know if she noticed them, but when I was presented to her she had touched the bracelet I was wearing, one made of replicas of old Greek coins, and asked to see it more closely, and had recognised each, giving the name of its city.]

My first ball also was at the Embassy, it was in honour of that royal guest, and in honour of her the Roman Princesses had brought out their tiaras from bankers' strong rooms. Of my few balls it was the most dazzling and glittering and brilliant; those at Buckingham Palace were more formal and less opulent. One at Government House, Calcutta, was a more beautiful sight, with its spacious whiteness of background, the rich colours of the native dresses.

On another day to be remembered we went to the Pope's reception at the Vatican and received his blessing, which he gave very solemnly. To us, indeed, he had given a special word and smile, because of the service my husband had done in Ceylon to his Church there, and because also of the gratitude of the priests and bishops in Ireland. I remember the pallid, fleshless face, dark eyes glowing as if with a fire that was consuming the wasted body. I had brought rosaries with me that I might give them to some of the devout old women at home, when they had received Leo the Tenth's blessing.

Athens looked very tranquil, lovely and serene after the

confusion of Roman streets and ruins, the low white marble temples were in harmony with the low violet hills. In the fields scarlet poppies were in flower. The ships in the harbour were decorated with flags for the Greek Easter. My husband had been a good friend of Greece in his Parliamentary days and so we received kindness from Tricoupis, the Prime Minister, and his sister, Sophie. Professor Rousopolis showed us the Antiquities; and Dr. Schliemann entertained us at his house, and gave me a "whorl" from the ruins of Troy.

I forgot whether it was before or after this that the almost tragic event happened of Schliemann being blackballed for the Athenaeum Club. He was in London when his name was coming up, and saw no harm in offering a tip, in Southern fashion, to, I think, the Head Porter who reported the offer to the Committee with as much indignation as that with which he had rejected it. By rule or pedantry, Schliemann was excluded and he went away very sore of heart from England and bequeathed the collection he had intended for the British Museum to, I think, Berlin.

Through the Ionian Isles to Constantinople; some pleasant weeks at the British Embassy; my beginning of a long and happy friendship with the Layards.

London again, and a short London season, dinners, receptions, the Marlborough House Garden Party, the Queen's Ball, the friendly faces of my husband's friends.

Then home to Coole; Gort is decorated, Priest and Archdeacon to welcome us, a bonfire at the gate, an arch with Cead Mile Failthe, goodwill everywhere.

The education through books was now in the background, another education was begun.

Sir William Gregory, a photograph taken soon after his marriage to Augusta Persse.

Lady Gregory's signature fans. Above: signatures include Sir Edward Malet, Lord
Houghton, Sir Arthur Sullivan, W. E. Gladstone, Robert Browning, G. O. Trevelyan
Sir Henry Layard, Wilfrid Scawen Blunt. The other side (not shown) includes
Sir Alfred Lyall, Lord Dufferin, Randolph Churchill, Lord Tennyson, Sir John
Millais, J. McN. Whistler, G. F. Watts, Sir Joseph Boehm, Max Muller and Arabi.
Below: this fan includes Henry James, Sir William Orpen, Bret Harte, Mark Twain
Thomas Hardy, Ellen Terry, Theodore Roosevelt, Antonio Mancini, Ramsay
MacDonald, Robin Flower, Augustus John, Rudyard Kipling, Lord Asquith
Fridtjof Nansen, G. B. Shaw, J. M. Synge, George Moore, Sean O'Casey, An
Craoibhin Aoibhin (Douglas Hyde), Jack B. Yeats, George Russell (A.E.), W. B
Yeats and Edward Martyn.

III

EDUCATION IN POLITICS: EGYPT

I WROTE to Wilfrid Blunt a while ago, asking if he had
any letters of mine written at the Egyptian time, and telling
him what I am now writing. He answers: "You talk of
having made your political education in Egypt, and so too
did I with you, for before that eventful year, 1882, I had
never played a public part of any kind or written so much
as a letter to *The Times* with my name to it, and we made
our education together over it."

I think there is no one in Ireland quite uninterested in
politics; I had noticed even after my first visit to England
in my girlhood that clergymen's and squires' wives had
talked of things of the neighbourhood, or their gardens and
servants and spring-cleanings, or if they had been to London,
of the portraits in the Royal Academy, but one might live
a long time among them without knowing whether they
were under a Liberal or a Conservative Government. This
has never been so in Ireland, for I remembered even from
childhood that on an afternoon visit one might usually
catch such words as "Dizzy may be sent for"—"Well he
deserves it" or "I would never trust Gladstone, he is a
Puseyite". The old words "Whig" and "Tory" were still
used, this last, as is well known, having been a nickname
for some especially wild robbers, so that I have known old
Thorpe, my cousin's maid, at the time of the Church's
disestablishment, puzzle English visitors by talking of "that
Tory Gladstone". But I myself had never given much heed
to politics, being less interested in newspapers than in books.

It was during that visit to the Embassy at Therapia in
1880 that I began to know anything of the Eastern Question.
I came back to London indignant at the wrong-doings of
the Turks and the sufferings of the Armenians. But at
London dinners, when I spoke of these with some fire, I
found but little response, and at least one politician said
to me, "But what do you think of the Hares and Rabbits
Bill? That is a *really* important question". I noticed the
same indifference to anything but Great Britain when an
election was coming on, and Sir William was asked to stand

for five different English constituencies. He was asked his opinion about several domestic questions, but not one about Egypt, which seemed to us such an exciting matter at the time.

It was in Egypt, where we spent the winter of 1881, that I first felt the real excitement of politics, for we tumbled into a revolution. We arrived there in November after the "revolt of the Colonels" of whom Arabi Bey was one. It was a restless moment; the story as we heard it was that early in the year Arabi, together with two other Colonels, Abdullah of the Black Regiment and Ali Fehmi, had presented a petition asking for an enquiry into the grievances of the Army and it was accepted. I was told that a month later, in February, these three Colonels had a summons from the Khedive to come to the Abdin Palace to receive orders for the arrangement of a procession in honour of the marriage of one of the Princesses. They were not without suspicion and before going to the Palace they left a message for their regiment, "If we are not back at sunset, come for us". As soon as they arrived at the Palace they were seized, thrown into a room, their swords taken from them, and the door locked. No one in Cairo thinks they would ever have been alive again but that at sunset the soldiers arrived demanding their officers, and then it was too late to do anything but to throw the doors open and let the prisoners out. Some who were there said the other Colonels seemed relieved and in a hurry to get home, but that Arabi had walked out "quite calm and unmoved". There had been no accusation made against him, but he had been looked on as "a man with ideas" who would be better out of the way. In September, the soldiers, who had learned the way to the Palace on the day they released their Colonels, appeared there again with a demand for a Constitution, which was promised them. And in December the Khedive made Arabi Under-Secretary of War.

I wrote at this time that Mr. (afterwards Sir Auckland) Colvin, the Controller of Finance, who had been with us at Helwan, "thinks Arabi Bey honest, but fears his being influenced by the European population, Italians, etc., who are discontented with the present state of things. The Khedive's hope is in Constantinople; Sherif Pasha is honest, and the only Turk in power who feels a responsibility towards the Arabs, but is indolent and has hazy ideas. There are 1,200 officers on half-pay in the country, owing to Ismail having increased and then reduced the army." There were certainly the makings of disorder here. Long afterwards, Sir Auckland, passionately calling out against the part we had taken, said "And I was not unjust—don't you remember at Helwan?" And I agreed that he had been fair-minded then.

My husband became interested in what he heard of Arabi and was taken to see him and liked him. Arabi did not deny that much good had been done by foreign officials, but he thought it unfair that his countrymen were kept out of any important office. He came to return the visit, and Sir William became more and more interested in his views and when he had seen more of him wrote some letters to *The Times* to make his views known in England. Mr. Blunt in his *Secret History of the Occupation of Egypt*[1] tells that he was urged to defend the Egyptian national case in *The Times* by Sir William Gregory, "who had himself sent more than one powerful letter in the same sense to what was then emphatically the leading journal of Europe. It is hardly possible to exaggerate the importance a letter on any subject had in those days when published by *The Times,* and the certainty there was if it was on any political question of its being read by the statesmen concerned and treated with full attention. Nor is it perhaps too much to say that Gregory's letters and mine—especially his—were largely the means of obtaining a respite for Egypt from the dangers that threatened her."

It was one day at lunch at the Fitzgeralds, we had met Wilfrid and Lady Anne Blunt, the beginning to me of a long friendship. And at this meeting Sir William had told us that many years ago he had seen a young Englishman in the bull-ring at Madrid, facing and attacking the bull, as outsiders were sometimes allowed to do, and had been struck by his extraordinary good looks. And asking who he was had been told he was an attaché from the English Legation, Wilfrid Blunt. He said to him, recalling this, "I wonder you were not afraid" and the answer was, "I was very much afraid indeed, but I would not give in". As to his good looks, I think when London fashion turned against him for his support of the Egyptian Nationalists, they were a positive annoyance to his enemies. All had not the good humour of Lord Houghton, who said to me in his whimsical way, "the

1 London, Fisher Unwin, 1907.

fellow knows he has a handsome head and he wants it to be seen on Temple Bar". He and Lady Anne were now living in the garden they had bought in the Heliopolis desert, near Cairo, and they were convinced that Arabi's revolt was right, that it would lead to the Turks, as well as the Christians being turned out from the control of Egypt. And beyond that they had the vision of an Arab Caliphate, an independent Arab race. Sir William did not go so far as this, though Lord Houghton mischievously declared that Arabi had said, "Blunt is a spy of Malet's, but Gregory is the real man". Then France and England sent that "most mischievous document," the Joint Note, promising support to the Khedive, and threatening armed intervention in case of disturbance. It made the National Party very angry. Arabi said to Mr. Blunt, "It is the language of menace, a menace to our liberties," and so indeed it was. I wrote of the gossip and rumours of the following days: "The Chamber (of Notables) won't agree to it, everything is at a deadlock" . . . "We met Colvin at tennis at Sir E. Malet's. He says, one advantage of the deadlock is that he has a little time to amuse himself. But he begs us to hold back W.S.B., and to say that if he had spoken to him rather sharply that morning it was because he had not breakfasted and was hungry and cross" . . . "We dined with Sir. E. Malet. He is very anxious. The Chamber refuses to yield on the Budget question, he says, at Arabi's instigation. We went on with him to the opera. The Khedive was in his box looking dreary enough. He said to Sir Edward when he went to sit with him, 'Well, they can't do more than take my head'."

On another day, W. S. B. came in Bedouin costume . . . "He says that the Chamber is right in holding out, that if England intervenes there will be a bloody war, but that liberty has never been gained without blood. In the middle of this, Mr. Villiers Stuart came in and began to talk of mummies and the covering of the Sacred Ark." Lord Houghton says, "Sherif has resigned and a Gregory-Blunt Ministry is talked of! "

3 February. "Sherif has resigned and Barody is forming a new Ministry. Rumours all day that Arabi drew his sword on Sultan Pasha and threatened to cut him in two if he did not obey his behests; that the bankers have sent their children to Alexandria, that troops are on their way from Constantinople, etc. Then Mr. Blunt's secretary comes in

and denies it all, says Arabi has refused to be named
Minister of War lest the people should think he was acting
for his own good; that the Chamber will still pay the interest
of the Debt to the Controller, but will insist on managing
the rest of the Budget for themselves. Then a mysterious
visitor with a message from Arabi that we need have no
fear . . . Lord Houghton in the evening, half inclined towards
the National Party, but still wishes Cairo to become Euro-
peanised.

"We went with Lord Houghton and Mrs. Fitzgerald to
see the Blunts at Heliopolis. They received us in Bedouin
costumes at the door of their tent. Two or three Arab sheiks
to luncheon—first sweets, nougat, etc., then incense burned
and coffee; then a bowl of boiled lamb and one of rice.
W.S.B. says the chief sheik is not what he would call a
robber, but ravages the villages near him. Lord H. says,
'Like a man, a friend of mine met out riding in the Far
West and asked his occupation, to which the answer was,
"Well, sir, I may say I am generally out on the steal."
5th. "We dined with Artin Bay. Everyone rushes off to
call on the new Ministers, quite proud of a gracious word
from Arabi and Barody. Consternation in the evening; a
telegram saying England will *not* intervene in case of
anarchy."
8th. "We lunched with Princess Said, in Turkish fashion,
Princesses Monssor and Nazli there; some dancing girls,
very young and pretty. Kiamil Pasha came in and announced
that ten thousand Turks were on their way here, and there
was consternation. We came back and found there was no
truth in it. Mr. Van der Nest (the Belgian Minister) had
been to call on Arabi, found him presenting the troops with
new colours and feared he was intruding, but Arabi said,
with much presence of mind: "I take it as a happy omen
that at the moment when the Army which has won such a
victory is receiving its colours the representative of a constitutional monarchy should come in.' We dined with Count
Sala. Sir E. Malet is more tolerant towards the new Ministry,
thinks it as well to give them a chance of getting on without
intervention, but says the Control is practically dead and it
might be more dignified to withdraw it. He has spoken to
Arabi about the abolition of the Slave Trade. (I asked him
to do this.)"
11th. "We dined at the Van der Nest's, and heard the
account of Arabi's reception at the Feast of the Sacred

Carpet in the morning. The people rushed to him, kissed
his hands, his feet, his knees, calling 'Long life to him who
has given us a Constitution!' His gloves were torn into
little pieces to be treasured up; the guards tried to beat the
people off, but Arabi stopped them and said: 'Go back, my
children" and without a word all fell back. The Khedive's
wife was looking on from a window and said, 'See how he
loses no chance of winning the hearts of the people'."

12th.   "We met the Duc d'Aumale at the La Salas and a
Count —— knowing the country well, who spoke of this
wonderful National movement, he says it will go beyond
the soldiers. Princess Nazli had heard the same account of
Arabi's ovation. We dined with Sir E. Malet, Lord
Houghton, Fitzgeralds, Sir. F. Goldsmid there, we quarrelled
over Arabi as usual, W. and I against the rest. Someone
spoke of Dickens and Lord H. said his grandmother had
lived as housekeeper in the family of Lady Houghton and
the children used to say no one ever told stories like Mrs.
Dickens."

17th.   "I met Arabi in the hall. I thanked him for the
photograph he had sent me with the words written, 'Arabi
the Egyptian; I present my picture to Lady Gregory as a
souvenir to preserve friendship'. He has the Slave Trade
suppression 'next to his heart' and will carry it out."

19th.   "In the evening at the Fitzgeralds. Sir. A. Colvin says
he thinks the Ministers are going too far with their military
estimates, but promises to come down from his pedestal and
try to work with them."

Mr. (afterwards Sir Gerald) Fitzgerald was one of those
with whom I carried on a good-humoured quarrel. He, like
so many others, had received some kindness from my husband when a young man in Galway town, and he did not
lose his temper with us, though as a well-paid and well-
meaning official he wished the Egyptian Government left
undisturbed. He would sometimes threaten to come in
return and wave the green Land League flag at the gates
of Coole. He had worked his way up since those Galway
days, and Lord Houghton had accepted him as a son-in-law,
though he had grumbled, 'this is not what I expected after
taking my daughter to every ducal house in England!'
Someone in the India Office told me that after the proposal
he had called and asked what they thought of Gerald Fitzgerald. They had praised his work and ability, but Lord

Houghton growled at this and said, 'Yes, but what I want to know is has he got *imagination*?'."

20th. "At dinner at the Moneys. Colonel Dulier spoke of Arabi, who was under him in Abyssinia, even then known and rather distrusted as a man with ideas. He used to gather the soldiers round him in the evenings, recite or preach or tell them stories. I asked Sir Frederic Goldsmid what was the exact truth as to his disagreement with Arabi. He says, 'It was last May we were sitting together on a military commission. I forgot what led to it, but General Stone said in answer to something said by Arabi: "Do you mean to say you would not take your regiment to any place you were ordered to?" "Yes," said Arabi, "if the order were not according to regulations". I felt a little nettled and getting up, said, "I belong to an Army that obeys its Sovereign's orders without a word, and if such language as this is used I think I had better retire". Upon this, General Stone got up and said, "I agree with what General Goldsmid has said and think we had better retire". Then someone said, "This is only a misunderstanding, no one meant to use insubordinate language". Arabi said something to the same effect, and the meeting ended amicably, and afterwards Arabi came up and spoke to me in a friendly manner of the difference that had taken place. It was, however, telegraphed to England that I had resigned, and a great deal too much fuss was made about a slight and trivial matter.' It is a comfort here to get the truth of any story!"

25th. "W. S. Blunt in the afternoon. He says Arabi and the others are so exasperated by the false reports of their motives in the English papers that they have now a very bitter feeling towards England, and it may lead them to some rash act."

26th. "The Blunts to lunch, and at three o'clock Lady Anne and I went to call on Arabi's wife. The house is new and unfurnished. She is a woman perhaps between thirty and forty with a rather heavy face but intelligent and honest. The room is bare, a few hard seats, a tiny table covered with a crotchet antimacassar, and on the walls photographs of Arabi in small black frames, and on her breast one set in diamonds. Her dress a trailing green, rather in European fashion. 'The Bey does not like my dress and my long train because it is of European fashion, he says he would like to light a match and set fire to it. But I tell him I must have a dress of this fashion to wear when I go and see the Khedive's wife.' She would like to send her children to Christian schools to learn languages, and would like to consult a Frankish Doctor for herself, but El Bey objects and his word is law. She is his third and only reigning wife. The last wife, she says, had nothing to recommend but that she was big and fat. Just a good bit of meat! His mother was there, a fine old woman in coarse clothes, her chin and hands stained blue. 'I am a fellah woman,' she said, 'and my two other sons are fellahs still'. We asked if she was very proud of her son. 'I produced him,' she said and her eyes lighted up and she told us how good he was. The children came in, three girls, two boys and a little one born last February, at the time Arabi was rescued, so is called (I forget the Arabic) Good Tidings. They had a meal cooked for us, and said had they known we were coming they would have cooked a buffalo! As we left we said, 'May God preserve you—and the Bey'. 'Inshallah,' the wife said rather sadly, 'but they say the Christian powers want to do something to my husband. Why should they? We cannot get on without the Christians nor they without us, why should we not live in peace together?' She told us of the attempt on the Colonels' lives in February, and how, when their swords were taken from them, the others were frightened but Arabi said, 'It is not God's will anything should happen to us,' and then afterwards when they were rescued and the others wanted to rise in arms, he had quieted them and said, 'That is not the way to work'. Lady Anne acted as interpreter.

"In the evening, Lord Cawdor and his daughter, the Duliers and Goldsmids came into tea with us. Sir Frederic Goldsmid says De Blignières (the French representative) makes no more jokes at Council. He says Arabi brings in a big sword with him and he thinks he had better be silent."

27th-28th. "The Blunts have left. W.S.B. writes in his *Secret History,* 'I decided to delay no longer my return to England where I could do more for Egyptian interests than I could at Cairo . . . I was estranged from those of my countrymen in blood, except Gregory, who formed the then little English Colony at Cairo. Following Colvin's lead, they had all gone over like sheep to ideas of intervention, for be it noted it was now no longer French intervention they talked of but English, and at once in English eyes the immorality of aggression had been transformed'."

March 1st. "Edmund Dicey says Mr. Money took to himself the sentence in Sir William's letter about 'incompetent and overpaid officials' but says 'you can tell him you meant his brother!'.

Mr. Gibson says his colleague in the Cadastre is notorious for his treatment of the natives, and that there are many abuses to which he himself would have called attention if he had not been afraid of hurting French susceptibilities."

19th. "A two hours visit from Arabi. We asked him if it was true they were making fortifications. 'No, only repairing them as we do every year. A man whose house needs repair would be laughed at if he let it fall down, and does not the same apply to forts and barracks.' About the Cadastre he says, 'We don't mean to abolish it, but it has been so badly managed that the cost of measuring has been as much as the cost of the land itself. We mean to send away no officials but those proved to be inefficient, and the Europeans set us the example already by sending away twenty of our Arab officers, sometimes without reason. The railways also and Customs are badly administered. The freedom of Europeans from taxes is unjust. We say all men are brothers, and the people say, then if the Europeans are our brothers why are they not taxed as we are? Slavery will soon be abolished. We have sent a decree to the Soudan saying no one can be bought or sold there in future, and the same decree is about to be made here. If any leave their masters the old will be provided for, the young sent to school, the girls married to soldiers.' 'You have made many enemies, there are strong interests against you,' W. said. 'Yes, but they will soon know that we do not seek our own advancement but the good of the people' . . . My last words, 'Chi va piano va sano'."

I wrote to Lady Anne Blunt, 23 March 1882: "Zohrab Bey has been to dine with us. He has a firm belief in Arabi . . . He told us that Said Pasha at one time ordered that the month of Ramadan was not to be observed by the army, but heard in a little time that some of the soldiers were fasting in spite of his command, so had them all called out, and passed along the ranks asking each one if he was obedient or not. One here and there confessed to having fasted, two or three hundred in all. Said was much displeased and was about to have them punished when one young soldier came forward and said very respectfully, 'Excellency, we have read in the Koran that we must obey God rather than man, and if we do not obey His command to fast how can we be expected to obey the command of your Highness?' 'What is your name?' 'Ahmed Arabi.' 'Take this man away!' His friends never expected to see him again, but next day he was released.

"I paid another visit to Arabi's wife on Tuesday, taking a Mrs. Schranz to act as interpreter. She begged me to kiss you on both cheeks, and the old mother sent you many compliments. They received me with great hospitality, and had a meal ready—but I made great friends with one of the children, Hassan, and fed him from my plate, so managed to avoid eating as much as they would have liked. Arabi had been made Pasha five days before. He had refused until the order came from the Sultan and then he had to accept. His wife looked anxious and harassed and says she is always in terror of harm coming to him. The Khedive is suspected of having instigated the attempted poisoning of Abdallah, which does not make them less nervous. I felt quite proud that Arabi had drunk coffee the day he was here! His old mother said, 'I cannot stop for a moment all day praying for his safety. I can't sleep at night till he comes in. The other night he was in pain when he came and I thought he had been poisoned, and since then I keep the water he drinks under lock and key, but nothing will frighten him. He says, "God will preserve me". We were happier in the old days when we saw more of him. Now he gets up early and has only time to say his prayers when there are people waiting for him with business and petitions, and then he goes out, and sometimes it is midnight before we see him again. Then he is abused because there are more robbers about the country than there were, but he can't do everything himself, and the Khedive won't help him in anything. I wish he would leave the slaves alone. They will all go away when they are free, and we must take European maids, and they will seduce their masters, and their children will be stronger than ours and drive them out. Ah, this has been a year full of trouble and anxiety for us all.' She is a good old thing and said she felt as if I was her sister, and my little friend, Hassan, said he liked me, but hated other ladies, and would come to England if he could, but that his papa takes the carriage every day so he did not see how he could get there."

24th. "Mr. Rowsell back from the country says there is an indefinite feeling of expectation among the people leading to disorder. He thinks Arabi is not enough of a brute to govern the country: lessons in brutality at 100 francs a week would give him a better chance."

28th. "Sir F. Goldsmid says Lord Granville asked him to write sometimes from here and he did do once, but thought it right to show what he had written to Sir. E. Malet, who he saw did not like it and as he was staying in his house he would not write again. He says there are four chiefs of Caisse each with £3,600 a year, and one man with £1,000 a year would do the work well. I must say for them that one day I went in and found three of them there: one was reading the paper, one sitting at a desk, the other walking about. I thought of Pickwick's visit to the Bank and Weller's question: 'But what has the eating of ham sandwiches to do with it?'."

We were back in London in May and on the 3rd, "at a reception at Lady Granville's, Dicey was attacking Arabi's character, the old story about house rent. The Sultan has refused the Conference at Constantinople. People are beginning to think W. not so wrong after all."

Sir William wrote to Mr. Gladstone, and he sent this reply from Downing Street (9 June 1882) in his clear handwriting:—

"I can assure you personally, and I think you will believe, that I view with satisfaction whatever there is in Egypt of a real movement towards institutions and local self-government. But I am wholly at a loss to view Arabi's recent conduct as having any relation to them. He seems to me to represent at this time military violence and nothing else. I may, of course, be in error but it is not for want of taking impartial pains to inform myself by hearing all sides, and I have no reason in this case for self-mistrust beyond the measure in which a sober-minded man ought to carry it along with him in all questions and on all occasions . . . P.S.—Will you be so kind as to breakfast here on Thursday at 10? or on another Thursday? I will not come down upon you with Arabi!"

"We dined at the Admiralty, and at an evening party afterwards, W.S.B. showed us a telegram announcing the reconciliation of the Khedive and Arabi. 'They walked arm in arm to the station, Colvin and Malet in mourning!'."

On 4 July. "W.S.B. has seen John Bright who says there is to be no intervention."

5 July. But next evening at Lady May's, Sir Erskine told

me Alexandria is to be bombarded tomorrow. "W.S.B. does not seem to mind; says there must be bloodshed before things come right." Then on the 11th, "A smart party at Lady Margaret Beaumont's, but Lord Northbrook showed me a telegram which upset me, saying the bombardment is to be continued tomorrow." And the next evening, "to the Admiralty and Lady Waterford's. Everybody rejoicing over the bombardment".

Next day, the 13th: "Garden Party at Marlborough House. The Queen very grey, the Princess not so pretty as usual, in blue and white. The news of the massacre and burning of Alexandria cast rather a gloom over the party."

The next day lunching with ——, "I had a long talk with Chenery (editor of *The Times*) about Egypt. I asked him why he, so sympathetic to the National Movement in Egypt, allowed his Egyptian correspondent to supply so incorrect an account of all that was happening there. After we had talked awhile he said suddenly, 'I will tell you. It is because of the influence of the European bondholders over *The Times*.' When I told Sir William, he said, 'Don't tell that to Wilfrid Blunt or he will have sandwich-men walking with it down Piccadilly tomorrow'. Lord Elcho says Beauchamp Seymour should have been strung up at his own yard-arm for causing the bombardment. Everybody is rabid, hearing called about the streets, 'Arabi advancing on Alexandria'."

There is an interlude of another disturbed country.

18th. "To Ireland. Arrived at Roxborough, my old home. Seven soldiers in the harness room 'drinking whiskey out of teacups'."

22nd. "Corporal comes in to report three soldiers missing. Mr. Taylor came from Gort and sent off the two worst soldiers with forty rounds of ammunition on their backs, and the oldest soldier of all, who had married a young wife and brought her to Kilchriest, was ordered six months' pack drill for being absent without leave. The day Algernon went to Coole with his three cars of soldiers and police he left one young soldier to guard the house. This youngster, the minute they were out of sight, came in to ask leave to go to Kilchriest and on being refused he sulked and went to bed. Algernon loads his revolver and carries it in his hand when walking in the garden, and when he and Fanny go out for a stroll they have five soldiers after them. The

Land League is not so powerful they say, and money falling."

After a fortnight I was back in London.

August 4th. "We dined at the Admiralty; Lord Cork, Lord Hartington, Sir T. Brassey. Lord Northbrook got a telegram from Sir Beauchamp Seymour after dinner, only saying 'all quiet, and Lieutenant Dechair well treated at Cairo'. Lord Northbrook says the Bedouins are all with the Khedive."

In August we went to Ems, Sir William had been ordered there. We had only news of the war in the German papers. He and Sir George Elliot brought them to me every day to be translated. But it was not until we arrived in September (16th) at Vienna that "I heard of Arabi's surrender and of his being stoned; and none so poor to do him reverence".

In London on the 22nd September. "The Guards marched past on their return from Egypt, a great mob to receive them. Edward Dicey came to tea, thinks there is no chance now of executing Arabi, which he much regrets. He thinks there will be no trial as too much has come to light that would implicate the Sultan and the Khedive, but that he will be exiled to the Andaman Islands.

"Then Lord Elcho telling me how Gladstone was looking at the entry of the Guards on Sunday in high delight at being cheered. He went down into the street and said, 'Here I need no detectives, I am safe among the people, and I should be safe in Ireland.'

"I lunched at James' Street with the Blunts to meet Ninet, who has arrived from Egypt. He says Arabi was absolutely innocent and ignorant of the burning of Alexandria. That he never expected to beat the English but only to keep them from reaching Cairo until favourable intervention had taken place, and some diplomatic arrangements been made at Constantinople. He was quite calm all through the war. *Même gai* when he gave himself up to the English."

The Times had given a telegram from its correspondent in Egypt demanding "exemplary punishment" for certain of the prisoners, including Arabi.

We did not think this extreme view of Egyptian officials would be taken by the Government, but on the 21st[2] Hayward brought me a letter he had received from Gladstone in which he mentions "the possible necessity" of putting

[2] October.

Arabi to death. I was very much troubled by this and
Hayward was also troubled: he thought Gladstone meant
it. He had written to him putting the case for mercy. For
Hayward, like Kinglake and many others, thought the
"Rebels" had been but reformers, made rebels of through
our intervention, and that they were being hardly dealt
with now. But there was an outcry if a word for the enemy
was said. I felt that my husband's letters to *The Times*,
and our sympathy, had helped Arabi to believe he would
find help for the reforms he asked for. One evening at
Cairo, when Arabi had been made Minister of War, Lord
Houghton had at dinner, in his mischievous way, teased me
to "give him up", and I said, "No, I supported him when
he was down in the world and I can't forsake him now he
is gone up". But now it was the other way about.

I don't remember if it was at Hayward's suggestion that
I wrote an account of *Arabi and his Household,* putting his
case. People had been interested when I told them of my
visit to the wife and mother, and now I thought this might
gain a wider sympathy for them. I took it to friendly
Chenery, and on the 23rd it was printed in *The Times.*

It really was a success. Sir William was pleased when he
went to the Athenaeum because so many of his friends,
Dicey and Chenery among them, paid him compliments
about it; and especially because when someone had said it
was so good that people would think it was written by him,
W. E. Forster had growled, "I know you didn't write it
because I know you couldn't." And Hayward came on Sunday
saying he had dined at Downing Street the night before to
meet the Granvilles, and they were all talking about it, and
Gladstone had said it was "very touching". And Greenwood,
writing in his *St. James' Gazette,* had said it "made every
woman in England Arabi's friend".

A little later, W. dined at the Athenaeum to meet the
Duc de Broglie. "Goschen was there and said, talking of
Egypt, 'We have the wolf by the ears and cannot either kill
it or let it go,' and all agreed we are in a great mess." For
there was a change coming in man's opinions.

In October, Sir William writing to Sir H. Layard says
"after having been the cockshy of London society during the
summer and been heartily abused on all sides, I find myself
greeted as a prophet. This will please you, as you always
stuck to me through evil report. Even Chenery, who I met
in Paris, told me he thought I ought to be highly gratified

at having opened men's eyes to the iniquities perpetrated in Egypt with our connivance."

W.S.B., in his *Secret History* writes in May: "Gregory has failed us." But that was not so. He never to the last gave up his belief in Arabi and his desire for a National Government in Egypt. In a long letter to Sir Henry Layard which I have given in his *Autobiography* he says, "I view all these matters differently from Blunt who pushes things to first principles, but I think that Blunt deserves great credit for the bold and indefatigable manner in which he has fought this battle almost single-handed. He has fought for Egypt alone, I have fought for England first and for Egypt also, I can well remember how I stood alone, or very much alone, in Parliament on many similar cases which were called my crazes—the Union of the Roumanian provinces, the complete liberation of Servia, the increase of Greek Territory." Immediately after the defeat of Arabi and his friends he wrote to *The Times* on their behalf and Mr. Blunt, writing to me on 1 October 1882, refers to it: "I have been too wretched since the taking of Cairo to write. Sir William seemed to have deserted us, and though I knew you had not, I had not the courage to send you my grief. I think Sir William's letter now will do good, as it seems to have been very well received by nearly all the newspapers."

On the 8th, "We were at Mrs. Gladstone's reception, Sir Garnet Wolseley there, looking joyous and covered with orders, everyone worshipping him. Gladstone spoke of Egypt, said 'How are we to get peace and quiet there again?' I said, 'Do what you like so that you don't touch my friend Arabi'. 'Ah, we don't want to touch him; if the charges can't be proved against him you need have no fear,' he said. I said, 'I have no fear, none at all, now that he is to have a fair trial'. 'And what do you say to the Sultan? What are we to do with him?' 'Oh, what you like. I give him up to you,' I said. Gladstone laughed and said, 'Oh, I don't want him at all. I am much obliged to you for the present.' Forster told me my letter had produced a strong reaction in favour of Arabi."

15th. "At dinner at the Jeunes. Lord Houghton was quite rabid about Egypt; wishes Arabi and Blunt had been shot but said, 'I don't wonder so much at Lady Gregory, but I wonder why Bruce and Randolph Churchill should take up Arabi.' I said, 'He is the pebble from the brook they put in their sling to slay the giant'. Mr. Beaumont says Gladstone never authorised the bombardment, that a subordinate at the Admiralty gave the order.

"On to Lady Hayter's. O'Connor Power said he had just congratulated Wolseley and added, 'but I suppose you are tired of congratulations'. 'Not from my own countrymen,' said Sir Garnet. Mr. Burnaby had just come back from a meeting at Manchester which wound up with 'Three cheers for Arabi'."

19th. "Kinglake came to see me, says I am quite right in thinking Gladstone knows nothing about Egypt; that he always leaves foreign affairs to the Foreign Office, and at the time of the Alabama mess he was the only one in the Cabinet who knew nothing about it. And Lord Elcho came in, glad to have his boy back safe from Egypt."

21st. "Evening, Lady Marion Alford's. Gladstone there, says he has seen no reason to change his first opinion of Arabi, but reserves his judgment, but that I have not seen, as he has, his letters to the Sultan. He hopes I don't mean to defend Toulba, who told Sir Beauchamp Seymour there were no fortifications, and the others. But he consented to write his name on my fan next to Arabi's. Mrs. Gladstone came hurrying across the room to see what he was putting his name to!"

Directly after Tel el Kebir and the fall of Cairo, Mr. Blunt had written me October 1st, "I have taken the precaution of sending out a couple of lawyers to see what can be done. My fear, however, is that Arabi may refuse my assistance. He has probably been told that I am quite out of favour with the Government and that my advocacy would only damage his cause, and I am prepared for a refusal . . . Even should he accept, the trial fills me with apprehension. It will be all but impossible to get evidence in his favour, or to refute the evidence they will bring, and the result will be determined not by any law of justice, but by the humour of the hour in England, and considerations of policy. I am anxious, however, that Arabi should take no undignified line of defence and resort as little as possible to the subterfuges of the law in his defence. This I believe to be his only safety and it has been to prevent his getting into unworthy hands that I have pressed my help upon him . . . This doubt (of his accepting) prevents me from starting for Cairo. Personally, I would give a very great deal not to go. To see Cairo back in the hand of Sherif and the Controllers

would be gall and wormwood to me, and all our friends will
be in gaol or in hiding or afraid to speak to us. However,
it is no use thinking of that. We are the rearguard of a
beaten army where there are plenty of blows and no glory
to be won. As to Cairo, what I cared most for in it is gone
beyond recovery. Egypt may get a certain share of financial
ease but she will not get liberty, at least not in our time,
and the bloodless revolution, so nearly brought about, has
been drowned in blood."

On the 24th he came to see me with a letter from Mr.
Napier (who was with Mr. Broadley conducting the case
for Arabi's defence in Egypt) saying "all is going well except
the expenses which are very heavy". He decided, though
disliking the idea, to write to *The Times* asking for subscriptions. I translated and gave him Dante's lines on the
good deed that had helped Provanzano Salvini in Purgatory,
and he took it away and used it in his letter: —

> 'Twas when, he said, I lived in high estate
> I did not shrink and I did not disdain
> To stand a beggar at Siena's gate
> That freedom for my friend I thus might gain
> To rescue him who lay in prison sore
> The pangs of wounded pride I gladly bore.

He came next day (Sunday) to lunch, "anxious W. should
urge Chenery to put his appeal in tomorrow, as he hears
the Egyptian Government wish to compromise".

I wrote that evening, 3 October 1882, "You had not been
gone half an hour when I had a visit from Chenery, and it
is all right, the letter will be in tomorrow. He says you
should have as many Liberal members and rich men as
possible on your Committee. He was very nice and said
he would put anything in *The Times* that could help you.
He does not think people will subscribe until they know
the Government are not going to pay and says a question
should be asked at once. Lord Elcho has just been here and
will do this, but has begged me to look through the reports
of the Session to see if there are any answers of Dilke's or
Gladstone's his question can be founded on. We have not a
back number of *The Times* in the house, but I will manage
it somehow and am to let him know before 2 o'clock. Albert
Grey (M.P.) has also been here, astounded to hear you have

been paying. 'What a noble fellow!' he said. I think everyone will put pressure on the Government to pay to avoid giving subscriptions themselves."*

And Chenery was as good as his word, for he not only printed the appeal, but wrote a few lines in a leading article in favour of it—I remember Dicey expressing his puzzled astonishment at this in next Sunday's *Observer*. The letter brought little money but some good names, Sir Frederic Harrison, Randolph Churchill, George Meredith, Kinglake. One of the subscribers was General Gordon, who wrote with his subscription, "I suppose Government will not pay it, Arabi himself will repay it in a year's time". (And again W.S.B. had a letter from Gordon saying, "Don't mind being abused, don't mind being praised; you remain yourself after it all". But he refused to write about Egypt because he says it is in the hands of Providence and he won't interfere.)

And I wrote in November, "Lord Elcho's first act on succeeding to his fortune has been to send his £20 subscription. I am keeping it for you. I think he will be a loss in the House of Commons."

I see in a letter written on 25 February 1884: "I am so sorry for poor Chenery[3], he was such a good friend; don't you remember how well he behaved about the Defence Fund?" And in 1883, on another Sunday evening, I had written about some letter Mr. Blunt wanted to have published in *The Times*, "I have seen Chenery today, and talked the matter over with him, but Lord Dufferin has been beforehand with me (!) having already seen him, and —as if he knew what was coming—persuaded him that any attack on the Khedive would add immense difficulty to the action of the Government just now; that whatever his faults may be, he has promised to support English policy, and that for the interests of the Empire, it is much better to let bygones be bygones, and that *The Times* is such a very important paper that anything that appeared in it against

---

*In a [W.S.B.] letter written in 1907 I see "the pamphlet is extraordinarily amusing . . . I had quite forgotten the drawing up of that schedule, but now I have a faint memory of an early morning spent in a Club before the members had arrived with some sleepy and astonished waiters watching me go through files of *The Times*. I rather think Lord Wemyss had promised to do something for Egypt in the House."

[3] Chenery died on 11 February 1884.

Tewfik would at once be made use of by the French and within two hours be telegraphed to the Khedive who would believe the Government and *The Times* were the same thing; that this is the time of change in Egypt, a new man being sent there, and a new start made, and the less stir made about what had already occurred there the better. This is also Lord Granville's view.

"Poor Chenery then had to listen to my appeal as to whether Arabi's name was never to be cleared from the slur cast upon it by Gladstone and Dilke in the House and never withdrawn, just to save the Khedive who no one has any opinion of; and he became agitated after reading your statement, and said that if it were true, the Khedive ought to be hanged; but that at the same time, for the reasons given before, he is very doubtful as to whether he ought to publish it, even as a letter from you. In the end he said that if you would modify as far as possible the personal attack on the Khedive and add a paragraph laying the crime more on the palace party than on him, and make it as much as possible a defence of Arabi rather than an indictment of Tewfik, he would see if he could publish it, though not binding himself by a promise, and if he could not, would return it to you in time to publish elsewhere, as I told him it must be out by the 11th. He was very kind and I think was really anxious to be amiable, and spoke most affectionately of you, and I don't blame him for not wishing to quarrel with the Government. Indeed, I was hopeless from the time I heard Lord D. had taken him in hand—what are we against him?

> Don't seek to hinder him
> Or to bewilder him.
> Sure he's a pilgrim
> From the Blarney Stone!

Chenery talked of your publishing it as a little pamphlet, but that was, of course, to prevent the little foundling being laid on his own doorstep."

But in the end, Mr. Blunt decided to pay the entire cost of the defence, some £3,000, having, as I believe, by his intervention saved Arabi's life.

And as the winter went on, and the expedition to the Soudan came as the war's aftermath, there were many who were sorry we had ever invaded Egypt. My notes and letters give echoes of this—"Sir Thomas Brassey, just back from

Egypt, says there is only a choice between annexation and
the return of Arabi". "Gladstone is determined to scuttle
out of Egypt (W.S.B. is told) and to resign if there is an
outcry. But he expects his colleagues to resign with him,
and this they won't do, as so many of them know they would
never get office again."

Then later, "We met Henry Monck at dinner. He had
been at Tel-el-Kebir, and had kept guard for twenty-four
hours over Arabi, who spent the whole night in prayer."
"I had a visit from Lord Wemyss in great distress, his son
having been ordered off to the Soudan. He is furious with
Gladstone—as I wrote to W.S.B., he is equally anxious to
smash Gladstone and the Mahdi." "W. dined at the Penders
to meet Hassam Fehmy, the Turkish envoy. A large party,
he sat next to Lord Derby. All crying out for Khartoum to
fall, with no idea what can be done then. Hobart Pasha, in
despair, saying they are bringing down the whole Mohammedan world on Egypt." And then on February 5th [(or
3rd)]: "I went down Sloane Street to buy some flowers, and
presently heard a boy shouting 'Fall of Khartoum—General
Gordon a prisoner!' I thought at first Wolseley had taken
him prisoner, so likely had it seemed he would have to do
so; but it is the Mahdi who has triumphed." Then on the
11th came news of Gordon's death.

A fortnight later we dined at Thomson Hankey's to meet
Gladstone. "After dinner asked William to sit with him in
the back drawing-room and talk about Aristophanes, who
he thinks above Shakespeare and above Molière in wit, and
then said, 'What do you think about Egypt?'

"W. 'I think it is a very serious matter.'

"G. 'Very serious indeed, but pray tell me, if you were
in Parliament, what line you would take?'

"W. 'First of all I would not go to Khartoum.'

"G. 'Will you give me your reasons for that?'

"W. 'First of all, there would be great difficulty in taking
it, you will want siege guns and it is strongly fortified,
and will be strongly defended.'

"G. 'Well, from the information we have received from
Lord Wolseley, I do not think the difficulty will be as
great as you anticipate, though I do not think it can be
taken till next year.'

"W. 'Then you have General dysentery, General fever,
and General ophthalmia fighting against you, and it seems
to me an immense waste of money and life and a foolish

one in view of all various other complications, and then comes my chief reason, what are you to do with it when you get it?'

"G. 'Ah, now you have hit it, that is indeed the difficulty; all the others are as child's play compared with this.'

"W. 'But when you have taken Berber, and after all these victories would it not be possible to negotiate with the Mahdi?'

"G. 'I would to God it might be done, but what do we know about him? Where can we find out his views and aims, and how can we treat with him?'

"W. 'Of course, Lord Wolseley can't do so, while he is holding a sword to his throat, but other means might be found.'

"G. 'But where are we to find a man who knows him and his people who would treat with him and yet be true to us?'

"W. 'There is such a man to be found.'

"G. 'Where? I suppose (laughing) you don't mean Blunt?'

"W. 'No, I don't mean Blunt—I mean Arabi.'

"G. 'But you and I differ diametrically in opinion about Arabi. You believe him to be a good man. I believe him to be a consummate blackguard.'

"W. 'There you are entirely mistaken. I believe him to be a God-fearing, upright man, and my confidence in him has never been shaken.'

"G. 'But I have had written proof in my hand that he tried to barter away the liberties of his country to the Sultan, the documents were signed by himself.'

"W. 'At what time?'

"G. 'About three weeks before the war.'

"W. 'I can well understand that; at that time he was driven by our interference into the Sultan's arms—who after all was his Sovereign; but I believe him, nonetheless, to be entirely worthy of confidence.'

"G. 'God knows, I wish I could believe that too—and I would *jump at him*.'

"And then Thomson Hankey, who had twice already tried to get him away, came in again and said he must not stay any longer.

"Mrs. Hankey told me she had noticed a yellow flag half-mast high at the Chinese Embassy and asked what it was. They told her it was mourning for Gordon—the only sign of mourning in all London."

We were away in Paris for a fortnight and when we came

back, March 11th, W. went to the Athenaeum to hear the news; found the Soudan completely forgotten. Who knows or cares whether they are going to Khartoum? And everyone excited as to the probability of war with Russia.

That was the end of my essay in politics, for though Ireland is always with me, and I first feared and then became reconciled to, and now hope to see even a greater independence than Home Rule, my saying has been long, "I am not fighting for it, but preparing for it". And that has been my purpose in my work for establishing a National Theatre, and for the revival of the language, and in making better known the heroic tales of Ireland. For whatever political inclination or energy was born with me may have run its course in that Egyptian year and worn itself out; or it may be that I saw too much of the inside, the tangled threads of diplomacy, the driving forces behind politicians. But I am glad to have been in that fight for freedom, and glad my husband took freedom's side, it was of a piece with his nature. And I honour Wilfrid Blunt for his generous and undying devotion to the cause he had taken up. (I wrote to him in 1912, "I have been reading *Gordon at Khartoum*[4] and you may imagine how it recalled those days and almost rekindled the fire of indignation and enthusiasm. But not quite, for so many who vexed one are gone. Malet and Colvin and Moberly Bell and Granville and the G.O.M., and one can't feel anger or triumph in a graveyard . . . I feel *The Wind and the Whirlwind*[5] is the real monument of that time.") And I like to remember also that I was of some service later on in making easier the circumstances of Arabi and his friends.

The terms of the compromise of the trial had not been put in writing, and the Egyptian Government had given but a bare living allowance to the exiles, and had seized small properties they owned. I had written to Mr. Blunt,

3, St. George's Place,
28 February 1883

"Sir William has had a very nice letter from the Governor of Ceylon, Sir James Longden, saying he thinks the allowance of £1 per day settled by the Egyptian Government 'painfully insufficient' and has written to Lord Derby to say so, and

[4] Blunt's *Gordon at Khartoum* was published by Stephen Swift & Co., London 1912.

[5] A volume of poetry by Blunt, published in 1883 by Kegan Paul, Trench & Co., London.

hopes Sir William will support him. I have copied the letter and sent it to Chenery, not for publication, but to show he will be justified in supporting Arabi's claim."

And again in July 1885, "My hopes are limited to an increase of allowance to the exiles, so please be practical and try what you can do". He had tried for this, and Sir William had written, both to the papers, and privately to members of the Government, on their behalf, but all our efforts had been in vain. I see in a letter of mine to Mr. Blunt, "I wish for poor Chenery's help now. I was looking yesterday at his last letter to me, in which he says, 'If the exiles' allowance is not increased it will be shameful,' so he would have taken a strong line."

On 2 February 1886, I wrote to W.S.B. from Government House, Madras: "This is our last day in India. At Calcutta we spent a week with the Dufferins before they left for Burma, and came in for all the gaieties given in honour of the foreign officers. Lord D. is taking India very seriously. I was generally next him at meal times, and used to begin some light conversation but he always went back to Indian politics, and was so anxious to know what we had heard and learned as we came along. And then he would go to Sir William afterwards to know if what I had been saying was quite accurate! We had a great fight about Egypt one evening, but at the end he volunteered to look into the question of the exiles' allowance, if I send him the papers about it, so I hope he will do something for them."

So when I went on to Ceylon and saw the exiles, I went through their household accounts with their wives and with English officials, and wrote a statement and sent it to Lord Dufferin.

I heard nothing more for a long time. But at last I wrote on 12 June 1886: "I dined at Miss Cohen's, a very good dinner and a very pretty woman . . . Just as I was going away, Sir Julian Pauncefote came over to tell me that at last, after such long efforts, the exiles have been granted some more money—in consequence of the recommendation of the Viceroy of India."

IV

FOLKLORE IN POLITICS:
MR. GLADSTONE AND IRELAND

WHEN, AS has happened, I have been reproached for having cast a slur on Ireland in my little comedy *Spreading the News,* I have thought how little such a theme can lay claim to any one home above another, and that the imaginary village of Cloon, where I lay the scene, might just as well be Piccadilly. There is as much folk-lore in London as elsewhere, as much myth in the making, myth that is always gathering in the air, always ready to descend upon, to cling around any high head. Was not Saul of the Witch of Endor and the Javelins shoulder high above the crowd? And, as I have said in my *Kiltartan History Book*—history as it is made by the people—while Charlemagne's height has grown through the ages beyond the height of man, and while his years are counted by centuries—"he is three hundred years old and when will he weary of war?" And Tradition in its caprice has turned the King of highly civilised Crete into a murderous tyrant owning a monster and labyrinth; while Mannanan, the great Sea-God of ancient Ireland, is transformed to a juggler doing tricks, and has been even hunted in the shape of a hare. O'Connell has already become the centre of grotesque legend, has been given a miraculous birth, is being endowed with the powers of a Saint.

I had not made this study or reflection in the years when Mr. Gladstone's Home Rule Bill was the cause of so great indignation, when he himself was looked upon as the Arch-enemy of the settled order. But of late, in looking through old letters, recalling old memories, I see that even then, myth was beginning to transform that militant and dominating figure, and may even yet, passing beyond those brilliant and forgetful drawing-rooms, be transfiguring his name in the little streets and lanes. That name may certainly in Ireland be some day joined with some strange shape or legend, for if our landlords abhorred him as the enemy of their order, the people learned to do so later as the destroyer of their leader. And so I have been told, "At the time of his death he had it on his mind that it was he threw the first stone at Parnell, and he confessed that, and was very sorry for it. But sure, there's no one can stand all through. Look at Solomon that had ten-hundred wives and some of them the finest of women, and that spent all the money laid up by Father David. And Gladstone encouraged Garibaldi the time he attacked the Vatican, and gave him arms. Parnell charged him with that, one time in the House of Commons, and said he had the documents, and he hadn't a word to say. But he was sorry for Parnell's death; and what was the use of that when they had his heart broke?"

I never saw much of Mr. Gladstone or had any intimate talk with him. When I first met him, pallid and his eyes aflame, there had come to my mind a thought of one Dante had met in his dream, and who was but a spirit and a shadow although yet dwelling upon earth.

"E mangia, e beve, e dorme, e veste panni."—And eats and drinks and sleeps and puts on clothes.—My husband had long known him but their chief bond was their intensity of interest in the Greek writers. I possess a postcard of his to my husband in reference to some controversy (May 1891) over a picture by Waterhouse in which the Sirens, as well as I remember, were represented by claws. "I entirely agree that there was no justification for identifying Sirens and Harpies, not only opposites but contradictions. Indeed, I think the Circe open to question on the ground that all golden hair in Homer is Hellenic. Circe, however, is Eastern rather than Southern, according to my own view of the geography." They always seemed glad to meet each other, I have already given a word of Gladstone's as to his pleasure in my husband's company, and I see in the postscript to a letter from Sir William to Sir Henry Layard, "Such a pleasant evening at Grillions. Sat next to Gladstone and we nearly kissed at parting. He is a marvel in conversation."

He was interested in so many things and could always turn the tide away from politics and this was often. One day at Dalmeny, during a Midlothian campaign, he would talk of nothing but the volcanic eruptions in Krakatoa, until at last, when W. said how fine it was of France sending a scientific expedition to investigate its cause, he quickly changed the subject, taking this perhaps as either a suggestion or a reproach. And Wilfrid Blunt, while his antagonist in Egyptian matters, wrote me of having met him at dinner, 'He is certainly in great form, and we had a debate on the

origin of the Arabian horse in which he displayed considerable research of an archaeological kind'."

At that dinner at the Hankey's, where he talked to us
about Egypt, he had made an outcry when the pancakes
were handed round (it was Shrove Tuesday) because the
sugar handed with them was white and not brown and he
had always been used to brown sugar with Shrove Tuesday
pancakes—(somebody whispered, it may have been myself,
that he was recalling the days when he had been a slave
owner). His indignation was loud and almost shrill. At last
Mrs. Hankey pacified him, promising to ask him to dinner
and give him the proper sugar when next Shrove Tuesday
came.

I think that power of rousing his own indignation,
whether real or unreal, was a chief foundation of his power.
One idle evening I was offered a place in the Speaker's
Gallery. The House was in Committee on the Franchise
Bill. The speeches did not interest me. Mrs. Gladstone
came into the Gallery and listened for a little time, and kept
whispering to me, "Can you see Mr. Gladstone?" "Is there
any chance he will speak?" "I want to get him to come and
have a cup of tea with Lady May. Do you think he has
been out for tea?" At last she tired of waiting, saw he could
not leave and thought 'it unlikely he would speak and
went away.

A little later some M.P., I think a Mr. Woodall, stood up
and proposed that a clause giving the franchise to women
should be added to the Bill. He made a short speech; it
seemed reasonable. I was not interested in votes for women,
but I began to think it might be a useful measure. Then
Gladstone got up. He was silent for a moment and then
I felt how his eyes gave out flames as he asked the House
if they were fully aware of what had happened. That at
this late hour of the night, and almost at the end of the
Session, an honourable member had, under the disguise of
an ordinary amendment in Committee, made a proposal
which, if adopted, would change the entire character of
England, the sanctity of the home. His whole figure seemed
shaken with indignation. When he sat down I found myself
thinking, "What a very wicked man Mr. Woodall must be
to have thought of doing such a dreadful thing!" Of course,
the amendment was not even discussed after that. I met
Mrs. Gladstone the next evening and said, "You went away
just too soon," and she said, in a heartbroken voice, "Oh, I

shall never get over it!" And yet when I had read the report of the speech it had seemed to contain nothing at all of note.

And I see in a letter of mine to Sir Henry Layard in December 1893, "On my last Tuesday in London I had a telegram from Miss Peel asking if I would like a place in their Gallery to hear the Navy Debate; so I went and heard Gladstone speak. It was a delight at the moment to hear such a fine oration, his voice so clear and melodious, and to see his fiery simulated indignation as he shook his fist at the Opposition, I saw no sign of age or failing power. I never heard him speak better. There was, of course, *nothing* in his fine sentences. I dined that night at Sir Alfred Lyall's, and everyone asked what he had said, and they suspected I had not listened when I told them he had only abused the Opposition for asking inconvenient questions and trying to force the House of Commons to interfere with the Executive, and had said they should know as much as was good for them in another three months: but I read his speech in *The Times* next day, and that was the whole summary."

And this is yet another impression of a debate on some forgotten controversy: 5 May 1888. "I went in the afternoon to the House of Commons, taking some friends, and when the questions were over I went in to have tea with Mrs. Peel, and fortunately came back, though nothing interesting was expected, and Mrs. Gladstone, who was in the Gallery, said there was no chance of her husband speaking. However, Tim Healy got up and attacked the Government for having given precedence to the King-Harman Salary Bill over that for National Defence the night before, which he compared to the boys in Oliver Twist being given a spoonful of treacle before they were allowed to touch their dinner. He spoke with great fluency and ease, his hands in his pockets, and the House filled while he was on his legs. Goschen got up to answer him, he was unprepared, and spoke with hesitation, and has not a good delivery. His contention was that King-Harman was the servant of the country, which benefited by his services, and that though the state of public business last year was such that they could not attempt to bring in the Bill, yet they felt themselves nonetheless bound to do so as soon as they found it practicable. Gladstone all this time was working himself up and the moment Goschen sat down he jumped up and said he quite denied the Chancellor of the Exchequer's premises that the country benefited by King-Harman's services, he thought on the contrary they were hurtful to the nation, while his appointment was a standing insult to the people of Ireland (tremendous applause). He also accused the Government of having delayed the passage of the Bill themselves by their speeches. This was contradicted, he appealed to Mr. Heneage as his authority. He, however, denied having said the Government made speeches,—he had only said they might have forced the measure through at half past ten if they had chosen; upon which Balfour said, 'Oh, now I see what is called obstruction. It is not our putting on the Closure at the end of an hour and a half.'

"Gladstone's voice was as clear and flexible as ever, and his speech as unhesitating, but he openly spoke for the Irish members, turning to them for applause at every point, and while Healy was speaking he leaned forward and listened with rapt attention, whereas during the other speeches he shut his eyes and folded his arms or read the question paper. Balfour got up to answer him and I could understand how the Irish members hate him, he looked so spruce and trim and smiling and so completely at his ease as he leaned against the table looking down on the G.O.M. opposite and saying in a caressing and bantering way that he was not surprised to find the Right Honourable Gentleman did not consider King-Harman's services beneficial—he was of the opinion that the members of the Opposition never did think the Government measures of benefit. For instance, when he had been in opposition he had never thought the services of the Rt. Hon. Gentleman were for the good of the country 'he thought so himself but he was mistaken, we all thought him mistaken, but we never came down to the House and moved the reduction of his salary on that account.' The G.O.M. grew first green and then black with fury, bending his head lower and lower, and Mrs. Gladstone in the Gallery looked no better pleased. Then John Morley got up and made a good point against the Government, saying they had declared they had felt in honour bound last year to bring the Bill in, but if that were the case, how was it that King-Harman in addressing his constituents at Margate last summer had 'thanked his God that he was not as the Irish Members were, who were paid by the maid-servants of New York—he served and was going to serve his country for nothing'. Great cheers, of course, at this. However, the Government victory in the division (on some side issue) restored their cheerfulness."

November, 1888: "Childers came to see me and told me of a speech at the Birmingham meeting, the enthusiasm wonderful and the stillness so great all through Gladstone's long speech that you hear a pin drop, but the speech itself disappointing, the G.O.M. having left out many things he meant to say. He said afterwards the effort of making such an enormous multitude hear had driven them from him."

He was well loved and well hated, and so as it happens to his like, folk-lore began to gather not only around him but about his house—and has not the wife of our own great Finn been turned in the stories to an enchanted faun? There were anecdotes always going around. One was that, anxious always about his comfort and at the same time, a prudent housekeeper, she made the hot tea he liked to have on his late return from the House serve a double purpose by keeping it in the jar that warmed his sheets; another that she had found some sandwiches at an evening party that he would enjoy and had put them in the bosom of her dress until the smarting of the mustard had forced her to disclose them.

Her care was for his ease of mind, as well as of body. Goschen told a story of Gladstone being hooted at Chester and that she had said, consolingly, "Never mind William, they are only gentlemen". I wrote on 3 October 1887, to Paul Harvey, "E.L.[1] had been at Hawarden two hours after the news of Mitchelstown arrived (September 1887, where the police had broken up a meeting by firing on the people, killing a man and wounding several). Gladstone was furious with rage till Mrs. Gladstone persuaded him to go and calm himself by cutting down a tree. Presently she opened a telegram which had just arrived and began wringing her hands and wailing, it was from Sir William Harcourt and E. asked leave to see it—'Pall Mall[2] reports bloody deeds going on in Ireland, you must go over at once' upon which she began to laugh and told Mrs. G. as the *Pall Mall* was the only authority, she need not be so unhappy." And I wrote elsewhere: "Mr. Blunt tells me when Lord W.[3] was at Hawarden, Lord Granville arrived unexpectedly on a cold day, all muffled and shivering. Mr. G. was out but Mrs. G. at once declared he must be put into a room with

[1] Enid, wife of Sir Henry Layard.
[2] *The Pall Mall Gazette.*
[3] Probably Lord Wentworth, afterwards Lord Lovelace, Blunt's brother-in-law.

a fire, and popped him into her own bedroom while she
went to prepare another for him. The G.O.M. coming in,
found the room occupied by Lord Granville, and Mrs.
Gladstone busy with a warming pan in the other. He
naturally looked astonished but Mrs. G., with charming
simplicity, thrust the warming pan into his hand and saying,
'Now William, you must keep it moving or it will burn a
hole in the sheets,' disappeared." Like the miracles worked
by St. Catherine herself, or attached to her by the folk,
all anecdotes were on the kindly side.

"E.L. told me she had taken a Dutch lady to a garden
party at Hawarden, 'A tree in the garden had been hung with
signed photographs of Mr. Gladstone to be sold for some
charity or benefit, but no one had taken notice of them
until our friend caught sight of them and was delighted at
being allowed to buy several as presents for friends in
Holland. Then others began to buy them, till the tree was
cleared, and when we were leaving, Mrs. Gladstone grasped
my hand and said, "That dear Dutch lady!".' She told
another friend that she had not known her husband nervous
except on the day Parnell was coming to Hawarden; and
yet another has heard there had been consternation in the
Hawarden household when Parnell was late for dinner and
didn't turn up at all for breakfast." It seemed as if she
represented the necessary reaction from his scathing intensity; no one was sure if her irrelevancies and simplicity
were natural or assumed. A country niece of Kinglake's
pleased him by summing up her impressions, "She has
always ends to the fingers of her gloves". The Hankeys
showed me a card in answer to a dinner invitation which
"having no date, or address, heading or signature, must
be from Catherine".

Mr. Gladstone's conversion or surrender to Parnell was
said to be sudden, but it had been growing, foreshadowed
for a while. My husband says in a letter to Sir H. Layard
in 3 September 1886, "I remember writing to you in
November 1882 an account of a conversation I had with him
at Lady Marion Alford's, in which he said, after extolling
Parnell in the highest degree, that he thought him the
ablest leader the Irish party had ever had. 'What, greater
than O'Connell?' said I. 'Well, perhaps not a greater man
than O'Connell, but I think the world will say by the
beginning of the next century that Parnell is a *more*

successful leader than O'Connell' was the answer." And yet Sir Algernon West, his private secretary, has written of him, "He thought O'Connell, except perhaps Mirabeau, the greatest demagogue that ever lived, and in that way not inferior even to Bright". And though I have not found the letter to Sir H. Layard my husband writes of, there is one to Lady Dartrey written but a few days after that conversation, on 22 November 1882 ("A year of sensational murders. One of the darkest periods of the land agitation in Ireland")*. I asked him what he thought of the news from Ireland. He replied, 'Good, decidedly good'. He proceeded to say that he was 'convinced the spirit of insubordination was fast subsiding in every quarter, and that before long tranquility would prevail. He was, however, perfectly prepared to hear at any moment of desperate outrages, the last struggle of the secret societies who were determined to retain their power of terror.' 'We must only meet these as best we can.' And strange enough, the following evening came the telegram on the attempt on Judge Lawson, to be followed by these other outrages. He then went on and said, 'it is clear from the attitude of the Irish members, especially of Parnell, that they know the game is up. He proceeded to the most enthusiastic eulogium on Parnell—he had most honourably fulfilled every intimation (not compact) he had given on being released from prison, and would do all in his power to restore tranquility. It was true that now and then he was forced to take a strong line in the House, but they quite understood his position and attached no importance to it . . . His strength of character and powerful grasp of a subject were astonishing, and he had great nobility of disposition. 'Do you know,' he said, 'he sent me word and offered to put the proposal in writing that if I thought it right he should do so, he would at once retire from Parliament'."

I remember that conversation and that my husband, as we came home, told me of it and that Gladstone had said with emphasis, "I cannot tell you how much I feel for *poor Parnell*".

But the "tranquility" of Gladstone's forecast was a long time on the road, and three years later, in June 1885, my husband says in a letter to Sir H. Layard from Dublin, "I have come up to be present at the swearing in of my old

*Barry O'Brien: *Life of Charles Stewart Parnell*, 1846-1891, London, Smith, Elder, 1898.

chief, Lord Carnarvon, as Lord Lieutenant. Poor fellow, he
is like the young bear with all his troubles before him . . .
What can he do? His chief has abandoned the renewal of
the Crimes Act, the only safeguard of the country, and he
will have, tied hand and foot powerless, to resist the organization which is in full swing, directed against property and
the British connection. Although Ireland is apparently
quiet, it is so for two reasons, first that the Nationalist
party with its committee in every district, is supreme. There
is no resistance to its decree. No man dare take a farm or
enter into an agreement with his landlord without the
assent of these bodies. If a farm falls vacant, though there be
twenty candidates for it, none may approach it unless the
rent be lowered to a scale which satisfied the notion of the
National League committee . . . the life of any offender
against the edict would not be worth a week's purchase."

And he writes to Sir Henry from Government House,
Calcutta, 2 February 1886, on the news that Gladstone had
lately come into power, but with Parnell holding its balance
is giving in to Parnell's demands. "This last episode of Gladstone's traitorism has utterly overwhelmed me. Dufferin
showed me a drawing of his house at Clandeboye today and
said, 'I had hoped to have ended my days there. I suppose it
will not be mine to enter even.' As to the alternatives of
Dynamite and Fenianism instead of Parnellism I do not fear
this one bit. They have tried them often enough already and
can any Fenianism be worse than the present unpunished
anarchy?"

Yet he and Lord Dufferin had always been liberal landlords, and as to my husband, he had been a land reformer
before Mr. Gladstone, for in 1886 he had joined with Sir
C. O'Loughlin in drawing up a Bill to give increased
stability of tenure to Ireland tenants. It proposed to discourage annual lettings and work for the granting of leases.
Where there was no written contract a lease of twenty-one
years was to be presumed, and compensation in case of
eviction of a yearly tenant was to be given, except in cases
of non-payment of rent. The Tenants' Associations of the
time were satisfied with it. He says in his *Autobiography*,
"Before I introduced the Bill I met Mr. Gladstone going out
of the House and I besought him to stay and hear what I
had to say, and to help me if he approved. He said, 'let me
look at your Bill,' and he ran his eye over the heading of
the clauses. 'Why you want,' said he, 'to interfere with the

management of a man's own property. I will have nothing
to do with it,' ejaculating these words with the greatest
emphasis. We failed in making any way with the Bill."

And Lord Dufferin had in 1854 brought in a Bill for the
compensation of tenants for improvements made by them,
and this also had failed to pass through the House. But now
far more than what they had asked was being given, as the
Nationalist Barry O'Brien says in his *Life of Parnell,*
"wrenched from the government by one of the most lawless
movements which had ever convulsed any country".

It was not for themselves alone they were alarmed; Lord
Dufferin writing after the defeat of the Home Rule Bill
(to Sir James Stephen) says, "had it gone the other way I
and every Irishman in my position would have been completely ruined, though that would have been an insignifi-
cant result in comparison with the ruin of the country itself
and for that matter of England too."

These may have been needless fears; but when such men
entertained them it is no wonder that London society in a
mass gave way to an exaggeration that leads, as I have said,
to the making of myths.

I, myself, no less indignant, wrote to Sir Mountstuart
Grant Duff from Ceylon on 19 March 1886, "We were met
on our return from a delightful week in the jungle two days
ago by the telegram announcing Gladstone's scheme of
expropriation," (probably a forecast of the Bill being prepared for the buying out of Irish landlords and creating a
peasant proprietory), "from the shock of which we have
hardly yet recovered . . . We met in the jungle an old man
who is wonderfully like *the* G.O.M. though he appears in
Society not only without a shirt collar but without a shirt,
his costume consisting of an immense Kandian hat and a
cloth round his waist. He is a real old schemer and was
known to be concerned in so many highway robberies that
he was appointed Head Man (I had almost written Prime
Minister) of the village, and since then he draws the line
at robbery and only exacts blackmail. Sir Arthur Gordon
was so much struck with him that when visiting the district
he had three chairs carried after him and placed for himself,
the Government Agent—and Gladstone! leaving everyone
else standing including Miss Shaw Lefevre who was directed
to 'try and sketch that noble head upon that noble neck'.
The consequence was that as soon as the Governor left, old
Gladstone took advantage of having been seen on such

intimate terms with his Excellency and told the villagers that the Governor had left orders they were without delay to clear the bed of a tank in the district. And as soon as they had gone so he sowed it with a fine crop of paddy for himself which we saw flourishing."

And I wrote to him from London in May, for unconsciously I had begun to learn the art of a folklorist, "Oh the turmoil of politics here! In three days comes the reading of the (Home Rule) Bill, and you may imagine the excitement we are in. Gladstone's manifesto has caused fury, not only among the "class" attacked, but the Irish members themselves say he has ruined their cause by his violence, and even Lord Northbrook said to Sir William 'it is the manifesto of a pirate who is going to blow up his ship'. The only person I have heard of as disinterestedly in favour of the Bill is Lowell, and he has been much cooled in his ardour by Healy saying incautiously to him, 'When we are governing Ireland our first Act will be to pass an Alien Bill to keep out those d - - - d Irish Americans!' We poor landlords with 'the sand running in the hour-glass' are resolved at least to die game. And though for peace sake one would gladly take any small sum and be sure of it, yet one has a feeling against selling one's child's birthright for a mess of hasty-pudding. Someone said to Lady Cook, 'You must confess, Gladstone is a Heaven-born statesman'. Then she said, 'I hope it will be a long time before Heaven is in the family way again!'."

21 May 1886. "Oh, how peaceful the thought of Madras is, with the flowers and the Southern Cross! and what a turmoil everything is in here. I fancy the tone of feeling in London must be something like that which prevailed in India toward the end of Lord Ripon's administration; there is such a bitterness of feeling and violence of speech. It was said a few days ago that Lord Ormond, meeting Lord Spencer in the street, refused to shake hands with him and said, 'You are a traitor and a liar'; and though this has been denied, it was believed and *applauded* for two days. Lord Justice Bowen says (with judicial calmness) of the G.O.M., 'He combines the irregularities of David with the inaccuracies of Ananias and Saphira'. Mrs. Gladstone, meanwhile, is serene, and meeting Lady Stanley at Marshall and Snelgrove's a few days ago, said, 'Mr. Gladstone is in wonderful health and spirits and carrying all before him. What a giant he is! People call him the Great Magician now.' Lady Stanley, his warm supporter of old, and even her son Lyulph, have turned

against him. She says, 'For the first time in the history of the world, the Stanley family are of one mind'. I was sitting next a German doctor at dinner the other night who boasted that he had restored Gladstone's voice last year. I asked if he would now find something to take it away. This, as Mr. Beaumont said, was a mild and ladylike wish, but the Duchess who is rabid, said, 'Oh, if we could find him out or insult him!'. Even our gentle Kinglake is roused to violence, though with him it is graceful violence. 'Imagine the folly,' he says, 'of that man proposing to cut a limb off the Empire and to trust to Parnell to sew it on again. He is a great advocate, and his name on a brief gives a chance of success to any case, otherwise no one would have thought seriously of the Bill for a moment'; while he accounts for the support still given to Gladstone in the country by the fact that the English people love to see anyone doing mischief. I am afraid from whatever cause it may be, the new voters will support him. I hear that in the country Joe Chamberlain and his cow are quite forgotten and Gladstone's name is the only one to conjure with. Mr. Mitchell Henry is treasuring a quotation to bring out about a certain King. When the people cried out, 'This is the voice of a God'— and what happened afterwards. Dilke is supposed to be sitting on a fence and can't decide whether to alight in Gladstone's office yard or Chamberlain's three acres. Somebody once said, 'A majority is sure to be wrong,' and I think it is that principle that will give the Ministry a majority in the country now.

"Lord Rosebery (then Minister of Foreign Affairs) being asked his real opinion of the Irish question said, 'I know nothing at all about Ireland. It is not a foreign country.'

"I see a letter of mine at this time to Lord Dufferin quoted in his *Life*: "At this moment no one will think or speak of any other subject than Ireland . . . you can hardly imagine the bitterness of feeling and of speech that prevail. If there is any act of absolutism or illegality that your Government wishes to commit, now is your time, for India is forgotten for the moment.' (Very spirited advice to give a Viceroy.)"

To Sir M. E. Grant Duff.

May. "We dined at the Wemysses'. Only Laurence Oliphant, Layards and ourselves, very pleasant. Sir Henry had been at a dinner where Gladstone did nothing but abuse Huxley about the scorpion, which he has discovered interferes with the Book of Genesis. 'D - - n his Genesis,' said Huxley aside, 'What I should like to see is his Exodus,' and so would many."

14 May 1886. "This is such an exciting week that I think I must write, though by the time this arrives all will be old history, and Gladstone may have failed and strangled himself in his own shirtcollar with rage, as some of his most attached friends seem to hope he will do.

"For the last two or three days before the opening of the Debate nothing was talked of but the probabilities as to whether Chamberlain would return to his allegiance or not. Labouchere was chosen as the go-between, and negotiated terms between the two statesmen, 'their country's pride' and was able to announce to Joe that G.O.M. had given way on all points and that the Irish members were to remain in the House of Commons.

"So, in the course of Gladstone's speech, Joe found he had been 'jockeyed' as he expresses it, to his infinite disgust, as he had telegraphed to a friend 'complete surrender', and the *Birmingham Post*, his organ, had published 'Triumph of Mr. Chamberlain'. His disgust was only equalled by that of Labouchere who says, 'This is my reward for trying to make terms between an honest patriot and a d - - d thief'. Gladstone shook his fist and banged his despatch box with rage at Lord Hartington during his speech and Lord H. actually trembled but spoke well afterwards. Mitchell Henry gave me this account of the debate. The day before yesterday Labouchere was talking with a Member who extolled Gladstone's greatness. 'Yes,' drawled Labby, 'no doubt he is a great statesman, a great orator and still greater in his piety, but I would rather not have him against me at whist. He would always have three aces up his sleeve and he would persuade himself and try to persuade me that they had been placed there by the Holy Ghost.' Laurence Oliphant, to whom I told this last night (and who begged me, when writing, to remember him most kindly to you), said this was the best instantaneous photograph of Gladstone he had ever heard of."

An undated half-sheet of a letter to H.P.H.[5] says (probably of a Foreign Office party): ". . . And diamonds and Royalties, and Lord Wolseley and John Morley jammed together (but not addressing one another) and Goschen and Chamberlain

[5] H. P. Harvey.

just come from dining with Gladstone (Chamberlain says
he has been poisoned by the 'dear old gentleman's champagne') and all the pomps and vanities that the heart of man
or woman could desire . . . At dinner on Monday I was next
Lord Wolseley, who is very strong on the Irish question,
says the Orangemen would sweep all the rest of Ireland,
and that they would be 'craven cowards' if they did not
fight against Nationalist rule. He *hates* Gladstone now, who
gave him his peerage and pampered him . . ."

To Grant Duff: "Chamberlain now will accept no terms.
'I have my foot on his neck,' he says, 'and I mean to keep it
there'. Mrs. Gladstone appeals for Divine aid, if the congregation of a London Church is to be believed in stating that
a little time ago this notice was given by the clergyman, 'The
wife of an eminent statesman requests that prayer may be
made that strength may be vouchsafed to her husband to
enable him to tread in the footsteps of Nehemiah'. Bibles
were instantly turned over and the allusion to the repartition
of land recognised in Nehemiah V. 7-13 (Then I consulted
with myself, and I rebuked the nobles and the rulers and
said unto them, 'You exact usury, every one of his brothers'.
And I set a great assembly against them . . . And I said unto
them 'restore, I pray, you to them even this day their lands,
their vineyards, their olive yards and their houses'. Then said
they, 'We will restore them, and will require nothing of
them'. Also I shook my lap and said, 'So God shall shake
out every man from his house and from labour that perform-
eth not this promise, even thus shall he be shaken out and
emptied')."

4 June 1886. "Still uncertainty and excitement, and still
though the Bill is considered doomed, some fear that he may
still have another card up his sleeve. And Oh! such bitterness
of speech. 'There will be no peace,' said a Scots M.P., 'until
one old gentleman sends for the other'. 'I wish he were cut
into cat's meat,' says one English gentleman. 'Don't say
that,' says another, 'he would poison the cats'. Gladstone
himself, meanwhile, says serenely to someone 'the educated
classes are against me, but not so the unlearned; and if the
opinion of all the men in England who can't read and write
was taken against those who can, I believe they would be
found nearest to the counsels of God'. (Kinglake says, 'this
is a dangerous practical application of the doctrine of Christ).
Chief Justice Morris says, 'If I am not for Ireland governing
herself, I'm for Ireland governing England, as she is doing

now. Look at her Generals and Governors' . . . It is curious, one used to hear the Academy worn so threadbare at London dinners, and this year only once, at Sir Henry Layards, have I heard it mentioned. The political interest sops up everything else."

I wrote elsewhere: "Chief Justice Morris to lunch with us. Cartwright says the reason Gladstone went for Papal infallibility was that he was jealous of the Pope having thought of it at first. We talked of the difficulty of finding a popular offer to make to the electors. I suggested the old one that every man's pint of beer should hold a quart, and the Chief Justice told of a clown he had heard, 'Every man of you will have his house built of stirabout and a spoon in his hand to make windows'."

31 May. "At a small party at Lord Northbrook's. News had just been circulated that Chamberlain and his followers have decided to vote against the Bill, so everyone was in good humour, even Lord Enfield, who has a bet of threepence on the Bill passing. Lowell came and sat by me and talked quietly about the charm of his daughter's home near Boston, and how he comes back from America more in love with democracy than ever."

1 June. "Frank Lawley was here, says there is to be a tunnel between Scotland and Ireland to settle the Irish question.

"He says Lady D.[6] boasts of her influence over Gladstone and that she can do anything with him, even took him to dine with absolute strangers the other night, which Mrs. Gladstone found out through a spirit rapper who was there having boasted of having performed before Mr. G.—and he caught it."

"Dicey said he had been asked to stand up in dispute against John Dillon at Oxford but had refused. I reproached him, but he said, 'Well, I am convinced he will invent facts on the spot which I shan't be able to refute, and I am, unfortunately, unable to do the same, for though a willing I am not a ready liar'. Sir William, speaking of Gladstone calling Homer colour-blind, Lord Selborne said, 'he himself is morally colour-blind'."

May 1886. "W.S.B. came after breakfast. Randolph had met him in the Lobby the other night the Bill was thrown out and offered to bet him £10 that Arabi would be back

[6] Probably Lady Derby. The original typescript has Lady D. but this is corrected and seems to be O., but the final version retains the D.

in Egypt before there was a Parliament in Dublin; a bet which Wilfred said he would be equally happy to win or lose.

"I dined at Lady Osborne's. A stupid old General next me, who had heard 'on good authority' of Gladstone, against whom he held forth, having ordered quantities of goods from Marshall and Snelgrove, which were counter-ordered later by Mrs. G. But these stories ought to be proved and published if true, and if untrue ought not to be repeated."

14th. "I came in to find Sir William and Wilfred Blunt talking amiably. Sir William had begun by extreme coolness but melted and Wilfred was under the impression he had converted him to Home Rule. 'What a chance you have missed,' he said. 'They told me in Ireland that you were so popular and so liberal you might have led the movement and been in Parnell's place.' He believes the Bill will get through in spite of Chamberlain. He came back to lunch, 'the last square meal he will get,' as he is off to Ireland again."

To H.P.H.: "Wilfred Blunt had been to a Court at Ennis, said the poor R.M.[7] looked unhappy, and the English deputation and Irish M.P.s sitting round criticizing, and a 'girl Graduate' looking over each of his shoulders, so that in his bewilderment he brought the wrong charges against the various prisoners and most of them got off altogether. I asked him how the Home Rulers would settle the Land question if it was left to an Irish Parliament and he says they would not bring in any purchase scheme but would arrange some sliding scale of rents, and so, as you know, the slide would be always down, until the bottomless pit was reached. I think we had better take any terms the English Parliament offers. Curiously, today we heard that thirteen years' purchase has been offered for the interest in the holding of one of our own tenants, a widow who has always been in arrear and is going to America, while they will not buy the fee simple at eighteen years and with borrowed money.

"W. dined with Labby who spoke of the Irish members and their quickness and cleverness and their deference to Parnell, who they all call Sir. The other night he was talking to Parnell in the Lobby and Dr. Tanner passed and Parnell said, 'Tanner, you are a doctor; I suppose you know all about the Army Medical Service'. 'No Sir, I know nothing

[7] Resident Magistrate.

of it,' said Tanner. 'Then go and make up the subject, for you must make a speech of an hour's length this evening.' (To delay the Estimates.)"

1886. "We dined at Lord Arthur Russell's, very pleasant. I sat near Broderick, George Howard and Sir L. Mallet; listened to and joined in the talk. A man called William Gladstone had been up in the Police Courts for cheating at cards, 'but never thought of saying they had been put in his hands by Divine power'. Lyulph Stanley, when someone said, 'I wonder what card the G.O.M. will next bring out of his sleeve,' said, 'let us hope it will be a P.P.C. card[8]'. Mr. Broderick, a great friend of Lord Spencer, says he accounts for his change by his being a man of not first-rate intelligence; by the Tories' behaviour to him when he came into office; and by Gladstone's speeches influencing him, which he thinks strange in a man having so little imagination. George Howard said these were just the men most affected by Gladstone; Lord Wolverton for instance. But Mr. Broderick says that Gladstone is equally influenced by Lord Wolverton, and thinks him a man of infinite knowledge of the world. They abused Randolph for his violent manifesto, but I defended him as being to the Liberal Party what the Salvation Army is to the Church of England. Reaching those whom reason would not reach by his sensationalism.

W.H.G. to A.H.L.[9], 1886: "I am told there is a young painter who calls himself Thaddeus, an Irishman, at Florence. He went there in the hope of painting Gladstone, and being a friend of Madame Kirkoff he got her to intercede, saying at the same time, that he was bound in honour to state he was an enrolled Fenian. Gladstone at first refused, but when Mme. Kirkoff confessed he was a Fenian, he rubbed his hands joyfully, 'A Fenian is he? That is good. Let him come by all means.' My authority is Miss Burke, Tom Burke's sister, who had it direct from Madame Kirkoff."

12th. "W. saw all sorts and conditions of men, all delighted at the elections going against the G.O.M.

"W. had a talk with Cardinal Manning, who has been much abused for his letter on Home Rule in *The Times,* but he says he only wishes that the land should be in the people's hands, and that is what we all wish, especially W. who was the first to propose it long ago."

---

[8] "Pour prendre congé."   [9] Sir Henry Layard.

17th. "The Dilke trial going on today. Gladstone's violent letter to George Leveson–Gower about the blackguardism of the Union causes great indignation among his friends, but is as good to his enemies 'as if he had written a book'." 7 June 1886. To Sir M. E.: "Feeble punning is indeed the order of the day. Someone in a speech the other day spoke of the Old Parliamentary Hand as an 'Old Parliamentary Leg'; and since the letters and telegrams from Hawarden, his friends quote sadly of the Irish saying, 'he never opens his mouth without putting his foot in it'. In allusion to his unwarrantable promise to the Liverpool labourers that the Irish will all leave England when Home Rule is granted, Lord Wemyss says 'at the last election they were offered three acres and a cow, but now only a cock and bull!'. The Marlborough House party was so bright and pleasant, I only discovered at the end it was from everyone being radiant about the Unionist majority in the elections." To H.P.H.: "When the Prince was taking the Queen round the gardens she stopped and patted the head of a little Singalese girl, a great friend of Robert's. It is odd to see good Liberals delighted at Tory successes. Only the defeated candidates looked a little bothered by the condolences of their friends. Oscar Browning, after his defeat, was followed through the town by a jeering mob who pointed at him in derision calling out, 'Poet! Poet!' (compare *Julius Caesar* III 3). He told this story to Robert Browning, who was not at all pleased at it . . . Kinglake says of Gladstone, and this is the most charitable view I have heard taken—'he is conscientious but his conscience is a diseased one'.

"We met Mr. Burrows at the Grosvenor and asked him if the story about Lord Spencer saying to him out hunting that if Gladstone asked him to cut his hand off he would do it, was true. He said he had never in his life either hunted with Lord Spencer or spoken to him on politics."

To Sir M.E. 1 July 1886: "How peaceful Ootacamund must be, contrasted with the violent storms of speech and abuse reigning here. Poor, gentle Hamilton Aide told me yesterday he has never witnessed such a disruption of society, that he is afraid to ask two people to meet each other lest they should fly at one another. At Harrow speeches yesterday, a boy recited a speech of Grattan's against the Union which was very slightly applauded, and then young Peel, the Speaker's son (who has won the Peel medal and many honours), recited a speech of his grandfather's against

Repeal, which was tumultuously applauded at every sentence by the whole assembly—rather hard on the boy who had the unpopular speech to deliver. I hear Bismarck said, speaking of Gladstone the other day, that a great orator seldom makes a great statesman, he is so taken up with finding words to convince other people, that he ends by convincing himself. George Howard amused us by telling of the speech of some Italian statesman who spoke of the 'transformism' of one of his fellow countrymen as distinct from the 'metamorphism' of Gladstone the other day, that a great orator seldom makes Wordster himself. I won't prophesy about the elections because it would literally be prophesying after the event when you get this, but old Lord Clonbrock said yesterday, 'We shall never let the Bill through, and the Unity of the Empire will be a cause for our House to die in,' and as you may probably be a member of the threatened Assembly, when the time for decisions comes, this is something for you to reflect on.

"Sir William met Labouchere at lunch the other day and was much amused by his account of a meeting at Islington the night before. 'Davitt and I were the two lions, and I advanced, holding Davitt by his one hand. The Duke of Bedford was mentioned and a voice cried "Shoot him!" but I said "No, we won't shoot him, we'll take all his property and divide it amongst ourselves," and the unanimity of the meeting was wonderful.'

The Blakes have arrived from the Bahamas, and the Duchess of St. Albans has come to town to meet her sister, but having come will speak on no subject but Ireland, so that the other day Mrs. Blake, having produced some double lanterned luminous beetles to exhibit (at lunch at Lady Dorothy's), the Duchess interrupted with, 'Have you read Gladstone's manifesto?' and Mrs. Blake turned on her, 'We're not talking of Gladstone, we are talking of beetles'.

"Mr. Beaumont is a curious Gladstonian Liberal. Agreed with me that he is in no fit frame of mind to govern or legislate just now, and that the land question and not the political one is the thing to be looked into. He says the English are wearied with Ireland; that is how he gained his election, by promising that Gladstone would get it out of the way."

To H.P.H. July, 1886: "Gladstone beaten by thirty. Isn't it delightful . . . Our agent writes today, 'Small tenants, and particularly those that have not paid their rent, expect great things from Home Rule, but the more respectable farmers rather dread it, as they think they will be tyrannized over by town-boys, etc. A tenant of W.S.-T's[10] at Monksfield refused to give up some of his land to be divided among some small squatters, and the tails of his cattle were cut off last Friday; and on the same night one ear was cut off a horse belonging to a man who had said he was right. Pat Monahan's pig was stuck for the same reason and died immediately, so this kind of work is giving the farmers a warning of what they may expect when the League has full powers.' Your bicycling expeditions must be pleasant, though I am rather of my countryman's opinion who said, 'I would as soon walk afoot as ride afoot any day'.

28 July 1886.   "We are leaving today for Ireland where we spend the rest of the autumn (Parnell permitting), so if my letters are few after this you will know it is because bog water (to vary Morier's phrase) does not make such good ink as London soot. Last week was a nasty one, the Dilke trial predominating. I find that our maids are extremely indignant with him on the ground of his infidelity *to Fanny.*

"Frank Lawley went to see Labouchere a day or two ago, saw a letter breathing defiance from the G.O.M. and on the table were many letters, both from him and Lord Wolverton. 'And indeed,' said Labby, 'I don't know which of the two is the greater fool''. Gladstone on being remonstrated with for his 'blackguard' letter to G. Leveson–Gower, said he was sorry the word had appeared in print, but were he asked to find a better word to describe the conduct of his opponents at the election, it would be 'devilish'.

"Parnell's visit to Hawarden at the moment when he is accused of untruth to Fenianism and Lord Carnarvon causes scandal.

"Kinglake says gently, 'St. Patrick, in driving the snakes and toads out of Ireland, seems also to have banished all the facts'." It was at the end of 1886 that Lord Randolph resigned. I have a note: "W. lunched with Lady Dorothy who had been at Hatfield and says the news of Dillon's prosecution came like a bombshell, Lord Salisbury not having had the slightest idea the Irish Executive were going to take such a step. Lord Randolph sat next her at dinner and was in a vile humour, saying, 'Bad dinner—cold plates—beastly

10 Walter T. N. Shawe-Taylor.

wine—' quite loud, but apologised to Lord Salisbury afterwards, saying he was in a bad temper."

And I see a letter of my husband's to Sir H. Layard written
December 28: "The resignation of R. Churchill was like
lightning in a clear sky . . . Whatever be Randolph's faults
of temper, he is the one man of genius among his party who
is clear-sighted enough to perceive that the old order has
changed, that the Tory mould must be broken up and shaped
into fresh combinations. We have to deal with Demos very
differently from our handling of the old constituencies, and
I am convinced that if Randolph had been allowed to have
his way he would have carried his party into power with an
enormous majority."

And again, "Lord R.C. lunched with Mrs. Jeune on Sunday and talked very freely about the matter. He was in
wretched spirits. Sir J. Stephens was present, I think the
only other person, and he spoke to him with deep solemnity
and even severity as to the danger involved by his rash
conduct. R.C. took it very well indeed, and at last said he
did not think his resignation would have been so promptly
accepted and that he hoped an offer might have been made
to him by Lord S.[11] to compromise difficulties. He added
that he wished he had consulted Stephens before he took the
step, but that the majority of the Cabinet were bent on
getting him out. This is true, but no doubt he treated them
like lacqueys. The mischief done at home and abroad is
terrible. In Ireland the general belief is that he is entirely
for the Nationalists. My brother-in-law writes that the
bellman had just gone through the town of Loughrea announcing that Lord Randolph had adopted the Plan of
Campaign."

4 December 1886. "Lord Camperdown came in the morning to see Sir William. He is pleased that Goschen has
joined the Government, but now there is an idea of Cross
and Lord Iddesleigh being kicked out, and Lord Northbrook invited to join and who that would strengthen I don't
know. Sir Wm. met the Duke of Cambridge afterwards and
he talked very sensibly about it, and said the only object
of putting Liberal peers in would be that in case of Goschen's
disagreement on any subject he might not feel quite alone.
But afterwards he met Matthews who said 'not the least
danger of any disagreement, unless indeed, Goschen thinks

[11] Lord Salisbury.

us too Radical!' Old Lady Stanley told me she had met Goschen in very good spirits the night before at dinner. She is furious with Chamberlain, Goschen and Trevelyan for 'touching pitch' in consenting to attend the Home Rule conferences."

1888 (Banquet 8 May): "Mrs. Green has been to the banquet given to Parnell by the 80 Club. She says Haldane in his speech, said by mistake, 'We have come to do honour to the chief of the Liberal party', upon which John Morley turned green, and someone whispered to Haldane, who then substituted the word Irish.

"W. lunched at Lord Northbrook's where much indignation was expressed at the Duke of Westminster's behaviour in cancelling Bobby Spencer's invitation to dinner because he had gone to the Parnell banquet. Mrs. Ford says lately she invited the Leckys and Trevelyans to dinner, and meeting Mrs. Lecky mentioned who the party was to consist of. Mrs. Lecky's face fell and she said, 'I must tell my husband Sir George Trevelyan is coming'. And next day she wrote to Mrs. Ford to say they had a prior engagement to dinner."

About another "banquet" to Parnell (in 1899), I wrote to H.P.H. February and March 1889. Coole. "The Parnell case seems to be going as well as anything can go after such a blight as Pigott's break down. Some of the Gladstonians were much put out at Parnell's avowal he had told a lie to deceive the House of Commons, and I have no doubt it was to counteract this, that Sir Charles Russell gave his famous dinner. He kept it a secret he expected Parnell. Wilfrid Blunt came to see me the day of the dinner and did not know he was to meet him; and Randolph Churchill told Lord Morris next day it was a regular trap, that he had never been told he was to be there. 'I know what I would have done,' said the Chief Justice, 'I would have written, "Lord Randolph Churchill presents his compliments to Sir Charles Russell. The occurrence of last night was Sir Charles Russell's fault. Should it occur again it will be Lord Randolph Churchill's fault".' The Chief Justice escorted me over on Friday night, and was most entertaining. Talking of Lord Zetland's appointment, he said it was quite true the Government had gone through the alphabet, offering it to Abercorn, Brownlow and Cadogan to begin with, till they came to Zetland, 'And sure,' he said, 'when I was a little chap I used to write in my copybook, "Z stands for Zany, who was a great fool"!'."

To H.P.H.: "Sir William was near Labby at dinner, he was most amusing, says he has thrown Parnell over and joined the 'Purity Party', and his cry is now, 'the Good Old Man, and the Good Old Book'.

"He abuses the South Africa Company, says it is all a swindle, and he is going to write it down, but will first get another £1,000 out of Cecil Rhodes for the Irish party as blackmail.

"Labby has such a queer cynical way of saying startling things in the meekest possible voice, he is most amusing. Many stories are told of his cool impudence when a young attaché. He was ordered from Brussels to Constantinople, but not given travelling expenses, at which he felt aggrieved. So he disappeared, and at the end of about a month, wrote to the Foreign Office, 'I set out on foot from Brussels and have now arrived at Berlin, but being rather footsore must wait for some time to recover, but hope to be able to continue my journey in a week or two'. When with Sir A. X., Minister at some German Court, and very stingy, Lady X, said one night, 'I wonder why people go away so early'. 'Because they are starved,' said Labby. 'But I ordered sandwiches,' said Lady X. 'There were three,' said Labby, 'but I ate two of them'. He likes to be considered the wickedest of mankind (not a laudable ambition) but he is really goodhearted, will do much to help a friend in need, gets up a subscription every year to buy toys for poor children and was the only M.P. who would say a word to help my poor Egyptian exiles."

November 1888: "George Howard and Costa, the painter, Sir Arthur and Lady Clay dined with us. I had to talk to Costa all dinner time in Italian, as he speaks nothing else. We spoke of Labby, and George Howard told how, after a speech he had made against the lending of carriages to Election Committees, on the ground of the horny-handed sons of toil having no carriages to lend, he had turned to him and said, 'And besides that, the horny-handed sons of toil lately borrowed two of my carriages for Herbert Gladstone, if you please, and sent them back in such a mess they had to go off to the coachbuilders'."

13 January 1891. "Dined at Sir Arthur Otway's and had some pleasant talk with E. Ponsonby and afterwards with

George Russell [12], who must regret he got down the wrong side of the fence. He says X is very unhappy because he went to see his constituents the other day, and General Booth was holding a meeting, and at the end some confounded fellow got up and said he would subscribe £100, and the thing spread like wildfire and others began subscribing their hundreds, and the General said, 'now Mr. X you must follow the example of your constituents,' so he gasped, 'I will speak to you in the other room,' and there gave him £20 and felt he was considered mean. X had asked him last year if he found his Home Rule views made much difference in his being asked out to dinner. G.R. said no, though he had been dropped by a few Unionists who used to ask him once a year. 'Oh, I shouldn't mind that,' said X. 'What I object to is that a great many Unionists come and dine at my house and won't ask me to theirs in return.'

"Mr. Ponsonby said he heard a discussion in the House of Commons smoking-room amongst Gladstonians as to the disaster their leader's death would be. But Labby said, 'Oh no, Gladstone dead would be far more valuable than Gladstone living. Wait till you see me trail his corpse! '."

That was the buzzing of the dinner tales, of the drawing-rooms. It is likely true that the unlearned, "the men who cannot read or write" saw with different eyes. And I find a note written in 1887, "I walked to Trinity Square, South-wark, except for a tram across the bridge. There was a crowd by the House of Commons watching the members arrive. A man said, 'They will wait till old Billy comes, and then they will go away'."

[12] The Rt. Hon. G. W. E. Russell.

V

AMONG THE POOR

THOUGH I liked and enjoyed the London life for a part of the year, I had soon begun to feel a certain barrenness in it; it was too much on the surface, one did not put out roots as on the Irish countryside. I missed the intercourse with the people, I wanted to become acquainted with the poor. But this was not so easy as to enter pleasant drawing-rooms; I had to grope for a while to find an open door. My old rule, "begin with what is nearest," failed me now. For St. George's Hospital being very close at hand and my husband one of its Governors, I took courage one day to ascend its steps and ask if I might be allowed to visit some of the inmates, and I was taken through wards, and spoke with some of the bed-ridden, and they seemed pleased and I asked leave to come again. But I was told that the visiting list was full, that I must wait until there was an empty place on it; and so I left my name, and there was an end of it, for no message ever came. And then, being known to the Matron of a Workhouse Infirmary, her father, a Resident Magistrate, being tenant of a house of ours at Coole, I went to see her, and she took me through the rooms. "They are clean and bright," I wrote, "there are flowers about, and the patients seem well cared for and have bath-chair drives in the Park. There are a great many visitors. 'Eighty ladies,' the Matron said, 'are making their souls by visiting here'. So I did not ask to be made the eighty-first. I asked her if her poor patients were pleased with the comforts they came to from their poor surroundings, and she said, 'They all hate it'. I understood this better when I went to a Christmas party there. In the bright light thrown on them, as they sat up in their uniform red jackets to drink their tea, they may well have felt they had left behind them any individual life of their own."

But not long afterwards I happened to meet Mrs. Dacre Craven, wife of the Vicar of St. George the Martyr, Holborn, and she told me there was much poverty in their parish and they needed help in many ways, but had never had it from outside, for the parish did not belong to the East End, where the slums were better known. She took me to see the schools, and Christmas coming on, I offered to provide a Christmas tree; and this I did for many years in succession with the help of friends. The tree itself always came from Wilfrid Blunt's woods at Crabbet. Some of my Athenaeum friends gave contributions, Kinglake even coming himself to see the little faces laughing over the gifts. Arthur Sullivan was another who came, and brought a hundred little boxes of sweets. And so, on many a Christmas Eve, there was a record such as this; the first: "Off early, and all day dressing up the tree with the help of the Master and some of the little boys, who thought most of trying the trumpets and drums. At four o'clock the children arrived for tea. Clothes distributed first, the names being on each; then the toy distribution, all the little hands going up when the dolls appeared, and great delight when it was found that there was one for each. A. Raffalovitch chose the lilac-spangled one for a little girl, Annie Smith, he was much taken with, and also gave her a looking glass." And I could not but feel touched when the other day, in looking over some of my husband's letters to Sir Henry Layard, I came upon these words about my work: "She was all yesterday and the day before organizing her Christmas tree for St. George the Martyr, and it was a perfect success, three-hundred children had clothes and were feasted to a surfeit, and all done by herself, without the slightest fuss or confusion. I really think had she been alive in the terrible times of the Crimea she would have brought order into the commissariat. She is now in Southwark where tomorrow and Saturday the same 'Function' is to go on with four-hundred still poorer children. The little wretches were very happy. They had none last year owing to her absence, and have been thinking of this for months. It is a good and Christian thing, in the right sense of the word Christian, to brighten the life of so many unfortunate fellow creatures."

There were also Mothers' Meetings, and some of my friends came and helped to make these pleasant. "With Miss Bowen and her Music to Great Ormond Street; it was a good evening to bring her, there was no lady there, and the mothers looked bored and dreary and were much cheered by her music, and the children by my sweets." "Bitterly cold and I went in the evening to Great Ormond Street and brought some warm things. Minnie Smithers' mother told me her husband had been out of work for five weeks, he was a licensed hawker but could not afford to renew his licence, and on Christmas Day she had neither a fire in the house nor a cup of tea, but Mrs. Craven had given her an order for half a ton of coal." "In the evening went to the Mothers' Meeting, and having been asked to speak to them, I told them about the growing and preparation of tea in Ceylon, winding up with an unexpected and improvised tea party, much enjoyed. The poor things had each two cups, hot, strong and sweet. One woman, Mrs. M., says her husband, a carrier, has been out of work for thirteen months. He had been twenty-three years in the same establishment until then. They have seven children, the eldest girl earns six shillings a week by filling pill boxes; the mother does washing from Tuesday morning to Friday evening and so gains a few shillings. They have two rooms." "To the Mothers' Meeting, and being the first of the year, I gave them a 'surprise tea,' which I fancy by the large attendance, was not altogether a surprise. They enjoyed it very much, poor old things. The Bowens, Cecil Smith, Mr. Holland and Lady Robinson came to help, and we had banjo playing."

I soon came to know another and yet poorer parish on the south side of the river.

My husband soon after our marriage had said he would come to church if I would take him to a different one every Sunday. For I never lost the habit of those early Killinane Sundays through the many changes of belief I have witnessed, or whose influence have touched me. I have heard a preacher say, as he looked around his Church, that he was confident that there was "not one in that large congregation who did not believe every word of the Bible to be literally and entirely true". I have already told of the doctrine taught in my early days, that to lose belief in any one story or statement in the Bible, is to deny its entire contents, its spiritual revelation. And going as I did into a society where intellect was in reaction against dogma, faith in me, as in them, was given a hard knock, was shaken and languished for a while. But for a while only; and for its recovery I thank in great part that "Correspondence fixed with Heaven," the beautiful Liturgy of our Church. So, one by one we explored first of all the City Churches, in their Sabbath quiet. I remember looking up and down Fleet Street at mid-day on one of those days when there was but one wheeled vehicle in sight, a little child's carriage drawn by a goat.

Some of the churches are well known and beautiful, as

St. Bartholomew's, Smithfield, and St. Helen's, Bishopsgate, and St. Saviour's, Southwark. In the less famous ones, the congregation was sometimes very small, as scant as in that Killinane church of my childhood; some had good music, and many the Wren architecture. The sermons in these were not usually very good. "St. P. . . . The preacher has been preaching for two years on the 'buts' of the Bible, and has two years more of them in his head." "All Hallows, where there are square pews and a congregation of forty-one and a beautiful old carved screen, and the clergyman announced that he too is going with the times, and will in future preach with a surplice." "Marylebone, service intoned and a sermon on adultery, I suppose in reference to the Campbell case." "Holy Trinity, a curious little city church, a good congregation for the city, though from the superior number of choristers (20) W. said it reminded him of MacPherson's raid, 'Four and twenty men and five and twenty pipers'."

And sometimes we went for the sermons: "Haweis preached the sermon that caused so great a disturbance at Oxford. On the text 'the letter killeth, but the Spirit gives life'. 'Nothing can move the Bible,' he said, 'from its supremacy in words and spirituality and one need not lose Christianity by looking on it as fallible, though inspired, and the history of an inspired people.' (In those days this seemed a heretical opinion. And I remember being told that the Crown Princess of Prussia, being asked to write a verse of the Bible in some book had chosen that text. This had been told us, with some suspicion of the influences she was under, of German heresy or unbelief.) We met Haweis afterwards at lunch at Lady Dorothy's and he talked to me a good deal on the subject, and *against* interfering with the faith of the young until we have something better to offer them, but that we must not teach what we do not ourselves believe. He spoke also of General Booth's scheme, which he upholds, saying that as men pick up cigar ends, and turn them into snuff as an article of commerce, or rags and turn them into paper, so he picks up the failures and the undeserving and turns them into good members of society."

Another day, in June 1886: "We went to Spurgeon's Tabernacle. The body of the church and galleries thronged with people, many men, all most attentive. A hymn was sung; 'And if there are some,' said Spurgeon 'who have no power of making sweet sounds, may God have pity upon their silence'. Then he expounded part of a chapter of Isaiah,

rather rambling, then offered up a prayer with a great deal
of imagery in the language, 'May we be anointed with oil;
may each of us give out a sweet perfume during the day;
May we be saved though it even be on boards and broken
pieces of the ship'. The only allusion to politics was a prayer
for the State now in very troubled water—(defiantly) God
save the Queen. We heard a man say afterwards, 'Well, it's
a great pity he has changed his political opinions'. 'Yes,'
said another, 'but we need not follow him in politics though
he is our minister'. His sermon was long and very eloquent
but one must be educated into the language to understand
the allusions to the Covenant, etc. It was about the Assyrian
camp and the lepers discovering its abandonment, and then
all the people coming out to plunder it, 'even those suffering
from rheumatism, even lame old ladies, stiff old men;' and
rather a far-fetched analogy to the soul that has been forgiven
sin, forgetting it all and beginning to enjoy its riches.
However, so large and attentive a congregation was better
than the very indifferent handful in most of the City
churches. The man next us lent Sir William his hymn book,
and at the end of the service grasped his hand warmly, as if
in fellowship."

My husband always liked to send a contribution to some
of the appeals for "A Day in the Country" for London
children. He yet remembered, he used to say, the joy of an
occasional holiday in fields and woods in his own early
schooldays. It was the love of natural history learned in
those days, he said, that had long afterwards taken form
when he had employed a Singalese artist to make paintings
of the wonderful butterflies (reproduced later in the three
volumes, *The Lepidoptera of Ceylon*). So one summer having
sent a guinea towards this fund to half a dozen poor parishes,
we took the church in each for our next Sunday excursions.
And among these we saw no neighbourhood so poor, no
church in which so very poor people were gathered as that
of St. Stephen's, Southwark. We stayed after the service and
spoke to the vicar and the Mission woman, and next day
I went to see them again, and from that time, and for the
rest of my London years, my hands were full. I worked to
help the helpers, for that is, I think, the best that a passing
visitor can do. Yet, I had also begun some new work of my
own, for it had happened in the Holborn Parish that when
Christmas trees were over, and as spring lengthened the
days, I thought of taking a party of little boys on Saturdays

to the Natural History Museum and giving them tea there. I made my plan with some misgivings, the boys might not care for it, they might run wild, there were unknown dangers of failure. I determined not to say anything to my husband about it until, the day over, the confession of a failure would be but a part of its humiliation, or I might after all have the joy of announcing a success.

The first party was to take place on a certain Saturday, but on the Friday evening, Sir William said, "I have asked a few people to lunch tomorrow, old friends, Sir Edward Banbury, the Shaw Lefevres; I want it to be a pleasant one." I was aghast. It was too late to put off either his party or mine. But when at last I was forced to make my confession, he told me with delight, with a little teasing, that he had seen a postcard for me, "Fifteen little boys will meet you at the Museum tomorrow," and could not resist inventing a mythical party with which to alarm us. And so we laughed together and he was as well pleased as I was when I reported on that and many a following Saturday that all had gone well. I had to read a good deal of Natural History and to be ready with stories of wild beasts and their ways, and snakes and crocodiles and the nesting places of birds; for I found that if the youngsters' attention flagged but for a moment they would begin to fiddle with the cases or finger the specimens, but while they were kept amused they never left my side. Indeed, we were sometimes followed by a train of grown-up listeners, even the policeman on guard now and again yielding a smile. Though I have found in a note about a party of fourteen very little girls that "one of the policemen in the room urged me to prevent them from touching things, that there one had hold of a crocodile's tooth and might easily have pulled it out."

I have other notes: "I took Robert to the Museum in the morning, to rub up my anecdotes, and then the boys from Southwark met me. We went first to the crocodiles and snakes, then birds, then tea, and wound up with wild beasts and humming birds. They seemed delighted and especially enjoyed looking for the nests of the birds, sometimes almost hidden as in nature. They were very poor looking, some with pinched faces." Another day: "A good dinner of stewed beef steak and potatoes and plenty of coffee and cakes warmed them up. I asked one what his father was. 'He is dead, and mother earns a few shillings now and again.' 'And what will you be?' 'I *am* a crossing sweeper. I go when

I leave school to a crossing near the Prince of Wales' house to earn a little to help my mother.' Another said, 'My father twists twine, I go with him at five o'clock and work till school-time, then from twelve to two, and after school I work till eight!' ('Not any play?' said Robert, when I told him.) Another, very ragged, had a shirt from the Christmas tree. They were pretty well up in the history of wild beasts and the foreign birds, from their school teaching, though knowing nothing of the British birds. The little crossing sweeper had been in a stable but was dismissed, not being tall enough to groom a horse." These parties, from one or the other parish, went on through the winters. "I met twelve boys, in charge of a teacher as poor-looking as themselves, a wire worker. One little boy said some verses about the 'Umming bird'; another looking at the rhinoceros and hippopotamus said, 'It must have taken thousands of years to get these together'. One little fellow I had expected last time had not come because 'his father had made him stand on the street selling haddocks'. Another little boy bites his tongue when he is tempted to swear. 'With ten little boys, one a rope maker's son, who goes with his father to work at five thirty and to school at nine. Most of them kept some of their cakes to take home to their little brothers and sisters. One asked to see a wolf, as his sisters had been nearly killed by one in Florida; another wanted to see the bear, his brother, who was with me last Saturday, had told him of it." "Thirteen little girls from Southwark, one the daughter of the man that I had seen with the sprained ankle. She has not got a situation yet, people think she looks too delicate, but Mrs. Hayes says that it is because she wants food. Another starved-looking little thing is the child of a maker of clothes-horses. I asked one what they had for dinner generally. She said 'What we can; no meat since Sunday'. 'He looks just like a gentleman,' said one on seeing the gorilla. Lady Darnley and her daughter joined us as we were going down the bird passage, she had never been there before and was interested in the birds as well as the children."

"To the Museum with a dozen little girls. They were pleased with the birds, especially humming birds. I don't think they liked the wild beasts as well as the boys, and they had not such good appetites. One girl aged fourteen is in an envelope folding factory from eight to eight, and is paid at the rate of three halfpence a thousand. Some days she can fold ten thousand, gets no Saturday holiday but she had asked for one today. Another works in an underclothing warehouse seven to seven. Another, with her brother and sister, is a chair caner. Poor things, they seemed to enjoy themselves, but I wished for something better than the Museum and if I had the fine weather, would take them to the Zoo for fresh air. It was the birthday of one, her fourteenth, and I gave her a bonbon box, then another little thing of seven found it was hers, and got another."

When the Colonial Exhibition was opened I took my parties there, "getting off 25% by taking 150 tickets at once. Eighteen came the first day, they were I think delighted, especially with the Jungle, and the Australian scene. They had sixpenny fish dinners, and tea and buns, and stayed, and I with them, from one o'clock till seven." Then "with another eighteen, 'ain't it nice'. One had an uncle who had been in India and brought a parrot back which one day when a bald-headed customer came into the shop called out 'Bald head stole the pickles'." "I spent the day with my boys at the Exhibition; smaller than the last and very happy, delighted with the Jungle, the Australian hut, and the Aquarium especially, even the wooden soldiers excited them. 'To think that we should have beaten those fellows,' says a little imp, looking up at a gigantic wooden Sepoy. When they were at tea, some working men at a table said, 'Well those little chaps are having a rare time, it's nice to see them; there's some sharp appetites there; they'll never forget this day'. 'My little chap,' said one, 'was at the Fisheries at a Sunday School treat, and he's talking of it yet, and that was three years ago'." And at the last party there, "nineteen boys, most of them little fellows, and I labelled them all for the Ceylon Court, so though we lost some, they were found again, and my mind was more at ease. Lady Arthur Russell, seeing little boys with blue labels to them, guessed they were mine, and by following them found me."

And all in good time I went to the Zoo, one day, "to meet fifty Southwark children. They came too soon and Mrs. Hayes paid for them instead of waiting for me and my tickets and I had some difficulty in getting the money back and in getting leave to take them out to the kiosk, where I had ordered dinner for them, and in again without repayment. However, at last all was done, and the little ones had a good time, they were ravenous at dinner; and then a roll and romp on the grass delighted them and then the gardens, especially riding the elephant and seeing the lions and tigers fed, and the monkey house; and at last, tired, back to the kiosk to tea and buns and another romp. And a Review was held just in front of us, as if on purpose, and the tulip beds glowed by our path, and all seemed perfectly happy."

Sometimes I went to a "Happy Evening" at the Southwark Board School; "the poor teachers seemed very tired, the children very lively. We romped and I learned a new game called 'Isabella'; we danced in a ring, chanting a description of different viands, then a little girl jumped up and kissed my cheek. 'What does that mean?' 'It means that you are to stand in the middle now.' But when the whistle sounded and we had a rest, listening to Cecil Smith's banjo with which children and teachers were equally delighted. I was very tired that night."

In February 1887, "We had a dinner at Southwark, 210 came to it, the old, the maimed, the afflicted, the hungry, the unemployed. During the evening, while smoking and singing were going on, and coffee and buns handed round, they became first cheerful and then merry. I would not have believed that the poor old faces could brighten so much. At first, I had only Miss Bowen to play, and Mrs. Campbell Praed's cousin to sing, but by Sir William Plowden's happy suggestion, I asked some of the men if they could sing, and found several candidates. Dibley sang 'The Old Armchair' with great spirit, and other songs with choruses, in which all the audience joined. They seemed delighted at some of their own number being called up. 'It is as good as half a sovereign to us,' someone said. Miss Gribell brought a friend who gave comic recitals and at nine-thirty Mr. Cecil Smith and a friend arrived with their banjos and gave nigger melodies, immensely applauded, so all went well and at ten we broke up. Each had a little tea or tobacco to take home, but they seemed to like the flowers best of all; as I divided them, hands were stretched out in every direction, so many old women begging for just one: 'it's so long since I had a flower,' but I had not enough to go round. The saddest visits were to the homes. In January 1887, "I took Lady Bowen to see some of these, guided by Mrs. Hayes, the Mission woman; our first visit was to a room, very small, very dirty, where an old woman was washing clothes at a tub. She lives there with her daughter, son-in-law, a grandchild; they all sleep on the floor. The man has been out of work for some weeks, the wife expects her confinement soon, she looks not more than eighteen. What they live on I don't know.

"Then to an old couple living in one room. They had once gone to the workhouse but were separated there, and after their long lifetime the loneliness told on them so much that they 'prayed to the Redeemer' to redeem them from their living death, and coming out, their son, a small tradesman in the firewood line, paid the rent of the room for them, and sends them an occasional sixpence or a bit of bread and meat. 'Do you live and sleep and cook here?' Lady Bowen asked. 'Oh, ma'am, it isn't much cooking I have, a cup of tea is my chief cooking.' But they seem not altogether unhappy, and a little rosy grandchild was with them. Then in another room an old blind woman and her son, a tinker, 'but work is very slow now'. They have two rooms, but live in one during the cold weather. I went upstairs, Lady Bowen declining to come, and at the top of the steep, worn stair-case we came into a room, cleaner and tidier than any I had been in, where a respectable looking young man in shirt sleeves was washing the faces of his three children. He is a labourer but has been out of work for five weeks. He went to the charity organization but it is not a case for them. This was the first case that looked in any degree hopeful, as he may get work again. I promised some clothes for the children and wife. A very old woman, eighty-eight, almost blind through an accident with a paraffin lamp. The room filthy, and her rags scarcely holding together, but she expected her grandchildren to come and clear up for her. She gets half-a-crown a week from the Parish and ten shillings a quarter from some charity. Then the old ex-bandbox maker I had sent a blanket to, stone deaf, but can read what is written on a slate. Her dress a mass of rags, Lady Bowen promised to send her one. She goes to church on Sunday evenings. Then a handsome young woman, the mother of five sons, from one-year-old to eight or nine. Her husband, a carpenter, has been down with rheumatism for three months. The parish gives 3/- a week and a little bread and tea. The rent of the room is 3/6. She has pawned all she can, bedding, even wedding ring. The boys looked clean, and the room tidy, and here also there may be some hope after her husband recovers. We left money to take her things out of pawn. We could not bear much more and my pocket was empty, but Mrs. Hayes said, 'just one more', and we went into another tiny tenement room where was an old woman whose husband was buried in the morning. He had died on Friday, and until Tuesday, by parish neglect, his body had been left lying on the only bed, in the room where she lived, ate, slept. Half-a-crown a week from the parish is her eager hope, the workhouse her terror. It is the loss of freedom they dread, and they feel that they go in there to die. Poor people, and oh, poor minister living among them and seeing always this hopeless dirt and poverty and misery, and the public house at every corner."

On another day with Mrs. Campbell Praed: "Three girls living alone, their mother dead, their father has almost deserted them, occasionally looks in and gives them a trifle. The eldest girl very pretty, though unkempt, supports them by picking rabbit fur. She could get a place, but won't desert her sisters, and they can't get into the workhouse because the father won't even go with them or pay for them there. The grate was fireless, panes of glass out of the window, the children almost naked."

Mrs. Campbell Praed afterwards told her brother-in-law, Mr. Herbert Praed, about these three girls; he told the Commissioner of Police, who sent an inspector who, finding the girls destitute, took the younger ones for a week to the workhouse (under the Industrial Act) and they are to be sent to a home five miles from London where their sister is to see them once a week, she meanwhile, going back to service.

"With Miss Gribell; a man out of work, aged fifty-nine. He had been employed on 'river work' for sixteen years, and turned off because he was getting old, and younger men came in plenty asking to be taken on. His wife does a little on collar folding. He looked starved, a very hard case. Next door a bricklayer was out of work, more cheerful as he will probably get work again when the weather changes. Both had been to the Charity Organization but they said they only helped the sick, not men out of work. He had tried to get work on anything, even sweeping the roads, but they said they had enough hands already. Then a blind woman, Mrs. Hall, very cheerful and her room clean. She had 4/- a week when her rent is paid, but has to pay a penny or a halfpenny to a guide whenever she wants to get out, so stays in and sings to herself all day. An old man who makes fourpence a day by sewing hooks and eyes on to a card from 7 a.m. to 8 p.m. His wife died the other day and his daughters are with him now. They can make sixpence a day each by hooks and eyes, but just now work is slack and they have not been given any to do.

"A man, Clarke, consumptive and asthmatic, finishes blacking brushes at fourpence a dozen, but can do very little now. Five children, wife with toothache. He showed me his rent book, two weeks in arrear. The landlord's printed rules say any tenant found removing goods for distress is liable to six months' imprisonment. A bitterly cold day."

March 1887. "I found Mr. Didge rather oppressed by an impending visit from the Rural Dean, who is sent to see that the church has all proper requisites, but not to provide them. He has already been ordered to provide a safe at his own expense at a cost of £9.

"Again with William Hozier to Southwark. He was softened by the sight of so much suffering, and generous in his gifts."

But more lasting help was needed, and I tried to find it here and there, so I wrote in March 1887: "A dark Sunday, and Sir William wouldn't come to church, so I set out for St. Stephen's. A good many poor in there, and I felt more at home than I had done in any London church, knowing almost every face, and so many of those that I had helped, greeted me. I see it ought to be adopted by a rich parish, and will at all events try to have it done. I ought not to despair of anything after getting the Exiles' allowance increased.

"I went off after breakfast to St. Philip's, Kensington, to gain information, having heard that it had adopted a parish, but after morning service (congregation of six including myself and the sexton), I asked the curate, and he said that they had never done so, and were not strong enough, but St. Jude's had done so. So I went on to St. Jude's, called on the Vicar, Dr. Forrest, Irish, and friendly, and he told me all that I wanted to know, how they had heard of the needs of a parish in Whitechapel, and began by paying a curate, and they sent lay helpers, and give in all £400 a year." "I wrote to the Bishop of Rochester, one effort made." A few days later, I had asked the curate of St. Stephen's to lunch at one-thirty. In accepting, he said, "I am sorry to say that I shall have to leave at four o'clock', which I was afraid to tell William, and trusted to my own ingenuity to get the visit shortened. And happily, in the morning, came a note from the Bishop of Rochester proposing to call a little after three; so I packed the poor curate off then.

"The Bishop was civil and kind, asked a great deal about the parish, doesn't see his way to doing much, but will ask Mr. Dodge to dinner and talk to him, and if he can, will help him quietly without exciting the jealousy of others. He told me to pray so that I might not forget St. Stephen's, and quoted, 'as ye have done it unto the least of one of these my brethren ye have done it unto me,' and thought the difficulty of getting an offertory a year out of other congregations would be very great. However, I feel more satisfied since I have seen him, but I think a private appeal for annual subscriptions would be good.

"Then three days later see Mr. Dodge, who has been asked to dinner by the Bishop—and refused—after all my trouble. But he didn't know that it was for any special reason, and was oppressed and ill with overwork, and thinks he cannot be spared for a day just now. He is very grateful for my efforts, but hurt that the Bishop calls the parish 'unimprovable' as already his congregations have risen from 22 on Sunday evening to 285, and on Wednesday from 27 to 185."

I proposed writing an account of the parish and its needs, and to this he joyfully agreed.

I wrote an appeal calling it *Over the River*[1] telling of the poverty of St. Stephen's and its need for help, and had it printed, and sent out a good many copies. I wrote in March 1887: "The first donation, I was told, was from the publisher's office, from someone who had seen it through the press, and this was a good beginning. Lady Osborne promised £15 a year for five years—a good encouragement. Kinglake wrote that it was written with a noble simplicity, and sent a cheque."

I wrote again: "I went to see Lady Burdett-Coutts. She was very kind and sympathetic, promised to try and interest people in St. Stephen's and to go there herself one day when the weather is warmer. She is dead against the church house and would not have subscribed but for some obligation she is under for the moment to the Archbishop, which made her unwilling to refuse. The Imperial Institute, if properly undertaken, would have her sympathy. She was much aggrieved by Mr. Burdett-Coutts having been called up to

[1] *Over The River*, London, William Ridgway, 1888. Another leaflet of the same title appeared in 1893 giving details of progress.

go to the House on the night of the long sitting. Though
he had paired, he had only come home at 4 a.m. I hope she
will do something, but I have more hope from less exalted
friends; Lady Henniker is very kind about Southwark, she
will try to get clothes from her working Guild."

We went in that April of 1887 for a few weeks to Spain.
I find there are notes in letters to H. P. Haeptar, those Southwark visits and Granada. "The Alhambra is, of course,
the great sight. India had spoiled us, for the Delhi and Agra
palaces in the same styles are much finer, besides having
the Indian sun to teach one to understand the merits of
these cool corners and colonnades. Still, it is a beautiful
building and one feels that the Moors paid for their time
of Sovereignty by leaving such traces of their dominion.
The Moresco Ambassadors who came here a few years ago,
visited the Alhambra, and when they saw the inscriptions
on the walls telling of past greatness, they cried big tears.
And at the hotel the cook, who knew a little Arabic, asked
one of the servants how he liked it and he said gloomily,
'It is no matter for jesting. I have still the key of my house
here, and will come back some day and turn you out again.'

"Here at Granada also there is a curious gipsy's quarter
where the houses are holes in the mountain side. They are
a dark, peculiar race, unlike the Spaniards, and keep their
own customs. Louis Napoleon, when young, is said to have
taken a girl away from them, and she was found one day
with a knife in her, having been followed by some of her
tribe.

"To return to Spain (which I hope never to do. The dis-
tances are so immense and it is not a lovable country like
Italy), our visit to Cuenca was a great success. J. C. Robinson
had told Sir William it was 'all Spain boiled down to a pint
pot' and Sir Clare Ford, hearing this, came with us. He
is an artist and the views which are lovely enchanted him.
He had given no notice of the visit, not wanting to be
bothered with ceremony, but when we arrived at the station
there were all the notabilities of the town, the Mayor,
Governor, etc., waiting to receive the Ambassador, the
Duc de Fries having telegraphed there. We were escorted
to our hotel and about the town by eight of the chief
officials, not one of whom spoke a word of anything but
Spanish. Whenever we came to a garden of any kind each
solemnly plucked a flower to present to me. It was still worse
next morning when Sir Clare was out sketching, they all

arrived again reinforced by the Officer in Command of the Civil Guard in full uniform. When Sir William, Mr. Ellicombe, and I had exhausted our stock of sentences I had then the conversations in *Murray's Handbook* to read. It was nine o'clock in the evening before we said farewell to them, but it is amusing to look back on. Here is Madrid. Sir Clare is adored by the young, but considered 'fast' by the old. But as somebody says 'that don't matter much as the old are going out of the world and the young are coming up'."

In Paris there was cold and sleet to meet us. We went into the Louvre in the afternoon and met Lord Clanricarde who walked round with us, very indignant with the sleeping-car conductor, who had borrowed his match-box and taken the matches. He had made himself amends for this by giving him no tip. We met also Sir Frederic Leighton[2], he has been at the Hague and is furious against the new Museum, which he says spoils the pictures. The salon here, he says, is not only execrable but ridiculous.

I wrote in passing through London on our way to Ireland, "I found Southwark pretty flourishing as Lady Tweeddale is going to set up a crèche there at her own expense, and Miss Gribell visits regularly and is going to give a tea to three-hundred children for Whitsuntide, and had got £15 from an old lady for coster barrows, and Miss Elliot has twice taken the children to the Zoo, and William Hozier has been visiting, but is a little out of heart at the result. I hope to turn him on to the breakfastless children at the Board School and get him to promise to go and see them." For I had written before this. "I took Lady Tweeddale to the Tabard Street Board School. 'Boys who know Lady Gregory hold up their hands.' A great many hands went up. Mr. Williams, the Master, told me that many of the boys were without breakfast, and he himself often sends out for bread and tea for them at his own expense. Mr. Dodge told me of a girl that came into the Board Meeting to prove her inability to pay the fee, her father being ill. They noticed that she looked pale and strange and it came out that she had not had any breakfast that day or the day before. Her father was very angry with her for telling this.

"They can not learn, poor little things. We consulted as to what could be done and decided to give the poorest

2 Later Lord Leighton.

children hot cocoa each day, but they are to bring their own bread. For, the teachers said, 'there is no one so poor he cannot give them that'." And this we found to work well. If any came empty-handed, the better provided children would share their portion with them, and the hot cocoa and milk nourished the little bodies. My friends were very good in helping. "Sir Hercules Robinson called in the evening, very proud of himself, having got £5 out of five city men to whom he had read my letter. I certainly never expected *him* to turn collector for me.

I left orders for some flower-boxes to be made and filled and placed on the school wall in imitation of Cordova, but thought there was a risk the boys would upset them. But I was told after the summer that they had not only not been meddled with, but that the boys had once captured and brought in a stranger who they fancied had been *looking* at Lady Gregory's flower-boxes in a suspicious way.

My work in Southwark went on, though less necessary than at the first, during all my London life, and in February 1891, my last year at St. George's Place, I wrote that I had been with "W. and Lady Tweeddale to the re-opening of St. Stephen's, a great day there, and a miracle to see the difference in the church."

The real helper, working there generously, unfailingly, doing far more than I could ever have done, was Julia, Marchioness of Tweeddale. In her hands I was able to leave the parish with a quiet mind when I went in the next year 1892, widowed, from London, which has never again become my home.

And before I left, I was able to write of increased congregations, of help brought to many in sorrow and want, a lessening of anxiety and perplexity among those workers who live among the poor. And I said also "The Inspector of Southwark Police Station bears testimony to considerable diminution of ruffianism and crime in Tabard Street during the last three years. He attributes this improvement to the continuous efforts put forth in the district for the people's welfare."

VI

LONDON TABLE TALK

"LITTLE boys should be heard and not seen; little girls should be seen and not heard." I was very well content to observe my part in that old saying in my early days, and my voice at least was not often heard by my elders, perhaps through the shyness I was long in outgrowing. For at my first dinner party, at Lough Cutra, I remember that the salt being out of reach I dared not ask my neighbour at the table to bring it within my reach, although he, the eldest son of the house, was not far beyond me in years and was no stranger. If I asked him and he did not hear me, so I meditated, no great harm would be done; but if he did not hear, and someone else did hear? What added savour could balance so miserable a confusion? In later years, laughing at the recollection, I told this to that gentle diplomatist who had been so unconscious of my need. And later again he said to me, in that fine manner that had gained him the affectionate nickname of Sir Charles Grandison among his colleagues, "That story you were so good as to tell me has been of the greatest service to many young ladies wherever I have lived, at Rio, at Stockholm, Rome, Berlin, Dresden . . . (It seems to me that he omitted Washington, where he had also been in the Embassy, from the list) for whenever one has been near me at dinner I have always made sure at the very beginning that she has been supplied with salt."

It was in that same shy winter that staying in a country house for a shooting party, I was taken into dinner for three evenings in succession by a very silent peer. For the first two evenings I did not say anything to him, or he to me; on the third he cleared his throat and turned towards me and I thought, "Now he is going to speak". And he said, "Are you going to eat your bread? And if not, may I have it?" I have sometimes met him in London since then, and though I have had a good deal more to say than in those days, it has not seemed to me that he has.

One winter a little later we stayed, my invalid brother and I, in a hotel at Cannes where there were only French people, kind and charming, not many of them from Paris but from the provinces. Every evening after dinner they used to sit round a long oval table in the salon, without books or newspapers or woolwork, their hands idle, simply clasped on the table, and talk. I don't remember that their conversation was very brilliant or witty (they were, as I was told, more flattering in their appreciation of me, and I still remember with vanity a phrase "chaque mot porte" spoken of the young stranger among them). I have a clearer recollection of everyone getting an opportunity, a turn, to give comment or opinion; as my husband used to say, to "put something into the pool".

Those French evenings came to memory in later years when I stayed in a cottage in one of the Aran islands near our Galway coast. When darkness fell friends would gather there, fishermen for the most part, and would sit in a half-circle round the fire. A pipe was passed from one to another, and each had his turn in speaking, the others listening, not interrupting; the woman of the house at her spinning in the background, saying her say if she had a mind.

I saw a yet different method later when we spent an evening in Parish at the salon of Ernest Renan, where we all sat in a half-circle, he alone in the middle of the room. He chose a guest (my husband) to come and sit by him, and we listened to that conversation for a while; and then Renan took all the talking to himself, and we all listened as he poured out an inexhaustible flow of words.

(And stopping as I read this the other day to Yeats, I asked if he remembered how his Monday evenings in Woburn Buildings used to be broken by his running down the three flights of stairs, each time there was a new guest at the door. Yes, he said, he remembered it, and that I had given him a better plan. For I had told one evening how in our Connacht churchyards the spirit of whatever man has been last buried is forced to await the entrance of another before he can go away to his rest. And so, I had said, might not whoever had been last to arrive on those Mondays be the door-opener for the next to come. So from that time each took his turn of service; it was only the first guest who would hear his host's rapid footstep on the stair and his hand on the latch of the door. But all had benefit in the end for it was to talk with him and listen to him we had come.)

There had, I think, been a somewhat similar fashion to Renan's in London, but when in 1880 I came there it had passed away. I don't remember having been asked to meet any supreme talker as used to happen. For I was told by Mrs. Kaye, the daughter of Henry Drummond, that Chief Secretary for Ireland who had startled landlords in more countries than one by a sentence "Property has its duties as well as its rights", that when after her father's death she and her sister had come to settle in London, they had feared it would be difficult, without large means or brilliance, to take their places in the society they wished for, and they did not want to entertain dull people. They told this to an old friend of their father and he took an almanac and wrote down his name in the blank space under four successive Thursdays and said, "I will dine with you on those four days and you may ask people to meet me". They did so, and with such a root of success that many years afterwards, when I came to know them, they were still giving weekly dinners, and although their house was not in the centre of fashion and their dinners were not very good, I never dined there without meeting interesting and distinguished people, and hearing some interchange of wit or wisdom. That was a fine gift for their father's friend to have bestowed on them, but that few would have like power to give; for he was the brilliant wit and talker, Sydney Smith. But when I came to London there was no Sydney Smith and no Macaulay to command an audience, and though there was good talk, it had, as Hayward used to say, "to be cut to the bone", and the little dinners used to remind me of the Pool of Bethesda; he only who was prompt to leap in at the right moment had any chance of success.

But extremes meet, and as it seems to me the conversation of France and that of the Irish cottage is constructed on the same lines, so is this "cut to the bone" condensed, quick-firing retort of the London dinners on the same lines as that of the two cabbies, the two 'bus conductors, one may hear shouting an epigram at each other as they pass after a momentary block in Piccadilly. The London talk may indeed, as it follows on its evolution, become even too rapid for words and become symbolic like that of the traditional 'bus man who looped his whip as he passed a rival and when asked what that signal meant said, "It is to show him I know that his father was hanged".

There was no welcome for soliloquy, nor for long discourse. I remember how disconcerted was a diplomatist, Robert Percy Ffrench, when coming back after many years of foreign salons, he found there was in London "no idea of conversation" to his mind in society, no space for it. "I thought I had offended in some way Lady Margaret Beaumont," he said to me, "because the other day she seemed rather cold to me before I left. But when I told this to Clanricarde (her brother), he said, "My dear fellow, in this country when you go to lunch at two o'clock people don't expect you to stay talking until seven". He grieved over this as over an uncivilised ancestral habit. Once indeed, at Aix, he talked to me through the whole of a wet afternoon, and when I went to dress for dinner, he came and continued his conversation outside the door. In London at one time I used to stay at home on Tuesday afternoons that friends might be sure to find me, and on one of these Tuesdays he came in and stayed. Other visitors came and sat for a half-hour, among them some kind old Galway constituents of my husband, and some gentle dark-skinned natives of Ceylon. And all through the changing sets of visitors Robert Ffrench continued his own subject, which happened to be the ramifications of the Esterhazy family through the different capitals of Europe. And yet he would often tell things worth hearing, as once of Bismarck, whom he used to know very well, and who meeting him at Biarritz before the war, said he would like to buy a house there to have as a refuge, as in case of the King of Prussia's death he would be exiled for high treason. The Queen, the Crown Princess "cette sotte" as he called her, and all the Court hated him then. "His first real struggle for supremacy was when the Emperor of Austria came to Frankfurt and invited the German Princes to meet him there as a kind of vassals, Bismarck said the King should not go, but he was very anxious to do so. They were on a journey and at the first place they stopped, at Baden, the King's sister (or his daughter), used all their influence to make him go. It came to the last day. Bismarck had the refusal ready written out for the King to sign, and brought it to him and stood behind him. 'And then,' he said, 'I think I magnetized him, for my hands were working with excitement as I stood behind him, and the instant he had signed I snatched the sheet away. It was a cold autumn night, but I hurried home, burst open the lock of my door and flung myself on the sofa as if I had come from a Turkish Bath, sweating.'."

Bismarck, he said, had spoken of races, "Europe is divided into two sexes, the female countries, Italy, the Celts, etc., have their soft pleasing quality and charm of a woman but no capacity for self-government. The male countries must take them in hand."

Once in my girlhood, I had heard an elder sister say she would never marry a clergyman, and another say she would never marry a widower; and I said to myself, I know not from what association or example, "I hope never to marry anyone I shall have to make small talk for". And while each of these sisters was led by circumstances to what she had protested against, my happier fate did even more than protect me from dullness, the forced creation of the chatter that may interest an unresponsive mind. Gladstone said to Sir Charles Tennant, "Sir William Gregory is a very agreeable man—I think the most agreeable I have ever known". Sarah Bernhardt, meeting him at dinner, spoke of him the next day as having more "esprit" than any Englishman she had ever met. Mr. G. W. Smalley, writing in an American newspaper an account of a house party at Dalmeny at the time of a Midlothian campaign, when he and Sir William and Mr. Gladstone were among Lord Rosebery's guests, says of him, "Gladstone liked him and talked to him. I was going to say, liked to hear him talk, but that is more doubtful. The great man was not always a good listener. He listened because his courtesy never failed him, but it was often plain that he put a restraint on himself in order to listen. He had so much to say for himself. Between him and Sir William Gregory there was never anything like competition, for one was as well-bred as the other. We used sometimes to wonder which of the two would give way. Both gave way and both were charming. Later I saw a good deal of Sir William, both in London and in the country. Wherever and however you met him he was always in the same agreeable, cultivated and convinced companion. If he had a subject he preferred it was Art, on that he was an expert, and he had the true Celtic notion of its importance; putting politics far below, as do all the races to whom Nature allots the artist's temperament. But on Art or life he talked with a sureness of knowledge and a vast experience and a warm heart."

So whether at home or abroad, with him I was always within hearing of conversation that was an endless delight.

But when, after my marriage, I found myself in that delightful society to which he brought me, the old shyness was still upon me, I found it hard to plunge into the Bethesda pool. And he, half vexed, half amused, would quote what was said of Goldsmith as a talker, that he had a thousand pounds in the bank but not a penny of small change in his pocket. It was not all my fault, for when he took me to see or dine with old friends, they would, after a kindly greeting to me, turn to him as was natural, and ask his opinion on this or that and gather round him to listen. I liked the large dinners best, no one could hear me except my neighbour; and now and then a happy chance would help me to confidence. I once quoted a sentence from Macaulay to an old gentleman whose name I had not heard, and he was pleased, and told me he was Sir Charles Trevelyan, Macaulay's brother-in-law. At another house, when politics were in the air and I was indignant with some of Gladstone's doing in Egypt or Ireland, I (though not going so far as Laurence Oliphant, whom I have heard say at a dinner table that he was the slave of his worst vices) spoke with considerable animation of his misdeeds to my neighbour at the dinner-table. And when we had gone to the drawing-room I was for some moments made miserable in being told that he was Sir Thomas Gladstone, the Prime Minister's brother. But our hostess said, "you need not take it to heart, for he stopped me as we left the dining-room to ask the name of 'that delightful lady'!" And after a while I began to take a pride in finding what would interest a stranger, in drawing him out of apathy or reserve; it was like playing a little game. One evening I found myself next Froude, I had never met him before. He turned his back and talked to an acquaintance on the other side for a while, and then grew bored with her and sat silent and gloomy, and when I made some remark, I know not what, his answer was "Everyone nowadays is so commonplace". I said, with some fire, "Not where I come from," and when he heard it was the West of Ireland all his gloom went away and he talked eagerly and with charm, and wrote to me the next day "it was a delight to meet you". And I think it was not insincere when a hostess to whom I said one night, "You put me next a very good talker," laughed and answered, "Haven't you noticed yet that whoever is next you talks well?" But it was only in our Egyptian winter and in the excitement of events there that I learned to take the leap, and one evening, coming from a small dinner at Sir Edward Malet's, where I had held my own, my husband made me very happy by saying he was content.

Of course, the small dinners when they went well, were

the most delightful of all. Our own table held but a dozen, and I see in a letter from Sir William to Sir Henry Layard that ours were pleasant. "We are not asking mashing-potato headed swells but people who can put something in the pot." But I noticed there and elsewhere that unless one is sure of one's guests there must be a little watchfulness, the breaking of *tête à têtes,* the danger that one guest may seize the conversation, like that Shah of Persia who seized and devoured all he could of the cucumbers on the table and put the rest in a bag to bring home. And sometimes the good talkers with a reputation to keep up may unconsciously struggle and each bring the other's wit to naught. There is an old Dublin story of two such men having been invited to dinner for the very purpose of seeing such a contest, by a mischievous host. One was Sir William Wilde, Oscar's father, the other I forget what Judge. But there was not much amusement after all, for the Judge at once took the lead and kept it, and Dr. Wilde ostentatiously fell asleep. I told this story in a lecture in America, and the next year it came back to me, exaggerated in the delightful American fashion: "Next morning they were found by the servants, one still talking, the other under the table—dead".

We were often at pleasant houses, for my husband had many friends. One evening that we dined at Millais's, I wrote: "It was very pleasant; the 'House Beautiful' looked very well at night, with Boehm's black marble sea-lion spouting water and in the drawing-room the curtains that had belonged to Amy Robsart. I sat next Millais, he is growing a little deaf, but pleasant and merry as ever, though he said he would not be good for much the next day, from eating and drinking a little more than usual. He won't dine out for three months before the Academy, and says his success is owing to his health and the care he had taken of it. If he is at all upset or had exceeded in any way his eye and hand fail and he can't point, though he could speak or write. When we see a picture of his that gives us pleasure we may know that he is in perfect health. He is pleased with his success, but thinks it a little hard that his pictures should go for so much more than he ever got for them, and that a Jew is making £800 a year by prints of 'The Huguenot', for the copyright of which he only got £140. On the evening we sat in the studio, a beautiful room with one Vandyke and many easel pictures about, and little mezzo-tints in black and gilt frames. He seemed proudest of a photograph of his daughter, Mrs. James. There was a half-finished portrait of her and of Lady Dalhousie and of his younger daughter in Gainsborough dress, and a very fine one nearly finished of Lord Hartington, and one imaginative picture, a mother and child looking at a bird's nest. He says his great men, Gladstone, Hartington, Rosebery, are punctual to the minute, but not those who have less to do; ladies are dreadful. He sent his love to Robert. "Tell him a man who has painted a few little pictures sends his love!"

Another artist friend was the sculptor who had made that sea-lion on Millais's staircase, Boehm. He had also made the statue of my husband put up at Colombo. Soon after my marriage we had gone to see him at his studio, and he had come forward to greet us, in his working blouse, his blue eyes sparkling and dancing as he told us, to our great amusement, that he had been dissatisfied with a statue of Drake he was making for the Duke of Bedford, to be put up at Tiverton, and the Duke also was not very well satisfied, there was something wrong. "And then I took your legs, Sir William, from the cast I made for your statue, and gave them to Drake, and the next time the Duke came he asked what I could have done to make such a man of him. So your legs will stand on Tiverton market place for ever as well as in Ceylon."

"I had a most amusing dinner at Boehm's, sitting between him and Burnand. I laughed so much! — but many of the jokes were *flashes* that left no traces. I said to Burnand that someone had been ordered to leave off meat and eggs, soup and sweets, 'so what can he live on now?'. 'On his friends I should think,' was the reply. Then Boehm said 'What is prestige?'. 'This dinner,' said Burnand, and we admired his quickness. I wish I could, but can't in writing, give you Burnand's account of an evening with Stanley, who lighting an immensely long cigar, began giving an account of Umtesa. 'Wal-wal-puff-puff-About Umtesa (drawled out as long as possible) and at about 2 a.m. he had only got to the description of the destruction of the army of Umtesa, man by man. So then Burnand, dying with sleep, proposed walking home with him but gained little by that, for Stanley put his back against each lamp-post that he might give each detail of his story with due emphasis.

"Then, Boehm declared, that of all the bores he had ever met, Gladstone is decidedly the greatest: 'He holds forth and expects no one else to while he does, and can't see a wine-glass without entering into details of the discovery of glass by the Phoenicians and the various dates at which theories as to its first use have been put forward. He had stayed at the same time with him at Balmoral, and they had been sent together to one of those picnics in which the Queen's heart delights, for herself and her household, when after a drive through drizzling rain they are expected to pick up wet sticks and light a fire and boil a kettle, which never boils, and partake of smoky tea in an open hut on the mountain side. On this festive occasion Lady Ponsonby happened to look at the mark on her teacup and said, 'I wonder what mark this is? Mr. Gladstone will be sure to know.' Gladstone seized it, and his opportunity, and said, 'It is a Chelsea mark of a period that only lasted two years,' then set off on a disquisition on china works all over the world. At last, when he was just coming back to Chelsea via Meissen, and the wind howling and the rain pattering, Lady Ponsonby innocently said, 'But, Mr. Gladstone,' upon which the G.O.M. turned on her, 'with a diabolical quiver', which it took Boehm's Hungarian face, animated by champagne to reproduce, and said, 'Will you be kind enough to allow me to speak!'. 'So,' said Boehm, 'I would not stay to hear that dear gentle little woman spoken to like that, and I went outside and walked up and down in the rain till it was time for our agreeable drive of thirty miles in a waggonette.'

"Burnand said he had once had the honour of breakfasting with the G.O.M. when he found the whole family circle assembled and also an Archimandrite who did not speak but had an insatiable appetite for muffins, and he never was so bored in his life. When he was leaving, Gladstone said, 'I only give dinners on Wednesday, Mr. Burnand, and I know your Wednesdays are always engaged, (and in a great hurry, lest I should say they were not), that is the reason I have [words missing] this by way of ingratiating himself with the [words missing].

"Burnand also told us that Irving had given a dinner to that same African explorer, but unfortunately, set him off talking at the beginning and he spun away about Umtesa, while Billy Russell and others were dying to talk, and at last Sala, in disgust, walked out of the room."

No doubt they would rather have listened to Billy (Dr. William) Russell, *The Times* correspondent in the Crimean and other wars. He was full of amusing reminiscence; good humoured and good natured. And behind the twinkle in his eyes there was much personal dignity. At the great Indian Durbar, the Prince himself had been obliged to ask him to forget some jesting word that had given him offence and driven him from the Royal table, before he would consent to came back to it.

He had gained great repute in the Crimean days and his letters reprinted was one of the books I remembered as a child at Roxborough. He told me that Arthur Sullivan, when unknown, had come to him, and asked him to write a song for him to set to music. "For," he said, "no one knows me, but if the words are by you it will be noticed." And now I do not think his name is known to many, while Arthur Sullivan's operas are being put on again and again.

I wrote, "At dinner at Mrs. Ware Scott's, Billy Russell was delightful, light and bright. He told us a story of the Prince's visit to Ceylon, when the Duke of Sutherland, wanting a brandy and soda late, sent his piper to ask the Singalese servants for it, and at the apparition they all bolted out of the window into the woods, and Sir William complained next day that some of them had not come back yet. He says when he was with Lord Wolseley in South Africa, the provisions failed and they had to live on tinned meat with no stimulant but tea. He never felt better in his life, and when he came back to Pretoria decided to go without wine, but found the excitement of the march being over he needed the artificial stimulant."

And at another house: "It was rather dull after dinner, the men were so long downstairs—'Sir William was explaining the Indian Corn Trade!' said Billy Russell.

"He also told of a shooting party at Colonel North's when the Colonel, who had spared no expense to get up a good head of game, quarrelled with his head keeper and gave him notice, whereupon the keeper collected a gang of poachers and had every pheasant carried off in the night. The Duke of Cambridge was the chief guest and his language when no pheasants appeared was very forcible."

He had once been taken to see Carlyle who asked if he was a Woburn Russell, and being told he was *The Times'* correspondent, said: "Well, sir, and do you still follow your detestable profession?" "Well, I write for money as you do, Mr. Carlyle." "Well, now I deserved that; but I thought you might only write for pleasure like Dicky Milnes" (Lord Houghton).

Carlyle said that once, going to some entertainment given by Cyrus Field, Houghton said to him at the station, "Come along, I'll give you a seat in my carriage". He then marched up to the Lord Mayor's (Sir H. Hanson) carriage and said he must have a place for himself and his friend, and two men already there were turned out for the purpose. He had said, "I shall only go twice more to Westminster Abbey before I am carried there myself; once after Gladstone, once after Tennyson."

Lord Houghton was another delightful companion. I met him at luncheon soon after my marriage, although all I can remember is that my interest in meeting him (and it was real because of his verses, *Strangers Yet,* verses that yet linger in my memory), was absorbed into a stronger one, for he spoke of having known Heine at the end of his life. And to have even touched that paralysed hand seemed a wonderful thing to me.

Later, dining with him one evening, "he and W. talked of old friends, of Lady Waldegrave's wonderful charm. As a girl, she and her father had been asked to tea at the Waldegraves', but arrived while dinner was going on. Lord Waldegrave and his brother, who had been drinking a good deal, said, "Bring Kitty Braham in here, she's a nice little girl', and she was put to sit between them. She told this to Lord Houghton, and said, 'And I knew then I should marry the two brothers¹'. When at twenty six she married, her husband was sixty two. 'Just the figures reversed,' she said. W. said the wine at her parties was not good. 'If I had good wine,' she said, 'A.Z. would get drunk.' 'Society has been left to two adventurers,' someone said to Lord H., talking of her and Lady Molesworth, but Lady Molesworth had never taken so high a place. Lady Morgan (the novelist) had hated her. She once said to Sir William: 'I happen to have a playbill by me announcing the appearance of Peg Carstairs in *Love in a Village.* That and an entry into Bath on a camel are the first things known of Lady Molesworth.' (It was she who was kept from old Richard Gregory's deathbed

---

¹ Frances Elizabeth Anne (Kitty), was the daughter of John Braham, a famous tenor. She married John James Waldegrave, of Navestock, Essex, the illegitimate son of the 6th Earl and on his death married the legitimate son, the 7th Earl. On the Earl's death, she was still in her mid-twenties and was twenty six when she married G. G. Harcourt, the son of the Archbishop of York, who was sixty two. On *his* death she married Lord Carlingford, who survived her.

by his servant, or she would doubtless have married him there and then.)

Lord Houghton talked of Dizzy's affection for his wife. "The first time he stayed at Windsor he was late for dinner and he had apologised to the Queen by saying, 'I have never had a man to attend me before; my wife has always dressed me.' She used to put his hair in curl papers every night. W. says George Smythe, once teasing him about 'Mary Anne', Dizzy turned on him and said, 'Young man, there is one word in the English language you have never heard of and that word is gratitude'. 'What can have been the charm about George Smythe?' W. asks. He was an ugly little fellow, but he fascinated women, whom he invariably treated badly. Mrs. Lennox insisted on marrying him on his death-bed in his Mistress's house. Mrs. M—— asked when dying that she might be buried beside him. Lady —— wrecked her life on him. He was only thirty-six when he died.

But Lord Houghton was sometimes rather irreverent in his wit. I remember going to a meeting for, I think, some plan of workmen's insurance, and where someone asked how the money was to be stopped out of the daily wage of a crossing sweeper or a man who holds horses and earns an occasional shilling; and an old gentleman who had been asleep woke up and asked, "What are you going to do with the money when you get it?" and one of the speakers answered "heaps of things". My reason for going had been that Lord Shaftesbury was in the Chair, and I wanted to see him, he had been one of the idlers of an older generation, my husband's mother and mine, and it was rather a shock when, as we came out, Lord Houghton came up and said, "I hope I may live to see Shaftesbury found out!"

And someone told me that at the time of the Irish Church Disestablishment Bill passing through Parliament, he had seen him go up to two Irish Bishops who were talking together on a hearthrug at the Athenaeum and say, "This time next year you two will be only a pair of Dissenting Ministers".

Lord Shaftesbury died not long after that meeting. His son, Evelyn Ashley, talking of his father's death, told us that he had suffered much in the last few days, and that the Queen had only once, at the very last, inquired for him; she had never forgiven him for opposing her being made Empress of India. He said the old Lord, his grandfather, who was quite of the old school and looked on his son as a Socialist, used to receive the rents himself at St. Giles, and when the tenants left the room he would say to the butler, "Simmons, do your duty," which meant, "Give them plenty to drink". On coming out of the room one evening, he found most of his tenants lying about dead drunk, upon which he seized his butler's hand and said, "Simmons, you have done your duty; the Lord will reward you".

I wrote to Sir M. Grant Duff: "Lowell says one dinner is just like another, except that at some you get ortolans". But it is not so, for Sir William has been at a quite original dinner at the Speaker's, to meet the working men M.P.s who have no Levée or evening clothes. He sat next Mr. Leicester, a glass-blower, who was much pleased because he recognised some glass of his own blowing on the table. He was a teetotaller, has put by all his life the money he would have spent on drink, and has bought himself a few acres, but still keeps up his blowing when not engaged in his Parliamentary duties. The butler came to him, 'The Speaker wishes to take wine with you, Sir'. 'No, I never drink wine.' 'But let me pour a little in your glass, Sir.' 'No, certainly not. Why waste it? Give me water.' J. Arch was there, with a benevolent open countenance. Mr. Leicester said, 'We all love him, but he is too soft, too easily taken in'. After dinner they adjourned to the drawing-room, and one of the guests said: 'Mr. Speaker, may I call upon Mr. Abraham for a song?'. 'Certainly,' said the Speaker, and Mr. Abraham stood in the middle of the room and without accompaniment sang, 'The Men of Harlech'. 'Chorus, Mr. Speaker!' he cried when the first verse was ended and they all sang it—in Welsh— Sir William included!

"The Bishop of Manchester told me a story that would have pleased you, about a young clergyman who, having been examined by Dean Stanley and the Bishop of London, had to wind up by preaching to them. He began his sermon, 'Every congregation is divided into two classes, those who are lost and those who are saved'. 'Stop!' said Stanley, 'and tell us in which category you place each of us'.

"I was at dinner the other night where a Colonel Campbell sat without saying a word all through dinner, but suddenly as the ladies were leaving, told us of an American he had heard called upon to return thanks for distinguished strangers at a public dinner. 'This is quite unexpected,' he had said. 'In fact, when I came into this room I felt much like Daniel in the lions' den. You don't seem to see it?

Why, when Daniel got into that place and looked around he thought to himself, "Whoever's got to do the after-dinner speaking, it won't be me"'.'."

This story had an Indian success, Grant Duff, delighted with it, told it next time he had to make a speech, inappropriate, as it seems, to a Governor. And Lord Dufferin wrote it to me in a letter a little later, having just heard it from Grant Duff!

I wrote of another dinner, "It is always pleasant to dine with a publisher. I dined at John Murray's last night. The house always charming, the staircase where Byron and Scott first met, the grate where Byron's MS. was burned; the screen made by Byron's fencing master under his directions, the corrected MS. of many authors. A speech of Peel's was much corrected for publication. 'I have never done anything of that sort,' said Gladstone when he saw it, forgetting a speech equally corrected in his own writing in Murray's possession and which he showed us."

At some other houses: "At dinner bi-metalism was talked of, and W. said that Everett, when told that Washington had thrown a dollar over the Potomac, had said, 'Well, I know the dollar went much further in Washington's time than it does now'. Everett had also said when a friend, meeting him in New York, noticed that he stuttered more than he used to do at Baltimore, 'But you know this is a much b-b-bigger place!'

"Lowell sat next me and we quarrelled over Ireland. He says we landlords must make up our minds to the spread of democracy in the nineteenth century and be the Jonah thrown to the whales. His cure for Ireland would be to send Davitt there as Chief Secretary, responsibility would make him conservative; he would be assassinated, replace him by the next leader, and so on.

"On to Lady Marian Alford's, 'small and early, like a seven months child,' says Elcho."

Spencer Ponsonby spoke of Landseer and said his works suffer by being seen together. He had sat next him at dinner not long before he died and had drawn a sketch on the menu of something they were talking about. Landseer caught sight of him and said, 'that's all wrong,' and taking the pencil from him, drew a line here and there and altered it. Towards the end of dinner Mr. Ponsonby took up the menu and put it in his pocket as a souvenir, whereupon Landseer was furious, flew at him, insisted on his giving it up and then tore it to fragments. His mania was that people wanted to make money by his works."

Lady Dorothy's luncheon parties were always amusing. "At one she asked riddles, 'Why can't you make Niagara into a lake?' 'Dam it you can't.' 'And why does it cost less to maintain a stepfather than a father?' Because ce n'est que le premier *pa* qui coute."

And again at Lady Dorothy's "to meet the Bishop of Emmaus and the Bancrofts. They talked of the imposition of beggars. Mrs. Bancroft had met in Portland Place a woman who asked the way to Finsbury Square and then lamented she had no money to pay a 'bus there, so she gave her some. But walking the same way some weeks later, she was accosted by the same woman who asked the same question. 'What,' said Mrs. Bancroft, 'haven't you found it yet?' The Bishop said one of his curates asked a woman he had helped what was her husband's profession. After some hesitation, she confessed that he was 'an asker'. He could do sixty streets in a day and it would be a very poor day when he didn't get a penny in each, five shillings, which he would find it hard to earn by honest labour. He says Chelsea is overburdened with charitable societies which do more harm than good. His principle is not to give to beggars, but to give tips liberally to cabbies or street sweepers who are working for their livelihood (and this advice has often been followed by me since then) or to set up costers with a stock in trade.

"The Bishop told of the footman who said he had given an evasive answer to a visitor he knew his master didn't want to see. And when questioned, he said the evasive answer had been—'you go and be damned'; Mrs. Bancroft told of the Prince's visit to Lord Tennyson. On giving his name, the footman put his thumb to his nose and said 'That's been tried on before!' And of an old man telling Lord Tennyson what a comfort his poems are to him, 'I just put my feet on the hob and am asleep in a minute!'.

"Mr. Jeune is canvassing Lewes, but in difficulties in consequence of having once pinned a consecrated wafer to his brief in some ecclesiastical case. The Ritualists have got hold of this and won't support him."

I used to think the great charm of London Society was in its unexpectedness; one did not know what new acquaintance or old friend one might meet—I had met Laurence Oliphant at Constantinople, and I wrote to H.P.H. in May 1886: —

"I am not always going to write so often, but I think you like a letter for Sunday, and Robert hasn't written his yet, as he only gets through one a day, and has begun with his grandma . . .

"At a pleasant little dinner at Lord Wemyss's, who is charming, very witty and amusing, there were only the Layards and ourselves and Laurence Oliphant. I forget if I told you anything of him. He was in the Foreign Office, a 'man about town' and a 'diner out', when he suddenly went off to America to follow a prophet, Mr. Harris, who gained the most extraordinary influence over him and the rest of the sect. They gave up their property for the time being. Mrs. Oliphant had to support herself by giving music lessons, some say by washing, and Laurence was sent off to Constantinople, on a mission to colonize Palestine with Jews. I met him there, and he was in the depths of despair because the Sultan had refused to allow the proposed Colony. Then came the expulsion of Jews from Russia, and he had his hands full, providing for them (still in obedience to Mr. Harris). He sent some to America but they don't like it much, some say because they have to eat pork. Now he has quarrelled with Mr. Harris, and his wife is dead, but he still sticks to the Jews, and lives at Mount Carmel, and a little colony has been formed of Jews who slip in, in spite of the Sultan, from time to time. But I don't think they will ever settle there in large numbers, the country is too poor, and agriculture doesn't suit them. One of the Rothschilds, when asked to join in a movement for the restoration of his race to Palestine said, 'I hope when we get there I shall be appointed Ambassador to London.' L. Oliphant wrote many years ago *Piccadilly,* a clever satire on London society and the 'Wholly worldly' and the 'worldly-holy' (with their meetings and bazaars). More lately he has written *Altiora Peto,* rather a clever novel, and *Traits and Travesties,* and now he has two books in the press.

"At a party at A. Raffalovich's. When supper was ready I found myself put into the care of Mr. T. P. O'Connor (of Tuam the Land Leaguer!). But before I had recovered my breath he said he remembered Sir William's election in his boyhood. I said, 'I hope you threw up your cap for him', and he said, 'Oh there was no need for that. All the people were with him'. And we got into pleasant talk on Irish politics and religion, without bitterness. He is a pleasant-faced young man, considered like O'Connell. I said to him,

'I hope Ireland will soon be quiet again'. 'Oh yes,' he said, 'in three years, when we shall have Home Rule'. But he seemed to agree with me that the Land Question should be settled first."

Mr. Thomson Hankey, an old friend of my husband from their House of Commons days, gave up formal dinner parties (such as that Shrove Tuesday one when Gladstone had no brown sugar with his pancakes) after his wife's death, but was seldom without guests at his house in Portland Place— a letter to H.P.H. says, "I met Goschen at dinner on Monday at old Mr. Hankey's, who is so punctual that he won't wait for anyone, so when the clock struck eight he gave me his arm and marched off, though the Chancellor of the Exchequer had not yet appeared. He (Goschen) told me his son, who was at Rugby, and is now his secretary, has just been making an American tour which he was delighted with. He has a boy now at Rugby, and I thought spoke rather coldly of Dr. Percival, saying he 'did not inspire enthusiasm'. Talking of the strikes, someone said, 'They say the Cabinet are going to strike'. 'Oh no,' said Goschen, 'there are too many blacklegs ready to do our work'."

Mr. Hankey would ask people informally, and I wrote some time later, "We had just finished soup when Sir Redvers and Lady Audrey Buller were announced. Mr. Hankey had forgotten he had asked them (but would not have waited dinner for them anyhow). It was rather awkward as there was hardly any room (his niece had to slip away) and food would have been scanty but for a joint of roast lamb. However, all ended well. Lord Herschell talked to me at dinner of the Manipur disaster, on which a light has been thrown by Mrs. Grimwood's letter about Manipur and said a fuss must be made and questions asked as to the truth of her story that the [word missing] was to have been arrested by treachery in Durbar[1], and also as to the mismanagement of the whole affair. After dinner, Sir Redvers Buller, who had been listening, came to talk to me on the same subject, said it was ridiculous to call the affair a 'massacre' that it was an ordinary frontier incident, and that Mrs. Grimwood's sister ought to be poisoned for having sent the letter to *The Times*. He scoffs at the idea of treachery, says that is the usual way of arresting prisoners, and they know quite well what to expect when they come to a

[1] The State Council.

Durbar (which apparently the [word missing] did, as he stayed away). And that no one would be so sensitive who had lived, as he had done, on a frontier, and seen hostile natives sitting on the doorsteps sharpening their spears and consulting as to which Englishman it would be most amusing to kill. No; 'foolish people like Lord Herschell's followers would doubtless talk nonsense about it'. A difference of opinion between the military official and Civilian Liberal.

"In talking of the Vandycks at the Grosvenor, Frederic Harrison said Vandyck was the true supporter of monarchy in this country by the sympathy he created for Charles I."

On 1 January 1887, "There was a New Year's dinner at the Jeunes; a large mixed party, Ouida, John Morley, three Bulgarian Delegates, General Willoughby, Envoy of the Queen of Madagascar, etc. The Bulgarians spoiled the evening for me, I had one at dinner and one afterwards. I was introduced to Ouida; she has a harsh, discordant voice and when I said by way of politeness, 'I suppose your influence had something to do with the unmuzzling of the dogs,' (the Order had taken effect today) she said, 'It was altogether my influence, with a little help from Georgie Salisbury'. The poor Bulgarians had met with sympathy but nothing more, and spoke of the misery of their first three days in London, Christmas, Sunday and Bank Holiday, one after another. I don't think anybody liked Ouida. Mrs. Lynn Lynton said she had given herself such airs at Mrs. Campbell Praed's as to make everyone furious. 'Speiring' at the dishes —'what is that?' and refusing to go upstairs with the ladies, she had sat in the cloakroom till her carriage came. She had met Irving at dinner and was most anxious he should be introduced to her, but when he was and said politely, 'I hope when you come to the Lyceum you will accept a box from me', 'I never go to the Theatres,' was her reply!"

One afternoon we went to Tristram Ellis's, where Mrs. Russell, an American, gave an address on "motion" and its speech, how one lady repulses you on coming into the room, another pleases you, and without speech, merely by movement. To move the hand and forearm only with "that's a fact", brings others into antagonism at once with you. But moving the whole arm and the fingers altogether is persuasive. One note of music played continuously is unpleasant; if all the landscape were red we should go mad; even plain red window curtains are maddening; but the varied tints of the leaves in an Indian summer are so healing that

doctors send their patients among them. So one motion, a
stiff nod for instance, is unpleasant, but a movement of the
whole body is full of grace. "I could give you a bow that
would make you feel small and of no account, or I could
give you one that would make you feel that I love and
esteem and reverence you, a bow that would make you walk
higher all day and feel good and wishing to be up to my
level." "The English, we have always heard, pride themselves on keeping quite still, and we tried to do so, but could
not, and we began to try and find out the meaning of
motion."

Then, again at Lady Dorothy's, "Mrs. Russell was lecturing
and much admired by Lord Lytton and others. She left out
the red curtain bit, Lady Dorothy's being of that colour.

"Paul[2] came from Rugby in high spirits with his 'Cap',
he came with us to lunch at Raffalovitch's. I sat between
Toole and Mr. Isadore de Lara. I liked Toole very much,
very grave, kind and quiet. He was very nice to Paul, he
had lost a son early, he thinks from the effect of a cricket
accident. I asked him if it was tiring playing the same piece
over and over again, and he said, no, because the audience
changed, it was like telling an anecdote to different people.
He likes a Scots audience very much, it is a little time before
they give you their confidence, but when they do, they stick
to you. The Irish are quicker but not so dependable.
Americans quick but don't like coming in a crush like the
English, which encourages the author.

"We dined at the Henry Reeves's, it was very pleasant. I
sat between Colonel Romilly and Lord Hobhouse, talked
Ireland and India, and afterwards I talked with Mr. Burrows
of Oxford, whose son is called 'Baedeker' at Anaradapura
where we had met him. So I made him happy by my account
of him; and then found it was Lady Elizabeth's son who had
written *New Guinea* and she was delighted with my appreciation of it. Lecky was more lively than usual, mildly
chaffy about Arabi, and Sir Montague Smith pleasant."

To H.P.H.: "Mrs. Hurburt told us of the offence the
German Emperor had given to the Diplomatic ladies at
Rome who had expected to be asked to dinner to meet him
as usual, but were left out at his special request, and their
husbands came from the dinner no better pleased, as by his
request they had not been presented to him. The Empress

2 H. P. Harvey.

Frederick always had want of tact, would say to one of the ladies at a reception, 'Ah, you are wearing an English dress, how much superior it is to any German one". And the Princesses always spoke of England as 'home', for which their eldest brother struck one of them one day.

"Last night we dined in a magnificent house in Carlton House Terrace 'smelling of money' as one of the guests said; the table covered with white flowers and gold plate, the carpets too beautiful to walk on. Sir William Drake, who was there told me that our host's father had arrived in London with half-a-crown in his pocket, had got a place in a City warehouse where he had to sleep under the counter, and had finally risen to be partner, and married the daughter of the house, just like Dick Whittington and the good little boys in story books.

"St. George's Place . . . We are cut away from the outer world just now, the wood pavement is being renewed, and no vehicle can drive to the door, and when we dined out the night I arrived we had to walk to the corner in the rain, and I lost my gloves, but apologised for arriving bare-handed as a refugee from Ireland, stripped and despoiled! The dinner was pleasant to me, I was next Sir Rutherford Alcock who lived in China and Japan, but I don't think we were a brilliant party, for some wretch asked what was the capital of Peru, and it went all down the table to Sir William who at last answered it. I hope you don't know! Sir A.B. told me of a house party he had been at where after dinner someone mentioned that Knowles gives Gladstone £50 for an article for *The Nineteenth Century*. 'Yes,' said Archibald Forbes, 'Gladstone and I are the only two men he gives so much to!'. But Mallock (*Is Life worth Living?*), who was there, said, 'He gave me £63 last week for one'. 'I don't believe you,' said Forbes, and a battle was kept off with difficulty.

"Our visit to Mentmore was very pleasant. Lord Rosebery looks about as old as you, and is very agreeable and merry, besides being what Sir William calls 'a statesman'. Lady R. looks like his mother and is very good natured and they got on very well. He is devoted to his children . . . it is nice to see how fond he is of them . . . the reception rooms are filled with costly and beautiful things, curtains worked by Marie Antoinette, a carpet that belonged to Louis XVI and what I liked best was Millais's portrait of little Lady Peggy. Sir William Harcourt is amusing, though he looks pompous, and another of Lord Spencer, 'as good as a play', and all the time there was pleasant witty talk. Great excitement, of course, about the elections, Lord Rosebery confesses he is pining to be in office again. . . . No one, even his late colleagues, can say a good word for Sir Charles Dilke[3], and the divorce trial is to come on in spite of his marriage which doesn't seem to have improved his position. I think they will have to take refuge in Paris, and you will find Lady Dilke in possession of your room, which your uncle so generously offered her.

"A dinner last night was pleasant to me because I sat next Sir Hercules Robinson, whom I like very much, though the dinner rather distressed me as a housekeeper, as we had lamb cutlets, roast mutton and roast lamb! I whispered to my neighbour, 'this mother and child were not divided in their death', and the same thing had just struck him.

"We had one day a very amusing lunch at Raffalovich's. I sat between Browning and the young officer in *Dandy Dick*. Browning, pleasant and agreeable as usual, but so unlike his poetry, which I knew first, that there is a kind of double identity about him which disturbs one. He is very proud because his son's picture has been given a first place in the Salon. Also Justin McCarthy, most respectable of the Irish members, Charles Wyndham (David Garrick!), Arthur Cecil, Lady Dorothy Nevill, Lady Monckton (who to Browning's indignation ate her lunch with her gloves on) and opposite to me, Grossmith, very nice looking and comical looking, and full of natural fun. The table was rather crowded and Browning called out, 'You look like Napoleon at St. Helena, as if you wanted elbow room', and he at once folded his arms in the Napoleonic attitude and looked the part most absurdly. Then he said he was going to give up the Savage Club because he was always expected to sing there (though he is most good natured about doing so) and that a friend of his, a lawyer, had said, 'I have joined the Savage on purpose to hear you'. 'Then you won't, said G. 'I don't sing for nothing. You wouldn't pass sentence on me for nothing.' 'But I suppose,' said his friend, 'you would sing if you were asked out to dinner?'. 'Certainly not. I don't eat more than eight-shillings' worth of food if I dine

[3] Sir Charles Dilke was cited as co-respondent by a Scottish Liberal lawyer by name of Crawford when his wife Virginia told him she had been Dilke's mistress since 1882. Dilke strenuously denied this, but later was forced to admit that Virginia's mother *had* been his mistress.

out. I think my song is worth more than that.'

"I haven't much to say, but old habit leads me to write my Saturday morning letter. Next term, however, you can take out the ones still unread, one for each Saturday—like the ante-dated *Christian Heralds* sent out with the Arctic Expedition—and I will spend my time in writing to some one with more courage in deciphering.

"The most amusing party of the week has been at Mr. Knowles (of *The Nineteenth Century*). He is a successful, popular, good-natured little man. He was an architect, built some rather ugly houses and while building one for Tennyson made great friends with him, and was introduced to various distinguished men. The *Quarterly* and *Edinburgh* were then the great magazines, but even when the writers in them were well known it was not etiquette to sign their names; and the idea struck Knowles that a magazine with signed articles would pay. So he started his *Nineteenth Century*, getting Tennyson, Gladstone and other celebrities to write for it, and it was at once an immense success, and I hear he clears £8,000 a year by it. *The Fortnightly* now runs on the same lines, and has a higher standard, requiring pretty good writing, as well as a good name, whereas Knowles doesn't care how rubbishy the articles are so that they are signed, and short . . .

"I am not much in love with magazines myself, they tempt one to dip into so many subjects and destroy the taste and consume the time for serious reading. And now *The Pall Mall*, with its interviews and summaries, takes the cream off everything.

"I hope your cold is all right. That camp must have been dreadful in this weather—such weather for the end of June! We were nearly perished at the Queen's Concert last night, waiting for our carriage, and as it was rather a dreary entertainment altogether, everyone in mourning for the King of Bavaria and no one venturing to applaud even Patti and Albani's highest efforts, Sir William declares he never, never will go to another, and waved his hand with, 'Goodbye Victoria' as we left."

"At dinner at the Lovelaces', Lady Tennyson told me that a lady had said to her husband at Oxford, 'I hear young Tennyson is here. Is he as great a fool as most great men's sons are?' He said, 'Quite'.

February 1891: "I went to Westminster Abbey in the morning to ask for a drawing order, and found a service

going on. At dinner at Thomson Hankey's I found the new
Bishop of Worcester with his wife and his son, and heard it
was his consecration service I had looked in at. He was
rather tired as it had lasted for three hours and Canon
Farrar had preached one hour seven minutes, chiefly on
drunkenness, which was unnecessary. The Bishop had to
take a glass of port to revive him, he was so tired out. Mrs.
Humphry Ward had been to see me in the afternoon asking
how to hold a Mothers' Meeting, etc. I asked about the
new 'University Hall' which has been opened with such a
flourish of trumpets, and she said it is a room with gymnastic
apparatus, newspapers, and lamps, where young men will
come in and spend the evening. This being just what there
is in St. Stephen's Institute, and no doubt many other
parishes. I was rather pleased at her having to borrow ideas
from Christianity, with all Robert Elsmere's inspiration at
her back."

George Moore called in the evening "perfectly satisfied
with his new novel, *A Drama in Muslin'*." At Mrs. Ford's I
sat next Sir John Fowler, who is pleasant. He knew an
Egyptian Mahommedan with three wives who said, "one
cooks and one keeps the house, but the other is young and
beautiful, the wife of the heart, she does nothing". "And
what do you do when they quarrel?" "Oh, if they make a
great noise I thrash the two eldest."

I used to dine often in later years with the Childerses,
who lived almost next door to us in St. George's Place. He
was Chancellor of the Exchequer, and it was at one of their
small round-table dinners that Gladstone had first met
Parnell in private life, and had made a compact with him,
giving some concession, I forget what, to the Irish party,
while Parnell agreed not to oppose an extra allowance to
the Prince of Wales (the late King Edward) for his children.
I used to propose putting an inscription: "At this round-
table Parnell was squared".

One night at our own dinner-table in London someone
was belittling Randolph Churchill, then a young man. But
Lord Morris said, "That man will succeed; he has been twice
caricatured in *Punch*". For, as W. E. Forster wrote to me once
when I had sent an Irish paper with some caricatures of him,
"In England we caricature our favourites; in France and
Ireland, the Celtic countries, only our enemies are
caricatured."

It was at another little dinner that someone who had just

been with Randolph Churchill, and advising him to moderation, told me his answer had been, "I have never done anything spirited that it hasn't been said by my friends 'Well, Randolph has done for himself *this* time!'. And yet I have kept my head pretty well up." And this was rather sad to remember later, when his political fall had indeed come.

I was lunching one day with Lord Morris's wife and daughters and sons, and then when he came in late I said, "We have been talking of beauty and they say you are no judge of beauty." "It's well for them I'm not," he said. But they forgave him for the sake of his wit. Lord Bowen was another witty lawyer I knew, but now his sayings are getting into print, how at a meeting of judges, he said to one of his juniors who contradicted him, "Even the youngest of us is not infallible[4]" and his definition of a metaphysician, "A blind man in a dark room groping for a black hat that isn't there".

I had first met Dr. Mahaffy at dinner at the Wellington Club in London. It was a dinner given by Lord Howth, and I was next him, but after a while (and this is an idea I think might well be followed now and again) he said he would change places with Mahaffy who was at the other end of the long table, as he thought we ought to make each other's acquaintance. I was delighted, for I had read his *Art of Conversation* and expected something very brilliant. But he began by talking of all the past Viceroys of Ireland's wives in turn and said of each (with more or less emphasis), "That was a charming woman"; and then he spoke of the Prince, and said what a bore it was when he came to London having to go so often to meet him at suppers and the like. I sat abashed, and after a while he dropped into really interesting talk. The same thing happened the second, perhaps the third time we met, and after that the prelude was dropped, and the good talk began at once. At first I thought it ordinary boasting, later I thought perhaps it was a testing of the listener. Once when we were staying at Howth Castle he came to dinner, and Lord Howth mischievously told me he wanted to see whether he or Sir William would hold the table. But one or two other guests, Miss Stokes with photographs of saints' cells, and some other

4 Another version was by W. H. Thompson, Master of St. John's College, Cambridge, "We are none of us infallible—not even the youngest of us".

woman, and a retired and apparently dull Colonel made the
dinner talk while we ladies were there rather scattered. At
the door as we left, Lord Howth whispered, "I'll tell you
what happens", and I wished I could stay and hear. But he
came in later, his sense of humour overcoming his disappointment, to say, "The outsider won in a gallop!" for the
Colonel had begun to talk the moment we left, and had
given no one else the chance to say a word.

I don't go out very much now, I am kept too hard at
work, but I have sometimes played my little game. It is not
so very long ago that I met Mahaffy again at a small dinner.
We sparred through dinner time on Nationalism and the
Irish language set on by a mischievous hostess. After dinner
I did not think he would come near me, yet he did so. He
began boasting of how he had once drawn a hopelessly dull
woman into conversation by praising her good-for-nothing
son. I said, "Oh that is nothing, you had some knowledge
of her before or of her son. Now I have a recipe for making
men talk. If all fails I try them by talking of their walking
sticks." He was interested. "Do you really do that? Did you
think of it yourself? I wonder why it should interest them."
Then presently he said, "Now *I* have a very interesting
walking stick that was given to me by King Edward, and
another that was lent to me by Queen Alexandra when I
was lame at Sandringham at one time, and another . . ."
"Yes," I said, "I knew my recipe would not fail".

To H.P.H. To go back to London: "Yesterday I found at
Mme. du Quaire's Sinnett and another psychist. They were
talking of Home the medium. Mme. du Quaire says the
Empress (Eugenie) told her that during an interview with
her he had said, 'Stay still, Madame!' and went up in the
air until she could see the soles of his boots, at which she
was so astonished that she let her hand fall to her side
suddenly and he came down with a bump and said angrily,
'That might have killed me'. The other man said that a
friend of his had been travelling with Home before he
became aware of his powers, and going into his room in the
morning found him suspended between his bed and the
ceiling and in a great fright lest he should fall.

"At dinner at the Arthur Russells', Dr. Abel said, 'the
reason of the immense number of German suicides now is
the atheism that prevails, the belief that there is nothing
after death, beyond death'. The state of Germany he describes as intolerable, the strain of preparation for war,

surrounded as they are by armies, intolerable. Bismarck has the Emperor and the masses with him, but three-fourths of the educated classes against him.

"Last evening Sir William was dining in the City with the Clothworkers, and I asked Solomon Reinach, who was in London for a few days, to dine here, and we went to the Exhibition afterwards. He didn't like the Indian art specimens, but was interested in the King of Ashanti's ornaments, reminding him of Etruscan, and in a little Indian god kneeling, which he says, as with Greek early art, is the expression of rapid movement, and that children often draw with the same idea.

"He cried when talking of Mrs. Lee Childe (daughter of de Triqueti, the sculptor) to whom he was devoted. She knew death was coming at the last but had made up her mind to die bravely and jested with it. One day she said it was very near, and the next, being a little better, 'Ah, you will say that is my pose! and that when I say I am dying je suis déjà vêtue pour la resurrection . . .' She died without pain, without breaking down, without seeing a clergyman, and we felt that a light had gone out. She had been very much attached to a small group of friends but used to say, 'I should not care if a great wave were to sweep away all the rest'."

Sometimes, not often, even at a dinner table, in a crowd, one hears a word, a sentence, that might have had its birth rather on the plains of Heaven than on the ridge of earth. "She is an old dweller in those high countries" someone in an old play says of his wife, "but not from me; here, she's here". There may yet be some in the crowd who hold converse as did our own saint Columcille with his guardian angel—"our loved one who spoke with Axel"—in the old days of the world. But it is the strange thing and the mystery that it is easier for us to get through the cloud that separates us from "those higher countries" than through the barrier made by the body that enfolds those fragments of the Divine "breathed into the soul of man at the beginning and the inheritance of man ever since"—(it was a poor man on Slieve Echtge who said that to me). Something holds us back from discovering that heavenly essence in one another; pride, shyness, humility. Is it not to make that discovery easier that Churches are formed, and Leagues and Societies? And even then are we not but as prisoners in adjoining cells, scratching a signal on the wall with a rusty nail, trying to wear away the stone, to work at an opening through it, to make it a little thinner; yet very seldom breaking it down or coming close to those who may be looking with us towards those high plains of Heaven. Yet sometimes from a stranger one may get that glimpse. I met once at dinner at the Leckys' a Dutch friend of theirs, an old man. I never met him again but when he said goodbye that evening he said, "We may meet again after death from this world". He said, among other things, "My mother would only when we were children read us the part of the Bible that was about Paradise, for she said, "Children always walk in Paradise; they can wait till later to learn of the world and its wickedness'." He said to me also, "We are on a journey home, and the ticket is taken at the moment we are born." I felt that he himself, whom I never met again, was an old dweller in those high countries.

It was also at Leckys' table that I met for the first time, sitting next him at dinner, Samuel Clemens, Mark Twain. I had lately been reading that wonderful book of his *Joan of Arc* and he told me how the mystical side or soul of that heroic woman had been as it were with him, in his mind, all through his life, so that he had written of her at the last. And he has written expressing that mystic side, that Divine in her, as no other writer has done. And he talked of the communion of mind with mind, even without words, telling me that once at a foreign hotel in a crowded dining-room he had noticed on the wall what he thought to be a portrait of the great Napoleon. And as his mind rested on it for a moment his wife said to him, "Do you remember what a shock it was to us hearing of the death of the Prince Imperial?" And presently he found the picture on the wall was of some quite other subject, and no portrait. It was the thought in his mind that had flashed to the mind of his wife. I saw afterwards that this was one of the marriages to which the secrets of heaven and earth were common, not one of those where the wedded hands are strangers' hands.

At another dinner, at Rome, the American chaplain told me that he had been attacked for going to Burne-Jones for designs for the mosaics for his church, on the ground that he had "no Christian feeling". And as a proof of how little we understand our neighbours he said that one day, looking through Burne-Jones's book of designs he came on a beautiful sketch of St. Francis receiving the stigmata. Burne-Jones said it was nothing and turned over the leaf, but then

he told that he had worked it out and painted a picture
from it and sent it to "that priest among the lepers" (Father
Damien), saying apologetically, "the idea of it took hold
of me".

And the story of the turning of a soul from one belief to
another was told to me one evening in a drawing-room with
guests talking and moving around us, by a man whose eyes
had revealed him as one who, in whatever Church, must
always have walked upon the heavenly plain. He said: "I
had been brought up in a strictly Protestant family with an
abhorrence of the Papacy. Then as a young man soon after
my marriage I came to Rome, and there I found that some
of the doctrines were not so false as I had been led to believe,
and I was struck with the wonderful way the Church had
preserved her faith through so many vicissitudes. I began
to fast in Lent and I did it so rigorously that I would only
eat meat on Sundays. But Cardinal Manning, then Archdeacon, noticed this and he said, 'I must take you in hand
and give you our regular rule. It will never do for you to
fast better than we Catholics ourselves do.' When my wife
and I went back to England we continued to think of the
doctrines of Catholicism, and to study them. We became
extreme Ritualists. Manning kept up his influence with me,
and a Catholic in the neighbourhood took my wife under
instruction. We were going to Switzerland, and we made up
our minds to spend every Sunday in a Canton where we
could attend a Catholic Church, but my wife took ill, she
required an operation, and we went to Edinburgh instead
for some months. I was about twenty-three at the time. My
wife was farther on the road than I was, though I was first
in the end. In packing up to go to Edinburgh I found in
an unused drawer a little book, placed perhaps by angel
hands in that Protestant house, on the errors attributed to
Rome. I put it in my pocket to read in the train, and I was
impressed by finding answers to many questions I had put
to myself as to Roman errors. I wrote to ask Manning what
book would best explain the true Roman doctrines to me,
and he referred me to Bossuet's *Histoire de la foi,* and I
bought it in Edinburgh, for ninepence. A little time before
that the Gorham judgment had been given, and I had been
startled at the doctrine expressed in it, that you might believe
in the Real Presence or not, in the Anglican Church. I went
to consult Manning about this and he said, 'It is either a
violation of all truth or it is a blossoming of the seed sown

at the Reformation'. These words, and the idea that I might be on the wrong side, gave me such a shock that my wife noticed that something had happened when I came back.

"In Edinburgh I used to take long walks with a High Church clergyman we had chosen as the best exponent to be found there of Anglican views, and I found sometimes that he was unable to answer the arguments in Bossuet. One Sunday I was going to church (I had before this begun confession) and to receive the Holy Communion, when my wife said, 'Ask the clergyman if he will come and administer the Communion to me tomorrow as an invalid—but I think it right that before he comes he should be told that I entertain some doubts as to the validity of Anglican Orders. I said, 'Whew!' and I confessed that there was the same doubt in my mind also. I told the clergyman what she had said and he flushed red and said angrily, 'What do you mean?' 'I mean what I have said.' 'Then it is a temptation of the devil. Tell your wife to receive—and the doubt will pass away.' But in the morning I had a letter from him saying, 'As you and your wife harbour these doubts I hold that you are living in mortal sin, and I will not receive you at the Lord's table'. When I read these words to my wife she looked at me half laughing and said, 'I think you have come to that corner at which you said you would have to enquire farther into the truth of the Church of Rome. We seem to be excommunicated from the Anglican one.' I said, 'I think so too', and I went to ask where a Catholic Bishop was to be found. I heard there was one within three miles and I came back to my wife and said, 'Pray for me, for I am going to take a very important step'. I set out to walk the three miles, praying all the time with might and main for grace and guidance. I had always been a praying lad. When I got to the Bishop's door I would not give my name, and in his presence I only said, 'I am an Anglican come to ask you some questions about the doctrine of your Church'. The Bishop said he would be glad to help me. We began by talking of the Real Presence, and very soon I found I had already believed in it for two years. Then we went on to the intercession of the Virgin. And then a miracle happened. A veil fell from my eyes. I could see nothing for a minute, and then I was dazzled by the clear sight of all the doctrines of the Church laid out before me as it were, and I cried out, 'Oh, I believe!' The Bishop said, 'Thank God!' Then we talked again and I said, 'But *must* I pray to the Virgin?'

The Bishop said she was in authority over the Saints whose intercession we need, 'and you will within a week be glad to pray to her'. That night I said a 'Hail Mary' for the first time, but just for that once from a mere sense of duty. When I went back to my wife I said, 'I have accepted the Catholic Church as mine'. She said, 'Oh, I am not ready for it yet'. But in a few days the Bishop came to speak to her, and within half-an-hour she too was a convert. He had to break the news to his father who was greatly distressed, but after a time saw he was sincere, and after his wife's death he went and lived with him."

I asked if he had ever been troubled by a doubt, and he said, "Only once, for about five minutes, and the thought then that I might have been wrong caused me intense agony".

(I read this to Yeats the other day and he said: "I am interested in his conversion in the presence of a Bishop. I remember a Singalese barrister saying to me once 'there is a saint in my neighbourhood who has not spoken for twenty years, but people go to live near him in the jungle, and by so doing get all they want'. Something is transferred as when the woman with the issue of blood touched Christ and was healed and He knew that virtue had gone out of Him.")

VII

ATHENAEUM FRIENDS I: A. W. KINGLAKE

AN OLD FRIEND of my husband told me he had said when he was meditating upon marriage that he was afraid a wife might not like his dining so often at the Athenaeum. But whenever we were in London he used to dine there on Sunday evenings, had we no other engagement, and that habit met with no opposition from me. It left the servants free, my own meal being of the simplest, and I always looked forward to the news and gossip that he would bring me; for he was as liberal at home, and with me as only listener, as abroad of that conversation made "the hours pass quickly" for others.

And soon it came about that many of his Athenaeum friends had become my friends, and he would come home pleased on those Sunday evenings when one or more had told him of having spent a pleasant hour or two of the afternoon in my company.

In 1895, while these memories were yet fresh in my mind, I wrote down some of them for *Blackwood*, calling them "Eothen and the Athenaeum Club"[1]. For Kinglake, whose book of Eastern travel *Eothen* is still well known, was the one that I had known best among that group of friends. And I said that club was now, as it were, peopled by ghosts. And quoting Heine's desire to bury a few sous under a paving stone of the Paris Boulevards because "where treasure has been buried there will the spirit return", I wondered if some of those that loved those rooms in their lifetime might perhaps have slipped some small coin behind the wainscot. And I went on to imagine their return, when midnight had struck. "Some listen with amusement, some with irritation as Hayward again shambles across the floor, proclaiming in his harsh voice how an Ambassador has asked him to review his book, or the wife of a Lord Chancellor to defend her husband's memory, mentioning dukes without a prefix, as, diving into a dingy pocket he brings out a letter from the reigning Prime Minister.

[1] In the December 1895 issue, pp. 797-804.

"Again the little round table in the north eastern corner of the dining room is laid for three, and we hear the gentle 'Heavens' of Kinglake, contrasting, as treble to bass, with the more forcible expletives of Hayward, who lays down the law, as one born a dictator, on some subject adopted as his own.

["It may still be some new work on Byron he reads in pieces: 'How dare any one attempt to say anything about Byron that I have not said? Why should anyone read dull and pretentious books giving no new information, pretending to defend him and leaving him with a worse reputation than before? How dare *The Times* review a book on that subject and speak well of it without consulting me?'

["Placid Chenery (the Editor of *The Times*) is roused to answer, but is met with 'I wonder you can venture to set up your judgment against mine. I knew Byron's most intimate friends; I knew M.M. and X. and Y. and Z., and Lady —— has answered every question that I set her, and no one else knows anything of the matter. Chenery hopelessly succumbs to such a peal of words; Kinglake's eyes twinkle with subdued malice, a delighted onlooker at all battles. Someone crosses the trail by telling of a letter on the subject in a weekly paper, and Hayward trots off to look at it, head down, grinding his teeth, still muttering threatenings and slaughters, while poor Chenery, relieved, leans back, gently twiddles his thumbs, and calls for an unaccustomed glass of punch.]

"Hayward's death was the first to break the circle, in 1884, and Kinglake's gentle presence was constant beside him during the long illness. Their very unlikeness seemed to bind them to one another." He wrote to me in 1884, "he is too weak to hold his cards, but not too weak to damn his partner". [But later, "His bodily weakness is now extreme, but he is easier in some respects than he was and suffers no actual pain". But soon after that he wrote:] "Yes, I was sure you would feel the loss of our long dominant friend Hayward. He was a great appreciator of you—and remember he was one that did not set up false idols, or even allow others to set up false idols for themselves."

[2]That was a true summary of Hayward's character. A little arrogant, a little overbearing, he had by intellect, by

[2] Although Lady Gregory states that she is quoting from her article, from here on she has revised the original version, but quotes as if she had not.

experience, by study, gained the power of forming an opinion on men and on books that had to be listened to. He knew that he saw to the core of politics and literature with a keener and clearer eye than is bestowed upon many, and it angered him when his verdict was not at once accepted. But there was a very kind heart within that bent form, and his eyes under that shaggy penthouse could flash sympathy as well as scorn. He liked letting his influence be known and [the dignified *Quarterly* was sometimes angry at finding that he had announced in the drawing rooms that the last voice of that oracle had been his own. But] if he laid a little too much stress on his own achievements in the discovery and recognition of genius, he would take equal pleasure in repeating praises by a friend that chanced to come to his ear. He would take trouble also in introducing someone he thought worth it to society that might be useful to him. Then should that friend speak of the assemblies he had been taken to as one used to them, (and Chenery himself had once been guilty of this) Hayward's wrath would explode "D—d—d—. He would never have been admitted to the *servant's hall* at those houses without me". [He liked to talk of the changes he had witnessed in his long life in London. I remember his bearing witness to the great increase in the efficiency of the clergy and in the respect paid to their devotion and energy, though he added with the touch of mockery he could seldom quite resist, "But I don't know when they accept Darwinism what they do with Adam and Eve". But he was no church-goer and I remember his coming to me one day to know if the text, "Whom the Lord loveth he chasteneth" was in the Bible. (Yeats says here, "I remember once seeing a quotation on a wooden shield on the wall of a National League Hall that I thought was from the Bible; and then I found it was from myself. It was in a poem that I had written on Parnell's death and that I hope has never been reprinted—something about his 'leading us from the tomb'." But not long after he had said this he was startled by seeing that poem, reprinted in full, in an Irish paper, as if a new one, and without Parnell's name; yet could make no remonstrance for it was put amongst the laments for Arthur Griffith's death.)

[He raged sometimes against society; poker playing had ruined it he declared, and the loud talking at dinner tables. But he held that beauty remained at its highest level, and I remember him at a party at Downing Street, seized with

أحمد عرابي المصري

Ahmad Arabi the Egyptian

for Lady Gregory October 1883

Wilfrid Scawen Blunt. A photograph taken at about the time he first met Lady Gregory.

a desire to present the Chinese Ambassador to Lady Dalhousie, just to see what would be the effect on him of her dazzling beauty.

[Even the Athenaeum was not sacred to him, and he would delightedly tell how on the yearly migration to the United Service Club its members "complain that the Bishops steal all their umbrellas". And Kinglake, with equal mischievous delight, had a counter story that when the librarian of the United Service was asked for, the answer was, "Please Sir, he's in the dining room carving the roast beef." They all at that time grumbled about the Athenaeum cookery. I remember someone saying to Sir William, "Why don't you get the Bishop to make a fuss?" and his answer, "What? Must I turn to the Bishop dining nearest to me and cry, 'O man of God, there is death in the pot?'." I wonder if such light words are ever heard in these days in those lofty rooms. As to Hayward's writings—("His writings," cried Yeats. "I suppose he was one of your statesmen authors. What did he write?" "His critical essays were reprinted," I said, but they were rather a disappointment to those who had been listeners to him. I know they were to Kinglake, who corrected the proofs. But his *Art of Dining* is very good, written with enthusiasm. I read it over again the other day with delight. His verses . . ." "Oh did he write verses? Now I know where I am. Let me at them." "No," I said, "they were but privately printed. He gave me my copy, I will not let you have it to tear to pieces. His translation of Faust is up there on the shelves. I don't know if it holds its place. It used to be thought a good deal of." "No one but Shelley has ever been able to translate Faust," said Yeats, "and he did but a bit of it. And as to criticism, there are too many of us. I have often said most of us ought to be sent off to civilise savage tribes. Just think what an effect Clutton Brock would have in Central Africa." "You should think all the more of Hayward's influence," I said, "if he was no great writer. But you professionals are like the plumber who cries out if the slater puts a finger on the pipes. And though I think his great moment had been when Lord Palmerston was Premier, he had still great influence in London when I came there, and he used it in a kindly way. There was a Russian Lady who came to England on purpose to see Gladstone and could not get near him till, as she said, "Un petit Juif bien sale nommé Hayward" took her to meet him at dinner at Mrs. Thistlewaite's. "Who was Mrs. Thistlewaite?" said Yeats. "I was forbidden to ask that question," I said, "when in my childhood by some strange chance a portrait of her found its way to the drawing-room table at Roxborough. But besides the beauty I still remember in that face I know she must have had tact as a hostess, from the account that I was given of the dinner, when Gladstone knew absolutely nothing about Russia, and thought a town was a sect. And then Mrs. Thistlewaite turned the conversation on the question whether arms or legs are of most use to us. So now I will read on about the Editor of *The Times*, Chenery.

[I wrote of him in that *Blackwood's* article, "His soul was that of a student and dwelt with the oriental lore he was so great a master of. His heart was large, wider than all the sheets of *The Times* . . ." ("Oh, stop," said Yeats, "I can't let that pass, it is the strained metaphor and hackneyed phrase of an amateur writer'. 'Well, that is what I was when I wrote it a quarter of a century ago,' said I. 'It was published, and I have put it in inverted commas. It would not be honest to alter it now.' 'Rubbish,' said Yeats. 'I found Wilde once writing his essay on Wainwright and he told me, "The chief difficulty I have is in rewriting my own quotations".' 'Well,' I said, 'I am not upholding the style. Indeed, as I read this after so many years and think how easily I might have gone on writing in the same way or worse, I paraphrase Wesley's[3] saying when he saw the criminal going to the gallows and say "but for the grace of Yeats and Kiltartan, there goes Lady Gregory". However, I will take out some of the very bad words.').")]

"Chenery had none of the pomp and mystery of an editor, though he served *The Times* well; he was very simple, learned and unaffected. 'He liked to entertain a few friends at dinner at his quiet rooms in Printing House Square, but bustling into the noisy world 'to keep in touch with it' was not for him. The Athenaeum gossips brought him such morsels of fact and criticism as were useful to his purpose. He was without malice. The hardest thing that I have ever heard him say was of some man that 'he could not think much of him since he found that he had a habit of binding his Bradshaws'. That is all I have written of him here," I said, "but he has left a book that everyone may admire, his great translation from the Arabic of *The Assemblies of El*

---

[3] Richard Baxter, not Wesley.

Hariri. There it is among the books given me by the writers." [And taking it down it opened by chance at a page where the first words that I read were in an ode on some Oriental ruler, "His friendship is as pedigree". And I said, "that is just what I feel about these, my Athenaeum and some other friends, they give my mind its ancestry".

["As to Kinglake", I went on reading, "Once in my girlhood, I who seldom heard of books and who grew up in a home without a Shakespeare and in a province without a bookstall, caught the words of one friend to another, 'What do you consider the most brilliant book of the last half-century?' And the answer that came was *Eothen,* and a sequel to the answer was the present to me of a copy of the book itself, with the frontispiece of impaled skeletons, afterwards brought up in evidence in the Bulgarian atrocity controversy. I took it to my heart at once and there it has since remained. 'Thank you so much for recommending me *Eothen',* a schoolboy friend wrote to me in after days 'and please tell me of some more books like it'. But he has grown to manhood, and the books 'like *Eothen'* have not yet appeared. So when I came to London and began to meet writers whose voices had reached me far away in the west, one of those that I was best pleased to meet was Kinglake."

Our real friendship began the following year, as we had only met at the time of the Egyptian war, in the autumn of 1881[4]. He often came to see me then to talk and learn about the revolution that had led to it, for as he wrote, "the truth is I am dissatisfied with myself for having since the Arabi time received ideas upon ideas with the carelessness of an irresponsible man".

[Some of the newspapers were clamouring for the execution of Arabi, and what seemed more alarming, Mr. Gladstone had written to Hayward, in reply to a letter saying that such an execution would of course be impossible, that he "hoped it might not be found necessary". *The Times* published an account of *Arabi and his Household* written by me in his defence and to gain sympathy for him, and Kinglake had been interested by it, writing, "I am horrified at the idea of there being really ground for alarm with respect to the fate of Arabi". He would like to help but could not write to *The Times* "as there is on their part (and not unnaturally) the strongest possible hostility towards me,

[4] This originally read "Our real friendship began at the time of the Egyptian war, or rather at its close in 1882."

arising out of what I had to say about them in my Crimean book". He subscribed towards the fund for the defence of the Arabi (the cost of which in the end was borne by Mr. Wilfrid Blunt) and though he would not write to *The Times* directly, he consented to write me a private letter on the matter with leave to publish. He gave me his promise but next day I had a note: "I have scrawled something in pursuance of my promise, but see to my dismay that there is not time to make a legible copy of it before the time that you fixed. I will write again to you." Then he brought it to me. But there was someone with me, I think Sir Edward Hamley, and in conversation some idea came to Kinglake of alteration or improvement of a sentence, and he took the letter away for one more rewriting. And so the moment had passed and the trial had been brought to an end by a compromise before he could return it. I could then understand his having had the proofs of *Eothen* back eleven times for correction, to the trial of his publisher's faith and patience. And I hardly yet understand how the eight volumes of his *Crimea*[5] ever saw the light, he was, even in an ordinary note, so fastidious in his choice of words.

"Blackwood wrote of him before he became his publisher, 'Oliphant tells me Kinglake is a monstrous clever fellow and a real good one but most particular and confoundedly fidgetty (sic) about what he writes'. He himself used plaintively to say while the *History* was in progress that he did not believe that he would ever be free of it He told me he had once, when staying in Scotland, strayed into a Free Kirk, and the minister at that moment said, 'Lord, send down thy quickening on him that be slow', but though he had whole-heartedly joined in the prayer it had been without result. [One day going out of the room he stopped and put his hand on my little boy's head and said, 'My little fellow, here is a piece of advice for you. If you ever think of writing a history, don't leap into the decision, but sit down first and write one half chapter as an experiment, and then you will know what sort of task that it is you are undertaking'.]

"When the last volume was out he joyfully said goodbye to writing and found himself too happy in being free from the bonds of authorship to think of venturing into them again.

In spite of his intimacy with Chenery he had a quaint

[5] The first two volumes appeared in 1863, and the remaining six at intervals down to 1887.

way of looking upon *The Times* as a sort of Juggernaut, irresistible and fateful. When I told him of the new editor, Mr. Buckle's, marriage, he exclaimed "Heavens. What brings *The Times* into relations with humanity?" "Never offend *The Times*," was his emphatic piece of advice. "A sea-captain told me that the cause of his failure in life was his having on some occasion refused to let one of their correspondents come on board his ship. From that time, whenever he distinguished himself, *The Times* mis-spelled his name—leaving out the first letter—which prevented his ever making any mark."

["It always seemed strange to me that so gentle a being should take such an intense interest in everything connected with war. Almost in his last days of weakness there came a vivid flash of delight when I told him of a soldier who on his return from Suakin was asked if the Arabs were not brave fighters and had answered 'I don't call that bravery, for they are not afraid of death'.

"He read the reports of the Soudan campaign with excitement. He wrote to me in 1884, 'Do not think too ill of your poor Egyptians on the road to Tokar. To enfold a convoy of baggage animals in a hollow square of infantry, and maintain it against bold cavalry—this is a triumph of valour and military coherence that is only made possible—one may say, after centuries of practice—by a perfected organisation and the presence of trustworthy officers. Considering that by Wolseley's stratagem of the night march they had been deprived of the power to use their main arm, the artillery, your poor Egyptians did really stand well at Tel-el-Kebir against that part of our line commanded by Hamley, which first attacked them. Hamley is an unpopular man but straightforward, truthful and a master of the business of war, so that I confidently accept what he tells me, with the result of being compelled to think better of the quality of the poor Egyptian soldier than I should otherwise do.']

"Then, turning to politics, he sums up, 'I am sometimes taxed with having said or printed that Gladstone was "a good man in the worst sense of the term," that there does not seem really good ground for saying that his management of England's Imperial tasks is tainted with amiability.'

"He did not look on General Gordon with entire admiration. He writes: 'There is something interesting in that device of sending out Chinese Gordon. I take it that he is a sagacious fanatic, so that it is practically sending out a

true prophet against the false prophet.' He said of him at
another time, 'Gordon has fits of sanity and then relapses
into lunacy'." And I wrote in February 1884, "Kinglake came
in the evening and sat with me a long time, very quaint and
pleasant, anxious I should write a clear account of Gordon's
mission, but I told him I had lost my admiration for Gordon
since his wishing to restore Zebehr and the Turks and Ismail,
all of whom he had written against so strongly, and this as
it seemed, to spite the Mahdi. One would not be surprised
at such a request coming from Baring or Dilke, but from
Gordon one felt a little like reading of David's treatment
of Uriah after a study of the Psalms. Kinglake laughed and
said, 'Yes, he is certainly a kind of divine weathercock.'
[After his (Gordon's) death, he said the country, having
failed in preventing his martyrdom, has a romantic desire to
seize the site of the crucifixion at Khartoum. Talking of
Tewfik's character he said, 'yet Gladstone seems to have an
acquired taste for him'. About Khartoum and the advance
on it, he quoted the Duke of Wellington, 'Always see what's
on the other side of the hill'.]

"In spite of his deafness, his quaint phrases made him the
most charming of companions. His words seemed to crystal-
lise into epigram as they touched the air. That deafness
was of late years a great privation to him, loving as he did
to hear and to join in the play of witty speech. Sir Edward
Hamley said, 'When I talk to Kinglake at the Athenaeum
everybody in the room hears every word that I say—except
Kinglake.'

"When I first knew him he lived in Hyde Park Place in
rooms overlooking a churchyard. When he had first looked
at them he said to the landlady, 'I should not like to live
here. I should be afraid of ghosts.' 'Oh no, sir,' she said, 'there
is always a policeman round the corner.' I really believe he
took the rooms on the spur of his delight at what he found
a truly British answer.

"Gout was the first malady to attack him, and to wean
him from his daily club. He had a fancy to try a doctor and
wrote to one to ask if gout was beyond her scope. She replied,
'Dear Sir, Gout is not beyond my scope but men are'. Then
he called in Sir James Paget because he had been very
much struck with a portrait that he had seen of him by
Millais. He went to Brighton for a change, and was there
brought into almost nearer relations with ghosts than in
the Hyde Park lodging. He was startled one day by a man

coming to him to say that his wife had appeared in a dream and told him to go at once and find out William Alexander Kinglake and convert him to Catholicism. He was evidently quite mad, and put on a surplice to speak in. Kinglake replied that even in Heaven there should be accuracy, and that his name was Alexander William. [This 'froze' the enthusiast a little, and then Kinglake, recalling the story of a young lady in a train who had quelled a madman by fixing her eyes on him, did the same, with the result of at last 'freezing' him altogether, and he went away in low spirits. He had once seen this man some years before for a few minutes, when he had come to say that his wife had run away, and to ask if Kinglake knew anything of her.

["Another afternoon he talked of Mrs. Carlyle and her ridiculous jealousy of Lady Ashburton, who only cared to have Carlyle at her house to tilt at words with. He would growl out something at dinner, and she would answer him wittily. And the house was most comfortable and it was impossible that Mrs. Carlyle had, as she complains, been forbidden a fire in her room. The groom of the chambers would have seen to that, it was he who looked after the comfort of the guests. 'The fact is,' he says, 'the Carlyles were like a pair of spiteful old maids, snapping at one another.'

["His *History of the War in the Crimea,* in its eight volumes, was his great work. The first volume especially is always a joy to read for the passionate energy of its indictment of Louis Napoleon. It was whispered that this although justified on public grounds was given its sharp edge on a personal ground; that at the time when Napoleon had lived in England they had both loved a beautiful woman and that it was the Emperor-to-be who was preferred.

["Though he had been so glad to say farewell to his *History* he was always pleased to talk of Crimean days. One Sunday he came in, just as my child and I had come from the Serpentine where we had been watching the fleets of toy boats, allowed the privilege of Sabbath sailing, forbidden to larger ones. And he told us how once in the Crimea he had seen a vessel come in under full sail, right under the Russian guns. 'They fired at her and missed, and she came in without wavering, though the crowds looking on waited to see her sink. A French officer standing by said, 'I hope the Queen of England will give the highest honour in her power, the Garter, to that brave captain'. But presently it appeared that she was, like the Serpentine boats, without a crew, empty and deserted.' He was very much excited over a story I had heard and brought him, that an English yacht had touched at the Crimea, the owner Sir John Pender, wishing to visit the scenes of the war, and that the authorities had refused to allow a Dean of the Church of England, who was on board, to land, as no priest of another communion than the Greek is permitted to set foot on Russian soil without special permission from the Emperor, which there was no time to obtain. He jumped up and his eyes flashed fire as he said, 'I have been in the Crimea at a time when we landed whom we liked without asking leave from Russia.']

"He grew angry in his last years about Ireland and the proposed Home Rule Bill. Like other gentle natures I have known, he seemed to lash himself into fury at the idea of what he considered 'the betrayal of a garrison'. He writes in January 1886, 'It was so kind a thought of yours to send me some sunshine from India. Your sunshine has cleaved its bright way through the mists of this London of ours, but also through the gloom of a political kind which during several days was not unmixed with alarm. The alarm I still think may be pardoned; for who could imagine that Gladstone would go over to the Home Rulers without having first satisfied himself by easy enquiry among his friends that he could carry his party along with him? And, supposing that he had become a Home Ruler after taking that precaution, the prospects of our country would have been such as to appal every man understanding the crisis, or make him school his mind for civil war. However, about the same time when your kind letter reached me, it began to seem probable that the leader had reckoned without his host, and this I now think is certain.

" 'But, heavens, the wickedness of Gladstone's escapade. I had hitherto sincerely believed him to be swayed by conscientious motives, though I saw that, like jackals, they acted as lion's providers. But I trust that in the happy time of May when you are once more at St. George's Place, there will be a United Kingdom to welcome you to.' "

[And as if half ashamed of his warmth he writes again, "The Irish Measure.] I thought myself a cool sort of fellow and know myself to be a lazy one, so that I am quite taken aback at finding that I have lost my temper and become savage."

And when May came his anger was still hot. On one wet

Sunday he came to see me, brimming with wrath against Gladstone, though he had never expected to be troubled with politics in his old age. "Gladstone has no imagination," he said, "he just wants to force his Bill through and can't foresee what will happen during the next few years, I never thought he was so silly. However, it has the good effect of showing how absurd and impossible repeal would be." And another day, "he wishes someone would compile a list of Gladstone's opinions, one of his first having been in favour of slavery, then the similarity between Helen of Troy and the Blessed Virgin; then at one time that Salvation was to be found in Bishops. He says there is something of Christ's idea in his present one that the secret of truth has been delivered to the unlearned, but is a practically mischievous one." And later again he came "still so angry with Gladstone and the 'revolution'. He thinks Gladstone's Edinburgh speech a wonderful word-torrent, but there is nothing in it that a man would tell his wife of when he came home." He says Lord Tennyson had written to Gladstone three months ago, quoting some lines to the effect that it is easy to pull down the work of ages, but very hard to reconstruct. Gladstone never answered until in writing two months afterwards to condole on Lionel Tennyson's death, he said, "I have had your words continually in my mind, but I feel certain that I have a mission from Heaven to settle the Irish Question. That only makes me take it up at my age."

In 1889, when things were going more quietly, he writes, "I am so constituted as to have a strong and painful feeling on the subject of the confiscation which seemed to be more or less annulling the ownership of the landlords and giving the soil—I won't say trenchantly to criminals, but to people bordering on crime; and in proportion to the gloominess of my thoughts on this subject is your truly welcome announcement that rents are being paid and prices are keeping up.

"Enforcing the law. That sounds simple, but what Balfour has done in that direction is a grand achievement."

But that year was to be a sad one to him, and to those who cared for him. He had once already been operated on for cancer, and now the disease had come back again. And this seemed especially cruel to one who looked so fragile and so feeble, as if a mere current of air might easily waft him away. He suffered much, but always with uncomplaining patience. His interest in outward affairs was as keen as ever, and in the party complications and tangles that followed the O'Shea v. Parnell trial, he liked to see me every day that I might tell him what was going on and "clear his mind". When he heard of the repudiation of Parnell by the Liberals on moral grounds, "Hypocrites," he said vehemently from beneath his covering, with the old energy and fire.

A little later I said in a letter, "Poor Kinglake's nurse came to lunch. I am to be sent two old Spanish duelling swords, as he wished me to have a souvenir. She says that he often spoke of me as beautiful in my charity . . . and said that at Hyde Park Place the servants and all in the house liked me better than any of his visitors. [Please God I may not grow bad, but earn a good opinion from others."] Here I asked Yeats: "Is that too big a compliment to myself to leave in an autobiography?" and he said, "No, I don't think so, I have just been reading *Benvenuto Cellini*". I said that as he had allowed me to give some compliments to myself I would ask him for a list of my faults, that I might put them in, or at least some of them as a balance. He said that would not be necessary, for one never could make a real portrait of oneself; he had not given much about himself in his own memoirs but had written chiefly about his friends. "But of course I can make a list of faults if you like. You are auto-cratic." "I suppose when you say that," I said, "you are thinking of such a case as when I found you and Synge shivering disconsolately in the Abbey scene dock, because you were kept out of the green room by the uncleanly habits of the stage manager's little dog, and you were waiting for me to come and turn it out." "If you argue like that over every fault that I give," he said, "how can I give any more? And I have plenty more on the list." "Oh," I said, "and when you first came here in your youth you said that I had but one fault: that was my enmity towards squirrels." So we did not go on with the subject that evening. Yet I have often felt a sort of gratitude to him and to one or two of my family, through whom I have never been forced to cry, as Wilfrid Blunt does, with the coming on of age, "Now then, Heaven help me, there is none to praise—or *blame*."

VIII

ATHENAEUM FRIENDS II: SIR FREDERIC BURTON

It was but a little while after my marriage that I went with
my husband to the London National Gallery, of which he
was a Trustee. The Director, Mr. Burton, not yet Sir
Frederic, walked round the rooms with us, and I forget
what other friends. They stopped before a picture of Mary
Magdalene and someone said she did not look altogether
repentant, and I, very shy as I was, murmured half
unconsciously, "Perhaps she did not grow quite good all at
once". The Director turned and looked at me through his
spectacles in an intent way I was to learn to know, as if
giving attention to some offered paintings or puzzling over
a new signature, and then burst into his sudden delighted
laugh, and I blushed disconcerted. But I think that laugh
had broken once for all the barrier of reserve, haughtiness,
almost of suspicion that encompassed him even amongst
acquaintances who might call themselves friends: "Are you
doing anything this evening?" someone, Humphrey Ward
I think, asked him at the Athenaeum and he drew himself
up with an indignant word and was hardly appeased by
finding that the object had been but to ask him if free to
a pleasant dinner. It is the way of the artist. I asked the
same question with that same intent to Granville Barker,
absorbed in a rehearsal of *Where there is Nothing,* met with
somewhat the same response and went away discomfited,
though next day the discomfiture was his, when some vague
memory awakening, he asked with contrition what he had
interrupted me in asking. And when he knew that had
patience allowed a hearing he could have dined with me to
meet Thomas Hardy and Arthur Symons he walked up and
down the stage, indignant with himself, reproaching himself
saying, "The one man of all others I want to meet is Hardy;
and as to Symons he was the first to praise some work of
mine and I would have liked to thank him." These were his
early days: he has been able to know whom he would since
then. But Sir Frederic, as the years went on, the sensitiveness
that is no part of reason causing him to shrink from the
reasoner's counsel to keep friendship in constant repair,

lessened rather than widened his acquaintance. At Christie's
sales he resented questions as to the authenticity or value of
pictures from even so gentle a rival as Henry Doyle; his
resentment at being asked an opinion was almost what it
might have been had one looked over his shoulder while
he was working at a landscape's shadows or lights. He was
affronted by sins of omission also, complaining of the "very
haughty housemaid" at Lady Layard's door who "said she
was away without saying when she would return", a question
his own haughtiness would not permit him to ask. Some at
least of the Trustees loved him, certainly my husband and
Sir Henry Layard, but they kept their places as advisers,
and never pressed advice on him or attempted to dictate.
"The Director is perfectly free to act in the purchase of
pictures. Even if he consults the Trustees he need not be
bound by them"—this is in one of Sir Henry's letters to
my husband, and again, "The Director has unquestioned
power to spend the money voted by the House of Commons
as he may think fit". He was very angry at one time with
Sir William, who with all his love of art protested against the
great sum of £80,000 being given for the Blenheim Madonna,
(and others thought later he was right in that, when the
Treasury had stopped the yearly grant of £10,000 to refund
the loan, and so during these years other fine pictures were
lost. It was little comfort to be told that this stoppage was
but caused by the mistake of a Treasury clerk.) But they
loved one another too well for that coldness to last long,
and in his last illness I was touched when he said to me,
"What a dear good fellow Gregory was; so kind-hearted and
such a gentleman. If he was a little hot sometimes according
to his nature, and I according to mine, we got over it afterwards because we were gentlemen." We were all proud of
our Director's good looks, the toss of his proud grey-curled
head, that seemed to surpass in distinction that other grey
handsome head of the other Sir Frederic (Leighton), President of the Royal Academy. We were proud also in Ireland
that two of our own countrymen were in control of the
National Galleries, he in Trafalgar Square, Henry Doyle in
Leinster Lawn.

    He was of a Clare county family, was a kinsman of Lady
Colin Campbell, whose battles he ever most chivalrously
fought; he had always been a painter, had exhibited when
but a lad of sixteen; had wandered in Germany; (a drawing
in sepia of St. Stephen of Hungary and another of a knight

in armour, painted at Bamberg always hung in his room as they do now in mine). And such travelling as I have heard Boehm say, "was in those days an education, a training, because artist or architect had to make his drawings of what he would keep in memory, while now he is but tempted to buy a photograph". He wandered also by the rocky coast line of his own county and by the quiet lakes and bogs of Connemara, painting as he went. Writing in 1901 of an exhibition of Mr. Jack Yeats' pictures[1], I contrasted these two painters of our western provinces, divided from one another by three quarters of a century, and wondered if the contrast came from a different point of view in the artist or from a change in the people themselves, in the life and thought of Ireland. "I have left at Coole," I said (for these early paintings had been Sir Frederic's legacy to me) "delicate shadows in still lakes; sweet shy peasant girls; comely serene women; men who are not strongly individualised. These were painted in the 'thirties, before the famine had set lasting furrows on the face of whole districts and left an eternal and tragic memory. The peasant of simple joys and easily healed sorrows we see in Miss Edgeworth's *Absentee* or *Castle Rackrent,* the peasant who hardly yet realised that his religion had been freed, or the momentous bearing of the Clare election, was the peasant painted by Frederic Burton. He sometimes even chose as a model, as in his Blind Girl at the Holy Well, some gently reared girl of his own class, for in his mind no type could be too refined or too delicate for the idealised peasant who did not understand himself and whom he did not understand. But I see traces of the harsh memories of famine, of banishment, of some unending war and some latent fierceness in the strong unflattered faces painted by Mr. Yeats. And in their energy and fire I see traces also of their knowledge of the "big change" the *Athrughadh Mor* that is coming, that is already begun; of the old world that is dying without pity and the young world that is growing up on its grave."

I have also a painting by him of a giraffe that had lived in the Dublin Zoological Gardens. He told me his tragic story. For some reason a new house had been built for him a little way from the old one, but when this was ready he refused to leave his old enclosure. The keepers tried to do

[1] This article was published as "At 9 Merrion Row" in the 2 November 1901 issue of *The Leader.*

by craft what they could not do by force; they enlarged or
lengthened the enclosure day by day, getting it nearer and
nearer to the old one, and tempting the giraffe towards it
by strewing his food there; then when it had come near the
new enclosure they threw them into one, closing the bars
behind him. But he would not forgive the trick. He would
not enter the new house nor would he eat, but lay down
and died.

But Sir Frederic, very learned in the history of art, had
never used pencil or brush from the time when in 1874 he
became Director of the National Gallery; a sudden renunciation. Happily, some of his paintings in water colour, as
were all his pictures, are in our Dublin National Gallery
now, among them *The Turret Stair* and the *Venetian Lady*
and the *Arran Fisherman's Drowned Child*. He told me that
two of his pictures had been burned in the Pantechnicon,
placed in it for safe keeping by different owners, the
Fisherman's Burial and a portrait of two sisters. Giving me
an engraving of the *Blind Girl*, he said his model for it had
been a daughter of Dr. Petrie. In telling me he had desired
his executors to give me the sketches made in Clare and
Connemara in 1839, he said, "I would like the sketches of
that happy time to be in your keeping". As to politics,
although all for the Union, he had once, as it were, touched
hands with rebels. I remember a day at Milan when Sir
William, he and I went together to the Poldi Museum and
that "after we had spent a while looking at the Savoldo and
a Rubens portrait which he might at one time have bought
but didn't, we had coffee at the cafe in the gallery, and he
talked of the United Irishmen." The frontispiece of *The
Spirit of the Nation,* that rebel song book of the 'forties, was
drawn by him, and when he was a strong Unionist I sometimes teased him about this, but he said, "it was Davis who
asked me to do it, and there was nothing I could refuse
Davis". Two pencil portraits of Davis drawn by him from
memory are in our National Gallery, and there is also in
the Gallery his portrait of Sir Samuel Ferguson, who wrote
the fine lament for Davis beginning—

> I walked through Bellinderry in the spring time,
> When the bird was on the tree,
> And I said, in every fresh ploughed field beholding
> The sowers striding free,
> Scattering broadcast forth the corn in golden plenty

In the quick seed-clasping soil
Even such this day among the fresh-stirred hearts of Erin
Thomas Davis is thy toil.

And surely Frederic Burton was one of those whose hearts he
stirred. And I am sure his heart was stirred, as was many
another's, by Davis's own lament on another lost leader:

We thought you would not die, we were sure you would
    not go
And leave us in our utmost need to Cromwell's cruel blow,
Sheep without a shepherd when the snow shuts out the sky;
Oh, why did you leave us, Owen? Why did you die?

Another portrait in the Gallery is one drawn by him of
Clarence Mangan, drawn in the hospital directly after his
death. Davis, he told me, had once taken him to see Mitchel,
perhaps with some such purpose of a portrait, "but I did not
like his appearance when I saw him. His skin was blotched
and he had ginger-coloured hair, he was a regular North-
erner and didn't make a good impression on me." He was
amused when I told him of Ingram's poem, "Who fears to
speak of '98" being made so much of during the '98
Centenary meetings, for he said, "he never was a Young
Irelander or sympathised with the movement, but one
evening he was roused by a speech of O'Connell's, throwing
disparagement on the '98 Rising and he went home and
wrote the verses."

He was slow to trust his own judgment, slow in decision;
that as a Director was his fault, and the Trustees would
murmur over his slow delivery of the new catalogue and
over masterpieces that might through his delay have been
lost. When I told him in his later years of Hugh Lane's
early rapid dealings he was silent for a moment and then
said, "I have never in all my life been able to have the same
confidence in my own judgment as that young man". It
may have been a safer fault in a Director who cannot rid
himself of his bad bargains than rashness; and I often heard
it said he did not make mistakes in buying, that his sins
were of omission rather than commission. But Sir Henry
Layard and my husband, both men of affairs, were often
impatient. Sir Henry in many a letter grumbles, half in
vexation, half humorously at "the Knight", a name scorn-
fully spoken by Lady Eastlake, the widow of the first Director
of the National Gallery, and whose nephew was now the

Registrar, and in her mind, the fitting successor of Sir
Frederic. They fretted when the new catalogue used the
time he might have spent looking for treasure. In 1888
Sir Henry writes, "the Knight was prevailed on after great
difficulty to leave his catalogue for a couple of hours
yesterday in order to dine with us. He made himself pleasant
enough, but rushed off like Cinderella when the clock struck
ten to his catalogue, which has deprived him of all sleep for
months if not for years," and Lady Layard adds, "when
Henry urged him to come out to Venice he merely cast the
Tu Brute look of reproach". "Burton was in rather a snappy
state," he writes again, "there is, I fear, but little chance of
dragging him out of his chair at the Athenaeum and sending
him on a pilgrimage to Florence. Your friend 'little Robinson' (Sir J.C. whom, however, Sir Henry abhorred) would
have been off within twenty-four hours." And in 1889, "the
Knight did not attend the sale of the Gatton pictures on
Saturday last, but Henry Doyle did, and with his usual
determination and good luck, purchased the five most
interesting pictures in it for less than £400!—a very fine
head by Eckhout (quite worthy of the National Gallery), the
misnamed Brecklencamp (which turns out to be a very good
de Pape), a female musician (an excellent signed specimen)
by Mytens, a girl by Cuyp, and a capital de Jimge. They
will be great additions to the Dublin Gallery. Doyle deserves
immense credit for what he has done for that collection."
And again, "Henry Doyle has just been to Belgium where
he purchased for a very moderate price a Rembrandt which
I have not yet seen, but which the Knight praises, so it must
be good. He is very fortunate, but then he takes trouble and
does not confine himself to an armchair at his club." (If
Sir Frederic had been given foresight I think he would have
been wise enough to join a Club other than the Athenaeum.)
    Yet they were ready enough with praise when it had been
earned. Sir Henry writes: "Burton was lucky enough to
purchase four splendid portraits by Moretto and three by
Moroni which Eastlake and I years ago endeavoured to get
out of the Finarola Palace at Brescia just in time for the
opening" (of the new rooms at the National Gallery) "the
most valuable addition to our Gallery". "Morelli spoke very
highly of Burton's catalogue." And Sir William in his turn
writes from London: —
    "He has grown so testy and *prepotente* that the least
contradiction throws him off his balance. Still, who is there

W. Kinglake. A portrait by Harriet M. Haviland. Courtesy the National ortrait Gallery, London.

Sir Frederic Burton, by H. T. Wells. Courtesy of the National Portrait Gallery, London.

in England who would have got together such fine things during the period of his office? I have always admired his courage in never being deterred by price from purchasing a picture if we wanted it, whereas Eastlake and Boxall shook in their shoes when anything expensive was on the tapis.

"I told our friend the Knight that you had lamented not having heard from him for a long time. He replied with a snort that resounded through the Athenaeum, 'I write to Sir Henry when I have need to write to him. I have something else to do besides *concocting* letters for him.'

"Lady G. mentioned to the Knight that I had not heard from you. He said with a snort, 'That is very extraordinary. I thought they never allowed a week to pass without communicating with each other. I only hope,' he added, 'that the correspondence will not see the light, for I suspect there would be many unpleasant observations in it on many of us.' Lady G. merely replied, 'I hope they don't say anything unpleasant about me'."

Sir Henry wrote in 1890: "Our Consul General at Florence writes to me, 'I never saw so undecided a man as Sir F. Burton in his movements,' which he may well say." And indeed, this indecision was a part of his being, and even in little matters. I remember at Venice the long, long choosing of a Mosaic brooch for his old housekeeper, and his coming away without a decision after all. And the kindred infirmity of procrastination that was growing on him nearly led to a real catastrophe in the end. The rule for the resignation of officials at the age of sixty had come into being and the Director of the National Gallery was not exempt. But an application for a further term of service was allowed, and the Trustees, unwilling to lose him, had asked him to make it. One day about Christmas time in 1891 he came to our door in St. George's Place in the greatest agitation. He had suddenly remembered that his sixtieth birthday was close at hand, and that he had never sent in the necessary application to the Trustees. And it seemed as if this negligence must lose him his place unless a meeting to receive and confirm the request could be held within the next few days. But the Trustees had left town, had gone here and there, Sir William was the only one of them within reach. This sudden awakening had been a terrible shock, and Sir Frederic looked white and shaken, aghast at the threatened ending of the charge he had no mind to resign. But Sir

William, always prompt in action, lost no time, but telegraphed to every Trustee who could be reached by that
means. Not one of them could come back to London, but
one and all empowered him to act in their name. (Sir Henry
wrote, "This 'age limit' appears to be a ridiculous Chinese
regulation. When a man is incompetent, whatever his age is,
he should be retired.") And before the few days had passed
away he had called a meeting at the National Gallery, and
alone, but for a not too well pleased Registrar, had proposed,
seconded and unanimously passed a resolution approving of
the extension of Sir Frederic Burton's time of office for
another term of years. So he was able to write to Layard: —

(2 January 1892). "I have just received yours of the 31st
and have thereby got the approval of all the Trustees to the
resolution I drew up and sent to the Treasury. I have heard
from Goschen and Burton has seen Sir R. Welby. The matter
will be arranged and we shall retain our Knight."

It was said, but of this I never heard him speak, that
another delay, the perhaps unconscious habit of hesitation
that was a part of his nature, had in his earlier life come to
a less happy end. He had been engaged to a charming girl
of gentle birth and beautiful, as some sketches he made of
her show. But he was poor in those days, and waited on a
turn in fortune's wheel. And when this came with the
appointment to the National Gallery, there seemed no
reason why marriage should be any longer deferred. His
devotion was no less than before, yet the moment never
came; the seasons passed—"and then she died". So the story
goes, and it would have been a subject fitting for one of
Henry James's finely woven webs, a tapestry of faint figures,
rustling, whispering in a morning breeze and then silent as
the dusk falls; figures that would have been as delicately
worked as the painter's own *Venetian Lady* or his *Turret
Stair*. Even his sensitiveness could never have imagined an
unkind touch in the benedictory presence of that writer.
("His play made sad fiasco at the St. James last Saturday,"
Sir Frederic wrote in 1895. "I am sorry for him. I rather like
him, and his own Chauvinist countrymen will rejoice at his
failure.") But they did not often meet outside the Athenaeum, for unlike him, and unlike Sir Alfred Lyall, interested,
even eager explorers of London and country house society,
Sir Frederic found his felicity rather in the recurrent pattern
of days, the mornings in the Gallery's routine, an hour at
Christie's salerooms, the afternoon at the Athenaeum. In

the evening, unless he dined with some near friends, the sanctuary of 43, Argyll Road.

He had friendships with other women. He had wandered with Margaret Stokes and her father among the ruins of Ireland's old civilization in his early days, and it was by her that some of his best pictures were bequeathed to the Dublin Gallery after his death, among them his portrait of Helen Faucit (Lady Martin) as Antigone. Another portrait of her hung on his own walls, and she and her husband, Sir Theodore Martin, were among his dearest friends. He writes in 1898 of this friend of half a lifetime: "Her rapidly failing strength foreboded the end that was to come. That end would be a relief to her, but to others would mean a final severance which no condition can very well soften. It came with the inevitable shock, and for a while I had not heart for writing."

Another friend to whom he had been devoted was George Eliot; he had made the portrait of her now in the National Portrait Gallery. One evening in Italy he spoke of her to me as "fascinating and brilliant, with a wonderful charm in her conversation and a great sense of humour; her own jokes always made with a little spirit of mockery; her eyes, though not beautiful, filling with beautiful expression as she talked. He has often looked away from lovely faces to her thin, pale, sad one, and seen much more to hold one in it than in all the others. Lewes also he liked very much, and Cross, who is practical and clever and a good man of business, which Lewes was not, so after his death she came to lean on him. He gave himself entirely to her service and being ordered abroad she married him, there being about twenty years between them."

One day in that long last illness I found him reading *The Mill on the Floss* for the first time, and that seemed strange to me because of his intimacy with her. But he said that in those days he was very much taken up with his art and that her novels excited him so much that they threw him off his balance and stopped his work. He told me again the history of her marriage. Lewes, a clever, witty man, (though much her inferior) living in a half Bohemian set, neglected his wife a good deal. Then he was enraged by finding she had been seduced . . . She promised amendment [and he kept her on,] but finding she broke her promise he put her away altogether. Then, being devoted to George

Eliot, who was alone and not much known, she consented to
live with him. She had no religious scruples, but felt in the
long run very bitter, having cut herself away from social
life. She was visited by great ladies when she became famous,
but could hardly ever be persuaded to go into society.
Though a professed unbeliever she believed in a spiritual
world, and she has said to me that the most stupendous
conception she knew of was the Redemption.

He was glad he had kept her books for these solitary days;
"they are such a delight to me now".

He had friends among poets as well as artists. He told me
of an amusing scene when "Browning was showing off his
son's first pictures—not very good ones—and Tennyson came
to see them and walked round in his cloak and hat, looking
much disgusted and giving an occasional growl, while
Browning cheerfuly and quietly did the honours. "Once at
Haworth he had met Tennyson who, having helped himself
to some cheese straws, suddenly began to dash them over the
table with his fork in a fit of petulance, saying 'beastly
things'. Carlyle had said of Tennyson to Lewes, 'It's a pity
to see that man wasting his great heart in bits of verses'.
'Why, what would you have him do?' said Lewes, and
Carlyle gave a great guffaw—his habit when he was taken
aback—and said, 'What's before him!'."

Henry James, in *The Outcry*, makes "The Prince" the
deus ex machina who gains the Mantovana masterpiece for
the National Gallery. But Sir Frederic, had he lived to read
that book, would hardly have acquiesced in that possibility
for he had all the pride of the artist, and was used to speak
with some resentment of the treatment of artists by Royalty.

He told me that some artists employed to decorate a kiosk
at Buckingham Palace returned the money given to them,
it was so little. Tom Landseer, the celebrated engraver,
was sent for to Windsor to instruct the Queen and Prince
Consort in etching, which they had taken up. He was shown
into a room and presently a flunkey arrived with a tray on
which was an etching plate. This he was requested to prepare,
and having done so it was taken away, and he was sent a
message that that was all that was required of him, and was
either offered money or asked what his charge was. He shook
off the dust of the Castle from his feet, absolutely fuming
with rage. A sculptor was talking to Prince Albert, who asked
him if he knew Threep, saying, "Oh, Threep is a very good
sculptor and cheap!" with a snap of the fingers. Carl Haag,

who was a favourite, gave me an amusing account of his first
day at Balmoral. He was summoned there to paint the Prince
Consort, and was deposited on the road-side by the coach
with his portmanteau. At last he found someone to carry it,
and having enquired his way, proceeded to the Castle. Next
morning he was sent for by the Prince, who said, "As I shall
not be able to sit until tomorrow, I would like you to paint
my two new dogs". These were then sent for and he began
to draw them. He was presently interrupted by a message
that the Queen wished to see him, so he took off his painting
garb, put on his frock coat, and was taken to the garden
where Her Majesty informed him that a photographer
having arrived to do some groups she thought he might
help in the arrangement of them. He proposed a couch and
Her Majesty thought this an excellent idea and sent for one.
But it never arrived, as no one could be found whose business
it was to bring couches to the garden. So at last some groups
were done without it, and then the Queen asked if he
would like to go and sketch during the afternoon at
Glenquoich[2], and a pony would be put at his disposal. Glad
to escape, he had set out on his pony with his sketch books,
etc., when he heard a shout, "Mr. Haag", and looking back
he saw a flunkey who said the Queen wished to see him again.
So he dismounted and came in, took off his riding things
and again got into his frock coat and was taken to the
drawing-room where Her Majesty received him with, "Why,
Mr. Haag, I thought you were at Glenquoich". "I was starting, but was told your Majesty wished to see me." "Who said
I wished to see Mr. Haag?" There was consternation in the
royal circle, and at last it was discovered that there had been
a discussion on some subject and she had said, "If Mr. Haag
were here he could tell us all about it", and some officious
person had rushed off for him.

   I see in a letter from Sir Henry Layard, written in 1873,
"Old Boxall is, I hear, very shaky, and I fear the Gallery is
at a standstill". And later letters tell that Leighton was
spoken of to take his place, and Solomon Hart and J. C.
Robinson, afterwards Keeper of the Queen's pictures. But in
the next year (February 1874), he writes, "I saw in *The
Times* that Boxall had resigned and that Burton had been
appointed in his stead. I know very little of him, but what

---

[2] Glenquoich is too far west, over seventy miles as the crow flies.
Perhaps Glenmuick is meant as it is only six or seven miles away.

little I know is on the whole favourable." Yet he is "afraid
that he will not have the social influence of position that the
Director should have". And again, staying with him in a
country house, he fears he is "somewhat wanting in vigour
and is slow to put himself forward". I had myself sometimes
in those later years when I saw much of Sir Frederic, wondered how with his reserve and aloofness he had ever attained
to that coveted Directorship. And on this I never questioned
him, but one day in talking of his life, he said he had been
persuaded to think of the place by Boxall, the outgoing
Director, and had consented "although I disliked the idea of
becoming a cockshy, chiefly to save it from becoming an
appanage of the Royal Academy. I refused, however to send
testimonials, though Boxall at Gladstone's request, begged
me to do so. Gladstone had a scruple against appointing me
because I was not a Royal Academician, and I had put the
thought out of my mind when one day a messenger arrived
from the Treasury, just as I was going out, bringing me the
offer. I had hoped and had been assured by Boxall I would
have time to go on with painting, but I've never been able
to touch a brush. The Gallery needed a great deal of
renovating. Many of the pictures were in a filthy state.
Boxall had had two or three cleaned, but was so intimidated
by the outcry in the papers that he had them rubbed over
with brown varnish. I waited till the arrangement of some
of them was being altered, then quietly had some cleaned,
and no one was the wiser."

The most fiery and independent of Directors, he had
determined to maintain the dignity and privileges of the
Gallery at any cost. I had often heard it said the Queen had
a grudge against the National Gallery, and that it was never
visited by Royalty; and he told me that was so and gave as
probable reasons: "It was in the first place because the Prince
Consort once offered it a collection of pictures he had bought
at a sale, and as they largely consisted of rubbish, Boxall
ventured to propose making a selection from it, which was
indignantly refused, and the offer withdrawn. Then immediately after my appointment (1874) I was sent for by Lord
Beaconsfield (my appointment was about the last act of
Gladstone's government) and when Boxall went to see him
at Downing Street about some final arrangement, he found
him just preparing to go and resign office to the Queen at
Windsor, and described his face as perfectly demoniacal.
There were some drawings left by Landseer for sale, and he

having been a royal favourite, the Queen had expressed a
desire that they should be purchased by the National Gallery.
The subject had already been brought up at a meeting of
the Board. Lord Hardinge had just been appointed a Trustee
and had tried to insist that this purchase should be carried
out in obedience to the Royal wish. He misunderstood his
position, having been Chairman of the Trustees of the British
Museum, where such a position carries weight, whereas with
us it is nothing, and he tried to insist on carrying this point.
I absolutely refused, first on the ground that there is no
money granted to the Gallery for the purchase either of
drawings or water colours, in fact for anything on paper;
these belong to the British Museum's department. And
secondly, I refused to entertain the idea because I thought
it would be a very bad precedent, and lead to many evils, if
we allowed ourselves to be dictated to on matters of art by
Royalty. It was then Lord Beaconsfield sent for me, and
though more courteously, conveyed to me the same request,
to which I made the same answer. When I was leaving and
Lord Beaconsfield was ringing the bell, I turned back, and
with courage at which I am now astonished, I said, "I hope,
Mr. Disraeli, that we quite understand one another. It is
quite impossible that I should entertain this proposal."
Dizzy, slightly taken aback, answered civilly, and never bore
me any grudge, as Gladstone would have done: but always
treated me with great consideration and liberality in all
matters connected with the Gallery."

IX

ATHENAEUM FRIENDS III: SIR HENRY LAYARD

I WROTE yesterday, 8 June 1922: "This morning I awoke early, very down-hearted about my book. And as I thought of it I almost wished it might be destroyed, although I had been so uneasy lest this should happen in case of a raid." But then in the afternoon Yeats came to spend some days here, and when we were sitting under the catalpa tree in the garden I told him of my discontent, that as I had thought in the still morning, in the clear light, of what I had been writing, it had seemed so far from what I wanted. I did not expect, I said, to make it a great book, or a beautiful one, but I had wanted it to be worthy to put beside my other books and not to be unworthy of faith, for it was he who had first urged me to write it. "And now," I said, "it seems in lumps without harmony, I don't know how I shall ever get it right". Yeats said, "that is often the way with what one is doing, I feel it myself sometimes, not perhaps with poems but with a play." "Oh, I can master a play," I said, "but a bundle of facts is different. In biography even of oneself, one is not free. I think of Mrs. Broderick in *The Jackdaw;* 'it's a terrible thing to be put in the dock and be bound to speak nothing but the truth'." "Well," said he, "you should remember the miracle of the five barley loaves and two small fishes, and that there were twelve baskets of fragments taken up. But it would have taken a yet greater miracle to turn those twelve baskets of fragments into two little fishes and five loaves." So being a little comforted, I said, "You have heard my first chapters, and now I want you to listen to the rest. I am not giving a history of myself from year to year, I think my book will have in it more of my friendships than of myself. It is by my friendships I should like to be judged. Your turn will come before the end of the book. I have been writing now about some more of my friends I made after my marriage. What do you know of Sir Henry Layard?" "Only that he enabled Rossetti to write his poem on the Nineveh bull," said Yeats, and he took down the volume and read: —

In our Museum galleries
Today I lingered o'er the prize
Dead Greece vouchsafes to living eyes,—
Her Art for ever in fresh wise
    From hour to hour rejoicing me.
Sighing, I turned at last to win
Once more the London dirt and din;
And as I made the swing-door spin
And issued, they were hoisting in
    A winged beast from Nineveh.

A human face the creature wore
And hoofs behind and hoofs before,
And flanks with dark runes fretted o'er.
'Twas bull, 'twas mitred Minotaur,
    A dead disbowelled mystery;
The mummy of a buried faith
Straight from the charnel without scathe,
Its wings stood for the light to bathe,—
Such fossil cerements as might swathe
    The very corpse of Nineveh.

The print of its first rush-wrapping,
Wound ere it dried, still ribbed the thing.
What song did the brown maidens sing,
From purple mouths alternating,
    When that was woven languidly?
What vows, what rites, what prayers preferr'd
What songs has the strange image heard?
In what blind vigil stood interr'd
For ages, till an English word
    Broke silence first at Nineveh?

"It is a fine poem," I said, "and it is time for you to learn
something about Layard. If you had been brought up on
Scripture history as I was you would have heard more about
the discovery of Nineveh. It happened just at the time when
Darwin was pulling nails out of Noah's Ark, and other stories
were being doubted, such as the story of Jonah who was
swallowed by the Whale when he was being sent to preach
at Nineveh. So when Rossetti wrote that

    Near the city gates the Lord
    Sheltered his Jonah with a gourd.

Layard was cried up in England as 'the man that made the
Bible true'. I had heard that much in my early lessons at
Roxborough. So when I had been only two months away
from the Sundays at Killinane church and had all this fresh

in my mind, it was a very exciting moment when the Embassy launch met us in the Bosphorus and took us to Therapia to stay with the Layards. So now listen to my chapter."

I have written in *Our Irish Theatre* of Enid, Lady Layard, as "Ambassadress at Constantinople and Madrid; helper of the miserable and the wounded in the Turkish-Russian War; helper of the sick in the hospital she founded in Venice; friend and hostess and guest of Queens in England and Germany and Rome. She was her husband's good helpmate while he lived—is not the Cyprus treaty set down in that clear handwriting I shall never see coming in here again? And widowed she kept his name in honour, living after him for fifteen years and herself leaving a noble memory in all places where she had lived and in Venice where her home was and where she died." She was my friend from 1880 till her death.

My husband's friendship with Sir Henry had begun long before, in their House of Commons days, although he had there "many a duel with Mr. Layard who was for the Turks *à tout prix*"; he himself doing all he could to free the Christians in the East from their dominance; while Layard in return accused him in debate of being "the mouthpiece of all the discontent in Eastern Europe". But Sir William told me that Greeks and Serbians, visitors to the House of Commons would whisper suspicions of treachery, seeing these antagonists walk home together after the debate in friendly talk—as likely as not about the National Gallery or some question of architecture or painting.

I was shy of him for some time. At meal times he would keep up a sort of humorous grumble at Lady Layard, rather disconcerting to a stranger, until when intimacy had grown I found myself treated in somewhat the same way. I never thought him at his best in general company. He would exaggerate his deafness. ("They say the waiter at Vigor's restaurant died of cholera," said he. "It was the cook," said I, "Of Croup?" says he, and so on.) And his habit perhaps also half humorous of grumbling against English politics and politicians was a pity, for those who did not know him would say it was discontent at not being kept in office.

I liked best to hear him talking with Sir William, when I could sit and listen. I heard him tell how coming to that same Therapia Embassy where he now ruled, he had been refused admission to the presence of the then Ambassador, Sir Stratford Canning. He had arrived from his first journey through Arabia, the bearer of news of great importance about the Arab leaders and tribes. But the haughty "young gentlemen of the Chancery" turned him away. They saw but an unknown young Englishman, rough-handed, travel-stained, wearing (and this was worse in their eyes than would have been any desert rags) a hastily bought blue frock coat, that was too small for him. But coming a few days later he had a different reception. The Ambassador, to whom he had meanwhile written, received him at once, and he was kept for hours talking with him, they two alone. And when he was leaving, the astonished Secretaries saw him escorted to the outer door by the "great Eltchi" himself, the fiery autocrat who had once drawn his sword on his French col-leagues. He was a good friend to Layard afterwards, giving him employment in the Embassy, helping him with a money loan to uncover those Nineveh marbles, and often making him his guest. One moonlit evening, as we sat by a window, Sir Henry laughed and told us how on one of those far-off evenings Lady Stratford had suddenly called out, "Oh Stratford, look at the moon!", and he, being interrupted in talk or train of thought, had answered with vehemence, "God damn the moon!".

They were wonderful days there, whether we went for rides in the forest, or to rummage in the Constantinople bazaars, or took our kettle across the Bosphorus and made our tea beside the "sweet waters of Asia". Guests would come in also, Hatzfelt, the German Ambassador, charming, and celebrated for his stretching of diplomatic privilege so far as to have had a cow sent him from Prussia in the Embassy postbag; Hobart Pasha; Laurence Oliphant, bent on getting support for what Sir Henry considered a wild scheme of planting a Jewish colony in Gilead. "He didn't think," he said, "that I had given him sufficient support, but he put a stopper on it himself by telling the Sultan's Secretary he was seeking to fulfil the Scripture prophecy that the end of the world was to come when the Jews were restored to their native land, and His Majesty had no desire to hurry that event."

And although Sir William refused to go and see, or allow me to be taken to see the Sultan saying, "I mean to pitch into him as soon as I get home", we went one day to see his Treasury, a wonderful vision of precious stones cut and uncut, heaped in gold and silver basins, where our eyes were soon dazzled. It was a very cave of Aladdin. While we

were there Sir Henry pointed out a couple of little china
cups studded with stones, of no great beauty, saying his
mother-in-law, Lady Charlotte Schreiber, a collector of
china, would be interested in them (I think they are now
in the South Kensington Museum) and took them up in his
hand. Next day a messenger arrived from the Palace with a
present for Lady Layard of these "horrid little cups", as
she called them. The Sultan had given orders that whatever
Sir Henry had seemed to admire most should be given to
her, and he had told that they had taken most notice of
these. He was vexed at being given anything; she was vexed
that as a present had been given it was such a useless one.
And later, when a cry against the Turks had become also
a cry against Sir Henry Layard, these "jewelled vessels"
were spoken of as a proof that he had been bribed.

"It was an unjust outcry, for although he had a real
affection for the Turkish people, the peasantry, he used to
say they lost their good qualities if ever they became Pashas.
And when he was there he was very vigorously working for
reform. He wrote to me long afterwards: "I had no sympathy
for the Turkish Government or the Turkish rule but very
great sympathy for the Turkish people who were ruthlessly
slaughtered in consequence of the humanitarian and anti-
Mahommedan crusade against them, headed by Gladstone.
Whether the maintenance of the Ottoman Empire was essential to the interests and even existence of the British Empire,
as all our great statesmen from Chatham to Palmerston
believed, is a question which will be decided hereafter. I
have not altered my opinion upon the subject."

I liked to listen also as he talked of his days in the Crimea
during the war; how it was to him that Bosquet said at
Balaclava: "C'est magnifique mais ce n'est pas la guerre",
how the correspondent of some paper bolted first thing at
Inkerman, but afterwards furnished a full account of it
which he got from him, but had written up some officer
who did less than nothing, and never mentioned Sir Collingwood Dickson who had threatened to kick him out of his
tent for impertinence; how cool Dickson was at, I think,
Alma, Layard found him shaving in his tent when balls
were falling all around and said, "Don't you know you're
in danger of being killed?" "Yes," he said, "but at all events
I would like to be a clean corpse". And how after the battle
he said to a poor lad, Denes, afterwards killed, who came
into mess, "Oh, we didn't keep a place for you, we made

sure you would be killed to-day". Sir William told of a letter
he had from Lord Dunkellin when he was made prisoner
and how, when he was lying in the sand under a redoubt,
a soldier told him there was a Russian standing firing at
him, and he said, "Well, I'll give you half-a-crown if you
bring him down, for I'm too comfortable to move".

Layard's blood must have been stirred by the visit. It was
another great memory in his life. Yet it might have been
better for him had he stayed at home, for as it happened
when he came back, his heart touched by the unnecessary
sufferings of the soldiers, he vehemently attacked in and out
of the House of Commons, the mismanagement in England,
the giving of high posts to favourites, the carelessness for
the comfort of the troops; and in the army and in the
Ministry this plain speaking made him enemies. And
another matter brought him real trouble. A private letter
he had written to Delane of *The Times,* from the *Agamem-
non,* a ship of the fleet on which he was a guest, had been by
mishap printed. In it he had found fault with Admiral
Dundas who was in command of the Fleet. He had thus
given a weapon to those who had a grudge against him, and
as is the way in politics, he had given further offence by
saying, after his explanation and apology, that if dared to
do so he would prove the charges he had made, of inactivity
and remissness and neglect. His courage and plain speaking
had helped reform, but it was at a heavy cost. Lord Palmerston had denounced him for untruth, and a nickname
"lie-hard" was given to him, one of the most honourable and
truthful of men. He had left Parliament for a couple of
years after these attacks, but as he himself declared, and as
was acknowledged, if he had suffered it was "on the side
of the people".

Little by little as I came to know him, I could see as it
were separate threads in his life, the weft and warp, luck
and ill-luck, warm friends and bitter enemies, woven into
the stuff by the good and the wicked godmother. The shining
threads came first, his childhood among artists in France
and Italy, the young years in London in his aunt, Mrs.
Austen's, salon, with its brilliant society of wits and writers,
among them Mr. Disraeli, 'that great political gladiator"
as he afterwards called him. Shining gifts also were the
headstrong energy, the lure of the East that led him to say
he would practise the law, if practise he must, in Ceylon
rather than at home and to choose instead of the common-

place sea voyage the roughness and danger of a journey to
India overland; his divination among the desert sandhills
that there lay under them a lost city; the fulfilment in its
uncovering. Then Parliament; the happy marriage; the
high diplomatic appointments as British Minister at Madrid,
as Ambassador to Constantinople. Yet the dark threads had
found their places in the web. In 1869 Mr. Gladstone made
him First Commissioner of Works; "the first expert to whom
the post had ever been given". He took the office with great
projects of making London beautiful, of building the new
Law Courts on the Thames Embankment, "the magnificent
plan of Mr. Layard, offering space and outlook for a grand
building". But a Committee decided on the Strand and that
was a choice I have often enough heard lamented. Sir Henry
says in a letter to my husband, who had supported him in
Parliament, "the design had to be altered, Fleet Street being
restricted in space, so that he had to give up the great feature
in his original plan, a great central hall accessible from the
Courts and a general gathering place of one great building.
Now it is but a number of buildings intended for different
purposes casually brought together in a street." And he wrote
to me (when I was editing my husband's *Autobiography*),
"I am much obliged to you for mentioning my connection
with the scheme for placing the Law Courts on the Embankment. The idea was entirely my own. The scheme failed
because Gladstone (out of pique I believe) opposed it.
Everyone now regrets that it was not carried out." Another
scheme he was set upon of decorating the Central Hall at
Westminster with mosaics was not approved. And how often
I have heard him and my husband, his constant supporter in
these schemes, lament that the Natural History Museum
had been built "sunk in a gravel pit" for want of £15,000
to make a proper foundation.

"What a city we might have made of London!" he wrote
to my husband from Madrid. "Such an opportunity can only
occur once in a nation's history."

And within a year when he was appointed British Minister
as Madrid, he was being replaced by Mr. Ayrton,
who as Parliamentary Secretary to the Treasury, had
done his best to thwart him, and who had said in a
speech to his constituents that he objected to public money
being spent on "painters, sculptors, architects, and market
gardeners". (This came to my mind of late years in Dublin
and I felt that Hugh Lane was not the first to see his dream

of a beautiful city knocked to pieces in much the same way.)

I think he was glad to leave Parliament after these rebuffs, yet Madrid was also a disappointment. He wrote to my husband in 1872, "This is no doubt a terrible banishment, but anything is better than the position in which I found myself at the Office of Works". And although he had tried to dissuade him from taking the Government of Ceylon—"If you leave the House who will there be to say a few words for art and public monuments?" he writes from Madrid to Colombo as if envying him: "It is something to find oneself in an independent position and to be able to mould things after one's own fashion. There is a tendency amongst people in general to identify one with the things which surround one and affairs with which one is more or less mixed up, so that while you will, and justly, be associated with the progress which your island is making, and the present wise and liberal government of it, I have the satisfaction of feeling that I can only be looked on in connection with this wretched (Spanish) Government and miserable intrigues which are every day bringing this country lower and lower."

He could not reconcile himself to Madrid. They were stormy and unsettled years there. He wrote (May 1875): "I ought not to remain here. The same Minister cannot serve with satisfaction to anyone or to himself, or even to the advantage of the public service, during such successive elementary-distinct governments as a Regency, a constitutional Monarchy, a moderate Republic and red ditto, a Dictatorship and the Bourbonic regime with which we are now threatened." Also his sturdy Protestantism from the day when, only eight years old, he had been all but drowned in the Allier at Moulins by his schoolfellows for refusing to bow to the Host as it was carried by, cried out against Catholic Spain. He writes in 1891 when the Religious Disabilities Bill was being brought in: "My Huguenot blood makes me revolt against any attempt to increase the power of the Pope and Catholic priesthood in England . . . I was a witness of what took place in Spain on the restoration of the Bourbon dynasty. The most energetic attempts were made by the Vatican to restore the mediaeval system of intolerance and persecution which was the disgrace of Spain before the revolution of 1868-69, and they were very nearly successful. I may take some credit to myself towards frustrating them . . . Then Gladstone, the old Protestant bigot, the author of the pamphlets on the Vatican degrees should now pose as the champion of the Roman Catholics, is a piece of audacious cynicism which could only be tolerated in a rapidly degenerating country." And a certain density or lack of understanding Catholic feeling gave offence there. Long afterwards I heard some who had been guests at the Legation in Madrid speak with vehemence of the anger roused by the sight of some ancient chalices he had bought from the churches used to decorate his table*.

Sometimes in those Madrid letters he wishes himself in Italy: "Anyone who does not recognise the enormous improvement which has taken place in Italy since the end of Austrian rule must be wilfully and incorrigibly blind". But above all, he wishes to be sent to Constantinople. "Turkey is going forward; this country backward." And at last in 1877, after years at Madrid, that hope had its fulfilment.

But now that he arrived at Constantinople in state and power, it was "much too late to do anything to prevent war" (between Russia and Turkey), "impossible to say what it may lead to except a shocking amount of carnage and infinite misery and desolation. Unhappily, the Russians have given it the character of a war of religion." He has (1877) "been misrepresented most shamefully" as encouraging the Turks in the war when "the one thing which every humane man must wish for is that the cruel war should be brought to a speedy end". He was able to be of use, although not in the way he had planned.

(September 1877). "The Embassy is turned into a great workshop; my wife and a number of allies and Secretaries and Attachés are rolling bandages and making things for the sick and wounded soldiers, and a very large sum has been sent to me for the relief of the fugitive women and children, Mussulman and Christian, many of them wounded, whose misery and sufferings are truly shocking."

When the war ended, the time for beneficial influence seemed at last to have come. He believed in the Sultan's good disposition and good intentions, and the Sultan showed him in every way confidence and friendship. Alas for that thread in the web! For the very reason of this friendship jealousies

---

*In January 1891 writing about the O'Shea v. Parnell case he says, "It is rather strange that England should have owed so much to a divorce Court—our Protestantism to the tribunal which broke poor Queen Catherine's heart, and the maintaining of the United Empire to this."

arose. His influence began to dwindle. The French Ambassador persuaded the Sultan to take a French doctor into the Palace; the French held to a monopoly for lighting the Palace that was against the Conventions. Sir Henry's audiences became less frequent, less familiar. Native advisers whispered strange accusations, and suspicion at last took such hold of the Sultan's mind, that a day came when the Ambassador, who had been his most trusted friend, was, although admitted to an audience, kept at the other end of the room lest he should try to assassinate him. And thus all hope of bringing a remedy to the ills he had hoped to cure was broken.

While we were yet his guests at Therapia in that May of 1880 Mr. Gladstone, who had just come into power, sent him an invitation to come back to England "to confer with the Government on some questions that had arisen". Sir William said to me when he heard this, "Layard will never be sent back here". And so it happened. Mr. Goschen was sent to Constantinople on a special mission, and Sir Henry was never again given employment or office.

If he had known he was so soon to be called back to England it is likely he would have kept the story of the Sultan's change of temper to be told by word of mouth. But he had written (and this was the cause of much trouble to him through coming years) a private dispatch to Lord Granville telling him of disappointed hopes, of broken promises and that it was impossible to believe the Sultan's word.

And as a private letter written from the Crimea had clouded and interrupted his Parliamentary life, so this other confidential letter put an end to his diplomatic life. It was published with a consent forced from him, and with this publication old and new enmities awoke. He was accused of having made that report through expediency to gain favour with the new Government, an altogether unfair accusation. He was not only given no new Embassy, even when the one he was of all men most fitted for fell vacant, that of Rome, but his diplomatic pension was ungraciously deferred. And this irked him because he was not a rich man.

The uncle from whom he had been named and who had promised to make him his heir had long before fallen out with him, reproving some romantic folly of his early life, a reproof perhaps too hotly spurned, and, offended, left the life use of his property to his widow; Layard in resentment ceased to use the name he had been known by, "Austin", and was a defiant "Henry" to the last.

With the same independent spirit he would not try to re-enter Parliament; he writes to my husband, "Nothing would induce me to go through the degradation of appealing to the ignorance and prejudices of the mob. I had quite enough of that in former days. I always felt heartily ashamed of myself after a canvass and hustings speech."

His friends yet believed that he who deserved so well of his country would be given a place in the House of Lords. He writes: "I should rejoice if I could do any good by making my voice heard and my influence felt. I have not the slightest wish to be a 'Lord' but as the House of Commons is closed to me I would like to have the opportunity of being of use in the Upper House." And again though he will make no claim when a Life Peerage Bill was being brought in (1888), he shows that such a claim could be a strong one. "I am a Privy Councillor and G.C.B. I have been an Ambassador and a Minister; twice Under Secretary for Foreign Affairs, and First Commissioner of Works. I obtained Cyprus for England; have made discoveries which distinguish the Victorian age, and am a corresponding member of the French Academy and an honorary D.C.L., an honorary member of I don't know how many learned societies, English and foreign . . ."

In 1890, the Jubilee gone by, when many peerages had been given, no offer of this honour had been made to him. A mystery hung about the matter. He was too proud to make or allow his friends to make any request. I do not know whether it was for good or ill that chance led me to try and undo the tangle. I wrote on 4 February 1888, telling of the guests at a dinner I had been to, "I sat next Lord Selborne" (the very Sir Roundell Palmer, who representing the convenience of lawyers, had done so much to upset that Law Court Scheme, but of late a warm friend of the Layards) "and talked with him all evening, and made use of the occasion by suggesting to him Layard's fitness for a peerage. He asked if he would like it, and I said, 'yes, it would crown his life, but he was so disinclined to put himself forward he would never ask for it'. He grew quite enthusiastic and said he did not pretend to have much influence, but would write to Lord Salisbury and propose it—and then I beckoned W. over and set him talking on the same subject."

Some little time after, Lord Selborne told Sir William

that Lord Salisbury had agreed with him that there was no one more deserving of the House of Lords, and that he would take up the matter.

It was a heavy disappointment, when yet later, we learned from Lord Selborne that the recommendation for a Peerage had been made to the Queen, but that she had refused to grant it on the ground that no Ambassador was justified in writing as Sir Henry Layard had done, in his letter from Constantinople, of the Sovereign to whose Court he was accredited.

A small committee had taken it in hand to place a bust of Sir Henry in the British Museum near the Nineveh marbles, a letter to Layard from my husband says, "Of course, you are the best judge how to act to clear Her Majesty's mind from disapprobation of your letter, but it ought to be cleared. And now again in *strictest confidence* I may tell you that when Sir Henry Thompson mentioned to the Prince that our Committee was going to place a bust of you in the British Museum, he said, 'You must not ask me to join. I have the highest regard and admiration for Sir Henry but there are reasons which I can't enter into. Don't forget, however, to ask my sister, she will join gladly.' (The Empress Frederick did join the Committee and subscribed.) Sir Henry Thompson replied, 'Sir, remember I have not made any request to you to join'. 'That is quite right,' said the Prince, 'I have not refused'. I did not know of the Queen's disapprobation till two or three days afterwards. This cleared up the somewhat puzzling words of the Prince."

Sir Henry, although hurt, took the refusal philosophically and with dignity. I think he was glad to have done with uncertainty and have the question set at rest. He writes from Venice, 28 December 1890: "I am now too old to take part in public affairs. I have no desire whatever to become a Lord, and am very happy and contented as I am. I live here to avoid the turmoil of English life and to escape the London fogs. Had I been put into the House of Lords I should have considered it my duty to reside in England, which certainly would not have contributed to my health or happiness. My only regret is that the Queen, from whom I have received much kindness, for which I am really grateful, should have acted with regard to me under a wrong impression . . . There was no 'letter' in the matter. I wrote,

as it was my duty to do, and as I presume every Representative of the Queen is bound to do, a dispatch giving a full
and complete report on the state of the Court to which I
had been sent. Such a dispatch would naturally contain my
opinion of the principal persons who administered the
affairs of that country, and especially of its Sovereign, and
of others who influenced its policy. It is essential for the
Government or its principal members to be informed on this
subject, and I wrote a secret dispatch without any reserve,
and with the honest desire of making those who were
recalling me, and to whom I was in no way indebted (but
quite the contrary) fully acquainted with the state of Turkey
and with the character of the Sultan, his Ministers, the
foreign Representation at Constantinople and others with
whom my successor would have to deal. Mr. Gladstone and
Lord Granville thought that the publication of this dispatch
was for the public interest and upon this ground they asked
me to consent to it. Under these circumstances I could not
refuse, although perfectly alive to the consequences—the
probable ruin of my career. It was for them to consider
whether the publication of a dispatch which was 'secret and
confidential' if ever a dispatch was, would be of advantage
to the public interests. In my opinion it was decidedly most
prejudicial to them. It was calculated to destroy all confidence of the Sultan in future in a British Representative,
and to be a fatal blow to the very great influence of England,
which I may say without fear of contradiction, that I had
succeeded in establishing at Constantinople . . . To me the
publication gave infinite pain, as I foresaw that the Sultan
would think that I had been a false friend to him, and had
betrayed the confidence which he had placed in me. He could
not make the distinction between public duty and private
friendship. I had experienced many acts of the greatest
kindness from him, and both Lady Layard and I had come
to entertain feelings of real affection for him. But if I had
allowed these feelings to interfere with my duty to the
Queen and her Government, I should have proved myself
unworthy of the trust which Her Majesty had placed in me
when she appointed me her Ambassador at Constantinople.
I was bound to the whole truth, and I may say without
boasting, that my dispatch did give a most faithful picture
of the state of affairs existing at that time in Constantinople."

His life was already a full one. The National Gallery had
already through a great part of his life been a chief interest;

it was in the long intercourse between him and my husband
that "third" so necessary a part of friendship. Even in 1869
when he writes announcing his engagement to "my relative,
Miss Guest, Sir Ivor Guest's sister" and asking for his
"support" as best man at the ceremony, he goes on to tell at
length of a loan of pictures from Hampton Court that had
been promised to the Gallery. He had looked after its
interests in Parliament, and had once while there been
offered a yet closer connection with it, as he writes (to
W.H.G.), "It is quite true that Lord Russell offered me the
Directorship of the National Gallery and pressed me much
to accept it. He was in a difficulty about finding a successor
to Eastlake, and thought that I might accept the place
without the salary—which as I was Under Secretary for
Foreign Affairs I could not, it was thought, receive. But I
was not disposed to entertain his views, and after consulting
Clarendon and the Attorney General I declined, and Boxall
was chosen to fill his place, an infinitely better arrangement.
But it is curious that I should have been offered it, and
that both Panizzi and Cole should have proposed me as
their successor in the offices they respectively held in the
British Museum and South Kensington."

But as a Trustee he was almost as much concerned with
its affairs as a Director could be. His letters are filled with
comments on pictures bought, or likely to be in the market,
or that ought to be added, or on its administration as indeed
were the answering letters from W.H.G. to him ("Oh! that
correspondence!" Sir Frederic Burton, the Director of the
Gallery, once cried out to me with a laugh that was something near a groan.) He was very proud of the collection.
And he found a special joy in the pictures he had himself
collected and that hung on the walls of Ca Capello because
of his intention that they should some day hang in Trafalgar
Square. He watched over its interests, raged over its want
of space, and then when new rooms were added is sarcastic
over their bad decoration: "Burton tells a good story. He
was one day looking at the proceedings of the sculptor who
made the friezes and lunettes, and who had prepared a most
ridiculous cartoon for a group emblematic of the triumph
of the Arts. The man, who evidently perceived Burton's
surprise, exclaimed, 'Pray, Mr. Burton, don't look at my
cartoon, for you know that I am a sculptor and can't draw!'."

The Treasury was the common enemy, threatening to
dump the Tate collection on to the only bit of land possible

to use for the Gallery's enlargement; stopping the grant
after the purchase of the Blenheim Raphael. Even Sir
Frederic Burton once entertained me with his indignation
against the Treasury, it having objected to repay £1 he had
given the butler at Blenheim when he went to inspect that
very picture.

I think, all ambition put aside, Sir Henry's last years
were very happy and serene. He was a good citizen of his
chosen home, Venice, helping and encouraging the Murano
glass-blowers, both in practical ways and in the finding of
models from which they could bring their art to the highest
beauty; encouraging in the same way the revival of the once
famous Venetian lace. He writes in 1890, "I have been
named Membre de l' Institut and I have been unanimously
elected by the R.A.s to succeed Browning as their honorary
Foreign Secretary". He belonged to the Athenaeum, though
I don't think he ever dined there or became a member of
any particular group. He clung to his home life as if in
reaction from the freedom of the desert tents in the adven-
turous Arabian days. Once he settled down it was for ever;
he would even hasten back from the Club to his wife's five
o'clock tea-table, to help her in the entertaining of her
guests. I remember her saying rather pathetically after his
death, when she was putting away letters, that she had none
of his to treasure, he had never written to her during their
married life, they had never been a day apart. Being
childless they clung the more closely to one another. In their
hospitality they were at one; I think they hardly liked to see
an empty place at their table or even an empty room in their
house. In London some of the many relations would come
in, they seldom dined alone. They gave more formal dinners
also, and there one was certain to meet good company,
friends marking, as it were like milestones, the different
epochs of Sir Henry's life. He had delighted to show the
wonders of London to Rassam the Syrian who had been his
helper in the work at Nineveh and told us with delight
how at a pantomime when a shining spangled ballet-dancer
was let down to the stage, Rassam, awed, had whispered,
"Could that be the Holy Ghost?" For the Oriental ideas of
our doctrines are as vague as ours of theirs, and Sir Henry
used to say that the difference between us and Mohammedans
is that they have one God and three wives, and we have one
wife and three Gods. At one of those dinners, to give an
instance, I met Percy Ffrench, his First Secretary of Legation

at Madrid; John Murray, his first publisher; Sir Collingwood
Dickson, whom we had known in the Crimea, and Mme.
Nietjens, a pretty Belgian, who sang very well, "though, as
Murray said, her voice was like a scimitar going through
one, but she looks music and Sir H. and W. are much
taken with her".

Again in May 1888, "I sat next Dr. Smith of *The
Quarterly*, who repeated an account he had just heard from
the Duchess of —— of the State Banquet given to the Queen
at Charlottenberg the other day. The guests were invited for
eight. The Queen did not arrive till nine and all had to
stand waiting. About ten minutes to nine the Emperor asked
the ladies to sit down, but even then the gentlemen were
left standing, including Moltke, aged eighty-seven. When the
long-awaited-for dinner appeared it consisted of soup, turbot
not very fresh; roast neck of mutton; lobster, woodcock, out
of season, and ice, and of this repast the poor Duke of ——
being on regime only took mutton, and that was whipped
away as he turned to speak to a lady after one mouthful.
Bismarck broke through all etiquette by holding forth at
the top of his voice and addressing the Queen across the
table, at which Sir E. Malet was aghast, but being Bismarck,
Her Majesty took it graciously. L. says the Empress has no
notion of housekeeping and that they were nearly starved
when staying at Potsdam—sour milk—champagne—stewed
fruit—fish served promiscuously and very little of anything.
Mrs. Smith came to return me thanks for having made
myself so agreeable to her husband!"

But it was at Venice that Sir Henry found his heart's
home. It was while he was yet living in Madrid he had
bought his palace on the Grand Canal and begun to lodge
his treasures there. "Live not where you do not love" is a
wise motto, and it came to mind sometimes as I saw his
whole nature, as it were, expand and ripen as he looked out
on the golden ripples from the wide windows of Ca Cappello.
His morning was spent in his quiet library; there he wrote
his memoirs or rewrote Kugler's book on painting, or studied
for some articles he meditated for *The Quarterly*. He was not
a wide reader. He writes: "I have so little time for reading
that I rarely, except when travelling I skim a French novel,
read any books except such as add something to the, alas!
very little knowledge that I possess on which directly
interests me, or bears upon some subject in which I may be
engaged. I have not read Mrs. H. Ward's book, nor shall I

probably do so, as those psychological novels somewhat bore me. I have been very idle since I came here (Norway), only reading some bad French novels and some of Dickens' early volumes which I had not looked at since they came out."

Anything concerning the history of Venice or Italy interested him and I remember his being very much interested in Creighton's history of the Popes[1]; and his praises made Lady Sophia Palmer read it, and she going on to Hatfield recommended it to Lord Salisbury, who thought it so fine a book that it first turned his attention to the writer, whom he afterwards made a Bishop. But reading was not much in fashion at Ca Capello. "W. is bored with the Patience in the evenings," I wrote. I myself used sometimes to bring down a book and read it while the cards went on, and I remember a sister of Lady Layard's, who was a sister-in-law of Lady Salisbury, saying rather with surprise, "reading in the evening! That is what the Cecils do at Hatfield."

Though Sir Henry did not hanker after London Theatres, he loved the Venetian amusements of the people. One evening when we were there we went with him to the Marionettes to see *Lord Byron in Venezia* acted. Lord Byron, in loose trousers and a huge watch chain, makes love to a "celestial creature", Margherita, but is disturbed by Lady Byron who arrives in a pink muslim dress and reproaches him, whereupon he falls on his knees and asks her forgiveness and goes off to Greece leaving Margherita in her tears. "Tell them when I die," he says to his secretary (Caro Shell), "that if Byron had faults, he had also virtues". One day, "I went out in the morning with W. and Sir H. and Burton. We went to a church to see an early Titian ... Then to the Foundling Hospital to look at the Moretto, which—a dead secret—is for sale, but I don't believe the Government will ever let it out of the country; *Christ in the House of the Pharisee.* Sir Frederic was very much excited and ready to give any price for it. We went then to see a Vittoria bust, and a staircase that is being carved for Lord Wimborne by a wood carver Sir H. has invented, and who has rewarded him by putting his head in the middle of one of his panels." For, though I don't think he gave largely to charities (he may like Morris have thought those poor "not my poor"), he brought money and fame to others besides this wood carver.

I have a note of having gone to an exhibition at Venice,

[1] *History of the Papacy during the Reformation* (1882-94) by Mandell Creighton.

I don't know how far his name has gone through the world. There were some who saw in him a new Benvenuto Cellini in the beauty and originality of his work and the whimsicality of his character. Sir Henry Layard had discovered him in Vicenza making counterfeit antiquities for the dealers, at small profit to himself. I have heard him tell how he used, having made a cabinet in some antique design, to load a gun with small shot and fire at his handiwork to thus imitate in a moment the wormholes of age. But Sir Henry divined the genius in him and gave him his opportunity.

Cortelazzo himself told me the story at Vicenza in his own villa, where I spent a day more than once with the Layards. I wrote: "It is the joy of his heart; it is in a garden full of chrysanthemums coming into flower, and sweet-scented verbena, and behind it are vines and bundles of maize drying in the sun. It is covered with frescoes, bold renaissance designs. His own portrait, life size, appears at the side, and on the front wall there are portraits of Sir Henry and Lady Layard. They are not very good, he says, for he only paid the artist fifty centimes for each. There is an inscription in the centre, 'No prophet has honour in his own country', and under it 'se vi é un Dio, Layard é il Mio'. He complains that his wife and coachman plant too many flowers about, and hide his architecture, so he is going to order 300 roses, in tin, painted, and people will say passing, 'Oh Cortelazzo has fine roses even in winter!'—just as they say now, 'What a fine tower he has got!'—not knowing it is only a half one! He showed us his tame eagle (which, because it eats a chicken in one mouthful, he calls the Minister of Finance), and his money, and all over his house, even to the granary; and his stable where he has two fine horses and a donkey, 'almost my brothers', and the little basket carriage he began with . . . the hansom he had built from a model Lady Layard sent him from London, and the brougham he has lately bought at Florence for £70. 'And the next I will have will be a brougham lined with blue satin in which I shall go to sleep'. Madame Cortelazzo looks on and smiles delightedly but won't promise to drive in the new carriage or wear a silk dress. The front of the house and the garden are decorated with statues he bought from an old theatre. The sitting room has a table-cloth formed of matchbox covers fitted together, and photographs of his work on the wall. In the kitchen, with its copper pots and its wide-raised hearth, is a tiny working bench where some of his later work has been done. I ask him which of his pieces he considers the best and he says 'the first, and points to the picture of the salver bacile made for Sir Henry, and tells me how he came to make it. 'I was working for the Antiquaries, making seals, and I got 15 centimes a day, and my wife and I lived in a garret where the rain came through the roof on to our bed at night. It was then that I came to know Layard. After he had talked with me, and I had told him I knew I could do good work if I had money to buy material to work on, I had a letter one day from Blumenthal, the Banker in Venice, saying I was to come to see him for he had fifty lire lodged there for me. I thought fifty lire would not go very far, for I have to buy gold and silver to work with, and the work will take a long time, and I and my wife must eat while it is going on and it would be better for me to keep to my work at fifteen centimes a day. However, I went to Venice and to Blumenthal's and he came to the counter and said, 'Here is the money I have to pay you', and he put down instead of the fifty paper lire I expected, fifty gold pieces one after another, and pushed them over to me. I looked at them and he said, 'Why don't you take them up?' and I said, 'Am I mad or are you mad?' for I had never known that the fifty lire would be lire sterling. I took them at last and put them into my pocket and went to the station with my head going round and round. And when I got into the train the idea of that bacile came to me—divide it into twelve, the twelve signs of the Zodiac, then so on—and so on—I saw it all before me. When I got home to our room my wife was there, and I put my hands in my pockets and pulled out the gold pieces and threw them down on the floor in handfuls, and then I lay down on them. My wife thought I had gone mad, and she often thought so after that, for I could think of nothing but my work. The designs I had made at first did not satisfy me, and even at meals I had the plans beside me and looked at them between my mouthfuls. Then I set to work at the plate. Sir Hudson (Lowe) came to see me one day and he was astonished when he saw what I was doing and where I was doing it, for the plate I was working at was bigger than my work bench.' "

There are pieces of his work now in Russia, in Germany and in England. When the bacile was seen, he had orders from Sir William Drake, Lord Wimborne, the Duke of Westminster and others. He had finished a piece for, I think, the Duke of Westminster, and he determined he would himself carry it to England; he would see the place whence his patron had come. He arrived in London, asked for the Duke's house, came to the door in his rough clothes, the masterpiece wrapped in Vicenza rags, and was refused admission by the stately servant at the door. He could laugh in telling this, but it had been no laughing matter at the time.

A yet more majestic door had been opened to him. He had been sent for to Windsor to show his work to the Queen. "Here, see this on my chain"—he triumphantly held up a hairpin bent into some fantastic shape, "it fell upon the carpet from the Queen's hair. I saw it, I hoped to pick it up —I did not dare. Then I was afraid some other one might notice it. I put my foot on it. I kept it there. Then the Queen went out. I stooped. I got it in my hand and had it! I have worn it ever since, the hairpin of the Queen of England!"

One evening he came from Vicenza to stay the night at Ca Capello and "he brought with him a bacile and tazza of very bold and beautiful design, made from a lump of white metal he had brought away from England after that visit. He had brought this to sell, he hadn't wanted to sell it but there was a debt he wanted to pay. I looked and coveted but did not think it would be possible for me to attain to. Then when I heard him say he only asked what would be in English money £40 my desire turned to hope. I had thought of having a velvet dress that winter, I had never had one before. But that thought vanished and I ventured to say, 'I will buy it'. It was not till long after that I heard that an English collector who was also looking at it, while professing indifference, had determined to have it, and that he was so much disconcerted as to cause amusement to the others present. So I carried off my trophy and have never been sorry for that purchase.

"Sir Henry Layard met us with his gondola and welcomed us to Ca Capello" was the first of many a like entry. And these visits stand out in memory with their days of delight, the sight of the passing boats, the rafts from the mountain forests, the sound of the water plashing against the wall at night, the cry of "Stali" as a gondolier turned the sharp corner from the narrow to the great canal.

Although the Embassy at Rome had been denied to him he seemed to be Ambassador in Venice, so great was his position and so deep was the reverence paid to that silver-maned head, for he was treated with ceremonious honour by those who recognised the value of his service to archaeology and art. He was free to exercise in his spacious palace the wide and liberal hospitality it may be he had learned in those early journeyings in Persia and Susiana and Babylonia, the gates of the East. His guests at Ca Capello were very many, but what avails a list of names? There was no one of distinction among his countrymen there whose gondola was not often at his door.

In 1888 Sir Henry writes, "Ruskin is here, and in very gentle humour, but in very low spirits. He speaks in his usual exaggerated way of the National Gallery and declares that it is beyond comparison the finest and most important collection in Europe. He came to see my pictures two days ago and expressed himself as much delighted with them. The Cima he pronounced the finest he had ever seen, and the Carpaccio, Luini, and Gentile Bellini 'entirely lovely'. He is very much aged and bent and has been half devoured by mosquitoes—the condition of his face giving you the impression that he is suffering from an attack of measles. He is a strange creature! Instead as I expected of denouncing Venice and all its works, he says that the penny steamers are in no way objectionable, that the restorations of St. Mark's have been carefully and lovingly done, that the new capitals of the columns supporting the Ducal Palace are so admirably executed that you would not tell them from the old, etc. On the other hand he declares that no one will ever see the Lake of Geneva again on account of the smoky haze generated by the steamers, which obscures the sky and turns the water from blue to brown, and that the only country worth living in is France, that the French are the best people in the world, and that he will settle at Beauvais to study French Gothic architecture which surpasses all others. Dolly Tennant is here with him, and conducts him about, and he is accompanied by two young men whom he calls pupils, to be instructed in the Ruskinian mysteries. We have also Browning, the poet, here in great force and very proud of his son having bought the Palazzo Rezzonico—the vastest on the Grand Canal, a proceeding which I consider the height of folly. I suspect young B. will find that he has more than a white elephant on his hands."

I had written at Venice that "the Brownings and Bronsons came to dinner, and after dinner all the English in Venice—

Max Mullers, Hammonds, Maxwells, etc., etc.—I talked to
Ainslie Bean and young Browning—who does not look like
the child of two poets; and Vigar and Max Muller who has
still a hankering for India, though he says there are no *old*
monuments there, the earliest date from about 300 before
Christ. Miss Hammond played the Zither (I so nearly wrote
the Jews harp!) rather feebly, and when she struck up
Home Sweet Home, Max Muller said so plaintively 'I think
I have heard that tune before', I could not help laughing
out. Muller said it was quite true the Japanese were in
search of a religion. An envoy from Japan was announced
one day and said, "I have only half-an-hour to spare; I have
come to say that we want a religion in Japan. I, you understand, am an enlightened man. I don't want a religion, but
for the people we must have one, and you Mr. Muller, you
have studied all religions and can tell us which is best—
(I have only half-an-hour to stay). We don't want Christianity,
that is tumultuous, but any other we are willing to try.' Max
Muller answered, 'You have a very good religion already,
Buddhism, try and live up to that . . .' There was some talk
about devil worshippers and Mrs. M. M. said, 'Then they
are not dying out?' and Sir Henry, who was getting rather
bored, said 'Oh, dear me, yes I'm afraid they are', in such
a lachrymose tone I could not but laugh again!"

Another evening, "The Max Mullers dined . . . He talked
of the old Emperor William and how, when he sees old
Stockman, who is eighty-three, he says, 'You march first and
I will follow'. Stockman replied one day, 'Your Majesty, I
hope we shall bring our shares to par', to which the
Emperor replied, 'Ah, you are no courtier or you would say,
at least, your Majesty, to a hunded and twenty'. Mrs. Muller
says the Princess does not get on either with the Emperor
or Empress, and that it was hard for her to get over
Bismarck's rudeness when he said in allusion to some of her
liberal ideas, 'You, Madam, have spoiled the blood of the
Hohenzollerns'. He has now alienated her son from her.
M.M. wrote his name in English and Sanscrit on my fan."

On Monday evening Hilda Montalba said, "I hope, I do
hope, Dreyfus is innocent", and I say, "In hoping that, you
hope that a great many are guilty", and someone says to
Admiral Hahn, "Do you believe he is innocent?" and
Hahn shouts across his imaginary quarter-deck, "I believe
de worst all round!" "Then Hilda Montalba said she was
dining at Kensington Palace with the Princess, and after

dinner they were going up to the Princess's room and she
was left for a moment, and a clear young voice said from
below, "Who is there?" She was surprised at anyone calling
this out in that place, and the Princess came running out
looking scared and said, "Did you hear anything?" and
when she told her, the Princess said, "Yes, others have heard
it too, it is George IV". "Ach!" says Hahn, "we hear stories
of ghosts and they are got up by people that want to keep
the place for shmuggling". (Kensington Palace!)

And at that table where the artist-artisan Cortelazzo was
honoured, there were sometimes royal guests, the Royalties
of Germany above all. The Crown Prince Frederick and the
Princess Royal of England, as she was wont to write her
name, had a love for Venice, escaping there from parched
Berlin, and once at least inhabiting a house opposite to
Ca Capello, lent to them by Mr. Malcolm, a devoted friend
of the Layards. They did not escape, even on those journeys,
the penalties of being in the succession of the Prussian
Kings. I wrote to H.P.H., "They travel with twenty-six
servants, 127 pieces of luggage and six dogs, two of those
being descendants of the Greyhounds of Frederick the Great,
without which it is not etiquette for a Crown Prince to
travel. And with all these attendants, the luggage was left
on the platform the other day, and the train had to be kept
back five minutes to have it put up, and the Princess had
to ask that the Layard's John might dust her umbrella which
her own servant had neglected to do. All the servants are
paid by the State, and they are often very careless and
unmanageable, as they can't be dismissed without a complaint being lodged at the Home Office, and long formalities
gone through. They sigh for the freedom of the Prince of
Wales, who visits Berlin with his son and an A.D.C. and
only one servant between them, and the Princess means to
begin many reforms when she is in power. She is not allowed
much at present and was much abused for her 'English
innovations' when she built a passage to her house at Potsdam
to prevent the maids walking through the drawing-rooms
with the slop pails, as Mr. Healy threatens to do in the
House of Commons."

I wrote elsewhere, "As to the Crown Princess, they say
she is very liberal in her views, 'too liberal for my position'.
She hates Bismarck—'He keeps me under surveillance,
knows who comes to see me at Potsdam, and if he objects
to my visitors I am remonstrated with. As to Herbert, he is

odious, ambitious, ignorant, presumptuous.' When she was
going to Corona there was some alarm of cholera there. Sir
Henry suggested her putting off her departure for a day.
'No,' she said in a sudden fury, 'I won't give Bismarck the
chance of sending me an impertinent telegram ordering me
home.' Everyone likes the Crown Prince, he is fond of
children, and when boys follow him in the street, will sometimes seize a cap from one of them and run after him. The
people, boys especially, about Potsdam are devoted to him.
He told the Layards amusing stories, one of having said to
a sentry, 'Have you seen the Kaiser pass?' The sentry
answered, 'Ja', so shortly and oddly that the Prince said,
'Is he drunk?' 'He did not appear to me to be so,' said the
sentry reflectively. Mlle. de Perpignan, a very handsome,
bright woman, has charge of the children and contradicts
their mother flatly at times. The Princess said to the girls
one day reprovingly, 'That is not like a lady, much less like
a princess', but Mlle. de P. took her up and said, 'Don't
say, and don't think, that a princess is brought up to be
ladylike, a lady is taught to think little of herself, to take
the lowest place, be unselfish and put herself in the background, but a princess is told "go, my dear, put yourself in
the best place, before everybody."

In Sir Henry's later years his friendship and his wife's
with the Emperor and Empress Frederick grew and increased,
and there was as close a friendship as is possible where there
is the never to be forgotten difference of royal rank. For the
Emperor was frank and lovable and the Empress was like
Sir Henry himself, a lover and student of many forms of
art, too energetic a lover as sometimes happened, when he
had to beg to be left at the foot of a hill or height climbed
by her and the laughing romping Princesses for the sake
of some ancient rook-perched church or castle. And there
was sadness in Ca Capello when the shadows on that Imperial
group began to fall.

I wrote from there in 1887 to H.P.H., "I received your
letter today and must try to write a very legible short letter
that it may not take too much of your time from Mommsen
next Sunday . . . Venice is beautiful but very cold, however,
we are well lodged in this beautiful palace and the Layards
as usual are the kindest of hosts. They have been staying at
a villa with the Crown Prince and Princess. She told them
what a dreadful time she had gone through with the German
doctors. When the Prince's throat was so bad they told her

suddenly that he must submit to an operation which very few have ever lived through as the last chance of saving his life. She insisted on first telegraphing for Dr. Morell Mackenzie, but the first telegram was sent in a cipher, the key of which had been lost in England, and it could not be read. Then she sent another, and then by mistake Dr. Mackenzie took a wrong train, slow instead of express, which increased the delay. Meanwhile, the doctors at Berlin had ordered an operating table from the hospital, and declared that if they delayed the operation after five o'clock when daylight began to wane, the Prince would not survive the night. At a few minutes before five Dr. M. arrived. Then the doctors wanted to insist on going on with the operation, merely allowing him to help. But he said, 'No, unless he were allowed to examine the patient thoroughly, he would take the next train back to England. After the examination, he said the disease was not a cancerous growth as they had said, but consumption of the throat, and he completely changed the treatment. Of course, there was no operation. The Prince is now much better, and Dr. Mackenzie says if he can avoid speaking and catching cold he will quite get over the disease, but that a cold would probably take him off. He feels so well that it is difficult to prevent his talking to his children and his friends, but he is allowed to see as few as possible."

In October 1888, after the death of the Emperor, Sir Henry writes, "Mlle de Bunsen gives a very sad account of the Empress Frederick's unpopularity during her short reign. She cannot help hoping that it is exaggerated. She makes out that the Empress never did anything right and offended everybody and that the only relief of everybody was that it would not last long. The Germans evidently hate her and are determined to find fault with everything and also hate England."

Then from Venice in October 1889: "The Empress Frederick and her daughters arrived here on Sunday last. We met them at the station and passed the evening with them. They spent Monday with us, lunching in Ca Capello (a party of eighteen) and we dined with them aboard the Lloyd's steamer which had been beautifully fitted up for them to take them to Greece. She was much depressed, with tears continually in her eyes, but most kind and indeed affectionate to us. She wrote her name in Enid's book, adding the well known lines of Dante: —

Nessun maggior dolore,
Che ricordare del tempo felice
Nella miseria.

I am afraid that her son, the Emperor, is not over kind or considerate to her. His taking the Empress to Athens to be present at the marriage, and thus placing his mother in the second place, is neither the one nor the other. Princess Sophie, the bride, is very charming, simple and unaffected. She has learned Greek and wrote her name and titles in Enid's book in an excellent Greek hand. All the Princesses are devoted to Enid, whom they call their aunt."

And in the next year, "Poor lady! She feels bitterly the treatment she experiences in Germany and more than all the manner in which her son treats the memory of his father, whom he never mentions and to whom he never refers. There is no reconciliation between them."

Then in October, "The Empress left, having spent rather more than a month here. She is as happy as she is, I fear, likely to be again, and the Princesses deplored having to return to boredom and etiquette. The Empress, in Malcolm's comfortable house, was freed from spies and newspaper correspondents who surround her at Berlin. I had many long and interesting talks with her. I fear that her son does his best to vex and humiliate her, especially by the way in which he endeavours to pass over his father and to lessen the reputation that his great qualities had gained for him in Germany. The young man has entered upon a bold career. The result remains to be seen. He may turn out a great man, for he has unquestionably great qualities; but on the other hand he may lead his country to disaster. Bismarck is, I hear, much alarmed at the state of Germany, especially as to the socialism that the young Emperor is favouring and encouraging."

Sir Henry had already written on the accession of the young Emperor, "I don't like his first issuing proclamations to the army and navy. This step can hardly fail to produce the impression that his policy is to be one of war and not of peace, as his father's would have been."

In 1856 young Henry Layard had written to his aunt, Mrs. Austin, from Italy, "I obtained permission at Milan to make tracings in the Brera, but had only time to make that of St. Catherine, placed in the tomb by the angels, in an exquisite work of Luini's."

In his last illness in London, where he passed away in 1904, the print of this picture made through the Arundel Society, one of the interests of his later years, hung where his eye could rest upon it to the last.

Rancour revived with the news of his death, and when his widow asked to see what had been written of his life in the London papers, I had already hidden such as I could of them away.

When I read my chapter on Sir Henry Layard to Yeats, he said, "It is not so good as the one you have written on Burton, because that gave a more living impression of personality, I think because you showed in it the irritability and sensitiveness of the man. You are too amiable—when you write. Your portrait would be stronger if you gave some of the faults."

But I said Sir Henry's faults were so loudly proclaimed by his public enemies I could not join in that stone throwing. I would rather show his virtues, and I think I have done this in telling of those harmonious and beneficent Venetian days.

Only last week, a sculptor as it happened, coming to Coole to make a medallion of Yeats, who was in his tower at the time with "no spare room to offer save a carpenter's shop", told me that once when he was but a young man, he had been put to sit next to Sir Henry Layard at a dinner given by a friendly neighbour, and he had talked with kindness and sympathy to the young artist, and had promised to help to make Venice pleasant to him should he ever come there. (And this promise had been redeemed by Lady Layard in later years, in her widowhood.)

Yet my mind, having been turned by Yeats from the advocate's to the judge's seat, went back to those days at the Therapia Embassy when one or two of the "young gentlemen from the Chancery", successors of those who had looked with cold eyes on the young Layard's blue frock coat, would be bidden, in its sense of commanded, to dinner, and would sometimes seem to be a little gloomy, a little bored, and were not drawn from their reserve by any gracious notice or geniality of their Chief, who indeed it seemed marked their names among the day's orders without personal preference or favour. He felt, unconsciously it may be, that a possible artist but not a possible diplomatist was of his own kind. And I came to know afterwards that these lads had often resented his command when they had planned some entertainment with one or other of their own friends, and yet were shy of saying so to their Chief, who had only meant to show goodwill to them through hospitality and was all unconscious of their discontent. And even his wife, beloved above all by girls, by a host of real and adopted nieces and godchildren, was never at her best, felt a little awkwardness, with young men, with boys.

So, one indeed of these attachés who had his dignity hurt, felt, I think, lifelong resentment, telling in his later years of how on his first arrival at that Embassy (and I am certain in befitting attire), he found the whole party having tea in the garden. And china having run short, and servants being it is likely out of reach, the Ambassadress had put an already used tea cup in his hand, saying in her deep voice, and certainly with the friendly intention of putting him at his ease, the never-to-be-forgotten words, new to his experience among diplomatists, "wash it at the pump".

A Note on the Intention of Testators.

In writing of Sir Henry Layard, a thought has often come to mind of that short, vivid life of Hugh[1] of which I have lately tried to give a picture, for with much unlikeness they were alike in their vision, their hope, of ennobling each his own city with the beauty of fine architecture finely placed; and that hope was thwarted in a not-unlike manner by that barrier of ignorance against which "the gods themselves strive in vain".

And I see a strange and yet closer affinity in that malice of fate which went near to upsetting the dearest intention of each of them, when dumbness had fallen on the lips whose one word would so easily have made all straight.

Hugh Lane, writing alone his codicil forgiving Dublin with a gift of the pictures he had in hasty anger taken away, made a mistake of omission, neglecting to call a witness to the name he had thrice signed; and his omission, as all who best know him declared, was not by intention or design. Sir Henry Layard, having his will drawn up by London lawyers, made a mistake of omission in another way. He left

[1] *Hugh Lane's Life and Achievement* (London, John Murray, 1921). *Sir Hugh Lane: His Life and Legacy* (Colin Smythe, 1973) contains this and other writings about him.

to the National Gallery of England his "collection of pictures"; in another clause of the will he left to a kinsman his "portraits". The National Gallery, justly appealing to manifest intention against the dictum of lawyers, held that in this clause he had meant the portraits of his family, that were not of sufficient value to hang on the walls of Ca Capello but had hung in his hired London house, and were no part of the fine collection of his lifetime that he had dedicated, not to the enrichment of any relative or friend but to the nation, to the Gallery in which he took such pride. I was myself asked to give testimony as to this intention and what I gave was thought to be of weight, for away in America a request reached me to make a declaration of what I had written before the Commissioner of Oaths. In the end, but after much sore feeling, the Treasury redeemed the pictures by paying a sum of money to the legal heir. In Hugh Lane's case we still look to see our bitterness healed, if not in that yet then in some other way. So have accident and friendship brought me to be by turn the helper and the enemy of that Gallery in Trafalgar Square.

X

ATHENAEUM FRIENDS IV: HENRY JAMES

20 NOVEMBER 1920. I am reading Henry James's *Letters*. They were sent to me by John Quinn, and I have written him in my second letter of gratitude, "I am just at the end of the first volume and feel there is a sadness creeping into the life. I think it comes from his having cut himself adrift from his own countrymen, from being as it were, 'in its pedigree'. He talks of the 'much cry and little wool' of London life, and the friendships that have faded away." That is akin to my own thought as I look back on that friendly and delightful society where I was made welcome and where I found enjoyment. Perhaps because England was not really my country, any more than his, I never felt that it was a part of my real life, as the Abbey Theatre has been or the parishes of Killinane and Kiltartan.

Kindliness, gentleness, are what come with the thought of Henry James to my mind. It was with a sudden rush of excitement I first saw him, just after my marriage, in Madame Waddington's salon at Rome. I think he was the first writer I had ever met, save one or two of whom I had glimpses, Emily Lawless and Aubrey de Vere, in my girlhood years; and the achievement of a writer was the one for which I had most reverence, perhaps because of some unconscious aspiration. And of all writers, Henry James was the one who had come nearest to the shaping of my life at that time. For it had happened that Sir William, then but a friend, having two or three months earlier said goodbye to me at my home in Ireland, he setting out for Italy, had sent me when he came to London a book that he admired, *Roderick Hudson*; and he had written with it, and in some way that thread of correspondence had kept him from going any further. And so, coming back to make me his wife, that journey that was to have been a lonely one, became the first of many in each other's company. So, when on that unlooked-for meeting with the author of the momentous book, Sir William said some charming words to him about it, my shyness kept me dumb. But now, feeling closer to that writer as I read his letters, I know that the story would have been delightful to him, and I wonder that I never told it in the friendliness of later years.

I often met him in London, but never got very near him, except in the one matter of our affectionate interest in a boy whose sister had been our friend. He liked to come and ask me about the lad's hopes and troubles, at school and at Oxford, (Grant Duff was amused when someone told him that being remonstrated with for spending a Sunday in going to Rugby to undo some early schoolboy tangle I had answered with a reference to those Pharisees who would not draw another's ox or ass from a pit on the Sabbath day). But when our schoolboy had become an attractive and eligible Private Secretary, with even a week-end cottage of his own, the undoing of more dangerous tangles took more than a day, and four hands were needed in place of two to draw our nurseling from the slippery edge towards which he was tending, half-willing, all relieved when the danger had passed by. He said that in such a time of crisis Henry James was a more comfortable guide than I, and this I can well believe, for guarding against the natural jealousy of a woman when another threatened to come into the life of even an adopted child, I weighed and balanced and tried to be just, looking on every side. "And what did Henry James say?" "He just said it was impossible, that I must put it out of my head." The best of advice, yet we can hardly imagine one of those beings who people his pages speaking on any matter, light or serious, in such brief and decisive words. But at another time he wrote, "I saw Henry James after you left. He said many things beautiful, so beautiful that I was too much taken up in admiring the way he said them to be fully conscious of what they were."

He was very gentle. He was the only one of my Sunday visitors, I used to say, who coming in would greet my little fair-haired child with a kiss. He was altogether a comfortable person to talk to; one had a conviction that he found interest in even the slightest shade of character of experience revealed or expressed. There would be a sudden flash of intensity in his look. I recall it when once, he having asked me what impression some young lady (probably setting her cap at our boy) had made on me, I began my answer with, "If I had seen her in an Aerated Bread Shop . . ." That word may have called up some latent picture, some possible *mise en scène*. Once sitting in the armchair in the drawing room (he always liked a comfortable chair and later gave one to "our boy" as a wedding present), he was very much struck with an elephant's foot I used as a waste paper basket. He admired its noble proportions, capacity, and the daring of the idea. Sir William as it happened, was in Ceylon just then on a visit and I wrote begging him to bring me one as an appropriate gift for so copious a corrector of manuscripts. It was a liberal thought that blessed at least the giver, for chiefs or hunters in Ceylon sent me, with prompt generosity, a present of not one but three similar trophies, each even finer than my first possession. I should have somewhere among my papers his letter of thanks, but I can only remember his calling it, amongst other descriptives phrases, "a picturesque luxury".

The other night I read his polished letters from America, revisited, and was interested and rather surprised to find him write of having given lectures "with enjoyment". And there came to mind a Western city, where once in my lecturing days I found myself placed at a table in an immense hall, amongst my audience-to-be. We all dined together (and I never could touch anything before speaking, save soup and a morsel of bread). The loud murmur of voices, and the knowledge of what was before me—and always that last half-hour was a terrified misery—and what seemed some echo in the room that made hearing difficult, troubled me; and then my nearest neighbour asked me if I had ever been told I resembled Queen Victoria . . . And while I was yet recovering from that bewildering comparison, someone turned my thoughts from it, saying that Henry James had lectured there not long before, in that room, to that same club or audience. He had not been very easy to hear, they said (and that I thought must be my fate also). Yet I feel sure that even on what he has spoken of as "that all-too gregariously assaulted lecture platform", his mere presence, his benignity, the harmony of his whole being with his writings, had well made up for any shortcoming to the ear. And in the handshaking it is personality that matters, the rush of life from the hand of one, another's healing touch.

As absorption in my work in Ireland drew me more and more from London I lost, or almost lost, sight of him for a while, yet I once found him in the stalls of the Court Theatre when we took our plays there, and he spoke some generous words. Later again, he came to my son's first exhibition, very gracious and kind to us all. And I have told in Hugh Lane's memoir of that staircase meeting in Lindsey

House—I can see it still, Hugh so alert, as little used to
ruminate in words as in action, giving me comical glances
over the shoulder as we listened to that crooning flight of
words, homing amongst all its intricacies with so certain
an aim. He had been already interested in Hugh, because
many people had thought a character in *The Outcry* was
founded upon him, whom he had never until that later day
even met. He liked him, I think, coming again to the house,
and writing to Yeats who was staying here at Coole in the
August after the *Lusitania* tragedy (and this was among his
last letters and written at a time of illness) he said, "I infer
from your address that you may be able very kindly to
recall me to the indulgent recollection of Lady Gregory. If
you can tell her from me with what a special tenderness of
fidelity and sympathy I thought of her a while back—and
still think of her—you will greatly serve yours and hers most
truly." Yeats had met him from time to time in these last
years, at the Academic Committee, and had given me news,
as of Maurice Hewlett, saying, "This is not very amusing",
and Henry James answering, one knows with what gravity
and what a humorous glance, "Hewlett, we don't come here
to be amused".

He wrote to Yeats in that same letter in which my message
came, thanking him for having sent at his asking some copy
of poems to Mrs. Wharton, "who I know will value your
extill (or whatever the proper name of your cluster of
rhymes may be) in a high and grateful degree. The great
thing is that you send it to her absent—and happy you
poets that can be present, and so present by a simple flicker
of your genius, and not, like the clumsier race, have to lay a
train and pile up faggots that may not after all prove in the
least combustible."

I once reproached him with having left one of his heroines
whose fortunes I had been following, with those fortunes
uncompleted, upon a doorstep. He said, "That is life, that
is just how we find that we have parted with so many we
have known—on a doorstep". And in one of his letters (to
C. E. Norton) there is an echo of the same thought. He is
"reacting against" many, many long years of London, where
he says, "Acquaintances and relations have a way of seeming
at last to end in smoke—while having consumed a great
deal of fuel and taken a great deal of time".

I have just now, moved by wakening memories, gone to
my cupboards and rummaged amongst some fragmentary

diaries, and have found, without too much loss of the sunlight of this short November day, a note I had written in
those London years. "In the evening Mr. James called. I had
finished and liked very much *The Princess Casamassima,*
and he himself likes it and thinks it one of his best. Paul
Muniment, he says, was getting tired of the whole thing and
meant to chuck it up and go into politics, having exploited
the Princess. We talked much of it, and another sad story."
And again: "There was tea and music at Miss Cohen's,
where in the intervals of music, finding Henry James beside
me, and being in the middle of *The Portrait of a Lady,* I
asked why he had let Isabel marry that despicable husband,
Osband. He said she was bound to do something foolish;
and I said, 'Yes, with all that money'. 'But without it,' he
said, 'where would have been the story? Besides, it is
delightful to a poor man being able to bestow large fortunes
on his heroines.' Mr. Samuels came and talked to us then,
and I happening to mention that bi-metallism is a favourite
subject of conversation in India, Henry James said he hoped
it would never be a popular subject here, as he knew nothing
about it. 'Oh, I'll have great pleasure in teaching you,' said
Mr. Samuel. 'Thanks,' said Mr. James, 'but you would find
me too stupid'. 'Oh, not at all, I have an excellent method.
I feel sure I could teach anyone.' And he buttonholed H.J.
who I am convinced will never more escape from him."

ㅅ

XI

ATHENAEUM FRIENDS V: SIR ALFRED LYALL

I HAD WRITTEN more pages than these upon Sir Alfred Lyall, a friend I cared for, and had given more quotations; but now I have read the whole chapter to Yeats, and he is impatient with some passages from letters, and in this he may be right; for as I read them aloud I felt that news of politics and movements that had been so welcome to me coming from London to the remoteness of Coole, had lost interest with the passing of time. And as to his poetry, he being of a newer generation will have none of it, calls it rhetoric, the rhetoric of a statesman, who has never known the toil of a craftsman, who has given his life to the trade.

Yet it was in part these poems that, as it were, set their writer above many rulers in India in his time and after his time. The little thin privately printed volume, *Verses written in India,* was the great literary treasure in any Anglo-Indian house that had the good fortune to possess it. Perhaps in it Lyall revealed to its readers something of the meaning of the dragging force that made them long to turn their back on the immense splendour of India towards even a dull existence at home. (It was in the Himalayas, while looking at the white summit of Mount Everest, that I could hear a high official murmuring questions as to the probable cost and comfort of a house in Cromwell Road.) Had not Pilate's wife in her exile in Judaea spoken of such an uneasy longing in one of these poems: —

> Ah let me go hence, let me go from this shadowy
> mystical East
> The phantoms that prophesy woe, from the wild-eyed
> menacing priest;
> From Gods that are strong and that dwell not on Earth
> nor are fashioned by hand;
> From the maze of enchantment and spell that is spread
> o'er the desolate land.

And as to the native Indian mind, even the succession of missionaries had not been able to reveal the questioning of the Hindu thinker, the spirit of melancholy that had come with the seeming abandonment by the old gods, as it was revealed by Lyall. And it seemed a strange achievement that one who had fought and commanded and punished in the Mutiny should thus gain the confidence of the conquered. He told me that the poem I had oftenest heard quoted, the "Meditations of a Hindu prince", had been put down by him almost word for word from the conversation of, I forget what Rajah, though it is likely such thoughts were helped to expression by intercourse with his own doubting philosophic mind; which had created that subtle and delicate analysis of Eastern religions in his Asiatic Studies: —

> All the world over, I wonder, in lands that I never have trod,
> Are the people eternally seeking for the signs and steps of a God?
> Westward across the ocean and Northward ayont the snow,
> Do they all stand gazing, as ever, and what do the wisest know?
>
> Here in this mystical India, the deities hover and swarm
> Like the wild bees heard in the tree-tops, or the gusts of a gathering storm;
> In the air men hear their voices, their feet on the rocks are seen,
> Yet we all say, "Whence is the message, and what may the wonders mean?"
>
> The path, ah! who has shown it, and which is the faithful guide?
> The haven, ah! who has known it? for steep is the mountain side,
> For ever the shot strikes surely, and ever the wasted breath
> Of the praying multitude rises, whose answer is only death.
>
> Shall I list to the word of the English, who come from the uttermost sea?
> "The Secret, hath it been told you, and what is its message to me?"
> It is naught but the wide-world story how the earth and the heavens began,
> How the gods are glad and angry, and a Deity once was man.

I think religion, even of the Churches, was always drawing him through sympathy, and again repelling him through reason. Long after he had left India and had become a part of London life, he wrote (I had written to him from Aran on a Sunday when I alone of the inhabitants of the island was outside the consecrated walls), "I have often that same touch of isolation whenever I stand apart from religious rites; one would like to be absorbed into some spiritual communion, it is connected with atavism—the mysterious survival of primeval impressions—which is always drawing us backwards."

He had no leaning toward Catholicism, though I remember a drive with him on his first visit to Rome, and when he was moved at the sight of the Vatican, so silent and enduring and immense. His comment was, "I wonder what the Pope thinks of Frederic Harrison"; and I fancy that his thought had gone back to the enduring East, looking on Europe as the passing show, its own patience as what is everlasting. Yet his mind, I think, insistently turned towards what he had called in writing of Tennyson's philosophy, "the signs and shadows of things invisible, the intimations of eternal Power and Divinity". His work in India had been the tearing of a rent in the veil behind which those Shadows pass, the discovery and disclosure of the mystic mind, of "the spirituality of the East"—that East in which, as he reminds us, every one of the great religions has had its birth. Had he belonged to France, more imaginative than England in its research, it may be that some special mission might have been created, sending him to continue that work in which he was pre-eminent. But as it was appointed by custom he had to return home, taking a place on the Indian Council in London.

I had first seen him as Lieutenant Governor of the Western Provinces in that wonderful Allahabad of mosques and temples and elephants, in what seemed almost regal state (for I had not yet lived under the Viceroy's more than regal roof): an added splendour falling on our visit's end, because the Commander-in-Chief had come as a fellow guest, and we left in a great clattering of horses and clanking of presented arms.

And our friendship went on growing in London, where he, like Henry James and so many of my friends, was a member of the Athenaeum. "Henry James dined with me a day or two ago. I think he must be polishing up a novel", I see in one of his letters. Yet I doubt that they were much in sympathy, he would have been more drawn to the elder

brother's philosophy. But they were certainly often in company in that welcoming London society that had already
adopted the American, and that at once took Alfred Lyall
on his return from India, with his poetic reputation, his
air of distinction, into its most brilliant and delightful
groups. There his pale slenderness flitted through the
drawing-rooms, and those strange eyes (in which the moon-
stone light so flashed and vanished that Indian culprits
brought before him would confess all, fearing most that dim
moment in which, to their fancy, his sight had gone in quest
of witnesses outside the bounds of earth) contemplated the
London scene with something of the dispassionate gaze of a
revenant; with a brooding detachment, not as of one sitting
in judgment but as one watching the balancing of invisible
scales. The "Souls" opened their doors to him; Mrs. Asquith,
writing of him as "having more bouquet than body" puts
him among the most delightful talkers she has known. He
writes of these "Souls" in 1892: "They have been in great
force during the last fortnight in town; flitting about to
each other's houses and showing that social gaiety and
delight in each other's company which certainly wins my
admiration; they know how to enjoy life. The ladies are very
angry because John Morley, in an austere mood, is reported
to have called them a frivolous set—they are much better
than that." He took full enjoyment in all this for a time,
for as he writes, "Talk is so much better than reading—
books are dreary inventions for the most part; good for study,
very bad for pastime or conversation". I think outside his
wide knowledge, the charm of his conversation lay in a
philosophy applied to what seemed trivial things. I remember
his being disturbed one afternoon at a house we had driven
over to, because we had come up on the daughter of the house
wandering away from garden to woods innocently enough,
with some young Cavalry officer. "One must not make little
of convention," he said. "It is the outcome of the experience
of centuries." There is no one more delightful in conversation than Mr. Birrell, yet the other day I listened to some
old friends round a tea-table in London as they quoted from
Sir Mountstuart Grant Duff's diaries a grumble that at the
Grillion Club, where he found himself next to Birrell, he
"was not able to listen to Sir Alfred Lyall who was opposite".
It amused him to stay in great country houses in England
or Scotland; at the Paris Embassy where he meets Clemenceau; in Dublin with the Commander-in-Chief; in Rome

with Lord Dufferin, the new Ambassador, his late Viceroy (almost *rais en exile* they may have felt themselves, guest and host. For I remember Augustus Hare apologising through me for not having shown more courtesy to Sir Alfred in a chance meeting among ruins; was "tired and didn't know who he was"; and Lord Dufferin saying that although he had been delighted on his first day of arrival with the freedom from state, and being "allowed to carry his own bag" he had felt a little disconcerted when Crispi, the Prime Minister, did not stand up when he went to pay his official visit, but received him sitting.) The dignified work of the India Council left him leisure for society, he was glad to find himself welcome among politicians and writers, though I don't think I ever saw him so much pleased, even elated, as when he told me that having gone down to Eton—he was himself an old Etonian—to put down rather belatedly his boy's name, the Head Master had walked back to the station with him. I said, "Very pleasant for the Head Master", but he was rather indignant, "You don't know what that means from a Head Master of Eton". "In London I dined with John Morley, Lords Spencer and Acton;" or "with Frederic Harrison and Jusserand". "I sat next but one last week to the G.O.M. who was in his usual force over literature and politics, though I hear he has grown irritable over Irish affairs." "I dined with Asquith last week and Mr. Bryce, who is troubled about the symptoms that the English people don't intend to abandon Uganda. I told him long ago that it would be so, but he and Morley never seem properly to realise the working of such matters in the English mind, which is always in favour of backing up missionaries and investments, whenever fresh markets are in the wind." But home politics did not concern him as did those of the vast Empire he had helped to rule. He wrote from the Isle of Man where he was on a visit to the Governor, Mr. Walpole, "Here one can study Home Rule in miniature. I am also interested as an ex-Anglo administrator who has had to do with large populations" (he had ruled over some forty million souls) "in observing the machinery required for ruling fifty thousand islanders." I think he looked even on English problems with something of the same observant detachment. History had ever been a favourite study and now he saw it in the making. He was but turning over another leaf.

He wrote in January 1899: "Barry O'Brien's *Life of*

Parnell is to my mind most interesting, it describes dramatically that very remarkable episode in the history of Ireland's
relations with England which terminated with the well
known romantic ending of a hero's ruin through a woman.
The Liberal Party has virtually been rushing into collapse
ever since that decisive incident. Gladstone is discredited,
and the subscriptions to his memorial are scanty—his place
is still vacant; Imperialism is triumphant; only John Morley
stands apart and denounces Omdurman. 'He kneels not
neither adores, but standing looks to the end', as Swinburne
says of the philosophic pagan . . . I myself am revising a new
edition of my *Asiatic Studies,* but the public mind in these
active times is not likely to concern itself about the religious
phantasies of the East."

Even during the Boer War he was not swept into passion.
"I myself have always been reluctant to see the two little
States utterly extinguished; but the Anglo-Saxon is in one
of his truculent moods and responds to the warwhoop of
Chamberlain. Undoubtedly, Great Britain is going wild with
Imperialism; we have so much surplus money and so many
men ready to go anywhere, that vast expenditure of both
men and money does not in the least deter us, but rather
excites the national imagination. In fact, any statesman
who will run us into a scrape is popular, because we have
all the tumultuous pleasure of fighting our way out of it,
and of course the newspapers are delighted with the harvest."

As to Ireland, he inclined towards sympathy with us for
a while. In 1900 he writes of an article I had written on our
national ballad poetry[1]. "It has always been to me a blot
against our name for intelligence and capacity that the first
land we English conquered beyond sea should still be the
least loyal to us, still eager to throw off our dominion and
ready to take arms if possible against us. The Irish and the
Poles are the two examples in Europe of complete failure
to reconcile subject races; everywhere else it has been more
or less done. And I agree that the verses which you quote
have an element of heroic poetry; though they have not the
power which affects the world at large, undoubtedly they
represent and serve to keep up an intense popular resentment, and it is no use for us to argue that much of it is

[1] Lady Gregory's article "Felons of our Land", in the May 1900 issue
of *The Cornhill Magazine.*

unreasonable . . . So far as I can see, we may now be in for
another century's estrangement between Irish and English
. . . Nor do I see what remedies we have to try, since Home
Rule has less chance than ever in the present temper of the
English who are becoming accustomed to the use of force,
and their determination to be dominant wherever they
dwell. This Boer war must, now having fallen into fierce
methods, leave traces that will last long, and we seem likely
to be driven to Cromwellian expedients for quieting an
obstinate resistance. The close reality of these things puts
me out of humour with my literary dissertations upon the
heroic poetry of ancient days, where distance lends enchantment to the stories of slaughtered men and burning towns.
There is, as you hint, nothing so truly heroic as a lost battle,
and no theme higher than the lofty spirit of defeated men."

Yet as my national feeling deepened, he did not give me
entire sympathy; although he told me it was his nephew,
Bernard Holland, who had written the Financial Report
declaring that Ireland had been over-taxed since the Union
"and Childers never saw it, and when Bernard was in
Devonshire House last week, the Duke said, 'Well, you've
put all the fat in the fire'."

But I wrote of an evening at Lady Lindsey's when we
wandered into politics and he was very angry at my saying
there is more love of country in Irish than in English men—
his eyes flashed and he indignantly denied it. Also he warned
me that we Irish must not speak ill of the Saxon for ever—
"We are getting a little cross about it—we will never let
you go. You are tied to us like a wife to her husband and
you must make the best of it." "Yes," I said, "but we want
our arrears of pin money." "Oh, you shall have that, indeed
you shall, and all you like, only try to be content and to
like us."

He had been pleased in India when I had written that
Robert Browning had spoken to me of having read and
admired his poems: "My generation, has so to speak, been
brought up on Browning". And he was pleased when these
poems were reprinted in England. "I believe they are selling
fairly well," he wrote; "Sir F. Pollock sent me a letter from
Swinburne containing some generous praise. So you will
behold me, if you receive me in London, wearing the
withered bay leaf that I carried away from Coole Park,
although I have now finally given up rhyming, having swept

Above: Sir Henry Layard in Ca
Capello; a portrait by L. Passini.
Courtesy the National Portrait
Gallery, London.
Left: Lady Layard. An inscribed
photograph she gave to Lady
Gregory.

Henry James, a portrait by John Singer Sargent. Courtesy the National Portrait Gallery, London.

out and closed that corner of my mind by the publication of that little book. I suppose middle-aged men find the sacred fire rather difficult to blow up, and yet what is the good of writing mild meditative poetry with retrospective glimpses of the storms one has passed through?"

In spite of a great admiration for Swinburne—I have a copy of the *Poems and Ballads* sent me by him—he said he liked Matthew Arnold's *Tristram* better than his. "It touches the heart more, though Swinburne is a better workman." "The Americans," he said, "will never produce a great poem because they are so passionless". At his own house one day, he said of Kipling, "He has gone down very low with 'Pay Pay Pay', and will lose his poetic reputation, though 'Recessional' saves it still." Sir S. Walpole, who was there, said "Pay Pay Pay" is all right, as it serves its purpose. I say a collecting box with a slit in it will do that, but it isn't poetry. Sir Alfred wonders why no great poetic voice has come from Ireland, which has had miseries enough to inspire it. I told him of the break in its literature caused by the change in the language.

And again at lunch with the Lyalls; we talked of Matthew Arnold's letters, which I had just been reading . . . Theodore Watts told Sir Alfred that Swinburne is much hurt at Matthew Arnold saying he takes a hundred words to say what could be said in one; and it was an ungracious thing to say in allusion to Swinburne having sent him a present of *Tristram of Lyonesse* . . . I had dreamed that Sir A. had said, "Matthew Arnold will be remembered when Nineveh is forgotten"—and the saying pleased him, as did another dream in which, as I told him I had heard it said, "Do not despise imagination; it is the corner stone of sympathy" . . . He wonders if Daniel really knew what Nebuchadnezzar's dream was, or whether he thought of it and conveyed it to him, hypnotised him.

Another day he talked of Tennyson. Once, when he was walking with him, Tennyson repeated one of his own poems, and Sir Alfred said, "I suppose you wrote that some time ago?" "I suppose you think I couldn't do it now," he growled. Watts told Sir Alfred that Tennyson had been one day to see him in a state of great depression, said he wished he had never written a line, he was only fit to be a civil engineer. at things as your own heroes would have done, King Arthur Watts said: "You should not give in but try to look bravely

or Galahad, or Ulysses", but for answer Tennyson pointed
to his knuckles and said in his sepulchral voice, "Gout in
the hand".

Sir Alfred's writings on oriental thought and history
during those London years were a part of his own thought
and harvest. But when in January 1903 he wrote that he
was leaving the India Office in that month, "when I shall
take up Lord Dufferin's life", I cried out against this new
bondage. I think he had consented to it less from inclination
than as a shield against what he imagined as indolence.
But he did not realise what actual waste of strength, of
creative force, there would be in working through so weighty
a mass of material as must gather round a long life spent in
great employments. When the end of it was in sight he
wrote, "What sort of work I shall have made of it I cannot
tell. If I get out of the business decently I shall be quite
satisfied."

I was reading this to Yeats today (17 August 1922) and
he said, "He must have disliked Lord Dufferin or he would
not have been so apathetic about a book that must have
dealt so much with his own life long interests—no, I was
wrong, If he had disliked him he might have written as
well as Smith, who wrote Nollekens' life because he had
left him out of his will. I daresay he neither loved nor
disliked anything." "It was impossible," I said, "for anyone
who knew Lord Dufferin well, as he did, or as my husband
did, to have anything but affection for him, if only for his
beautiful courtesy." I went and hunted out a letter written
by Sir Alfred from Clandeboye saying, "What an example
he is to those who suffer their outward behaviour to be
modified by their inward feelings": "that is a weakness I
myself try vainly to overcome," I said. And then I went to
talk of that courtesy, saying Dufferin had used it as he would
any other natural gift, knowing its value. And that he had
told me how on his arrival as Viceroy at Calcutta he had
been warned there would be some hostility among the
English there, they had been ruffled by Lord Ripon's
encouragement of native claims, though they themselves had
been made little of at the Viceregal Court and were inclined
to let him see it. "Then," he said, "I spoke to my A.D.C.s.
I said the popularity of a Viceroy does not depend on himself but his staff, you must use all possible courtesy; and not
only when you find it pleasant to do so, but especially if
any guest should come, who is unattractive or uninteresting

or plain, that is the one I expect you to be attentive to, to make the evening pleasant for, to set at ease." (I said I had noticed their being very nice to me.) And as he spoke, I had felt sure that was a lesson he had set for himself long before he had passed it on to them.

And to give another example, I went on to tell Yeats that three of the Governors we stayed with that winter were very shortsighted; Sir Mountstuart Grant Duff at Madras suffered this, for he was sociable, kindly, appreciative, a lover of conversation, and loved collecting for his "Diaries" new facts of nature or history or observation, he was a man interested in nature and in books. Yet at his receptions at Madras he would stand or move about depressed and silent, just because he did not recognise people there or realise to whom he was talking. He would be envious when I told him something of interest I had heard perhaps from some young Civil Servant from the jungle he had not noticed or recognised. And that Sir Arthur Gordon, who was in Ceylon, was even more unlucky; Lady Gordon said to me, "I don't think people would be so much offended with Arthur if they knew that at our own balls he had shaken hands three times with me." But he did give offence, because it was his habit to look indignant (though no doubt with himself) if he found out his mistake. Whereas I had known Lord Dufferin in the same case "turn his defeat to a victory", saying as he discovered his mistake, "I knew you would not mind giving me your hand again!".

"No," I went on, "if Sir Alfred did not write the life with enthusiasm it can't have been on that ground. But it is hard to keep up enthusiasm when you are writing a sort of official life, a record of official triumphs." Yeats said, "Vasari wrote the most vivid lives outside Plutarch, but he had to stop them every two or three pages to give a list of paintings or statues. Couldn't the official triumphs be put into a summary, that could be skipped as easily? Or better still one might do as Standish O'Grady did when he wrote his *History of Ireland*. He had gone to consult Freeman about some historical question, and Freeman had to consult Freeman's *History of England* before he answered. 'I thought it a dreadful thing,' said O'Grady to me, 'that a man should write a book and not have it all in his own head. So I went to Dublin and bought a bottle of ink and went into the country and wrote the *History of Ireland* without a book in the house, and as I didn't consult a single authority I had

never to mention a fact that wasn't so interesting that it
stuck in my head.' The result was his very picturesque and
spirited history." "I suppose," said I, "that explains why
two of the world's best books were written in gaol. *Don
Quixote* and *The Pilgrim's Progress*. If Cervantes had been
free he might have addled his head by consulting tales of
chivalry, and Bunyan his by listening to sermons." "Probably," said Yeats. "But," I said, "I think it is the length of
the book that does the mischief. Even one of Plutarch's noble
Grecians mightn't have carried his nobility through two
volumes. And I think what biography needs is a challenger,
a devil's advocate on the one side to call down all the blame,
and a champion—a lover—on the other; a sort of battle of
the kind that, as the country people tell us, is fought over
the roof of a dying man by invisible friends and enemies.
When Forgaill made his great praise of Columcille, the
devils took his eyesight from him in revenge, but the poem
of praise lives still—'he was eager, he was noble, it is high
his death was; we hope great honour will be given to him
on the head of these deeds'." Yeats said, "Yes, and if there
is no one else to be had, the biographer must split himself
into two parts".

So I being full of my subject and vexed at the criticism
of Lyall, went on, "It is all wrong. If a complete chronicle
is wanted of events—births, marriages, occupation—that
could be put down by a clerk without waste of a writer, and
then even a half-dozen lines added with, as you say, love or
hatred—with energy and fire. Many a life has been kept in
memory by a phrase. The foreign centurion in the New
Testament: 'He loveth our nation and hath built us a
synagogue'; Clarendon's Mr. Nathaniel Fiennes who 'had
spent his time abroad in Geneva and the Cantons of Switzerland where he improved his Disinclination to the Church,
with which Milk he had been nursed.' Bunyan better still
with his Mr. Fearing, 'Some must pipe and some must weep;
now Mr. Fearing was one that played upon the bass'. (But I
think a champion is needed for his 'young woman whose
name was Dull'.)"

Then I went on to read my last paragraph.

And whatever may be the difficulties that beset a
biographer, they are made greater when he is watched by
the affection, the suspicion of kinsfolk. Reginald Smith, the
publisher, told me that Barry O'Brien lamented this when
he was writing Lord Russell's life, and that to save him

from pious interference he brought him into hiding as his guest at Hyde Park Place, saying, "No one will think of looking for you at your publisher's". G. W. E. Russell told me of his difficulty when he was editing Matthew Arnold's letters: "Whenever I had found a sentence that was particularly good, or characteristic above the rest, some relative would cry, 'that must come out!'."

But it is not as a reader I criticise biography. In America it was the first thing I looked for on the bookshelves of any house where I stayed, and so I learned American history as I went on. I only grudge a fine player to be put to do the scoring when he might be running it up with his own bat and ball.

And as I think again over Yeats's criticism, I see it is but a natural outbreak of the revolt, the reaction of the new generation against its forerunner, as well as of the craftsman against the amateur.

And I remember an evening long ago when I asked him and Sir Alfred to dinner that I might make them acquainted with each other, and the younger poet ran wild, poured out conversation on Stephen Gwynn, their fellow guest, though he said, when they had gone, in half apology, "I talked too much, I know I ought to have asked him questions about Indian idols." And, alas, when the conversation had become general, it had fallen not upon Indian idols but upon "In Memoriam". For Sir Alfred had written eleven pages on what he considered "Tennyson's masterpiece" and Yeats, though he admired some of the other poems, hated it. And Sir Alfred, though he wrote that he would try to help the young poet to "come out of that Celtic Twilight" in which he fancied he was obscured, said a few days later of some other Irish acquaintance "like our young friend the other night, he talks too much".

But now Yeats has his revenge, for though the *Asiatic Studies*, that subtle analysis of Eastern religion, will, I believe, always hold its place, the memory of Alfred Lyall's work, his histories, his poetry, has already begun to fade. Again I am being asked, as at the time of our first acquaintance, if he was not a geologist. Yet this but shows how great must have been the personal magnetism, the charm, that made thinkers and writers and statesmen take delight in his company, and many brilliant and beautiful women proud to be known as his friends.

VIII

ATHENAEUM FRIENDS VI: ROBERT BROWNING

AT THE PRIVATE view of the Royal Academy in one of my
first years in London, I admired very much the picture of
a pig, by young Browning, hanging over a doorway. I felt
quite enthusiastic and spoke of it to people that I met in
the crowded rooms, among them Boehm, the sculptor, who
said he also had thought it extremely good, and that it ought
to have been better hung, but it had been Alma Tadema's
little joke insisting it should be put over the door of the
refreshment room.

It was soon afterwards that I met for the first time Robert
Browning, and he greeted me very warmly, because he had
been told that I had praised "Pen's Pig". It was at lunch
at Mrs. Ford's I met him, and besides this greeting I only
remember that when someone spoke of an attack Hutton
had made on Swinburne in *The Spectator,* he said "Hutton's
nose ought to be rubbed in his own articles."

After that he would dine with us sometimes, and come
to see me on a Sunday afternoon. One afternoon he brought
me a photograph of himself and one of his sister, Sariana,
who lived with him. They had been taken he said, by a lad
who had been in their service, who had come from the
country and been very clumsy in housework, so they had
advised him to try something else, and he had gone into
the studio of Hollyer the photographer. And now he had
called on his old master, had become quite an accomplished
photographer, and had asked leave to take their portraits.
It reminded me of my mother saying that everyone was
good at some one thing, and that she had asked a footman
she thought quite useless to fold up a newspaper one day
for post, and he had done it quite beautifully. But I am
afraid that did not open up so many possibilities as were to
be found in helping Hollyer's fine work.

I don't think one could have paid Browning any personal
compliment he would have valued so much as one to his
dear Pen. I wrote of going to see him one day. "He and his
sister received me with outstretched hands. His son's paintings are about the room now, and the table as usual covered

with books sent to him. He showed me a pen wiper of wash
leather and said it had been sent to him from America some
time before with a request to use it for a while and then
return it. There were words embroidered on it, 'Extracts
from the pen of Robert Browning'. He had been half amused,
half vexed, but as it lay on his table he had made use of it,
and then he found that he was no longer worried by little
threads getting into the nib of his pen as used to happen,
so when he sends this back he will ask his sister to make his
penwipers of chamois instead of cloth." (I took a lesson from
this, and henceforth have used for my own pen the gauntlets
of discarded Swedish gloves.)

I found him kind in what he said of people, and very
pleasant and genial in society, seeming, as I thought, to
suffer fools gladly, or at least escape without discourtesy.
Yeats tells me that once when a professional biographer of
poets had got him into a window corner he made his escape
with the courteous words, "I must not monopolise you
any longer".

One evening in London, "he was sitting next me at the
Smalleys' where he had dined, when an American actress,
who was just beginning to be known, gave a recital of the
poem[1]. She gave it too dramatically, pawing, if not snorting,
like a war horse, panting at the end. Browning was furious,
he could not keep still, but kept saying to me under his
breath, 'absolutely wrong—she has no idea of how it should
be given—she makes it artificial—I meant that poem to be
spoken as quietly as possible'. I have heard him read it one
afternoon in that quiet unaffected way. He said of Kingsley's
poem 'Lorraine', which she also recited, that Kingsley had
first written the refrain now Lorraine Loree as Br--um
Br--um Boree, he meant it to represent the hum of a fair."

I think that among poets there was no better lover of
Venice than Browning, and there was seldom a year when
he did not find his way there. He sometimes stayed with the
Curtises at their beautiful apartment in the Palazzo Barbaro.
Mr. Curtis told me he had been troubled for a while in
spite of his love for the city because he could not find a
place where he could walk alone, he wanted exercise and
solitude for some part of the day. But then they sent him
each morning in their gondola to the Lido, and he took his

[1] Probably his "How they Brought the Good News from Ghent to
Aix".

walks happily on its level shore. Mr. Curtis had asked him
what he did if an idea came to him at night, if he got up
and wrote it down, but he said, No, he wrote poetry for a
couple of hours every morning and at no other time. He
had written "Childe Roland" in one morning, at a time
when he had resolved to write a lyric every day, but he had
failed to keep this resolve. He told Mr. Curtis that the
reason he and Alfred Austin disliked each other was that
he made "Austin" rhyme with "sauce tin" in some poem;
and also that long ago at a riding school they both attended
there was a young lady to whom Austin was making up,
and when she snubbed him—as she did—he got it into his
head, though quite erroneously, that it was through Browning's interference, and never forgave him.

One Venice afternoon we went with the Layards to hear
Browning read his own poems at Mrs. Bronson's. (It was at
her beautiful villa at Asolo that he wrote later his last
volume; and his son built a house in the village there with
a wonderful studio.) "The Storys and Max Mullers were
there," I wrote, "I enjoyed the reading, though the audience
was not a very sympathetic one and there was no copy of
a volume of his poems to be found in the house, and he
said he could not remember a single one by memory. (I
don't think that this was quite true, for once at his own
house when he had given me an autograph for a daughter
of Sir Alfred Lyall, I asked if I might have one for myself
and he wrote out for me at once, and without hesitation, the
poem beginning, 'All that I know of a certain star'. However,
the slight nervousness caused by an audience, however
friendly, may have disturbed his memory; it is so with Yeats."

Mrs. Bronson at last discovered, or confessed to, an American pirated edition, and from this he read "Andrea del
Sarto", and "Youth and Art", and "The Statue and the
Bust", and then "Hervé Riel" very simply and with spirit,
and told us at the end that it was quite a true tale. Sir
Henry Layard said it reminded him of another true story,
of a ship that was burned and one boat crew saved by the
exertions of a midshipman who behaved very gallantly.
When he got to England he went to *The Times* office and
gave Delane an account of it all. Delane was much struck
with him and said, as he was going, "Can you think of
anything I can do for you?" Upon which, the middy said,
"I would be much obliged if you could get me a free place
at the Adelphi Theatre".

"I said to Miss Browning afterwards how much we had enjoyed it, but she said, 'It was very kind of you to listen, but I myself prefer my dear sister-in-law's poems. And I'm sure that you'd much rather come and have some tea.' For she adores her brother much more than his work. Then Browning introduced me to Pen, who came in after the reading. He was pleasant enough and clever, but I was disappointed. He did not look like the child of two poets."

Browning never became rich. He told me once that there was no profession that he could have chosen, even that of making matches, that would not have brought him in more money than writing poetry; but he said it without rancour or regret. He was a little sore, I think, at the want of public recognition. Tennyson was the great figure, and all the honours were for him. There was nothing but friendliness between them for all that. I remember his showing me a sketch made at his house by Rossetti of Tennyson while he was correcting the proofs of *Maud,* though he said, "Tennyson's reading is now quite impossible to understand, it is like the booming of a gun".

But at some Royal function at Westminster Abbey, Browning's invitation was only sent at the last moment and he was hurt and would not go. And when, to make room for a railway, the little house on the Regent's Canal was to be pulled down and he was turned out, he had set his heart on building a house for himself just inside Kensington Gardens, where Lord Carlisle already lived. But the Board of Works or their representatives in the Government refused permission. He said to me, "It is the only favour I ever asked of the nation".

It was a great joy to him when Pen, making a rich marriage, bought the Palazzo Rezzonico at Venice, and it was in that splendid palace, and while that happiness was still new to him that he died.

He once told me that when he had first come to Italy he had come by sea all the way from England in order that his first sight of Venice should be from the sea. It happened that when my son and I made our third Eastern visit to Italy, Yeats came with us, for his first visit. We had chosen Florence and Siena; and then to please that student of Castiglione's *Courtier* we drove across the Apennines to Urbino, and descended to Pesaro and Ravenna. Yeats had also set his heart on visiting Ferrara, that is on the way to Venice; and I, having in mind what that other poet had said, arranged an easier voyage to the same end. And leaving Ferrara one May morning we went by rail through fields that as we drew nearer to the Adriatic changed to reedy swamps, and passed by little towns showing traces on the architecture of their Queen city. Then taking steam-boat at Chioggia we came before the sun had set to our haven, not to the jangle and uproar of the railway station, but to set foot first upon the very threshold of the city's beauty, the steps leading to the Grand Piazza, to the Duomo, of St. Mark.

XIII

LETTERS TO AND FROM WILFRID BLUNT

7 AUGUST 1921. That Egyptian revolution was the beginning
of my friendship with Wilfrid Blunt, the longest friendship
of my life, for it has lasted forty years. We fell out of
sympathy for a while in the Land League days; "property
blinds all eyes," he wrote, and perhaps it may have been so.
But I see by the letters I have been looking through that we
must quickly have made friends again, for I was able to be
of some use to him through the Visiting Magistrates when
he was imprisoned in Galway Gaol, for holding a meeting
of protest against the denial of the "right universally claimed
by our countrymen to speak where grievances exist". A piece
of oakum unravelled by him "from a tarred rope with a good
healthy smell" as a part of his daily task in his cell makes a
marker for my copy of his prison poems, *In Vinculis* (and
he had entrusted the proof of this to me to correct). And
many years later in thanking me for my little play *The Gaol
Gate,* he wrote, "I am particularly glad the scene is laid in
Galway Gaol; I have very tender memories of it, and of you
in connection with it".

His *Diaries* have given the story of his later years, and
there are diaries of his yet to be published and I think of
even greater interest, being more personal, so there is little
for me to tell. He begged me a couple of months ago to
write in his place (for he was suffering from illness and the
summer languor), a preface for the edition of these *Diaries*
that is now being printed in America, and in it I wrote that
he had said the other day, "I have lived my life in full", and
he had written, as I remembered, "No life is perfect that
has not been lived, youth in feeling—manhood in battle—
old age in meditation. And no life is perfect that is not
sincere." And that on the very same day I had that talk
with him someone said to me in London: "His life has been
lived for freedom". And I wrote that he had been called an
"enfant terrible of politics", and that he had justified that
name, in having kept to his resolve of "pleading the cause
of the backward nations of the world" in and out of season.
"He has never given up his right of protest against injustice

in Egypt and elsewhere, denouncing the floggings and hangings of the villagers of Denshawi in 1905—calling out
against the hanging of Dingra, the Hindu political assassin
in 1909; against the Italian massacres of Arabs in Tripoli in
1911; against the hanging of Roger Casement in 1916, and
against the lawyers' arguments used in the British Cabinet
to urge and justify the late war. An unusual and gallant
record for a Sussex gentleman of many acres, of inherited
wealth and ease." And I said that "the life of love, the
romance of travel, the delight in woods and skies and fields,
the pride of ancestry ascribed to him by those who knew
him; the many gifts, the mastery of living, seem to belong
to the heroic ages of the world, and show him out as one of
Plutarch's men."

Yet, though the doings of his life need no new record,
I may give some record of our friendship in the letters, his
and mine, written from town or country through many years;
and this I may justify by one he wrote three years ago when
I thought to begin putting down something of my own life
history: "Cockerell was with me and we were talking of you
when your letter came yesterday, and I told him of your
thought of memoir writing which he greatly approved. I
have found it a great and consoling occupation of my later
years, for it does not need imagination, which is the fault
that age robs us of, and if we have letters and diaries to
found our writing on it is quite easy work. I have finished
my memoirs now and got them (the political ones) ready for
bringing out the moment peace is declared, and the price
of publication becomes more normal. Of your letters I have
several bundles which I will look through and see what they
contain. But it will take some little time as they range over
thirty-five years and are not very legible, almost always
without dates. My diplomatic education fortunately taught
me always to date mine and it is the first thing I should teach
my child to do.

"Also it has been of wonderful use to have kept a diary.
Reading mine brings my whole life back to me and those
who are dead once more alive precisely as they were. If I
have any skill in writing prose it is entirely due to the habit
of diary keeping which I began fifty years ago and have
continued, with some gaps, ever since."

So in a little time he sent me back some bundles of letters
written and forgotten long ago, trivial many of them; and
as I look at those concerned with politics, his and mine, I

wonder to see them flat and empty, wrinkled balloons, full
as they were then of the angers and hopes and disappoint-
ments of the day; wasted hopes and angers. I was better
pleased to find some written during my London days of gay
talk and pleasant acquaintanceship and gossip that I have
called folklore; and some from my remote and quiet spaces
of time at Coole. Both dwelling houses were delightful and
both necessary; different sides of one's nature called out—
call even now—for one or the other in its turn. But when I
had of late endeavoured in writing this story to give the
contrast, the picture, of one and the other side, I had found
it hard to put down a vivid outline, to recall the past
intimately. So it was with joy I found in these letters what I
had needed; and could see the writer, as she is now, in the
drawing-room or library, looking out at the enclosing woods,
the tranquil clouds floating from the Atlantic that lies
beyond the grey barren hills.

Here are some of my letters from Coole: —

20 September 1883.   "If you had chosen to devote yourself
to Irish politics you might have been here to-day and not
unhappy, for the weather is lovely now, and our lake as blue
as yours at Crabbet, and this is the first day of the partridge
shooting, for in that as in other things, civilisation, etc.,
we are supposed to be content to be some way behind
England.

"There is not much to say of Ireland, for there is a
strange lull in the agitation of the last few years. The people
for the moment are busy with the harvest, and I fancy
Parnell is trying to keep things as quiet as possible until
the next session, when Gladstone has, I believe, promised
a very large measure of Home Rule, much more than his
colleagues approve of. He may, however, have been converted
since he has been entertaining Royalty and the Emperor of
Russia. Landlords are not yet considered quite out of danger,
and Revol" (my French maid who had lived for many years
with his cousin, Mrs. Percy Wyndham) "wept on Sunday
when she saw my brother drive up with an escort of four
policemen. She was consoled, however, when they came in
to tea, thought one of them 'très bien' and I think rather
regrets that we are not threatened. Old Lady Gough who
lives near us, told me that the spirit of the people is certainly much better, for the old woman who keeps her gate
told her that her daughter who died a little time ago gasped
with her latest breath 'To hell with Parnell'. (I wrote this

to W. E. Forster and he answered "Ireland will be topsy turvy when peers do not hear pleasant things from their gatekeepers) . . . I have no idea where this will find you. If in Egypt, shed a tear for me. Is it not as someone said of human life, 'a comedy to those who think, a tragedy to those who feel?'."

Coole. (4 October 1883). "Sir William writes to me from London that you are credited with having gone to India with the intention of overthrowing English supremacy and establishing Mahommedan rule and rapine throughout the Peninsula, so I think you have still a chance of Tower Hill! Kinglake in particular has been lamenting over you . . . I have been quite alone for some time except for little Robert's company, he is quite happy running after rabbits and picking up horse-chestnuts. Sir William comes back on Saturday, and I am expecting my mother who has never been here since my marriage. I shall feel like a child again and expect scoldings when she is in the house, though whereas she scolded me very often when I was young and a model of goodness, now that I am not particularly good she never finds fault with me. Such is life and such a thing it is to be the mother of the favourite grandchild. I feel rather proud of myself just now, firstly because I went to help the Goughs to entertain a superannuated Bishop, and did so with such success that they said I must have been making a special study of Bishops, and his family said he had not eaten such a dinner for weeks as my agreeable conversation had helped down! And secondly because I received a cheque for £5 from the *Fortnightly* (for an article on Portugal)[1] and it being my first *earned* money. I feel very proud even of being valued at a quarter of you; and thirdly because a mouse having disturbed my rest and baffled cats and traps, I devised a trap of my own, a biscuit floating in a paper boat on a basin of water, and in the morning a floating corpse was found (illustration). I give you the receipt in case you should meet a mouse in your travels (for Max Muller announces that he has discovered from Sanskrit roots that my mouse, though not the cat, was known in the East before the Aryan separation).

"Have you read Max Muller's *India*? Parts of it remind me of verses in your poems, the comparison of the wisdom of the East and the West. He says there are hemispheres in human nature, answering to North and South, and while we

---

[1] "Through Portugal".

have developed the active, combative and political side, the people of the East have developed the passive, meditative and philosophical, and that if we call their notions of life dreamy, unreal, unpractical, they may look on ours as 'short sighted, fussy and in the end most unpractical because involving a sacrifice of life for the sake of life'. Here, I am glad to say, our combative politics have not been developing themselves lately, though at a picnic on the hills of my old home the other day a police officer appeared and begged my brother to be more than ever careful and not stir without his escort, as fresh plots had come to light, and outrage was beginning again in the neighbourhood. It strikes me curiously, after England, how in paying a morning visit to a neighbour, the conversation naturally turns on politics, Gladstone's views on Home Rule and the strength of the English Radical party, and American sympathy, make such a practical question of domestic interest in plans and expenditure.

"Revol is rather pleased with the country, though she can't get over the want of shops and there not being a chemist within reach, and is astonished at the unpractical and roundabout way in which things are done. For instance, last week the kitchen pump broke down, and the gunsmith was sent for, as the only person in the neighbourhood likely to be able to mend it. But it being the first day of the partridge shooting he was out poaching, and we had to wait a day or two for him, and when he came he patched it ineffectually. They having heard meanwhile of a real plumber, drove miles off to look for him, and found him in a field engaged in digging potatoes, and he came next day and patched it again, and the cook was so pleased at his having come 'riding his own horse' that she was quite satisfied with his handiwork . . . Forgive me for writing nonsense. If I were in the East with Lady Anne and Sabin I would write you such interesting letters! So don't forget me, and if my letters bore you, tell your agent to forward only every second one or third."

Coole. 16 December 1883 . . ."Your letter from Madras came a few days ago . . . Your letter in *The Times* appeared the same day . . . Sir William tells me to say how extremely good he thinks it . . . All the philanthropists will be down on the Government for allowing Sebehr, the king of slave dealers, to be sent back at the head of an army, it will be just the thing for those benevolent beings Randolph and Labouchere

to take up . . . We have had several "old friends" of Sir
William staying here, and one was in low spirits and cried
all day, and one thinks he should have married her instead
of me, and one he had not seen for twenty years has grown
hideous and is stone deaf, and my head is so bothered with
'unprofitable chat' I shall be glad of a little silence."

Coole. 1884 . . ."Sir Wm. left Ceylon yesterday. He introduced Arabi to Lord Rosebery who was much taken with
him."

1 August 1884 . . ."The borage you gave me is a fine plant
now and in flower. "I borage give courage" says the old
rhyme, so it is a useful herb in one's garden. All is quiet
here; prices are low for stock, in consequence of the failure
of turnips in England (see the evil of British connection, the
Land League will say), so we may expect some difficulty
about rents, though it is rather hard that we never get any
more in good years."

9 September 1884 . . ."We have wet depressing weather here.
I am entertaining some relatives of Sir Wm.'s to whom I have
to show all the civility I can to make up for Robert's birth,
which has cut them out from the doubtful good of succeeding
to an Irish estate. I am also suffering from servant worry,
the footman having taken to drink, and the coachman having
been detected in malpractices left at an hour's notice, and
there has been trouble at my old home and things are not
very bright. But to make up the average of human happiness
I have had all the Gort Workhouse children out to spend the
day, and the poor little things who had never been asked
outside the walls before managed to enjoy themselves very
much."

Coole. 4 October 1884 . . . "I must send a line of congratu-
lation in the 'Ideas about India' in the *Fortnightly* of this
month. It is more forcible and interesting than even the
first instalment . . . Sir William is enthusiastic about it, and
says he will write to you. He did a great deal in Ceylon to
put the natives on an equality, both officially and socially,
with the English, and I think succeeded in a great degree.
An Anglo-Indian I met the other day,* a Mr. de Morgan
from Madras, said he could hardly believe it possible when
he went to Ceylon a little wh'le ago that the natives of a
country so close to India could be so differently treated, a
fact he was not inclined to profit by, for he was a typical
A - I, and it did me good to hear him say in a sudden fury,
'I HATE Mr. Blunt'. Your name is evidently a byword out

Alfred Lyall. A portrait by J. H. Hudson after J. J. Shannon. Courtesy of
National Portrait Gallery, London.

Robert Browning. A portrait by M. Gordigiami. Courtesy of the Natic
Portrait Gallery, London.

there. As I am repeating compliments, let me give you a sentence of Mr. Lee Childe's last letter: 'I am glad the Blunts are happy. People that create a great deal of mischief generally are. May the Lord give them what they deserve! Amen.' "

12 March 1885 . . ."We arrived here two days ago, the weather is cold and even the horse-chestnut trees hardly give promise of a leaf (just three weeks behind Paris) and I was so tired by travelling and unpacking that I have not yet recovered my energy, but half dormant take up my old occupations and buy flannel and make cough cures for old women. But little Robert is bright enough for two and as happy as the day is long . . . "

14 April 1885 . . . "We came here a little too soon and the landscape looked as hard and dry as a Hobbema, but now it is as soft and mysterious as a Corot. We spent last week in Dublin to manifest our loyalty. The Royal visitors (the Prince and Princess of Wales) have been so far a 'great success', that is to say, they, and also Lord Spencer, were cheered through the streets all through Dublin. Whether that means much I can't say, it is an excitable population, and I saw a man who walked through the cleared space carrying two large bandboxes cheered as much as anyone. 'St. Patrick's Day' when played at the laying of a foundation stone was cheered more than anything else, but the Prince was equal to the occasion and waved his hat as if it was meant for him. He looked very fat, the Princess very pretty and not more than five-and-twenty at the Ball, in her white dress and diamonds. I took a seat in a commanding position and felt as if the dancing and display of beauty and diamonds was all done for my benefit. The Marchionesses were most admired, Lady Kildare, who I refuse to believe is rouged, and Lady Ormond as pretty as Millais has painted her, and Lady Conyngham in the stolen Crown Jewels . . . The waltz of diamond tiaras was very dazzling, and I feel that I have seen a crystallization of the pomps and vanities of this wicked world enough to last for a long time. As an antidote, I spent today in visiting some of our own poor people; it is the best part of living in Ireland that they are always bright, intelligent and witty. One old woman asked me to come and see a sick man. 'He was a real gentleman,' she said, 'if I asked him for five or seven shillings he never said "I haven't it", and if he went out to cut his corn he never raised his back till the sun went down' . . . Another said she

had at first sight taken me for the priest's sister and was
going to say 'How's Father Considine?' when she recognised
me and said (I hope meaning a compliment), 'Aren't we very
happy to have such a plain lady?'

"You will be very tired of Ireland if I write any more.
You see, I am now home keeping and have only homely
thoughts, but I wish very much to know how you are and
what you are doing, and what you hear and what hope you
have for the triumph of good and the punishment of evil-
doers."

May 1885 . . . "I have been reading only now Gordon's
Journals, and think you ought to feel very proud and very
glad that your name seemed so sometimes to stand between
him and injustice—'I shall have Wilfrid Blunt making a
nice row about this.' . . . I believe you could get in as a
'Tory Democrat' easily enough, [word missing] at the Government to please an English mob, which enjoys hard hitting as
a substitute for prize fights.

"The days are very uneventful, the poor women who come
to sell flannel are almost my only visitors, but for once I
enjoy seeing the beauty of the spring. I have never spent a
spring in the country since some primeval period when I
was in my teens, and the blossoms on the trees and the daily
unfolding of the leaves are new and delightful to me. The
marsh marigolds remind me how good you were last year in
bringing me a quantity and how glad I was to get them.

"Robert has now a pig which he calls Wideawake, and
a puppy which he calls Pompey, and is very happy."

15 May 1885 . . . "Very many thanks for the sonnets, it was
delightful your sending them to Gladstone; nothing gratifies
me so much except your having sent them to me."

June 1885 . . . "Randolph for India! I can think of nothing
else, it amuses me so much, the idea of Colvin's face when
he heard it, and Lord Dufferin taking his orders from him,
and Lord Reay who went out in the strength of Gladstone's
name. Will he be able to do any good I wonder? One must
never expect too much of people in office . . ."

June 1885 . . . "As for you, you will never be able to support
any Government but will always be in opposition, you have
too much the courage of your opinions to be ever a 'party
man' . . . I gave the workhouse children a day in the woods,
which was my chief excitement, and I am nursing a little
nephew who has a weak spine, and doing good works, and

reading Gibbon's *Decline and Fall* by way of relaxation, and begin to feel rather Pharisaical.

". . . The newspapers and officials say Ireland has never been so bad as now, but living here one meets with nothing but pleasant words and good wishes."

3 August 1886 . . . "I had some baskets of fruit picked and drove to the Workhouse with Robert and divided it amongst the children, an agreeable interruption to their lessons. Then I bought some toys for the school feast. When we came back there was a woman muffled in black at the door. Presently Boswell came up to say she wanted to see Sir William. He sent down to ask her name and business, as being a stranger he thought she was begging. No answer came up and in a little while I went to see if she was still there and found her in tears. I asked who she was. 'I cannot tell my name,' she said, 'but I have this to give Sir William—and it was sent by a dying hand', and she held up a steel chain purse full of sovereigns. I went up to W. and sent him to speak to her, and they had a long talk. She gave him the purse with twenty sovereigns in it and said, 'This was confided to me by a dying man to give you. I have come from America with it and now I have put it into your hand I will go again.' She would not tell her name or any circumstances connected with the message, but she knew Coole and Roxborough and the neighbourhood well, and she had left before the famine, when she was 18 years old, and never been back since. She refused to take money even for her expenses but W. at last forced five pounds upon her by refusing to take the rest unless she accepted it. He told her, at my suggestion, that he would give the money to the poor and she said she was quite satisfied now and happy. She was most struck on her return with the dirt of Ireland. 'We are so proud of our country and always like to hear a good word spoken of it, but we have forgotten the dirt and disorder and the laziness—Oh, it is dreadful to see!' She said at last, perhaps she would write from America, and our kindness she would never forget, and so, nameless still, she disappeared." (We never heard of her again nor ever had any clue as to whom the money came from.) "Sir William says that once before the Fenian outbreak, he was standing by the roadside watching the draining of the Kiltartan bog. A man dressed in light-coloured frieze, and not the frieze of this country, stopped and spoke to him and said, 'This is a fine job you are making of this, Sir, but couldn't you leave it to your steward

to look after it for a little time?' He said, 'I suppose I could, but why should I?' 'Because,' said the man, coming close to him, 'it is time for you to leave'. W. said, 'I am not afraid. I have complete confidence in my people here.' 'Yes and you may have,' said the man; 'and they wouldn't hurt a hair of your head—but there are those coming that would.' 'And why do you tell me that?' said W. 'Because you once did a great kindness to a friend of mine and it may have been a friend and it may have been a brother; that's all I will say. And for three days past I have walked the roads to get a chance of giving you this warning.' 'And why did you not come to Coole?' 'Because if it came to be known that I went to Coole and spoke to your honour there are those that would not leave me living for one hour. Now will you go?' 'No,' W. said, 'I won't leave my people. I will stay by them whatever comes.' The man's face grew dark and he thundered out *'Manam an diabhal,* your blood on your own head!' But W. said, 'Don't part with me in anger. I thank you very much for your warning, but I can't take it. Shake hands at all events.' And they shook hands and parted."

The Workhouse parties were generally twice in the year, one in the autumn when the nuts were ripe.

"Paul Harvey drove me to the Workhouse and to choose toys. The Temperance Band were parading up and down Gort playing. This was to intimidate bidders from buying Morony's house which he had taken for an hotel, from being a Land League rendezvous.

"The next day was so stormy it was not fit for the party so I drove into Gort with Harry and Robert and took one of the big cakes to the Workhouse that the children might not be too much disappointed and distributed it. My hat was blown off and down Crow Lane and pursued by the inhabitants. But yesterday was fine enough at last, so I sent in for the children and they came out, four loads of happy little paupers. The boys took them out in the boat first and the rest of the day they spent in the nutwood. Then tea, cake and toys to take home. The idiot boy Malachi, when he got back, rushed up to the nuns and gave them cake and nuts from his bag saying, 'If *herself* had come sooner we'd have had a fine day before this'." And in July 1887: "The Layards are staying with us . . . The Workhouse party was a great success yesterday, tea in the wood, then swinging and nutting and climbing trees, and the lame boy as happy as a king, driving the little ones in the donkey trap. Sir Henry crooked down nuts for them and Enid sang for them and played with them. Lord Gough and Miss Arbuthnot came to call and found them so employed."

(Pleasant visitors came to stay with us sometimes; one summer Mr. Cordery who had entertained us when he was Resident at Hyderabad. "He and W. spend each morning in going through his translation of *The Iliad,* which W. had been annotating . . . He stayed on to meet Lord Northbrook who 'has come in search of knowledge!' He said he would like to spend all his time in the garden (as John Morley had said he would like to spend all his life pacing up and down the long walk there)—it is looking very bright and pretty—but W. took him and Cordery off to Lisdoonvarna for two days' driving round by the coast." Chief Justice Morris came to stay also, and when Lord Northbrook went on to see where the Clanricarde evictions have been taking place, "Those English," says the Chief Justice, "want to see everything! Sure, he might as well look into the next potato garden!"

July 1888 . . . "Sir William gave me the songs found in Lord Edward Fitzgerald's room on his arrest, which had been given to his grandfather, the Under Secretary . . ." The days slip by very quickly with housekeeping and correspondence and teaching Robert and the boys to play croquet, and attending to the poor, and seeing to the garden; and I took up an Irish grammar by chance the other day and am puzzling over the pronunciation and growing ambitious to learn.

To W. S. B. Mentmore, August 1885: "We crossed from Ireland last night in a storm, arrived in London this morning, and came here this afternoon to spend Sunday. I thought I should have had time to call at James Street to ask for news of you, but had to accompany a little nephew who was to choose presents for his eight brothers and sisters which took time. Lord Rosebery asked me if I understood your politics, and I had to confess that as far as your English views are concerned there are some points I need enlightening on, so I expect you to explain them very clearly to me!"

These letters are from India, where we spent the winter of 1885-86:—

Government House, Ganish Khind. 3 December 1885. "It was a great blow to me yesterday when we landed at Bombay, to hear the result of the Camberwell election, not so much for your sake, for you will find better work to do and be saved a great many dreamy days and drowsy nights, but I had looked forward to seeing you face to face with the G.O.M., and asking him unanswerable questions . . ."

"We arrived in India yesterday and came straight here from Bombay. The house is beautiful, the gardens and situation are very fine, but I feel already that we shall see very little of *India* from Government Houses; one is surrounded by a cordon of sunburnt officers with fair moustaches whose ideas on all subjects are as much alike as the cut of their hair. Lord Reay is up in the hills for a few days . . . I enjoyed the voyage out (after the Mediterranean) the sunset and the moonrise and the starry nights were so beautiful, and my little armchair on deck became quite a home. My chief amusement was lending your *Ideas*[2] to Anglo-Indians, and watching the explosion that immediately came. Some said the book was 'a mass of falsehood', others that it was 'a lie that is half a truth and so the blackest of lies', but all agreed in regretting that there is not a common hangman in India by whom it might be burned."

Bombay. 21 December 1885. "A doctor has been talking about the salt tax, he is indignant and says, from a medical point of view, it is most disastrous. What first drew his attention to its iniquity was meeting two Parsis collecting the tax, and finding they made 1,500 to 2,000 R. per month, as their percentage on what they collected, so of course they squeezed the people well . . ."

(I had written to him in 1883: "I have been talking about India with my brother, Colonel Persse, who has just returned. He says the horror of the salt tax cannot be exaggerated. What first made him think of it was hearing one native saying to another, 'he is a very rich man, he eats salt every day'.")

Aurungabad. 23 December 1885. "At a great dinner here I sat next an admirer of yours, Mehdi Hassan, Chief Justice of Hyderabad (aged 22) who says every word of your chapter on the Native States is true. It was the first I had heard anyone venture to say so!

"We have just come from Hyderabad, and I think you may be interested in hearing about it, though I have not a very satisfactory account to give. The Nizam and Salar Jung have fallen out and for months have hardly been on speaking terms, at least His Highness will hardly speak to the Minister,

2 *Ideas about India* (1885) London, Kegan Paul French & Co.

in consequence of which there is great difficulty in transacting business, and affairs are nearly at a deadlock. I believe it all began about a woman (the Minister being the successful wooer) and the opportunity was seized by intriguers on both sides to make a lasting breach; and they have so far succeeded in doing so. All the nobles are jealous of Salar Jung! and his health is beginning to fail from worry and indigestion, he hardly eats anything and is growing thin. He used to come to Mr. Cordery a good deal to consult about important matters, and now H.H. is growing jealous and has decreed that no one may go to the Residency without a special permission from him, and as he (the Nizam) sometimes does not look at a paper or transact any business for days together, that will not help the deadlock. No one has a word to say against the Minister, except that he is rather indolent and has not very good business habits. I felt for him very much, so young to begin the troubles of public life, and it was very painful when twice at breakfast and dinner, I sat next the Nizam and Salar Jung was opposite. H.H. talked to everyone but him, to make his displeasure more marked. Mr. Cordery is worried by it all, and I think would be honestly glad to see peace restored, but his heart is less in Hyderabad than in the proof sheets of his new edition of Homer. The little Nizam gets the credit of being intelligent and quick, but childishly fond of amusement and with an exalted idea of his own power. I think if this block goes on much longer the Government will be taken over by England. Lord Dufferin is expected soon, to put things to rights. I enjoyed my visit very much. Mr. Cordery, as you know, is a very good host and all the dresses of the people are so bright and picturesque I was never tired of going about the city either in a carriage or (once) on an elephant, or watching the big people coming to the Residency (they knew Sir William's good name from Ceylon) and the escort drawn up, the horns tootling, and Mr. Cordery giving his arm to some old gentleman in a dressing-gown. We breakfasted with the Nizam and dined with him at Golconda after some sports in which he and some of his nobles took part. He rides well and looks much more imposing on horseback than in ordinary life, and has certainly very good manners and a great deal of dignity. We dined also with Salar Jung (an Arabian nights entertainment) and we are now on a picnic given by him to Mr. Cordery. He wanted to come himself but yielded to advice and stuck to his post.

We are in tents here, spending a very pleasant Christmas
week, the last two days we spent at Ellora exploring the cave
temples . . . Sir William was very much struck with Hyderabad, and to find these great Mohammedans sitting down to
dinner with us, and you are certainly right in saying that
even the poorer people are more to be admired than those
in British parts—at least they don't scowl at one as the
Poona people do."

The Residency, Jeypore. 13 January 1886. "We have been
having a very pleasant time at Baroda, Ahmedabad, Oodeypore and here, and certainly in one thing you are right, that
in the Native Protected States the people look happier, and
much more amiable than in those directly under England.
Oodeypore is the most lovely place in the world, I think,
only rather unreal, like the illustrations of poetry books, the
lake surrounded by mountains and bordered with white
marble palaces and temples and palm trees, and the blue
sky over all. Sir William caught a 16lb. fish in the lake . . .
The general formula when we sit down to a meal is that
we are not to think, like Mr. Blunt, that our hosts live like
this every day, it is only for guests the 'imported delicacies'
are opened!"

I may put in here some letters I wrote to Paul Harvey, to
whom I had promised to report what I could see in that
Indian winter of the advantages or drawbacks of its Civil
Service, in his mind at that time as a possible profession.
And at that time also he had some thoughts of trying for a
prize to be given at Rugby for an Indian essay. But though,
or perhaps because, I wrote more than I have given here of
the country's history, that idea was abandoned; and the
home Civil Service, which he chose instead of that of the
East, brought even wider and more various interests than
he could have found in the presidencies, leading him as it
did on the country's service to Athens, to Salonika, to Egypt;
giving him work of great responsibility and in which he
carried and won honour.

Hyderabad. 15 December. "I see I must write very often
if I am to tell you anything, but my letters are only a text
for you to hang your Indian essay on . . . We left Ganish
Khind after a great dinner of farewell to the Commander-
in-Chief (forty men all in uniform, ten generals among
them, only four ladies), a very brilliant sight. Our next
stopping place was Bijapur. It was once a great Mohammedan city, and after the hideous Hindu idols it was

refreshing to come to a place where the one God is worshipped. There are innumerable mosques and minarets
to be seen, and what has a very striking effect, though the
city walls are left the city itself (it was probably one of mud
huts) has completely disappeared, only some straggling
villages left, and you look upon a green plain, covered with
tamarind and pepul trees and amongst them domes rising
in every direction. One larger than St. Paul's . . . Only in one
is there still a Friday service. The Hindus, having no idols
there are reduced to worshipping a great gun, into whose
tiger-shaped mouth they stick little bits of coconut and
flowers. Tradition says this gun was only fired off once, and
then the soldier who lit the match was so afraid of being
burned that he prepared a tank of water to jump into, and
did so, and the heat of the explosion made the water boil
and he was scalded to death! The city was besieged and
sacked several times, but now what remains of it is peace-
ably governed by five Englishmen (two of whom are away
on leave), who have no military force or European politation
wherewith to keep order, yet do so over the whole district.
It amazed me to see these three men in such absolute
authority over a population (including large gangs of con-
victs) of a different nation and religion. That is what makes
the Civil Service interesting, having so much individual
liberty of action, but of course, there is loneliness to contend
with. One of these three, a quite young man, was going off
to live in a tent for some months to listen to complaints
and settle disputes, but he gets plenty of sport and seemed
quite cheerful. All the five live in beautiful houses, which
were palaces or mosques in the old times (most of them
built about 1550 to 1556). We stayed with the Collector in
an old arched Court of Justice.

"Here at Hyderabad we are magnificently lodged in the
Residency. Our host, Mr. Cordery, is a most charming
entertainer. He, I must tell you, is a brother of Mrs. Jex
Blake, and there is also staying here a brother of Mr. Lee
Warner, so Rugby is in the ascendant. This is the most
enchanting place I have been to yet. The streets are full of
bright colours and all the men wear arms, sword or dagger,
and it is quite common to meet an elephant or camel in the
street, sometimes with a little one trotting after her. We
breakfasted this morning with the Nizam in great state, a
troop of black Abyssinian soldiers at the gate to salute us,
and some native troops in gorgeous uniform inside. The

Nizam is only twenty, very small, dressed in a check suit with high black cap, and gold tuft; long black hair. He handed me in to breakfast, I was the only lady present, several of his nobles and retainers. He was rather hard to talk to as he says 'yes' to everything and relapses into silence, and only at the end he began to get over his shyness. Salar Jung, the Prime Minister, sat opposite. He is only twenty-three but looks older and is very big. I had met him when he was in England three years ago, had sat next him at dinner, and he had been very much excited at seeing Arabi's name on my fan. He dined here last night and I said, 'Do you remember meeting me at Lord Northbrook's?' 'Yes,' he said, 'and you had a fan'. So we made great friends and he is sending his elephant tomorrow for me to have a ride on . . . The weather is delicious, never has been too hot, and the roses and other flowers are beautiful.

"You know this is the largest native State that is independent, not quite absorbed by England only 'protected' by her . . . Mr. Lee Warner is in the Civil Service and I have been asking him his opinion of it as a profession. He thinks that, on the whole, it is as fine and interesting a one as any young man can choose, if he has a little money of his own to retire on in case his health breaks down (he himself is very unwell and is trying to keep on, and his wife is also ill). He says, and others say, one must not judge of India in the winter, that in the hot weather everything is different, and everyone's temper bad, and that we travellers see only the rosy side and the luxurious living of the Civil Servants, but that the other side is to be seen when in some lonely station you come upon a little grave where some official has buried his child who died for want of a doctor's help. My impression up to this is that it is a very good and fine service for unmarried men, but after marriage comes the grief of having to send the children home, and often that of the wife's health breaking down. When one comes to be a high official like Mr. Cordery, with a palace and an escort and aide-de-camp, and such immense power and influence (Adviser here, and Controller of Berar, which is in pawn to England) no life can be better worth living, and prizes like this dangle before every Civil Servant's eyes. Now you will say this letter is as bad as a holiday task, so good-bye."

In camp, Aurungabad. 23 December. "Now we are on a picnic given to Mr. Cordery and to us by Salar Jung. He could not come himself, but his private secretary is acting as host. We are lodged in sumptuous tents, I have a beautiful yellow and black one to myself. Another tent is furnished as a drawing-room, another as a banqueting hall. We travel with four horses and an escort of Lancers and mounted Police, and Mr. Cordery never having been here before, the town has been illuminated in his honour, oh! so beautifully, with garlands of tiny little oil lamps all through the streets, and the public gardens are festooned with lamps shaped and coloured like tulips. At a great dinner given by the town notables I was taken in by the Subar (the Head Man), a most charming old Mahommedan, a great admirer of Arabi, so we have sworn eternal friendship; and at my other side was the Chief Justice of Hyderabad, Mehdi Hassan, aged twenty-two (they know how to appreciate youth out here!) and we made such friends he has sent me a work on the administration of justice, written by himself, and both he and the Subar say they intend to write to me . . . But this is not *history*, so look in your Biographical Dictionary for Aurungzebe, great Mohammedan conqueror, and you will find that he founded Aurungabad, and the camps of his followers became its suburbs, and Chinese Ambassadors brought him blue china, still to be found there, and he built a magnificent tomb for his wife, but he himself was buried in the little town of Roza 'in the shadow of a saint's tomb' by his own desire—rather hard on his wife—and being a good Mohammedan he would have no roof or slab over his grave, but as the Koran commands, left it open to the air and dew.

". . . Near this there is a wonderful rock fortress and a deserted city, Daulatabad . . . Salar Jung's secretary told me that last year, looking from the fortress, he had seen a panther spring upon a calf inside the city walls.

"We spent a couple of days exploring the cave temples of Ellora . . . most wonderful, all carved out of the rock . . . There are three series of caves which form a sort of first, second and third reading book of the religions of India. The original religion (as, no doubt, every Rugby boy knows) was Brahminism, but about 600 B.C. Buddha, a King's son, began to preach that there was no caste, and no transmigration of souls, and that a life of pure morality led to Nirvana, 'the city of peace', something very near annihilation, and this caught the ear of the Hindus, and Buddhism became popular. These are the first caves, those of the Buddhists (but not very old, all after Christ), they are very

simple, with no image but that of Buddha over and over
again, and one very touching little carving of three figures,
one pursued by fire, one by a sword, and one by a snake,
and each turning to Buddha's image carved at the side
('from fire, from battle and murder and from sudden death
—Good Lord, deliver us! '). Well, after a time, the Brahmins
seeing they were losing so many followers, began to popular-
ize their religion chiefly by adding new gods and fables, and
so brought back India to Hinduism again, and their temples
are carved all over with figures (all repulsive) of Brahma the
creator, Vishnu the preserver, Siva the destroyer, and many
others. But in all their allegories it is Siva, the destructive
power, that triumphs, and this is the key to the Hindu
religion; they worship what they fear, like the big gun at
Bijapur, rather than what is good.

"The Jain temples are the last, very slightly different
from the Brahmins—the Jains were Buddhists and have
become half Brahminised, and their sect still exists, but pure
Buddhism is banished to Ceylon. I hope you will get this
before you are back at school or you will never read it in
time for your Indian essay . . . I hope to hear you are in
the Sixth."

Oodeypore. 8 January . . . "We began the New Year at
Baroda, an independent Mahratta State under the Gaekwar,
whose history is rather romantic. The last Gaekwar turned
out badly, tried to poison Sir Robert Phayre, and the English
turned him out and sent him off to Madras (where he died
just in time to make room for Theebaw). Then an heir was
wanted for the throne and on searching the records it was
found that in one of the villages there lived a boy with
royal blood in his veins. They say he was acting as cowboy,
but at all events, like David, he was helping to tend the
flocks. So he was brought to Court and educated, had a
good English tutor, and now he is twenty-six and a model
Prince, thinking more of educating his people than of
arena sports and illuminations, though he had to go through
those at his wedding the other day. He gave a State banquet
on New Year's Day to which we were invited, but with all
his liberal principles he is too strict a Hindu to break bread
with a Christian, so he only came in at dessert, to propose
'the Empress's' health. He sat next me and is pleasant to
talk to, and his diamonds are magnificent—one necklace
worth £320,000. We came in for some of his wedding festi-
vities, sports at which a hundred men pulled 'tug of war'

against an elephant, and won. (The elephant would have won had he not sulked.) Then we went to Ahmedabad (English), there are beautiful mosques and tombs, built at the time when the Mohammedans were supreme. We stayed with the Head of Police who told us exciting stories about Dacoits (wild hill robbers). There is a famous one still at large, 'Mowar Sudwani'. Our host, Major Humphreys, had sent two men a little time ago to spy out what he was doing, and Mowar got hold of them, suffocated one with a handkerchief and cut the other in pieces. The son of one of the murdered men came to tell the story, bringing with him a little wild ass his father had caught and meant for a present for Major Humphreys, a very pretty little thing, it is to be sent to London, to the Zoo.

"Now we are at Oodeypore, it is one of the smallest and oldest of the Rajput states and is independent, though it was saved by the English from destruction by the Mahratta and other native antagonists. An English resident lives here, and 'advises' the Maharaja on all subjects and, of course, the advice is always taken, for without English support the native army (five regiments, the Commander-in-Chief of which began life as a circus rider) could not even hold its own against the hill tribes. For all that, the Maharaja 'porte sa tête comme le Saint Sacrement', for he is of the oldest of all Indian families—one of the 'children of the Sun'. His ancestors reigned here in 728 A.D. but can trace their descent for some centuries before that, and when the other Rajput chiefs had to bow to the Mohammedan Emperor of Delhi and give him their daughters in marriage, the Oodeypore Rana did neither one nor the other, and for many years even refused to intermarry with the families of Rajahs who had so disgraced themselves. The father of the present man refused the Star of India—'What honour could a star confer on the Son of the Sun?' He is a strict Hindu as all the Rajputs are. He has just sent to say he would like us to have a dinner at his expense and will send it down this evening, and his carriage and horses brought us and will take us back our seventy miles to the station, so we must speak well of him."

Government House, Calcutta. 29 January.   "You can't think how delighted I am at the good news in your last letters, from Paris, about your prizes and your remove . . . As to the Indian essay, my letters are only a kind of sign-posts telling you where information is to be found . . . It is very good for

you to have to go into French society and keep up your
knowledge of the language, it will be a great help to you,
whatever profession you choose. I found the A.D.C.s at
Bombay in a great state of mind the night the foreign
officers were to dine, for not one in the house except Lord
and Lady Reay could speak French with ease; and once at
Ceylon, when Sir William had the officers of a French
man-of-war to dinner and sent out to look for French-
speaking Englishmen in Colombo to meet them, *one* was
to be found.

"Even here at Government House, at the great dinner the
other evening for the foreign officers who have come on the
Delhi manoeuvres, when Lord William Beresford came with
the list of names to ask the ladies who we would choose to
go in with, we all with one voice cried 'The American!'
But as we could not all have him, and the Italian Consul
had been heard talking to me in his language, I was given
General Saletta and found him charming."

Government House, Madras. 15 February. "I have just
been with Mrs. Grant Duff to call on Queen Soopyalat (Mrs.
Theebaw). Theebaw himself is not allowed to see visitors.
She is a pretty Japanese-looking little woman, wearing
magnificent diamonds; and stayed sitting down all the time,
and what had the most odd effect, the maids-of-honour and
the interpreter are obliged to lie all the time with their feet
close to the floor, or move about on their knees, but never
get up. It was ridiculous to see one of them coming in on
her knees carrying the baby; I thought they would both
have tumbled down. Her Majesty gave me an immense
cheeroot made by her own hands. They are not very happy,
poor people, and miss all the ceremonial of their Court."

Government House, Madras. 23 February. "We came back
yesterday from a pleasant tour in the South, to Madura,
where there are immense Hindu temples and where you
may imagine yourself in the old Pagan times, as the High
Priest presents you with garlands and you are allowed to
look into mysterious shrines at grotesque idols . . .Idolatry
seems engrained in the people's nature; the Judge we were
staying with showed us a stone under a banyan tree which
all his gardeners worship. They have a theory that there is
a sacred snake in the tree which only comes out on Fridays.
They are a gentle people 'made to be ruled' and there is
not an English soldier south of Madras now . . .

"On our way back we spent half a day at a dak bungalow

with a young civilian. Poor young man! Hardly had I seen
him when I thought now is the chance of getting information
on the Civil Service for Paul—for he looked about your age,
though very small and meek, and has only been four years
in the country; so I proceeded to cross-examine him. He likes
the Civil Service very well, much better than he expected,
the work is so varied, though he has been for nearly a year
quite alone at a country station, except for occasional visits
to headquarters. The first six months were the worst, as he
was home-sick, and only learning his work with the Collector.
He had not much to do. Now he is Assistant Collector, and
in a position of great authority over about a million and a
half of souls. He spends a good deal of time in camp, moving
about his servants and tents in bullock carts, he riding. The
villagers come to him to make their complaints. One who
has had his house burned down accuses his neighbour;
another says his boundary stones have been moved, and he
must examine into each case. Then he has magisterial func-
tions, small cases are brought before him; a man has been
found making salt illegally, or stealing firewood, or assaulting
an enemy, and he can sentence them to a fine or imprisonment. An immense responsibility for a mere boy, it seems.
He has £350 a year to begin with; keeps about eight servants;
his cook excellent, as we found out. He works till late,
reads during meals, and goes to bed early. This year he is
going home on three months' leave. There is plenty of snipe
shooting to be had but he is not a sportsman. I think this is
a pretty fair account of the first year of a young civilian's life
here. In the army you would have more society but less
interesting work. So now, good-bye, this is our last day in
India, we sail for Ceylon tomorrow."

To W.S.B.:—

Colombo. 2 March 1886. "I send this to reassure you about
Arabi. He has not taken to drink, but looks I think better,
younger and handsomer than when I last saw him in Egypt,
or perhaps all those libellous photographs distorted his
image in my mind. Seriously, it has put me quite in good
spirits seeing him again, for he looks as if he had so much
good work in him yet, that I am sure he is not meant to
remain here all his life looking over the sea. I have had no
talk with him yet, because he came with several others, only
he looked eloquent while his son made a little grateful
speech to me, but I am going to make an appointment with
him for tomorrow. Today I visit all the wives, and next day

we go to the Gordons at Kandy. Great preparations were going on at Madras for the Viceroy's visit (and, oh! my best travelling dress was spoiled by the new paint on the pier), but fancy the consternation—the natives have refused to decorate or help—'You would not help us to welcome Lord Ripon, and we won't help you now' they say, and as you know, natives are always expected to take the brunt of these kind of flare-ups.

"As to Toulba, he is like a fat schoolboy, quite a new lease of life he has taken, and sat on the edge of his chair with patent leather shoes with little bows, whereas the others wear boots; and the tassel of his tarboosh over his ear instead of hanging down behind. He is quite proud because his wife brought out last year a baby of 'two and a half *months* old, but I trust he *meant* years.''

19 March 1886. I wrote to Sir M.G.D. "I am delighted with Ceylon and its flowery trees, and of course, it is a great pleasure to me to see how much my husband did of good work while he was ruler here. One district we visited was when he first came a desolate jungle, the people dying of starvation and bad water; deserted villages to be seen everywhere. Now, chiefly through the repairing of old tanks by him, the people have taken heart, and jungle is disappearing and paddy fields are visible in all directions; and while the villages are filling up and the market is overcrowded, the hospitals are almost empty, that terrible disease 'parangi' having disappeared.

"The rock temples have struck me very much, especially the first I saw, in an almost inaccessible place. It was just a cave hollowed in the rock, and in it one sleeping figure cut out of the rock, the head resting upon a lotus. A yellow-robed priest who appeared from some cleft pointed to it and said, 'this is Buddha, how he died'. The same simple figure repeated over and over in each temple is far more striking than the monstrous idols of the Hindus . . . There is beauty in the worship here, for however early in the morning we visited some lonely shrine, someone had been there before us and had laid fresh flowers on the stone.

"An engineer told me the other day that his horse-keeper having been much mangled by a crocodile (from which he saved him) he went to see the poor man next day, and found him in bed and hung round with clothes, though the heat was suffocating. But on his remonstrating, the coolie in charge had pointed to some lizards on the wall and said under his breath, 'The big crocodile has told these little crocodiles, his brothers: there is a man I tried to kill and he was taken from me; you kill him for me—and they will spit poison at him, so we must keep him covered up.' The man recovered, he said, and is only a little lame."

London. May 1886. "Don't court-martial Lord Dufferin just yet, for in a letter to me by last mail he says, 'many thanks for your letter and especially for the sonnets (*Proteus*) I have read a great number of them and quite agree with you in thinking that they are very good, full of music and feeling.'

"Curiously, in India the only man we met who seemed uneasy about Burma and against its annexation was Lord Dufferin, but the fear of French intrigues there I fancy decided him. I slept in the room at Oodeypore where the 'trigger was pulled', from which he sent his telegram ordering the war to begin. But I was not so much touched by the sight of Soopyalat in her diamond chains at Madras as by my poor Ceylon exiles."

But later in the year I fell out of sympathy with W. Blunt. 26 September, to Sir M. Grant Duff . . . "Oh, and I must tell you that Wilfrid Blunt, who has been moonlighting in Ireland in the interests of the Land League, had to leave suddenly because going there in Lent, as a good Catholic he was expected to fast like his entertainers, but just like the stork and the fox, they made up with whiskey punch, while he (being a Mohammedan teetotaller) was set down to salt cod and cold water, and even on feast days he was not much better off as he won't touch the flesh of the pig, on religious grounds. So having lived on tea and toast for a fortnight his nerves broke down, and he has had to make a rush for Paris, and spend his time at the best restaurants, and now he feels well enough to begin a fresh campaign."

But a little later from Coole I wrote to W.S.B. . . . "I am glad that you are concerned with foreign politics on which I can agree with you better than on Irish, though I rather suspect we are at heart agreed, only we have never quite patience to get below the surface. Perhaps some long winter afternoon we may talk it out if you are in England next winter. We go to London on the 1st November. Here, we are rather at the back of the North Wind, reading exciting Irish news in the papers and living such a still, peaceful life, we are yet on most cordial terms with our people—but we mustn't boast too much till rent day comes.

"I have been entertaining schoolboys all the summer, my most welcome guests, and have never been a dozen miles away from home since we arrived . . . I hope your new poems are soon to appear, Lord Dufferin in another letter to Sir Wm. writes very appreciatively of them. I fancy he is having rather a bad time about Burma, but I really think it had to be annexed, as almost all India was originally annexed, to keep French fingers off. I wish you would write some more sonnets instead of joining Irish spoilation societies."

And in October. Coole . . . "I hope, some day or other—on the other side of the hill—we shall be in sympathy again . . . We are going to Italy for the winter. I am sorry to leave Ireland, which I love better than you do England."

From 3 St. George's Place. 29 November 1886. "I have not liked being so long without news of you, but I have been too anxious about our Irish affairs to write without mentioning them, and since you have taken your place 'in open rank with those who love me not' (as a landowner), I could not expect your sympathy.

"However, I had a telegram 'all right' from our agent on Saturday when he was to meet our tenants again (we had offered 15 per cent. out of excess of goodwill on the very low rents, and after the rise in prices, and they had refused, after a speech of Dillon's, to pay unless they got off 28 per cent.) so I hope all goes well, and that we shall avoid war, which we should go into, perhaps with heavy hearts, but certainly with clear consciences.

"I must condole with you on not being in Ireland just now, you would have such a good chance of imprisonment. They would hardly refuse to lock you up if you took Dillon's place and made violent speeches, and as Kinglake observed of you yesterday 'there is a fire about Mr. Blunt which must command a following'. And think what letters you could write from prison, and you would have time to finish all your poems! I shall never believe in your renunciation of politics, you must come back to them and to hunting as the excitement your nature needs. Perhaps even in Italy you may find a secret society—you, 'the sworn poet of every rebel the world over'—to take your place in! . . . One hears little here, except the scandals connected with those cases the Campbell and S., and everyone concerned in them seems to have hands not over clean—that encourages them, perhaps, to throw so much mud at each other.

"Lady Dorothy Nevill was at Hatfield a few days ago and

met Randolph Churchill, who was in the most vile humour. He had to apologise to Lady Salisbury afterwards by saying he was in a bad temper . . . Neither he nor Mr. Matthews nor Lord Salisbury had the least idea that Dillon was to be proceeded against, the step was taken quite independently of the Irish Executive. I doubt that it was the wisest step to take, but it was necessary that something should be done to prove the existence of a Government. I hear the Vatican has suffered so much by supporting Legitimacy and Conservatism (Bourbons, etc.) that it is going to throw its lot in with revolution in future, so you will be quite in your proper sphere in Rome! . . . I am busy with good works, my Saturday Natural History parties for little Southwark boys are a great success, and I have as usual a Christmas tree on my hands. I shall miss your beautiful Crabbet tree this year. We dine with the Wentworths this week and I may hear something of you. I met your cousin, Mr. Webb, at dinner but I don't think he is in your confidence.

"I won't write any more now, as you may have taken a vow not to read letters, for aught I know."

11 January 1887. "Lord Randolph's resignation was a tremendous excitement. He had not been having his own way in the Cabinet and says that, though Lord Salisbury always supported him, Smith and the others wanted to shove him out. He had threatened to resign but was not believed until the night when he arrived at *The Times* office, asked to see Buckle and announced his resignation. Buckle instantly had every door locked, and no one was allowed to leave the office until morning, lest any other paper should get hold of it. The Queen first heard of it from Princess Beatrice, who read it in *The Times,* and Lord Salisbury got the telegram announcing it, in the middle of a ball at Hatfield, when he was sitting on a sofa by the Duchess of Marlboro', who has been in tears ever since. Randolph will be able to turn it to account with 'the masses' that he resigned in the effort to save them taxation, but he is at present very low and Lady Dorothy says she wishes he would resign every day, he is so gentle and pleasant. Sir Fitzjames Stephens gave him a great rating in her presence, and he took it very well and said 'if anyone had spoken to me like that before I had taken the step, it might have prevented me'."

(At a little dinner at the Ricardos' someone who had just been with Randolph and advising him to moderation, told me his answer had been "I have never done·anything spirited in my life that it hasn't been said by my friends 'Well, Randolph has done for himself this time'—and yet I have kept my head pretty well up." This is rather sad to remember now.)

"I hear Goschen is very happy in having at last found a place to suit him. Sir William said to Matthews, 'I suppose he ought to have some other Liberals in the Government to back him up should he disagree with you'. 'No danger of that,' said Matthews, 'he knows all our intentions and approves of them—unless, indeed, he may find us too radical!'

"I had a pleasant letter from Sir Alfred Lyall yesterday. He is one of the very few officials who confess to regret on leaving India."

11 January 1887. "I am the most ungrateful of women in not having written long ago to thank you for the beautiful tree which duly arrived for Christmas, and which became a centre of happiness for 600 children. For having, with only Kinglake's help, given my usual entertainment to my 300 Holborn children, I felt like the man whose gun only wanted a new stock lock and barrel—for there was the tree and it only wanted complete refurnishing to give a happy Christmas to 300 other children of a wretched Southwark parish which I have very much in my heart; so having been offered some help for my first tree, I refused it for Holborn, but took it with the other hand for Southwark, and both were very successful. I had a good deal of hard work, however, and had to sit up till the small hours making sweet bags and dressing dolls, and my correspondence was interrupted for a time. Lady Dartrey says there is something distinctly immoral in Penny Dinners, both Lady Colin and Mrs. Craufurd have been interested in them, but that Xmas trees are quite harmless. I hear the Duke of Argyll is determined to bring the C.C.[3] case on again, and the Queen has refused a knighthood for Butt, who had his name down for it, in consequence of his partial summing up. Six of the jury were for and six against her, but when they were locked up two of the latter were the first to grow hungry and went over, and the others saw no good in holding out. The Duke of Marlboro' says plaintively, 'It seems that in future I am to be the John Doe of the Divorce Court!'."

3 March 1887. "'What do people say about Egypt?'

3 Lord Colin Campbell's divorce case was heard by Mr. Justice Butt.

Nothing, it has for the moment been completely forgotten; you know what London people are, how one idea only can occupy their minds, and that idea is now in politics, Ireland, and in daily life by what excuses they can best get off subscribing to the various Jubilee funds. (You, I know, are exempt, belonging to the White Rose League.) But perhaps by the time you come back there will be an opening to speak about Egypt again . . . There is but little news. Lord Salisbury is said to be getting into bad health, eating a great deal and taking no exercise. Parnell is said to have cancer in the stomach, Trevelyan to have been well rated by Chamberlain for his weakness. In fact, there is no Happy Warrior anywhere in politics, unless it be the G.O.M. himself, who was lost the other night but unfortunately found again—in a fog.

"Nothing startling from India, the Mohammedans are growing fashionable there, Lord Dufferin and others write of their loyalty. You see the Nizam has been given another dry nurse, and Cordery is staying on another year to superintend his education.

"I wonder if Egypt will be opened to you. I don't see why you should be shut out of it and allowed to go to Ireland." January 1887. "Lord Iddlesleigh's death has been the great and only sensation. I went to see Kinglake, who was laid up with gout, and I said 'the papers are so hard up for news they are placarding a speech of the Prince of Wales in the Imperial Institute'; and an hour later, on my way home, Lord I's death was being cried. The real truth was this: all the Ministers had offered to resign and facilitate negotiations with Goschen, Lord Salisbury decided to accept Lord I's, who was really growing as unfit for the work as Granville always was. He went home intending to write and break it to him, but feeling tired, said 'I'm not up to it tonight, I'll do it in the morning'—(a warning against procrastination). In the morning it was in all the papers, and Lord I. saw it hours before he received the official intimation. Lord S. said to J. Northcote, 'Oh, your father won't mind, he's so kind'; but he did mind, and Mrs. Jeune tells me she had a most heart-broken letter from him after it. It was tragic his bringing his death to Lord Salisbury's door, and Lord S., a curious thing at his age, had never seen death before, and was terribly upset.

"Lady C. has been to dine at Mrs. Jeune's, where all the

men looked at her as if they wished they had been co-respondent. Ouida was invited but refused indignantly, remarking
that in her opinion 'Lady C. was an *edition de luxe* of all
the deadly sins' . . .

"My mind and time are a good deal occupied with the
troubles of the poor in that wretched Southwark district
where I had my second Xmas tree. Our Irish poor, with
their potatoes and turf and flannel and wholesome peat smoke
are in luxury compared to these wretched creatures, living,
whole families, in one tiny damp room with no fire in the
grate and no food in the cupboard. It is not fashionable
like the East End and has had little help from outside.

"I have just seen your letter in *The Times* . . . I told you
the Pope was going to make friends with Democracy. There
is always something that awakes sympathy with Communism
—at a distance. I have a feeling even for the Socialists here;
but I would be glad to save my child's heritage from
covetous hands in Ireland."

Ca Capello, Venice. 29 October 1887. (After his arrest) . . .
"Oh, I can jest about it in writing, but the whole troublesome time is very near my heart. I remember you once
saying when we were hopeful about Egypt, 'Fancy the time
coming when there will be no Egyptian news in the daily
papers!' Will the time ever come when Ireland will have
no dark column?"

Rome. 10 December 1887 . . . "I am more sorry than ever to
have left Ireland, as I should have had the pleasure of seeing
you at Coole and saved you from that Gort Hotel—but
perhaps after all it would have compromised you to have
slept under a landlord's roof! . . . I am sure this long
canvassing of the English voters (who are not so responsive
and quick-witted as those of Ireland) must be wearing . . .
In spite of your bringing one more Gladstonian vote into
the House, I should like to see you there at last, especially
as I don't think you will always be a rose in the G.O.M.'s
buttonhole but rather a thorn in his side. Who would have
believed three years ago that 'les étrangleurs d'Egypt' would
have been your supporters now? But I don't think the better
of them for it, feeling it is all for the sake of the party.
Oh! how grateful we should have been in those days for
one word of the sympathy that is lavished on you now!

"I have little to say of myself, I always hate this trans-
planting process, and have not put out any roots here yet,
and Ireland and my child are very near my heart, which

Rome has not touched . . . What a wretch Clanricarde is,
and can't you spare us a little pity for having him held up as
a typical Irish landlord? My little Robert is in Galway, if
you go there free you must go and see him."

Rome. March 1888 . . . "This is only to welcome you from
prison to the free air! When it has been wet and cold I
have thought how dreary your cell must be, and when the
sun has shone I have wished that you could enjoy it, and
Oh! I shall be so glad when you are on the right side of
the wall again.

"For Deptford what can I say? I confess that my first
thought when I heard of the defeat was not for you but for
Lady Anne. I had lain awake on the polling night, *feeling*
her anxiety and the strain on her mind . . . Fancy the
whirligig of time having brought Mrs. Gladstone to Deptford
to canvass for you."

Coole. 5 June 1888 . . . "I am glad my sketches (of his cell)
pleased you. I had great difficulty—even I—in getting into
the prison. There are very strict anti-visitor rules enforced
now, but I was determined to see your place of abode. There
was a young man in your cell for three months, for assault,
picking oakum and looking pretty cheerful.

". . . I met Lady Anne Daly, wife of one of the Visiting
Justices, yesterday and she told me that her husband had
gone to see you in Galway Gaol fully determined that you
should suffer the utmost penalty the law admitted of for your
misdeeds, but he had come back quite fascinated by you,
and others have told me the same thing. See what a dangerous enemy you are to have as one's dearest foe!

". . . I have had a very troubled week, for the night before
my return the police made a raid and several supposed
moonlighters were arrested, and every day brings some of
their relatives to my door appealing to my sympathy and
expecting me to effect a release in some way. Two of them
are our tenants, and one at the door of Galway Gaol after
a 'Star Chamber' inquiry called out to his brother in the
crowd 'Go to Lady Gregory to help us!' But I had already
done what I could, for I think he is innocent and every day
I hope to hear of his release." (He was released, and when
his mother asked him if he had been frightened when he
was in the dock, he said, "Not at all, when I saw the Magistrate reading a letter with Coole Park, Gort, on the top—.")

Coole. 29 August 1888 . . . "I scarcely say what I have
been doing . . . For one thing, trying to have as tempting

dinners for Sir William as those produced by our late cook,
who had twice the wages, more than twice the help and not
half the work of our present one (for we have followed the
prevailing fashion and reduced our establishment); and
spending much time with Robert searching in the long
grass for his lately lost pocket-knife . . . The poor people
come to the door daily, believing that I can cure them of all
diseases, including poverty, and I mix their cough-cures
and buy their flannel and dye it with madder in an iron
pot, and altogether I am at present one of the happy people
without a history. I asked Robert, 'why will your knife be
like a Land Leaguer when we find it?' and he replied,
'Because it will be Blunt', and so it will if this rain lasts.
The winter evenings, with fires and window curtains drawn,
have begun *before* dinner now, and yesterday I found a
Christmas rose which had mistaken the season and put forth
a flower . . . Now duty calls me, in the rain, to go and call
on the wife of a 'Removable Magistrate' just arrived. I
suppose I should escape that under Home Rule."
St. G.'s Place. 14 November 1888 . . . "Not much new at the
Parnell trial. I heard from someone who was in the house
with Sir R. Webster last Sunday that he is very much pleased
so far with the course it has taken. Sir G. Russell, on the other
hand, loses his temper perpetually and the President has
had to give him toko. They say he is the best man in the
world to win a case, but a very bad man to lose one, as he
loses control of himself also; but it is also said that he
irritates the Judge on purpose, so that if he does lose the
case he can say it was tried before a partial tribunal and
point to the snubs given him as proof . . ."
24 November 1888. "You show great confidence in me in
having your prison poems entrusted to my hands. Should I
not be doing a notable service to the Unionist cause by
mutilating them? The poems themselves read extremely
well and I am sure will be a great success. I like the most
personal of the sonnets best, such as the contrast between
your own reception of your guests and the reception of you
in prison, but I like best of all the later part of the Canon
of Aughrim . . . Sir William says the Canon is wonderfully
good 'and will do a great deal of mischief', which I know is
the compliment you will really care for! Kegan Paul sent
me the etching of your portrait a few days ago. I took it
back to him and said I thought it a libel. It looks like a
picture of a villain, but that you wouldn't mind, but the

lip projects in an extraordinary way, as if you had been in the habit of smoking a long clay pipe that had caused a permanent malformation. K.P. was horrified when I pointed it out though he hadn't noticed it before, and said it should be remedied . . . I don't think London would amuse you much now . . . The witnesses in the Parnell case have grown monotonous, their one idea is to give as little information as possible, and wisely, for the priests read the evidence aloud after Mass to the congregations in Ireland when a neighbour has been examined. I hear that when Gladstone was on the war trail he had all the secret evidence connecting the League with the murder collected and printed to be made use of later, but when he turned to 'love his enemies', he destroyed all the twenty copies printed except three which had disappeared, and of these one has been sold to *The Times* (what a subject for a picture, the G.O.M. consuming them at his midnight fire!). Labby says, 'I can't make up my mind about the letters. I asked Tim Healy if Parnell had written them and he said, 'The cur—he never had the pluck'. Sir Henry James came from the House the other night to dinner where we were (Lord Northbrook's) and said Healy had been making a very eloquent speech, and after the plaudits had said to a friend, 'the mistake this Parliament makes is taking us seriously', which indeed there is some truth in. Balfour told Billy Russell that when this Irish trial is over he means to leave Parliament and politics altogether and study theological questions. However, you and the G.O.M. have made similar resolutions and I don't expect the three will ever meet in a monastery . . . Randolph had an immense meeting of his constituents because they expected an exciting attack on the Government, and were indignant when he only blessed it.

"We dine out a good deal, and I find pleasure in the shifting society and quick interchange of speech, if not of ideas, in London life after the long absence. I met several Anglo-Indians at dinner at the Tennants' the other night, Sir Alfred Lyall, Sir Lepel Griffin, Sir Redvers Buller, Sir Edwin Arnold, etc. I don't think any one of them liked meeting the others. Edwin Arnold was near me and grumbled, said he liked small dinners better. 'The other night I was at a dinner where we were only five. Three of us were duchesses!'

"Kinglake came to see me the other day from Richmond and is the first person I have met who is excited over the 'revelations' in the Parnell trial, which seem very ancient history to us. He had been losing his hold on the news of the day during the later years of his history, and now that he has done with it, has taken to the newspapers, reads every word of the Commission and thinks it a most extraordinary thing that Ireland should have been in such a condition for so long, and expects the English electors to be stirred to the depths by such startling disclosures! Wentworth Beaumont told me of a dinner last year, at I forget whose house, where the Gladstones and Z's were among the guests. When dinner was announced, the G.O.M. was seen violently remonstrating with his hostess, and after some confusion they went down, Lady M. Beaumont, to her surprise, being handed in by Gladstone instead of Lord Crewe who she had expected. It turned out he had absolutely refused to sit next Lady Z. on the ground of invincible dullness!

"Laurence Oliphant you know, is very ill, cancer in the lungs, and is pronounced incurable by the doctors, but under the treatment of a mesmerist, who has come to him from Haifa, he has (for the moment) made a wonderful recovery and expects to get to Syria again. I hear from Rome, on rather good authority, that the Pope's intellect is at last being touched by old age (so the Galway priest who said, 'Sure, they say he's doting' as an excuse for not obeying the rescript against boycotting wasn't so far wrong); and that he has an absolute mania about having a Legation in England, and is very sore with the Government for doing nothing towards it.

"We have summer weather still, a great thing for the poor. I take my Saturday ragamuffins to the Natural History Museum still, and am already preparing for Christmas trees, a double labour now I haven't poor Revol to dress dolls, but I can't bear to see children toyless in London at Christmas, when the shops are made so tempting.

"Poor Laurence Oliphant was not saved by his Syrian. I hear he was confident of recovery to the last, and was amusing himself by drawing the doctors out and keeping a daily diary of what he considered their quackery. It is sad for the Grant Duffs having a death in their house when their children are home for Christmas.

"I heard last week the two worst speeches I have ever heard in my life, at the opening of a sale of work. One was delivered by Lord B. and was as awkward and ungracious as it was possible to make it, however, it was mitigated by a cheque for £10. The other speaker was the new member, and never have I had such a belief in the strength of Unionism as in beholding him. Lockwood, Q.C., said of him that he is like 'a hearse horse at a pauper's funeral'. I asked the clergyman there what the inducement was to the very poor inhabitants of his parish to vote with 'the classes', and he says they have a great horror of the Parnellites in themselves and say, 'We don't want to have anything to do with those fellows'.

"... The Wentworths dined here the other day and were very pleasant, he especially. He said of you that you are a 'warm friend and placable enemy'. No social news, except that Courtney is setting the fashion of a reform in evening dress by appearing in a blue coat and buff waistcoat, but the result doesn't tempt imitation."

St. G's Place. 16 December 1888. "Many thanks for your Euboean letter. I am sure the calm of your visit did you good after the storms of the last year, but I thought you would have managed to take up some thread of Grecian politics and unravel it for the world. Princess Sophie is learning Greek, in preparation for her marriage, and when she received a Greek deputation the other day she had learned a sentence by heart, 'I hope to meet you all again', but her courage failed when the moment came and she could only look hopelessly at her mother and stammer in English . . .

"Mr. Hurlburt says somebody has called Boulanger 'le grand ressort de la mécontentement du pays', rather a happy expression; but he thinks he must be going to lose, or you would not have taken up his cause! Everyone is talking of Lord Salisbury's 'black man'. The indignation it has caused in society shows how much more interest has been taken of late in Indian affairs, Lord Northbrook deplores it as, coming at the same time as Lord Dufferin's speech, it looks like a deliberate attempt to irritate the natives. One or two 'black' friends from Hyderabad, Mehdi Hassan and Moureddin, have been to see me and are furious about it, and I have to sympathise and say how aggrieved I had felt when Lord Salisbury called us Irish 'Hottentots'. I was at an amusing debate on the vote for the Irish Police on Monday, all the 86 attacking Balfour who was quite alone on the Treasury bench and seemed rather to enjoy it. I thought O'Brien's oratory more suited to rouse a mob than Dillon's. And Mrs. Peel, whom I had tea with, agreed and said, 'When I hear

him speak I feel that if I were an Irishwoman I would go
out and break windows'. It struck me that the Irish members
listened with hardly concealed contempt to the laboured
speeches of their English allies on their behalf. They had
said the same thing so often and so much better themselves.
G. Lefevre gave a long account of his experience and wound
up by saying a school inspector in Ireland had been reprimanded from the Castle for having had an interview with
him. Balfour, in answering, said he had never heard of the
occurrence, and if he had would certainly not have
reprimanded the inspector 'but would have considered it
had carried with it its own penalty'. This was received with
roars of delight from the Tories and a sympathetic grin
from the Irish benches. I have also been to the Parnell trial.
It was very touching to see our poor western peasants
brought straight from their cabins to the turmoil of the
court, to tell of the cruel mercies of the countrymen. One
poor man told of the murder of his son by Moonlighters, but
the pathos of his story didn't save him from being tormented
by his examiners. But perhaps you wouldn't mind! Childers
dined here last night and says when he was staying in the
house with you he heard sentiments that shocked him from
your lips. But he is a very mild Home Ruler, never approved
of the Plan of Campaign, and says he told his colleagues it
was wicked, which they didn't mind, and that it wouldn't
succeed, to which they paid more attention. We dined at the
Wentworths a few days ago very pleasantly. She was beautifully dressed in white watered silk, and didn't yawn once,
and Sir Wm. was very much taken with Lord Wentworth's
charming, courteous manner, just like Lady Anne's. G.
Lefevre tells me Lady Anne was much more popular
amongst the Irish Nationalists than you, they thought you
'too aristocratic'. I was interrupted here by a visit from Sir
Edwin Arnold, he says he has just written an article for
The Telegraph imploring the Government to treat with,
rather than fight the Arabs. I was quoting those verses of *The
Wind and the Whirlwind* to him: 'Thou wentest to this
Egypt for thy pleasure; thou shalt remain with her for thy
sore pain' (which is being translated into reality these days)
and he spoke very warmly of you, your poetic talent and
your having defended Arabi at your own cost. He dined last
night at the Tennants to meet Gladstone, who talked of
nothing but the Divorce Laws and is against divorce, but
thinks if allowed by law it should be for men and women

alike. Sir J. Mackinnon, the head of the East African Company, was there to meet him, and they tried to draw him on that subject, but he refused to speak of it, saying, 'I can't have a finger in every pie'. He said very solemnly to Miss Tennant, 'Dorothy, when I render up my account, I do believe it will be a clear one and that I have always fulfilled my duty'. I hear Mrs. Gladstone said the other day, 'My husband is so extraordinarily accurate and precise in his statements that if it were not for his flashes of genius his conversation would be quite dull at times'. I met Frederic Harrison at dinner at Mrs. Humphry Ward's. He said they had enjoyed your visit so much and you were the most delightful companion."

St. G.'s Place. Christmas Day 1888.   "This is a good day to write and thank you for my charming Xmas present, *In Vinculis,* which arrived a few days ago. I wrote to order some copies to give away (one for my mother) but it has been withdrawn for a week because of the dropped letters on page 36 . . . I think all the possessors, present and future, owe a great deal to me for having persuaded you to put the prison portrait in, it adds so much to its interest and value. It is very much improved from the first etching.

"I met Mr. Haldane, M.P., at the Arthur Russell's, and he announced as great news that you were bringing these poems out (Kegan Paul had showed them to him) and that some of the sonnets were extraordinarily good. I am looking forward to the reviews."

St. G.'s Place. 6 January 1889.   "It seems rather like writing into the air 'to one in Heaven'—imaginary letters—writing to you, as I have not heard of your arrival in Egypt . . . Colonel North, the Nitrate King, is the star of the firmament at present, and no wonder there should be a rush for the honour of his acquaintance, Sir William's solicitor asked him to dine at his Club, and the Colonel in return gave him 'tips' by which he cleared £2,000 within a week. Randolph Churchill has £20,000 shares in his undertakings and is going out to Chile with him, and invited a party to meet him at dinner, including the Prince of Wales, George Lewis and Arthur Balfour, and the Prince and his satellites have all taken shares in nitre. Needless to say, this is a far more absorbing topic of interest than the Soudan or the E. African question.

"It is you who brought Boulanger into fashion! From the day your letter appeared he has been taken more seriously,

and recognised even by Blowitz. It is a comfort the G.O.M.
is away.'

St. G.'s Place. 27 January 1889. ". . . We have heard from
Lord Dufferin at Rome. He found the Embassy looking very
small and dilapidated, every chimney smoking and no door
shutting, but now he has formed plans for its enlargement
and embellishment, which no doubt, for *him* the Treasury
will carry out, though they wouldn't spend a penny on poor
Savile . . . Old Bismarck is working heaven and earth to get
Morier out of St. Petersburg, to Rome, to which however
Dufferin intends to cling . . . I met Gennadius, the Greek
Minister, at lunch today, he told me how well you and Lady
Anne had been received at Athens.

"There are rumours of a break between Stead and the
Pall Mall, but I believe the truth is that on account of the
side he took in the Trafalgar Square riots, the chief trades-
men withdrew their advertisements from the paper and
Yates Thompson told him he must go. But he asked for six
months' grace, and it has been extended ever since, but the
sword is hanging over his head. It is curious what an admiration he has for force, and how he can't resist paying
compliments to Balfour at intervals. One of the sub-editors
described him as 'a cross between Cromwell and the penny
a liner' . . . People who have been staying at Sandringham
say nothing could equal the imprudence of the Empress in
abusing Germany and the powers that be in the presence
of the twenty eight guests in the house and the numberless
servants . . . A cold, and a long visit from Childers, must be
the excuse for the want of imagination in this letter, which I
feel is rather like the paragraph in *Truth*."

10 February 1889. "I wonder where you are now; in
warmer climes than these, I hope, for it has been snowing
all day and I have been looking out of the window at horses
slipping and at the processions marching into the Park to
protest against coercion, with portraits of the G.O.M. looking
very cold in a white shirtfront on some banners and 'Down
with Balfour' and 'Liberty and Equality' on others.

"You have really done more to divert sympathy from
William O'Brien than anyone else. I heard Lord Knutsford
—and many others— say, 'If Wilfrid Blunt didn't complain
of the clothes, why should he do so?'

"Last Sunday we spent at York House with the Grant
Duffs, where poor Laurence Oliphant died. They say his
passing away was so peaceful and painless it was a beautiful

experience they are glad not to have missed. His grey-haired wife of fifteen weeks nursed him tenderly and regretted him sincerely, but it was only a marriage of convenience for the good of 'the cause' and it would have lent a more poetic completeness to his life if they had only been associated with his beautiful first wife.

"Prince Rudolph's death has been the last sensation. (They say it was prophesied by Zadkiel—Lady H.L. in repeating this, said by *Ezekiel*.) All sorts of rumours fly about."

3 St. George's Place. 5 March 1889. "Even in the desert the excitement of the Pigott episode must have made itself felt. Here, as you may imagine, it has been a Gaboriau episode translated into reality, and all moved so fast from his first appearance to his tragic suicide that one still feels in a dream. It really seems as if the solid earth had melted beneath one's feet—the respectable, cautious, reliable, old *Times* having walked into the business and declared over and over again its ability to prove the letters genuine with no better witness than Pigott, so long discredited by all who knew him in Ireland, to bring forward. Delane would never have fallen into such a pit, he was an Irishman, and too clever.

"Chenery would not, for he would have consulted Sir William, who has always been dead against the whole affair . . . Walter had never been allowed to meddle with the paper by either of the two last editors, and so appointed Buckle, a young untried man, thinking he could have his own way now, and so he has! Lord Carnarvon says Walter and Buckle both drove over to see him last autumn and the former was in a state of nervous excitement, his pockets filled with papers which he said would enable him to win his case triumphantly but Buckle, on the other hand, was very low and didn't half like the business. We met a good many of *The Times* Counsel, etc. one evening at the Duchess of St. Albans' just before Pigott had appeared . . . The extreme Gladstonians talk of something worse than stupidity, but that is nonsense, for a plot would have been more skilfully laid. The extreme *Times*-ites on the other hand say that clearly the first batch of letters is genuine. That Pigott obtained them (he did go to New York for them, they have his ticket) just at the moment when there was a split between the extreme and Parliamentary parties, and the extremists wanted to discredit Parnell. That he tried to buy them back just at the time when the Exreme party had patched upon the difference with Parnell and had resolved to support him for the present. That from the very day of the appearance of the facsimile in *The Times* the Parnellites said it had been forged by Pigott, which they could not have known, though they did know that Egan had given him the letters and so guessed where they came from. That Labby sent Pigott to Madrid, not knowing that extradition had been quite lately introduced into a treaty, and that he had bargained for *The Times* telegram being sent as a blind. That the letters to Pigott, from which he is supposed to have traced the others were in reality the forged ones, being traced from the facsimiles. In fact, Pigott's word not counting one way or the other, one may adopt any theory that suits; but of course *The Times,* having no evidence at all, save the experts to rely on, had to abandon that part of the case, and it is thanks to their own folly that by their facsimiles and handbills more attention has been drawn to the letters than anything else, and many voters who have never read another word of the proceedings know them off by heart."

Rome. 26 April 1889. "I think this is as interesting a place as any to write to you from, and I have not your gift of writing beautiful letters from the desert. We have been here for a week, which I have enjoyed very much, partly because I have for the first time seen Rome under a blue sky and partly because I have done my sightseeing with so charming a companion as Sir Alfred Lyall . . . I hear that the Pope's mind is decidedly weakening, and that (perhaps in consequence) he is lending a more favourable ear to the Irish Revolutionary party. Also that the quite predominant influence is French, which is of course anti-English, so it is possible that Moonlighting may yet have his consent and blessing . . . The Italians are perhaps a little less inclined to trail their coat in defiance than they were. It is said that the Emperor of Germany rather snubbed them and their army, but for all that their army is very much improved and officers better educated and men better disciplined than before, and they have been making an astonishingly strong fortified port south of Sardinia, where three fleets can shelter at once and sail forth to dispute the Mediterranean with all-comers. Lord Dufferin is very unsettled and uncomfortable at the Embassy; is alone but for Sir A. Lyall just now. We have dined there and seen a good deal of him and I think he is equally bored by his diplomatic duties and by the society, both Italian and Anglo-American, though he politely says he likes Rome, and only yawns behind his hand. He felt an immense relief and delight the day he had left Bombay and found the burden of Government fallen from his back; and enjoyed the first landing in Italy and being allowed to carry his own travelling bag. But the King and Court seem very small and one-horse to him after his own royal state.

Coole. 7 August 1889. "One of our horses has put its shoulder out, very unfortunate, as we have some enquiring English tourists here who want 'to see everything for themselves' and if not taken about think we are keeping them from native opinion, like Cordery with Lord Ripon.

Coole. 28 October 1889. "I suppose you have heard Sir E. Malet is to marry Lady E. Russell . . . He proposed and was accepted at the Marlborough House party. Bismarck, given the choice between him, Thornton and Morierand, chose *natürlich* the one with least bone and gristle—most easy to assimilate . . . I suppose we shall find London thinking of nothing but the Franchise and the Lords.

". . . Sancho Sanchez is splendid. Sir William reads it over and over and says it 'smells of Spain' . . ."

Coole. 2 October. "I have been in Galway and thought of you when I saw the gaol. Dr. Kinkhead enquired for you. He says W. O'Brien is growing fat in prison. I told him Balfour would, no doubt, give him a baronetcy if he brought him out with doubled weight! Summer has passed away very quickly and now I am living in terror of the first touch of frost, which will spoil the purple and gold of my garden. We had a nice week of Sir Alfred Lyall. His visit made up for many uninteresting tourists on the warpath."

Coole. 29 December 1889. "I admire O'Brien more than any of the revolutionists. I always feel as if Dillon was trading on his interesting white face and dark eyes. Perhaps, as Lord Houghton used to say of you, 'the fellow knows he has a handsome head and would sacrifice it if it could be shown off at the gate of the Tower'. Our 'Removable Magistrate' was here yesterday and gave me a vivid account of the infernal machine at Woodford. He was one of the party who opened the door, and for whose destruction it was set up. (I see George Lefevre, who wasn't there, denies its existence.) Don't our Irish politics seem very microscopic compared to those of Africa? What strange glimpses one gets of the conquering army with 'flames coming from the point of their spears'. Is there any communication between Egypt and the Soudan now?"

London. 5 February 1890. "I came over with Sir William at the beginning of the month and while he is on his way to Ceylon I am staying on till Easter with Robert that he may attend his day school . . . Happy you to be in sunshine. We have perpetual rain and yellow fog, and everyone is, or has been, or is going to be, ill . . . One of the few bright days was utilized by Lady E.B.'s marriage . . . As the bridegroom has already seven children for her to begin life with, the hymn which was sung praying that she might be as fruitful as an olive tree seemed rather superfluous."

Sloane Street, London. 10 March 1890. "I spent Sunday with the Grant Duffs at Twickenham. Lady G.D. was much excited at hearing of Mrs. Laurence Oliphant's marriage. A young 'disciple' used to come and see her when while Laurence was dying, and she persuaded him to break off with some girl he was engaged to, saying it would not be for his good, and now she has married him herself, she being fifty and he twenty five and very rich, the son of a carpet manufacturer.

"I sat next Lord Alcester at dinner the other night. How indignant I should have been some years ago at having to do so! and how one's feelings calm down with time. He has lost his teeth, literally as well as figuratively, and is very inarticulate . . . Having been so long in Ireland I am enjoying society very much, and cling to the London pavements with affection. I spend the mornings drawing at the Tower, with occasional lessons from an insolvent artist, a new and very fascinating pastime to me, and I haven't time for it when I have a house and husband to look after. Robert gets on well with learning and thrashed a boy bigger than himself a few days ago for calling him a liar. 'Quite right,' said Thomson Hankey, 'the only place you may stand being called a liar is in the House of Commons'."

Coole. 20 September 1890. "I am sure your thoughts have turned to Ireland now, though not to me but to Dillon and O'Brien. I am sorry the Government thought it necessary to arrest them, but I suppose it was impossible to avoid it, as they had been trailing their coats very defiantly for some time. It is quite new having to think of political things again, we have had such a quiet summer . . . Potato blight has not visited us, though I see the *Review of Reviews* has shaded us with black famine lines. Two days ago I heard that John Morley was coming to lunch. I never quite know how to treat these wandering enquirers, if we starve them they will go away in a bad humour; and if we feast them they will say, like you in India, 'The poor *ryot* was really my host!' However, I thought I couldn't go wrong in ordering the potatoes to be sent up in their skins to show how absolutely free from disease they are. But I have an engineer brother in the house, and his first request on hearing of the distinguished guest expected was 'pick out bad potatoes for him and perhaps he'll give us some money for public works'; so I find it is hard to reconcile all interests. John Morley's visit was a pleasant episode. I had never met him before. He listens to all one has to say as if quite convinced by one's arguments, but I fancy keeps his own opinion quite unchanged all the time. (And he said he would like to spend his life pacing up and down our long garden walk.) We had another enquirer. Parker Smith, M.P., the week before, but he is a born Unionist and his opinions also got through the enemy's country unscathed.

"You would not wonder at my writing such a dull letter if you knew how the rain is coming down, and the two visitors I have to entertain for the rest of the afternoon, an hysterical and aggrieved widow, and a frisky young matron whose ideas of a visit to Galway are founded on Lever's novels . . . I am trying to write a local story[4], but don't think it will come to much. It is easy enough to write 'situations' or conversation, but the trivial parts are the difficulty, getting people up and down stairs, or in and out of the house gracefully."

3 St. George's Place. 16 November 1890. "I arrived a few days ago from Ireland, and have had my hands full, chiefly of soap and dusters . . . The house had been inhabited by Lady L. and the Duchess of M., and the walls, echoed by the voice of our old housemaid, tell wild tales . . . The day after I arrived, Lord Carlisle proposed himself to dinner and I had to go out and buy tumblers, he being a water drinker. Not a single tumbler had survived the American regime. I wonder what they drank out of at the last, each other's slippers? Or if they shivered all the glasses at their last banquet that they might not be touched by other lips.

"I am in the hands of dressmakers and too shabby to pay visits, and the hall door is being painted and the bell handle

[4] It is probably the one called "Peeler Astore", which does not appear to have been published.

is off, so that visitors have to be very enterprising to gain
admission, but I hear echoes from the world without. Stanley
is in great disgrace for his revelations, so many people disliked him personally that they are delighted to have an
excuse for turning on him. No doubt, if he had been a *real*
Englishman he would have held his tongue . . . Even you
will hate the idea of the French gloating over these revelations of English barbarity, but they may do good in the
long run; explorers and settlers are let run ahead too much.
Sir Arthur Gordon says English deeds in the South Sea
Islands beat Jameson hollow . . . The undefended Parnell
case came as a surprise . . . I am amused by the *Pall Mall
Gazette* with its high moral tone, saying we mustn't connect
private actions with public life after all . . . The real
excitement has been in the City, where it was just touch and
go with Baring's Bank . . . I think they have tided over the
worst now, owing to helping hands, but as an impecunious
undergraduate said to me today, 'It is really very serious for
where are we to put our money?' . . . My first visit here was
to dear old Kinglake, a very sad one. He has been attacked
again with cancer, and suffers a good deal, morphia having
lost its effect, and one's hope must be that his strength will
fail before the disease has time to develop itself more cruelly.
He is so frail and wasted, and looks as if a gust of wind
would take him away, it seems cruel that nature should take
a sledgehammer to kill him with."

3 St. George's Place. 3 December 1890.   "You ought to be
here in the middle of this exciting fight! Parnell is going to
win, ought to win. What do you think of Dillon and O'Brien
having thrown him over at the bidding of a foreigner? . . .
I think the Radicals already regret their high moral tone
. . . I remember you saying, when the G.O.M. took up the
Irish party, 'I hope he will live to be found out', and I
thought of it when he was hissed at Cork. Anyhow, Home
Rule is knocked to pieces for some time to come, and we
whose homes are in Ireland look forward with hope to a quite
unexpected horizon of peace and quietness. And Land
Purchase will be growing while politics are sleeping, and by
the time the Home Rule idea comes up again the peasants
will be 'Haves' instead of 'Have-nots', and may safely look
after the interests of this country as well as their own. The
Government are only afraid that the H.R. idea has been so
completely smashed that the Opposition will lay it by and
take up Socialistic measures, more popular with the English

mob. The Gladstonians confess themselves too disheartened
to make any fight at all about anything . . . Parnell's friends
still declare that he has in his possession letters of Captain
O'Shea which prove connivance, but that Mrs. O'S. won't
allow them to be produced lest the Queen's Proctor should
intervene and the divorce be prevented . . . Parnell must win
when it comes to the payment of members, for he will get
more from the Clan na Gael than the dissentients will from
Childers and John Morley . . . Fog here today in which I
nearly lost myself in a charitable tour in Southwark . . ."
16 December 1890. "I don't think you could resist plunging
into the fray as a Parnellite if you were here. I am sure
O'Brien will either join him or throw up the sponge. He
could never bear to be less revolutionary than Parnell and
take the side of loyal moderation. The Raffaloviches say he
has been for some time anxious to give up politics and lead
a literary life in Paris, where he is made a great deal of.
His wife has quite forsaken them and thinks only of tying
a handkerchief round his neck when it is cold, and giving
him egg flip when he is hoarse. The Anti-P.'s are furious
with Healy, and say all could have been arranged but for
his violence. What he actually called out at the meeting,
that made Parnell so angry was 'The Queen's Proctor won't
let you have your Kitty after all'. Gladstone confessed to
Knowles last week that he is fairly bewildered by the Irish
question now; and the members of his ex-Cabinet whom he
was supposed to have consulted before writing the letter,
have turned on him and say they know nothing of it, only
thought there was to be a hint quietly given to Parnell that
his withdrawal would be acceptable. Rich Gladstonians are
afraid of being asked for subscriptions and are cooling off.
George Lefevre came to see me on Sunday, looking so cast
down I had not the heart to tease him. He confesses thirty
of the Anti-P.'s were paid members, and there is only enough
money in hand to support them for six months, and though
he and others would subscribe to an evicted tenants' fund,
they are unwilling to do so for a Parliamentary one. He is
rather offended at your not having sent him a 'New
Pilgrimage' or called on him in the summer. I told him I
would tell you. John Morley goes to Ireland this week as
witness in the Police v. Harrison case, and the whole
situation is farcical—he is going (or was) to abuse the Police
who will now probably have to protect him, and to assert
the innocence of 'the stripling Harrison, who Parnell has

just announced to have choked three policemen in Tipperary."

Coole. 13 July 1890. "I see in our local paper that even a late leader of the Land League who used to attend the meetings on horseback, 'a drawn sword in his hand and a green sash over his shoulder', has grabbed a farm and yet lives . . . I hope I shall see your play some day, what a different birthplace it is having from that of the prison sonnets. You are at home in more places than anyone I know, prisons and palaces and deserts. I think where you are quite out of your element is in trying to feel fellowship with English Radicals."

3 St. George's Place. 26 January 1891. "The Wentworths dined here last night, I like him very much indeed, he is so very much in earnest and thinks a subject out so thoroughly, I was afraid he might be put out by Lord Morris's denunciations of the Nationalists, but he took it very good humouredly (he said to me afterwards 'I could never be put out by anything that is said in this house') . . .

"It was extraordinary, the Duke of Bedford's suicide being kept a secret for so long, even his brother, Lord Arthur, did not know it till he read it in the papers. Sir Henry Thompson says he suffered terrible pain and had often said to him he would rather put an end to himself than continue to live a life of pain. And Sir Henry probably encouraged him, as he approves of suicide in cases of hopeless illness, and was telling me a little time ago that a friend of his who had an incurable disease, confided to him that he was starving himself to death, and he advised quicker and less painful means; and next morning his friend was found dead. Poor Kinglake used to say to his nurse, 'Don't let me linger at the end', but the last ten days of his life were painless and almost unconscious. The last time I saw him he wrote in the evening, 'I am in bed and in pain but cannot yet quell the glow of my gratitude for your visit this morning and the delight it brought me'—and then for the first time his words grew rather wandering, and the nurse had to end it.

"His executors have sent me two of the swords—Spanish duelling swords—from his little collection, by his wish. I went to the service before he was taken to Woking, but though in theory I approve of cremation my feeling all day was a terribly painful one—it seemed as if violence was being used to destroy the helpless body, and for days after I could not get it out of my mind.

"I heard from Lord Dufferin yesterday. Very proud of having come in one of four at the death after a run on the Campagna—one of the best he ever had in his life—seven rail fences—two stone walls. His horse rolled down a bank, but his Irish blood was up and he left most of the field behind.

"We met Labby at dinner . . . He affects a mock sanctimonious manner and says he has joined the purity party, and that his cry is now 'the good Old Man and the good Old Book'.

"It is curious how unpopular X.Y. is. Freddy Leveson dined here the other night and said he wondered at our asking wicked Gladstonians like himself and George Russell. I said we had not quarrelled with anyone all through the struggle, not even with X.Y. He said, 'That fellow. I have often felt inclined to quarrel with him myself,' and George Russell told me, with great gusto, that X.Y. was bitterly complaining of having been asked to take the chair at a meeting of General Booth's at Bradford lately, which he did to please his constituents, and the General was so eloquent that 'some confounded fellow' got up and promised him £100 and others began doing the same, and then the General said, 'Now, Mr. X., you won't be outdone by your supporters' and he could only gasp and say, 'I'll speak to you after the meeting' and then gave him £20, which looked mean, yet was more than he liked parting with . . . I am sure the secret of Booth's success is his absolute faith, first in Christianity and then in himself and his mission, just at a time when the Church of England clergy are a little shaky as to how much they believe he attracts, as a solid body has more power of attraction than a nebulous one. The spread of agnosticism is very rapid, so that there is difficulty in finding good University men to fill the ranks in the Church; and I notice from year to year even that unbelief in revealed religion is avowed more and more in society—a great pity, for why disturb the faith that remains? I called on Mrs. Lynn Lynton the other day, and during a mere morning visit she made a violent attack on Christianity and even its moral teaching, but not many go as far as that, and I hope never to see her again. There was something ridiculous—if it had not pained me—in her asserting with perfect confidence that there was no mystery in our being and no divinity anywhere, and that she could confidently assure me that this visible world is *all*.

Coole. 8 October 1891. "The proofs of the Morris book arrived this morning and I now return them. Don't think I have not read them with a careful and critical eye by my finding so little to correct. They are beautifully printed and I see you have already searched them. On page 13 'Exstasy' should be either 'extasy' or 'ecstacy'; Spenser uses the former, Shakespeare the latter, but neither 'xs'. See also 'exstatic' on page 19 . . . The volume will be beautiful in itself . . . Sir William took Robert over to school and is just back. I was almost broken-hearted at losing him, everything is so silent without his bright little presence, I could not bear to stay here and paid some visits; one to Lord Morris, on the Atlantic coast. I met there Lord Ashbourne's eldest son, who has just become a R. Catholic, a curious result of the study of philosophy at Oxford, which generally leads to agnosticism."

Coole. 27 May 1891. "I am so glad to have had that day at Crabbet . . . Those young ladies seemed much pleased with their visit and said they would have liked to stay a week. Poor Lady Anne if they had—though I am sure she would have been as gracious and charming and self-forgetting as she always is to her guests . . . I am afraid Judith would despise me if she knew I liked looking at her better than at the horses."

Coole. 25 August 1891. "All our county is for Parnell, as far as words go, but they will probably vote with the priests. I am reading through John Morley's biographies—they charm me—but certainly he and the priests are strange bedfellows to have been brought together by circumstances . . . Robert is clamouring for me to bowl to him, but only indoor cricket today, there is heavy rain.

4 October 1891. "Parnell's death and funeral impress the imagination, and I should think will drive O'Brien from politics (had Zimri peace who slew his master?), though Dillon is more tainted by his intercourse with English politicians and may hold on. Parnell may not be beaten yet but we may 'see a dead man win a fight' as happened before now."

St. George's Place. 29 November 1891. "I feel as if I ought to write and condole with you on Lord Lytton's death, you will miss him so much and feel the severing of your long friendship. That appreciation he wrote (in the *XIXth Century*) and you valued, did you good in the eyes of the world, though as a poet he was far behind you; but as Dr.

Johnson said gratefully of someone, 'he praised me at a time when praise was of value to me' . . . You had been staying so lately at the Paris Embassy too, it must have been a shock to you . . . Everyone is wondering if Dufferin will take it. He had been telling his friends he would not, but that was before the vacancy."

3 St. George's Place. 6 December 1891. "We have had such warm weather here we might, had we sunshine, be as well off as you in Egypt, but the mud is dreadful, though I find the long dresses now in fashion are easier to keep out of it than the so-called short ones. Your tail over your arm; a frill round your petticoat and your poultry yard round your neck, and you are in the height of fashion. I met Lord Wentworth at the Victorian Exhibition, such a vulgar, dull collection; the pictures of Royal weddings and baptisms really the most cheerful part, as they make one think good looks are really more prevalent than a generation ago.

"I am resting a little from charitable work just now, and have been out to lunch and sat between Froude and George Russell, Froude comfortably chuckling over Lecky's poems with something of the 'Oh, that mine enemy had written a book!' feeling. G. Russell was cutting at John Morley, says he won't quarrel with the G.O.M. as he is completely subservient to him. I said, 'What would he do if Gladstone wished him to come to early Communion?' and he said he would even do that, and he hears it said his religious attitude has quite changed under the influence of his leader. Mr. Edward Ponsonby, the Speaker's secretary, has just been here, believes the Government will dribble time away till Easter, then lay their Local Government Bill on the table and dissolve, as they are as strong now as they are likely to be and don't want to waste time quarrelling with their own supporters, as will be the case over that Bill . . .

"I sold Irish blackthorns, 'in view of the approaching General Election', at a bazaar at Holborn, with great success. Princess Louise bought one, I hope she used it on Lord Lorne for the bad opening speech he made."

3 St. George's Place. 19 January 1892. "Have you shed a tear over poor Tewfik's grave? I can't be sorry for him, though I fancy he was well punished in his last years of bondage for his early stupidities. His death is rather welcomed here as a ladder down which Gladstone can scramble backwards from his evacuation speech."

3 St. George's Place. 27 December 1891. "You have been
lucky being in sunshine during this past week. I never
remember five consecutive days of fog before . . . It was hard
on Robert, too, in his holidays, but we got to St. James's
Park for skating and I sat on an iron rail with my feet on
the ice, while he flashed past me now and then and disappeared in the fog. I had your beautiful tall tree from
Crabbet, and it did duty first at Southwark and then at
Holborn."

Here are some of Mr. Blunt's letters. They at least are
very legible; his clear handwriting has never needed the
intervention of that machine which Henry James finds so
many strange and elusive ways of avoiding to name (yet
when once I said to him that I thought people were ceasing
to be offended at receiving a typed letter he answered, with
unusual vigour and directness, "whether they like it or not
they will get nothing else from me"). But although Wilfrid
Blunt wrote once with some indignation of a letter from
Yeats (and of which I myself had been the guilty typist)
that while liking the matter, "the manner of it, typewriting,
rather 'enraged me'"; he never grumbled when I myself, in
my later years, took up the new fashion.

And it was not only to date his letters he learned in his
diplomatic life. He gained in it the intimate knowledge that
has been of so great use to him in his work for troubled
nations, of the inner springs and wheels, the power of the
Chancelleries and their weaknesses. He went early to this
school, almost straight from boyhood, to be at attaché at the
Court of the King of Greece, of a Queen Regnant of Spain,
at the Tuilleries in the third Napoleon's shining days. And
so, he has ever found old friends and comrades in European
capitals to give him a helping hand, as did those Wyndhams,
Curries, Bourkes and the rest, of whose cousinship he has
made good use at home.

Wilfrid Blunt's letters.

He recalls the trouble of youth:—

Crabbet Park. 17 April 1883. "When I was at Cintra I was
in my most poetical phase—very unhappy and very desirous
of being happy. I was constantly expecting a letter from a
person to whom I was attached, which did not come, and I
consoled myself with running about the hills with some
young ladies, or carousing on the Peña with Don Fernando
and his unmarried spouse, the intervals being spent with
Lytton, a most charming companion, and writing verses. He

was the first person who ever told me I was a poet—and I really think that he (and I suppose the young ladies) saved me from committing suicide from the top of the pinnacles, so very unhappy I was. I can smell the musty damp walls of Mrs. Lawrence's hotel now as I write, and hear some children who used to drive me distracted by singing under the windows. On the whole, I don't regret youth. I am far happier now.

"You must not mind if I write about myself. If I stopped to think what I should say about other people and other things you would have no letter. We have had bright, sunny weather ever since you left, a little cold, but pleasant, and today it is heavenly with a soft south wind. There are sixteen nests of rooks now, and Judith has just caught three fish with me in the boat. You don't know what it is to be the father of an only daughter, so you will not understand how I am wrapped up in this child. She is the only person I feel afraid of, and I suppose that is the reason."

He turns from politics to poetry:—
Crabbet. 3 April 1883. "I am at sea without you what to do about Arabi . . . It is useless my trying, as questions in the House of Commons are worse than useless, and I cannot move anybody to bring the thing forward in the House of Lords. Lord Wemyss could do it, however, and you could move Lord Wemyss . . . I am in the meanwhile living at home very happy with Judith, and making a pretence of writing poetry. But the wheels of my chariot are so rusty from disuse that I have actually done nothing beyond planning my poem. The plan, however, is something and as I have not promised to finish it by any particular date I do not yet despair. It is to be a tale of love and politics in which the politics will be more passionate than the love and the love more philosophical than the politics. But we shall see —unless it all ends, as it very likely may—in a vast number of sheets thrown into the fire because of the impossibility of getting things to rhyme. I have been reading at Knebworth to my great satisfaction Mrs. Carlyle's letters. I think them quite the best ever written in English except one or two . . ."

The Wind and the Whirlwind.
10 James Street. 18 August 1883. "Since I wrote last I have been at Knebworth and Buckhurst and other places. At Knebworth I read my 'Egyptian' poem to Lord Lytton and he gave me a title for it which I think is a good one. *The*

Wind and the Whirlwind, and as such it is being put in type, as you will see by the specimen page just sent me. As there is so little of it it will be large type, and Lytton says it will do an infinity of harm! ... Arabi has just sent me his answers to my questions which are very satisfactory, as it appears from them that Dufferin took the few sensible ideas in his famous dispatch from Arabi."

The same.
Naworth. 27 August 1883. "I am enjoying myself much here as there is a very large and very cheerful family, and I am allowed to write from morning till night if I feel so inclined—or I can take diversion shooting or driving or conversing . . . My poem, however, they think would do harm. But I intend in any case to have it ready to fire off on the proper occasion. I have written two new verses, or rather rewritten verses omitted. They are to insert after verse 38 as follows: —

> Did ye not hear it? From those muffled windows
> The sound of wailing rises and of mirth.
> These are our daughters—ay, our sons in prison
> Captives to shame with those who rule the earth.

> The silent river by those gardens lapping
> Tonight receives its burden of new dead
> A man of age sent home with his lord's wages
> Stones to his feet, a gravecloth to his head.

He would follow the swallows:
Crabbet. 11 September 1883. "These are my last hours at home, and as I have a few minutes to spare I employ them in wishing you good-bye. I confess I am not sad this time at the thought of going. I have been so long away from the East that I feel as the swallows are doing at this moment, and could go with or without that provision of Daddy-long-legs which Judith assured me they carry with them under their wings when they go. Only, this cheerfulness must certainly be an evil omen, and if I had not made a new codicil to my will and rearranged my papers I should feel certain that I was going for ever."

His illness in Ceylon:
Madras. 20 November 1883. "I wrote to nobody, from Colombo. I was really ill and at one time hoped to die there and be made a Mohammedan saint. But this was not to be,

and I got well, through the influence of a little bag containing some verses of the Koran rolled in a peculiar gum and tied round my arm by Arabi . . . I left Colombo in a blaze of fireworks and the odour of sanctity which I never felt before but which was real . . . Sir William has an immense reputation in Ceylon, equalling that of the late Lord Mayo in India . . . I am setting very quietly to work to get information, and I shall say nothing or express any opinion till I have been through the three Presidencies . . . There is no doubt the English rule has done a great deal of good in past years, but the child has almost had enough of schooling and some of his clothes are quite too tight for him."

An Indian Parnell.

Calcutta. 18 December 1883. "What a capital idea sending the *Wind and the Whirlwind* about the world. I am distributing it here to convert India—but India wants no converting. They all believe in Arabi as a hero, Hindus as well as Mohammedans. You cannot think how successful our tour had been hitherto. Wherever we go the people come up to us in spite of the officials . . . I am to see Lord Ripon privately tomorrow. I fear, poor man, he is rather weak-kneed after all, and will require a good deal of backing to make him stick to his point. He has gained a great reputation among the natives because he has tried to help them, but in reality he has done nothing, nor can do anything, with the people at home pulling him by the coat tails. There is a grand opening here for Randolph Churchill or Sir William or any M.P. to step into Gladstone's shoes as the friend of the people here. They don't believe in Gladstone or any of the liberal leaders, for they understand our politics just as well as we do. If I was in Parliament I could be an Indian Parnell, but in Parliament I shall never be. You must forgive me if I write about myself. These politics take up all my thoughts."

A threatened arrest:

Crabbet. 29 March 1884. "We arrived yesterday in good health and spirits. I was threatened by an English Lt.-Colonel with arrest in Egypt on my way through the Canal, and have got a capital case to make out of it for Randolph. At Paris I saw Lord Lyons and advised him to repudiate the debt in Egypt."

Friends at Therapia.

Therapia. 17 October 1884. "We have been received with

the greatest amiability, Hugh Wyndham now in charge, being a cousin of mine. I have made acquaintance with all the Corps Diplomatique. The Russian Ambassador, Nelidof, I find is an old friend of mine. The wife of the German Ambassador I knew as a young lady seventeen years ago; Mme. de Radowitz. She is probably coming as Ambassadress to London; Costi, the Italian, is an ancient acquaintance of Anne's; and Mme. de Noailles, the French Ambassador, is a Pole to whom we had introductions from Poles in Poland."

The Embassy at Constantinople.

Constantinople. 24 October 1884. "Private. Dufferin is away, I should have liked to have a few words with him on the Mohammedan side of the Indian question. I fear, as far as this is concerned, he is not the best man in the world for his new place, as there is probably no man more disliked in the Mohammedan world, unless it be Malet or Gladstone. With all the flourish of trumpets about his diplomatic talents I find him looked upon by everybody here as a failure. He never at any time had any influence with the Sultan, and was only saved from an entire checkmate by the bombardment and Tel el Kebir. Since then he seems to have given it up as a bad job, and for the last six months never went near the Palace. The English Embassy is entirely in Coventry, being snubbed even by the Vizier, and can hardly get a civil answer to a letter. It seems to me that with Egypt on our hands and discontent in India this state of things is rather dangerous, and they will be well advised to send an Ambassador who shall be able to take new ground. But who can it be? Layard is entirely out of favour on account of the publication of that last dispatch of his, which the Sultan will never forgive, and I hardly know anybody who would be a *persona grata*."

The Stage of Contemplation.

10 St. James's Street. 18 October 1886. "Your letter found me at Castle Howard where I have been spending a fortnight preparatory to leaving England. I am getting weary of politics and feel the third stage of my life—the stage of contemplation—rapidly approaching, and I doubt whether I shall ever take an active part in the world's ways again. As a first step I am going to spend a few weeks or months at Rome in ecclesiastical retirement, and shall take my poetry with me and my memoirs. These should be sufficient to

occupy me for the rest of my intellectual life; and in the night of things I may perhaps aspire to an even higher Nirvana."

A holy place.
Hotel D'Europe, Rome. 15 December 1886. "I have taken no vows yet, and can, therefore, answer your letter, though I am in a kind of retreat here from the follies of the world. I needed something of the sort very badly, and for the first few weeks I was really ill, which did me good. But now I am well again, but still enjoying that quiet mind which seclusion gives—seclusion in a holy place, where I can write and read without thinking of the flight of time. I am writing a good deal—principally my political memoirs which I find are very interesting, though whether they would be wise or not to publish I cannot tell. I wrote things as they really were, without respect of persons, and when I come home I shall ask you to help me where I have had to leave gaps. This takes me away from current politics, and indeed I can do nothing here. In Ireland I should be very happy to help, but Englishmen cannot be of the same use Irishmen themselves could, and my time is not yet come . . . So too with Egypt, it is all going on now without me—and better than I could have hoped, though it will take some time yet to get Lord Salisbury quite out of his pigheaded ways. Anything is better than the old stagnation and as long as they are kept moving they must go in our direction. I shall do nothing now but wait events. With regard to coming back to England, I hardly know when it will be. As long as I am able to write I shall probably stay on here, for I know from experience that I cannot write in England in the winter on account of the darkness. Here, the weather is like heaven, or rather like the desert, hot enough to burn one's face riding in the Campagna. I am glad you got your rents. Good landlords need fear nothing; but don't let your agent play tricks with the tenants. I know it is difficult to keep agents straight. Did mine send you a Xmas tree?"

He revisits Cairo.
Cairo. 30 January 1887. "I think you will like to get a letter from Cairo, short though it be and bad the writing, for my hands are numb with cold. The English occupation has spoiled the weather as well as the rest. We came here by a sudden inspiration, getting leave from Lord Salisbury by telegraph, and have been five days at Cairo without

either the Nile or the town taking fire. I am surprised to
find how little changed it is in all outward things. Except
that the European shops have crept a hundred yards further
up the Mouski and that there are more hotels and grog
shops, one would not know that Arabi was not still in the
Kasr-el-nil. But the life has gone out of it all for me, and I
shall not stay a day longer than to settle the affairs of my
garden, that is to say a week or so at most. As I am most
probably watched by spies who will take this letter to Baring
to read, I will not allude to politics except to say that everybody here seems to consider evacuation certain, though
what is to come after nobody can tell . . . We went yesterday
to see the British garrison engaged in 'its great work of
humanity and civilisation' on the Gezirah race-course—
teaching the Egyptian youth how to compete in 'egg and
spoon races', 'brandy and soda' races and other Christian and
athletic sports. Sir Evelyn Baring was there, with footmen
running before him, in a white hat, and he came up to me,
nose to nose, as I was talking to Armar Corry, but I had
the presence of mind not to see him, and as he will probably
read this letter I shall not say how much like a grocer he
looked. I hope and trust his reign here is nearly over, as
Randolph will be Foreign Secretary before we are many
weeks older and he will sweep the place out of the old gang."

*He visits Ireland to help the Land League and is put under
arrest.*

Crabbet. 5 December 1887. "I was as near as possible paying
you a visit at Coole, only you were not there, by accident,
for I was wandering about one night in a car, and by accident
was taken to Gort where I had to spend the night . . .
Everything is turning out exceedingly well for me politically
as you may see by the papers. Think of old Pussy subscribing
£15 to my defence fund, and my stumping the North of
England with Schnadhorst and Harcourt. Even the G.O.M.
has 'yet to learn' that I have never been wrong in my political
doings. I am, nevertheless, exceedingly weary of it all. The
happiest time was the night I passed in prison, and even
you must envy me the privilege of being the first Englishman
locked up in the Irish cause. Now I am divided between the
hope of beating Balfour on the appeal case in January, and
the fear of being at liberty in January and February to
canvass Deptford. As a first class misdemeanant, with leave to
edit a new volume of poems, I should be absolutely happy."

St. James's Club, Piccadilly. 23 March 1888. "I have been too idle since I came out of prison to write letters, but yours has lain on my table every day, and now I thank you for it. My principal visitor at Galway was your cousin, Mr. Persse, who used to look in about twice a week and talk horseflesh to me, breaking thereby the prison rules. This did me more good than if he expounded to me many Scriptures. I found everybody who came to me exceedingly kind, the visiting justices doing everything that was in their power. I felt quite *attendri* when I left the prison, but I am writing my prison pamphlet, and you shall hear all about it. I wonder if you are still at Rome. I shall send this letter there on the chance . . . You will find me much altered when we meet. It seems to me several years since last October."

Crabbet. 9 July 1888. "We spent two pleasant long days at Galway and saw your mother, who greatly delighted me, for she has the sacred fire of wit besides being a personage pleasing to look at."

20 April 1888. "I have been in much perplexity of mind lately about Ireland. I had almost decided to throw in my lot with your nation and propose myself to Parnell for the next election, but circumstances prevented me, and now Randolph has come home and offers to find me a seat, and I am writing him a letter on the subject so as to find out whether I am a Tory democrat with Nationalist tendencies or a Nationalist with Tory democratic tendencies, and on his answer my position will depend."

Lord Randolph Churchill.
10 James's Street. 18 July 1885. "I hope great things of this new Government, in spite of Lord Salisbury's speech. They are all very polite to me now and I go to see Randolph whenever I like at the India Office. He is great fun and quite unchanged. 'They will never make an official of me,' he said last time I saw him, and I am sure they won't. In spite of this the officials adore him, for with them he is as serious as a judge and asks their advice in the most engaging way. He is very pleased, however, when he is left alone and then his face relaxes. He will lead them a dance yet. Not that Randolph is not really quite as serious as they are—indeed, I have always said he was the only serious politician I have had to do with. But he hates the red boxes, and means to do things, instead of writing about them."

His poems written in prison.

Paris. 14 November 1888. "This is a word of good-bye before we start on our serious travels. It is settled now that we go first to Greece, which Lady Anne has never seen, and then to Egypt. It has been fairly pleasant weather here and I have gone through the usual round of plays with my cousin, Francis Currie, who lives here. This always gives me a new start in life and I shall be able now to think nothing at all about serious matters till my return in the spring. The poems (*In Vinculis*) are already in print and the first proofs corrected, but the second are to be sent to you, and I have left you my representative with Kegan Paul . . . Here, nobody thinks of anything but Boulanger and war, and I am beginning to believe in its probability . . . Nobody at Paris thinks of anything more about Egypt, and for the moment it is against Italy that there is the principal anger, but we are so cordially detested that it is quite on the cards that the war, when it comes, may be against us rather than the others. I don't know, however, why I should write to you about politics, seeing that I have renounced all such. I trust to you to give me news from time to time of what is being said and done in London. I know you will do all things needful for the book."

His life at Sheykh Obeyd.

27 December 1888. "I have just been reading your last letter in my hermitage here, for the air of Cairo under British occupation disagreed with me, and I have escaped from it and my family to live alone in my garden. It is great fun being here for I see all sorts of people, and the weather is hot enough for it to be very pleasant sitting in the verandah of the house doing nothing. We have had the gardener's house done up and it really makes a quite inhabitable place with four bedrooms and a large space roofed in and open on one side which I use as a drawing room. There is no furniture, but I have had the floors strewn with fresh white sand and I put a carpet down wherever I want to sit. I have got a square chicken coop for a divan and another for a table. My servants are all old friends, a man from Nejd who cooks and recites poetry and plays the rebeck. My own camel Bedouin from Mount Sinai, another whose home is in the hills between Cairo and Suez and who scouted for Arabi during the war; and lastly as head gardener (only do not repeat it for we conceal his identity), Arabi's own body servant who fled with him on horseback from Tel-el-Kebir.

So we form a little community of free-minded people and of
people who have been in trouble. I think it says well for
them all, that the fact of my having spent two months in
gaol (for 'raising a rebellion' that is how the case is presented
to them) has made me much more popular than I was before
in the neighbourhood. A touch of nature makes the whole
world kin, and in Egypt as in Ireland a prison record is no
slur on a man's character . . . I am interrupted by Zeid's
wife who helps in the cooking and who has come with four
live pigeons (one shilling) and forty one eggs (one shilling)
asking me to pay, as I am keeping house myself and laying in
supplies. This seems to me very cheap. Zeid too has brought
a dozen round flat loaves and some white sheep's cheese . . .
and there is not a soul for several miles round who has the
smallest connection with Europe, or so much as a garden
nearer than Matarieh two miles off . . . I have been reading
Gordon's journal again these last few days. It is a strange
medley, but full of consolation to the political outcast. The
fun he makes of Baring and the F.O. is exceedingly wholesome, and I am in sympathy with all except the fact that
he was fighting on the wrong side. It is a curious thing that
he did not see this, though now and then he seems very
near it. It strikes me more forcibly than when I first read it,
as the writing of a man of genius. If he had not been a
soldier he would have been altogether a good man, but the
world would never have found it out. What they liked was
his insisting on fighting when Gladstone wouldn't. All the
rest would have gone for nothing."

Lord Dufferin.

5 May 1889. "We have been talking (Bertram Currie and
I) about Lord Dufferin, which has reminded me of your
letter. What you say interests me for I have always followed
his career with a kind of affectionate regard bound in old
memories of my extreme youth when I had a romantic
attachment, if I may call it such, for his mother. What
ancient history it sounds! I suppose his viceroyalty in India
was no great success, and it does not surprise me, as he was
always an idle man, capable of great things for a while and
then tiring of them. Lytton in some sort over again. But I
doubt if men of genius are suited for governments except
in very exceptional times. Thinking over what he did in
Egypt I feel a kind of gratitude to him now for his good
intentions (so few people in public positions have these)
though none of his promises have had any fulfilment. Balfour

and his like would have hung Arabi without trial and so would Malet."

He has found felicity.

Sheykh Obeyd. 7 February 1890. "You see I date from Sheykh Obeyd—not 'the town' or 'the man' (see Gordon on Baring) but the garden, my own beloved garden near Heliopolis. For the first time in my life, I think, this winter I have been absolutely and entirely happy. The feeling that I have finished with the vain European life of fret and worry never leaves me and is like the dressing-gown and slippers one puts on after a day's hunting and finds the best part of the sport. I have come exactly to the point where I was ten years ago when the East was a romance to me and not a sphere of influence, and I am able to enjoy it better now, having ransacked the other treasuries of life. I go very little to Cairo, but see a number of interesting Eastern people who come from all parts of the Arabian world to this garden which stands convenient for them as their first *menzil* in Egypt, and as I provide them with coffee all day long they stay on. I have built a house on the Arab plain, half of it for guests and half for the family, and in this way my visitors are no trouble and I see as much or as little of them as I like. This is to me the ideal life for old age, and I feel quite prepared for it, if it has not come already. Anne and Judith too are very happy, Judith is blessed with the gift of perpetual happiness, and we have our donkey rides in the garden and rides on horses outside and she finds it all delightful. It has been a lovely winter and to-day is the first of the sand storms which come at this time of year. The garden is a mass of apricot blossoms and in another fortnight the oranges and lemons will be in flower and the pomegranates. We mean to stay on till the middle of April if not driven away by the heat . . .

"Truly, people must be arrant cowards at heart to fall down and worship courage of the Stanley sort. Doughty's travels in Arabia were a hundred times more perilous and made by a man more capable of understanding what he saw. But because he shot down nobody and had only the courage of patience nobody recognised him as heroic. I would give a good deal to have the hanging of Stanley and I think he is the only man in the world I should much care to hang, for his multitudinous murders."

His poems are being printed by the Kelmscott Press.

Crabbet. 5 October 1891. "Here are the proof sheets of the

first half of my new book. I shall be very much obliged to you if you will look through and return them if possible by return of post. I leave home on Saturday for Paris and I want if possible to get this printing business off my hands before I start. The second half of the volume will consist of the old *Sonnets of Proteus* reprinted with twenty-five more, some of them suppressed in the earlier editions and others new. You are the only person I know whom I can quite depend upon to read carefully, with a view to corrections, and any errors you may find I will ask you to note on a separate slip of paper. The parts underlined in red will be printed red, and the copy will be sold at two guineas, but I will send you yours. I am not quite satisfied about the longer pieces, which were written long ago. But these will not be very prominent, and nearly half the book will be a reprint. I was obliged 'for private reasons' to suppress the best long piece. But Kegan Paul is going to bring out another volume for me next year.

*This refers to *The Love Lyrics and Songs of Proteus*: Kelmscott Press Edition. The only book from the Press in which the initials are printed in red.

XIV

THE TWELVE YEARS ENDED

MR. FRANK LAWLEY, in the recollections of my husband I have already quoted from, says some kind words of his marriage to me, and that my "little salon in St. George's Place soon became one of the most agreeable in London". He says also during the concluding years of his life offers from divers constituencies poured in upon Sir William, but in vain. He was equally deaf to overtures made to him by Secretaries for the Colonies that he would accept another Governorship. And that these his latest years were "undoubtedly the happiest that he had ever passed". And then he gives a letter received from him a few days only before he was in the grip of his last illness.

It is dated 4 February 1892: "I have to thank you for your review of Lord Rosebery's *Pitt,* which is a fine biography, and the style admirable.

"On the whole, despite the delightful style, it is one of the saddest books I ever read. It is the struggle of the most noble-minded patriotic Englishman that ever lived to establish a wise fiscal policy, to abandon the old insane foreign entanglements, to pacify Ireland by wise and feasible measures, which would have rendered her a glory to England and no longer a shame to humanity. In all these aims he was arrested, thwarted, and beaten back by the powers of evil. You should not have concluded your critique without Rosebery's noble final sentence: 'From the dead eighteenth century Pitt's figure still faces us with a majesty of loneliness and courage. There may have been men abler and greater than he, though it is not easy to cite them. But in all history there is no more patriotic spirit, none more intrepid, none more pure.

"I am as ill as a man can well be. I went to Bournemouth for ten days, but came back much as I went. The doctors are quite *au bout de leur Latin,* but one of them says there is a chance of heat bringing me round. We start, therefore, on Thursday next at 3.00 p.m. and arrive at Marseilles next day at 2.30. Is not that wonderful? I remember travelling five days and nights from Marseilles to Paris, to be present at Coronation's Derby."

But that journey to Marseilles was never made, and it was in his own house, on the sixth day of that bitterly cold March, he passed away.

I have little to say of the sad months that followed, the last I spent in the little house that had been so gay in its outlook on the riders and carriages in the Park, so pleasant in its changing visitors and friends within, in the joy of affection and delightful companionship. I had much bitterness to attend to, many letters to write; I was helped through all by much kindness. Then I returned to Coole; to the empty house and the tenanted grave.

XV

THE *AUTOBIOGRAPHY*

EASTER and summer brought Robert home for his holidays, and I say in letters to Lady Layard: —

Easter 1892: "I go over with Robert on the 21st to take him to his new school, Elstree. His last master, Mr. Rawnsley, seems to regret him very much, and for my own ease of mind I would have liked to leave him at Park Hill, where he was so well and happy, but he had got quite to the top of the school, and his father had decided that when that happened he must go to a larger one. He is delighted to be here for his holidays, and quite happy with boat, catapult, donkey and a retriever puppy."

And again: "We are alone this time and live out of doors. The weather has been lovely and Robert is very much taken up with the two new dogs, and his old one on a visit, and a new gun that has been given him by Edward Martyn. Last night we were not in till near nine as the dogs discovered a hedgehog and we had to capture it and carry it home in R.'s hat, to put it out in the garden."

All through his school years I brought friends or cousins near his own age to be his playmates and companions, and the holidays were the bright weeks of the year. So I wrote from time to time: —

"And again it has not been easy to do any reading or writing, I am so surrounded by schoolboys. Tony and Wyndham Birch have been spending the holidays with us, one from Eton, one from Marlborough, (their poor mother slowly dying at Wimbledon and Sir Arthur not able to leave her) and all these six weeks I have heard of little but fishing-flies, and worms, and rods, and cartridges. They are both very nice and bright and enjoy shooting, fishing, ferreting and all other country sports, and were a great help to me at the school feasts and workhouse party, which I have resumed this year.

"I have been helping Tony Birch to stuff a 10 lb. pike he caught, from a book on taxidermy. It looks very grand at present, but I have fears of the skin shrinking. I am so glad to be able to turn the place into a summer run for them

all, though they are a good many to feed and think for . . .
I got from London an 'understudy' for my house and parlour
maid, who arrived looking like a Maori dressed in a missionary's cast off clothing, with fuzzy head, a white shirt front
and black cravat, and who got a fainting fit as the result
of tight lacing, so I speedily said 'good-bye' to her."

And on 14 October 1894: "We had the Morris boys for
a part of the holidays, Charlie and Edmund; then the Birch
boys and Una. I was delighted to make the house so cheerful
for Robert, feeling it better for him that it should be filled
with his contemporaries than mine. I took Tony to Galway
one day, and he caught seven salmon, and I had him photographed contemplating them. I feel so glad that, another
summer having gone by, we are still on good terms with our
people. We had the school feast (122 children) and the
workhouse party, and all the people are nice and cordial
and bring little presents for Robert as of old.

"Robert made the most of his holidays to the last, shooting
and ferreting the last morning till it was time to start. Our
poor little new dog, Russ, was thrown from a car, the pony
having shied at a flock of starlings, and died the day the
boys left. As he was such a newcomer we did not bury him
with the other dogs who have their little headstones, but
under a tulip tree near. My sister says it is like poor Prince
Henry being interred at Whippingham and not at Windsor!

"We had our school feast on Friday, 122 children, and a
fine day, and food and presents held out well. I am always
so thankful when it is over, partly because of the trouble it
gives me but chiefly because it marks another year of being
on friendly terms with our people, and I am so anxious that
should last till Robert is grown up. We have no evicted
tenants in this neighbourhood and I can hear of no excitement about the rejection of the Bill."

There were lonely months also—I wrote in the summer
of 1893: "The arrival here is always sad and depressing, the
silence, and one's responsibilities coming on again—but
work is the best cure.

"We have had a few showers but the ground is dreadfully
parched. However, our people have good potatoes, and pigs
are very dear, so they won't be badly off, and are behaving
very well about rent paying. Sometimes they do so by selling
stock at a sacrifice, and then I have to set them up again
with presents of little pigs, etc., and altogether it is a much
less satisfactory way of getting one's income than simply

drawing dividends . . . My garden looks tolerably well. I have been preserving immense quantities of gooseberries for school feasts, etc. and strawberries and raspberries for Robert and his friends. My drawing-room is really very pretty now with some handsome things from St. George's Place, and all rubbish put away. But the house is terribly silent and lonely, and the wind whistles round it at night."

And in winter: "I am planting some larch and silvers to see if the rabbits will be more merciful to them than to those we plant in the autumn. I have planted a bare place with larch, spruce, silver and evergreen oak, and renewed for the third time the Insignis by the nutwood path." For through all of these twenty two years[1] indeed, planting has been my work and anxiety and joy. When I came home, before the nursery of little grandchildren began, I would run out to see the last little trees we had put down, and then on and on to the earlier plantings that might need help against stifling or rabbit or squirrel. So the trees became companions, their enemies mine. Often when some letter or newspaper has brought tidings that have made me angry with or without good cause, I have taken my little hatchet and slashed at choking ivy or woodbine or even hazel that has thrust itself between the sunlight and my nurselings, and have come in placable, amiable, at peace with the world.

For through all these twenty-two years of widowed life, Coole has continued to be my dear home.

And so the months passed, and after a while I wrote: "I have read in Stanley's life of 'the loneliness of the selfish man'. I must try to avoid that, and am likely to do so, for already the poor are at my door. Little K. has knitted a petticoat, a moth-trap, but I had to buy it at a fancy price, her brothers and sisters being down with the measles; old Davy Boland has died, his wife and children all away in America and the burial falls on me. F.'s children are said to be left destitute, and Curtin, W.'s old Kinvara bailiff, writes from the workhouse hospital for help."

I sometimes went for a visit to my mother, who then lived near Galway. "The morning sermon by a curate, who said 'the celebrated Germans; Strauss and Renan' had become infidels entirely by *want* of study. And in the evening another curate came and there was controversial gossip. And after prayers he got up from his knees and said there had

[1] Twenty two years takes Lady Gregory up to 1914. It is probable that this passage was typed as early as this date.

been great mortality lately, no, not from influenza, but from the extreme unction advised by the priests on the smallest excuse, the effect of which was to make the patient die and put death dues into their pockets! . . . There are some ecclesiastical quarrels going on. The Rector has lessened the size of the napkin over the 'Elements' and Mr. M., the hotel keeper, refuses to come to the Sacrament till it has reached its proper size again . . . The Rector in his sermon yesterday said, 'I suppose there is not one person in this church who does not accept every statement of the Scripture as literal and absolute truth'. I wonder if I shall ever hear that said in any London congregation."

So I wrote on coming back to Coole in 1894: "In spite of stormy weather, I enjoy the free and silent life here. I have elbow room to write and liberty of thought which had been denied me of late."

While I was yet in the schoolroom I wrote one or two stories and sent them to a magazine, but they were refused. I was disappointed, but I am glad now, for they were not good, and one at least, as I remember, had a sort of moral intention, that might have made some paper that gave sermons veiled in fiction my customer, and have put me into bonds. During my married life I had written one short article that was printed in *The Fortnightly,* and a little story without my name appeared in some weekly paper, and that was all[2].

I wrote in the summer of 1893: "I have worked at intervals at my husband's memoirs and have sent them to be typewritten."

I had begged him in one London winter to write something of the facts of his life, because he had no sisters or near relations to keep its circumstances in mind, and in case of my death there would be no one to tell Robert of what he had been and the good work he had done. And he had set to work, to please me, and meaning it to be but a family record. But it had grown into so full a narrative, that even as he wrote and I copied, I had hoped it might some day keep his memory alive for a while, after we were both gone. And so the editing of it was a chief occupation of that lonely

[2] Not accurate: Lady Gregory wrote two articles for *The Fortnightly Review* before the death of Sir William. "Through Portugal" appeared in 1883, and "Glimpses of the Soudan" in the following year. She also wrote "The Philanthropist" which appeared in *Living Age* in 1891 among other articles.

first year. Sir Henry Layard had sent me the letters to him, and allowed me to use his own; and it was a sad task reading through these and copying out a note or passage here and there.

When I had done my best with the manuscript, I sent it to John Murray. In about ten days it came back with a note, saying some parts were slightly too long, but if I would alter these he would make me an offer. So I went through it again, and the offer when it came was satisfactory, he would publish at his own risk and expense, giving me half profits. I was very glad for Robert's sake also, "a good name is better than riches" and is no mean part of the heritage of a son.

Then I said to Murray that I would like to have the manuscript gone through by someone more in the world than I was, who would strike out anything likely to give pain or vexation. I suggested Sir Henry Thompson, who knew everyone and whose little "octave" dinners had proved his many-sided sympathies and friendships. But Murray preferred Sir Henry Layard, and to this I could not but agree. Sir Henry was extremely kind and took the trouble of reading the typed copy closely, and he proposed my taking out a few sentences here and there, and this I did willingly.

I wrote to him in February 1894: "I am very much obliged to you for your corrections and suggestions. I had left out so much of general interest, because it was too personal, that I began to fear that Murray would find the whole thing too short, and so left in after consideration some passages I had some misgivings about, but from having been through the MS so often (I had copied it all out twice!), I felt I could no longer judge clearly in the matter. I have written to Murray to say that he need not send me the MS again as I am quite content that anything marked by you should be omitted, except in the passages relating to Ireland, for I attach great importance to the breadth and sincerity of his views on Irish questions being remembered."

But before the book had been published, Sir Henry Layard, my husband's friend and mine, had himself passed away.

I had, when I gave up the house in St. George's Place, received a very kind letter from the Layards asking me to look on their house in Queen Anne Street as my London home. And after the Christmas holidays of 1893, having taken Robert back to school, I spent a few weeks in that

house and began to meet friends again. "I went to the
Grant Duffs at Twickenham for the weekend; the Godleys
and Lord Monkswell there, and the pleasant talk and being
made welcome helped to restore my courage." I spent a day
at Southwark, seeing the dinners and breakfasts, cheered by
the welcome of the children and all. "People were very kind
to me, the Layards first of all, and the Lyalls and Arthur
Russells. I had waited on the Layards when they came home
and on my last day I had a morning visit from Lord Wemyss,
and lunched with the Duchess of St. Albans; and Lord
Selborne and Lady Sophia and Sir Henry Thompson came
to dinner to meet me."

But in 1894 Sir Henry had come back to London, very
ill—I stayed to help in taking care of him for a while, and
then seeing how unlikely it was he could ever leave England
again, I determined to find a little independent abode for
myself. I had been considering the matter for some time
and had written, "I think, money permitting, it would be
unwise to give up London. I have at present many friends,
but there of all places one must keep one's friendship in
'constant repair'. I should lose sight of our old friends by
staying away, and I should like to keep them for Robert . . .
Then I have found it impossible to pass the winter alone at
Coole, the long evenings when it grows dark at five or six
are too trying, and I cannot eat alone, and both appetite
and sleep desert me. So I have decided that it would be
better for Robert, as well as for myself, to use my 'two
talents' and spend part of the year in town."

And then: "I have found nice rooms at Queen Anne's
Mansions, which suit me very well. My friends helped to
furnish them, Lady Layard giving me a Florentine carved
chair, a set of tea things that had belonged to Sir Henry's
aunt, Mrs. Austin (Disraeli may have made use of them!),
Paul Harvey gave me a Chippendale chair, just the right
height for my writing table, Sir Henry a print from his
portrait, Sir F. Burton a large drawing, Lady Lindsay three
beautiful rugs and a cabinet. The Burmese silk curtains from
St. George's Place came in very nicely. The other day, driving
down Knightsbridge I caught sight in a dealer's window
(Arthur Smith) of the picture by Longhi, a lady renouncing
her worldly goods, which I had sold at Christie's for £21
and regretted ever since. I went to ask about it, and they
wanted £50, and said they had an offer from Mr. Freshfield
for £45. However, I wrote to A. Smith himself, and he came

to see me and after some conversation let me have it for
£28, and I was glad; for it and the curtains give my rooms
a look of home." And so I set up house, and liked the
independence and the absence of housekeeping.

And in October 1894, when I came home again to London,
"the little flat looked clean and cosy, with fires and a new
Belgian housemaid."

My husband's book was about to appear and I wrote from
day to day: 16 October—"I went to Murray's and found the
Autobiography ready and to be published in a few days. It
looks very well got up and is attractive to look through."

19 October.   "I called at Frank Lawley's. He came up, saying
he had only two minutes for me, as he had to write at once
three columns on Randolph Churchill, having heard there
was a telegram saying he was not expected to live. However,
he promised to review the *Autobiography* for the *Daily
Telegraph* if sent to him before Sunday, and talked over it
a good deal. And then we talked of Randolph, and he was
delighted I had come, as I happened to know something of
his success in administering the Famine Fund in Ireland,
the passionate attachment of his sisters to him, and above
all his great success at the India Office. Also the very good
impression he had made in India during his tour there, by
the sympathetic interest in the affairs of the natives, and
prudence, dignity and reticence, rather unusual in any
travelling politician.

"F. Lawley says that though Lord Rosebery is so inscrut-
able and unconfidential to his colleagues, he has made
himself so popular at the Foreign Office that the very dogs
wag their tails at the word 'Rosebery', his kindness extending
to the messengers, while to young clerks and secretaries he
is most generous and gracious, encouraging their interest in
art or archaeology and asking them to Mentmore.

"And that the Empress Frederic said to someone that the
death of the Czar, which seems very near, won't be such a
great loss after all, as he is nothing wonderful, and his son
has quite enough brains and will have the cleverest wife in
Europe. Not that the Empress's own talent did her poor
husband much good, as far as public life went."

20th.   "I went to Albemarle Street about F. Lawley's copy,
found only Hallam there and no one knowing who had got
copies and who had not. But he said they were most grateful
to me for doing so much, as many authors left all the trouble
to them . . . I sent a copy to Sir W. Harcourt, in gratitude

for his kind thought of asking Robert from Park Hill for the first Sunday after his father's death.

"Going home after a little shopping I met Lecky and stopped to speak to him, and he as usual, with his head carried like a giraffe's, never saw me, and a man looked derisively at me, thinking apparently that I had accosted Lecky and been rejected!"

On Sunday I went to St. Margaret's, Westminster. "An immense crowd to hear Canon Farrer's sermon on St. James. It was eloquent, but not much in it save a few moral exhortations. At lunch at the Robinsons', Lady R. said they want Sir Hercules to go back to the Cape. Cecil Rhodes writes by every mail urging him to do so.

"Lady X. gave me but a poor account of Sir X., interspersed with complaints of his obstinacy in not giving her a new kitchen range."

22nd. "Very anxious, it being the eve of the publication of the book. Dined on a piece of bread and a pear and went to bed early."

23rd. "Awoke early and flew to *The Times,* and was relieved to find a review in; rather a dull and unappreciative one, but still in a good place. Then in the reading room I found F. Lawley's enthusiastic article in *The Telegraph;* a fairly good one in *The Morning Post,* and one in *Daily News* giving plenty of quotations. And at Murray's I had got the *Standard* notice which had come out a day too soon, which made *The Times* angry, but is very full, and all are kind, and none have discovered the mistakes in Greek and elsewhere. So I felt a load roll off me, I should have taken it to heart so terribly if the book had fallen flat. Now it has had its good start, and must stand or fall by its own merits. I have also nice letters from the houses I have sent it to, and the Murrays are most amiable."

24th. "A wet, stormy day, and I was rather pleased at the excuse to stay in and arrange my little room. I dined with the Birches, Sir A. asked if I did not feel three inches taller at the success of the book. I said no, but ten years younger, which is true. They had a copy from the library with notice 'This book being *in great demand* it is to be returned as soon as possible'."

26th. "To Mudie's. The foreman told me there was a great run on the book and he himself had not been able to take it home to read, and they had just sent for a further supply.

A nice letter from Lord Dufferin who will send me his mother's poems in return."

28th. "To Twickenham for the night. Grant Duff asked me what was thought of Rosebery's speech against the Lords. I said I had not heard, but that my own feeling was akin to that awakened when the Emperor of China the other day, after long silence during which he had seen his armies shattered and his fleets sunk, had at last spoken to announce his resolve of depriving Li Hung Chang of his yellow jacket. G.D. thought this a most delightful idea."

29 October. "The day began with nice letters from the Prime Minister and the Chancellor of the Exchequer (Rosebery and W. Harcourt) and a present of his mother's poems from Lord Dufferin, from the Paris Embassy. Lord Rosebery writes 'it is a most fascinating and sincere specimen of a class of literature, generally fascinating and almost always insincere, the autobiography. If everyone wrote his autobiography we should want no other library or literature.'

"Pouring rain all day. Albert Gray came to see me, and I dined with Lady Lindsay, only Henry James there, cheery and pleasant as usual."

3 November. "A telegram from Julia Peel asking me to Sandy for the Sunday. I accepted and had a very pleasant time. The Speaker very well and charming, the three girls nice and cordial, Mr. Gore from Oxford (he had been in the railway carriage with me and I had been struck by his saintlike face, and then found him in the brougham waiting for me) and Sir Thomas Wade from Cambridge, full of China, on which he had just been giving a lecture."

4th. "Sunday. To church and heard old Mr. Richardson preach on the death of the Czar! Pleasant walk in the woods and talks. Such a treat to hear what is going on in the world of thought. The Speaker very full of Froude's *Erasmus*. Then talk of poets, Sir T. Wade all for Scott, the Speaker all for Wordsworth, Mr. Gore for Browning. The evening ended by Mr. Gore reading from *The Flight of the Duchess*. The Speaker read *Rugby Chapel* most beautifully, interrupted by family prayers, and his as beautiful reading of a chapter of *Micah*. He had been reading the *Autobiography* aloud to his daughters, and all were delighted with it. I asked who he thought the best of our Irish orators. He said for mob oratory, O'Brien. Then I asked who was the best orator he had ever heard and he considered a minute or two till I suggested Bright, and then said 'Yes, *facile princeps*'."

5th. "Back to London, and lunched with the Morrises. Lord M. looking much altered by his illness, with a white beard and haggard eyes. (The policeman at the door of the House of Lords had not recognised him, but he exclaimed 'Wha-at!', and the policeman said, 'I beg your pardon my lord!'.) He still takes a pessimistic view of Ireland, thinks we have not touched bottom, that the new land bill will pass, and Morley appoint the new Commissioners, and property be sliced away by degrees.

"There is a good review in the *Spectator,* and also in the *Athenaeum;* the classical errors noted, but not unkindly."

6th. "To Southwark Board School and saw Mrs. Hills, Mr. Dodge was out, but I have written to ask if I can help in any parish work. In the afternoon I had quite a party, Sir A. Colvin, Mr. Grenfell, Lord and Lady Morris, Mr. Ball. Lord M. says Rosebery is just like his horse Lades, they both began by winning the blue ribbon, one the Derby, the other the Premiership, and neither has distinguished himself by doing anything since. Father Healy, when Lord Bishop Plunket, who was talking of the validity of orders, asked, 'What should I do if two of your priests came to me for ordination?' promptly replied, 'Make them take the pledge!' When he found Matt Darcy arranging his library of books bought for ornament, which he called his 'old friends', he said, 'I'm glad to see you don't cut them'.

"Mr. Grenfell said that Lord Carlingford would like some small alteration made in the part about Lady Waldegrave, if there is a second edition, but he was pleased with the mention of her on the whole."

7th. "To Newman Street and joined the drawing class for I must break through my present idle habits and work at something. I began at the Clytie, and was surprised to find I could get it tolerably on to the paper . . . Tea at John Gray's, where I talked to H. D. Traill. I was rather vague as to what he had written, but noticed he rather winced when I said John Morley was the best biographer of the day, and I find that he has written some lives."

8th. "Had tea with Sir A. Lyall, the first time I had seen him since his illness. He said Lord Dufferin is put out at the story in the *Autobiography* about Mrs. Norton (having sold the news of the Repeal of the Corn Laws to *The Times*) and denies it, but that Spencer Walpole says it is absolutely true. Then he, by way of consolation, said, 'The responsibility is not yours, as the Memoirs were so evidently written for publication', I having so expressly stated they were not."

9th. "Henry James, whose visit is always benedictory, and then Paul, just made private secretary to Sir Ralph Knox. Then I ran round and dined with Lord and Lady Morris. The best and most tranquil evening I have had for a long time."

10th. "To Elstree. Found Robert with all the boys at a football match, and spent the afternoon watching it, balanced on a board to save my feet from the wet grass. R. looked well and we had tea with Mr. Wilson, who speaks very well of him. All the masters seem kindly men, and I think my child is in good hands. He was told to bring a friend to tea, and I was glad he chose his rival, Barnes."

11th. "To Christ Church, Victoria Street. Very empty; very full of millinery; green altarcloth, green markers, green banner and the curate, who had greenish hair, preached in green bands, on the means to 'catch men'. Lunched with Lady Dorothy, where were the Frederic Harrisons, H. H. Johnston, Sir H. Bulwer and Bret Harte, who is quiet and modest, and was much interested in hearing of the Isles of Aran. He says California is too civilised now for romance. F. Harrison has improved in appearance, his hair grown grey and his beard. H. H. Johnstone, the little pocket travel-ler, quite charming, with his gentle quaint sayings and look of power. His hope is to colonize Central Africa with Indians. He spoke of the want of nurses, but he said he would prefer male ones, as the 'Sisters' want to flirt, and if you resist flirting and getting engaged to them they write books abusing you. He sent me afterwards his 'unexpurgated Blue Book' to read, with some remarks about erratic missionaries."

12th. "To opening of the Gibbon Exhibition at British Museum. Grant Duff opened it, and Frederic Harrison showed us the chief treasures. Rain came on, and I stayed to study the Elgin marbles and came to the conclusion that while the Greek debt is in such an unsatisfactory condition it is a comfort to think we have held on to them. Dined with Raffalovich, sat next H. D. Traill who talked to me all the evening pleasantly enough . . ."

14th. "Dined with the Morrises. Lady M. and Maud went to the play, so I sat with Lord M. and had a long talk about Edmund O'Flaherty (mentioned in the *Autobiography*). etc. He said O'Flaherty's father was an old Peninsular officer. 'Many a time I tried to pull the sword out of his scabbard. They lived close to my father's house, and I used to be mad when Edmund came back for his holidays, because I used to have the loan of his pony to ride while he was away. His mother was a daughter of Burke, the hairdresser, who preceded Hayes. He was always drunk, so that as boys we were sent to have our hair cut early in the morning for fear he would cut our heads off by mistake in the afternoon.

" 'I was in the hustings with my father in the year 1807 when he proposed Daly, that was afterwards Lord Dunsandle. In the old days a priest was obliged to wear a stamp in his hat to show he was allowed to officiate by the civil power. One day, an old priest was much vexed in the streets of Galway by being required to take off his hat and show his stamp, which everyone was allowed to require him to do. Daly, when he saw this, went and took his arm and walked up and down with him for an hour to see if anyone would venture to make the demand, but no one did.' He told me objections had been made to my putting the story about Mrs. Norton in the book, but that he had defended me on the right ground, that of its having been already published in *Diana of the Crossways.* And when I came back I found a letter from F. Lawley saying all South Carolina would be up in arms about the tarring and feathering story; and all the Foreign and Colonial Office about the Queen not having been told about the Ceylon appointment. However, 'better are the wounds of a friend than the kisses of an enemy'."

15th. "Gibbon lecture in the afternoon. Grant Duff spoke and then F. Harrison, whom I didn't think a sympathetic speaker. I gave a little dinner in the evening, Grant Duff, Leckys, Bret Harte, Lady Morris and Fischer Williams and ——, whose dullness is poison. I don't think I will have more than six again that I may keep them all in hand myself! "

16th. "I saw H. Murray in the morning, and he said a second edition might be wanted at any moment, and I must have corrections ready, so I went off to F. Lawley for his copy, in which he said he has marked sixteen mistakes. But he wants it for the next day or two to write an article for *Baily's Magazine.* We made friends and I withstood him about Carolina. I found a note from Murray on my return, saying that they had another order during the day, which increases the probability of a reprint being wanted, so I spent the evening over corrections."

17th. "I was just going out when a messenger arrived with a note from Murray saying things were going so well that all corrections must be sent straight to the printer at Beccles on Sunday night.

"I went as usual to see Sir F. Burton, and then the Tennants and Mrs. Lynn Lynton. Dined with the Childerses, only the O'Conor Don and Sir N. Chamberlain."

18th. "A Sunday of rather hard work. I spent the morning over corrections as best I could, but F. Lawley, who had promised me his marked copy, wrote at the last moment that he wanted it, and besides, I might not like to see the marginal notes he had written in it! Albert Gray sent the Ceylon corrections and I had been given others by various people. Lunched with the Robinsons, Sir Hercules said the book had kept him up for two nights till two o'clock.

"I had, ever since reading Lord Dufferin's memoir of his mother, felt some remorse for having published the story of Mrs. Norton, which I had before looked on as so far away and so well known that there could be no indiscretion in publishing it. And I had heard that 'some people' had said I should not have left it in. While sitting with Sir Frederic I spoke of it, and he thought it ought to be modified, so on leaving him I went to Sir A. Lyall, and said the new edition had been called for, and I was not happy about the Norton story. He said he had just been on the point of coming to see me on that very subject. He and Spencer Walpole had been examining it that morning and found discrepancies, and that it did not agree with the account in *The Greville Memoirs,* and Henry Reeve would be sure to attack it in the *Quarterly*. We did not think it could be left out, having no matter ready to take its place, and Sir Alfred tried to alter it, but found that impossible. So we decided to leave out the cheque part, and to add a note saying that so many discrepancies had been pointed out to me that I felt sure that if my husband had himself revised his memoirs with a thought of publication he would by enquiring into details have been led to doubt the truth of the story.

"Then home to meet Mr. Grenfell who brought pages of amendments of Lord Carlingford's to be inserted! Then Paul came to dine and help me, and we were till near midnight trying to get the corrections into order, he correcting the classical mistakes. I was really ill by this time, and all my bones aching, but we got the corrections off by post."

19th. "A tremendously strong letter from Lecky by first post on the Norton story, almost *commanding* its withdrawal. This would have made me wretched had I received it at first, when I did not know there would be a second edition, or if I had taken no steps of my own accord. Directly after breakfast I went to Murray. Luckily, John was there. He at first said it would be impossible to make the omission altogether, but when I showed him Lecky's letter he said at once, 'We must leave it out', to my great relief. We tried to fill the page in with a bit from *The Greville Memoirs* but found it impracticable, and then we settled to alter the paging of the chapters, and I added a note withdrawing it. It is curious that Sir Henry Layard, though objecting to some small and trivial anecdotes, never made a remark on this.

"Then I had to go to F. Lawley to find out what some of the mistakes noted by him were, (chiefly very trivial). He attacked *The Greville Memoirs* and said they gave a false account of his own 'ruinous episode', which was really the most creditable one of his life, and rapidly gave details from which I gathered he had tried to screen his friend A.Z. but I did not clearly understand either story or the refutation. Back to Murray. Then to Sir F. Burton . . . Visitors till past 7.00, and then dressed in a great hurry to dine with the Grenfells and meet Lord Carlingford. I was so depressed by the Norton episode I dreaded him, but he was very nice, thanked me warmly for the 'tribute' to Lady Waldegrave published, but produced a long note to be inserted, chiefly clearing the character of one of his predecessors, Lord Waldegrave. This, to my relief, I found would be possible and rather interesting. He says Lord Northbrook tells an excellent story, the inaccuracy of which I forgave as it is so good. It is that I sent him a copy of the book, saying he might like to have it as some members of his family were mentioned in it (I really said because W. had been his guest at the Durbar which he described) and that when he looked in the Index all he could find was 'Bruiser Baring, card-sharper'!"

20th. "To Lord Carlingford for some alteration in his note, and to say I must state he had given it to me, at which he hesitated, saying in that case he must examine into the facts more closely! He had no objection to my becoming responsible for them. However, I insisted. He showed me the portraits of Lady Waldegrave and spoke much of her, 'You

have no idea what life with her meant', and wished so much
I had known her. I asked leave to publish the story of her
rebuking Lord Normanby, but he thought it better not,
'though tempted', as he had never heard it and thought 'it
might lead to questions'. He is evidently feeble, and living
on her memory. In the evening (I having with some little
difficulty got Murray to again alter the page, which makes
a delay) he sends me a quantity of further alterations to
make!"

21st.   "To the Stores to send a hamper to Robert, and to
Sir F.B. And called on Mrs. Murray and found John there
who I thought would have hated the sight of me, but they
had just written to ask me to dinner. He says he has never
known an author who has given away so many copies of his
book as Lord Dufferin, which indeed I believe, having seen
it on most tables."

22nd.   "Lunched with Knowles. He was astonished at my
withdrawing the Norton anecdote, says it was quite true,
and he has not heard a single person object to it! But had
I heard from the Vaughans? They were likely to object to
the duel story. Voting for the School Board going on, great
squabbling and excitement and much bad feeling over the
fourth R., Religion. Then to Sir Frederic, and Lady A.
Russell, who asked me if the O'Flaherty family objected to
the account of his misdoings! Dined Leckys'. He serene
and kind; Lord Reay, white and shadowy; Miss X. rather
prepotente, probably from association with Moberley Bell.
I would say 'with *The Times*' but Sir D. Mackenzie Wallace
was also there, quiet and modest as ever. Also the Nether-
lands minister and his wife, and at one time the conversation
on one side of the table went on in Dutch.

"The Dean of Westminster (and I had not sent it to him)
wrote to me of 'the great delight' with which he was reading
the book—'very slowly, as I only allow myself to read it at
night before I finally put out the lights—in bed, and cutting
the leaves as I go', and he asked if in future editions 'could
a little map of Ceylon be introduced? . . . I know how we who
have not gone through Board Schools often need assistance
of the kind!' And again a little later he wrote, 'I have
finished the volume . . . But I cannot say how interested I
have been, and I have already begun to read it a second
time, the best proof of what I have gained from it'."

24th.   "Had to go, with headache and pains in the bones,
to open the sale of work at Southwark, made a short speech

and bought something at every stall, and the second day the
stuffed globe-fish. Coughed all night."

29th. "Called on Mrs. Humphry Ward, who is very proud
of her son having gained the Balliol. I was able to congratulate her on this more sincerely than on the success of her
books. *Marcella* in its eleventh thousand."

30th. "Dined Murrays, a very pleasant dinner . . . Mr.
Lidderdal in great spirits, the Baring affair having that
day come to a happy end. Lecky prophesies I shall go on
writing, says it is 'like drink'. The Murrays rather in a
state about my book, the second edition can't be out till
next week, and they haven't a single copy left of the first.

"Dined with the Lefevres . . . I only found at the end of
the evening that Wemyss Reid was there, whom I should
have liked to talk to. I had Mundella next me, and after
dinner Frederic Harrison came and talked, very much
pleased with the *Autobiography*, which he has been reading."

6th. "The chief event was tea with Sir. H. H. Johnston
at the end of my passage at Q.A.M. His drawing-room
beautiful and very interesting, and he himself such a modest
tidy dapper little creature to rule so much of Africa. We sat
at his little tea table, and he poured tea from a little teapot,
and spread a little napkin over his knees lest any crumbs
should fall, and on the walls were some rather terrible
pictures of vultures and men hanged from the 'tree of death'.

"I asked how he had taken first to Africa, and he said
from his childhood he had intended it, and wrote a story
when he was about nine which turns on adventures there.
When he grew up he took to art, and went through an artist's
training, but his health was so bad he went abroad, to Tunis,
which awoke all his desire for Africa again. He tried to
get a consulate, but he looked so ill and fragile that no
one thought him worth getting a post for. Then he persuaded
his father to advance him money (like the Prodigal Son),
and set out for the Congo on his own account. When he
came back he published his book on it, and easily got a
publisher, whereas he had never before been able to find
one. And he has stuck to Africa ever since and is as strong
and well as possible. He hopes to be allowed to visit India
on the way back, about renewing the Sikh contingent, and
wants to go by Rome and Constantinople that he may see
the Pope and the Sultan. Such great mind in little body!
He came back to my rooms and sat a long time, a most
interesting talk leading into larger worlds."

7th.   "Hugh Lane to lunch."

8th.   "Second edition out to-day, at last."

12th.   "Dined with Mrs. Kaye. George Lefevre told me that John Morley said to Lord Rosebery, 'I should like to review your *Pitt*'. 'Then why don't you do it?' 'If I did, you would probably never speak to me again!'."

XVI

SCHOOLS AND HOLIDAYS

I wrote in the early summer of 1893 from Chenies, where I was spending Saturday and Sunday with the Duchess (Adeline) of Bedford, "Robert is with me, as he had an exeat from Elstree for the Eton and Harrow match. Enid Layard is here, a little better, the Duchess very kind and charming, a large-hearted, large-minded woman, very attractive. On Sunday she showed me the Russell monuments in the old church; a great deal of English history to be learned there. I felt so much for her, and indeed for Enid, as we three widows sat together at morning service, Robert the only child amongst us. He was delighted with the trout in the streams and the perch in the pond, and the great dog, Aleuse, and it is a comfort to see him so free from self-consciousness, with a nice simple manner, though very merry."

I had written in 1893: "I went to see Robert at Elstree on Sunday, and we had a nice walk and chat together. I meant to send him to Harrow this autumn but Mr. Royle begged me to leave him at Elstree till Easter, to try for the entrance scholarship and after consultation with Paul and Fischer Williams I have consented, especially as Mr. Bowen could not receive him at his House at Harrow till Christmas. Mr. Royle says he ought never to be lower than second in the school if not first, but that he drops if not taken notice of and stirred up, and that Harrow masters will take more trouble with him if he enters as a scholar. I trust I am doing right. I took thought and counsel before deciding."

And now before Easter 1895, I wrote: "I am anxious this week about Robert going up to Harrow for the scholarship. His masters speak so well of him I sometimes think he must get one, and then I remember his little careless ways, and the excitement he will be in about coming home, and hope dies."

And on April 15th: "All Tuesday and Wednesday I was miserably anxious about Robert and his exam., not altogether lest he should fall, but that the strain of two such long days would be bad for him, and then if he failed there would be nothing at all gained to make up, and if he won it would not be worth the sacrifice of health. Tuesday was not so bad, for I drove to Kinvara with F. who went to inspect the castle of Dunguaire, which E. Martyn went to make safe, and I sketched, and the drive was nice. On my return, first came Father Fahey to see me, then E. Martyn. Next day I was alone, and was out till dark cutting ivy from the trees, and could not read or sleep at night. On Thursday I thought if there was any good news I should have a telegram before 10.00 o'clock, but none came, and each time I passed the front windows I looked out in vain. At last, at 11.20, just as I was going to start to meet Robert, I saw 'Johnny from Gort' coming to the door. I had not courage to go down, but stayed on the stairs and Marian—looking scared—brought me three telegrams. 'Gregory first classical scholar. Heartiest congratulations', was Mr. Sanderson's (Head Master of Elstree) and then one from Harrow and one from Mr. Richardson, and all had arrived in Gort before 10.00 o'clock and had been delayed there. I was quite upset by the reaction and relief, and Marian rushed down and told Johnny from Gort, who calmed me by demanding 'something extra for bringing good news' and also that I would forgive his son who was one of the tree-cutters in Inchy the other day, who were to be prosecuted. Then to the station, where I greeted my little man with the news when he stepped out safe and sound, rosy and more solid-looking than usual—and pleased to hear of his success, but much taken up with Croft (his retriever, who having got out of hand and killed a Crannagh goose, had been banished to Galway), who had met him at Athenry, on loan from the postman, to spend the holidays.

"Many congratulations ever since. Dr. Welldon (Head-master of Harrow) writes that he 'passed a brilliant examination'; Mr. Bowen, that he was 'clearly first—some of the Greek was too much for him, but his Latin excellent, the Latin verses capital'; and Mr. Sanderson writes that he hears the Latin verses carried the day, the last stanzas especially being excellent. And he is as merry as if he had never opened a book, romping with Croft and Jap and China, and making acquaintance with Rover, and to-day making a kite, and he is as obedient and affectionate as ever . . . Easter Sunday we went to the workhouse after church with tobacco for the old man, oranges and sugar stick for the children, and the old women, and there was a poor little smiling mite, Thomas Corless from Kinvara, who had fallen over a stone wall and was much injured. We gave him what we could and again this morning drove in to see him, and brought him the kangaroo game and other toys and sweets, etc., and I left him £1 to take home. I have been in a very liberal mood since R.'s return. So much the better for the people's seed potatoes!

"And after all my torture during the two days' exam. I find it was all thrown away, as R. enjoyed himself extremely, the morning drive to Harrow, and seeing racquets played for the first time, and says 'when you got interested in the work the time simply flew and the two and a half hours of Latin verses seemed like twenty minutes'. He was evidently not nervous, and not the least intimidated by being marched into a small room with Dr. Welldon and asked to define such words as 'plagiarism' which he did not know and 'demur' which he defined as 'to object to a thing, and want to do it, a sort of shirking'. He also did well in the subjects of the *Waverley* novels; but could not give the reasons for Disestablishment of the Welsh Church . . ."

16th. "He is very much taken up making a new kite, that of yesterday having flown away. This is an improved one with pink eyes, gold spectacles and a brown paper beard. He shot a rat last night, and is now trying for a pigeon . . ."

30 April. "We left Coole after a very bright open-air holiday. R. low at leaving, and we had a storm going over, I had never been so knocked to pieces.

"We went to Cheapside in search of a cricket bat, not, however, to be taken to Harrow, as that is 'swagger' but to be left in my charge till sent for . . . To Baker Street . . . Poor R. looked a little sad at making such a plunge into the unknown, and though he met two or three boys he knew, they were also low, and didn't seem particularly glad to see him. I came back sad enough to my empty rooms, found Paul waiting for me, very kind, and his visit helped me, and then having dined off two cucumber sandwiches, I very gladly turned into bed."

3 May. "I went to the Academy private view; a fine day and I enjoyed seeing so many people and hearing so many voices again; lots of friends and acquaintances. Lady Haliburton congratulated me about R.'s scholarship, and said it was his mother's talent coming out, and I said, no, it was like the book, I took no credit, I had only edited both; and Billy Russell took off his hat with a low bow and said

'Bien dit'! Then to lunch at Sir John Pender's. I was warmly congratulated by Lord Duncannon and the Duchess of St. Albans upon R.'s success."

Then in December 1896. "Robert has shot his first woodcock, his first cock pheasant and his first snipe, but yesterday he was out ferreting and as the ferrets were a long time coming out, he put his gun against a tree and went on all fours to bark at the cows like a dog, and they came behind him and knocked the gun down on a stone, and it is badly dented. Such a baby for the Fourth Form! (he did well, was third in the Exam. and gets his remove to middle division) and I had been quite anxious about his brain the evening before, he was so intent on chess problems, though mastering them in a moment."

25 January. "Robert very happy until the last moment. He and the other boys went out shooting and ferreting before they started. I saw them off, then went to the workhouse, saw the Master who says the old men are delighted with the *Freeman's Journal* I am taking for them. Sister Xavier has been roused by my saying the men look dull, and is going to start a bookcase, and I am to give her some books . . . I was left quite alone, the house so silent that when I went up to dress for dinner I thought I was going to bed; and turned the lamp down. But I am glad to be alone for a time to 'possess my soul' and look life in the face."

The new Land Bill was then going through the House of Commons and I write: "I feel that this Bill is the last of 'Dobson's Three Warnings' and am thankful that we land-owners have been given even a little time to prepare and to work while it is day. It is necessary that as democracy gains power, our power should go; and God knows many of our ancestors and forerunners have eaten sour grapes and we must not repine if our teeth are set on edge. I would like to leave a good memory and not a 'monument of champagne bottles', and with all that, I hope to save the *home,* the house and woods at least for Robert. John Morley last week in his speech on the Land Bill quoted from the *Autobiography* the account of the Kinvara tenants, and spoke of Sir William as one who had never been a harsh landlord."

Mr. Blunt had written 1 April 1903: "I also wanted to know your thoughts about the new Land Bill. I think it excellent and a certain road to Home Rule. It will bring all the landlords too into patriotic ideas. I met Redmond only this morning and he asked me about you, whether

you were a Home Ruler. He had just received a letter from
Roosevelt about your *Cuchulain,* and he took out of his
pocket the little paragraph for me to send you, though I
daresay you will have already seen it."

Then came Mrs. Pat, I had visits from tenants very often,
with a long story of a projected lawsuit with the Quinns
about a right of way, and wanting a letter to the Magistrate
or the lawyer, or anyone in fact, and a pair of boots to take
her little girl to Court. I preached peace and arbitration,
refused the loan for the boots, but promised to give a pair
and also the £1 already spent on the lawyer in case of
arbitration.

Sometimes I myself took a holiday at Venice, staying with
Lady Layard at beautiful Ca Capello. She loved it better
than her London house and continued so far as she could
the same life as in her husband's time, welcoming his friends,
all of whom had become her own; and with all her simple
kindliness, keeping up the same dignity and stateliness as
before. What "Henry would have liked" was often on her
lips. Childless and with sufficient wealth, she had no anxieties
such as mine, and her interests did not widen as mine did.
Yet she was the nearest of my women friends, and our
affectionate friendship was never broken; so long as she
lived Venice was to me as a home.

I wrote to them from time to time.

20 May 1896. "Robert's birthday; fifteen years old. I have
looked forward to this birthday as an epoch, because my
first real recollection of myself is at fifteen, and because I
first knew Paul when he was at that age, and know how well
we have got on ever since, and that I have not bored him
but been friends, so I hope it may be the same with my
little son.

"I went with Lady Layard to Passini's studio, where her
portrait was being done, and looked through a portfolio of
his sketches. He said 'Ah, Madame, ce n'est que mon
hôpital"; and I said, 'Ah, Monsieur, je vois que vos malades
sont en train de commencer leur vie d'immortalité'!"

7 June. "Count Seckendorf has been here for a few days,
a pleasant guest. He leaves to-day to meet the Empress at
Trieste. He says the Emperor was led on by his advisers to
send the congratulatory telegram to Kruger, and is now very
sorry that he can't go to the Cowes Regatta, and wanted to
do so all the same. But he is very *rusé,* and is already trying
to make friends: has invited a large party of English naval

engineers to Berlin, and sent one of the officials who did most to egg him on against England to meet them at Hamburg. He is only afraid of one person in the world, that is his mother. He can wind the Queen round his little finger, and is *aux petits soins* with her. She said to Seckendorff, 'I am afraid the Empress does not know how to manage her difficult son, but I understand him quite well.' He persuaded her to become Colonel of one of his regiments, that he might in return have an English honour of the same kind, and is especially proud of having been made an English Admiral, and when he comes to stay with his mother in the country, comes down to dinner in a naval jacket. Seckendorff laments that the Empress's daughters don't care to look beyond their own affairs, and are no companions to their mother. Princess Charlotte thinks of nothing but playing with her babies, and is entirely under the dominion of her nurses. Sir E. Malet is not lamented at Berlin, but was harmless, never did anything. The Empress complained that he was no resource to her, and she would never have been treated so badly if Lord Ampthill had been there. He would have gone to Bismarck or the Emperor and said it would not be allowed, but Malet actually *shook* before them. Seckendorff dined with the Malets pretty often but never met any men worth meeting or of any distinction, except an occasional passer-through . . .

"Enid said to Admiral Canavaro (who had lived five years in England) in talking of duelling, 'you know we get on without it in England'. And he answered, 'Oui Madame, mais c'est différent; vous avez le boxe'!"

8th. "Countess Pisani, Passini and Belmondo to dinner . . . Some interesting talk as to how the Crown Prince of Austria had come by his death. Passini says his brother saw the dead body and said that, whereas a suicide's head is usually just pierced by a ball, his whole skull was smashed. Sir C. Euan Smith afterwards . . . He says he went to Windsor when he came back from Zanzibar, and the Queen said, 'I am afraid you have had a good deal of trouble with the Germans'. He bowed. Then, 'And with the Missionaries'. He bowed again, and she said, 'I have been talking over religious matters with my Munshi, and have come to the conclusion that, difficult as I have always found it to understand the doctrine of the Trinity when explained in my own language, I should find it impossible of explanation in any other'. He says she is completely in the hands of her Indian servants.

Lady E.S. says there is a terrible fever at Zanzibar, in which after death the temperature goes up to 115°. 107° is death."

And later . . . "About the Cretan question they spoke of the German Emperor's domineering ways . . . He was so indignant at the Duchess of Sparta joining the Greek Church that he ordered her never to come into Germany again, that if she did he would have her arrested at the frontier; upon which she took the first train and came; knowing he would not dare to carry out his threat!

"We have been from Saturday to Monday at Vescovana, Countess Pisani's, an amusing change, a great farm on the plains, fat and fertile, tilled by white oxen. The Countess full of energy, looking after every detail on the farm, having the 'bed-sores' of the oxen washed before her eyes; but also full of enthusiasm for art and literature, could not sleep one night because Don Antonio had been reading us the story of Ginevra from Boccaccio. A talk with her opens the windows of the mind. Yet I think love is lacking, she has no good word to say of the people she lives amongst. We are happier at Kiltartan.

"Taxes very high. Mrs. Eden says it is a charity to take a little packet of salt to a poor person. It costs so much they don't eat enough of it, and madness is sometimes the result. Coffee also very dear, and sugar, and petroleum, a pint of which costs as much as a quart in England. And the conscription takes all the young men away for at least a year and sometimes when they come back there is no place for them in their old workshops, and they suffer distress for a time."

October 1898. "The Strongs came to lunch. He is the Librarian of the House of Lords; he says it was in great disorder, and the Lords don't read much, but Lord Acton comes sometimes to consult an encyclopaedia which is not to be found at Cambridge. He spoke of Dublin—thinks J. F. Taylor very brilliant, and has recommended him to Lord A. to write on Philip IV. He has a great admiration also for John O'Leary, thinks it a privilege to know him, and says he lives for the ideal. He thinks the Trinity College body a very brilliant one, but that they live on board ship and have no current of communication with the country."

1898. "A gala day, all Venice decorated, the King and Queen having come to see the Emperor and Empress of Germany off. The procession on the Grand Canal passed this house. The Queen looked handsome and dignified though very stout, and her hair now bright gold. The

Emperor fat too, but has a pleasant face. He recognised Lady Layard on the balcony and waved his hand and touched his hat two or three times. The Empress looks rather a *hausfrau*, with a hideous black hat. They were all so amiable to each other, the Emperor carrying the Queen's parasol . . . one wonders if they will ever be at each other's throats."

And later: "People came in last evening, old Count Mocenigo, who is said to be the real possessor of Cyprus, and declared himself to have had a romantic attachment to Lady Dorothy Nevill!

"Venetian society has been excited by the infatuation of the Emperor for the Countess Morosini, said to be the most beautiful woman in Italy. He went to see her and stayed an hour and twenty three minutes, the mob waiting outside on the traghetto and counting the time. He ended by asking her to the private lunch that was to have settled the triple alliance, to meet the King and Queen, and after lunch gave her his arm and marched off to show her the ship, leaving their Majesties to the care of the Empress. But there is happily no scandal in the matter."

The Emperor paid a later visit to Venice, when Lady Layard was asked to meet him, at I forget what house. As she sat down she kept her umbrella in her hand, and he came and begged her to let him put it in safety in a corner, as it might be broken if she let it fall. She said she would be especially sorry if that were to happen as it had been given to her by one of the Princess's sisters. He had come to see her at Ca Capello, and had said he was anxious to have lectures given in Berlin on Sir Henry Layard's discoveries with photographs of the Nineveh marbles reproduced on screens. It seemed to her he had changed and softened very much.

XVII

LONDON AGAIN

I HAD SOMETIMES entertained a few friends while alone at the Layards' house in Queen Anne Street. In a letter to Sir Henry of December 1893 I say, "I have just given a successful little dinner here. I will enclose the menu that Enid may see what a grand cook I have in Hannah! (the housemaid). She really did extremely well, but I got in the soup from Verrays; also the cold beef and ice pudding. The pheasants were a present from Norfolk and the snipe from Ireland. The guests, Grant Duff and daughter, Sir Alfred Lyall and ditto, Mr. Alfred Cole, Mr. Fischer Williams, and Oswald Craufurd, who is now editor of *Black and White,* and it went off very pleasantly. We sat in the library afterwards, it is always very much admired. I have also had a little tea party, Emily Lawless, Clara Grant Duff, Mrs. Middleton (the Professor's wife), and Lisa Stillman came, and Sir M. Grant Duff, Henry James, Sidney Colvin and John Gray, a poet. I had been to tea with Miss Lawless the day before, and she had only one man, so I felt proud of my superiority! Old Lady C. lies on a sofa, a mass of black lace and affectation, she always speaks of you as 'those nice people with a balcony'. I dined with your friend, Mrs. Kaye one night . . . Kegan Paul was next me, he is agreeable enough but had behaved so badly to some of my friends (as a publisher) that I was pleased to find Mrs. Kaye had made no provision for fasters, and, it being Wednesday in Advent, he would not touch meat, and so was reduced to a diet of potato-chips and tomatoes, and grew very cross. Sir A. Lyall says it reminded him of a convert who wrote from Rome during Lent that 'there was nothing to eat and a great deal to swallow'!"

When I settled into my little flat in Queen Anne Mansions I missed the Queen Anne Street spacious library, the fine surroundings, and my guests had to miss that luxury of game from woods and bogs; but I had no trouble as housekeeper or provider, I had but to order a table to be kept for me in the restaurant. So very soon I was able to write that to my first little dinner there came Lady Layard, Sir Arthur and

Lady Clay, Sir Auckland Colvin (our old opponent in Egypt), Sir Frederic Burton, and a new acquaintance, Mr. Wardle of Leek, the dyer and silk manufacturer, and it was "very bright and pleasant; Mr. Wardle made a novelty and was able to talk to Enid and Lady C. about embroidery silks and to Sir Auckland about Indian silk worms; and Enid and I teased Sir Frederic.

"My next, for the Cecil Smiths, was Lord Carlisle, Hallam Murray and Sir A. Clay and Dorothy Stanley—also a success. The next I did not care so much for, it was for 'Armede Barine' Madame Vincens, whom Lee Childe had asked me to be civil to, and I got it up in a hurry. I had Mr. Cross (as A. Barine had written on George Eliot I thought she might like to meet her 'relict'), Edward Martyn, Albert Ball, Sir A. Birch to talk city to Cross. I had a more successful lunch for Madame Barine, T. P. O'Connor, who had never met her but had been devoting columns of the *Weekly Sun* to her last book *Bourgeois et gens de Peu,* and Oswald Craufurd who had showed London to Zola. I took Madame B. to the Temple afterwards, to see it under Nevill Geary's guidance."

I had another little lunch, to give Mr. Bennett, editor of the *Times of India,* an opportunity of meeting Sir Alfred Lyall, whom he had never seen. I also asked the Whites to dine, Australian friends of the Layards—Mr. White had an immense admiration for Sir Hercules Robinson, so I had him to meet them, and Wilfrid Blunt, and Mr. McBride (from Ceylon) to meet Sir Hercules, as they were all "horsey" and that also was a success. Mr. Blunt entertained the Whites and McBride at Crabbet the next Sunday.

And I went to some pleasant little dinners, "One with Wilfrid Blunt to meet Lord Carlisle and Lady Lytton; at the Childerses', where Sir Barrington Seymour, who sat next me, began by reading his menu with his back to me, and ended by inviting me to stay at his house in the Isle of Wight! Another with the Blakes—Sir Henry has brought some luminous beetles from Jamaica and Lady Blake wore them in her hair sometimes at night. Sir H. gave Robert two when he came for his exeat, and they were the cause of great anxiety and excitement, had to be fed on sugar and given damp bark to nestle in. We had to take them to Chenies and back again, and after all our care left them on the platform at Euston! So next day I had to start off in search and found them in the Lost Property office, and sent them on by post and one arrived alive . . .''

Another evening, I sat next Edwin Arnold. I confessed to not having read *Light of Asia,* and he said, "Oh, you will enjoy that, just listen to the opening stanzas", and repeated several pages! He told me of his reception in all parts of the world, how in an American village the post office clerk, when he asked for his letters, had cried, "Are you indeed Edwin Arnold?" and produced the *Light of Asia* from his pocket—and the old story of the Buddhist priests in Ceylon having read him an address. He did *not* tell me as G. A. Sala had done, who was present on the occasion, that in welcoming him as the exponent of Buddhism in the West, they had coupled his name with that of Madame Blavatsky, to his great indignation! Then he gave me his religious views, told me there was no real death or separation. "Lady Gregory—I myself have been married to two ladies, each of whom was a liberal education. They have both died —am I sorry? Not a bit!" On my other side was Lord —— who talked very modestly and intelligibly and puzzled me by his knowledge of the West Indies, till I found afterwards he had been a schoolmaster out there, and had succeeded to the title on the death of his cousin, who had married a South African Hottentot according to native rites, which marriage has been disallowed by the Courts in England. Stanley I met for the first time and was agreeably surprised. I saw very little of him, but he gave me his arm downstairs, regretted not having had more talk with me, he had heard so much of me, and we parted with mutual compliments.

I wrote of other houses from time to time. "The evening at Mrs. Bradley's was rather pleasant. Canon Gore took me out on the leads to see the Abbey roof by moonlight. Dean Bradley gave a little discourse in the Jerusalem Chamber."

"Tea at Lady Lindsay's, where I met Coventry Patmore. And with Lord and Lady Morris at the House of Lords to make acquaintance with old Colonel Talbot, the 'Pat' of Lord Talbot's letters."

"I dined with Alfred Cole, a very pleasant dinner. Mr. Welldon, Head Master of Harrow, Mr. Lyttelton, Head Master of Haileybury, Mr. and Mrs. Thackeray Ritchie. Welldon very amiable and pleasant. I had met him before, one day I came to Harrow and was sitting on the cricket field he came over and sat between R. and me, and talked for a long time, and seemed to have been much struck with the *Autobiography,* especially the story of the Soldier of the Cross."

I went to lunch one Sunday at Lady O'Hagan's, only Dr. Klein and Professor Dicey there. Klein gave an account of a Gipsy encampment in Wales he had once known, the Queen of the Gipsies was there, and her consort, who came from Waterford, and who complained that if his wife slept indoors she got fever and if he slept outdoors he got cold. Dicey said he had been asked to stand up in argument against John Dillon at Oxford but had refused. He said, "I feel convinced he will invent facts on the spot which I shan't be able to refute, and I am, unfortunately, unable to do the same, for though a willing, I am not a ready liar!"

"I met at dinner at Mrs. Kaye's old Sir Leopold McClintock, who I thought had died in past ages. It was reading articles by him in the *Sunday at Home* long ago that gave me an interest I have always kept in Arctic Voyages. And at the same dinner there was a young Mr. North, whose mother I found I had made acquaintance with one day when waiting at Waterloo Station for Robert. She had told me that when her son went to school, aged eleven, he did not know how to read, but was now a leading member of the Junior Bar. He and the rest of the company were much amused to hear this."

"On Sunday, Enid L., Sir F. Burton and Sidney Colvin dined with me. S. C. was much struck with the print of Pitt I had brought over to be framed, says it is very rare, he does not think it is in the British Museum, and those of Fox and Burgess he also thinks very good."

15th. "I met at dinner Mr. O., who is tutor to some of the Royal children, and says his lot has fallen in pleasant places, though F. declares he is no better than an upper footman. I had heard a story of him, which he confirms, that one day when the Royal children were having tea at Balmoral, little Princess Ina of Battenberg was very naughty, and he said, 'I wish I could go and lunch with the Queen and see how you behave there'. Next day at lunch Princess Ina said, 'Gan-Gan'. 'Well, my dear,' said Her Majesty. 'Gan-Gan, Mr. O. says he would like to lunch with you.' There was a dead silence, the lady-in-waiting horrified. Afterwards, Her Majesty asked what was the meaning of this, and fortunately someone had been present and was able to give the correct version. A few days later, Her Majesty invited him on an expedition, and they had tea together, a party of six, and he had to explain to her the difference between Rugby and Association Football." . . . "Mlle. de Perpignan says the old Emperor said to her he would rather sit in the saddle for four hours than listen to Wagner's music for two."

As to good works, I did not quite neglect the old women's Monday meetings, had one very successful one, gave them tea and had Lady Layard, with her guitar, and Cecil Smith, with his banjo, and at other times went alone. I also had from twelve to twenty Southwark children on several Saturdays to picnic on the grass in St. James's Park, row on the lake, and fish with their mugs on its edge. Once I borrowed Lady Layard's carriage and took the teachers for a drive in the Park to their great joy. I also went and helped at "Happy Evenings" at the Board School.

"I met Lecky in the street and stopped to give him my good wishes for the election. (He was standing for Dublin University.) He is low about it, says he did not want to stand, but was begged to do so, and that he would rather not get in at all than by a very small majority. And he refuses to give his religious opinions, says they are a matter for himself. I went on afterwards to Lady Arthur Russell's and Flora told me of a lady at Dr. Vaughan's, who asked who that very tall man was, and was told Lecky, the writer. She asked what he had written, and on hearing the *History of Rationalism,* said 'Then this is no place for me!' and marched off. Sir R. Meade came to tea, rather exhausted, Chamberlain having come back from his tour in a preternatural state of energy and keeping them all at the Colonial Office up to the mark."

8th. "I called on Mrs. Lecky, who is anxious and eager about the election and worried about all the letters they receive, some asking questions, some for subscriptions already."

6 May. "I had a letter from Robert, a little down-hearted, I think, 'finds Harrow very different from Elstree, as you have to find out everything for yourself from other boys, and the masters hardly tell you anything'. He invites me to go down and see what is wanting for his room, and this of course I jumped at. And in the morning the housemaid brought me the African butterflies H. H. Johnston had promised to leave for R. and had I thought forgotten. So I flew to the nearest framer and persuaded him to put them in a case at once for me to take.

"I found him at the station gate, rather shy in his little

tail coat and flat little hat . . . He had been a little lonely at first, the only new boy in the House and rather 'out of it', feeling in the way in their games, but is beginning to settle down, is getting on better in work and likes his drawing. We went out shopping and got a little clock and some plants and a blotter and stuff for new curtains, and the room looked much more home-like when we had arranged it and taken down the fans the last boy had put up. We also went to a grocer, 'where if you spend seven and sixpence you get a book of American views'. I went in to see Mr. Bowen, his Housemaster, a quiet elderly man, though as alert at cricket as any schoolboy. He was kind and pleasant but has not the brilliance of his brother. (Yet, while Lord Bowen's witty phrases will long be quoted at the Bar and have been put on record in print, the memory of the other will be kept fresh, as it seems for ever, through his School Songs, 'Forty Years On' and the rest, sung so delightfully on Harrow Speech Days, though it may be remembered later with heartbreak by some who heard them.)

"I came back late and fagged with the heat, but happier about my child, on the whole."

I went to Waterloo Station to see the Robinsons off to the Cape, both more cheery, Lady R. pleased with the bouquets and bustle, Sir Hercules hoping to come back very soon, thinks there will be some little tangle that wants undoing in a year's time, "just about the date of the Derby!".

10th. "I went to see *Trilby* with Paul . . . Lord Dufferin was sitting a little way behind, and I went and spoke to him and hoped he had forgiven me. He said, 'Quite' and held my hand, and said it was Murray's fault; but I refused to agree to that. But he said the effect was good, and that it was Lord Aberdeen who had let the secret out, as he has now discovered by making researches. He has had a letter from Lord Stanmore saying this. I asked if there would be anything about it in Sidney Herbert's *Life* and he said quite probably."

At dinner at the Leckys', Sir A. Lyall was startled at hearing I had written an article about the Athenaeum Club*. But I told him I had been discreet and had not put in about the member who takes off his boots before the fire, or the one that steals the soap. He asked if I had told of the one who, on being spoken to by a member he had not been

* "Eothen and the Athenaeum Club" in *Blackwood's Magazine*.

introduced to, rang the bell and said, "Waiter, I think this gentleman wants something. He is speaking!" Lady Victoria Plunkett told me Lord Dufferin had been delighted with *Trilby* the other night, and had gone to sup with the actors and actresses afterwards. Then Lecky talked to me, more resigned about his election, but says if he gets in it will interfere with his literary work, and he wished to write about the beginning of this century in Ireland, after the Union. Mrs. O. told me she had heard Gladstone at a dinner party talk the entire time on asparagus, which he planted, divided, cut, till everyone was bored to death.

16th. "At lunch at the Haliburtons. I sat next Sir Redvers Buller, who says Mahaffy is tormenting his life out to be made an English Dean. Old F. Leveson Gower has just been staying at Hawarden, where he found the G.O.M. extraordinarily well, but Mrs. Gladstone a good deal broken. When he was leaving, Gladstone said, 'So glad to have got you here, and I hope you will repeat the visit *every year!*'

"I took E. Layard to Southwark Board School and made the children have a Scripture examination that she might see they are taught the Bible. And they sang 'Jesus, Lover of my Soul' and 'I heard the voice of Jesus say' . . . I hope she will get interested in place."

"I was at C.P.'s[1] wedding at the Plymouth Brethren Hall in Welbeck Street, a shabby-looking place, a little table with green altar cloth representing an altar; some flowers on the chimney piece above it. She looked nice, fresh and good-humoured, and her dress, white silk, fashionably made. First we sang a hymn, and then a 'brother' gave an extempor-ary prayer, 'Lord, provide the wine for this marriage feast'; 'Amen,' from the bridegroom, etc. Then he read with a running exposition, passages from the Bible bearing on matrimony, but was interrupted by the Registrar, a shabby-looking man, who had taken his seat at the green table, and who pointed at the clock, ten minutes to three, and said that if not celebrated before three o'clock the marriage would not be legal. So the bridegroom repeated a form of words, something like this: 'I promise that I will live with this woman as her true and faithful husband, according to the principles laid down in the word of God'. And she repeated the same form, and the ring was put on as a memorial of this. Then they signed their names in the register; then

[2] Cecy Parnell.

another hymn and an address on the bad marriages of the Bible—Abraham's wife was ninety, Moses married a black woman, etc.—with application that Christ in wedding the Church is ready to wed sinners. Then extemporary prayers were requested from the congregation, and one or two men responded—one prayer for 'her ladyship and all the family and also the aged mother of the bridegroom'; and after another hymn all was over. It was less solemn than a church marriage, and I think its simplicity would have been impressive if only the text, the promise of fidelity, and a hymn had been given, but the ramshackle prayers and address spoiled it. The reception crowded, so I only stayed a minute, and went on to call on Miss Lefevre, who was excited over John Dillon's marriage which had taken place that morning at eight o'clock, to exclude friends and the Irish Party. Miss Matthew is very bright and clever and had been in love with Dillon for eight years, but he would not marry while there were any evicted tenants.

"Madeline Lefevre has become member of a school board, and is astonished to find how much religion is taught, and she has persuaded the clergyman who had been holding aloof to join, and he is also astonished, and confesses he could not do the instructing much better himself. I took E.L. to a Southwark 'Happy Evening' and taught the children 'Fly away pigeon' and 'Earth, Air and Water'.

"Sir A. Haliburton says he is taking one of the War Office men to Brighton for a change, as he has been completely knocked up by all the work lately, and especially by a new envelope that has been issued, into which the paper used will not fit without extra folding—this has got on his brain. What a horrible idea!

"At tea at Mrs. Humphry Ward's I told her I was amused in Matthew Arnold's letters at the serious way he speaks of croquet. She laughed and said he was a wretched croquet player, but quite happy to spend hours knocking the balls about on a steep slope on which they played.

"Mrs. Lecky is very anxious about her husband's election; she had a telegram saying the nomination had gone off well, but the uproar so great the speeches could not be heard.

"I dined at the Walpoles'. They apologised for a small party as they had four put-offs at the last, but I was well enough off as I was next my host, who is so agreeable and a mine of knowledge. I told him of Morley saying in his M. Arnold article that there are probably not more than six

men over fifty now living in England whose lives will be
worth writing, and he tried to pick them out, but only got
to Gladstone, Lord Salisbury, Herbert Spencer and Lord
Dufferin. But he said a very good hundred pages could be
written about Lord Peel.

"I went with Martin Morris and E. Martyn to the Carlyle
Centenary meeting to hear John Morley speak, which was
a great delight, hearing instead of reading for once his
luminous sentences. He spoke of Wordsworth and Goethe
having 'a radiant sanity of vision, a serene humanity'. Then
A. Birrell spoke, very well and brightly, with jests and
epigrams, and it was good to see Morley's enjoyment of it.
Frederic Harrison proposed the vote of thanks not very well.
Morley said he hardly believed anyone now living had read
through *Frederick the Great,* but E. Martyn and I, we two
Galwegians, said simultaneously to each other, 'I have done
so'. John Morley comes nearer my idea of an inspired teacher
than anyone I have heard or read of living writers, and
makes one at least grope after the 'radiant sanity of vision'
that we want so much in poor Ireland. I bought a *Pall Mall,*
and saw that Lecky was elected all right; and sent a telegram
of congratulations to Mrs. L."

7th. "I saw Mr. Woods at Christie's about the Waithman's
Velasquez. He said to me, 'Well, I must say you are a lady
with a great many friends'. (He believes it is genuine
Velasquez but doesn't think the public sufficiently educated
to give much for it.) Then I went to Jean Ingelow, whom
I thought a good deal changed and broken, rather inconse-
quent in talk. She has given up writing for some months.
She is always cheerful and says she had no reason to complain
of literature or of her publishers, as she has made a good deal.
She is reading M. Arnold's letters, and thinks them 'rubbish';
but had liked him and Mrs. Arnold, and used to stay with
them. Browning's poems she thinks 'vulgar' but liked Mrs.
Browning's. When I mentioned Lewis Morris, she asked, 'Is
that the shopman?' Poor thing, I hardly think I shall see
her again."

At Mrs. Kaye's I sat between Lord Lingen, who was
interesting on educational matters, and Mr. Barry O'Brien,
a Nationalist, sub-editor of *The Speaker,* and very sensible
and moderate in conversation. He believes in Home Rule,
but thinks there is no chance for it until all the present
members are swept off the Board. He says he has been talking
to one of the writers on the *Freeman,* who has been travelling

in Ireland, and who says the only thing in which all parties are agreed is the failure of Morley's government. He (B. O'B.) believes A. Balfour is the only man who has any understanding of Ireland, and believes he would have swept the whole country if he had gone over and made a speech against Cromwell, whom he is not an admirer of, when the Liberals proposed to erect a statue to him. We agreed on the extraordinary stupidity of even enlightened men like Morley and Bryce in Irish affairs, in having ever thought the Irish would let such a proposal pass.

9 December 1895. "Dined at the Humphry Wards' . . . Du Maurier there, he told me he had been astonished at the success of *Trilby,* he had written it 'in corners' to amuse himself; and that he himself prefers *Peter Ibbetson,* but his new book contains quite a different heroine.

"This morning I had a beautiful bouquet of game sent by Dr. Moran, nine snipe and two teal . . . and then 'Mr. Spencer Walpole' was announced, and had come to ask me to dine, to meet Sir West Ridgeway, and luckily I was free and had been wishing for something to distract my thoughts in the evening, and he sat and chatted pleasantly for a little. On over-reading, he said that Lord Acton had read eighteen books on a Saturday to Monday in the country. No wonder his lecture on History had such an undigested effect! . . . Very pleasant dinner at the Walpoles', three ex-governors of the Isle of Man. My host, West Ridgeway and Lord Loch, with Lady Loch, Lord and Lady Rendal, and the Lyalls, and Wentworth Beaumont."

15 April. "Lunched Lady Dorothy's . . . C. spoke rather sneeringly of Lord Morris, and said 'he doesn't take his Duchesses as his daily bread!' Frank Lawley paid me a long visit, delighted with my Kinglake article[2]. He gets the wrong end of the news sometimes, and had heard a few days ago such alarming news of Lord Salisbury's health that he had written an obituary notice of him. Also that the one 'leader of men' in the Ministry is Lord Lansdowne. He said he had met Cecil Rhodes in the summer, and he had said his chief relaxation is having translations of the classics read to him, that his sight is going, and in a year he will be quite blind. But he said, 'I am not going to be like your old chief, I will still keep the helm in my own hands'!"

And garden party at Lambeth, where I stood admiring the

[2]"Eothen and the Athenaeum Club."

poor Archbishop's courtesy and good looks, standing the whole long afternoon to receive his guests that none might miss his greeting . . .

4th. "At dinner with Sir Harry Johnston. I sat between him and 'Mr. Guthrie', who only at the end of dinner I felt must be Anstey, he was so original and pleasant. I also talked to Orchardson, a rather Don Quixote-looking lanky figure, very quaint and agreeable. Sir Harry said, 'We used to be very hard on him in the life school at the Academy and he says he is proud of it, as it did him so much good'.

"At the Leckys' I sat next Lord Loch, who had been to hear Cecil Rhodes examined by the Committee, and thinks he came badly out of it. His answers were not straight, and he had not even read the Blue Book, and Lord L. is very down upon Flora Shaw, who he thinks seems to have precipitated the revolution."

Sunday . . . "I had a long visit from Lecky, very kind and pleasant, more lively and less mysterious, I thought, than in his pre-Parliament days. He said that when his *Rationalism* came out it was much talked of and sold quickly; the *Morals,* which he had always preferred himself, lagging behind. But of late it has been coming on, and they are now all but abreast as far as the sale goes. He had divided his history of Ireland from that of England, because it had grown so out of proportion, and though it has far more original matter in it, the English has been selling very much better. He disparages his *Leaders of Public Opinion,* only wants to keep the O'Connell, and to re-write that. He is anxious, if he ever finds time, to write on the Famine and the Tithe War, so little comparatively is known about them."

XVIII

MR. GREGORY'S LETTER-BOX

IN OCTOBER 1896 I wrote to Lady Layard: "I have had a fortnight of complete solitude and freedom. I have been very much out of doors, looking after woods and gates and fences, and have much enjoyed the lovely weather and the changing tints of the leaves . . . I have begun going through the box of old Mr. Gregory's papers, which W. and I once or twice began to do together, but did not persist in. Some of his early letters from Harrow to his grandfather are there, dated sixty years ago! . . . I live literally 'looking before and after', back over his life, forward to Robert's" . . .

For when I first came to Coole my husband had shown me a large iron-clamped leather-covered box containing letters to and from his grandfather, another Rt. Hon. William Gregory, who had been Under Secretary for Ireland 1813 to 1830. We sometimes talked of going through those letters, once we even began to read them. But it happened that almost all we took out of the first bundles were from men of no great account begging for places, to be made Magistrates, Baronets, Stampers, Tidewaiters, Landwaiters and Chief Constables. And after a few days' work we put off the task, and now, when I came back to it, I was alone.

There were letters, many of them intimate and even affectionate, from the Viceroys and Chief Secretaries of the time; Lord Whitworth, Lord Wellesley, Lord Talbot, Lord Anglesey, the Duke of Northumberland, Sir Robert Peel, and him who was later known as Lord Melbourne. Although prints of these hung in the breakfast room, I did not know much about them or about the history of their time; the years of the fear of a French landing, and of the fight for Catholic Emancipation. I was more interested in some little rebel songbooks "found in Lord Edward Fitzgerald's Apartments in Leinster House" at the time of his arrest. But as I went through the letters, most of them written in a clearer hand than those of present-day politicians, the character of each writer began to show itself out dimly; and then having come to the bottom of the box, I went to Dublin and read histories of their time in the National Library, and even collected "folk-lore" from memory or tradition about some of the personages of that day, until having rubbed away some of the dust of time, they stood out clear in my mind.

I wrote while in Dublin: "I dined with old Mr. Henn and after many efforts extracted an anecdote of O'Connell from him and one or two of Lord Plunket. And his sister, Mrs. La Touche, gave me a nice recollection of Daniel O'Connell."

I learned of present-day notable people also.

"I had a pleasant dinner at George Morris's. He has served under twelve Chief Secretaries, and Arthur Balfour shines among them all. 'He was vexed if you didn't give him your own opinion. He'd say what he thought and lean back against the chimney piece and turn up his coat tail and say, "Now tell me what *you think*". I declare if that man had given me a kick, I'd almost have been ready to say thank-you for it'."

(Yeats interrupts here: "When I first met Arthur Balfour I wrote to my father describing his conversation, its hesitation and lack of emphasis, and he wrote back, 'You have described a born leader of men'. Men would not feel when they met him the presence of a rival egotism but the presence of some truth.")

And I wrote, 19 February: "I stayed in Galway for a while —there, I got a dear little pup, "Rip", for Robert and I went and saw Sir Thomas Moffett at the College and he not only lent me several books useful to me, but told me anecdotes of Lord Whitworth and Lord Talbot, etc., which will be a help if I publish."

Then I set a good deal of what I had already written out, in typewriting, Lord Talbot's letters and others. These I sent to Lord Peel, to ask him if I might use them without indiscretion, and he said, yes. Then I wrote a narrative in which to set the more interesting of the letters, and when I had done the best I could with the material I sent the manuscript to John Murray. It was a disappointment when he refused it, not thinking it had in it enough new material. But this was all for the best, for I worked at it again, cutting out some dull parts, and then I found some material that was new. For I remembered that Sir William had been asked to lend all letters from Sir Robert Peel to the Trustees who were arranging for his life to be written. So I wrote again to Lord Peel and asked if I might have these letters, for they had never been returned. He gave leave, but said there were twelve hundred of them and I would have to get them from Mr. Parker, who had for a long time been writing the *Life* and had not yet brought it to an end. But when I applied to Mr. Parker he wrote once, twice and three times that he had done with the letters, but that they were put away—I think in a cellar—with other papers he had used, and that it would be a troublesome matter looking for them. But I have learned how much more valuable one grain of original matter will be than any amount of reproducing, so I clung to the hope of my twelve hundred letters. And at last, by a happy thought, I wrote saying that, as I wanted to save him any possible trouble, I would call the next day at his house, and with his leave, would myself make the search. And the next morning I had a hurried note from him saying I need not take the trouble of coming, I should have the letters at once. And so, on 23 March 1897, "I had a visit from Mr. Parker, bringing the letters at last. He was very kind, and stayed a long time talking. He told me Peel had been fond of pistol practice at Harrow, and also of shooting. He and a friend kept guns at a house some distance off. One day, after they had left their guns, a master met them and asked where they had got the birds they were carrying, and the friend said, 'Oh, Peel is such a wonderful shot with a stone!'. He thinks he will have one volume ready by Christmas, the next six weeks later, but they have not yet got leave, or asked it, to publish his letters to the Queen, and now he hears she is herself writing a book and may say, 'I will publish what is proper to appear and the rest must be left unpublished!' He has heard that Peel once apologised to someone he had affronted by his coldness, for his unfortunate manner."

And after my own book was published and he had seen in it a letter referring to Peel having had the whooping cough, Mr. Parker said to me regretfully, "I meant to print that one, but Lord Peel said, 'I think we had better not mention the whooping cough'."

I now sent my manuscript to Smith Elder and was asked to call there. The first day I came I was not known in the office and was looked on, I think, with suspicion; I believe they thought I was a poetess. But upstairs Reginald Smith was charming and we had soon settled matters, for though they would not publish at their own risk, I was ready to take that. (And I did not lose in the end, it paid its way.) That was the beginning of a pleasant acquaintanceship. I remember in that first conversation I made some allusion to "wicked publisher" and he interrupted, "Are there not wicked baronets also?" and I said, "but they are in fiction whereas . . ." and we both laughed.

And on the 6 March I wrote: "My book comes out to-morrow and I am getting anxious about it. Smith says it has been fairly well subscribed, but much will depend on the reviews." I was dining with the Leckys that evening and he had not spoken of it (although he had given me at the outset very good practical advice, to begin by buying a quantity of very large envelopes for sorting my material). "As he put my cloak on in the hall I noticed a parcel from Smith Elder and knew it was a copy I had ordered to be sent him as to other friends."

Next day (Sunday): "I lunched with the Lyalls, and Sir Alfred thanked me for the book, I had sent him a copy, and I said, 'I don't suppose Irish Politics are much in your line'. 'Oh yes,' he said, 'it sent me back to Lecky'. Then he said he thought I was wrong in saying Napoleon flourished his cane at Lord Whitworth. I said my authority was Sir Thomas Moffett, President of Queen's College. Then he said it was badly bound, in which he is right, and that I ought to speak to Smith, and he noticed the date on cover being different from that on title page. This not very encouraging and I went home rather low. Lady Blake came in for a talk, and then Sir Henry Cunningham, and then Mr. Lecky, who when the others had gone, spoke with enthusiasm of the book. He said, "We know so little of that period, all is known up to the Union and after the Famine, but that is a blank." I was quite cheered, for I was more anxious for his good opinion than for any other. He thinks me a little hard on Plunkett and that he was not a proselytiser, because he remembers a saying of his to his son, the Bishop of Man, "Leave the Catholics alone" . . . He also thinks I am a little severe to George III. But Sir Frederic Burton, who came in afterwards, said, 'I am glad you have come down on the real culprit, King George III, and quoted one or two people who had said his obstinacy was the real cause of so many of Ireland's troubles. He is much pleased with the book (I have already told of our little talk at that time)."

"The next day, after rather a bad night, I looked at *The Times*, no notice at all in it, but a very good one in the *Chronicle* . . . In the Reading Room I found a fairly good article in *Daily News*, a poor one in the *Standard*, which wants to know who I am! An old gentleman had got hold of the *Telegraph* and I had to wait a long time before I could get it and see Frank Lawley's gushing notice, but the *Chronicle* was much the most interesting . . . Smith thought I ought to be very well content with four reviews on the first day. And I had a charming letter from Lord Rosebery, 'I only received the book yesterday afternoon but have been unable to lay it down; the picture of Lord Talbot is the pleasantest: soft in heart (and I fear in head) but extremely loveable. Perhaps I am naturally moved, however, by his description of Dalmeny! The picture of Lord Wellesley is not less faithful: One can never understand how he played so great a part in India; Sir Robert Peel's letter on 1 July 1829 is most valuable, because so much more succinct than his other defences.' And he shows how carefully he read the book by pointing out a mistake in a date, 1 July, on Peel's letter, which ought to have been 1 February (he had written January and then put a scratch to make it February, which made it look like July) . . . Other nice letters, liked one from old Mrs. Martin saying her grandfather, Chief Justice Bushe, had never been done justice to before, and quoting a saying about him I should have liked to use, 'he shrank from giving pain with the same instinct other men do from feeling it'. Then I was told by A. P. Graves that—a great compliment—Lecky was reviewing the *Box* for the *Spectator* and on the 19th he wrote that this article 'takes the first place'. I should have recognised it, anyhow, both by what he blames and what he praises, he is a very good sincere friend.

"I am glad he has seen it, for I remember him once saying that in all his writings he had never had any help from the landowning class, they were indifferent to history, so I feel that reproach had been taken off Coole. Then, going to buy a *Spectator* and looking at the *Athenaeum* I found it also had a first page review, very good, and I think more likely to attract readers than the others, though it criticises the 'brilliant unorthodoxy' of my editing, and is down on me for the wrong date of the title page, though it is really the cover, for which I am not responsible, that has the wrong date, and the *Athenaeum* itself which heads the article as the *Letter Box*, has in the table of contents immediately above, *Mr. Gregory's* Post Box, so *it* needn't call out against inaccuracy!

"And dining at the Morrises', Lady Morris says she could not get Lord Morris to bed last night, he was so taken up with it. I sat between Lord Denbigh and Sidney Colvin. Lord Morris was in great humour, praising my book (so it must be a success) and is sending a copy to Lady Londonderry, and Willy Peel who was there, says Lord Acton was very full of it at Trinity. I say the worst of the *World* review is that people will expect me when I dine out to be as amusing as Lord Morris. 'So you are,' says Lady M., and I say in return that it was necessary for me to have good reviews or Martin (he had just published an amusing book on America) would not acknowledge me, but his lordship says, 'Ah'm sure Martin's is only a tuppeny halfpenny ephemeral sort of a thing, but yours is a book of importance. As Lecky says, it deals with a time that has passed out of memory, but has not passed into history.'

"Then a nice letter from Lord Peel and a cheery one from Robert who says, 'I have begun to read your book and like it very much, though I did not think it would suit me'."

I am glad I did that work just then, I could not have taken it up later, when creative work came my way. It tidied up that mass of papers that one felt ought to be gone through and so saved trouble to those who may come after me. It put on record good work done by little Richard's great-great-grandfather. The last time I saw it mentioned in a newspaper was, I think, in an article by Roger Casement in America, saying that until the publication of those letters there had never been any idea of the serious anxiety of the government in those years as to the dangers of a French invasion of Ireland and a Rebellion.

But my real connection with intellectual work in my own country was now about to begin—

XIX

THE CHANGING IRELAND

I THINK it was in 1896 that I suddenly became aware of the change that had come about in Ireland in those first years after Parnell's death. My twelve years of married life had been the years of the Land War, tenant struggling to gain a lasting possession for his children, landlord to keep that which had been in trust to him for his. All the passion of Ireland seemed to be thrown into that fight, it obscured the vision beyond it of the rebuilding of a nation. Then, at last, had come the breaking of Parnell's power and his death, the quarrel among his followers that pushed politics into the background, and with the loss of that dominance of his, there came a birth of new hope and interests, as it were, a setting free of the imagination. First among the builders of the new Ireland I had already set the name of Douglas Hyde, the founder of the Gaelic League, when I saw last year (May 1922) that Michael Collins had thus written of that League under the title of "The Greatest Event" and "It restored the language to its place in the reverence of the people. It revived Gaelic culture; while being non-political it was, by its very nature, intensely national . . . Irish history will recognise in the birth of the Gaelic League in 1893 the most important event of the nineteenth century but in the whole history of our nation. It did more than any other movement to restore the national pride, honour and self-respect. Through the medium of the past it linked the people with the past and led them to look to a future that would be a noble continuation of it." I think he has not said too much, and that the small beginning, in Galway first of all, and then other Irish-speaking places, the bringing together of the people to give the songs and poems, old and new, kept in their memory, led to the discovery, the dis-closure, of folk learning, of folk poetry of ancient tradition, to an upsetting of the table of values, to an extraordinary excitement. The imagination of Ireland had found a new homing place. Douglas Hyde's vision, as he founded that League had been one of those "solid announcements" of the poets that, while looked on as dreams, come true.

Horace Plunkett was another of those first builders. He had led that unloosed imagination to practical uses, like the farmer in the old folk tale who set his sons to dig in search of a treasure to be found in the field, he urged the better cultivation of the soil, the better management of dairies, of farms; above all, he brought about that friendliness and strength that comes from working together, rather than in isolation. He began that co-operative farming that England and America have not been too proud to take a lesson from. Yeats, on the other hand, forming a Literary Society, speaking on literature, had called for the freedom of the individual from the long tradition of patriotic poetry of propagandist writing, which to criticise was to lay a hand upon the sacred Ark. He would never have any truce with a poet who was content with less than the perfect form, whatever national cause he might be trying to serve.

These were the men I was happy enough to meet after I had tried here and there in my lonely months to find work to do for my country. I did not find it in a moment. As usual in my parochial way, working at what was close at hand, I was brought through Gort Convent into connection with the "Irish Industries". I had taught the nuns or their pupils to embroider with linen thread upon linen in the old Portuguese style, and when they had made some very charming blinds and counterpanes they asked me to take them to the London sale, together with hand-woven flannel and linen, and even "tennis dresses" made from a distant view of some tennis parties seen from the convent windows. My letters telling of having slept on the eve of a sale "with a pyramid of parcels in the middle of my room . . . And at the sale the "tennis dresses" recalling those of the wives in the Noah's Arks in our childhood lay despised till Lady Fingall slipped them one by one over her own dress and sold them off triumphantly.

But I didn't like the sales; I didn't think they "brought dignity to Ireland". I was not sorry when a break-down in the convent on the business side, set me free.

I went on with my quiet life. In the February of 1895 I wrote to E.L.: "The garden is like Italy, warm sunshine and many flowers out, wallflowers, grape hyacinths, violets and in the woods, primroses. I did a little ornamental planting yesterday, putting out copper beeches and laburnums raised from seed in my own nursery. I hope, if there are ever grandchildren, they will be grateful some day. Our people are paying rents and paying very well, and a policeman who came from Gort in the holidays to cut the boys' hair said he was glad of the distraction, as they have absolutely nothing to do about here now." And then in August: "Paul Bourget and his wife have been at Duras, de Basterot brought them over one day to lunch. Bourget was interested in oriental things but most of all in a photograph of Parnell, the last taken of him, which I had put in a frame, writing at the back the words of an old ballad—

> Oh, I hae dream'd a dreary dream
> Beyond the Isle of Skye:
> I saw a dead man win a fight
> And I think that man was I.

He held it to his breast and walked about the house with it, struck by the tragedy of the dying face. Edward Martyn had also poets with him, Arthur Symons, and W. B. Yeats, who is full of charm and the Celtic revival. I have been collecting fairy-lore since his visit and am surprised to find how full of it are the minds of the people, and how strong the belief in the invisible world around us." I remember the first day Edward and his mother brought them out to lunch with me, I showed Yeats a letter from Bret Harte, to whom I had sent his *Celtic Twilight,* and saying, "I am reading it during my only really intelligent and lucid intervals—in bed, at night! Then I have time and leisure to enjoy what I am reading, and it is, after all, not a bad thing to drop off to sleep with the fairies! I think I am particularly delighted with a certain Mr. Montgomery who doubts the alleged fact of his wife's ghostly reappearance on earth, on the grounds that 'she would not show herself to Mrs. Kelly! She with respectable people to appear to!' This seems to me to add another sting to death! Let us hope that we may all live such a life in this world that we shall be able to reappear in it hereafter to the most respectable people, and in the best society."

The Sligo legends in that little book made me jealous for Galway, and the gathering of legend among my own neighbours became a chief interest and a great part of my work for many years to come. The gathering was for the most part mine, but as it had been begun so it was continued under Yeats' direction so to speak, so far as the lore of vision was concerned. The folk history and folk tales and poems came later and made a foundation for many of my plays;

I found suggestion, inspiration, and the means of expression there. Is there not a tale of a King and his Court who went through the world looking for a wonder worker, a saint or healer, they believed to be living in some far place; and it was when they had returned after years of the vain pursuit they found he had sat all the while hidden under the rags of a beggar they had seen daily sitting at the door. And I know that even as a child my heart would feel oppressed at some rare moments with emotion, as I saw the snipe rise sidelong from the rushy marsh, sunset reflected in its pools, or the wild deer among the purple heather of the hills from which I looked on distant mountain and sea. That feeling came again and again in later years, when some olive-belted hill, or lovely southern plain that well satisfied the eye, filled the heart with a hunger, a pain of longing, I knew not for what. I know now it was the artist's desire to capture, to express, the perfect. And although fulfillment has fallen far, far short of vision, I know how barren one side of my life would have been without that poetry of the soil, those words and dreams and cadences of the people that helped me to give some echoed expression to that dragging driving force.

But folk-lore was only one among Yeats' interests at that time. He was tumbling now and again into politics. He wrote to me from Manchester in that autumn of 1897, "We had a long and exhausting political meeting this morning and will have another tonight . . . Miss Gonne and I went to the picture gallery after the meeting to see a Rossetti that is there . . . This is a very feeble letter, the sort of thing one writes when one is ten years old. It is a fine day. How are you? A tree has fallen into the pond. I have a new canary, and etc. You know the style. But I have been chairman of a noisy meeting for three hours and am very done up. I have a speech to prepare for tonight. Everything went smoothly this morning in spite of anonymous letters warning us to have a bodyguard at the door. Perhaps the disturbance waits for tonight. I find the infinite triviality of politics more trying than ever. We tear each other's character to pieces for things that don't matter to anybody."

And I had written in that summer, "One evening Hanlon brought me in some trout he had caught at the Natural Bridge, and as next day was Friday, I drove over to Tillyra to offer them to Mrs. Martyn. There I found W. B. Yeats just arrived from Dublin, white, haggard, voiceless, fresh

from the jubilee riots which he had been in the thick of,
having been led into them as escort to Miss Gonne. However,
he had by main force and lock and key kept her from
reaching the mob when it had come into collision with the
police. Black flags had been distributed and windows
broken. It was not a very dignified proceeding and he himself disapproved of it, not because of respect for the Queen
for he thinks it was right to make some protest against the
unhappy misgovernment and misfortunes of Ireland during
her reign, but that he thinks that the impulse should come
from the people themselves and not be thrust on them from
above. Some episodes were amusing. He heard "cheers for the
French" and then some men cried "and boo for the
Germans", and another said: "Why do you boo the Germans,
don't you know they're the worst enemies of England now?"
"Are they so?" said the other, "then hi for them!" And
going into the Theosophist Society afterwards he saw a tall
Theosophist, whom he had last seen lying on his face on a
hillside striving after unearthly visions, sitting in triumph
with a thick stick by his side, with which he had just
knocked down a policeman; somebody whispered to Yeats,
"We saw him carried away to the hospital".

But even my growing friendship with Yeats did not bring
me into that National struggle in which he had a hand,
although my feeling against Home Rule had gradually been
changing[1]. It is hard to say how the change of mind came.
There was preparation for it in my husband's liberal views,
(though he, too, had cried out against Gladstone's proposals)
and in my friendship with Wilfrid Blunt, and my always
friendly and affectionate intercourse with the people. Perhaps
also in that work on the *Letter Box* which had given me a
more intimate knowledge of Irish history. But I felt less
and less interest in politics as other interests came in. I had
soon laid down a formula for myself, "Not working for Home
Rule, but preparing for it", and this, by adding dignity to
the country through our work. But it is hard to keep quite
clear.

And in the summer of 1897, I wrote: "I have been a little

[1] In 1895, Lady Gregory had been sufficiently anti-Home Rule to get
published anonymously her *Phantom's Pilgrimage or Home Ruin*,
which showed what terrible things would happen to Ireland if the
Bill was passed. The Earl of Wemyss drew a cartoon for its
frontispiece, which was not used: it shows a ghostly Gladstone seated
on top of a railway engine steaming into the night.

in disgrace myself about the Jubilee. George Gough had ordered a bonfire to be lighted at Lough Cutra, and then had written to all the neighbours calling on them to do the same. I refused on the ground of the Queen's neglect of the country. (The Prince told Sir William in Ceylon she had even prevented him from coming when he wished to.) W. Shawe-Taylor wrote and refused on the ground of turf being dear. Edward Martyn wrote that he had no turf himself but he hoped those of his tenants who had bogs might see their way to lighting bonfires. George Gough was sadly grieved by my refusal. On Sunday his wife asked me if I had received a 'dreadful letter' from him. I said, 'No, it was only a wail over a lost soul'. In the end the As and Zs (who have English wives) lighted bonfires but the people did not go near them, or take any notice. Next night, St. John's Eve, the mountains alight with fires and the people in crowds around them."

Yeats came over to Coole several times. It was then that we had begun making our plans for a theatre. And in the next year at the end of July, a week before the holidays, W. B. Yeats came to stay with me, the first of many visits, bringing his friend, George Russell ("A.E."). He had told me he had described him as "Michael Robartes" in *Rosa Alchemica,* and when one Monday morning I had a letter saying that they would be with me by lunch-time I looked at the passage and read "with his wild red hair, fierce eyes and sensitive lips and rough clothing, Michael Robartes looks something between a peasant, a saint and a debauchee", so I was rather apprehensive and went down to meet them feeling quite shy, but to my relief found a quiet gentleman, perfectly simple and composed. Yeats told me that eight years ago he was the most promising student in the Dublin Art schools, but one day he came and said, as well as I understand, that the will is the only thing given us in this life as absolutely our own, and that we should allow no weakening of it, and that Art, which he cared for so much, would, he believed, weaken his will. And so he went into Pim's shop as cashier, and has been there ever since, and Pim says he is the best cashier he has ever had.

He works till six in the evening, had £60 a year, out of which he not only supports himself, but helps others poorer than himself. He edits *The Theosophist*[2], writing a great

---

[2] Actually *The Irish Theosophist.*

part and has formed a little band of mystics believing, I think, in universal brotherhood and reincarnation. Yeats says his poems are not so good now as when they were dictated by the spirits, he only paints now on the white-washed wall of his lodgings, as he is sure it will be all white-washed out when he leaves it, and to paint anything that lasts would be "a bond upon his soul". He signed his poems Æ, but the publishers insisted on separating the letters, a great grievance to the writer, who says that the dipthong exactly by its sound expressed the mood of his soul . . . He said one evening, "This life bores me, I am waiting for a higher one". His *Homeward Songs by the Way* have gone into a second edition here and have a great sale in America. On Saturday afternoon and Sunday, his only holidays, he goes to the Wicklow Hills and wanders there, sometimes lying down and seeing visions of the old Celtic Gods; of these he has done some beautiful pastel drawings; the first afternoon I took the two poets across the lake to the cromlech, and there they sat until A.E. saw a purple druid appear. Next day we went to Burren hills to Corcomroe, a grey day but it pleased them, and we heard fairy-lore from a young man there.

W.B.Y. had written to me before they came. Rosses Point: "George Russell has made drawings since he came here of quite a number of supernatural beings. The resemblance between the things seen by him at certain places and the things seen there at a different time by a cousin of mine has been very curious. They have met, however, and so, as we say, 'may have got things out of each other's sphere', although they did not talk about them."

1922. Yeats said the other day: "Do you remember that I brought Russell to the old castle of Balinamantane, where old Mrs. Sheridan has told us about seeing a drawbridge across the river there, and ladies looking out from the windows, but A.E. hated to be put to see anyone else's ghosts and wandered about in a discontented silence. Presently I said, 'Don't you see anything, Russell?' and he replied, 'Oh, yes, I do, but they are a low lot'."

One evening they talked about Shelley. Yeats is writing his essays on him, and A.E. says, "It will make people angry to be told he had a meaning because what people go to poetry for is to escape from conviction." Yeats said, "Shelley was not a political reformer, but a prophet with the eternal vision that is never welcome, for people want reformation, not

revelation, which offers nothing but itself." A.E. doesn't like
The Water of the Wondrous Isles, which Yeats delights in;
he says it is wallpaper, a mere decoration, and that it is an
imitation of Malory. Yeats says it is no more imitation than
Rossetti is imitator of early Italian pictures, the individual
soul comes through, and that there could be no art at all
without tradition. A.E. doesn't like Swinburne, says, "There
is nothing but words; nothing behind, while Wordsworth
had faith behind him".

And as to their acquaintances, Yeats declared George
Russell was always looking about for a clothes-horse on which
to hang his superfluous ideals and would rend to pieces those
to whom he gave any praise; "A. has good ideas but is
long-winded, and getting at them is like laying out an
old-fashioned tea service." "B. is rather an overwhelming
patron of a society. He is like the elephant that when he
had put his foot on the old partridge, said, 'Never mind, I
will be a father to the young birds!'." "C. has a formula
and one always gets tired of people with a formula. You know
what they will say on every occasion. Bernard Shaw has a
formula, but he knows it, and takes as much pains to hide
it, as a dog burying a bone." "D. will be a very good sort of
wife for E. A nice kind sort of woman, who will always be
ready to take up an idea that has just died." "F. as curator
of a gallery—a sort of man whose knowledge exists to give
courage to his ignorance." "G. has the genius for the inexpe-
dient." "H. is ponderous in the chair and getting him to
propose a resolution is like setting a whole army to peel
a potato."

Mr. Russell left in a few days, having to go back to his
cash office but Mr. Yeats stayed for two months—a most
charming companion, never out of humour, gentle, interested
in all that went on, liking to do his work in the library in
the midst of the coming and going. Then if I was typing
in the drawing-room suddenly bursting in with some great
new idea, and when it was expounded, laughing and saying:
"I treat you as my father says, as an anvil to beat out my
ideas on". We searched for folk-lore. I gave him all I had
collected, and took him about looking for more, and whoever
came to the door, fisherwoman or beggar or farmer, I would
talk to on the subject, and if I found the stories worth having
would call him down that he might have them first hand.
His healthiness, both of mind and body, increased while

with us, so that he wrote afterwards: "My days at Coole passed like a dream—a dream of peace."

"Standish O'Grady came to stay with us, but during dinner the first evening he had a telegram calling him away as Revising Barrister to Belfast. He had mistaken the time by a month. He is a fine writer. He is now a little over-excited on the financial movement. Next day, after his early start, another of my best country men arrived, Horace Plunkett. He is working himself to death in his agricultural organization movement but he is doing a great work in Ireland, teaching the farmers to get over their suspicion of each other, and to manage their own affairs. We had asked the farmers to meet him, but it was a fine day after long rain, and very few came, we had to call our workmen and even F.'s driver to fill the background, but he came and talked to them, explaining the methods with so much courtesy and earnestness, that he won their hearts. His quiet manner, with so much enthusiasm underneath, strikes one very much and he was a pleasant guest, played cricket with Robert and talked with Yeats. Edward Martyn stayed with us for his visit, and will help his co-operative work. I saw Mr. Plunkett off in the morning, taking him to the convent on the way to the station. He saw the work being done there and promised a loom for the weaving."

And some months later I wrote, "Sitting idle, the shop-keepers are," old O. says, "for the people are getting the worth of their money in manure and seed from the Organiza-tion. And before this the shopkeepers had to work hard to spend all the fortune they were making."

Horace Plunkett is quite with the Celtic movement, asked E.M. and Yeats to the Agricultural Organization dinner and made Yeats speak—a charming little speech, he said, "like a rose leaf falling among a lot of agricultural implements". And he has been very kind about the theatre and went to see the Attorney General on its behalf, and to see me about it in one day over here. And he has taken George Russell out of Pim's and made him an organiser of rural banks.

As to the work that has held me through so many years. I need say but little here. I have given its history in *Our Irish Theatre*. I tell how in this year, 1898[3], Edward Martyn,

[3] Elizabeth Coxhead, in her book *Lady Gregory: A Literary Portrait*, points out that this date is incorrect, as it can be seen from Yeats's letters to Lady Gregory of November 1897 that the project was then already under way. See *The Letters of W. B. Yeats*, edited by Allan Wade (Hart-Davis, 1954) pp. 288 and 290-291.

having written a play, *Maeve,* lent it to Count de Basterot, and I read it while staying with him on the sea coast at Duras, and admired it very much. And then one day, when E. Martyn and Yeats had come to spend a day with the old Count, and rain came on, I had a talk with Yeats as we had tea together in the steward's office, and the idea came to us that if *Maeve* could be acted in Dublin instead of London, or Germany as E.M. thought of, and with Yeats's *Countess Cathleen,* it might lead to a theatre in which plays by Irish writers might be given in Ireland. It would help to get rid of the stage Irishman, and help to restore dignity to Ireland. This seaside talk was the practical beginning of all that led to the Abbey Theatre, to the dramatic movement.

Twenty-five years have passed since that talk by the seaside, that planning of a Theatre where Irish plays could be performed in Ireland. I have told in my book of the building, the difficulties, of the generosity of friends, the attacks of enemies, the battle with the Castle, with the Crowd—so I will not repeat it here.

The Abbey Theatre still endures. Through that quarter of a century it has won and held a good name. William Peel has said in public that it "has revolutionised other theatres and will be spoken of in a hundred years to come". Theodore Roosevelt, that it has "not only made an extraordinary contribution to the sum of Irish literary and artistic achievement, it has done more for the drama than has been accomplished by any other nation of recent years". C. E. Montague praising its method of acting says that actors "come at an effect of spiritual austerity. They contrive to reach past most of the futilities; they take a fresh clear hold on their craft in its elements." Ford Madox Hueffer says, "I don't think there is anything like it in the world". And many people ask in other words the question in the Aran Fisherman's song, "What way has your little curragh come to land when the big ships have gone away?".

When I was asked that question in America sometimes by students of a University—as that of Pennysylvania for an instance, I said I thought one reason of our success was a rule that had been forced on us, of limitation. A clause had been forced into our licence by the jealousy of other Dublin theatres limiting us outside foreign masterpieces to Irish plays. We had less than half a dozen plays with which to begin our enterprise, two by Mr. Martyn and two by Mr. Yeats. Without that clause we might have been tempted

for convenience sake to borrow from England, but with it
came the necessity to encourage every attempt to welcome
every writer who showed he had the dramatic idea. My own
comedies were written simply because at the time comedy
was so much needed.

"And then," I said, "necessity put upon us the limitation
of expense. Managers are slow to put on new .work unless
they are sure of a big return because of the heavy cost of
staging that is expected. We had by necessity to use the
same cottage scene for a dozen or so of the peasant plays, and
our set of hangings, our kilts and fillets for heroic ones. I have
seen 'The Faery Child' in Mr. Yeats's *Land of Hearts Desire*
dancing across the stage in a dress I had myself made some
time before for Synge's *Deirdre of the Sorrows*. So a new play
even of Kings and Queens did not rob us of many pounds.
A roll of dyed sacking and a stencil will furnish a palace
wall. And as to Irish subjects, I must myself be grateful for
that limitation, and so may we all. Our windows should be
open to Heaven, but the floor of the house of *our own* earth.
Every work that we take up in that home we should be able
to work out by the light above us and not be ashamed of the
work. I believe it is in what is closest to us we find our
best inspiration. Whitman has told us that, and so has
Turguenieff when he says of his country, Russia, 'She can
do without everyone of us, but not one of us can do without
her. Woe to him who thinks he can, and woe twofold to
him who actually does without her! The Cosmopolitan is
a nonentity, without nationality is no art nor truth, nor
life, nor anything. You cannot have an ideal face without
an individual expression; only a vulgar face can be without
it.' Synge had done no good work till he came back to his
own country. It was there he found all he wanted. Fable,
emotion, style. Whatever I myself have written that is, as
our people would say, 'worth while' has come from my own
surroundings, my own parish, my own home."

And when the students, who had been very patient, asked
me for some rule of choice as to the plays they put on, I
said that in the Abbey Theatre we had chosen nothing that
we had not hoped to revive from time to time, thus keeping
out plays of merely passing interest. And I said, "We have
some plays on our list that reach so high a standard we
should feel it unfitting to put vulgarity in their company."
And then I told them how in my husband's Oxford days a
dealer had tried to persuade him to buy a beautiful line

engraving of Leonardo da Vinci's "Madonna of the Rocks" and he had refused, saying, "I like the picture in my room". But the dealer said, "I will lend you the picture for a month, sir; it will drive the others out". And sure enough before the month was over that picture had driven away the prizefighters and ballet dancers, and he bought others of the same beauty to put with it, and all now hang together at my home." "And so," I said, "put on your stage some one play at least of the highest quality, even if you must borrow it from the great masters, and test every play you choose afterwards by asking if it is worth to claim comradeship with this. We want to have a base of reality, and an apex of beauty. I think we have even in our roughest comedies some quality of imagination or fantasy or some sincerity of purpose that makes them fitting to be given in the same season at least with Yeats's *King's Threshold* or Hyde's *Nativity* or Synge's *Riders to the Sea*. Are not the story of the procession of beasts into the Ark and of Jonah swallowed by the great fish bound within the same cover as the Revelation of St. John the Divine?"

But it is hard to lay down fixed rules, and often when I was asked how to make a theatre, I would say "by beginning to make it". I was talking once to Bernard Shaw about a new manager, an untried one, and he said, "He'll learn. You and Yeats knew nothing about the Theatre when you began, and you've done it better than anyone."

And then another enriching influence came into my life. "Dr. Douglas Hyde came one day to Tillyra, where I was staying, pushing along a broken bicycle, because instead of coming to the station by train, as had been expected, he had got out at Craughwell to look for folk-lore. That afternoon I took him to the cromlech at Crannagh, and he talked in Irish with Fahey, who to my pride came out with legends of Finn and the Fianna. Hyde was full of enthusiasm and Irish. I was able to find for him later some manuscripts containing Irish poems, from a man who had left Galway a year ago, and whom I traced at last to a butcher's shop in Oranmore." . . . I have written elsewhere how once in my childhood I had been eager to learn Irish, I thought to get leave to take lessons from an old Scripture-reader who spent a part of his time in the parish of Killinane, teaching such scholars as he could find to read their own language in the hope that they might turn to the only book then being printed in Irish, the Bible. But my asking, timid with the

fear of mockery, was unheeded. Yet I missed by a little an
opportunity that might have made me a real Irish scholar,
and not as I am, imperfect, stumbling. For a kinsman learned
in the language, Standish Hayes O'Grady, the translator of
the wonderful *Silva Gaedelica* had been sometimes a guest in
the house, and would still have been welcomed there but that
my mother, who had a great dislike to the marriage of
cousins, had fancied he was taking a liking to one of my
elder sisters; and with that suspicion the "winged nymph,
Opportunity", had passed from my reach.

This same Standish Hayes O'Grady had refused, Yeats
tells me, to join the Irish Literary Society or the Gaelic
League, declaring them both Fenian organizations. But yet
he was so little English that he boasted to me near his life's
end, that though he had lived forty years in England, he had
never made an English friend.

After my marriage I had bought a grammar and worked
at it for a while with the help of a gardener. But it was difficult, and my teacher was languid, suspecting it may be
some hidden mockery, for those were the days before Irish
had become the fashion.

But in 1897 I had written after Yeats's first visit and A.E.'s
and Horace Plunkett's, and the beginning of our Theatre
projects, "The result of this little national literary stir was
that Robert near the end of the holidays said he wanted to
learn Irish. We tried in vain for a teacher, many speak but
none know the grammar, so we began with a primer and
mastered the first exercises, taking them out to Mike to get
the pronunciation right. But the partridge shooting interfered at the end. Robert's first chance (which he owed to the
Jubilee extra week), was also his last. He was pretty successful, getting a good many birds at Coole but making his
biggest bag at Tillyra. The Birch boys had come at the end
very glad to find themselves back again."

But I went on working and learning, and I found the task
far easier than when I had first taken up a grammar. "For
that young priest Eugene O'Growney (I have still a little
Gaelic League badge sent to me by him), sent from Ireland
to look for health in California, had used the short span of
life left to him in writing simple lessons in Irish grammar
that made at least the first steps easy."

I was given renewed enthusiasm by that meeting with the
Founder of "the Gaelic League, one in the first three of our
"Mighty Men". And a little later I was spending ten days

very pleasantly at Spiddal with the Morrises. Fine weather
had come at last, a sort of Indian summer; the Atlantic was
beautiful . . . I ran down when I could to the school and
had an Irish lesson and gathered some folk stories . . . Then
Yeats came and I arranged an interview with a witch doctor
for him, of which he will doubtless give an account. I stirred
up the master of the school to collect folk stories, and offered
a prize for stories written down in either English or Irish
. . . The school children have already sent me eleven . . ."

And again, "I spent a day or two at Spiddal, the Leckys
there. I had a talk with Lecky about compulsory purchase,
which he thinks likely, though from his usual balancing
mind, it is hard to say if he approves or not, (I have heard
his Athenaeum friends complain that it is very hard to get
him to give a definite opinion on anything they ask him).
At dinner I had a fight for the Irish language. Lord Morris
says he never spoke against its being taught in the schools,
for he never heard any proposal at all made for it at the
board—if he had he would only have laughed at such an
absurd craze. Lecky, defending his Trinity Professors,
sneered at me for calling Irish a modern language. I said,
'Yes, just in the same way as modern Greek'; and Lady
Morris told him it is spoken all round Spiddal; and I told
him the people's songs are still composed in it, which
disturbed him. Lord M. gave some Irish phrases, which
luckily I understood, so I came pretty well out of it."

And later, "I went to Galway with W.B.Y. to support the
Gaelic movement, very glad we went, for none of the
'classes' were there to support it unless priests can so be
called."

Grealey, the young schoolmaster, gave a recitation with
great vigour, and as Daly, the other master, was giving the
next, W.B.Y. asked Grealey what they were all about and
he said: "Both poems are called 'Thoughts on Ireland', my
one tells how the Sassenachs murdered us a while ago." Very
characteristic "Thoughts on Ireland"!

In a letter written to Lady Layard in the Christmas
holidays of 1898-99 I said, "they have passed very cheerily
so far. Douglas Hyde, LL.D., an Irish scholar, was here for
a week, spent the days shooting with the boys, and I captured old men with songs and stories for him to interview
in the evenings; and we have started a branch of the Gaelic
League. Miss Borthwick, the Irish scholar who had been
giving me lessons in London, is staying here and has classes

every afternoon at the gate lodge, about eight girls and
thirty to forty young men alternately, some walking as far
as three miles to attend. They get on very quickly, knowing
the spoken language; it is just the reading and grammatical
construction they have to learn; a splendid educational help
to say the least, and they will be able to appreciate in the
end the dignity and beauty of our own literature . . . The
Theatre project has now been announced, and I hope all
will go well with it."

We had done other things besides the classes for the
language: "On Thursday I took lunch to the boys who were
shooting at Inchy, and in the afternoon had a meeting at
Kiltartan school, Dr. Fahey in the chair, and a branch of
the Gaelic League was formed . . . Dr. Hyde made a very
eloquent speech in Irish, not that I understood it, but it
roused the people. Then he made one in English in which he
drew attention to the inferiority of the vocabulary of the
English peasant to that of the Irish. All very good, except
that he came a little too near what may be taken for
politics in saying, 'Let English go their road and let us go
ours, and God forbid their road should ever be our road'."

And then I wrote of a great climax, the first performance
as I believe of a Punch and Judy show in Irish! "On Friday
the Christmas tree, very hard work, a holy day, and the
boys went off to shoot Tillyra and took the Mikes (keeper
and steward), so I could get no help but Murty's to set up
the Punch and Judy show. And when I proposed to decorate
the tree I was told it was still in the woods! However, John
Rourke appeared and dug up a small silver fir, to be planted
again. We had a good many children, over a hundred, more
than usual at Christmas; however, provisions and presents
held out, some of the latter, Italian pottery, I had brought
home from Venice. The Punch and Judy, a great success,
first Wyndham Birch and my niece, Frances, did it in
English, and then Dr. Hyde and Miss Borthwick in Irish,
and this brought down the house; his chastising of the
baby was much applauded—the children's own chastisement
had probably been accompanied by the same words. He
made only the 'peeler' speak English, and said the *páistín*
has fallen out of the window of itself . . . A success, but very
tiring, twenty-five guests in the breakfast-room afterwards to
tea. Old Diveney says 'that gentlemen has very good Irish,
only his tongue is a little hard and sharp because he's
Englified. But I am a common labourer and so I speak flat.'

On Saturday—the boys to the bogs, but didn't get much, but R. and D.H. got a pheasant and two woodcocks when they got back.

"On Sunday. After lunch I took D.H. across the lake to Fahey's and left him there but he didn't get much except my story of Usheen and says mine was just as good in English and very accurate. Fahey says, 'Father Fahey has good Irish but he's that talented the people can't well understand it'. He also says they can't understand more than half what he said in English. Miss Borthwick found about sixty pupils at the gate house.

"At the Convent. Sister Frances tells me that last year £2 was sent for the poor, after their appeal, with a letter written in a strange language. They puzzled over it, and thought the signature was a Turkish one, so the Reverend Mother thought it must be a gift from the Sultan, sent through the Turkish Ambassador in Paris and wrote to thank him (the Ambassador) (for it has never been forgotten that the Sultan sent money in the Famine years 'And that is what the Queen never did'). His Secretary wrote back to say His Excellency knew nothing of it. Then they took the letter to Dr. Fahey who burst out laughing, for it was written in Irish! They have begun teaching the little boys their prayers in Irish!"

"Tommy Hynes came last night and D.H. got some songs from him, the best was by Raftery 'Mary Hynes of Ballylee'; and there was 'Mary Brown' and 'Raftery and death', too long to be all taken down. Miss Borthwick had thirty young men at her class and they got through fifty pages! The boys shot the bogs and got a nice mixed bag."

29 January (1899). "The holidays over, all gone, 'Fade an la gan Cloinne Uisnigh' (It is long the day without the sons of Usnach). The workmen have made a bond only to speak Irish when together, and John Burke knows the first book by heart and has sent for the second; and Mike says 'there isn't a child you'll meet on the road now, but will say "God save you" in Irish'." It was also in that year, 1899, there is an entry—28 June—J. M. Synge came from Aran.

And so I found my work in Ireland and could claim comradeship with other workers. The threads of new interests began to be woven into the pattern of my life. The theatre, the folk legends, the language. And as to this last, I sometimes think with a little pride that when Michael Collins and Eamonn de Valera were in their short jackets going to school or marching from it, I was spending time and money and energy in bringing back the Irish among my own people.

And the meeting of Yeats and Horace Plunkett at Coole had an influence on the fortunes of another guest of that summer. I remember once in London that brilliant talker and writer of reminiscences, George W. E. Russell, being surprised one evening when dining with me to hear there was another George Russell known as a writer, rather amused at the idea, a little scornful. Yet, in later years he had some time to write to strangers to explain he was not the George Russell whose fame had grown, and letters for whom often found their way to him. But as to him who is better known now as "A.E.", Yeats wrote to me from Dublin in November 1897 that, "There is a possibility of his becoming of all things in the world one of Plunkett's organizers. They want a man to organize agricultural banks and I suggested him. He seems to combine the three needful things, business knowledge, power to make a speech, enthusiasm. He is at this moment asking his flock if they can get along without him for most of the month and on their answer depends his decision. I would not have urged him to give up a certainty like Pim's for an uncertainty like Plunkett's, did I not know that he was going to leave Pim's in any case. The American Theosophists have been asking him to give up Pim's and write for them, and have promised him some small income. This, as I think, would be a much greater uncertainty than Plunkett's and I am afraid his conscience would compel him to write too much. He would feel bound to be very propagandist . . . It would give him a great knowledge of Ireland." At first he refused on the ground of its being impossible for him to leave the little Dublin group of mystics for so long a time. I brought some of the mystics to him, and they all promised to hold together and work on while he was away, and now I think it is all right. His work will be organising co-operative banks in the congested districts of the west.

He was from the first a fine organiser, he put his mind to the work. When he stayed with me again, I wrote: "Thought him happier than at Pim's but he won't allow it—says 'he had renounced life, and now has come into it again'. In Pim's he says he found five mystics, 'five avenues into eternity'. He looks much better than in the summer and is full of life and energy, evidently doing his work well and feeling that he is doing so." And I wrote again: "Horace

Plunkett is enthusiastic about A.E.'s work—'the highest ideals and more practical than any of us'." Yet he had ups and downs. "Yeats has had a very downcast letter from A.E. and asks me to write and find out if he is permanently depressed or if it was only a passing mood. He finds what responsibility there is in trying to help others."

I wished to give here some letters written by him at that time of transition and when I had copied out such passages as I wished to use I took them to him and asked his leave. He cried out against any making public of what he had written with no such thought, but at my pleading he took them to look through. And next day, when with rather a sinking heart, I climbed the high staircase to his official room, his kindness had triumphed and he gave me back the pages, brown pencilled, indeed, but leaving enough to enrich my story of the changing Ireland. And I may use as a further enrichment a letter he had just written me, in which he says, "I have crossed out things in the letters. I must not be taken to agree that what is not crossed out is worth printing, I do not think there is a single thought in all worth quoting in a book. But if you wish to quote you can take anything from the parts not brown pencilled. My own view of myself is that at times I fall into a depth of my own being, when I feel there is some spiritual illumination. When I do not speak out of that depth what I do is commonplace or only superficially intelligent and I would never attach the 'A.E.' to what is written or said, and as for the personality, George Russell, I hope it never will be remembered, and my friends will please me best by never talking about it."

So I went away very well content, and I believe for all he may say, both names will be remembered in more home-steads than the one he edits in the time to come.

This is a letter written in October 1897, before he had joined the Organization: "I still have in my mind the scents of the woods at Coole, and all the west has been clamouring to my soul for months. I hunger more after my cottage and make poems to it and finally I know I must go: —

> A cabin on the mountain side hid in a grassy nook
> With door and windows open wide where friendly stars may look.
> The rabbit shy can patter in, and winds may enter free,
> Who throng around the mountain throne in living ecstasy.

And when the sun sets dimmed in eve and purple fills the
    air,
I think the sacred Hazel Tree is dropping berries there
From starry fruitage waved aloft where Connla's Well
    o'erflows;
For sure the immortal waters run through every wind that
    blows.

I think when the night towers up aloft and shakes the
    trembling dew,
How every high and lonely thought that thrills my being
    through
Is but a ruddy berry dropped down through the purple
    air,
And from the magic tree of life the fruit falls everywhere."

And again—"As I get further away from my holidays
every year my verse gets less robust and more metaphysical
and only faintly tinged with the colour of the earth. I wrote
a "Call of the Sidhe", however, which I was brooding upon
when I was with you: —

Tarry thou there yet, late lingerer in the twilight's glory:
Gay are the hills with song: earth's fairy children leave
More dim abodes to roam the primrose-hearted eve,
Opening their glimmering lips to breathe some wondrous
    story . . .

When his journeys began I sometimes sent him a book
for companionship and he writes from Ballina in January
1898: "I believe I have not done so badly (three banks)
from the external point of view, but the soul in me has
never spoken once since I started . . . The extracts from
Johannes Scotus Erigena were translated by Larminie, who is
the most spiritual of all of us." And again from Ballina,
"Thoreau is an old friend of mine but I am very glad to
have a copy of Walden. I do not know where various copies
I had are gone to. He nearly started me long ago on the
tramp, emulous of his lonely joys. But I think I must make
peace with the Gods before I get my cabin. Otherwise, it
might happen with me, as he slyly admitted after a while
'there was a little langour in the afternoons'. This is a delightful way of putting the real cause of his departure. I have
gathered a few stray fragments of fairy belief since I have
been in the west, but very little of the beautiful in them,
though this may be my own defect of vision. I must get a
long way from any incident before I can make anything

out of it. I have let it sink for months into my heart before
it will reveal any beauty. Perhaps a year or two from this
I may find an inexhaustible fund of ideas in the acquisitions
I think so carelessly about. I notice with amusement that I
have the materials for a mob orator somewhere about me,
and can now stand up and face a crowd of five hundred
people without my heart being somewhere in the toe of my
boots." Then from Crossmolina: "I have been reading
Tolstoy's *What to Do* in the hope of finding something
which might throw light on the problems here in the West.
He has such penetrating vision into the real obstacles to any
improvement that I feel inclined to wonder 'Can I do anything except live among them and be one of them?' For I
feel that what they really want is the stimulating presence
of people with infinite courage, hope and enthusiasm. If our
co-operative societies will not help them I do not know what
will. I refer, of course, to permanent help in the material
sense. I have an instinct against giving money as demoralis-
ing, but do not see often how it can be helped, for the
poverty is frightful in some places. I stayed with Father
Augher for four days and I have counted as many as sixty
people before his door at one time wanting relief. I could
hear all day long passionate pleading voices, 'The white sun
in Heaven does not look down on poorer people than this
man and myself', I heard one say who came from a lonely
mountain place. The other man, thin, spiritless, with a
frightful despondency in his eyes, only gnawed his fingers
and said nothing. I felt ashamed to listen to those who came
to their priest telling him their sorrows as if they were telling
them to their own hearts. I felt night in my soul all the time
I was there. If I had money I would give it to him. He is a
good man and I could trust him. He employs the money
he gets from Manchester and elsewhere in making them
improve their own holdings and drain their fields, and it is
wiser than to give the money in charity. He objected to my
giving it and I feel he was right. They have been demoralised by many years of 'doles' and the main thing to consider
is how can they be made to help themselves, for this is the
only thing which seems to have been neglected in trying
to assist them. Neither at Attymas, Crossmolina, Gumsco,
Buniscarra or Labaradane was the distress so evident. I speak
only of those places I have been in. But I go tomorrow to
Carna in Galway, which I hear is indescribably poor and
squalid, and after that I think I will go to the Aran Isles.

I may see things there as bad or worse than Aughoes. But
I would not think it a good thing for a stranger to give
money on a hasty superficial investigation of poverty. Those
who are locally intimate are the best dispensers of relief as
a rule.

"Henley's poem, 'Invictus', is long in my mind. I have often
repeated it since I first read it some six years ago. It repre-
sents a fundamental feeling in my own soul, but to tell the
truth, I generally dally with an intellectual despair before
I take up that condition of inflexible resistance . . . The
country round here is a miracle of pure light and dreamy
colour. The snow is glittering on the hills round the world,
and that mighty Nephin half purple and half white, over
the pale green of the fields, is really not of this earth at all,
but of the hills of dreams. I have been trying to write some
of these vague stories I hear, in verse, but have not yet got
quite at home in them (enclosed is the poem beginning, 'It's
a lonely road through bogland to the lake at Carrowmore')."

Then in June: "I am afraid I will never get the 'economic
peasant' out of my mind, and I will never be able to write
about him or make poems on him—not for ages to come . . .
W.B.Y. ought to keep clear of me, for I am devoid of anything
mystical just at present, and know more of the price of eggs
than of what is going on behind the veil. I am really interested more and more in this movement, and see the promise
of great things for Ireland in it, and am doing what I can to
understand it and the principles at the back of it. Meanwhile,
literature and other things lie over. I am drifting altogether
out of old habits of thought and the wheel is hurrying so
far and fast that I hardly would understand anyone who
came and told me my own thoughts of a year ago. Whatever
I take up I must take up altogether, and I am afraid Willie
would only be bored by the new dyes of my mind." Other
letters in that year say: "I find it difficult to survey Ireland
and its people at once from the industrial and artistic
standpoint. All these things, beauty, magic, spirit, underlie
eternally the simplest things, but it is for *that* we must look
and not for anything else if we are to see and express it.
While I have found myself dried up and devoid of inspiration amid my late rambles in the West, I have never doubted
the ever-living spirit behind all things, only if I had put
myself into the mood which interests me more than any
book I have read for a very long time. I quite understand
Willie's admiration. There is a certain spiritual arrogance

which is quite in the same vein as the sentences he is so fond of quoting from some modern French mystics." "I am glad you like 'From the Irish Hills'. I like it myself, as well as anything I have written. You would have been delighted with a meeting at Whitecross, Co. Armagh, Mr. Anderson and myself attended a couple of days ago. We spoke to a crowd of men, women and children for three mortal hours and they were not tired; spoke of the ideals of the movement, brotherliness, justice, the good of Ireland, and they seemed to like it better than ever the idea of earning a few pounds extra for their cows. I felt proud of my countrymen, for I am a County Armagh man, and my earliest and most vivid remembrance of it was a conflict between Orangemen and Nationalists, and sticks descending on each other's skulls; and my last is of the parson proposing the Priest as president, and an Orangeman seconding it, and of a Priest saying, 'What matter does religion make? It is the best men we want.'

"I have not read *The Workers*[4]. If it is a serious attempt to deal with the question of the workers I would like to read it. To me economic schemes mainly resolve themselves into human problems and the scheme is of less importance than the men who work it. Everything in the long run, success or failure, springs from the perfection or imperfection of the men and women who are engaged in managing and communities. I hate tinkering at the outside of things." "I have received, a few days ago and read with much interest *The Workers*. His experience seems to have rather inter- fered with his analysis. He evidently wrote down his imme- diate impressions and did not wait long enough for a really deep impression to be made on him. Every new situation conquers us at first, we receive only surface impressions, and to be of value to others these impressions must have passed through the soul. The article by Tolstoy is splendid. I boiled down as much as the *Homestead* had room for and sent it to Mr. Plunkett, who was delighted with it." "W.B.Y. turned up last night in good form, and much concerned and enthusiastic about bad spirits. He has a new theory about a Fomorian King whose name pleased him (Altheir) and he is

[4] Walter A. Wyckoff wrote two books, *The Workers: an Experiment in Reality. The East* (London 1897) and *The Workers: An Experi- ment in Reality. The West* (London 1899). Lady Gregory is probably referring to the latter.

building a gorgeous intellectual structure on the strength of sundry visions.

"Whatever his mind touches, even if it is only a name, that thing begins to send its flames up to the Heavens, a Jacob's ladder up and down which pass the unearthly ministers to his imagination. His uncle's old servant, Mary Battle, told him before he left Sligo that if he was not married when he came next to Sligo he never would be, an oracular statement . . . He has profound confidence in her seership and he has the funniest story about the way his magical operations react on her mind. He had dreamed of the union of Heaven and Earth, and the next morning Mary Battle had a dream that the Catholic Bishop married an Honourable Miss Somebody, and all the clergy were going to follow his example."

There is no need to give any record of Mr. Russell's later work. As Editor of the *Homestead* he speaks every week to the Agricultural Societies, to individuals through the whole country. His office is visited by men from England, from other countries, looking for knowledge from his wisdom, his intuition; now and again he has been summoned to London to be consulted by the British Government (someone who met him at lunch at 10 Downing Street told me of his talking to the Prime Minister of the day "like a father"). He wrote passionately against the harshness of the Government in the dark winter of 1920-21. And in his pamphlets he has given us the other side, not with equal sympathy but with equal justice. And through all he is a painter, a poet. He has never lost either his sanity or his vision.

XX

NEW THREADS IN THE PATTERN

I wrote on 6 March 1899, "It is seven years to-day since my husband's death. The years have gone by more happily than I could have expected. No serious cause for anxiety. Coole peaceful, and we are I think on closer and more sympathetic terms with the people. I have found happiness in new interests joining with the old. I feel that if there should be still some years before me there is work for me to do, and I think Robert will always understand and care for his people."

There had been no break in my old London friendships, there is no place where I have met with greater kindness. And when I went back now and again to my little rooms in Queen Anne Mansions new guests would come there, and sometimes I would bring together old and new.

I wrote in March 1897, "Horace Plunkett, Barry O'Brien, author of *Fifty Years of Concessions to Ireland*, and the *Life of Parnell*, and W. B. Yeats dined with me last night; there was some interesting talk. Barry O'Brien arrived first, and said he would be so glad to meet Mr. Plunkett, as all sections of Nationalists of late have been agreeing that he is the only possible leader to unite all parties. Yeats, just back from Dublin, corroborates this. He has been trying to reconcile conflicting committees in the matter of the '98 Centenary, but there is a great deal of squabbling. He said 'Every man who has time on his hands and a little industry has a secret society of his own'. Then Mr. Plunkett came and we went up to dinner, a little tentative conversation first. Then Mr. Plunkett said his grudge against Parnellism is that Parnell so mastered and dominated his followers, as to crush national life instead of developing it, as has happened when there has been a national awakening in other countries. Mr. O'Brien says it was necessary he should dominate for the campaign and that he was a good General. I say, we see Mr. Plunkett's contention is true, by the helpless disorganisation parties have fallen into since his death, and ask Mr. O'Brien what he would do at this moment in Ireland if he had power there. He says: 'I would make Mr. Horace

Plunkett our leader and follow him.' Mr. Plunkett is evidently touched, though his quiet manner is unchanged. Yeats asks him how far he would go, and he says, to a large measure of local government, but not separation, and not yet Home Rule; they are not ready for it. We urge him to make his speech strong. Mr. O'Brien tells him how he said to a Cabinet Minister: 'No Irishman ever gets anything from you till he goes to you with the head of a landlord in one hand and the tail of a cow in the other.' Mr. Plunkett is delighted, says if he would say things like that he might indeed think of being a leader.*"

We come down and have coffee and I give them cigarettes and we talk of our taxation—the financial grievance—. Mr. O'Brien's point is that it ought to be rubbed into the Government that it was their own Protestant colony they destroyed in destroying trade. My point is that the Liberals, and indeed the Government, have confessed already the enormity of England's conduct in the past, and by way of making up, gave liberally of the landlord's money, the Church money or anything they could get at the expense of others, but as soon as it comes to their own money and the case is put before them, they say, "Oh, now we must have another commission, and button up their pockets". Mr. O'Brien is much pleased at my saying, "It is not getting the money that is the important thing—it is getting all Ireland into line".

Mr. Plunkett wonders Redmond hasn't made more way. Mr. O'Brien thinks it is the difficulty of succeeding such a man as Parnell. I think it is the dual weight of the priests against him, they were afraid to resist Parnell until England did so, but tried, by way of make up, to crush Redmond with all their force. Mr. Plunkett never met Parnell. He

---

*He used these words in the House of Commons later with Mr. O'Brien's leave. As to the taxation matter, a Royal Commission had been appointed in 1894 "to enquire into the financial relations between England and Ireland". In 1896, "The Jury found a verdict for Ireland", deciding "that the Act of Union imposed upon Ireland a burden which, as events showed, it was unable to bear; that the increase of taxation laid upon Ireland between 1850 and 1860" (when Mr. Gladstone extended the income tax to Ireland and trebled the spirit duties) "was not justified by the then existing circumstances". Great efforts were made to recover some of this money paid in over taxation. Lord Castletown among others had taken up the matter and had made a vigorous speech in which he made allusion to the tea thrown into Boston Harbour in 1773.

once had an appointment with him about the industrial scheme, but he did not keep it and wrote afterwards to say he was going to Ireland and would be hard to find there. Mr. Plunkett thinks he was quite unlike an Irishman, but Yeats says it is quite Celtic to have that strong will. The Englishman, he says, is reserved, because of his want of sensibility. Parnell was reserved in spite of it. When he was taunted by Foster in the House he answered with no change from his usual cold manner, but afterwards it was seen blood was streaming from his hands, wounded by the clutch which had driven in the nails. The Irish are a feminine nation with masculine ideals; the English, a masculine nation with feminine ideals. The English novel shows this—compare Balzac and Zola with Thackeray and Dickens—the English novelist knows nothing of the tenacity that makes a man write forty novels in sequence, or that made Balzac keep himself awake with coffee for a week while he wrote. But England would never like a masculine nature, Napoleon or Parnell, as Ireland would do. He said also, "In Ireland we care too much for action, to succeed in literature. We are not satisfied to sit down and meditate, we all want to be doing something. I myself had a faint feeling of satisfaction the other day when a man in the street said, 'How are you Mr. Redmond?'."

The party did not break up till 12.00 o'clock, Mr. Plunkett going first. I gave Mr. O'Brien his agricultural pamphlet and gave the Froude notes I had made for his speech in the Financial debate to Mr. Plunkett and asked O'Brien to send him his little *History of Ireland* and I gave Yeats my folk-lore pages, so I think I did my best for them all.

Mr. O'Brien looked at Yeats when he left and said, "We could go far with that man as a leader", but is a little sad that he doesn't go in more for Home Rule, yet confesses it is wiser to stick to Agricultural Co-operation for the present.

Dined with Mr. Horace Plunkett—Fingalls, Castletowns, Alfred Lyttletons. I was next Lord Castletown and had some financial talk as to relations between Ireland and England. He says he is no Home Ruler but is a Nationalist; he believes, from an Imperial point of view, Home Rule would be a mistake and also that it will never be granted. I told him there was disappointment that his House of Lords speech was so much milder than his first, and he says it is impossible to speak in the depressing influence of the House of Lords. Lord Salisbury had said to him as he came out: "This was very different from your tone in Ireland", and he said: "Yes, and I have known you speak differently on the hustings to what you do in this house." His object in that violent speech was to attract the attention of the people and get their confidence and bring them into line. I asked what we are to do now we are fairly in line, it is no good making a general agitation, we should get to some point, and insist on its being granted. Mr. Plunkett, talking of Irish tactics in Parliament, told us how one night there was a naval debate and Redmond got up and talked for twenty minutes and took a division on every motion. Afterwards in the Lobby he asked Redmond, "Now, do tell me as a friend, what pleasure it gives you to keep us all out of bed and what the Navy estimates matter to you; what are you aiming at?" "What I'm aiming at!" said Redmond, "is that I want to have a boat slip at —— and for this he was impeding the whole Imperial business.

Again: "I had an Irish lesson from Miss Borthwick and went in the afternoon to 18 Woburn Buildings to meet the father of Mr. W. B. Yeats who was there sketching him, and not very successfully, probably knows his face too well. He has been at this for three days. W.B.Y. had written that 'it was very difficult to make him begin and now it is still more difficult to make him leave off'. His sitting-room is very nice, large and low, looking on a raised flagged pavement where no traffic can come, and the bedroom, very small and draughty, looking out on St. Pancras Church with its caryatids and trees. But I wish he could be a little better waited on; his sitting-room had not yet been done up, and remains of breakfast (cooked by himself) still there. He received me with the announcement he had 'lost his coals' and the fire was going out, but at last, when his father left, a bucket of coal was sent in and stowed away. One cold night when he dined with me I asked him if he would find his fire in when he went back and he said, no, he had carefully raked it out so that the landlady, when she came, might make it up for lighting next morning, or otherwise he would have to make it up himself and the mornings are so cold for that. His father has to set out for Dublin in the evening to paint Standish O'Grady's portrait, but I heard next day he had gone to the station, then found he had left his sketch book and gone back for that, and just as he had taken his ticket at Euston the train steamed off. So then he decided to go by the next train and left his things at the cloak room and went back to Woburn Buildings. When he set out the second time he again left his sketch book, the other one, and had to return. But still he was in pretty good time at Euston, and they changed the ticket, but when he went into the cloak room he had lost his luggage ticket and had to make a declaration, and while it was being made the train went off, and then he was ashamed to go back to his family and so went to the hotel for the night and has been no more heard of."

February 1897. Lecky came to see me. He thinks we have a financial grievance, but that ninety millions is too much to ask. Then in came Sir F. Burton, looking certainly aged, but in very good humour; delighted with my fairy-lore—he does love Ireland—and so does Lecky.

"Sir A. Lyall came to see me in the morning, says his nephew, Bernard Holland, wrote the financial report, and Childers never saw it; and when B.H. went to Devonshire House last week the Duke said, 'Well, you've put the fat in the fire'."

And then I went to the Irish Literary Society, my first introduction to it, to hear a lecture on Clarence Mangan. The lecturer tried to be sprightly and tried to make a "funny man" of poor stricken Mangan, quoting only his "funny" pieces and a scrap or two of his translations. Yeats read *United Ireland* for a bit and examined and admired his new blackthorn. Then Rolleston made rather a prosy speech, and read a slightly better poem. Then J. F. Taylor, disappointing as I had heard he was an orator, but the audience was too much for him. Then old McDermot, the last of the '98 men read what was supposed to be an unpublished life of Mangan he has written, but so toothless it was difficult to hear him. Yeats had grown desperate, asked me for pencil and paper. I had only a blank cheque, which I gave him, and he jotted down some notes. Then when McDermot sat down he sprang up and said: "I entirely disagree with Mr. Rolleston and I entirely disagree with Mr. Taylor, they claim too much for Mangan in claiming a mass of fine poetry for him. He did not do many fine things—he did two or three that were very fine. "Dark Rosaleen' and 'O'Hussey's Ode to the Maguire' I do not look on as perfection but I look on them as near perfection as anything that has ever been written. The poetry of Ireland is ballad poetry and in the ballad poetry of all

countries few men have written more than one or two of
the best, and the rest has been rubbish. It is absurd to claim
for Mangan that he kept up to the high level of Shelley or
Keats. In England there is a tradition of literature. In
Ireland this had had to be created in later years. Mangan
was one of the first creators. By these few fine ballads he
inspired Poe, who inspired so much in modern French
literature, and in England. He was the creator of a new
style. And I disagree with Mr. Taylor in his ideas as to the
end of art. Art should only be used for its own sake. In
literature the art that aims at moral ends in the copybook
and the headlines—in Ireland many have an idea that
literary art should be used for political ends, and this would
lead us to Spirit of the Nation after Spirit of the Nation to
the end of time. Art should be for its own sake only—Art
is the reflection of the heavenly vision, and its end should
be, for peace . . . It is often my misfortune to have to combat
with the enthusiasms of my elders."

He spoke with such life and vigour that he put life into
the assembly, but he says it was "lifting a dead weight" all
the time. Strachey was in the chair and had been listening
with contemptuous intolerance, but his expression changed
when this speech began—he told Yeats afterwards he was in
full agreement with him. Stephen Gwynn, usually his enemy,
stood up and said Mr. Yeats had expressed his own ideas
better than he could have done it himself, and all ended well.
Yeats came back with me, still excited with indignation at
the poorness of the speaking, and read me 'Dark Rosaleen'
before he left.

At another meeting of the Irish Literary Society a lecture
by Stephen Gwynn on Irish Humour: "Before the lecture
two funeral orations on the late Lord Russell of Killowen
were delivered by two Judges, introduced in a cheerful
patronizing way by Edmund Gosse who was in the chair.
Gwynn's lecture, rather good, was chiefly to prove how little
humour there is in Ireland. This annoyed the audience and
Graves made a long speech quoting humorous anecdotes, or
what he considered as such. Yeats made a fighting speech,
sat on Graves for telling as an Irish story one that had been
current in India before the Christian era (three monks
speaking at the end of a year) and did not agree with Gwynn
that Swift was un-Irish, as wherever he was born his humour
was the humour of insult, which is so much in the Irish
nature, 'The humour of insult has given us Swift, Mitchel,

Tim Healy; the humour of servility has given us Handy Andy . . . Tim Healy is only divided from Jon Swift by an abyss of genius'."

Another evening: "Miss X. to dinner (to interest her in the little movement) Yeats, Willy Peel, Sir Alan Johnson (uncle to Lionel), young Comyns Carr, who has just left Oxford and is going in for literature. It was very amusing for W.B.Y. was excited by Miss X.'s dogmatic ultra-English mind, and let off fireworks all the evening, declaiming against men of science, 'they are poor and paltry in every other subject; they are but a [bore?] on their own discoveries —a man of letters like Goethe, of all-embracing wisdom—so different . . . Yes, Parnell was a representative Irishman, he lived for an idea; Englishmen will only live for an institution . . . Sir Frederic Leighton ought to have been King of England, and the Queen President of the Royal Academy.' 'Oh,' says Miss X. seriously, 'but do you not confess she is an excellent constitutional monarch?' Sir A. Johnson rather amusing. He meant to crush Yeats about Mme. Blavatsky, of whom he had heard some stories and said: 'Do you infer Mme. Blavatsky was an imposter?' 'Well,' Yeats said, 'as to her being an imposter, it is like Newman being asked if he believed that the sun really stood still in the valley of Ajalon', and he said, 'There were so many ways of interpreting the words *stood still* that it must remain an uncertain question.'

"Miss X. when leaving said pityingly, 'He's very young'. I asked Sir A. Johnson if his nephew Lionel talked like that and he said: 'Not to me, but I daresay he does when they're together', which amuses W.B.Y. very much, Lionel being the most gloomy, serious and discreet of men, save and except when he is drunk. Then he draws on imaginary reminiscences, including a conversation of an hour with Gladstone at Oxford, which he never varies—his family, who are Tory, disapprove of, but at the same time, are proud of this interview."

But Yeats says Sir Alan is a very tactful man. "He went to see a lady, a relation of his, of whom everyone was afraid, including himself. He sat down in an armchair, crushing to death a kitten that was asleep in it. He knew he could not bring it to life again, so he carefully and secretly tucked it into his tail pocket. The old lady has never yet discovered what happened to that kitten."

Again at dinner, Nevill Geary, Yeats, George Moore, Miss Childers. We talked of J. F. Taylor, whom B. O'Brien is asking to write a pamphlet on the financial question. Yeats says he is the best orator he has ever heard, that he is very quarrelsome, will never join any party, but if any party joins him he immediately secedes from it. There was, or is, some debating club in Dublin where there was one surviving Unionist, who was carefully preserved and invited, for the sake of argument, and one evening when Y. went in, he heard Taylor roaring at this unlucky member: "Sir, have you got your head in a bag?" He and G. Moore rather scoff at A. Beardsley's conversion. I was afraid to tell them I had found Raffalovich and his friends rejoicing over it. They said it had just been effected by a Jesuit priest at Bournemouth. He is dying of consumption and was unhappy at the thought of leaving life so young, but now is quite peaceful and happy, though wishing to live a little longer to look at things in the new light cast upon them by Faith. Raffalovich has sent him to the Riviera at his own expense. George Moore came to see me yesterday, very much pleased with his own *Esther Waters* which he has been reading again. He said, "You are quite right. It is a great book. I did not agree with you when you said it but now I am sure you are right."

I had been sincere in saying this to him, for I had said it to others, and meeting Lady Sophy Palmer at dinner she said she was delighted with *Esther Waters,* which she read because she heard I thought so much of it, and then she recommended it to Lady Salisbury, whom she was going to Hatfield with, and who tried to buy it at the Hatfield station, but the stallkeeper said, "Oh, we would not take that book"; upon which Lady S. picked out *A Yellow Aster, A Superfluous Woman* and *The Heavenly Twins* and said, "Then how can you with any consistency keep these?"

14 February. "I had dinner here. W. B. Yeats, Sir H. J. and Lady Johnson, Sophie Lyall, Alfred Cole, Barry O'Brien, Sir A. Clay, very pleasant, at least I enjoyed it myself very much, liking them all, and they got on well. There was an argument at dinner as whom Conan Doyle had meant in a speech the night before by 'the greatest man this country has produced'. B. O'Brien was for Napoleon, Sir H. for Darwin, Yeats for Goethe, A. Cole stirring them all up; but as none could agree on the premises I had to intervene at last."

One Sunday evening, Yeats, H. Plunkett, Mrs. Emery, E. Martyn and Mrs. Dugdale came to dinner. Pleasant talk, and Mrs. Emery read E. Bronte's *Remembrance* and a poem

of A.E.'s, and Yeats read from *The Love Songs of Connacht*.
H. Plunkett is quite for the language movement now. I think
A.E., of whom he speaks with great enthusiasm, has inspired
him with the idea of a spiritual nationality. He says my
article ("Ireland Real and Ideal"[1] in *The Nineteenth
Century*) has been a great help to him, especially in America,
where it had been a good deal read. I teased him about his
bull, that the best organizer was "'an ex-firebrand who has
sowed his wild oats'". He says A.E. promised to do a picture
for the *Homestead* of the firebrand sowing them, and the
crop that resulted! He told a story of Mahaffy complaining
that he had once been birched for speaking the truth, and
another Professor of T.C.D., I forget who, squashed him by
saying, "Well, you must confess it was very efficacious!"
Mrs. Dugdale mentioned Gladstone's beautiful oratory, that
once when he spoke of finance, he said "loan" with such a
pathetic inflection that it sounded like solitude!

Another evening I dined at the Lovelaces', sat between
Strachey, Editor of the *Spectator*, and "Mr. Fortescue", whom
I happily asked if he was related to the writer of *The History
of a Red Deer*, and found it was he himself who had written
it. The other day I had heard Mrs. Severn say Ruskin was
delighted with it and had intended before his death to write
and tell him so, and this much pleased him as he is a disciple
of his. Strachey, condescending to men of low estate—is
always glad when the Irish upper classes join in a movement
for it shows it is over; is of course against the Irish language,
and in favour of a tunnel. I talked to Lecky afterwards, he
is very down on Yeats for removing the chairs set for the
Viceregal party at Miss Stokes' lecture at the Literary
Society*. I made the best defence I could, that the Society
only recognised intellect, not patronage, etc., but he was
unconvinced, and murmured "silly" at intervals. Lady
Lyttelton and Lord Welby also there, and I drove Wilfrid
Blunt home. He is now enjoying society and giving a series

[1] This article appeared in the November 1898 issue.

*Yeats had written to me in January 1903, "Lord Castletown is to
address the National Literary Society on the Pan Celtic project and
explain his programme. The thing may do some good. Miss Stokes
got the Nat. Lit. Society to ask Lady Cadogan to his lecture tomorrow;
as it is a custom to ask anybody a lecturer wants asked, it thought it
had to do so. Now the Society is tearing its hair—that is to say, our
part is tearing the other part. She is coming incognito—and they are
doing their best to keep it out of the papers. I told the President
I am going to the council meeting on Monday to see what happens."

of dinners. "To Jack Yeats's exhibition, sketches of the West of Ireland, very good, I bought 'The Returned American'. I wrote an appreciation of Jack Yeats's sketches and sent it to the *Dublin Express* hoping it may be an advertisement."

(The Saturday issue of the *Dublin Express,* at that time edited by T. P. Gill, was a sort of literary supplement. My little article on the pictures did lead to good, for it was seen by John Quinn of New York, and he wrote to Jack Yeats and bought some of the pictures. Then when he came to Ireland later he asked him to join him in a run through the west, and they stopped and drove from Athenry to the gathering at Raftery's grave and I brought them back here to Coole. That was the beginning of a long friendship for me, and for others in Ireland.)

Then "Dinner at John Murray's; sat between Buckle, Editor of *The Times* and Lord Eustace Cecil. Buckle has been *materialised* by *The Times.* I remember his advent as editor, slight and eager and intellectual . . . I, as usual thinking if there was any friend I give a life to, cried up Horace Plunkett's work, and he seemed impressed and said he had been told it is 'mostly talk'. He probably heard this from Lord ———. Lord E. Cecil was charming, knew W. so well when they were in Parliament together and had sometimes asked news of me from Sir A. Birch."

27th. "I met at Lady Lindsay's Lady Shrewsbury, who asked me to let her see Lord Talbot's letters, which Lady Londonderry has returned. She told me some curious things about him. That when Lady Talbot died he did not like to tell the children it was in consequence of her confinement, so said it was from eating too much peppermint; and that not many years ago Gerald Talbot had told her his mother had died through eating too much peppermint, having believed this all through his long life. Also she says that Lord Ingestre's body was not recovered for a long time after his death, but this was not told to Lord Talbot and he sent one of his other sons to bring the body home, and he had to bring an empty coffin, which was interred with great solemnity at Ingestre. When the body was found afterward, it was buried at Vienna. I went on to see Lady Haliburton and Lady Dorothy came in, very smart, having entertained the Prince at lunch. He had proposed himself on short notice, wanted Mrs. Brown Potter and others to meet him. She got her, but Lord Onslow, whom he wanted, could not be found. 'And what did you give him to eat?' said H. 'Oh,

there was the difficulty. Those wretched servants! I ordered
what he was sure to like, boiled beef and chickens and bacon
and beans, but I told them to bring up the beef and chickens
together, and they thought they knew best and brought the
beef first, and he said, "No, I am going to have chicken",
and he had to wait till it came. Then he always likes bacon
and beans, that I always have for him, though of course
there are only flageolets to be had now; but he likes them
on separate dishes, and that wretched cook squashed them
on the same dish.' However, he stayed from ten minutes to
two till a quarter past four, so must have enjoyed himself.

"I dined at Reginald Smith's (Smith Elder), Canon Page
Roberts, a nice old man, Humphry Ward, Lord Robert Cecil,
Miss Millais. Pleasant enough, but not so pleasant as
Murray's dinners. Smith says John Morley took up Barry
O'Brien's *Life of Parnell* in Bain's shop and looked at a page
or two and said, 'Three lies already' and put it down. Lady
Westmeath came in at tea time to see me, talked of the
badness of the people and the hopelessness of the country,
and is afraid the study of the language may create bad
feeling.

"I had tea at Wilfrid Blunt's. Herbert Spencer has written
to beg him to write a poem against war and killing, an outline of which he sends me. Satan wandering about and
arguing with men, not much of an idea, but H. Spencer's
letter interesting—says that though an invalid since 1853
he had (I think) in 1882 joined Frederic Harrison and John
Morley in getting up a demonstration against bloodshed,
and had permanently ruined his remaining health by the
effort. W. Blunt thinks Mr. Harcourt has resigned leadership
because of the —— of the whole Liberal, as well as Conservative party, the Liberals are worse if possible, and there is no
one but Labby to say a word against it. He had written to
Harcourt and had an answer: 'Dear Blunt, like yourself
I live out of jail and rejoicing in my freedom.' He says W.
Harcourt is quite in earnest in his Church letters. He was
much disgusted at the way bishops are appointed. He knew
that the Duke of Devonshire had recommended Page
Roberts for a bishopric, not that he knew him, but someone
had asked him to; however, he was not appointed. When the
Duke asked Lord Salisbury why he had not done so he said,
'Why, that was the man who denounced us at Walworth!'
He had mistaken him for Page Hopps! Wilfrid said, 'Well,
that shows the Holy Spirit is looking after the Church, or it

would have gone to wreck long ago with such Government.'
(Mr. Blunt tells this in his diaries, but without his own
comment.)"

28th. "A lunch at the Verekers'. Lord Gort was pleasant
enough but could give me no legends of Harrow, though
his father had been Byron's fag there—'Didn't I tell you
I can remember my own family history?' Dinner at home.
Mrs. Vere O'Brien, Yeats, Sir Henry Cunningham, George
Russell, extremely agreeable and amusing, quite in the vein,
anecdotes, poems, rhymes of all sorts. He told us of
Gladstone's want of humour, that he had showed him a
funny letter from a clergyman asking for preferment, oddly
worded, and saying it was an old promise of Lord Beaconsfield, and that his wife, 'the only child of an Earl', was now
dead. Gladstone only remarked, 'What a curious thing he
should expect me to keep the promise of Beaconsfield'. Mrs.
O'Brien said Forster used to say Gladstone had a sense of
humour, for that at a drawing-room he had said, 'There's
someone standing on my wife's train and she doesn't know
it', and Gladstone had gone into uncontrollable fits of
laughter over this. G.R. was at a meeting where a missionary
told them that in the dialect of his district 'cousin' and
'enemy' were synonymous terms. Yeats gave them an
interesting account of the other George Russell (A.E.)."

1 March. "Marwood Tucker, with whom I lunched, has
been staying with Gerald Balfour and Lady Betty at the
Chief Secretary's Lodge for the tableau, *The Countess
Cathleen,* and says they were very good. She was surprised
to find the Balfours and Lady de Vesci taking the Nationalist
spirit in Ireland so seriously, and so anxious about it.

"I went on to see Grant Duff, I had seen his *Indian Diaries*
in which he gives several not very brilliant bits from my
conversation. I repeated to him another version of the
Moschus lines he quotes; and he liked it and made me
promise to send it to him. I had read it long ago, in my
girlhood, and remembered it ever since, I don't know who
it was made by: —

> Alas, alas, when swallows fly, when wintry tempests kill
> The light-leaved tender parsley and the curly scented dill,
> They die and come to life again and bloom each coming
>   year.
> But we who are the lords of all, we men of wisdom clear

> So strong and great and crafty in dying once die out,
> And lie forever in the dust, dark, quiet, wrapped about
> With sleep that has no waking up.

"He is very anxious about Lord Halifax's statement at the meeting of the Church delegates that they will not submit to any authority but that of their own Church; he thinks there will be a large secession to Rome and an intolerant High Church party as a result. He showed me some sapphires and moonstones just come from Ceylon and told me to choose a sapphire from among them. (The one I chose was given by me afterwards to Robert for Margaret's engagement ring.)

"Dined at Sir Arthur Clay's. The electric light had just gone out when we came, so we groped, but I got next Sir A. Lyall in the chimney corner and we sat there placidly. At dinner I was next Strachey; he was delighted with the old election ballad about the Raphael Rent made at the election when we fought O'Connell.

> Oh, what happened all the rent? says the Sean Van Voght
> What happened all the rent? Ah, none knows like them
>   that spent
> The curious ways that went! says the Sean Van Voght.

"Some pleasant talk with E. Ashley, it was like a resurrection meeting him again and Mrs. H. Reeve and old Freddy Leveson. All the better for the outing.

"At dinner with the Grant Duffs. Sir Wilfrid Lawson was enthusiastic about the *Life of Parnell,* so I asked him to meet Barry O'Brien and Yeats one evening at dinner, and he came and we had very pleasant talk. B. O'B. told us that Lewis told him he had gone to Brighton to take Parnell's directions about the case, and Mrs. O'Shea came in and interrupted and gave her opinion. Lewis said, 'I was employed by Mr. Parnell', but she said, 'he will do as I wish', and Parnell sat there meek and mild.

"E.L. has been to Buckingham Palace to see the Empress; she is not at all well, and is much worried about Greece and Crete. She has had a letter from the Duchess of Sparta saying Greece must have it. She says Lord Salisbury is furious at the hundred M.P.s having ventured to send an address of sympathy to the Greeks; says he ought to be left alone to arrange the Cretan business, and criticized afterwards. All very well, but it may be too late then."

11 March. "Dined Haliburtons', a large party; sat between Sir Edward Bradford, such a gentle quiet little man to be over all the London police, and a Mr. St. John, a future Lord Bolingbroke. Also Lord and Lady Morris, Lord Poltimore, Lady Duncannon, Sir F. and Lady Jeune, Lord and Lady Harris, Rider Haggard. Lord Morris in great spirits abusing the House of Lords, 'Sure I have to be pa-aid to sit in it. Sure if I'd known in my young days I'd ever be in it I'd have practised making speeches in a graveyard. (On one of the first days on the Court of Appeal in the House of Lords he had come to ask me if I could tell him the difference between the doctrines of the Oriental sects, the Shiahs and Sunnites, a case concerning them had come before him. 'Always fighting they seem to be—about religion. I give you my word I thought I was in Belfast! ')"

12th. "At Archibald Groves', I sat between Sir John Ardagh and Mr. Lucy, Sir John was in Turkey during the Russian War, says Sir H. Layard was a complete dupe and did very badly! He is very anti-Greek and Cretan, and above all anti-Cecil Rhodes and all his works. I said to Mr. Lucy what I had said to others, that the best support the Cretans have had yet is from *Punch,* with the cartoon of the 'kind Turkish policeman' who is to take care of the weeping little boy. He says it is a great difficulty to know beforehand what cartoons to have; that it must be Crete next week, and they don't know what turn things will have taken.

"Lady Betty Balfour sent a messenger asking me to bring Yeats to lunch: 'I know he won't go to an official residence but thank God we are not official here, and my husband would like so much to meet him.' However, I was engaged, and not sure if he would go, and knew he was busy, so made an excuse of this.

"Dined Lovelaces'; sat next Leonard Courtney and had some pleasant talk. After dinner when the men came in, Henry James and Lord Lovelace sat down one on each side: one at a time would have been better, as common ground was not quite easy to find, but we got on to the Byron letters which Lord L. is editing; a pleasant evening in those beautiful rooms."

Then Coole. April 1899. "Jack Yeats and his wife have come on a visit. He is too good an artist to leave to Devonshire. I want to keep him to Irish things."

24 April. "The County Council election has gone by; the people have kept the power in their own hands, and this is

best, they will learn by responsibility . . . A great exodus to America, Bridget D. just come to say good-bye."

12 July. "There was so much to say that I have not said it. The Literary Theatre: well it is in the newscutting books." (But these which I had kept with such labour were lost in America on the Company's first visit there.)[2]

28 August. "Emily Lawless has been here and Geraldine Beauchamp; John Eglinton, Douglas Hyde and his wife. A.E. who left today, W.B.Y. is writing *The Shadowy Waters* and has finished an article for *The North American Review*, which has given him £40, and is writing a little article on Raftery, 'Dust hath closed Helen's Eye'.

"Robert has said good-bye regretfully to Harrow. Mr. Bowen has written highly of him, A.E. has done a portrait of him in pastel; Arnold Harvey, holiday tutor and cricketing companion is a great success. We spent some days at Chevy where I got a good deal of folk-lore, and I go on with Irish but slowly. We have beaten Ennis at cricket."

4 September. "Mr. Ussher, Irish teacher, has arrived to teach at the school and I am taking lessons."

31 December 1899. "All but I left in October, but after two or three weeks W.B.Y., Geraldine and Hugh Lane came back for a fortnight; then I was alone again.

"I spent my time alone chiefly in collecting materials for an account of Raftery. I found his place of burial at Killeenan, and borrowed a MSS. book of his poems, and went to the lodge by moonlight each evening to translate them with Mulkere's help; and then wrote my article.

"On the whole the year has passed well . . . Robert has begun his Oxford time happily; no trouble with tenants; was able to help W.B.Y. by his long stay here, which was in itself a pleasure. The Literary Theatre was successful; on good terms I think with neighbours. I have been a little too long at home, however, and am tired of housekeeping and entertaining and welcome Robert's suggestion that we should go to Venice for Easter."

These are a few passages from Yeats' letters, they help to fill the outline of these years, 1897-1904.

---

[2] It would appear that the press-cutting books referred to are still in the Abbey Theatre Archives. There are certainly some there for the first decades, which were written up by Lady Gregory.

Biddy Early, the Witch Doctor.

Dublin. November 1897. "There was a man at the Contemporary Club whose uncle was Biddy Early's landlord. He evicted her and she cursed him, and presently a house he was in caught fire and fell on him and burnt him to death. I also got a curious story from another man there about a way of cursing by making fire of stones and bidding the curse stay until the stone was burned."

He is grieved for a friend's troubled life[3].

Paris. April 1898. "I would not so much lament but if things remain as they are she will never leave this life of hatred, which a vision I made her see years ago told her was her deepest hell, and contrasted with the life of labour from the divine love which was her highest heaven . . . Whenever things are going ill I find myself thinking of my peaceful months at Coole . . ."

An Introduction.

11 January 1898. "Your letter came last night when a visit from Symons had suspended this letter. He came to read me a review and I took the opportunity of introducing him to Raspberry Vinegar, which he had never heard of. He wanted to know if it was intoxicating. I told him very, but when he tasted it he recognised a drink he had drunk in Paris and thought entirely a French product. O drink of our grandmothers!"

Death is the beginning.

30 March 1898. "I did not write to you because I always think one can say nothing when anyone is dead. The best one can do is to be silent. Much of one's old beliefs have gone from one, but one thing becomes more certain to me every day that death is the beginning and not the end."

A.E. as Organizer.

Paris. 25 April 1898. "I got a letter from Russell a little before I left London. He had a mild fit of the old gloom through having to dine with parish priests every night. He was going to dine the day he wrote with a Bishop and was hoping to have a theological argument. 'That is a bright spot in my future,' he said . . . My host is a Celtic enthusiast

---

[3] The typescript has 1899, but Yeats was not then in Paris, although he had been there in February 1899 and April 1898. The reference must be to Maud Gonne.

who spends most of his day in highland costume to the wonder of the neighbours."[4]

In general hot water.

Sligo. November 1898. "My uncle is just at this moment in one of his bed fits, owing to the fact that I am in general hot water and the inhabitants attack him as they can't get at me. He brought me to a Masonic concert on Thursday and somebody sang a stage Irishman song—the usual whiskey-Shillelagh kind of thing—and I hissed him and lest my hiss be lost in the general applause waited till the applause was done and hissed again. This gave somebody else courage and we both hissed. My uncle defends me, but admits that he makes a poor hand of it and gets beaten, as I can well believe."

The best one can give.

"M.N. has been to see me. She has ostentatiously taken up with a notorious rascal she must share with a score of casual loves. Lady X.[5], remembering her own adventures in the Divorce Court, meant to be tolerant, but finally cut her for making such a choice. I am about the only person who belongs to the orderly worlds she is likely to meet from this out . . . It seems to be a point of pride with her to observe no disguise . . . She is in love, and because she has some genius to make her thirst for realities, and not enough of intellect to see that temporal use of unreal things, she is throwing off every remnant of respectability with an almost religious enthusiasm. Certainly the spirit 'blows where it listeth' and the best one can give its victims is charity."

A Wager.

Dublin. January 1901. "I saw Mrs. Pat Campbell's manager yesterday. He told me that the reason why the *Independent* made that amazing attack on Maeterlinck was that it was written by big Manning, and big Manning had just lost a wager to some of Mrs. Pat's company. They had bet they

4 MacGregor Mathers, the senior figure in the Order of the Golden Dawn, the English branch of which, under Yeats, separated from Mathers when he brought Aleister Crowley into the order. See *The Magicians of the Golden Dawn*, by Ellic Howe (Routledge & Kegan Paul, 1972).
5 M.N. is in all probability Althea Gyles and Lady X., Lady Colin Campbell. See the letter from Arthur Symons dated 15 September 1900, quoted by Ian Fletcher in his article "Poet & Designer: W. B. Yeats & Althea Gyles" *Yeats Studies*, No. 1, p.69, Irish University Press, Shannon, Bealtaine 1971.

could produce among themselves a taller man than Manning, and they did—he beat Manning by half an inch. Before that he had praised everything.

"I have just heard an American saying to some English Officer about the African war that the English have as much chance of catching De Wet as a Lord Mayor's Procession of catching a burglar in Hampstead."

The Woman clothed with the sun.
London. January 1901. "Do you remember Mr. and Madam Horus who took in Magregor? A poor lady of no very great intelligence but of much benevolence came to me yesterday in distress. They and three friends had planted themselves upon her and were running up bills in her name, and she was in too great terror to send them away. The poor lady had been in some remote part of the world when the English Reverses with Africa began. She explained to me yesterday with great *naiveté* that she asked herself, 'What could have caused them—how could the English be defeated unless by Black Art?' Then suddenly she thought—'It is Magregor! Magregor is doing it', and she came to England to get some mystic to stop him. In England she met the Horus' fresh from rooking the terrible Magregor himself, and all went well until they told her that she was the woman clothed with the sun, and that the world was not convex but concave with the sun in the middle—and then she doubted. She is a good soul, and felt that the world might have what shape it liked but that she could not believe that St. John had made all that fuss about her."[6]

I bring him a lute from Cattaro.
13 April 1901. "I am delighted about the one-stringed lute. One string should do much to restrain the irrelevant activities of the musician."

Hostility in Dublin.
Sligo. May 1901. "Last Saturday to my great surprise I met Bullen in Dublin . . . He has been trying to sell copies of my books there. He told me that he was amazed to find the hostility to me of the booksellers. Gill, he declared, seemed to hardly like to speak my name. *The Secret Rose* was strange to say particularly disapproved of, but they spoke with hostility of even *The Shadowy Waters*. Memory of the *Countess Cathleen* attacks account for a great deal. Bullen

6 See Ellic Howe's *The Magicians of the Golden Dawn.*

found the Protestant booksellers little better, and asked
Magee, the College publisher, if T.C.D. disliked me. He
said, 'What is he doing here? Why doesn't he go away and
leave us in peace?' He seems to have suspected me of some
deep revolutionary design. As Bullen was rather drunk when
he told me these things I asked his traveller, whom I saw
on Monday, and got the same account. He had tried to sell
a book of Carleton's, too, and said that Carleton and myself
were received with the same suspicion. This was of course
because of his early stories.

"I imagine that as I withdraw from politics my friends
among the Nationalists will grow less, at first at any rate,
and my foes more numerous. What I heard from Bullen
only confirms the idea that I had at the time of the *Countess
Cathleen* row, that it would make a very serious difference
outside the small cultivated class.

"My uncle, who is High Sheriff this year, has had a hint
from people here that I must not go near the Constitutional
Club, where I have no desire to go. This because of my
letter about the late Queen. Between my politics and my
poetry I shall hardly have my head turned with popularity."
Rosses Point. June 1901. "My uncle has rheumatism and
the way he is groaning and sighing about the house fills me
with rage. Mary Battle, who is always praising him, always
ends up her praises by saying, 'It is such a pity he never
thinks of anybody but himself!' She says this, I think, in part
because whenever she is ill he takes no notice, as he is
convinced it is bad for her to encourage her to speak about
her illness. He himself has scarcely another subject."

He has given offence in a speech.
London. November 1901. "How Moore lives in the present.
If the National Theatre is ever started, what he is and what
I am will be weighed and very little what we have said or
done. A phrase more or less matters little. Yet I suppose we
would both be more popular if I could keep from saying
what I think and he from saying what he does not think.
You may tell him that the wisest of men does not know
what is expedient, but that we can all get a very good idea
as to what is our particular truth. The more we keep to that
the better. Cajolery never lighted the fire.

"I forgot to tell you that the bottle of champagne that had
survived my illness blew up, and Mrs. Old, who was quite
close to it at the time, said, 'I could better have spared the

St. Pancras Church'. (She does not approve of the Church of
England.) And she and her husband have disputes on future
punishment. She says hell is an accusing conscience but he
says, 'Flame's flame and there's an end of it'.

"I have found a great increased friendliness on the part of
some young men here in Dublin. In a battle like Ireland's,
which is one of poverty against wealth, one must prove one's
sincerity by making oneself unpopular to wealth. One must
accept the baptism of the gutter. Have not all teachers done
the like?

"I have been written to by some Socialist society in France
asking me to give my views as to the future of Socialism and
the way in which Art should associate itself with it. And not
feeling inclined to work at an article for them I wrote,
'Socialism by the end of the next century will have put a
number on the back of every man. It will be the function
of Art to secure that the colour of these numbers be in tone
with that of the jacket.'

"Miss Purser tells me that the difference between me and
my father is that my nose is broad at the top and my father's
is narrow; and people with the nose broad at the top are
effective and those with it narrow are ineffective."

London. November 1901.   "I saw Bjornson's *Beyond Human
Power* today. It is manifestly an unbeliever's account of
belief. The hero, a parson who works miracles, or what
seem miracles, through his faith, is made talk like any
common, jealous, gnashing preacher. One feels that Bjornson
does not take the religious genius seriously, though he wants
to. He cannot understand that the religious genius like
every other kind of genius differs from mere zeal because it
is perfectly precise. His parson would have occupied himself
with nothing transcendental, but probably with the housing
of the working classes or the like. He is even not a little
vulgar, and one is not happy until he is gone from the stage.
Apart from this it is a really absorbing play, and Mrs. Pat
Campbell plays it beautifully."

A lecture on Robert Emmet.
New York. 2 January 1904.   "I lecture tomorrow night in
Carnegie Hall. My big lecture, the most important of the
whole lot. I wonder what sort of an audience I will have,
for the hall is too big. I have been down practising my
oratorical passages in the empty hall, that I may not be put
out if there are some empty benches. I got one compliment.

I had just finished my peroration when I heard the clapping of hands in a dark corner. It was the Irish caretaker. You remember my old organ peroration, the one I wound up the speech with at the Horace Plunkett dinner? Well, there is a big organ on the platform at Carnegie Hall. I turn towards it meditatively and then, as if the thought suddenly struck me, speak that old peroration. It was this piece of extemporizing that pleased the caretaker. I am working at this speech as I never worked at a speech before."

But when I asked Yeats later if he ever now took such pains about a lecture, he said, "Oh, I take pains enough, but only of the arrangement of my thoughts. I had to pick my words then because I was going to speak to a half-educated Irish audience. I didn't know what was wrong with me that I couldn't do better, but I know now and take great care never to speak anywhere where I cannot speak out of my habitual thought and in my habitual language. I am done with diplomacies."

From a letter to a friend in England: "But seriously is it not the poor black-coated man in the street who is absurd and not we in a brief moment of splendour? You in England and we in Ireland have different kinds of humour; your kind sterilizes the will, for you are always afraid of being absurd; our kind stimulates the will on to action, for it makes us delight in all fantastic energy; you laugh with scorn, the laughter which Shelley thought marked the death of nations, but we laugh from affection. You laugh at others, we laugh at ourselves, and yet it is our laughter and not yours that is the laughter of triumph. It is like the hundred eyes of the peacock."

These are some Yeats sayings, written down by me or remembered: —

"There are strange juxtapositions in history. The Protestants opened a road for the intellect, and Catholics opened a road for the expression of the emotions."

"All the Churches are in danger, and they ought to unite and stand together like cows in a storm."

"To try and write a lyric is like settling oneself to look intently at a little spot of light, and that is tiring after an hour."

"In writing the best work is never done through observation but through experience."

"Goethe has a great genius, occasionally impeded by restless fits of intelligence."

"Someone said, 'A woman after twenty years of public life is a ruin'. Oscar Wilde said, 'And a woman after twenty years of domestic life is a public building'."

"My father says, 'The Englishman has good principles and a bad heart; the Irishman has bad principles and a good heart'."

"Those turkeys look as if each should have an embroidery frame before it."

"The modern wit is the only representative of the old hero. Wit is never vanquished; and courage is an essential part of it."

"H.G., like other children of great men I have seen, gives one the impression of a pew opener."

"To Croft (a dog) the Universe is a series of delightful smells."

"We should go through life like a soldier through a battle, not feeling our wounds because of the strength of our energy."

"It is not the past that urges us, it is the future."

"The Goncourt Academy—how is it to be kept up unless they admit some theologians? The business theologians always set themselves to trying to explain away the intentions of the founder."

In argument with a French Countess who expressed horror in an exaggerated way at "the dirt of the Irish people". "Well, they are pious. You can't have piety and cleanliness together. Would you have them heretics like the Dutch? Cleanliness and infidelity are always on the one side." She was speechless and De Basterot delighted.

Someone said, "No use arguing with you. You are a projectile and the gunner out of sight." Yeats said, "A projectile is always confident and does not think where it is going to strike. It leaves that to the gunpowder."

"We never love the woman we like, or like the woman we love, for she whom we like gives us peace, and she whom we love gives us unrest."

"When enthusiasms go out of the door, greed comes up from the kitchen."

About Z.'s conversion. "Catholicism is the last liaison of the decadent."

He saw in a dream a stone that had been in part carved and left unfinished "because the man who was carving it so greatly loved the rough uses of the stone."

"Moonlight is like mob oratory."

"In questions of taste, it's no good to use argument, one must use force."

E.M. says, "You would like to be mad but you can,'t", and W. B. Yeats, "I have just enough enthusiasm to make me my own butt". He said to Miss G., "I can organise, but the minute I begin to act I see the ridiculous side."

"The object of games should be to lend an excitement to idleness."

"I admire pikes and rifles in the abstract but to use them would be sectarian."

"Turkeys have always a look of being related to the county families and living on a reduced income."

"In the search for folk-lore one finds things with infinite reverberations into the past."

"Yes, it is a fine sunset but too rhetorical."

"Literature is the forgiveness of sins."

XXI

THE BOER WAR AND THE THEATRE

THAT IRISH Theatre, Literary Theatre as it was first called, planned on that day at Duras by the sea, had come into being in 1899, when we gave for a May week *The Heather Field* and *The Countess Cathleen*. And now in its second year we were in London for the rehearsals of *Maeve* and *The Bending of the Bough* and *The Last Feast of the Fianna*[1]. For in these first years we brought over actors from London; we had not yet discerned what fine players we were to find or to train nearer home.

The Boer War had begun to bring unforeseen sorrow and anxiety into England, and although this seems to have been but a shadow of what was to come fourteen years later, it had yet in one way a more bitter edge. For in the war against Germany those only were objectors who believed all war wrong, while there were many who saw that war against the Boers as an unjust one; and so temper rose and old friendships were shaken. And even our Theatre did not escape trouble. For the war led to the Queen's belated visit to Ireland, and letters written on that account brought an accusation of political intention against the scheme that had been launched with no such thought. All this will be better understood if I give some of the gossip written in or from London from time to time.

I wrote in January 1900: "Yeats came and stayed to dinner but had to go on to some mystical meeting. *Shadowy Waters* is on its way to America for the *North American Review*. He had received an unexpected cheque, 25 guineas from the *Academy,* a prize for the best book of poems in the year, and is as pleased as a baby, especially as some fortune-teller had foretold he was to come into some money he had not earned. He brought me the cheque to be changed and is going to buy a new suit of clothes and some books. He believes a new period of political activity is coming on in Ireland but does not think it will be agrarian, because of

---

[1] *The Countess Cathleen* by W. B. Yeats was performed on 8 May, *The Heather Field* by Edward Martyn on 9 May. *The Bending of the Bough* by George Moore and *The Last Feast of the Fianna* by Alice Milligan were performed on 19 February 1900 and *Maeve* by Edward Martyn the following day.

the strength of the artizans in the towns. His occult ideas make him think there may be a revolution coming on, and Miss Gonne believes that she has been 'sent' to stir up disloyalty, and though he thinks her hopes unreasonable, he thinks a prophet is an unreasonable person sent by Providence when it is going to do an unreasonable thing.

"I found Enid Layard busy making 'fisher caps' for sick soldiers, and sewing little Union Jacks on to various garments. Of course she is, like the rest, in a frenzy of rage with the Boers. There is no use saying anything, people think it is because one is Irish and wishing for the downfall of England, and to state one's reasons is, as Biglow would say, like 'giving a tract to a Bull of Bashan'. I went on to lunch with the Morrises, who are by no means in that line. Wolseley, they say, is going wrong in the head and forgets things, so no wonder the War Office is in confusion, especially as a chief official is so cross at being forbidden by Lord Lansdowne to make any more cock-a-hoop speeches that they are hardly on speaking terms, which impedes work. I was telling Lord M. about Buller being identified at Lisdoonvarna as 'the man who drank most of the champagne', and he says he has taken quantities out with him. He says also that he was on a Committee of Grillon's Club with him and there was an accumulation of money to spend, and a discussion arose as to using it for portraits of members, etc., but Buller insisted that it should be spent on champagne at £1 a bottle . . ."

22 January. "I went to Yeats's Monday evening to meet Miss Milligan whose play, or a part of it, is to be performed. But there was nearly a quarrel, as George Moore, who is resolving himself into a syndicate for the re-writing of plays, wanted to alter hers, and she refuses to let any hand touch it but her own. However, that calmed down; then an explosion about Mrs. Emery, who W.B.Y. thought had been promised some parts, but G.M. has given them to someone else."

23rd January. "The Barry O'Briens, G. Moore, E. Martyn, Yeats, came to dine with me. G.M. has been writing an article on the decadence of England . . . B. O'Brien says it is coming out more and more clearly that the Prince of Wales was concerned in the Raid[2]. Hawksley as good as told him Chamberlain was in it (and our Primate in his official prayer returns thanks that we are not guilty of the 'crimson sin' of having begun the war!); they went on to a discussion on

[2] The Jameson Raid which took place on 29 December 1895.

Caesar and Bonaparte. O'B. says Pompey was a better general
than Caesar, but Caesar had more character. G.M. said it was
striking to read Tolstoy's account of Bonaparte's efforts to get
to Moscow, and the Russian efforts to keep him from reaching it; and if he had not reached it he would not have lost
his army. said it was like the anxiety the Boers had for a
seaport, and the determination of the English they should
not have one, though wise Sir Hercules had advised it, and
now the great advantage to the Boers is their having no
place that the British navy could reach.

"At lunch Lord Haliburton said Wolseley is no good for
office work, and Buller shines there, but in war Wolseley
has imagination, which Buller is lacking in, and could see
'what is on the other side of the hill', while Buller can only
look at the hill doggedly and get to the top. The taking of
Spion Kop was announced.

"A rehearsal of *Bending of the Bough* 12.00 o'clock to
3.30. It was very amusing, Delange, the stage manager, a
splendid general drilling them all, letting nothing pass.
Moore watching closely, and near his temper. E. Martyn,
who has been requested by Moore not to make any more
comments, made them only in depreciating whispers to me.
Yeats suggesting new alterations.

"Posters announce, 'Spion Kop abandoned'.

"I met Lord Duncannon at dinner, furious with the
Salisbury-Balfour regime, both in Ireland and South Africa;
wishes for Chamberlain with a free hand, and Rosebery to
help him. He says last May he dined at Lady Selkirk's, 'and
Montague White was there and had a long talk with him
and told him of the Boer armaments, and that they would
take the field in October because they believed the independence of their country was threatened. And if he knew and
was ready to tell that, why did not the Government know it?
And the same way with the Raid. F.G. on his way out to
South Africa wrote home from shipboard that the rising at
Johannesburg was to take place at such a time, and why did
not the Government hear it? And who is responsible, the
Government or their military advisers for the insufficient
preparations and inadequate guns. Evelyn Wood is under
petticoat influence, and the whole W.O. more or less under
it.' He has seen a letter, ready for publication, giving a list
of officers sent out at the bidding of certain ladies. And he
was told by the mother of a young officer that 'he was anxious
to go but couldn't get leave, but a lady who had taken a

fancy to him said she would manage it, went down to the W.O. and at once he was attached to a regiment going out. Then she took a fancy to go out herself, took her ticket, asked him if he would like to go out in the same ship. He said he was under orders to sail a week earlier. She said that didn't matter, went again to the W.O. and he got orders to go in her ship.' "

28th. "I dined with the Grant Duffs, but the news, which I brought, of the retreat of Redvers Buller across the Tugela, depressed Sir M., and the others were chiefly miscellaneous girls and young men. Sir M. agreeing that the Boers had been badly treated but very bloodthirsty for all that."

29th, 30th. "Geraldine (a niece) came up, and we set out together to Oxford to see Robert. A great delight seeing him there, well and happy in his own snug little rooms. I would rather have had him to myself, but such a treat for G. I worked in the morning at an article for *Beltaine,* our new theatre magazine."

31st. "I spent the afternoon at Savile Row typing my article. Enid was excited about her scheme for a Villa Hospital at Madeira for officers. My belief is they would not stay there, within four days of friends and home. And then she went off to have safety pins made with little Union Jacks on for Tommy to fasten his bandage with. I dined with Lady Shrewsbury to meet Lady Londonderry, Lord Morris, Edmund Gosse, Mr. Cockerill and Bishop Rendall; very pleasant, though the talk too much of the war to be really good. All friends of Buller, but Lady L. wanting to know why he changed his plans when he went out, what pressure was brought to bear on him. Lord M. says a man in Galway said to him, 'We are for the Boers, but we are not for the Orange Free State' (looking on it as an Orange foothold!)."

1 February. "I went to see Mrs. Frederic Harrison, who says her husband's anti-war lecture the night before was very successful and well received. She says it was dreadful before the war began how all women in society were urging it on, but now there is a feeling rising up against it.

"I lunched with Sir A. Birch, who rails chiefly against Rhodes, says it was he who clamoured for war, assuring the Government that the Boers would cave in as soon as attacked. I asked if Chamberlain had really known the raid was coming, and he said 'They all knew it; I did for one'. At Mrs. D.'s Mrs. R. (Miss B. of long ago) came in and they talked of the war. One young fellow lately killed had lunched with

Mrs. D. before he left, looking so well and handsome. It seems rather cruel to his family that the report sent back to them says he was found two days after the battle, dead, (Magersfontein I think), and the wound was such a slight one he could probably have been saved if it had been attended to in time. An officer's wife told Mrs. D. that her husband had written a terrible account of the flight of the Highlanders. They ran over him and trampled him, they were howling with fright, some of them on hands and knees, quite demoralised and terror stricken.

"At dinner at Reginald Smith's he spoke of the indignation felt against the Dean of Durham for his sermon against sending soldiers out drunk, and showing that he disapproved of the war. The Lord Chancellor as well as Lord G. have abused him for alluding to politics in the pulpit, well and good if it were applied to all—but I have had to sit under our Archdeacon with his 'rebellion of witchcraft' and R. Smith had heard Canon Farrer preach at Canterbury this winter on the war, which he declared to be an absolutely right one. He said in his sermon, 'And what shall we say for the noble boy from this town who killed three Boers with his own hands?' I told him of Sir Alfred Lyall saying the only thing that makes him believe in eternal punishment is the existence of Farrer."

4 February. "Fog, but I went to Westminster Abbey. Horace Plunkett came in the afternoon, full of cares of his new Board, and I think more Unionist than before his illness, seems to think the grant for the Board in part satisfied our financial claims, and that we ought to be grateful. I say no, if we are owed the money let us have it, there is no question of gratitude, and we ought not to have to sit up and beg for it every time.

"Hugh Lane came to lunch, he tells of his successes, how he sold on Saturday a Cuyp for £40, which he had bought in Dublin for 15/-. With Geraldine to rehearsal of *Maeve*, to take Peg Inerney's costume, and to show 'Maeve' G.'s red Galway petticoat, E. Martyn wishing her to wear one. She, however, rejects it, saying Maeve was supposed to have a sense of beauty! The rehearsal went well and the play gives just the impression I had when I first read it in MS., of taking one into a beautiful dream world.

"G. Moore came in with a wild scheme for having *The Shadowy Waters* translated into Irish for next year's theatre, that he may make the announcement in a speech he is going to make. But I will hold to its being acted next year in its own beautiful words. I believe what gives him his force is his power of only seeing one thing at a time; at the moment he only sees the language, whereas I see the Theatre is the work in hand and our immediate duty. *Shadowy Waters* in Irish! It would appear to the audience as 'Three men in a Boat' talking gibberish."

9th. "There was a lecture on Gaelic literature at the Grosvenor Club. Alfred Nutt lectured, read extracts from Bricriu's Feast, etc., the audience were looking for jokes, and when he spoke of Celtic chivalry, and told how Cuchulain sent a part of the herbs brought to heal him across the ford to his wounded enemy, all burst out laughing—such a joke!

"Barry O'Brien was at the war debate and said Tim Healy's speech was wonderful. He led the House into a trap, telling how the *Morning Post* had published a letter from Winston Churchill giving an account of the splendid courage, coolness and bravery of the Irish soldiers, and saying that they were the finest infantry in the world (cheers). This had been copied into nine English papers, 'yes into nine English papers'. But in every one of them the word 'Irish' had been left out! Gloomy silence, and the House at the end of his speech 'sat cowering as if it had been whipped'.

"Snow and slush. I went to see Yeats who had been coughing terribly yesterday. He said Symons, who had dined with him the night before, had discussed the question as to whether any man with self-respect could wear goloshes, as he, like Yeats, arrives at the house he dines in with muddy boots. I went on to lunch at Savile Row, Lord Robert Cecil was there, so I consulted him, and he said snow-shoes were the thing now. He is very sorry for himself, having joined the Volunteers in a moment of enthusiasm, and not liking the drill. Enid said she had joined a ladies' Volunteer regiment after the Crimean War, and practised shooting, she forgot at what—something white. I suggested a flag of truce . . .

"She had asked Soveral, the Portuguese Minister, why we had all the nations against us in this war, and he said, 'Because they think, as many people in England do, that it is an unjust one'. She gasped but made no answer.

"At dinner at the Birches, I sat between Sidney Colvin and Sir Mansfield Clark, who was Commissioner in Basutoland. He said there is a good deal to be said for the Boers, the real bitter pill to them after annexation was sending Sir

Owen Lanyon, who had black blood (his grandmother was a negress), which they have a horror of, to lord it over them. Sidney Colvin abused G.M. (for Stevenson's sake) and Symonds (for Phillips's sake) and is full of Phillips's praises—'he is so fine and athletic and reads poetry so beautifully'. I consulted him on the golosh question, and he said he had arrived at dinner in a pair, and 'I think them good enough for me—let alone Symons!'

"I dined with the Haliburtons, a banquet. The Lord Chancellor and Lady Halsbury, Lord and Lady Cork, Duncannons, Mr. Watts Russell (Tony) as a young man for the Halsbury girl. I sat, well guarded, between the Chief Commissioner of Police (Lord Wolseley), Sir Edward charming, and pro-Boer in principle, but would like to kill them himself now we are at war, Lord Wolseley amiable, but grew cross and excited talking of the Boers, so I left him to Lady Duncannon. 'Dirty, ignorant, odious, uncivilised, never have a flower near their houses—not a flower!' He doesn't think much of the Madeira Hospital scheme. He looks much aged, his face shrunken; protests he has not a drop of Irish blood in his veins, and abuses Irish soldiers, 'hard to manage and drunken'."

Then came the performances of our Irish Theatre, February 1900.

17th. "Up very early and off by 8.30 train to Dublin with George Moore and Yeats. G.M. had brought his speech for us to read, very forcible in its paradoxical way, his point that the English language has been exhausted by all that has been written in it, and especially by journalism, and that the literature of the future will be in the languages that are not used up, Irish, Welsh, Hungarian, perhaps Basque! A very pleasant journey and comfortable lunch in the train, the scenery lovely going through Wales, snow on the mountains and the sea as blue as the Mediterranean. A fine crossing. Yeats came and dined with me and went to the Literary Society party. Douglas Hyde there, between amusement and uneasiness at his new disciple; Rolleston delighted with *Bending of the Bough* which he has just read. Yeats gave a little address on the plays."

18th. "To see Jack Yeats's pictures at Leinster Hall, a great improvement in colour from last year and so full of energy and imagination . . . Yeats has told Rolleston he must do something that will violently annoy the upper classes to redeem his character."

19th. "I had sent cards for the first afternoon of Jack Yeats's show for 2.00 o'clock. But at 2.30 no one had come. At 3.00 o'clock 'a gentleman' appeared, but it was to ask if we would buy a Thom's *Directory,* or if we wanted any advertisements put in. However, about 4.00 o'clock people began to come, Mahaffy, Lady Fingall, Lord Powerscourt, Sir George and Lady Morris, Lady Arnott, Martin and Redmond Morris, Douglas Hyde, Lyster, Miss Stokes, Dr. Fitzgerald, and many I didn't know; the pictures much appreciated and admired. It was dark and the gas was turned on, and some people said they would come again and see them by daylight.

"Then the anxiety about the plays began. We found the Gaiety very well filled. A box was kept for the Committee and we had it to ourselves. Douglas Hyde, who was in the stalls, came now and again to talk to us, and Magrath, writing for the *Freeman,* came to consult about his report. Miss Milligan's little piece was well staged, but Finn and Usheen both very bad . . . *Maeve* didn't begin very well, the long dialogue, and once the audience tittered, I think at old O'Hegan's fear that the rich son-in-law would not come back. But then things improved, and it went very well, the anti-English touch being much applauded, and the little anti-hissing helped. Edward Martyn called for at the end three times."

20th. "People in to tea, and G. Moore very nice, walked round with Jack and gave practical criticisms of the pictures, at the same time praising what was good, and I think looking at him with respect when he found he worked from sketches and not models. This, Moore says, was the method of the old masters but it is a lost art; Whistler could do nothing at all without a model in his studio.

"I went to *The Bending of the Bough* in some trepidation, the last rehearsal had gone so badly, but need not have been afraid, it went splendidly."

22nd. "To the lunch given by the National Literary Society to the Literary Theatre. Dr. Sigerson handed me down, but I told him he was to have an actress on each side of him, on which he exclaimed, 'God bless my soul!'. I found myself next Mr. Oldham and opposite John O'Leary, G. Moore's great speech went off well. When it began, the wretched waiters were rushing about with coffee cups, making a disturbance. Yeats made a fighting speech, calling on the M.P.s to use all their old methods of obstruction if necessary, when the amendment to the Education Bill comes

on, to insist on the teaching of Irish. He attacked Trinity
College as provincial, 'which the Literary Society is not; and
the Gaelic League is not; we must fight against provincialism
and die fighting; that as Heine wished for himself, a sword
may be laid upon our graves.'

"Some of the people came into tea with me, Magrath of
the *Freeman* for one, who introduced a young man on the
Irish Times. I remonstrated about the very bad, even ferocious notice of the plays the day before, and he said it was
not the desire of the *Irish Times* to show hostility, but that
the writer of the notice was a 'crank' and they were all vexed
about it. He said they couldn't eat their own words but
would put in a polite paragraph next day, which they did,
so my tea party did so much good. I told him it was like
the American paper which, when some man remonstrated
at having been put among the deaths, said 'we will be happy
free of charge to put you among the births to-morrow
morning'.

"George Russell sat a long time in the afternoon with me,
a great pleasure, telling me of his new poems and talking of
Larminie's death, and his own boy, and our friends and
their work. Then Miss Borthwick and Miss O'Reilly came
in and I had a Gaelic League talk with them and found
them amiable. Then the people from the matinee began to
arrive, and I was whirled off from them by E. Martyn, to the
library round the corner about the Deputy Lieutenant
business. The story is, at a charity concert at Tillyra it was
suggested 'God save the Queen' should be sung, and he said
No, but without giving much thought to the matter. Archdeacon Daly, however, and others chatted about it. (When
I met Mrs. T. in Dublin she said, 'Is it true Mr. Martyn
refused to allow "God save the Queen"?' I said 'Yes, and
much worse than that, he would not have "The Absent
Minded Beggar"!' which she took seriously.) Lord Clonbrock (Lieutenant of W. Galway) came up to E.M. in the
smoking room at Kildare Street Club the other day and said
he had heard of his refusal to have the National Anthem
in his house. Edward said yes, he did not like songs that were
party cries, and that someone else might have objected to
the Wearing of the Green. Clonbrock gave him a lecture and
said he should remember his oath as D.L. and J.P., Edward
said, in that case, he had better resign both. Clonbrock got
frightened, begged him not to think of doing so, and talked
of other things. Next morning, however, Edward sent in his

resignation to Lord Ashbourne. In the evening, Clonbrock came to him, said he had met Lord Ashbourne who was very much put out at his resignation (no doubt had rebuked Clonbrock) and would write a letter to him (C) to show Edward and give him a chance of withdrawing. This letter had now come, enclosed in one from Clonbrock, begging Edward to 'reconsider his determination'. He came to consult me, but said he wished to resign, that he never wished for the D.L. or J.P. and would be freer without them. I was personally against his resigning as we are short of magistrates. . . . Still, it is intolerable that in one's own house one should not be allowed to choose one's own line in politics, and I begged him if he did resign to put it on definite grounds and not leave his motive at the mercy of every chatterer's invention. He made me write down what I proposed, and said he would bring a draft of the letter the next day.

"Then back to the Gallery, full of people, Walter Osborne among them. My teas have certainly been a success, a help to the Theatre, and to the Gallery, in making the pictures known.

"George Moore wants E. Martyn to write a column and a half in the *Freeman* showing up the landlords and officials and declaring his political convictions. Edward says, 'My political convictions are those of the company I am in. I have no convictions but religious ones.' This settles the question."

25th. "Sunday. The week over and well over, for though there is financial loss we have gained rather than lost credit, have justified our existence and come into touch with National feeling on its best side, the side one wants to develop . . . Then back to Edward and his letter. He begins by stating his position something like this: 'When I was made a J.P. and D.L. I was a Unionist, I had been brought up one, and in ignorance of the history of my country and of its language. Some years ago my eyes were opened by reading Lecky's *History of Ireland in the 18th Century*. Since then I have gone on and developed a dislike of England, I refused to have "God save the Queen" and "The Absent Minded Beggar" performed at a concert in my house, because unfortunately in our country Mr. Kipling's name has come to mean the same thing as the Union, and the extinction of our distinctive nationality. If I am not free to act upon my convictions without being liable to be called to task in however friendly a manner by the Lieutenant of my county I have no alternative but to resign the J.P. and D.L. I am, however, no politician and do not wish to take an active part in politics.' So Clonbrock has succeeded in pushing him over the border. I am sorry, for I hoped we might all keep out of politics."

London. 1 March. "Saw flags flying and knew Ladysmith was relieved. I began translating Douglas Hyde's poems. I dined with E.L. and listened to a great deal of war talk. Her enthusiasm for the Madeira Hospital has rather faded as only one officer was got to accept a berth there. 7,000 beds have been offered in England for convalescent soldiers, but only 40 have been found to accept them.

". . . To see M.S., but she is like gunpowder, all nerves and irritability, and indeed one is afraid to disagree with blood-thirstiness for fear of being hit with umbrellas, like the people at last night's meeting.

"Dined Lecky's; he rather cross. Took me down to dinner and said first thing, 'What silly speeches your Celtic people have been making!' 'Moore?' I said, 'Yes, and Yeats, oh, very silly.' He is in bad humour because Blackrock, which he has known and knows to speak English all his life, has sent him a copy of resolutions in favour of Irish. In revenge, I told him how a Deputy Lieutenant was proclaiming himself a Nationalist on the ground of having been converted by his history. He shrugs his shoulders and says 'People in Ireland are so one-sided and only take up one part of one's argument. I say I have a comfortable feeling I can be as one-sided as I like, because the Irish average of impartiality will be kept balanced while he exists.'

"Afterwards I talked with Mrs. Clemens and then later with 'Mark Twain' himself . . . Then to Carson, Q.C., genial and shrewd. He had congratulated Redmond on being chosen leader, and he had replied gloomily, 'I hope you may be able to congratulate me in three months' time—' Then a talk with Mrs. Lecky about the war. She is a little bitter about the papers and intolerance here—houses wrecked last night at Stratford because their owners were suspected of pro-Boer feelings."

4 March. "Mark Twain and Mrs. Clemens dined with me, and W. B. Yeats and Kathleen Morris. I asked George Moore but he refused on the ground of hating humorists, however, he came in after dinner, and though I had been a little anxious, it was to me, and I think to all, a very pleasant evening. Clemens, rather slow in getting things out in his American drawl, but always got to the point at last. Yeats

read translations from the Irish after dinner, Hyde's and mine, which Clemens seemed delighted with. G. Moore was enthusiastic about Benson's uncut *Hamlet* at the Lyceum, and contrasts its length and exuberance with our fear of boring an audience for one single moment. He abuses the scenery of *Midsummer Night's Dream,* says people won't look at a Velasquez for half-an-hour without being tired; and why are they called to look at a badly painted wood for two hours? Clemens, however protests, 'I like that wood, I like to see a wood on the stage that looks like a wood, and I like to see a moon get up and act like a moon!' G. Moore and Yeats stayed on till after 12.00, Moore adding to his speech to make an article for *New Ireland Review,* putting in the evil effects the Boer War will have on England, how she will be smothered in South Africa. Yeats says, 'She might have been Greece and she has chosen to be Persia!'

"I walked over to Hugh Lane's Gallery, and to Christie's, as there were Simeon Solomons to be sold, one a lovely little thing of a musician I set my heart on—within bounds. However, it went up to £14 so I am trying to forget it, and Hugh sent me to make up a present of a beautiful painting, by Poussin, of a blind laurel-crowned poet-fiddler. Raftery of course! the eternal bard: Homer wandering through the ages.

"Then with Yeats to Benson's *Hamlet.* The unabridged text lasting from 3.30 to 6.30 and then from 8.00 to 10.30. A wonderful play, well as I know it I had never known its extraordinary richness and variety before, and was never tired for one moment. And the acting did little for it. And as to the utterance, as Yeats said, verse is considered of no account, they don't even try to give it, many lines were quite unintelligible. I am all the more anxious about *Shadowy Waters,* that it may be perfectly clear. (Yeats says an actor once told him that in *Hamlet* especially it was unnecessary for the audience to understand what was said, because they knew it already.)"

8th. "I dined with the Clemenses, taking W.B. and Jack Yeats. Only themselves and two daughters, a quiet pleasant evening, all friendly. Mark Twain gives the impression of genuine goodness and kindliness. Jack came out and told anecdotes, and did a sketch of George Moore from memory, which delighted them; and Willie read Mary Hynes and some other poems of Raftery's. Then they wanted to hear one of his own poems, and he couldn't remember one, and I wrote out 'Wandering Aengus' for him to read.

"Mark Twain told us some American anecdotes, and these I have heard Jack Yeats repeat sometimes, exactly as they were told. I asked him the other day to put down one or two for me and he did so, reminding me that 'they were told by him in a long slow drawl which at the right time got longer and slower'. They made us laugh very much at the time. 'There was a young man years ago in Natchez, and he took the steamboat and went down the river to New Orleans to get brushed up socially. But the very first night at the hotel he nearly ran up against a snag.

"There were finger-bowls—

"Now in the South it was the fashion at that time to float geranium leaves in the finger-bowls. The young man was very thirsty. But an old gentleman used his finger-bowl for the purpose for which it was made—and the young man was saved.

"After a few weeks he returned to Natchez, and he told most, if not all, of his adventures in New Orleans. Well, he talked a great deal to another young man in Natchez, and the second young man got fired with the ambition to get brushed up socially. Wall, he went aboard the steamboat and travelled down to New Orleans. In a few days he came back, and I had the privilege to be standing in front of the post office hotel and main stores of Natchez when the second young man who went to New Orleans came up from the landing stage and met the first young man who went to New Orleans. When they met the second young man caught the first young man with his right hand and with his left he hit him repeatedly under the ear and every time he hit him he said 'I'll give you geranium tea', 'I'll give you geranium tea!'

"Willy asked him if on going back to America after a long absence he noticed much difference. Mark Twain said, 'Wall, it's like this. When I'm going on a lecture tour and come to a town where I have been years before, the secretary of the reception committee meets me at the Depot and he says 'Well, Mr. Clemens do you notice much change in our little burg since you last visited it?' Wall, if I'm in a bad humour I say "I've forgotten all about it". But if I'm in a good humour I say "I shouldn't have known it"!'

"The streets crowded with people to see the Queen. The announcement of her visit to Ireland was made today, and also that Irish soldiers were in future to wear the shamrock on St. Patrick's day. I met Miss Purser in Bond Street and she said, 'Well, what do you think of the shamrock? Rather hard isn't it, on the undivided Trinity in whose honour it has heretofore been worn?'

"Mrs. Courtney is sad about the intolerance over the war. She says someone mentioned the other day there was a letter in the papers saying the Boers had treated the English prisoners well, on which a lady got up and walked out of the room.

"I saw the Queen drive past on her way to Paddington; great crowds and great decorations and shouting. One could just see a dab of pink, her face, and a dab of white, her hair, and white feathers. (Someone had said, seeing her white hair, 'When the snow melts the Flood will come'.) Dublin will look very small and dingy after this triumphal progress."

11th. "To Westminster Abbey, and met Hallam Murray at the door, who said he had been hearing of Robert from the Dean of New College, Spooner, and that he spoke very well of him and seemed to have a great regard for him; this was pleasant.

"To lunch I had Mrs. Martin (of Ross), very blind and tottering, with a sun hat and white veil, and old Mrs. Aylmer Gowing in point lace and feathers, very deaf. And during lunch George Moore came in. However, he had known Mrs. Gowing of old, and paid her compliments on her knowledge of Greek and French. Then I went down with him to look at a letter he has written on the Queen's visit to Ireland— moderate for him, only calling for 'chill politeness'. I said it would no doubt make many people over here angry, but that he says he does not mind; Ireland cannot be expected to give a warm welcome to the head of the English State, and she has never shown sympathy to Ireland, even in the famine time. (I remember my husband telling me that in those midnight talks in India the Prince had told him he had always been anxious to be more in Ireland and always prevented by the Queen . . . It used to be said by gossip long ago her dislike to Ireland had arisen from the Prince Consort having caught a cold in his head on their visit there.)"

13th. "Shopping and paying bills and taking tickets for Rome . . . Lady Poynter came in, also Yeats with an article on Mohini for the *Speaker,* and delighted with my new translations from Hyde. John O'Leary has written asking him to write on the Queen's visit and he thinks of doing so, suggesting that the M.P.s, as natural leaders of the people, should organize a meeting at the Rotunda, expressing disapproval of public welcomes, as otherwise the demonstration against signs of rejoicing would fall into other hands, and lead to riots.

"At dinner with the Lyalls . . . Sir Alfred asked me about the Queen's visit to Ireland, thinks it a mistake 'such visits must be political'; and if he were a Nationalist he would object to expressions of welcome. Speaking of critics, he quoted a sentence from Coleridge, 'Critics are the eunuchs at the door of the temples of the gods'."

14th. "I went to see E.L., rather afraid to face her because of G. Moore's letter in *The Times*, but happily she had not read it; however, she talked a good deal of the war. She says of course Lord Roberts must have a dukedom, the Duke of Wellington got one, and Lord Roberts has done much more than he did! Very flattering to the Boers.

". . . George Moore, Philip Comyns Carr and Yeats came to dinner. All abused Kipling's letter to *The Times*, calling for the hanging of Cape Colonists. G. Moore said how much better a writer Bret Harte was, and I think it a just comparison as to prose. Talking of the Queen's visit and the impossibility of its being non-political, G.M. said it reminded him of Gladstone being asked to take part in some procession or meeting and saying 'he would be happy to take a *small* part in it!'."

17 March. "Walked across St. James's Park to lunch with Enid, the whole place like Birnam Wood marching— shamrock bunches as big as cabbage heads and tied with Union Jack ribbons on every ragamuffin! I wore an ivy leaf (Parnell's emblem) feeling I must give up the poor shamrock till this calamity of vulgarising is overpast, but found E.L. very proud of wearing one, 'so kind of us'. I said I could not wear one for fear of being taken for a cockney— great indignation on the part of E.A., who like all the A.s connected with Lord Salisbury give the impression 'l'Empire c'est moi'. After lunch I put my ivy leaf under my cloak, pinned with my diamond wheatear, thinking it really distressed Enid. We went off together to the Mansion House sale, a crowd there, and bunches of shamrock. I went later to see the Haliburtons. Lord Haliburton decorated with shamrock said, 'Don't you think this shamrock business will settle our difficulties in Ireland?' I said, 'I doubt that this sentimental affection will outlive the financial debate of next

week'. On the Queen's visit he, like all intelligent men, is reasonable, able to separate the personal from the political aspect. Home, and as I was taking my things off I found that my diamond wheatear that fastened the ivy leaf had disappeared; and as I had been so much about all the afternoon I felt low and that there was not much prospect of seeing it again. Yeats brought a draft of his letter to the papers on the Queen's visit. He had adopted my idea of having a meeting on the ground of denouncing the Union rather than the visit on this its centenary, if dates would fit in. And as luck would have it, 2 April, the day the Queen will leave Windsor for Ireland, is the very day the Union passed through Parliament. His letter slightly modified is good, and if his advice is taken there will be a dignified protest instead of window breaking. I asked Symons why *Paolo and Francesca* was so much cried up; he says 'because it is the nearest approach to poetry people are able to understand'. Home, and found my wheatear awaiting me, sent in from Savile Row, so am comforted.

"In the afternoon Knowles came in. We talked of the Queen's visit, I said there would be disturbances, or at least some expression of opinion against it. He was indignant at the idea. I said I hoped it might be turned into an expression of opinion against the Union, which would be justified and dignified; but that did not please him any better, there should be nothing but a gushing reception, or England would be in a state of fury. Horace Plunkett and Lady Fingall then came in, and Lady F. echoed Knowles and declared there would be nothing but loyalty and 'at all events there are plenty of police', which gratified him. And he was pleased at meeting a new Countess, and invited himself to Killeen, and pleased H. Plunkett by asking for an article, so all went off well. H.P. pretty sure of losing his seat, because of having appointed a Nationalist (Gill) to the Board, and doesn't know what to do; he would not get a northern constituency as he is for a Catholic University, or a Home Rule one. I advised him to read Lecky's *History* and then turn Nationalist like E. Martyn."

19 March. "Packing, and R. came from Oxford, and out shopping with him . . . I met Wilfrid Ward at dinner . . . His horror is great at Lecky having said to his wife at dinner one night, talking of Mrs. Craven's *Life,* that 'to have religion as she had it was a disease'. He asked me if Horace Plunkett was not Secretary to Gerald Balfour—"

20 March. "Off at 11.00 on our journey. Monotonous France didn't give R. a good impression of the Continent, but next morning we had some lovely hours . . . till rain began on the Italian side . . . and we got to Milan in rain. We saw an announcement of *Lohengrin,* which he had never seen, so went there after dinner and saw a fairly good performance in the splendid Scala. So R. saw Lucerne, the Alps, Milan and *Lohengrin* all in one day.

"In Rome . . . De Basterot gave us a delightful drive, showing St. Peter's to R. and then out of the walls to S. Paolo, and by great good luck there were Croatian pilgrims there, in national costume, walking in procession and kneeling and praying . . . R. did some sketches.

"There has been a paragraph in *The Times* about Yeats's letter on the Queen's visit, and also about Edward Martyn resigning his D.L. This last much annoyed De Basterot.

"De B. says, 'the peasantry are the fountain of the world; the upper classes get worn out!

"Evening to the Embassy, Lady Currie very cordial and a very pretty party. It is curious that my first great party and Robert's should be at the same Embassy. The old Duke of Cambridge looking apoplectic, but making himself agreeable to beautiful, at least beautifully dressed ladies . . . I felt like a revenant, but very proud of my fair-haired son.

"When I went to say goodbye to De Basterot he was out and I waited and his servant lighted a lamp and brought to amuse me Cicero's *Letters,* and four volumes of Mahon's *History of England.* I looked into this, and found what I had not known or had forgotten, an account of Dublin in I think 1753, when there was a rumour of a proposed Union, and the mob rose and seized Lords and Members of Parliament, and made them swear in the streets they would never agree to it. Then De B. came in, and said that he was very cross with Yeats's letter, which he had just been sent; but I think I made him understand it was written to keep the mob from violence, not to egg them on to it . . . ."

4 April. "I looked at *The Times* and saw that Mr. Lecky has withdrawn his support from the Irish Literary Theatre in consequence of 'the discreditable conduct of Mr. W. B. Yeats, Mr. George Moore and other prominent supporters of the movement'. It will do the Theatre no harm, rather good I think, resting it again on a literary basis not helped by outsiders; but that little want of courtesy in his decision being sent to the papers with no private notice to me hurts

me. On the other hand, I see that Parliamentarians and the Dublin Council (including the Lord Mayor!) have passed a resolution denouncing the Union, on the date of its introduction to the English House of Lords. So my suggestion that this and not the Queen's visit should be the point of attack has borne fruit.

"We dined at the Embassy, Countess Passoloni was there, and I was taken into dinner by Sir L. Alma Tadema, and had a clever Italian who is over the excavations at the Forum on my other side. R. found that one of the attachés had been at New College, had had his rooms and his scout, a great bond of union. Pleasant enough, and we drove Alma Tadema home, as cabs were scarce and rain had begun."

8th. "A new letter of Yeats calls to those who don't approve of the war to refrain from cheering as the Queen passes. He quotes Mirabeau's sentence, 'the silence of the people is the lesson of kings'. He writes me that he has just met Swift McNeill who says, 'you will pay for that letter, Yeats—they will remember it against you for years'."

30 April. "To Paris, where Robert and I parted after a very happy five weeks . . ."

"E. Lee Childe called and took me to see Salomon Reinach, and I had a long Celtic talk with him. He was in Ireland with the ignorance of French in Ireland; astonished that neither Colonel Plunkett nor Mr. Coffey could speak Irish; and at the hostility of Trinity College to Irish things—'It is an English fort, nothing else, there is no chair of Irish literature or Irish archaeology, no lectures on them.' 'Its garrison, the students', had gone out and broken the windows of a newspaper office while he was there. He had spent an evening with Mahaffy, who had been much astonished to find that he was no longer taken up with Greek things, finding Irish antiquity so much more interesting. He was delighted with the National Gallery, especially the Machiavelli picture and gave me a pamphlet he has written on it.

"I went to the Exhibition again to see the reproductions of Irish antiquities which Reinach had told me were ready. Then to the Ceylon Court, and seeing Mr. Davidson's name on a door I knocked and found him and he was very glad to see me, for he said he had been thinking so much of us, knowing that, of all the people, Sir William would have been the one most interested in its success. He showed me the exhibits and brought up the goldsmith Mulabya and others to introduce to me, and they welcomed me with such warmth and affection for my husband's sake, that I felt as if I had suddenly put on a crown!

"My 'Felons of our Land' was sent to me in *The Cornhill*[1], and De B. read it, and gave me a little lecture in the evening, complimenting me on the style, but thinks I am going too far away from the opinions of my husband, and my son. I told him I am convinced my husband would have been with me in all I have done so far; but that I had already determined not to go so far towards political nationality in anything I write again, because I wish to keep out of politics and work only for literature; and partly because if Robert is Imperialist I don't want to separate myself from him, so he preached to the converted. He wound up by saying in disgust (about the ballads I had quoted from), 'that sort of patriotic doggerel makes me sick'.

"I took Mrs. Lee Childe to tea at the Ceylon Court, and Synge came also. He is working on a book on Aran, and has sent an article to *Harper's,* which if taken he promises to get Jack Yeats to illustrate."

3 May. "London. Yeats has written nothing but his essay on Symbolism and a little article on Loyalty and Disloyalty in the *United Irishman,* taking high ground. I wish that all those who have read his letters on the Queen's visit could read this—but it would not make much difference. English people are in a fever, and every attempt at reasoning acts as an irritant.

"G. Moore had said sadly that he had thought his Queen letter splendid while he was writing it, but once written he thought it poor and flat. Yeats said, 'That is how Nature works. She holds out a lure before you. Nothing would ever be done if that lure were not held before us. Thence when our work is done, it vanishes, withdrawn. If Nature had not her lure would you ever get up out of that armchair?'."

(28 May 1919. That is the difficulty about doing a memoir or any form of autobiography, I don't feel any lure, see any mountain top so far. And there is a play running to and fro in my mind luring me . . . yet I will hold to this for a while, Robert thought it ought to be done.)

28 May 1900. "Stephen Gwynn says he was fighting his way into the Imperial Hotel in Dublin through a crowd shouting

[1] The *Cornhill Magazine,* Vol. 81, No. 47 New Series, May 1900, pp. 622-632.

for the Boers, and being hustled by the police, and when he got in he found the correspondent of the *Chronicle* writing an account of the reception and saying how enthusiastic all the people were, and said, 'Had you not better go out and see what is going on outside the hotel before you finish that?' But he answered, 'Thank you, I have quite enough material for my article'."

3 June 1900. "I went to see Horace Plunkett about the Gort Convent, as the nuns want to turn it into a Co-operative Society, and have me on the Committee, and I wanted to know if it would be genuine. He begged me to help, as he says his department will have to fight with them, and I will be so reasonable to fight with! He lamented the Queen's letters, 'She is so nice and says the right thing, and it is so sad the "real and ideal" Ireland cannot work together. Yeats had made such a beautiful speech that time they had an Agricultural dinner, and he had hoped we would work side by side.' I defended Yeats, and on his persisting I said we could still all work together. 'You made a speech on the war that made angels weep, but we have not given up the effort to help you because of that.' He said his speech on the war had offended some of his South Dublin people by not being strong enough; and then he vexed me by saying, 'It is just as Balfour said in the House of Commons, the Irish would be against England in any war'. I said No; extremists would be, but I never heard of a war like this, in which our small farmers felt that the small farmers of another nation were being exterminated. It vexes me that he should take his opinion of the opinion of Irish farmers from Balfour. However, we parted friends."

Sunday 6th. "I went to Oxford to spend the afternoon with Robert. His little room looked very nice. We walked in the gardens, and went to evening service in the beautiful chapel . . .

Dined at Lecky's; he is kind but does seem to be going backwards, I think from want of faith. When talking of F.M.'s reception in the convent and its being a life of prayer, he said, 'and prayer is so unnecessary' . . . this from the representative of Trinity! He is sad at Ulster having compulsory land purchase, thinks it will impoverish the country, sees no hope anyhow for congested districts like 'that incurable optimist Horace Plunkett'. When saying good-bye I said, 'I will try to behave well in Ireland, and he said, in his plaintive voice, 'please don't do anything incendiary in

Ireland'. I was afraid to mention my candlesticks" (the book
of essays by various writers called *Ideals in Ireland*[2]).

7th. "I went in to tell the Morrises I could not dine with
them, and Lord M. called me into his room, and I sat talking
with him a long time. He is angry with E. Martyn for
persisting in his resignation after Lord Ashbourne's amiable
letter. However, he had silenced Clonbrock, who had talked
to him about it, by telling him he had 'no more right to
interfere with him as Lieutenant of the County than any
crossing sweeper' . . . He says the Queen determined on going
to Ireland quite by herself. Lord Salisbury told him that
when he went to Windsor, Princess Henry came into the
room and said, 'I am going to Ireland!' and that was the
first he heard of it. Lord M. thinks it was the Irish massacres
in the war that got on the Queen's mind—the Inniskillings
going into action and coming out with five officers left out
of thirty; forty men out of five hundred. 'A member of the
Royal family' told Lord M. that it was John Brown who
kept the Queen from coming before. Whenever she spoke
of it he would say, 'Oh those Irish are good for nothing;
come to Scotland, that's the place for you.'

"G. told me, on the authority of Miss Stokes, who was
present at Mahaffy's presentation to the Queen, that he
affably said, 'I am very glad to see your Majesty. I met one
of your nephews a little time ago.' The Queen glared at him
and he withered up by degrees, and now he says the Queen
is 'a stupid old woman—doting'.

"Sir A. Birch says they are abusing Lord Roberts now for
having lost the waterworks and for other mistakes. He saw
a letter from an officer out there abusing the infantry, and
another *vice versa* and both the artillery; and meanwhile
the terrific weekly expenses are mounting up."

I had written in London, I went with Lady Layard to call
on Sir Frederic Burton, who braver than I, ventured a word
in favour of the Boers. He wrote to me later, "I have ceased
to keep account of days. This war is killing me. It is the
worst affair I recollect. It is utterly inglorious—otherwise
there would be some compensation for our losses—for

[2] *Ideals in Ireland,* edited by Lady Gregory. Written by "A.E.", D. P.
Moran, George Moore, Douglas Hyde, Standish O'Grady and W. B.
Yeats. London: at the Sign of the Unicorn, 1901. The "candlestick"
was an iron rushlight holder given to Lady Gregory by the daughter
of a blacksmith who made it in 1798. A reproduction of it appeared
on the front cover.

incompetence—for errors—for unforseen and inevitable accidents. But every man chosen and cracked up by the War Office commits the same mistakes as his predecessors. Equally brave, equally without brains, he dashes his men against stone walls, confident in the success of mere force and chance. I grieve especially for our brave Irishmen, whose lives have been squandered to no purpose." And as to that purpose he was not confident, for he says though believing that if the choice had come between the government by the English or the Boers, that of England should be preferred, he writes, "on the other hand no generous mind could refuse ample sympathy to a courageous community struggling for independence, for the rights of their forefathers and for their languages, and moreover, smarting under the wrong that has been inflicted upon them from time to time, though it was probably more the result of blundering policy here, or of that sort of contemptuous neglect that is apt to characterise English doings by small nations, than of any deliberate intention to act unfairly."

Wilfrid Blunt wrote from Newbuildings. 24 June 1901: "I came down in the train with G. and his wife who talked anti-English treason in a loud voice to me all the way, much to the astonishment of certain old-fashioned Sussex people in the carriage with us. I have become so respectable now that I felt rather compromised by his language, though I was pleased to find his Irish literary Toryism taking that line. I have always considered that the true test of Irish nationality was hatred of England. The Boers delight me beyond measure with their pertinacity. I consider that they have already saved the Eastern world from any new aggression from us for a generation, and if they go on a little longer will go near to breaking up the British Empire altogether. But for them, we should have been swallowing half China by this time, to say nothing of Abyssinia, whose conquest was intended and planned for last year. As it is, the Chinese have been able to score against United Europe, including us. They have really got the whole object of the Boxer movement at a very low price, having frightened every European missionary and nearly every European trader out of the country, and put back their clock of civilisation another fifty years. Our violence in South Africa, imitated and exaggerated by the Germans at Pekin, has worked its own revenge, and China has been saved at the cost of less than a million of its inhabitants—a million it is fortunately well able to spare."

Then I spent a day in Dublin on my way home. I saw A.E. and had a long talk with him, and he asked me to come in the evening and see his drawings. He has written a fine article in *The United Irishman* putting the question on a high level, and one feels how futile ordinary newspapers or drawing-room criticism is in dealing with it.

And then I came home to Coole . . .

"Edward Martyn came over yesterday bringing Bishop Healy and Gill. A man said to the Bishop, 'Isn't Mr. Martyn a grand man? Sure, he cut the Government adrift.' Just off to church to face the Archdeacon and Lord Gough. I hear I am held responsible for Edward's action, and my nephew, Arthur Persse, having been made D.L. in his place, lends some colour to this.

"I got a side of bacon for old Farrell, and Mrs. Farrell, when I gave it to her for him said, 'It will rise his heart after the bad news that is after coming'. 'What bad news?' 'The Boers being beat!' (that is the relief of Mafeking just known).

"I lunched at Lough Cutra. Lord Gough anxious to know how we can encourage recruiting. He is surprised that none of the tenants followed his brother George to the war, thinks one might make the family at home more comfortable, and make a hero of the soldier. Fallon, from across the lake, hopes the English may win the war, 'because if not we'll have more taxes, and they are heavy enough as it is'. He understands that the Boers have been preparing for the last fifteen years against the English, making portholes and setting traps.

"To Chevy for the day. I went to see old Mary Glyn, who says, 'I hear the neighbours, when they come in to light their pipes, saying there's a power of the Queen's soldiers killed. And I have asked Pat Diveney to make a little cabin in the wood where I'll be near him when the war comes here; but he says the wood will be the first place they will try. They say it was the fault of the Queen beginning the war. Well, wasn't it foolish of her, and she so old, up to eighty years, but she knows that herself is safe from slaughter, whatever may happen to anyone else.'

"I have been collecting and putting together some of the ballads that are being sung at fairs and markets, or are printed in the corner of the weekly papers. At Galway

Railway Station the wives of Connacht Rangers setting out
for the war bade their husbands 'not to be too hard on the
Boers', and the small farmers have a special sympathy for
them : —

> Those Boers can't be blamed, as you might understand;
> They are trying to free their own native land,
> Where they toil night and day by the sweat of their brow
> Like the farmers of Ireland that follow the plough.

And another ballad "The Boer's Prayer" shows the same
sympathy : —

> My back is to the wall;
> Lo, here I stand.
> O Lord whate'er befall
> I love this land!
>
> This land that I have tilled
> This land is mine;
> Would Lord that thou hadst willed,
> This heart were Thine!
>
> This land to us Thou gave
> In days of old;
> They seek to make a grave
> Or field of gold.
>
> To us, O Lord, Thy hand
> Put forth to save;
> Give us, O Lord, this land
> Or give a grave!

At home. An old miller talking to me of the Fianna of
old times said, "Finn hadn't much luck himself? Well, that's
true, he didn't, or much good out of his life. That's the way
with people that set their minds on fighting and on taking
other people's goods. Look now, though I don't like to be
saying it, look at the English, the way they went against
those poor Boers to take their living from them and their
land, and they with plenty of their own before. Covetousness
led them to it, and curiosity. They thought to go shooting
them just as if they were snipe or woodcocks. And it wasn't
long before they were stretched in the field, and the Royalty
of England along with them, and not a knocker in London
town without a bit of crepe on it."

XXII

WORK AND PLAY AT COOLE

ONE EVENING in New York in the winter of 1911 I was driving back to my hotel from the Theatre, where our Irish plays were being given, when Mr. Roosevelt said to Mr. John Quinn (our good helper in all work for Ireland), for they were both with me, "You must write something about Lady Gregory for the next number of *The Outlook;* we are printing one of her plays, and I will write about her Theatre; I want it to be a Lady Gregory number." Mr. Quinn, a much occupied man, protested; but who could refuse when Roosevelt commanded? I will give some of the memories put down by him of his first visit to Coole and of the interests and harmony of the workers there in those fruitful days: "I was away from New York when the Abbey Theatre company of Dublin first came here, and I did not see them play until the end of their first week. In writing to a friend to explain who they were and what they had accomplished, I pointed out the perfect naturalness of their acting, the simplicity of their methods, their freedom from all distracting theatricalism and stage business, their little resort to gesture, the beautiful rhythm of their speech, the absence of extensive and elaborate scenery and stage-settings, and the delightful suggestion of spontaneity given by their apparently deliberate throwing away of technical accomplishments in the strict sense of the word. I said that too many theatres have costly scenery and expensive property to cover the poverty of art in the play or the players, just as poor paintings are sold by dealers in big glaring gold frames; and that their acting, in comparison with the acting of many theatres, had the same refined quality, not always apparent at the first glance, that old Chinese paintings are seen to have when placed alongside of modern paintings by Western artists.

"As I observed the fine craftsmanship of the actors, without a single false note, each seeming to get into the very skin of the part that he impersonated, my thoughts went back some eight or nine years to what were the beginnings of this whole enterprise.

"On a Sunday in August 1902 I travelled with Jack B.

Yeats, the artist, from Dublin, through Mullingar to Athenry, and thence by side-car to Killeenan, in County Galway. On the way from Athenry to Killeenan we passed little groups of bright-eyed men and women, always with a hearty laugh and a cheery word 'for the American' and 'a pleasant journey to you'. They were on their way to a 'Feis' (or festival) that was to be held that afternoon at Killeenan, where the blind Connacht poet, Raftery, was buried. The Feis was held on rising ground in a field beside the road. There were, perhaps, a hundred side-cars and other vehicles and five or six hundred men and women at the meeting. On a raised platform sat Douglas Hyde, the President of the Gaelic League; Edward Martyn from Tillyra Castle; Lady Gregory from Coole; and others in charge of the Feis. W. B. Yeats, the poet, and his brother, Jack B. Yeats, the artist, and myself stood in the crowd and watched the spectacle.

"Yeats told me that Lady Gregory had heard some time before that there was in the neighbourhood a book in Irish with songs of Raftery. She had found it in the possession of an old stone-cutter near Killeenan. She got a loan of the book and gave it to Dr. Hyde, and he discovered in it seventeen of Raftery's songs. Douglas Hyde has since edited and translated a book of the songs and poems of Raftery, and he gives many interesting stories of the bard. He told me that Sunday that it was to the kindness of Lady Gregory that he owed many of his stories of Raftery. She had got, from a man who, when he was a boy, was present at Raftery's death, a full account of it. The poet was buried in the old churchyard of Killeenan, among the people whom he knew. In August 1900 there had been a great gathering there. Lady Gregory was the chief organiser of the gathering. She had raised a high stone over Raftery's grave with the name of the poet in Irish upon it. It was she who had thought of doing it, Dr. Hyde told me that Sunday afternoon, and it was upon her that the cost, or most of the cost, had fallen.

"Prizes were given at the Feis for Irish singing, for the recitation of old poems, the telling of old stories all in Irish, and for traditional Irish dancing, flute-playing, and Irish music. A little girl from the Claddagh, the fishermen's quarter of Galway, took two or three of the prizes, and a week or ten days after, in going through the Claddagh, I saw her and spoke to her, and she remembered seeing me at the Feis. There was an old man there, and it took much persuasion to get him to mount the platform and tell his

story. He hung back diffidently for a long time, but finally
a lane was opened in the crowd and he got his courage up,
and marched bravely to the platform, and, gesticulating with
a big blackthorn stick, made a great speech in Irish. Hyde
translated parts of it for Yeats and me, and told us how the
old man had boasted that he had been at Raftery's dying
and had 'held the candle to him'.

"Over the platform was a big green banner with letters
in Irish on it and a picture of Raftery as an old man
remembered him, painted by a sympathetic artist in the
neighbourhood. The Feis continued until some time after
nightfall. It was black night when the lights of Coole welcomed us . . . I wish I could picture something of the charm
that hangs around Coole, of its tangled woods, its stately
trees, the lake, the winding paths, the two beautiful old
gardens, and the view of the distant Burren hills. There
seemed to be magic in the air, enchantment in the woods
and the beauty of the place, and the best talk and stories
I ever found anywhere. The great library was to me a delight,
and Jack Yeats told me that Lady Gregory had made a
catalogue of it herself. She seemed to me to have a strong
sense of property, and took great pride in keeping up the
fabled 'Seven Woods of Coole', planting every year trees for
the coming generations.

"Every summer for some years Yeats had spent at Coole.
He is the best talker I have ever listened to, and he does
love to talk. So long as he can amuse himself and interest
others with good talk he will not write. Lady Gregory
devoted herself to his work. With infinite tact and sympathy
she has got the best out of him, and the world of letters
owes it chiefly to her that in the last ten years Yeats has done
so much creative work and has been able to devote himself
so fully to the Irish Theatre. At Coole he had leisure and
delightful surroundings which in London he could not have.
He was able there to dream out and plan out his poems
and plays . . .

"One of the chief charms of my repeated visits to Coole
lay in the stores of good talk and anecdotes by Yeats and
Hyde, who were there at the time of each of my visits, and
in my interest in the genius and personality of Yeats and
Lady Gregory. During the whole time of our visit the
sparkle and brilliancy of the conversation never failed. Lady
Gregory's interest in the people about her was untiring . . .
She had the faculty of laying aside her work and making all

her guests enjoy to the full the pleasant side of life . . .
Those who came in contact with her—Yeats, Hyde, Synge,
and the rest—became or were made her helpers and
associates.

"One morning Lady Gregory, Dr. Hyde, and myself, wandered through one of the beautiful old gardens. She named
over the names of this, that, and the other flower until
Hyde said that if she just wrote down the names there
was matter for a sonnet ready for Yeats. Yeats was very
happy there, and he had just finished a poem on 'The Seven
Woods of Coole', and he was so pleased with it that he kept
murmuring it over and over again, and these lines from it
have remained in my memory still: —

> I have heard the pigeons of the Seven Woods
> Make their faint thunder, and the garden bees
> Hum in the lime-tree flowers; and put away
> The unavailing outcries and the old bitterness
> That empty the heart . . .
> I am contented, for I know that Quiet
> Wanders laughing and eating her wild heart
> Among pigeons and bees . . .

"Yeats, Hyde, and I used to sit up every night until one
or two in the morning, talking, it seems to me, about everything and everybody under the sky of Ireland, but chiefly
about the Theatre of which Yeats's mind was full. These
were wonderful nights, long nights filled with good talk,
Yeats full of plans for the development of the Theatre. The
mornings were devoted to work, the afternoons to out-of-
doors, and the evenings to the reading of scenarios for plays,
the reading of short plays in English by Lady Gregory and in
Irish by Hyde. Lady Gregory and Hyde read out to us from
time to time their translations of Irish songs and ballads,
in the beautiful English of her books and of Hyde's *Love
Songs of Connacht*. Yeats and Lady Gregory made a scenario
of a play and Hyde spent three afternoons 'putting the Irish
on it'. She has written how one morning she went for a long
drive to the sea, leaving Hyde with a bundle of blank paper
before him. When she returned in the evening, Dr. Hyde
had finished the play and was out shooting wild duck. This
play was *The Lost Saint*. Dr. Hyde put the hymn in the
play into Irish rhythm the next day while he was watching
is extinct become a new race. He thinks them inferior to us,
'He giveth his beloved sleep' is really 'He gives to his

for wild duck beside the marsh. He read out the play to us in the evening, translating it back into English as he went along, and Lady Gregory has written how 'we were all left with a feeling as if some beautiful white blossom had suddenly fallen at our feet'.

"I was there when Lady Gregory was at work on her two great books, *Cuchulain of Muirthemne* and *Gods and Fighting Men*. In these two books she brought together for the first time and retold in the language of the people of the country about her, in the unspoiled Elizabethan English of her own neighbourhood, the great legends of Ireland. She did for the old Irish sagas what Malory did for the Knights of the Round Table, and fairly won the right to be known as the Irish Malory.

"When Synge was writing his plays, poems, and essays he came often to Coole. Other guests there were George Russell, the poet and writer, 'John Eglinton', the brothers Fay, George Moore, and Bernard Shaw, and Lady Gregory's home really became a centre of the literary life of Ireland of the last ten years.

"From this old house, the house in which were stored up so many memories of statesmen, soldiers, authors, artists, and other distinguished people, with its great library, its pictures, statues, and souvenirs gathered from many lands, nestling in the soft climate of the west of Ireland under the grey skies and surrounded by the brilliant greens and rich browns of west Ireland landscape, or bathed in the purple glow of the air as the sun declined, I carried away two vivid impressions: first, the realization of a unique literary friendship between the chatelaine and the poet Yeats; and, second, of the gentleness and energy of this woman . . . who has, at the cost of infinite time and pains, proved herself to be, with Yeats, the directing genius of the new Irish Drama."

While still a little doubtful as to whether I should use praises of myself given by this and other friends, I came upon a passage in one of the Lady Bessborough's letters of over a century ago, which I may take as giving me counten- ance: "You must have thought me excessively vain for repeating to you all the fine things that were said to me, and as I always do it on every opportunity perhaps you do. And you are quite wrong—there is no surer sign of humility than boasting of compliments. A vain person thinks them

their due, and would as little boast of this as being called
by their proper title."

I was happy in my guests during those and later years.
In the old days also we had not been without guests who had
done good work, as Lyall, Layard, Henry Doyle, Cordery
who brought his translation of the *Iliad* to go through for
my husband's criticism. But there were also in those days
acquaintances, distant relatives, who would come by habit or
custom, and for whom it was necessary to find some amusement or distraction to fill out the days. A drive to Lough
Cutra, with its owners' kindness and the beauty of its lake;
to Tillyra where one might ascend the tower; to Castle
Taylor with its fine gardens; a dinner party or two; these
were a necessary part of entertaining. It was all in the day's
work and I took it cheerfully, but I was pleased when someone told me Sir William had said, 'Augusta deserves to have
good company, she is so splendid at entertaining bores'. But
now my guests found their own employment; schoolboys
with gun or rod or cricket bat. Wilfrid Blunt wrote from
Gros Bois in October 1894, "You are quite right to fill your
house with young people. The pleasure of life is to live
with the old when you are young and with the young when
you are old. The united age should always be about sixty."
Painters were happy in the woods or by the lake, and for
poets there were paper and pen enough, though I did not
quite approve of Yeats's suggestion that Pater had written
so well through writing every sentence on a separate sheet
of paper. It was here Douglas Hyde wrote his *Twisting of the
Rope* (*Casadh an t-Sugáin*) the first play ever given in Irish
in a Dublin Theatre, and his *Lost Saint,* and *Nativity.* His
plays are better known I think than his poems, for these
were published in Irish only. I gave translations of some
of them in my *Poets and Dreamers.* Here is one he called
"The Three Devils": —

> There are three fine devils eating my heart—
> They left me, my grief! without a thing:
> Sickness wrought, and Love wrought,
> And an empty pocket, my ruin and my woe.
> Poverty left me without a shirt,
> Barefoot, barelegged, without any covering;
> Sickness left me with my head weak
> And my body miserable, an ugly thing.
> Love left me like a coal upon the floor,
> Like a half burned sod that is never put out,

Worse than the cough, worse than the fever itself,
Worse than any curse at all under the sun,
Worse than the great poverty
Is the devil that is called "Love" by the people.
And if I were in my young youth again
I would not take, or give, or ask for a kiss!

But he was really at his happiest with a gun in his hand.
Mrs. Hyde declared he brought in so many strange birds that
she had to insist that nothing must come into the house
unless he was prepared to eat it. (When some elderly ladies
heard there had been a gentleman at our covert shooting
who had talked in Irish to the beaters they had said, "He
cannot be a gentleman if he speaks Irish.") And he was yet
happier when looking for a snipe on the bogs, he could go
in at dusk to some cottage and gather wild stories that had
come down from ancient times. And I saw him once in
eager conversation with a young farmer who was standing
above him on a half-made hayrick, and it pleased me to find
they had been talking in Irish of some old Irish poems that
had been published by the Irish Texts Society. His name
was and is well known and loved through the country, "An
Craoibhin Aoibhin" "the Delightful Little Branch; and it
was of him some member of his League said to me in a sort of
ecstasy 'he should not be in the world at all or doing the
world's work'!" Yet the feeling against the revival of the
language was so strong among a certain class that it was
gravely declared and believed that he, gentlest of men, a
good churchgoer and good Christian, had publicly hoped he
might one day "wade through Protestant blood". It was here
also that the fine portrait of him was painted by J. B. Yeats,
that now hangs in the Municipal Gallery.

I wrote in the summer of 1900, "We went to Galway Feis
on Thursday; more competitions and more people and more
life than before. Robert came with me and Douglas Hyde
and Yeats. Old men in flannel bawneens recited poems,
some of Raftery's, one 'A talk with Death', who told us
how he had swept away great people, among others the
Queen of England. The old man stopped to say 'and that
wouldn't be much loss' at which there was great applause
among those who understood Irish. I found I understood a
little more than last year but still not much." And again
"The piper, Corly, came and Hyde talked with him and
took down some verses. He had spoken much of the change

in E. Martyn and what an ordeal it used to be going there
in the old days 'with fear in your heart and weakness in
your feet, and a sixpenny or maybe a threepenny thrust out
at you through the window. All the country talking of the
change and I have it in my heart and in my conscience that
it is the woman of this house that has been the cause of that
change'." "I left Hyde at a meeting at Labane, and called in
at my Irish class on the way back, and we had asked a few
men who are in earnest about the language to come and
meet him, and they came . . . Hyde proposed his Beal
Direach (Straight-Mouth) League, and they put themselves
under *geasa* not to speak any English amongst themselves or
with any except 'uneducated people who cannot understand
the language of Ireland'. They are the first members of this
League."

I had written to Lord Gough in 1899: "Jack Yeats is
staying here now with his wife, for though he is Irish they
have made their home in Devonshire and I grudge him to
overpainted England and want to keep him in touch with
our neglected west country. He paints peasant life with a
kind of dramatic fervour . . . There is quite an awakening
in Ireland in art and literature—such a comfort to have done
with politics for the moment."

And I wrote in the summer of 1900: "Jack Yeats and his
wife, Mr. Harvey and the Russells are with me, A.E. being
only able to get his holiday now. The baby Brian Russell,
a dear little fellow, very friendly and merry, is with me at
this moment, as I am acting chief nurse—A.E. and Mrs.
Russell being on the lake, Robert, and Jack Yeats and
Harvey at Athenry where the County is playing Kiltartan.
Poor Kiltartan!

"A.E. is doing wonderful pictures, he has begun oils which
have not the same charm as his pastels but are of course
more lasting. The deep pools delight him. He has painted
two figures raising a cup, and seven figures holding a sword
(at the deep hole) and a Queen and some landscapes—I
asked him what he thought these spirits are that he so
certainly sees, and he said they are earth spirits that have
not yet taken animal forms, but will probably when our race
is extinct become a new race. He thinks them inferior to us,
chiefly because, though more beautiful, they have not the
look of being capable of complex emotions or of understanding the nature of sacrifice. Anyone could see them, he

says, who can detach the mind from the ordinary business of life and wait for them. He is surprised I cannot see them by the shadowy pools, but I say I am like Martha, careful and cumbered with much serving.

"His idea of our life is that we are making a daily sacrifice consciously, but that the consciousness only comes in sleep, and cannot be remembered afterwards; and that the verse 'He giveth his beloved sleep' is really 'He gives to his beloved in sleep'. Even a drunkard is making a sacrifice in having consciously taken the nature of a drunkard to work off the evil of the race (but this I don't follow quite clearly).

"Russell and Yeats drew the big tree at Raheen. Yeats made a charming sketch. Russell a charming one also, but with a rather dreadful figure with long ears under the tree. He says it was not very nice, but he would like to stroke it. When a man passed it shrank up, as if it would climb the tree backwards. I showed it to Maurteen who says his own brother-in-law had work to get his horse past that tree, one night, but he is surprised that Mr. Russell can see these things in the daytime."

26th. "All sketching. Evening A.E. and Yeats tease each other. A.E. tells how Yeats found a 'clairvoyant' in Miss S. and put her to look in a crystal, and invoked the Angel Gabriel. She looked and saw a Golden Palace. This was puzzling but she looked again, and saw a white-armed figure at the palace window. W.B.Y. was delighted, and prepared questions to put to the Archangel. But a rationalist who stood by observed that the shop opposite had had a lot of gilding about it which was reflected in the crystal and that there was a man in white shirt-sleeves cleaning the window, who was the archangel. W.B.Y. says then in return that he once said that one of A.E.'s group dropped his H's, A.E. replied that 'he functioned in a higher sphere'."

1 August. "They had a fiery argument in the woods yesterday on the sword, whether it was the symbol of fire or air, and 'called each other all the names'; but were good friends in the evening.

"Y. has finished his lyric on the *Withering of the Boughs*. (At Chevy a woman had said to me, 'If you tell your dream to the trees, fasting, they will all wither.) A.E. has done, besides his spirit and landscape drawings, a charming little picture of Baby Brian for me. He says if he had money, he would go all over Ireland to look for the two men who are ruling its destinies at present. He has seen them and others have seen them in vision. One lives in a cottage beside a single-line railway, a log of wood in front. He is oldish, with a golden beard. The other, young and dark, lives in a park alone. There is a third but he is vague; perhaps not in a physical body. The first time he saw them he was filled with energy and life, so that he worked without effort and with joy for a long time after. I suggest they were symbolic of the new spirit in people and landed gentry, but he declares they were real.

"On Monday we went to Athenry for a cricket match, and beat the County again. Our men immensely proud."

For cricket went on all the time. In the match at Athenry, Kiltartan beat the County by three runs, a great triumph. R. made top score, twenty-seven.

R. dreamed that Yeats wanted him to go with him and A.E. and see visions and he was going, and then he thought "If I see visions it will spoil my eyesight, and I won't be able to play cricket", so he turned back.

A cricket match here, Ennistymon came and was ignominiously beaten.

Another match—Ennis v. Kiltartan. Then a report went out that "the pick of Ennis" had arrived. Our men were nervous and went down like ninepins, till Shaughnessy, the quiet and teetotal publican went in, and he looked on the visitors only as possible customers and strode about the field, didn't do very much but looked as if he did. R. redeemed the game, played with great composure and style, made twenty-two—and we beat them, to our great satisfaction. Meade gave instructions to the umpire, scooped up some gravel and cried: "Can't you take five stones in your hand, and can't you put them one after another into the other hand according as the balls go?" The Ennis captain, very fat, said when going in: "Don't expect me to run." "Is it a caravan you want us to get for you?" cries one of his side . . .

Miss Q. says to Miss G., "Are there eleven on each side?" "Oh, dear me, on each side, what a very strong team!"

Miss Franks asks Robert: "Why have they been beaten? Why did you beat them when they had come so far?"

My guests were not all of the one way of thinking. Emily Lawless who visited us one summer was a Unionist, though her poem "With the Wild Geese" almost set her on the other side. I had been grateful to her for her books, *Hurrish* and *Grania,* that were published in those Land League days of the eighties. For in London the usual greeting to one coming from the West was a question about rents or outrages or politics and it was a boon to find these novels take their place as a new Irish topic for a while. And Gladstone himself was said to have been deceived into believing her much finer book, *With Essex in Ireland,* was an original Elizabethan document. But though Yeats admired *Essex* and she his poems, they did not get on very well, they always turned to some subject they could not agree on, and I find in a letter written after her visit that "after acquaintance with Emily Lawless he had a dream that the argument was still going on, and that he said, 'I don't know why it should be considered more essential to know the component parts of the air than to know the component parts of Biddy Flaherty's family. What is the good of knowing that we are made up of oxygen and hydrogen or the names of Biddy Flaherty and Micky Flaherty and all the little Flahertys?"

George Moore, as he tells us in his *Hail and Farewell,* worked here with Yeats on their *Diarmuid and Grania* that was produced in Dublin by F. R. Benson in the third year of our Literary Theatre, that is now the Abbey Theatre, and has its own company of Irish actors.

I wrote: "G. Moore has been away in Dublin and has just come back. We read the first act of *Diarmuid and Grania* to Russell, and Russell was indignant, thought the character of Diarmuid and of the Fianna was being taken away. So, Moore having written on Wednesday that the act was thin, and the Fianna were to be made more turbulent, wrote on Thursday that they were to be endowed with all the virtues. I telegraphed to him to come back, that he and Yeats might arrive at some conclusion and work together. I had a busy week. Yeats was rewriting the 2nd Act . . . the play being altered a good deal."

I had written in London in 1900: "Yeats came back from the Gibsons with a very bad cold, quite ill. I dined with him on the Monday to entertain a new admirer who had sent him some books, a Mr. Masefield."

I remember so well that evening the beginning of a most pleasant friendship. Yeats was not well enough to come in to dinner, and Masefield in his gentle and quiet way told me of his hardships and wanderings in his early life, and his search for work in America, and was listened to with delight and sympathy by me but with evident disapproval by Yeats's old housekeeper as she changed the plates. Her back stiffened and her nose went up higher as she caught fragments of the reminiscences of one she no doubt considered to be no better than a tramp. He came to visit us at Coole afterwards. That is one of the pleasant memories of the place.

I was proud when later he dedicated to me his edition of *Dampier's Voyages,* a book in which I take delight. He wrote in March 1906: "I send you a very bad photograph of William Dampier, the buccaneer, pirate, sea-captain and hydrographer whose works I am editing for you. The portrait is in the National Portrait Gallery. It is by a man called Murray. The photograph does not do justice to the painting, for it misses the colour which is bronzed and glowing, and destroys all the peculiar refinement of the face, which Coleridge noticed. It is an attractive face even in the photograph but there is something lacking in it which the portrait supplies." And in October: *"Dampier* is thriving now. He should be out this year. If he will only sell well I will follow him up with another buccaneer, or a whole volume of lives of pirates. They are attractive. They weren't recognised by the Government, and everybody is ashamed of them, so that they are really like so many geniuses, with a piratical knowledge of seamanship thrown in." And then in November: "I had hoped to send you the complete work, but the second volume has been delayed so I can only send one. I hope that some little bits of him may amuse you, and that the lives of his associates may help you to understand how hard it was for him to approach his work in the comic spirit . . . I hope that the book may lie upon your shelf to remind you of our first meeting, now six years ago."

And yet later, in sending me a little pebble brought from Oisin's grave in Antrim, he says: "I have parodied one of your translations to tell you how fine a land it is—

> It's my grief that I am not a little wild bee
> For then, maybe, I could fly to Ireland of the clover,
> For it's sweeter the clover is there than the red roses of
> Hereford town;
> And it's Hereford is the poor place after a sight of Antrim.
>
> It's my sorrow that I am not a nimble minnow in the
> pool,
> For it's then I could feel the warm sea lifting me
> And watch the sheep in the grass, high up, where the
> gorse is,

And maybe Pat McCannell would be there in the dusk,
and he playing the pipes.

It's a pain in my heart to me that I was not born Irish,
With a sweet tongue in my head and a pleasant way with
me,
For it's then I could have written the fine songs for Mr.
Yeats, the great poet, and for Lady Gregory,
And written them strong and comely in a warm speech
like the dear noise of the bees."

Almost all of the friends who stayed here had cut the
initials of their names in the bark of a great copper beech
in the garden, those I have written of here and others who
came later; John and Innes among painters (John had
climbed up and cut his at the very top of the tree); Sara
Allgood; "G.B.S."; "Martin Ross"; Ian Hamilton. Jack
Yeats, the beloved of all, schoolboys, poets, day labourers,
whose figures come into many of the sketches he made, put
a little figure of a donkey over his; Dr. Ethel Smyth cut a
note of music alone.

Synge was the first of all that company to pass away and
leave his signature but as a sad memorial upon that shining
bark. He had stayed here several times, not touching pen
or paper, wandering in the woods while others were at work
or play, it may be gathering thoughts for his Deirdre's
twilight wanderings "when beech trees were silver and
copper, and ash trees were fine gold". He was a comfortable
guest, good humoured, gentle, a quiet looker-on, a good
listener. Once in his illness, Yeats found him reading
Lockhart's *Life of Scott,* and he said that in reading it he
was often reminded of me, writing and keeping power of
invention in the midst of so many activities. I said in a
letter to Yeats after his death, "I like to think that he stayed
here, I suppose the only country-house in Ireland he came
to . . . I sometimes wondered whether much of my liking for
him did not come from his being an appreciative listener—
he would take out his cigarette and have a long comfortable
laugh, and then put it back again. I think you and I supplied
him with vitality when he was with us, as the wild people
did in the Blaskets." And again, "You did more than anyone
for him, you gave him his means of expression. You have
given me mine, but I should have found something else to
do, though not anything coming near this, but I don't think
Synge would have done anything but drift but for you and

the Theatre. I helped him far less, just feeding him when he was badly fed and working for the staging of his plays and in other little ways, and I am glad to think of it, for he got very little help from any other but you and myself. I wonder if he was ever offered a meal in Dublin except at the Nassau . . . I feel very down-hearted for it is such a break in our very small circle of understanding friends. One never had to arrange one's mind to talk to him. I had got to know him much better in his last year's illness."

And I wrote later: "As to writing about Synge, I should not like to do it. I have nothing to say that you are not saying, we knew him together so much. Indeed, I would like you to give some impression of that, of the theatre years in Dublin when none of us saw anyone from outside, we just moved from the Abbey to the Nassau and back again, we three always, and the Fays or two or three others sometimes."

Yeats wrote from London after one of those summers: "I had a wonderful voyage, I never had such a crossing, a slight mist, and as we came into Holyhead, the sun getting golden for sunset—everything shining, and porpoises showing their fins. Somehow it made me very homesick for Coole, for it was like the evenings there by the lake, and last night I dreamed of Coole and the sea and Sligo all mixed up in strange shining pictures. I am always full of thoughts of Coole every year when I start on the winter destination."

I had just now finished writing this chapter, in March 1923, when news came of the death of one of the gentlest and most joyous of our schoolboy guests of those days, "Tony" as we knew him, Arthur Egerton Watts-Russell of Biggin Hall, Oundle, and late of the Coldstream Guards. Our scrapbooks hold many of his merry sketches, one of that first Gaelic Punch and Judy, and of journeys to the bogs, and of Yeats "being punished by the fairies for enquiring into their habits". All here who knew him grieve for him. And one of those nearest to him writes: "He always spoke of Coole as if it were fairyland or Paradise"; and another, the nearest of all, "He told me all about Coole the first time we ever met, long before we were engaged, I always felt I knew his beloved Coole Woods and the lake as he did. He remembered every minute of them and nothing dimmed the perfect happiness of those days brought into his life."

XXIII

THE EPICS

WHEN YEATS had first come to the neighbourhood I showed him a folklore article I had written for the *Spectator*[1], but he was not much interested. He was more interested in hearing of an old man near Ballylee, Diveney, who spoke continually of the fairies. He wanted to see him, so one day he came from Tillyra to the foot of the lane at Lissatunna and I drove there to meet him, and we talked to the old man and listened to him.

While we were walking home that day I remember asking Yeats if there was anything I could do to help in Ireland, and he said, "Buy Irish books". But although by these he meant books in English there were not then many to be bought, and I felt rather disappointed. But I went on gathering folk-lore, that being the work nearest at hand, and being a help to his own.

If I had not met Yeats I believe I should still have become a writer, because my energy was turning to that side, and I had got a certain training in the editing of the *Autobiography* and the *Letter Box*. But I might never have found opportunity or freedom; I might have become a writer of middle articles in literary papers, or one of those "dull people who edit books" I was once in the early days of our acquaintance rather hurt by hearing him speak of. He is a severe critic of himself and others. He was slow in coming to believe I had any gift for writing, and he would not encourage me to it, thinking he made better use of my folk-lore gatherings than I could do. It was only when I had read him one day in London my chapter the "Death of Cuchulain" that he came to look on me as a fellow writer. From that time I read him each chapter or story as it was finished, and even when he did not criticise, the feeling that I was putting it to the test of his criticism was my greatest help, and I was glad when his prefaces to those two first books gave them his sanction and benediction. He showed

[1]Possibly the anonymous article "Irish Visions" which appeared in the issue of 10 July 1897.

his faith also by giving me his Hanrahan stories to rewrite in the Kiltartan style.

And it was not long until I found other work to do, for that is one great advantage in Ireland, there is room for dreams to be turned to reality without fear of overcrowding. It is not like that London hospital where I was put on the waiting list.

The memory of battles fades, and I can but half remember the anger, the passionate resentment, we who were workers in the Gaelic revival felt against the attacks made not only upon the "barbarous language" (the study of which I myself was accused of having taken up through disloyalty, or desire of popularity, or being "'quite mad") but upon its ancient literature. Trinity College had ignored it, although Germany and France were working at it. Then, Dr. Atkinson, its Professor of Sanscrit had publicly said of that ancient literature in his evidence before the Commission of Inter- mediate Education: "It is almost intolerably low in tone— I do not mean naughty but low; and every now and then when the circumstance occasions it, it goes down lower than low . . . If I read books in the Greek, the Latin or the French course, in almost any one of them there is something I can read with positive pleasure . . . but if I read the Irish books I see nothing ideal in them, and my astonishment is that through the whole range of Irish literature that I have read (and I have read an enormous range of it) the smallness of the element of idealism is most noticeable . . . And as there is very little idealism there is very little imagination . . . The Irish tales as a rule are devoid of it fundamentally." Dr. Atkinson was an Englishman, but Dr. Mahaffy, led astray by his companions in office, took his word for it, and himself said in public and in a rash moment, that all the Irish literature he had ever seen was "either silly or indecent or religious". This had been a throwing down of the glove. Meanwhile, Miss Hull's *Cuchullin Saga* was of very great use when it came, awakening interest by making known some of the tales translated by various scholars old and new; and Standish O'Grady's Homeric paraphrases had long been an inspiration and a delight.

On 19 October 1900, I wrote: "I have had an idea floating in my mind for some time that I might put together the Irish legends of Cuchulain into a sort of 'Morte d'Arthur', choosing only the most beautiful or striking; but I was uncertain about style, one could not copy Malory, yet they should be in some style answering to it. Now I think of putting each story into the English spoken by the Irish people, which keeps so much of the idiom of the Irish original. I consulted Yeats, and after a short hesitation he thinks the idea very good, so I will try to carry it out, and am provided with work for the rest of my life."

I was not scholar enough to read ancient manuscript, but the Irish text of most of the stories had already been printed, and I worked from this text with the help of the translations given. The text of "The War for the Bull of Cuailgne" had not been printed as a whole, and I worked by comparing and piecing together various versions; (and when Windisch's great literal translation into German came out later, I found but little to add or alter for the next edition). I added but a connecting sentence where necessary, but I condensed and transposed, and I left out some passages that have changed their meaning. For when we are told of Cuchulain's "distortion" one knows that the meaning was that the battle-anger upon him made him different from his fellows, transfigured him to something above and beyond the ordinary, the natural man; "His feet, his shins and his knees shifted themselves and were behind him; his heels and calves and hams were displaced to the front of his leg-bones that their knotted muscles stood up in lumps large as the clenched fist of a fighting man . . . his lion's gnashing caused flakes of fire, each one larger than the fleece of three-year-old wether, to stream from his throat into his mouth. The sounding blows of the heart that panted within him were as the howl of a ban-dog doing his office, or of a lion in the act of charging bears." (The translation by that cousin of mine, Standish Hayes O'Grady, banished in my childhood, a friend in my later life.) Traherne, telling of his own childhood, says of its soaring thoughts, "Sometimes I wondered why men were made no bigger. I would have had a man as big as a giant, a giant as big as a castle, and a castle as big as the heavens." And it is so that the strong, the usual, were pictured in the childhood of the world. There were redundancies also to cut out. It was not the work of the scholars to do this, but it was mine. When I was preparing a new edition, I asked Kuno Meyer, one of the great scholars, if he had criticisms to make, and he said I ought not to have left out the description of Etain's naked body when King Eochaid first caught sight of her beside the well. But to do that I should have had to give up her purple cloak and dress of green with its clasps and embroideries. One picture may be more beautiful than the other, I told him, but you cannot have both together in that sudden vision. So in the many legends of the fate of the Sons of Usnach I could but choose one story of Deirdre's courtship and but one of her death.

The four years I spent in working at this book and the one that followed, *Gods and Fighting Men*, were happy ones. It was work that delighted me. It was in a way like that I had spent on *Mr. Gregory's Letter Box*, far as that was behind it. My ignorance when I began was as great, I had as gradually to build up personalities, for Cuchulain and Conan and Usheen are as real and individual as Lord Talbot or Lord Wellesley or Sir Robert Peel. And the beauty of the lyric poetry coming through the mists of a strange language was a great excitement and joy. I spent some time working at documents in the British Museum and the Royal Irish Academy. My old knowledge of German was now of great use to me, for German scholars had taken up the task despised by our own Trinity professors. I used to spend all my day at the British Museum, and sometimes dine at the neighbouring Austrian Restaurant (that vanished at the outbreak of the war) and work again until 9.00 or 10.00 o'clock. It is a curious thing that I had never cared for Dickens; but at this time, coming back one evening to my little rooms, my mind full of the imaginative beauty and nobility of the epics, I by chance took up *Bleak House*, and found an immense relief, a sort of warmth and refreshment in its humour, its humanity; a reaction no doubt from those hours in that ancient world of heroism and of dreams.

So this was another thread to weave into the web among those of less importance and colour. My usual life went on at Coole.

December 1900. "A telegram from Father Considine to say he will send Conolly, the Irish teacher from Aran, tomorrow, so I sent for Preston (the National School Master) and talked to him and wrote to Father Fahey about classes at the school . . . F. came, and we talked tenants, and how to settle the Cunningham case without an eviction.

"Had a quiet wet busy fortnight, starting Conolly with classes, marking trees for tenants who can't get turf from the wet bogs. Ceaseless rain. Gillane says it is 'heart-broken weather'. I had lessons from Conolly, rather disheartening, I understand so little by ear.

Robert came . . . Is working for Mods. at Greek sculpture

and Greek plays . . . and really interested in his work, but very much enjoys the shooting.

"Douglas Hyde came for shooting . . . He rather snubs my idea of the Cuchulain book. I think his feeling is that only a scholar should do it, and he is bewildered at my simple translation. I had got Conolly to put the Death of Cuchulain, of which I had only the English version, into Irish, and had translated it back literally into English. 'Of course an epic should not be translated in colloquial style,' he says, which accounts for his translations of bits of epics being heavy and formal, quite different from his folk-tales and peasant poem translations. However, he gave his consent, which is all I wanted, though I don't yet know if the task will be beyond my strength and time.

"He had seen Moran (Editor of *The Leader*), who told him he could not make head or tail of Yeats, or understand a word he said or wrote. However, he promised not to attack him (though he has not altogether kept his promise). Hyde hinted that it was unwise to attack any but enemies, but Moran would by no means agree to this. 'Your enemies don't mind what you say, but if you attack your friend, he's the boy that will feel it!' But he has already made a great change in Ireland by *The Leader,* and helps in the building up of the nation better than anyone else has done from the industrial side.

"Christmas over, and has left me alive, though with an empty pocket. A busy time, the poor at the door.

". . . On Sunday evening Mulkere came down and we went through some of Raftery's poems, and a little bit of the Cuchulain translation . . .

"I am in pretty good heart at the beginning of the new century. So many of my anxieties about R. are over, he is safe through childhood and school . . . Whatever turn his ideas take he will always I think be fond of home and Ireland, and have a sense of duty to his people."

The *Ideals** not out yet. I got a little nervous about them, but I think I was right in publishing, to show how strong the national spirit can be, without those who feel it being of necessity followers of William O'Brien or Tim Healy. The passionate love of Ireland is the foundation to work and one of the best things that has been done for some time is Moran's attempt in *The Leader* to turn the hatred of

Ideals in Ireland (London and New York 1901).

England into a hatred of "the works of the flesh" that come from outside.

14 January. "On the 3rd, Richard and Alec came (nephews from South Africa), and Harvey and they and Robert have had a pleasant time since then, only one wet day, constant shooting.

"A.E. came for one day only, full of life and fire, much more National than he used to be. He declares his psychical state has been injured for all time by all the Agricultural Organisation lectures he has had to give. He is so openly pro-Boer that I was a little afraid of a row with Alec, who is rather 'permanent official', but they got on fairly well, and he was delighted with Richard who has hedged by saying he tried to join the Boers first; and who said in his simple way, 'I don't see that the war was necessary. Why couldn't Chamberlain have said, "We want the goldfields; what will you take for them?" It would have cost less than the war is costing.' His brother, Aubrey, was fired on in an ambulance waggon by the British, who mistook it for a Boer ambulance!"

26 January. "All gone now. A very quiet week, bad rough weather . . . I was out a good deal planting with the men. John Farrell says 'Nurserymen are more crafty than any other men within the four walls of the world'. Conolly went to Tillyra, I was rather glad to get free of my Irish lessons, being at work on an article on Irish folk ballads, and also translating Deirdre as an experiment towards my Cuchulain . . . The place so still that I felt as if sudden gaiety had begun one day because the sheep had been put in the back lawn and I could see them from the windows; the old black sheep that always seems so friendly because W. knew it, and the cuckoo lamb in its absurd last year's coat . . . Excitement enough elsewhere, for the news of the Queen's illness was quickly followed by her death on Tuesday. Poor old Queen, good in England, callous to Ireland . . . Maurteen regrets her because he 'has been told that the Prince of Wales has said he will rule Ireland with a rod of iron.'!

"This very stormy day has been a good one, for Yeats writes that *Ideals* is out, is good, and has been quite well taken by Dublin booksellers, Eason is taking a hundred . . . F. writes that Cunningham has settled, will pay two years' rent and accept the valuation made. I am most thankful for this for he seemed perilously near eviction. Mike says it is my help to his wife while sick that softened his heart, I don't know, I was afraid he would look on it as yielding to him, but had to help the poor thing."

31 January. "Sunday was very stormy, no church; just as well as I hear the Archdeacon preached a funeral sermon in which he came down on those who did not sufficiently reverence the Queen, and said 'O'Connell had done so, but O'Connell was a gentleman and came from County Kerry'. This of course aimed at Yeats, Moore and Martyn. Conolly walked over from Tillyra with a couple of Irish ballads he has been sent from Aran. I went out in the storm to look at my little trees."

3 February. "Busy with 'Children of Usnach', and making a translation from the Irish, and with my 'Folk Ballads', and out tree planting. I found that snow having come on, rabbits had killed some larch in the night. Capel tarring them delicately with the point of a stick. Patrick very boozy, holding silvers very sideways while Maurteen planted them. I got some more of the rabbit mixture and stayed out till 5.00 o'clock in the snow seeing it put on, and came home soaking. Worked at Deirdre . . ."

In February I wrote from London: "I went to see Lady Haliburton at tea time. She says there has been great squabbling between the Earl Marshal and Lord Chamberlain, the Windsor funeral muddled. Poor Lecky was there and nearly died of cold and hunger and said the seats at St. George's Chapel were not half filled . . . I saw Mrs. D. also, who said the Kaiser had won all their hearts, 'So clean cut and rigid', and the King had 'risen to the occasion and looked like Henry the Eighth'.

"On Sunday I read Yeats my translation of Sons of Usnach, and he was enthusiastic, says I must go on, and that it will be a great book. So I was encouraged, and on Friday I went to the British Museum and asked for a reading ticket. The clerk asked what I was working at, I said, 'The Cuchulain Saga', and as that did not seem to convey much, I said, 'Ancient Irish History'. He asked how long I expected to be at it. I said I didn't know, perhaps two years, at which he jumped, having expected me I think to say two hours. Then he said I must make formal application and have a reference. I asked if Mr. Sidney Colvin would do. His respect increased and he said if I would go to him I could get my order at once. So I found him and he was affable about my ticket but not very sympathetic about my scheme, says 'the difficulty about harmonizing is that there are so many different stories'. I

said, yes, that is just why it is necessary. Then he objected
to the Sons of Usnach having been overcome by enchantment,
and he broke off to say Herbert Trench has got more of the
Celtic spirit into 'Deidre Wed' than any of our other poets,
'though he is not in that set'. Also he thinks Yeats has gone
off. (He wrote next day attributing this to the influence of
Arthur Symons.)

"Then Sir Edward Thompson, the Librarian, came in,
an old acquaintance, and gave me a reading order which
made all the clerks bow before me like Joseph's sheaves, and
after a great many instructions I got the books I wanted—
I never would have known how to get them, but Yeats
arrived and helped me.

"I worked again at the Museum, getting on nicely. I met
Miss Kinkead, she is doing coloured woodcuts, so I have
asked her to teach me that I may pass on the knowledge to
R. This seems to be a working visit to London . . . Going to
Sussex Place I found police, and the street lined rather
thinly with people, and came in for the King and Queen's
public entry, their first. He was fat and smiling, she bowing
coldly but looking pretty under her veil. 'Mrs. L. whom I
met at dinner at the Lyalls, speaking of the Queen's beauty,
said, "It is all my loyalty has to hang on to now". That is
why so much is made of it.' Wilfrid Blunt says he has heard
no one speak seriously about Edward VII. The ladies of
his acquaintance call him 'Edward the Caresser'.

"Bernard Holland, who had been to Pretoria on Concessions Committee, says the war has been the triumph of the
amateur, the Boers are amateurs and so are all the soldiers
who did best. Poor Tommy was nowhere, though he would
do a task set him well enough.

"People are kind, and I had a good many dinners to go
to, but somehow I have lost my interest in society for the
present . . . the Boer War still dominating conversation—a
special correspondent at a dinner takes the place of the
captured peer we used to laugh at."

March. "The reaction beginning against the war shows
itself in the absurd excitement over 'An Englishman's Love
Letters'. This I heard discussed at many houses, but did not
trouble to read it till after I had left London. Had I done
so, I could have settled the question as to their having been
written 'many years ago' for in one of the earliest is quoted
a line 'my share of the world' 'from the Irish peasant poet
who drops from absurd exaggeration to this.' It is taken

from my translation of Mary Hynes, published by Yeats in *The Dome* less than two years ago."

April. "When the Oxford vacation began we went to Venice . . . then to Trieste . . . Later we went down the Dalmatian Coast and to Montenegro, a very pleasant time."

12 May. Coole. "The little larch trees I last planted are doing well everywhere, but the silvers and spruce have withered up in the cold.

"I am working very hard at Cuchulain; have done the fight with Ferdiad and Birth of Cuchulain, and am now at Bricriu's Feast."

18 May. "I have done Bricriu and am still at the second part, the championship of Ulster, very fascinating work. Hyde has sent a bundle of "Irische Texte" and other books, and a manuscript.

"On Sunday there was a meeting at Kiltartan to establish a branch of the United Irish League. M. attended; says Mr. Duffy, M.P. from Loughrea, and Mr. Lynam, evicted Portumna tenant, spoke well, but 'the same old story ever since we were born, abuse of the landlords and Cromwell'. Some landlords were denounced . . . however, we were not mentioned.

"Yeats has been to the Royal Irish Academy and seen the manuscript translation of the *Tain* I had heard of, and thinks it will serve for my purpose. A great relief, for I was beginning to feel the want of the great central tale to work at, and if I could not have got the *Tain* all my work would have had to lie by."

Sometimes I got a word or two from tradition. I wrote to Yeats: "An old woman in Galway Workhouse told me Queen Maeve was very handsome and she used the hazel rod which her enemies could not stand against. But after that she grew very disagreeable, 'It's best not to be talking about her. How do we know it is true? Best leave it between the book and the readers.' She had evidently some scandal about Fergus in her mind."

This was rather a long day, I walked to Kiltartan to see Treston about Irish teaching, and he has done nothing, Father Fahey being away; then round to see the elms planted in the winter and a good many have failed. Tim makes complaints of rats which are eating the peas, red lead and all. I had a pleasant little talk with Mulkere, who is mowing, about an Irish singer he had heard in Gort, and about old manuscripts he has heard of; there is one with Raftery's

poems he thinks can still be had. Then came in, and found
a letter from R. which had been left in the postbag all day!

"Work as usual—a little tired of the Championship of
Ulster"—the first I have got tired of.

29 May 1901.   "I had a nice Sunday at Killeaden with Miss
MacManus, and saw old men who remembered Raftery, and
young men from Kiltimagh chartered a car and came to
greet me. On to Dublin Monday.

"At the R.I. Academy, and saw the MSS. of *Tain Bo*
which I think will do quite nicely. I am to apply for leave to
have it copied . . . A.E. came and spent the evening with me,
and told me his scheme of an Irish mythology. He had met
Massingham who says he is convinced that the moral
influence of England is injurious to the world."

6 January 1902.   "These last eight months have been very
busy ones. Summer holidays passed pleasantly as usual. Yeats,
Jack and his wife, Geraldine Beauchamp. The W. Gibsons
for some days. Violet Martin for a couple of nights. Harvey
about a month. In October we broke up. R. went back to
Oxford. I went to Dublin for Literary Theatre . . . It was a
success, quite respectable, even *Times* and *Irish Times* gave
us their blessing. Benson undertook *Diarmuid and Grania*,
and Hyde's *Twisting of the Rope* (I have carried off the real
Sugain [straw rope] as a trophy) was a real and immense
success . . .

"I stayed on for a while to read at Irish Academy and
National Library. I worked very hard through the summer
at *Cuchulain*, and finished it in the autumn. I tried to find
an Irish publisher. But one did not answer my letter at all,
and the other sent someone who asked me how many words
there were in the manuscript, which I told him as near as
I could, and 'what length the words were' which I could not
tell, and that was the end of the business. So then I sent it
to Murray who kept it a month, then sent it back with a
rather disparaging letter from some wise man he had consulted, the point of which was that I should write it more
in the manner and to the level of Jacob's fairy tales, (and
also prefix it to a history of Ireland and especially of Ulster,
at that time!) I indignantly refused this suggestion and sent
the MS. to Yeats to dispose of. Then Murray wrote that he
didn't mean to refuse it and was willing to publish at his own
risk . . . So it has been arranged and I am already revising
proofs."

And then in March 1902, after an Easter at Florence

with Robert, "I left London for Coole on the very day *Cuchulain* was published."

I had done what I wanted; something for the dignity of Ireland. The reviews showed that the enemy could no longer scoff at our literature and its "want of idealism".

When I consulted Yeats about giving some of the letters that were written to me about *Cuchulain* here, or if they looked too much like Hyacinth Halvey's testimonials, he said, "You should give them for our nation will be but partly educated for a long time to come, and a half-educated man thinks he should hate all that he has just risen out of. Many and many a young man who might have got the beginning of culture from these books has been kept from them because he thinks that there is something low about the country speech. When Hyde sent the first chapters of his *Religious Songs of Connacht* to a Dublin magazine thirty years ago they were as beautifully written as his *Love Songs of Connacht,* but the clerical editor insisted on his turning them into the style of the newspaper. 'You must be either Irish or English,' he said, and Hyde has never had an English style since. If Ireland were a mediaeval principality and I its prince I would forbid all forms of English in the schools except the old English of the country places. But as we can't do that, the next best thing to do is to get such a consensus of authority in commendation of a fine use of that English that no sensible man henceforth will think that he should renounce it when he puts on boots.

"That's what your relation Hayes O'Grady thought when he translated fragments of the epics into preposterous Latinised English. His hero 'ascends to the apex of an eminence' and there 'vibrates his javelin', while the heroine 'fractures her heart'." "No," I say, "he invented a thunderous majestic style of his own, it is original, he carries it all through, he doesn't just choose dictionary words instead of usual ones." "Well," said Yeats, "I don't see how any decent man could write 'colossal ocean's superfices' when the literal translation is I believe 'the hillsides of the great sea'." So I am giving some of the letters that came from my friends among writers.

Mark Twain wrote from Riversdale on the Hudson, in March 1903: "I have been marvelling along through your wonderful book again, and trying to understand how those people could produce such a literature in that old day, and they so remote (apparently) from the well-springs and inspirations of such things. Or so remote, I am perhaps meaning to say, from the culture and training whence such fine literary art proceeds, such fine literary form, such force, imagination, expression. It puzzles me so; and then the chariots, the jewels, the sumptuous raiment, the carvings, metal work, suggestions of advanced architecture, and all that when they hadn't experienced a Roman occupation (I suppose), and the like had perished from the neighbouring island for centuries and been forgotten. But never mind about those things. I can't guess them out. But we've got the stories and that is the important thing, and we are grateful to you for that. And we should always be grateful, even if you had given us the Fate of the Children of Usnach alone, that moving and beautiful tale, that masterpiece!

"There's great imagery in those stories! After all these centuries we can't surpass it—not fling it on the canvas with an easier grace nor a surer hand either. It is indeed a wonderful book.

"I recognise that I have said the like of this before, last year, but no matter, I wanted to say it again, and thank you again—and Mrs. Clemens said 'go on and do it—and give my kindest regards and cherished remembrance to Lady Gregory and Mr. Yeats'. It is from her sick-bed where she has been lying seven months. It is nervous prostration. I see her twice a day, twenty minutes each time; one of the daughters stands the afternoon watch with her; no one else is ever allowed in the room except the doctor and the trained nurse. We think she makes a little progress. We can't exactly *see* it but we do *believe* it . . ."

Professor York Powell wrote from Christchurch: "Murray has sent me your *Cuchulain*. It is masterly. It is really a beautiful piece of English as well as a beautiful story and subject. You have the gratitude of everybody who cares for poetry of the highest kind, and the noblest tradition of Epic story. I hope to see your Finn McCumhail ere very long. Your *Cuchulain* is an abiding joy. Cuchulain is most beautiful; the Deirdre part one of the most beautiful stories in the world I should think now. How odd it is that no one in Greek times ever idealised Helen and Paris! All the poets speak of them with some severity, and most with definite hatred." And he wrote to me that he had sent out copies of the book to friends in Australia, "who I am sure will receive the same sort of impression, almost an impression of pride in the Irish mind, as I received myself . . . It opened up a great world of beautiful legend, which, though accounting myself an Irishman I had never known at all."

Professor Eoin MacNeill, whom I then knew as a profound scholar, generous in his help, and who later was a leader of the Volunteers of 1916, and when back from prison became President of the Gaelic League and later the Speaker of *An Dail,* sent me the most charming compliment of all . . . "It is late to acknowledge it now, but late as it is, it is still early in the life of the book, and I congratulate you sincerely and heartily on its arrival. It is the truest representation of the Irish heroic age, as our forefathers had it in their minds, that I have ever seen in English. A few more books like it, and the Gaelic League will want to suppress you on a double indictment, to wit, depriving the Irish language of her sole right to express the innermost Irish mind, and secondly, investing the Anglo-Irish language with a literary dignity it has never hitherto possessed."

And Sir John Rhys wrote to me again in December 1903: "Just a word to wish you and your son a merry Christmas and a happy New Year, also to tell you that when the Moseley Education Commission was received by the President of the United States at the White House, I had an exceptionally long conversation with him all about Irish, and especially your book on Cuchulain. He was exceedingly interested in your work, and anxious to learn the pronunciation of the hard names in it. He did not tell me how he came to be interested in Irish questions, but he seems to be a great student whom neither the chase—for he is a great hunter—nor politics prevent from reading. I have been told that he is of Irish descent on the mother's side, but that is mere hearsay; at all events he is deeply interested in Irish and fond of reading your book on Cuchulain, as he is also of Dr. Hyde's works."

I had already heard of President Roosevelt's interest, for my nephew John Shawe-Taylor had ridden over one day to Coole with a paper in which was printed a note from him to John Redmond (who had sent him shamrock for St. Patrick's day), in which he said: "I have just been reading Lady Gregory's translation or paraphrase of the old Erse epic *Cuchulain of Murmethne* (Heaven forgive me if my spelling is wrong)—and I am delighted with it." He himself afterwards wrote to me that after he had read it, he had sent for all the books on Irish literature he could get hold of, to take upon a journey to the west.

And Yeats wrote in 1904 from New York: "Did I tell you that I lunched with the President and that he asked much about you and wished that you would go to America that he might entertain you."

Irish writers also welcomed it with generous praise.

Synge, whom I did not know so well then as later, wrote from 90 rue d'Assas, Paris, saying he had received the book the day before and "I have been reading it ever since with intense delight. *Au fond* I am a somewhat squibbling spirit and I never expect to enjoy a book that I have heard praised beforehand, but in this case I have been altogether carried away. I had no idea the book was going to be so great. What puny pallid stuff most of our modern writing seems beside it! Many of the stories, of course, I have known for a long time, but they seem to gain a new life in the beautiful language you have told them in. There are a very few details that I would like differently managed—I will tell you about them if I may when I see you again, but the success of the whole is so triumphant one has not time to think of them. I told old Jubainville about what you were doing a few weeks ago, and he was very much interested, but I am afraid he looks at Irish things from a too strict point of view to appreciate their literary value as fully as we do." . . . And two years later he wrote to me: "Cuchulain is still a part of my daily bread".

In Ireland there were some criticisms and these are hinted at when J. B. Yeats writes to W. B. Yeats: "I had expected the style to be studied and affected and odd—my judicial mind I suppose had been alarmed by your eulogies—besides I had heard it abused (not by Douglas Hyde, who is quite of your opinion). I think, however, the style is absolute perfection and the *most perfectly natural* thing I have ever read."

And "John Eglinton" wrote: "The style which you adopt I think you more than justify, and I take leave to congratulate you on having produced what will no doubt be the 'authorised version' of the 'Irish Old Testament'."

A.E. wrote: "I never thought I would like to read anything about Cuchulain after O'Grady's old Epic, but you have swept away my prejudices by a dream wind of beautiful pictures.

". . . It is the document of a people's past, and like Rousseau with the book of his *Confessions,* they can bring it before the throne and say 'such were our thoughts, such were our acts."

And a young man I didn't know, one of the Tennysons, wrote: "It is seldom one comes upon a book nowadays that makes one want to shout!"

As to my next book, it was my intention to give only the story of Finn and the Fianna. But as I gathered fragments here and there I came to feel sure that Finn was not, as we were usually told, the head of an army within chronicled, even Christian times, but that he went back to even an earlier day than Cuchulain.

I wrote to Yeats: "I began in Dublin to read up the gods. Then I found the material too scanty to make a whole volume and turned to Finn. I found him hard to understand —why should the sacred knowledge of the Hazel Tree have been given to a mere militia captain? Then I reflected that he wasn't given the knowledge, he took it without leave like Eve the apple, and as I think, the gods had a grudge against him for it. I feel sure he was before Cuchulain's time, nearer to the spirit world. Anyhow I will work at him from that point of view, in connection with the gods.

I have written, I utilised O.'s idleness at the Academy by getting him to correct Tomas's story for *The Gael*[1], but had to spend half-an-hour this morning listening to an exposition on his mistakes delivered with great vehemence. "That use of d. e. in the plural is a custom introduced by the Gaelic League, and is simply *infernal*. As to the letter *a* in *beag* which was only put there in the seventeenth century, it is no more wanted there than in Mullins", where it certainly does not seem to be wanted. Count Plunkett was hovering about and the happy thought came to me of telling him I had gone round the second-hand book sellers yesterday trying to get the six volumes of the Ossianic Society, as there is so much I can use in them it would be worth buying them to take home; and he said, as a member of the Council, he could give me leave to have the copy in the Academy on loan, volume by volume, at Coole. So I think I shall get home very soon, as with that and *Silva Gaedelica* I have plenty of Finn material for a time." And then Mr. Eoin McNeill let me see the proofs of the cycle of poems, *Duanaire Finn,* he was editing and translating for the Irish Texts Society, and there I found that Finn was of the near kindred of Lugh of the Tuatha de Danaan, the people of

---

[1] T. O'Niell Russell published three articles in *The Gael* in 1903 (in the May, June and October issues) giving translations from ancient Irish manuscripts.

unearthly race who drove out the Fomor, the people of darkness and evil; and that the shield he owned had been soaked with the blood of the Fomor King, Balor, whose terrible eye brought death on every man on whom it looked. So with my belief thus confirmed I set to work, and what I could find of the history of the Gods, that is chiefly in the old writings, made a preface for the living legends of Finn. And although I worked again in the British Museum and the Irish Academy I found more news of the Fianna nearer home.

I wrote again after a visit to a workhouse: "I didn't get much new about the Fianna except a little verse that says they were nice and mannerly in their going out and in their coming in." And "an old man who came to the door told me the story of Finn and Grania 'and wasn't it a queer thing that she married him in the end? It was with enchantment he coaxed her to marry him'." Again, "A blind piper told me, 'Some say Grania was handsome, and some say she was ugly, there's a saying in the Irish for that'. But the old basket-maker was scornful and said, 'Many would tell you Grania slept under the cromlechs, but I don't believe that, and she a king's daughter. And I don't believe she was handsome either. If she was, why would she have run away?' At Moycullen I was told: 'As they were passing a stream the water splashed Grania and she said, 'Diarmuid never came so near to me as that'." I heard many stories of Oisin also, of his journey to Tir nan Og and his arguments with Patrick and his conversion "and as soon as St. Patrick converted him he was in such a hurry not to lose a minute but to baptise him at once that he struck down his spear on his foot without seeing it, and pinned him by the instep to the ground. And when he saw a stream of blood coming from the instep he said, 'Why did not you make no sign when the spear struck you?' And Oisin said, 'I thought it was a part of the rite of baptism, and I wouldn't begrudge a little drop of blood to God Almighty'."

And from Galway: "I have just come from a long day at Clare-Galway, looking for Finn legends. I got at last a good many written out in a MS. book, an old man has lent it to me. I was at Oughterard for a night and go again to-morrow. An old man in the workhouse there has a long poem, but very few teeth, and the Moycullen priest, an Irish expert, is coming to help interpret it."

So *Gods and Fighting Men* was published in 1904.

Sir John Rhys writing that "the wildness of the stories is most absorbing and irresistible" and had made him forget all his correspondence adds: "I wonder what Professor Atkinson was thinking of when he complained of the lack of imagination in Irish literature."

And I was quite sorry when in 1908 Dr. Atkinson died.

This is a charming letter from John Masefield: "I write to thank you very much for your kind gift of *Gods and Fighting Men*, a most beautiful book, full of golden poems, which makes me sick at heart that I am not Irish, and of the folk to whom the hearth is still an altar. I have not much to complain about, perhaps, as I was brought up near woods, and taught by sailors, and spent three years working with my hands. All my boyhood I was near the earth and water, among folk who held some old-world beliefs, and a few threadbare stories, so that, for an Englishman, I was given a large measure of the best things the earth has. But I cannot tell you how I envy the ragged Irish boy, with his wits unspoiled by a school, and the green earth beautiful about him, and such tales as those you have garnered, to tell him of the grand folk who once trod those hills he sees, and lie buried beneath the grey cairn where his goats go browsing.

"I think there can be no little lad in any cabin but must be helped unspeakably, even if the help be a thing hidden in the heart, only showing in some chance sympathy or subtlety, by such tales as these. And I feel that had I had the fortune to be born to these tales I would never have gone a-roaming without a hope that among the fern I would come across the cave where Finn lies. I would never have heard a fiddler in the tavern, singing some old song of Ireland, without thinking that maybe the fiddler was Finn come back, and the song some secret message to the sorrowful hearts that waited for him.

It is my grief that I am not a shepherd of the hills,
In a blue cloak, lying among the fern, the sheep cropping
    at the grass,
With the wind blowing keen and steady, the wind full
    of sighs, full of songs, full of beautiful folk,
And I there, lying lonely, watching the grey town and
    the sea.

For it's great wool my sheep would have, eating the
    pleasant grass with no ivy near
It would be warm wool, white wool, wool for a queen

For a king, for a golden poet, for a woman that is the
    beauty of the world
It would bring me gold and white silver those pleasant
    fleeces,
The way I could buy all Lady Gregory's books, and the
    books of Mr. Yeats,
And do nothing but read them till the day I died."

In 1906 I wrote to Yeats: "I am full of strength and
energy and walk miles in various directions, but it is a little
lonely sometimes, there are so many things I want to talk
to you about. However, I am really getting the saints into
shape, and they were worrying me, I want to get them clean
off my mind. I think I shall have seventy or eighty pages of
very quaint or beautiful stories and hymns, but I must read
all to you before putting into final shape."

My *Book of Saints and Wonders* has not the outline of
the others. It is perhaps of less value for what it gives than
for what it leaves out, those accumulated fragments from
the lives of many saints and of many miracles that had been
brought in Christian times into Ireland and overlaid the
primitive legends that I tried to disentangle and make clear.
I had but little trouble with this in comparison with other
books. For as I worked at them I had met with many of the
stories of the Saints that I used afterwards. And as I gathered
folk-lore concerned with the visions of the people, and the
nearness of the invisible world, I heard some of the most
lovely of the Christian stories. That of "The Soul and the
Body" which tells of St. Patrick's visit to a cottage where
death had come and where the soul three times as it departed
came back to kiss its farewell, because "that soul was sorry
to leave that body, because it had kept it so clean and so
honest" was told to me by a poor woman under a ragged
thatch beside a narrow road of Slieve Echtge.

In working at these three books and in gathering the
folk-lore that was to appear later in *Visions and Beliefs* all
seemed to bring into a whole, into harmony, the beliefs of
old Pagan times and of ancient Christian times and of today.
It seemed to me that Ireland had never lost the vision that
it is likely all ages have possessed in the early days of faith;
that she can claim continuity of vision, a thread that has
never been snapped. For there was no violent break in
belief; the gods came first, and with a changing theology
many of their attributes were carried on, were conferred

upon the Saints. When Lugh of the Long Hand came in a time of need from beyond the world to free the people from the tyranny of the Fomor, the powers of darkness, "the people were not able to look at him, for the brightness of his face was like the setting sun, and he was riding a horse that was as swift as the naked wind of March." And I think after Christianity had sent the gods out of fashion some of his attributes were given to Saint Columcille who "was called the Golden Moon by reason of his high race and his wisdom", and who on being told the poets, the men of imagination, were being driven out from Ireland, went back and insisted this should not be done, standing up against the king. That sounds more like radiant Lugh than a saint of later days. He was proud and when Axel the angel offered him gifts, what he asked was that he might die in his youth and so escape the ugliness of age; and at the last it was to the Chief of the Poets rather than the Church that "an angel came riding a speckled horse with news that Columcille was dead". Another amongst the gods was Brigit, the Fiery Arrow, a woman of poetry, and poets worshipped her, for her sway was very great and very noble and she was a woman of healing along with that. And although as a Saint she does not disdain to restore the eyesight of the poor, appearing as I have been told "very nice and loughy in the shape of a little fish", it is as a Saint she was seen when Strongbow called out on his deathbed that it was by her, by Brigit of the Gael, he was being brought to his death. Heaven itself, the other world, had been foreshadowed in the ancient stories long before news had come of the *Revelation* of St. John the Divine. Those who heard those wonder voyages where Taig or Laegaire in Manannan's Islands found ever-lasting apples upon an ever-blossoming tree must have felt that the vision has been carried but a little farther when he told of the heavenly city of the fruits and flowers upon the Tree of Life. When an old wrinkled woman told me of a strange unearthly visitor who has said to her "Tir-nan-og is not far from any one of us" I felt that through the ages, alike to Brendan, or Blake, or Kiltartan dreamer, heaven is about us and may be our present abode.

It was after he had read *Saints and Wonders* that Masefield wrote to me, and having said that The Old Woman of Beare made Villon's ballad seem a poor thing, a thing of rags and patches, went on, "Next to that I think I like Columcille's song about Doire; one feels like that about every place where one has been happy; and perhaps if there were more of such poems and if more people knew them, our holy places would not be desecrated, and our holy places not trodden down by the feet of the despiser. Perhaps that is what moved me so deeply in all your stories and poems; that reverence for the dead, as the home of those who were once great or beautiful; and that peopling of the land with august and holy shadows; so that one could hardly tend sheep upon a hill without passing where a hero passes; or drink at a brook without thinking of the young men who drank there before going to their death. In England these things are not remembered. The hero of the English hill is the last highwayman who happened to be hanged there; and I remember as a boy looking out day after day upon the Welsh hills, and the hills nearer to me, and all the border country, so alive with passion and sorrowing, that no one could tell me any story at all about anyone at all who had ever lived there, or about any of the hills or woods or brooks, or about any ghost, or murder, or why an old thorn was called the Dead Man's Thorn; or why two little round hills were called Robin Hood's Butts. All of the stories I like very much; and it is difficult to select one as better than another. Perhaps 'Tuan Son of Cairell' moves me most; but the breaking of Columcille's guarantee is another I am fond of; and I love the story of the woman who saw the civil little fish the time St. Brigit cured her blindness, and that other story of Columcille keeping the Feast of Pentecost . . . It would be a good deed to make, little by little, the sagas of all the saints and heroes; and to publish them with maps of their countries (as Morris in his Icelandic sagas) and if it could be managed with pictures of the places they made famous, or sacred, as they are now."

In 1903 I published *Poets and Dreamers,* chapters or essays upon Irish poetry and legends, and with translations of some of the songs of the wandering poet Raftery, who had died in 1835, before the famine years.

It shows in what ignorance of the mind of the people I, in common with others of my class had lived, that Raftery's songs, of which I had never until then heard, had been not only known through the west of Ireland but had been taken to Australia and to America and had been heard "even in a trolly" there. Archbishop Carr wrote to me from Melbourne that he knew a man who had come out there forty years ago, and "although he cannot read or write can repeat Raftery's poems".

Critics were kind to all these books, and in a little time the English papers were giving quotations from long-forgotten Raftery and his kin.

There was more of my own writing in *Poets and Dreamers* than in anything I had yet published. I felt it more my own. The chapter especially on Raftery had been an excitement. As I heard of him in many thatched houses his image grew. It was almost like Browning's excitement, "Ah, did you once see Shelley plain?"—when some memory of him was given by some old labourer or withered hag. I seemed to be sitting in a mart with treasures coming in. And when tramp or beggar gave me his garnered store, my hands were often filled to overflowing. In the midst of household duties and duties of hospitality, and cricket lunches and letter writing, it took some determination to sit and write down while still fresh in the memory all I had been told by perhaps a beggar at the door. And I could not do this during the telling of the story, or it would have become dry and laboured on the teller's lips. I had to train my memory till it could hardly make a mistake. I think one may boast of industry for it is one's own; those who possess genius should not boast of it, for that is the gift of the Gods.

XXIV

SEVEN YEARS: 1903-10

I wrote at the end of 1909: "Five years interregnum. What has happened in these last five years?

"Robert's marriage in September 1907.

"Before that, a beautiful month in Italy with him and Yeats. Birth of Richard (the darling). This is a great happiness and Margaret is charming and beautiful, and I am quite satisfied with Robert's choice.

"I have worked very hard at the Theatre, its splits and quarrels.

"I wrote my *Seven Short Plays* and *Kincora, The White Cockade, Dervorgilla, The Canavans* and in this last year *The Image.*

"J. M. Synge's death this year a great sadness." But from the beginning of the century I find no clear record. It was work begun or finished that marked the passing years.

Lately (1922) I have been looking through some letters of Yeats to me and of mine to him written during that time. And as I read I marvelled to find how much of time and energy was not only used, but as it seems squandered, on the endless affairs of the Abbey Theatre, almost crushing out, as it seems, other interests; the effort to maintain discipline, the staging, the reading of plays, the choice of plays, the quarrels among players, the suspicion of politicians and of the authorities, anxieties about money. I am glad to have given a sufficient outline of that story in my book on our Theatre, I need not tell it again*. Nor will I give any account of the difficulties Hugh Lane met with and our endeavours to help him in making the Dublin Municipal Gallery, for that story I have also told†. I will but borrow from the letters some passages that the bare outline of these years may not be left quite empty.

As to play-writing it came as if by accident. I think my

* *Our Irish Theatre* (Putnam 1913.) [3rd edition enlarged, Colin Smythe 1973.]

† *Hugh Lane's Life and Achievement* (Murray 1921). [Now included in *Sir Hugh Lane: His Life and Legacy* (Colin Smythe 1973).]

preparation for it had been in great part that London life, that education in talking. For what is the substance of drama but conversation clipped and arranged? I have also told in *Our Irish Theatre* of my preparation in working with Yeats. "He who loseth himself findeth himself", for I had no thought of any personal benefit to myself when I helped in his work.

I have just been looking at the old copybooks in which are the first versions of *Spreading the News* never much altered, and a little bundle of paper figures with the names on them of Mrs. Tarpey and Tim Casey and the rest, that I had used in grouping my characters and arranging their entry and exits. I will not write anything about the success of these short plays, for they are still being given in many countries and it is not the critic but the audience that is the test of failure or success. The writing of these was a real joy, being the first entirely creative work I had done. These are some scraps from my letters, chiefly to W. B. Yeats: —

From Dublin. "Your father has been here making a nice drawing of me, a sort of Mother of Sorrows with tearful eyes. I like it at all events and won't let him come for a third sitting as he is anxious to do.

"He had been to the C. Club on Saturday night and gave such a funny account of it . . . X., 'the great man there', read them Moore's interview, which they had not seen, and proceeded to ask 'who is this George Moore? Where does he come from? Who asked him to come here? He seems to me a very vulgar fellow.' He then went on to abuse *Diarmuid and Grania.* Your father after some time fired up and said how enthusiastic he had felt and the people about him each time it was performed. X. however, would not agree, and gave his idea of what a play should be. He would like to see all Ireland in uproar, wars going on all round, and the Four Masters sitting quietly all the time, writing their annals. This idea he sets out at great length, without however getting beyond the tableau stage.

"They went on to Horace Plunkett, and decided he was weak, vain, greedy, ambitious, and wants to be Chief Secretary. Someone feebly said he believed he gave back his salary to the work of the Agricultural Organization. There was silence for a moment, and then another said 'If he does it is very irregular. I would not believe in a man who would do such a thing as that.'

"Your father says he expects you to change very much in

old age, you will become much quieter, and your mother's characteristics will come out. I asked what they were, but he said it was hard to say that, but that he often told her he must take her affection on trust, for she never showed any sign of it. But you are also very like his father, who used to walk up and down the room when talking as you do and rub his hands. You are also very like your sister Lolly who will never go to bed till Lilly sends her there."

Dublin. 1902. "A splendid *Oireachtas* week! If all the delegates feel as much on fire as I do, something will come of it.

"I went with Edward Martyn to the Pro-Cathedral this morning to hear his choir, which I thought beautiful. We were given two seats between the altar and the Archbishop's throne, and the Archbishop sent afterwards to say he would be "greatly disappointed" if I did not come with Edward to lunch. So I found myself at lunch, on His Grace's right hand, the Lord Mayor at his left, and various ecclesiastics making up the party. The A.B. was very pleasant, asked how my book was getting on, and talked of Raftery's poems, did not mention the theatre except that he had read *Twisting of the Rope.*

"How the Craoibhin is alive after this week I don't know, he is a wonder, and he went to service at Trinity College Chapel this morning. Traill asked him if it was to consult the oracle. A.E. had a talk with Moran last night and asked why he attacked you, who were doing such good work for Ireland. He put it on religious grounds.

"Father Dineen is rather sad over your letter; is not afraid of your writing anything very wicked yourself, but 'if literary men are to think they may write just what they like what will the end be?' I said I didn't know what the end would be.

"I really think you ought not to send your own books for review to Irish papers in future. They have evidently an idea they should be a sort of truffle dog where you are concerned and scent out heresy wherever concealed.

"If Literary Theatre breaks up, we must try and settle something with Fay, possibly a week of the little plays he has been doing through the spring, at the Ancient Concert Rooms. I have a sketch in my head that might do for Hyde to work on."

1904—to W.B.Y. at St. Louis. "Saturday night brought a larger audience to the Molesworth Hall, who were quite astonished at the beauty of *Shadowy Waters,* and some giggling young men behind me were hushed almost at once, and I heard them saying afterwards how beautiful it was. I liked it better each time. I should like to hear it once a week through the whole year.

"Saturday . . . Last night the plays went off even better than the first night. *Twenty-Five* was much better done, the actors being less nervous. Sir Anthony McDonnell was there and enthusiastic. He asked me straight out if a performance could be managed before the King, I said I thought not, but would consult Fay. I am rather vexed, he had hinted at the matter to your father privately and he had already proclaimed it to five of the company! Colum was sitting near, and I brought him into the conversation and he said presently he saw the eye of some important member of Cumann-na-Gael fixed on him in suspicion. Sir Anthony said he himself would be under suspicion if he were seen talking to two such rebels! Many thanks for the San Francisco papers, the portraits rather bewildering, the descriptions like those of criminals taken by the police. I expect to see an impression of your thumb in the next!

". . . If I come round to the Gaelic scheme I should be inclined to work it up in Galway, writing plays for them instead of for production in England. I might be more useful to the country. But I won't till I feel the want is a real and not an artificial one.

"Old Hayes O'Grady talks of my last book, *Poets and Dreamers,* as *Poets and Schemers!*"

February 1904. "I am distracted trying to get Synge's 'properties' together for staging *Riders to the Sea.* I luckily took the flannel myself to the Gort dyer, and found he was going to use Diamond dyes instead of madder, and only 2 lbs. arrived. No real Aran caps can be got so far, or tweed. I am trying to stir Synge up to go to big shops and look for something near it, and get as little as possible for this time and the real stuff after, for *Riders to the Sea* will probably be a stock piece for a long time and ought to be well staged. However, I am promised a spinning wheel tomorrow."

25 February 1904. "We, Synge and I, are still struggling with the things for his play. He has to deal with Aran Islanders, I with nuns, and I do think they might run a race backwards! However, yesterday, 'An ass and car went into the country' and brought back the spinning wheel in triumph, and it has been sent off by the nuns, but the red petticoats aren't ready yet, and the pampooties will have to

be made in Dublin, a very good thing too, there is no object
in bringing local smells into the theatre. I have had a very
sad letter from Mark Twain, from Florence. His wife is
wasting away. He asks about you and is very sorry not to
have been in America to welcome you."

1905. "I have had a letter from Synge asking me to go up,
as he wants dresses, etc., for *Well of the Saints*, looked after,
so of course I will go tomorrow."

Dublin. 1908. "Henderson in this morning, has just seen
Professor Cole who proposed that the Reception Committee
should take the Abbey for one evening, giving free seats to
the whole British Association . . . Henderson proposed
Kathleen and *Well of the Saints*, but he chose *Hour Glass*,
'said it was someway more scientific, *Riders to the Sea* and
with *Rising of the Moon* or *Spreading the News*. I think it
will take *Spreading the News* to cheer them."

December 1905. "I think my bad stars were justified at
White Cockade. The audience from patriotic motives would
applaud Sarsfield and almost hissed King James, who retired
in a sulk and wouldn't appear at first curtain. And Hugh
Lane came, in very bad humour, is having some gallery
worry, and abused the wigs and the costumes and said the
whole thing was like a charade and couldn't get it into his
head that King James wasn't meant to be serious. He says
Mrs. Duncan told him that Gerothwohl came on Wednesday
to lecture on Victor Hugo, and Markiewicz arrived and said
'This won't do, this room is wanted for rehearsals' and turned
him out . . . I am going to a rehearsal of *Hyacinth* bye and
bye."

In my work at the Abbey Theatre I had often to act as
peacemaker. I find a copy I had sent to Yeats of a letter to
an actress who had taken some offence. "If you have been
vacillating and have taken offence easily I believe it is
because your health has not been good and that you have
been overworked and overstrung, and I feel that so much
of that work was helpful to the enterprise we have at heart,
besides a great personal pleasure to the writers whose plays
you interpreted, that you should be treated with great
gentleness and consideration. I cannot believe that Mr.
Yeats's letter was an 'insult', I think you must have misread
it. He is impatient sometimes—all men are so, they have a
different nature from ours; we are born with a capacity for
the nine months childbearing, for the endless child rearing.
But I think you will confess you tried his patience, indeed

you must have tried it very much to drive him to anger
sweet Fedelm against beautiful Dectora . . . Whether you go
on acting for us or not I should like to see you some day
in our 'Seven Woods', making friends with squirrels and
the birds."

And to Yeats about some other trouble: —

". . . You must talk the whole matter out with Fay. I do
not want him to threaten to leave. I feel sure you should
talk to him as you would to me (only with more of the
harp string in your voice). I believe he is quite reasonable
when not suspicious."

Again: "Your letter was a relief. One forgets what a baby
she is, however greater personages are as silly. R. says Patti
refused to sing at a concert unless her name was put on the
posters twice the size of some other artist's, and then the
other insisted on having his name enlarged, and when the
posters came out they were fit to be read by giraffes.

"Oh, this theatre! 1.00 o'clock now, and I have been
writing on its affairs ever since breakfast time.

"I came round before matinee. M. wanted to speak to me
'to tender his resignation' in consequence of Miss N. having
insulted him during *Cross Roads* last night, before the
stagehands, asked him what the devil he meant because he
had missed his cue . . . Also he was knocked down in *Cross
Roads* by O. instead of being choked sitting in a chair, and
this he seems to think was revenge, because he had at some
previous time hit O. with the pipe he throws at him in
Workhouse Ward. I spoke to Miss N. who accuses him of a
variety of small offences connected with cues . . . P. has been
up a few minutes ago asking for a rise of wages. On my way
back to the auditorium I met Miss Q. and asked her about
the quarrel. She says M. is desperately in love with N.
He has been much worse since Mr. Yeats did her horoscope
saying she was to marry a fair man. He walked up and down
saying, 'I am that fair man'. She went to him the other
day and told him he was foolish and ought to put N. out of
his head, but at the end he said, 'I know very well that
you are in love with me yourself!'

"Anyhow, I am like Mr. Pickwick between the two
armies at the sham fight, and am afraid to come behind.
However, a clergyman last night turned to me after *Rising
of the Moon* and said: 'That is better than ever—I have
seen it many times and always liking it better' and after
to-day's matinee a man passing out said, 'You ought to be a

proud woman, a proud woman' . . . The sun shone in at
rehearsal and I felt quite sick of thinking of Coole and all
I have lett there, and the last flowers of the garden, and
little grandson holding out his tiny hands . . .

"All lambs at present however long it may last. Miss B.
came yesterday quite amiable . . . C. came in before she
had left and they did not speak to each other or recognise
each other's existence. When she went I told B. that my
sister, Mrs. Waithman, and I used to have quarrels when
we were children until our mother insisted on our kissing
each other afterwards, and we disliked that so much that
we gave up quarrelling. If it goes on I think I must
supervise a reconciliation.

"S. wanted to be let off his fine for unpunctuality on the
ground of having been kept late through attending Mass
on the Feast of the Circumcision, I refused, saying he could
claim compensation in the next world, which he agreed to!
I wonder if it would be possible to let the chief actors have
a turn at production? It would keep them very much alive,
working in competition, and I fancy we could get respect
for producers *pro tem* . . .

"I had not read Gerothwohl's speech till after you left
and thought that sentence most excellent about the theatre
he was connected with, having worked 'for Art and a thinking Democracy'. It is just what we set out to do, and now
we are giving in to a stupid Democracy. I think the sentence
should be used when we can."

1909. Coole. "I will spend all January at the Theatre but
I must be back 1 February to do some planting here. I am
quite alone with December and the bareness of the boughs."

A.E. says C.'s plays won't be taken in London "unless he
sells his soul—Buchanan sold his soul and got £8,000 a
year for it", but I am afraid managers will ask for other
goods besides the soul! He is anxious about Sinn Fein, as
A. Griffith is overworked and there is no one else to do
anything. He thinks the Gaelic League is losing ground,
and three different people have told him it is because the
vital element in it would have been those who were ready
to fight the priests, but whenever such a fight was proposed
Hyde came and smoothed it down, and so Hyde is being
accused of having killed the League.

1908. "The Company know very well that parting with
Fay meant parting with American hopes, so we are not at
all responsible to them . . . I don't grumble for myself,

because I am only a play-writer by accident, and I don't mind about Synge, because he was always against America, and because he was so wrong at Christmas in putting off the crisis, but I feel very much that your reputation has not got the heightening it would have got in America if we could have kept together."

I had been translating some of Molière's plays and wrote from Galway, 1908: "I am very sorry, but I am afraid *The Miser* may not be ready in time. If I get very well so that I can work all day I may run it through but I have still three acts to do, besides starting to type what I have done from the beginning now the business had come. I shall know better tomorrow. I am ashamed, for I have never failed before to be up to time, but these last days I have gone to pieces, from want of sleep chiefly, and could do nothing, so I came here last night to try a change and landed into a headache, so this is a lost day, but tomorrow I expect to be quite well."

Dublin. January 1909. "Just back from rehearsal and cheered up on the whole. *The Miser* goes very well and will be quite safe when Wright and Power, the servants, have been given a little business. Synge says it was quite different tonight, they all waked up in honour of me . . . As to *Baile's Strand* it will be splendid . . . The only real blot at present is the song. The three women repeat it together, their voices don't go together . . . one gets nervous listening for the separate ones. I got Miss A. to speak it alone, and that was beautiful . . . W. Fay most enthusiastic, says you are a wonderful man, and keeps repeating lines—says, 'There is nothing like that being written in London.' Miss — seemed very low, W. Fay is anxious to give her another 2/6d. or 5/- a week . . ."

St. Stephen's Day 1907. "I went to the workhouse yesterday boldly with my toys, tobacco, etc., and was received with great glee by the inmates*.

"The Sister told me that the old men had refused to decorate the rooms until they were assured I would not be kept out. A very old woman asked Margaret if she knew me, and when she said yes, the old woman said, 'If you know Lady Gregory, God is with you'."

---

*The workhouse children had not been allowed to come for their usual day at Coole because I had refused to take off Synge's *Playboy* during the riot in Dublin.

To Robert Gregory—22 February 1907: —

"*Jackdaw* is being rehearsed and is as dreary as morning rehearsals of a farce always seem."

24 February. "We were quite astonished at the success of *The Jackdaw*! It was splendidly acted. Fay quite a new character and an astonishment. F. Fay very good as Tommy Nally, but all good. There was great laughter, especially towards the end, then great applause and actors applauded once or twice; then cries of 'Author!' till I bowed from the stalls, but they would not be satisfied, went on applauding and shouting 'Lady Gregory' till at last I had to go round to the stage and had a great reception. I daresay it was partly to show we were forgiven for *Playboy*.

". . . Magrath, whom Yeats found in a lively state towards the end of the evening, said with great enthusiasm, 'This is not a farce like *White Cockade*—this is a comedy—a high comedy like the French!' The actors in great humour. Fay quite deferential to me."

Coole. 25 February. "Here I am, a lovely day to arrive, but the weather has been very bad. All looks well so far, Sarsfield and Roosevelt with their ribs well covered. Sandy, Tim says, 'was sitting just like a fairy on the top of the steps all day long knowing someone was coming'.

"I had been often envying you of late, being able to paint your pictures without depending on others in any way, but when I saw my sketch so well filled out the other night, I felt there are compensations."

To W.B.Y. 1907. "Margaret writes me from Paris some 'most flattering and exciting' compliments paid to Robert's work by Blanche. It will help to give him belief in himself, which is all he wants. She says, 'Blanche said (which of course Robert argued) that like all English drawings it lacked construction and was probably nothing like the model, but it had reached the high-water mark of artistic and intellectual merit, and that it would do credit to any old master', and he snubbed unmercifully one of the students who said it was unfinished; and said it was an absolutely finished work of art, but not crowded with meaningless detail.

"A Professor at Johannesburg sent me Transvaal papers yesterday containing some chapters of a translation into Dutch of *Spreading the News*, which was to be performed in Pretoria on 6 December. They are forming a theatre on the lines of our Irish National Theatre, and have acted

Medea, done into Dutch verse from a French version. He quotes in the paper your determination to keep the theatre non-political. It is really encouraging to find appreciation so far off. W. Fay is now enthusiastic about *Rising of the Moon* and wishes it had another act. I have finished and typed second act of *Scapin* and begun the third. I think it will go very well . . ."

April 1908. "*Scapin* was a real success. There was a fine pit, and fair stalls, and the laughter and applause was constant and genuine, and the few I spoke to were quite astonished at it. To begin with the scene (your doing) was very good, pleasant to the eye and something new, and the costumes looked well. Sinclair was splendid, quite a revelation, not so triumphant in the sack scene—for it would take a very experienced actor and a lot of rehearsing, but in other parts he was wonderful, he seemed a Manannan in disguise playing with mere mortals, such an easy consciousness of inexhaustible power. Power also splendid; in his stamping scene the dust rose in clouds, which increased the effect . . . It was very encouraging. Carton wanted to know what is the original of 'Blobby tears'. D. was patronizing at the beginning but rushed round to congratulate me afterwards . . . I am going tomorrow morning to rehearse *Workhouse Ward*, to be produced 20 April . . .

". . . I spent yesterday morning at theatre, rehearsed *Workhouse* and changed cast of *Hyacinth*. Synge lunched with me. He is most enthusiastic about *Scapin* (not being by a contemporary) and thinks it would do for London . . .

"C. is frankly wanting a larger audience to see his plays. He reminds me of King James, his mind 'unalterably fixed' on sitting on the fence. I think we must press on sixpenny seats. If we had a good pit the actors would be pleased and we could leave the stalls to natural growth. If we 'paper' strangers we shall offend our friends, and if we 'paper' our friends they will never pay again."

August 1909. "I came early to Theatre . . . I was depressed by the rehearsal of *Blanco Posnet*. One can't judge much of the acting as they don't know their parts but the positions are as bad as they can be. Feemy sits at centre table in the old heraldic attitude, and is unmoved by all that passes . . . I said she must try to be a little wickeder, and put out her tongue at, or make a face at, Posnet, and that she should stand with arms akimbo and only sit down in defiance when he has insulted her . . . however, I will do my best to get something done . . . They all stand in a row or sit in a conventional drawing-room attitude . . . I must get at Blanco alone and try to waken him up. I don't think there is any chance of getting home tomorrow.

"Poor T.W.[1] What a comfort he isn't in Ireland to add to the general languor . . . I enclose his letter, a discontented meandering here and there . . . I myself am rather a withered branch, I think I had lived on hard work in Dublin, and being out of the shafts brings collapse . . ."

Galway. 1909. "I got in the young carpenter I saw here one evening and asked him to do a bit of his part for me to see. He could only remember a speech of Dinny O'Dowd, which he did fairly well. Then he said what he really liked was such a part as he had in Deirdre—Deirdre by someone I had never heard of. He acted a bit, a dreadful play—'What ho!' literally, and he did it in the most dreadful manner, like the worst recitation possible, has been taught by an engineer who stage-manages here. He would like to come to us, as he feels all time wasted that is not acting. He says he is steady as a rule but sometimes a bit foolish on a Saturday night . . . A bone man has just been singing in the street and I had him in to learn to do the bones—they are just bits of ribs from a butcher's—it would double the singer's effect in Dervorgilla if they could do them.

"We can get the theatre here for Whit Monday and Tuesday. I asked the proprietor if the people drank as much that day as on Saturdays but he said 'No, they take it very light on that day'.

"I wouldn't give that play this season, I think we have given our peck of dirt, but it is vigorous and might be useful in the autumn, especially if we keep verse and classics going. If we don't, we shall end like the Literary Society, with an audience only for variety entertainments, and Henderson will have to engage that conjuror he took there last year.

"And I don't think we ought to let it be said that we were kept out of politics. We were not political at any time, we have never put down the red carpet or put up the green flag; as to our independent action as to Playboy and Blanco, we did not consult anyone at any time as to our attitude . . . it was your principles laid down in Samhain we were to be bound by, not any utterance of others."

[1] T. W. Rolleston.

My home life went on much as usual: —

"A tramp told me yesterday there is a star coming that will burn up the world on the fifteenth of May, 'but I don't believe it myself, for if God had a mind to burn up the world what would he want with a star?'

"I have backache today and had to get up at 6.00 o'clock and walk about the room it was so bad, but my prospectus says one mustn't mind pain coming in extra places. It is the medicine roaming about in search of the enemy!"

To R.G.: "I came home yesterday—a deluge of rain as I arrived, but it is fine today. Sarsfield looks well and quite fat. The puppies Tim and Fan also look well. Togo is in Mike's house. Mike John has an exciting story of a fox which carried off one of Murty's traps in the skirting, and which Pat found in the wood, where all the trees are down from the storm, a week later when out with Mike looking for a woodcock. It was under three trunks of trees and was 'terrible wicked, biting at the trap', but Mike heroically climbed up in a branch and shot it dead—unfortunate beast.

"Now he says a fox carried off a trap 'from the hobble field on a Sunday night, and in the morn he was met by Tommy Hynes that was bringing the post, running along with the trap on his leg. Tommy Hynes told Jim, and Jim went to the yard and told Murty, and Murty sent to tell Tom, and Tom came to the House to get Sandy (the terrier), but Sandy was with myself in Inchy that day, the day I got the three brace of cock. There was no word of him Tuesday or Wednesday, but on Thursday at 2.00 o'clock a little brother of John Healy's saw him near Raheen. He told John of it Thursday night, and John told me Friday morning, and I got Pat and Sandy and rowed over in the boat, and went to the place John's brother had seen him and searched about for half-an-hour, never expecting to meet him. At last I heard Pat in full cry, and I thought it was a hare he was after and I put Sandy on the trail, but when I got to the field beyond, by Jove, there was my brave fox, himself and Sandy rushing at one another. Pat came upon them and the three of them had a wrestling match for a while, and they would have killed him but that I called them off and shot him myself.' His only regret is that he forgets the day of the month but thinks he can find it out in consultation with Mike."

To W.B.Y.: ". . . Dublin doesn't seem to improve, and

won't till some vigorous new life sweeps the idlers and
triflers away. I have just been in the garden, it is more lovely
than ever in this Indian summer, but now I am going to
church, I have two souls to think of, for Margaret said she
would go if I did.

"I am out nearly all day at the planting, in spite of
rheumatism, and am cutting and compressing *Image* in spare
moments.

"My idea of a play is not advanced enough for anything
like writing. I must wait to hear music and see plays, and
for London to make my blood circulate and go to the brain,
I have been out on grass for too long.

"I am trying to work, but only just ploughing a field,
and not very confident of any crop from it . . .

". . . Hyde has come on from a meeting at Ballina in
tremendous spirits. Two years ago when he was at a meeting
at Castlebar he had to take a room and entertain himself
with a mutton chop. This time the best room at the hotel
was put at his disposal for nothing and he was entertained
by priests at a dinner, which began at 4.00 o'clock and
ended at 7.00 o'clock, began with champagne and ended
with punch, after which he says he made the best speech
of his life, but he says he has not seen it reported yet. All
the priests abuse William O'Brien and the U.I. League, and
declare every grass farm to be had is snapped up by the
U.I.L. officials and that £50 was sent to one publican to have
free drinks going on one occasion . . . One of the priests, a
young Father Z., was full of a discovery he has made of
Shakespeare having been written by Bacon; declares that
he has found the anagram. He recited innumerable verses,
rhyming, made out of Shakespeare's blank verses, and he
says he has discovered that a great many of his characters
are from real life and a great many symbolical. Hyde asked
him who the two grave-diggers in Hamlet were, and Anne
Hathaway and Ben Jonson; Horatio is falsehood, Hamlet
truth, and they were friends till death, because falsehood
and truth always go hand in hand. He says a great deal of
Shakespeare's inner life also comes out, and that he has
discovered that Anne Hathaway was Ben Jonson's servant,
and also his mistress, which Shakespeare didn't know till he
had married her, and then they blackmailed Ben Jonson
till he died. He is anxious to publish his discoveries, but at
the same time is afraid to leave his MS. with a publisher,
lest they should steal his secret. All this quite unexpected

from a priest at Ballina . . . Now off to church and then Hyde is afterwards to address a little meeting at the gate.

"If they are going to run the Irish Literary Society on political lines where will the literary element come in? The Society will die of respectability and lie in a respectable coffin . . . The Sunday Hyde was here he asked me at lunch if I knew the proverb 'Ma's maith leat, etc.', 'If you wish to grow old you must drink hot and cold'. I told him it was the text I had taken to meditate on during the Archdeacon's sermon, for I take it to mean if you want a movement to succeed you must use all sorts, and I had applied it to the I.L.S. and its intolerance.

"It is very sad your friend should have taken such a step for what seems so slight a motive. It shows how hard it is for any of us to escape from our surroundings. What did it matter to her what Paris people thought or to me what Gort (Galway) people think, and yet there is an imperceptible influence closing round one all the time—a net to catch the feet.

"We have had a flying visit from A.E., only one day and night, and by ill-luck it was wet, so he was disappointed of sketches, only began one or two which he may finish afterwards. It was a great joy to see him, though he says his agricultural lectures have dimmed his soul for the time . . . He has not had time for writing himself of late . . . His chief indignation is turned just now on some smart ladies, who wanting to get up a presentation to Lady Betty Balfour, asked Hughes for a design of a figure of Erin, a statuette. He sent it in, Russell says, a beautiful little figure, sitting— but someone said the head should be looking up, not down, and someone else suggested the figure should be made standing up and they wrote and requested Hughes to attend their next committee meeting and receive suggestions, which of course he refused to do; so she has been given a piece of lace instead. This is what they consider the encouragement of Irish Art!"

1903. "Dr. Bonn, that little German, who was doing a book about Ireland, is back and says the Gaelic League is becoming a most dangerous political organization.

"Russell is delighted to hear of MacGregor's downfall. He never could think much of a man who had to look at his watch to know what was going on in the other world.

"To-day I am having the school children (a Christmas tree—and Heaven has sent a bleary-eyed piper from the county Donegal who will enliven the proceedings . . . I see a great troop of children 1.00 o'clock) and must go out to them.

"March has come like a white lion, for the ground was covered with snow this morning. The poor lambs who were born on primroses don't know what to make of it. I am 'holystoning' the deck to-day but working through accumulations of letters and trying to answer some of them . . . You know the sailor's commandments, 'Six days shalt thou work as long as thou art able. On the Seventh holystone the deck, and scrape down the cable—! ! '

"I noticed an elm tree looking rather ragged, and found the ground under it piled with twigs and blossoms nipped off. I looked up and saw a squirrel with a twig in his mouth. He growled with rage as he dropped it. Will you ever say they are harmless again?"

A.E. had written to me in August 1902: "Tell Willie that the thing I prophesied to him has already come to pass. A new generation is rising, to whose enlightened vision he and A.E. are too obvious, our intelligence backward and lacking in subtlety. The first of the new race called on me a couple of days ago. He wanted to see whether I was he who was to come or was he to look for another. He is going to look for another, but he sat with me up to 4.00 a.m. telling me of the true inwardness of things from his point of view. He is a young man aged twenty-one whom we shall I think hear of later on. He writes well, too well indeed for such a boy, and his reading ranges from the mediaeval saints and theologians to the sacred books of the East. He seemed to quote with equal fluency from Ibsen in the original and the early Franciscans. His name is Joyce. I will hand him over to Willie as one of his men when he comes up to town. He is too superior for me. I belong to a lower order of thought than this spectre of fastidiousness . . . I will hand him over to Willie who may be the Messiah he is looking for. I am not."

15 November 1902. "I have seen Joyce who came up to see me last night. His mind is quite made up for Paris. I think from any ordinary standpoint his action is wild, but with boys like Joyce there is always the overshadowing powers to consider. I think he has genius of a kind and I like his pride and waywardness. I have written to a friend in Paris about him but cannot be sure if anything can be done by him. Joyce's father is too poor and I think Joyce

can only gather up money together to pay his fare over and keep him for two or three weeks. I think it likely if he could hold on for six weeks that he could find work. He is well educated, knows French and German and Italian and has a degree here. The cost of a medical degree in Paris is much less than in Trinity and if he could get tuition he would be able probably to pay his way. He can live cheaply and I can, through art students, put him in the way of finding financially possible lodgings. I hope he will be all right. The more I know him the better I like him, and though I wish he could remain in Ireland still I would like to see him prosper somewhere. I am sure he will make a name somewhere."

I wrote to Yeats from Coole in 1902: "Joyce has been writing to me of his plans and I have him much on my mind. I am afraid he will find it hard to make a living by lessons in Paris, where there are so many English teachers. But I daresay Paris may be a good place for him—there is not enough give and take in Dublin—everyone, as Magee says, gets into a clique or two (perhaps he includes us!)."

And again, "I wonder if Joyce has written to you. Poor boy, I am afraid he will knock his ribs against the earth, but he has grit and will succeed in the end. You should write and ask him to breakfast with you on the morning he arrives, if you can get up early enough, and feed him and take care of him and give him dinner at Victoria before he goes and help him on his way. I am writing to various people who might possibly get him tuitions and to Synge who would at least tell him of cheap lodgings . . .

"It is a pity I can't go to Dublin to see about the *Hour-Glass*. I was allowing myself to think of it as a pleasant break before I began to roll my heavy Christmas snowball uphill. But it can't be helped, and I must console myself by counting the extra words of Finn I am able to do. I know you think that makes up for everything!

"Robert, Tony and Harvey have gone to shoot at Tillyra and I have done a nice bit of Finn, though interrupted by a visit from cracked Mary looking for a Christmas box, and from the Loughrea clockmaker who you may remember carried off all the clocks the day he came in the summer, and has only to-day brought them back! We must be working for eternity here, for we are certainly not working for time.

"A woman yesterday said, 'God save the mark!' I don't remember that before in living speech."

1908. "Very sorry indeed to hear about poor Z. It is a terrible fate for any man who had any pride of intellect. And you will feel it though you did not see much of him of late. One misses any of those who know and understand what one is doing. Understanding seems sometimes even better than sympathy.

"I rather tremble at the idea of the rewriting of the sermon in *Where there is Nothing*. I have just come from A. Daly's. He preached on the race course and theatres and intends next Sunday to preach on materialism, 'a difficult subject but I hope to make it easy enough for the mind of the youngest child here to understand'. I was just watching a little child about five in the choir, fidgetting till the turkey feather in its hat went into Miss G.'s face. I wonder if he will make it understand materialism."

16 April 1903. "I have just come home. The place sadly changed by the storm of 26 February, the accounts of which had disturbed me in London; ten lime trees down between house and stables, and the big lime to the left (greatest loss of all) and the big evergreen oak on front lawn, and some parts of the wood laid flat. Many thousands of spruce and larch down."

To A.: "A quiet Easter. R. busy reading for Greats. Yeats here, busy and I busy helping him with scenario of *Seanchan*[2] and arranging all the folk-lore. I did a little Finn but hadn't time for much.

"On Easter Sunday R. and I had a talk about his profession. He would have tried for the House of Commons Clerkship to please me, but his heart was in art. I told him he should choose as he liked; and he has chosen art. I am glad he has so strong a bent towards anything, and especially so high a profession, though the temptation to take work easily may beset him. But I believe he will succeed. He has imagination and love of this countryside which has not yet found its expression.

"It is a nice beginning to a dark day getting your essay, a great many thanks, I have cut it and played with it, and tried how it looks in the bookcase next *Paul* and then brought it back to the writing table . . . But is not *rythmous* on p. 336 a misprint? The motto for to-day in the almanac

[2] The earliest title of W. B. Yeats's play, *The King's Threshold*.

is 'What boots it at one gate to make defence and at another to let in the foe'—which I think is applicable to proof reading.

I did 700 words of the Sons of Usnach to-day, 900 yesterday, but I have just been counting that I still want 6,000 words, so there is plenty of work before me. I only work at it when quite fresh, but I do a lot of odds and ends to prevent the house from becoming some day a pyramid of waste papers. Store lists today, and I am going to Mulkere about an Irish class for the people. Puppy has killed a goose and two hens and we have administered a whipping and are watching the effect. 2,500 little trees just arrived to supplement those we have."

May 1905. "Estate business has settled down, but I have had a very bad fortnight and could not have left home for a day, I just prevented war with the grass farmers, and I am very much in want of sleep.

"All well with the tenants, a very nice letter from Father Fahey. He says, 'through your great kindness we have the old kindly relations preserved. I can assure you of the gratitude of the tenantry and of mine.' I am managing the sawmill at present owing to trouble by M.M. I have just written a long letter to Redmond about preservation of trees. I want to get those along Kiltartan road, for instance, vested in a rural council, that tenants when they purchase may not cut them down."

1907. ". . . A slight nervousness about the advent of Margaret, happy as I am about her it must make a difference, I had been so free and unquestioned."

1908. "I drove home last night from Athenry in a 'heavy frost' and felt rather like the camel taking up its burdens again. The little trees in the nurseries have been planted slanting and will get a permanent bend, the tenants' cases re. revision of rents, are to be tried this month. Two of our tenants nearly killed each other yesterday; a man was killed outright near Gort on St. Patrick's Day (all land) all the malefactors were let off at Assizes except the man in woman's clothes who fired two shots, and he has only been given two months."

1909. "I am sorry to say I shan't be able to get over for the performances . . . I was just ready for plays and talk and sociability, but I must think of Finn's music (the music that is best with Finn is what happens) and keep my courage up . . .

". . . I had a faint hope of getting to the plays tomorrow but it is quite impossible. I have to be out all day with my woodmen or things go wrong, the silvers are put on stony ridges and the Scotch in the shade and the wrong sized trees everywhere. I am getting rather tired of outdoor work, and the weather is boisterous and the Burren hills are covered with snow . . .

"Sarsfield yesterday 'beat Mayo, Clare and Limerick and a part of England getting his first two prizes'. Amongst those beaten by him and Robert were two new English M.F.Hs.

"E. tells me that before Gort Horse Show, where as you know prize animals are decorated, the Kilbecanty priest preached on Sunday on the immorality of bulls and stallions being dressed up with bunches of ribbons."

To R.G.: "John Shaw-Taylor came over yesterday afternoon, and the evening came on so stormy that he came back from the stables after saying goodbye, to say he had ordered his horse to be put up and would like a bed. We had quite a nice evening, going through the clauses of Sinn Fein policy. He has full belief still in the Reform Association, but I can't say I think much of it . . . Such a funny creature appeared the day before yesterday, a young man, hair curled, apparently with tongs, moustache, gold eye-glasses, black suit, black worsted gloves, cloth cap . . . I found Marian discoursing to him at the door, evidently not knowing what room to conduct him to. He was a Gaelic League organiser in Gort, quite intelligent but with a nervous laugh. He has got up a class of 200 in Gort, and was quite interesting to talk to, has been reading *Cuchulain* and asked leave to put some of it into Irish. I felt rather proud in the end that Ireland was capable of producing such a completely new type! He had worked on his father's farm till about five years ago."

To A.F.: "Y.X. has been talking of the Maid-of-Honour's life. She gets a nominal £300 a year, really £270 because of Income Tax. This barely pays half the clothes she must have; she had to get twenty-seven dresses for the Empress's visit. The old Queen's maid-of-honour said she couldn't dress on it, and she gave them £100 extra each out of her own purse, but the present Queen can't afford that. They must go to the Queen in the morning, put in photographs or do odd jobs, or if there are people staying, must show them round, for in the evening visitors are examined as to what they have seen, china, etc., and if they hadn't seen enough the Maids-of-Honour catch it. In the afternoon they may be

wanted, but if they don't hear by 4.00 o'clock they may go
out. They used to have tea-time free or have it in their own
rooms but some asked so many guests and gave trouble that
now they must have it with the Queen. They go to balls
with her, but mustn't dance before supper, and she leaves
after supper, but then when they have seen her home they
may go back to the ball with anyone they like and enjoy
themselves. After the opera also, having had supper with
the Queen, they may go to balls. She 'loves' the life but
gets bored sometimes, and Ladies-in-Waiting have been
resigning, Lady Z. whose husband can't bear her away, and
others who have daughters coming out. Lady A. is in disgrace
for having talked so much after she left and Lady Y. who
talked after she had resigned and said she refused to 'sit
with the servants'. They have often to sit in the waiting
room with the pages because of the Queen's unpunctuality.
She is so deaf she reads the movement of the lips, and hates
people putting their mouth near her ear, for then she can't
see it."

1909.   "We have bitter weather still, a wind, like steel
knives and think if it would change little Richard would
be quite well—he is really well except for a sneeze or a
cough now and again, very seldom, but each time having a
curious physical effect on me, as if all my bones had gone
or melted . . . However, I stayed all day with the planters
yesterday.

"Froissart is going to be a joy, and there's plenty of dialect
in it, Miss G.'s favourite 'for to' for example . . . I look
forward to *The Golden Helmet* very much, there is joyousness in it that the verse will bring out. I was thinking last
night we ought not to be discouraged by the difficulty of
getting a shape to our plays, when even God makes so many
clumsy bodies for so many a poor soul."

1908.   "Oh yes, I can idle, but in the right place. I idled
more than you in Italy, and only wanted to exist and look at
the olives. But at home one must work or die or one's mind
must, and I am lucky in having changes of work, in and
out of doors. I have been helping to carry little Richard
round a sunny field this afternoon.

"I went to *The O'Flynn* in London; Tree baffles description. Fay looked so distinguished, the only gentleman in the
play, though it was a poor part. I do think we have killed
the Stage Irishman and that this was his wake. There was a
poorish audience."

Yeats wrote sometimes from Dublin giving news of the Theatre: —

Dublin. December 1904. "There was a strange scene last night. After the plays were over R. took off his coat to fight young W. because W. had not put a mattress on the bed in *Shadow of the Glen* and his bones were sore from the bare boards. Fay imposed order in great style and to-day there is peace.

"Synge is taking the reorganization very much in earnest and will I think make a good director. He has a plan for bringing a Gaelic company from the Blasket Islands, we will have to consider it presently. Synge would stage-manage it himself.

"Fay says our company is in great humour and already takes great airs and looks down on all amateurs. H. said yesterday that he had noticed that ours is the only Dublin Theatre with an audience of mainly men."

February 1908. "Sean has settled the business of his pipe for himself. He has weighed in his mind the pleasure of smoking against the pleasure of preventing those who hire the theatre from doing so, and has chosen the more intellectual pleasure. I am pleased.

"M.'s play still continues to puzzle and to bore audiences. Hyde was there last night and after abusing it vigorously raised a loud cry for author. I said, 'What are you doing that for?' He answered, 'I have never seen him, I want to know what he looks like'. He kept on till he got some applause out of the benevolence of the pit. The author said to me presently, 'How well it went!'.

"Someone writes offering us a play which 'unlike those at the Abbey', he says, is so constructed as to admit any topic or a scene laid in any country. It will, under the circumstances, he says 'do good to all'. I am sending him *Advice to Dramatists*.

"I saw Martyn to-day and explained what we wanted of him . . . He says he approves of us, admires us, but that he would have to interfere with us if he were Lessee. I asked if we had done anything he objected to and if he had disapproved of *The Playboy*. He said, 'No, nothing that Synge or anybody else said about the women of Ireland could annoy him in any way'. He then said he had disapproved of our fight over *Blanco*. He said he thought there was nothing wrong in the play or in anything we said or did, but that large numbers of people went to it because they thought it was an improper play. He said he couldn't approve of that. He thinks Horace Plunkett would do it but says that everyone will say Lady Gregory is the proper person to be Lessee."

12 February 1909. *"Kincora* got a good reception. It thoroughly satisfies me. I did not like it when you read it to me but now I delight in it. It is a fine play, noble and beautiful.

"I have written little of late, I have been reading Nietzsche, that strong enchanter. I have read him so much that I have made my eyes bad again. Nietzsche completes Blake and had the same roots. I have not read anything with so much excitement since I got to love Morris's stories which have the same curious stringent joy.

"When A. P. Watt rather advised Bullen, and not only on *The Celtic Twilight,* but for the new books, I told him that Bullen was anything but steady. A. P. Watt merely muttered something like 'the better they are the more they drink' or 'the better the man the more he drinks' or something equally surprising, coming from such a white-haired Father Christmas.

"You will remember *Mosada,* a bad early play of mine— which is in the Usheen book, and which was printed in a shilling pamphlet long ago in Dublin. Well, a shabby relative of mine has prosecuted a borrower and got £5 for *Mosada* which the borrower had lost. I wrote a letter for the prosecuted man, who called on me, saying it was worth, so far as I knew, nothing (I said I thought there was no demand). However, my miserable relative got Elkin Matthews to say it was worth £10. I heard nothing of the case until the borrower came to me on the morning of the trial.

"My alchemist is very anxious to have a look at that book of Magic. He says it is really valuable. Could you bring it when you come? He has just made what he hopes is the Elixir of Life. If the rabbits on whom he is trying it survive we are all to drink a noggin full—at least all of us whose longevity he feels he could honestly encourage.

"I have been writing hard at Spenser and think it will be done in a few days. I am only using what I dictated to you as what Moore calls 'a smoky ceiling'. It is full of suggestion and has fine passages I think but it is too incoherent. I am basing the whole thing on my conviction that England up to the time of the Parliamentary Wars was the Anglo-French nation and that the hitherto conquered Saxon

elements rose into power with Cromwell. This idea certainly
makes my essay very striking, it enables me to say all kinds
of interesting things about that time.

"He was bound to marry some kind woman with a confident will. For I have noticed that every woman who sets
eyes on him wants to see that he gets regular meals.

"I saw *The Vikings* last night. I liked Ellen Terry in it
and liked moments of the play altogether, and it all
interested me. Craig's scenery is amazing but rather distracts
one's thoughts from the words. The four verses I made for
them are spoken with great energy but are quite inaudible.
There is a kind of lyre to which he is supposed to speak,
and out of that amazing lyre comes the whole orchestra,
wind instruments used and all, and every one of them makes
the most of its unnaturally loud voice. I suggested that the
fortunes of the theatre might be restored (house was nearly
empty) by their imitating *The Times* and having a prize
competition, and £5 a piece for words heard anywhere. This
amused Miss Craig, who had tried to get the verses properly
spoken. The play is not, I think, a really very good play.
One constantly finds, when one pierces beneath the stage
tumult, that the passions, or rather the motives, are conventional. There is a touch of melodrama in the characterization.
These heroes alternate between impulses of very obvious
Christian charity and more barbaric energies in the sudden-
est way. I felt that Ibsen had not really grasped and unified
the old life. He had not clear thought or emotion about it.
Of course, however, the play is better worth seeing than
anything else that has been here this long while and for that
reason is failing. Ellen Terry, whom I saw for a moment
after it, said, 'Well, it is a fine play to have made a failure
with'. She added that everybody there had got a good living
wage out of it and so it did not matter—everybody but she
herself who would get nothing. She impresses me a good deal
by her vitality and a kind of joyousness."

May 1903. "I am sorry about Mrs. A.'s stupidity . . . If one
is doing anything, one always rouses anger somewhere or
somehow among the people who are not. If for no other
reason than that every movement of life is a movement
against platitude, and platitude is their breath of life. I
dined with the L.'s (East Indian) last night, and it seemed to
me that our Irish movement has for a chief privilege that
it has all the platitudes against it. Somebody said, 'What does
Ireland want? Why does she not tell us what we are to do?

She cries out and yet, though we are anxious to do whatever is right, she does not tell us.' I said, 'Nothing simpler. Clear out.' The conversation languished after that for a little, until somebody began by saying how bad politics were for a country and so on. Then somebody spoke of the poverty of the Irish people being caused by their large payments to the priest; I said that the land laws and over-taxation had something to do with it, but the speaker who was Lady L. stuck to the point, because she had once known a butler who came in for £300 and she concluded he gave it to the priest 'because nobody ever found out what he did with it'. I behaved well but would not have been able to do so much longer. I was fortunately going on to Clifford's Inn where I lectured to a fine audience on the Psaltery."

London. May 1905. "I saw *Beckett* last night. The Beckett scenes are good, though not so good as I thought, but the rest is sentimental melodrama, with nothing to act, and therefore no acting. The worst and most sentimental melo- drama scene rouses the audience to enthusiasm it seems, it was the bit where Beckett appears from behind a tree in time to keep Queen Elinor from stabbing Rosamond. There was a child, and a garish wood and much sentiment, and I heard the people behind me saying from time to time 'How beautiful'. Irving played finely but I think more out of manner and habit than in old days, and all the rest—well, they were a good deal below our level. With good parts they might have done well. The construction of the play is childlike and the character drawing of the stage.

"All the papers have been abusing Ben Jonson's *Silent Woman*, which I thought the most joyful, laughable, wonderful cup of youth—my uncle was not less delighted than I—it was all so simple and radical. I wish you could have seen it, it is even nearer to folk than Molière. He even went so far as to say, 'Why, this would be a success in the town of Sligo'."

15 January 1907. "Masefield's play is still a standing horror here. I said to him last night I heard people crying and he replied, 'Oh, so did I, but that's nothing, a lady in the Upper Circle was sick'.

". . . I have had an always growing desire to get away for a time every year from Ireland altogether, that is to say, from all that moves me to criticism. I am still living on thoughts got in Italy a year ago, and letters from Normandy. My imagination is full of Ireland when I no longer see it, and it is always the worse for every sight of Dublin . . . My work seems changing, all of recent work, including the new lyric, is grotesque, almost comedy. I hear Mrs. Old on the stairs and so must stop."

London. 16 June 1906. "Nearly all my time in Edinburgh I was absorbed in Mrs. Traquaire's work and find it far more beautiful than I had foreseen—one can only judge of it when one sees it in a great mass, for only then does one get any idea of her extraordinary abundance of imagination. She has but one story, the drama of the soul. She herself describes it as captivity, the divine descent to meet it, its liberation, its realisation of itself in the world of spirit. She is herself delightful, a saint and a little singing bird. For a time she was forbidden to paint, and some of her most beautiful work, a wonderful mortuary chapel at a hospital, was done in stolen hours, painting at the greatest possible speed because the hour was short. After dinner everyone sat listening to Mrs. Traquaire, who as it were, sang a little happy childlike song. I have come from her work overwhelmed, astonished, as I used to come long ago from Blake, and from him alone. She differs from all other modern devout painters but him in this supreme thing. The nearer she approaches the Divine the more passionate become the lines—the more expressive the faces, the more vehement is every movement. To the others the world is full and the spirit empty."

July 1906. "I hear that Swinburne has made a wild attack on me in *The Athenaeum*. I have not seen it and I daresay I will not as I don't mean to reply and don't want to annoy myself uselessly. Ellis wrote something perfectly polite and just—he is a Swinburne enthusiast—in the big Blake book about Swinburne not understanding some doctrine of Blake's. Swinburne thinks I am the author of this passage, and now he, in reprinting his own Blake book, avenges himself by a furious attack apparently upon everything Celtic. He says, Cockerell tells me, that the Celt has no imagination and puts the emotions above the reason, which is a curious complaint for him. I have had a most indignant letter from my father about it, in which he tells how, in the old days, Swinburne could not read out one of his own poems without bursting into tears three or four times. There would be no use replying, for it would only lead to more violent rhetoric of the sort there is no reply to.

"I went yesterday to the New Gallery and heard Rothenstein praise the Mancini portrait of Lane; a man who was with him disliked it. Rothenstein said: 'If I were wearing seven hats I would take them off before it'. He then said, 'It is horrible, it is like a bad Italian building, something baroque, but all the same it is magnificent, inimitable'."

December 1907. "I send one of the John etchings. I admire it very much as an etching and shall hang it on my wall with joy, but it is, of course, a translation of me into tinker language."

December 1908. "I had supper with Mrs. Campbell last night. Sometimes she says fine things. (She had been talking of poor S.), she said, 'The difference between men is not manners, or good breeding even. It is that some seem to have loved princesses and some sluts.' And then a little later she said, 'I could walk to the cannon's mouth, but I could not endure a husband who bored me; that would be heroism', and she added, 'a great Duchess said the other day, "I married my husband out of curiosity and endure him out of politeness.'"

2 March 1909. "There has been a friendly long note on latest volumes of my collected edition which says, 'the stories in volume five are as good as any of the poems'. These stories are the Hanrahan set*. Did I ever tell you that Masefield told me that a comparison which he made between the style of the first and later versions caused him to alter his own style completely? It taught him to make his style simpler and stronger. He added, 'modern style is like a steaming marsh, full of rank words', or some such phrase."

25 November 1909. "Last night I was put next the Prime Minister and had a god deal of talk with him, or rather I chattered a good deal about nothing and pleased Gosse by doing so. I imagine I was selected as the most unpolitical person who could be found. My start in the evening was bad. Gosse whispered to me, 'Mind, no politics' and then introduced me to Lord Cromer, whose first sentence was, 'We had a very interesting debate in the House of Lords this afternoon', to which I replied, 'Oh, English politics are to me what a racecourse is to a child. I take sides by the colour of the jockey's coat and I often change sides in the middle of a race'. After that, conversation rather languished, and somebody told me afterwards that Lord Cromer has no interests outside politics. However, this was before dinner, and at dinner the Prime Minister began by questioning me

*Every word in *Red Hanrahan* by I.A.G.

about Stephen's poetry which he has been reading, and then
about our *Blanco* fight. The other questioners were the Lord
Chief Justice, Alfred East, some other Academician whose
name I forget, Anthony Hope and Austin Dobson."

December 1909. "A.T. thinks Gosse wants to discuss the
matter of a pension for me. I said, 'Tell him that if the
French land in the West of Ireland I won't undertake not
to join them if they want me, so there will be no deceit
about the matter.'

"I am writing in the British Museum where I have been
trying to read Swinburne. Even the things that once excited
me beyond measure seem to me mere rhetoric, but I know
I must be deceived. I suppose that one tires of all over-
abundant things.

"X. has done measureless mischief in this business. He is
a logician and a logician is a fool where human life, which
is a thing of emotion, is in question. It is as if a watch was
to try and understand a bullock."

May 1905. "I am very sorry about the land trouble. This
must indeed be very painful to you but do not allow
yourself to act weakly for the sake of peace. Life in its last
analysis is a war of forces and it is right it should be, for
it makes us strong and I think that is the root of happiness—
certainly not to fear is.

". . . A day comes in everything almost in which one has
to fight, and wisdom is not in avoiding it but in keeping no
bitterness when the day is over. Of course, one should do
all one can for peace and see that one is just, but after
that—firmness and an easy mind."

22 May. "I certainly do not think you have been weak, I
think you have done entirely right. I should have known
that your alert will would find some positive thing to do—
that you would never merely be inactive. I am always so
afraid of the sensitiveness created by imaginative culture
making one over-yielding, that I perhaps push things the
other way. I have always been anxious over this purchase
question, afraid it would bring you trouble. It is a relief to
know all is well for the moment."

Dublin. January 1909. "The day I left London Mrs. X.
amused me. I said something about having a long play to
do, and being rather tired of plays. She replied, 'Yes, sir, one
has to take fortune when it comes, it never comes twice. It
came to me and I let it go. The richest gentleman in our
village said to me, "If you won't marry while I live I'll see

you never want". But I married and here I am with an old
man to support, and he only lived thirteen months, and my
mother sees me but she says, "You *were* a fool!".' She grew
up a long way from Father Fahey."

12 March 1909. "L.[3] says of the ghost I am to investigate,
'I saw a furniture van arrive at the house one day, in ten
days the house was empty again. Miss Mitchell passed early
one morning and saw an old woman, the caretaker, out on
a window sill clinging to the window sash. The ghost had
driven her out, and a policeman was trying to get her down.
But pious Protestants say it's not a ghost; the house is
opposite a convent, they say. And it's the young novices
screaming that is taken for a ghost."

February 1909. "Last night at the Arts Club I found Orpen
and some others sitting down to dinner and joined them and
we talked. Presently they got up to go and I was startled to
see a clean knife and fork and no plate before me, I appealed
to the attendants to know whether I had eaten my dinner
or not. One said yes and one no. Presently they came to say
that they had both come to the conclusion that I had not.
I then ate my dinner and was rather late at rehearsal. I am
not yet certain on the point, however."

4 February 1909. (Written during my illness.) "On Friday,
after I had been thinking all that day and the day before
of what the world would be without you, I made a little
scrap of verse. I mean by sickness and the scales that when
one we love is ill we weigh them against a world without
them:

> Sickness brought me this—
> Thought in that scale of his:
> Why should I be dismayed
> Though flame had burned the whole
> World, as it were a coal
> Now I have seen it weighed
> Against a soul?

. . . After this we will all work that you may rest. You have
laboured for us all with uncomplaining heart.

"I begin to think of you again with a more peaceful mind,
I am only anxious when I say, 'I know she is working'. I
wish little Richard were old enough to look after you[*].

"When the burden is too much you should leave to others

---
[*]He was four weeks old!!
[3] Either Lily (S.M.) or Lollie (E.C.) Yeats.

the finding of a remedy. Everyone is at his best in an emergency, and a certain number of emergencies are necessary to shape a soul."

6 March 1909. "I saw Synge to-day and Hyde. Synge looked very very ill. Hyde is nearly well again. He said he once congratulated Martyn (then President of Sinn Fein) on being leader of a party and Martyn said, 'I don't like it at all, I want to do my own work'. Hyde said (President of the Gaelic League), 'And so do I', on which Martyn said, 'And the worst of it is that we would not be left there for five minutes if those fellows thought we liked it'. Do not force yourself to work. Ah! If I could only give you my gift of idleness!'"

8 March. "I saw Synge again, very pale and thin but not, I thought, gloomy. He gives me an impression of peaceful courage whenever I see him, yet I thought he was certainly doubtful of the result. He says the doctors tell him very little. He has asked them if they mean to operate again but they do not seem anxious for an operation."

23 March. "I have just met M. in the street and I saw by her face that she has had bad news. She told me that Synge is now so weak that he cannot raise himself on his arm in bed and at night he can only sleep with the help of drugs. For some days he has been too weak to read. He cannot read even his letters. They have moved him to another room that he may see the mountains from his bed.

"Now I am going to the St. Enda school for the plays, as that is one of the few places where we have friends . . . (Later) I have just come from St. Enda's, both *The Lost Saint,* and O'Grady's play were very well staged, and O'Grady's play *The Coming of Finn* really touched me. The waiting old men of the defeated clan seemed so like ourselves."

24 March 1909. "You will have had the telegram Henderson sent. In the early morning Synge said to the nurse, 'It is no use fighting death any longer' and turned over and died. I have seen Mr. Stephens, he says Synge wanted to see me to make some arrangements about his work. He says he wished that his shares in the Society should be divided between you and me . . . I am to speak on Synge at the Club tonight and have no thought of what I am to say.

"I have been busy all day about poor Synge's affairs. I went down to Kingstown at the request of various people to get leave for a death-mask to be taken with a view to a bust, but the coffin was closed . . . I left orders for wreaths, one from the Company with 'To our Leader and our Friend, Good Bye', and one from myself with 'In memory of his courage and his gentleness' and this sentence from Proclus, 'The Lonely returns to the Lonely, the Divine to the Divinity' . . ."

Sligo. 20 September 1909. "I write while I am waiting to set out for my uncle's funeral, I think there is much real sorrow. My sister told me that all day the workmen and pilots were coming . . . They had come to see 'Master George' their imagination going back to the time when his father lived . . . Jack has been telling me that George knew every man in his employ and had the gift of getting discipline without ever being harsh; that men would be let back after a time if they had done wrong and so on. That he would as it were degrade a carter to the ranks, he would take his whip from him and hang it on the wall and then when the man was penitent give it back and the workmen understood this way and liked it. Every case was decided as an indepen-dent case and with sympathy."

Dublin. 29 September.   "The funeral was very touching, the Church full of the working people, Catholics who had never been in a Protestant Church before, and the man next me crying all the time. I thought of Synge's funeral, few there, after some two or three who were not enemies drawn by curiosity or conventional images of gloom. The Masons (there were eighty of them) had their own service and one by one threw acacia leaves into the grave with the traditional Masonic good-bye, 'Alas my brother, so mote it be'. Then there came two who each threw a white rose, and that was because they and he were 'Prince Masons', a high degree of Masonry. It was as George would have wished, for he loved form and ceremony."

In May 1909 I had a holiday and wrote to Yeats from Ca Capello, Venice, Lady Layard's house, "I am in my old state room, at the corner of the water floor, looking through four ivy trellised windows at the sunlight on the water, and only hearing the splash of cars and a gondolier singing. The room is full of beautiful furniture, and when I came in last night, at midnight, from the long dusty journey and found the Italian housemaid who has welcomed me for twenty-five years, on the steps to kiss my hand, and other servants bringing Chianti in a flask and soup in a silver bowl, it felt like fairyland!

"Yesterday, Ascension Thursday (and Robert's birthday), as Lady L. and I came out from church, there was a sailor on the landing with a note from the Royal Yacht which had arrived, asking if the Queen, the Empress of Russia, Princess Victoria. a party of twelve altogether, might come to lunch at 1.00 o'clock. Lady L. said, 'Impossible'. I said, 'Possible'. She said, '2.00 o'clock'. I said, '1.30', and so it was. We came straight back and rushed to the kitchen, and the cook wasn't fussy and said it would be all right. Then I took the gondola and went to ask for the loan of the Curtis's servant, and sent to look for flowers. At 1.30 they arrived, the Queen looking younger than when I had seen her a year or two ago, not only her complexion, which one could understand, but the modelling of her face so good. Her hands, however, are knobby and her voice is very deep and guttural. She shook hands with us all and is very unaffected. She was very simply dressed, a white blouse, black and grey skirt, small hat with purple bird's wings. A Russian Prince (attending the Empress) was next me at lunch, and the Queen next him, and she talked to him in French about the noises of Naples and the quiet of Venice. Then, when eating some, she stooped across and said, 'What lovely peas!' and she admired the wild strawberries. She leaned across again and said she was so glad the Campanile was being built, it made such a difference on arrival seeing even a bit of it up. A little later, talk was flagging, and someone noticed the dessert plates, and I turned mine up to show the Cantigalli cock, and then the others turned theirs up, and the Queen was indignant that there was not one on hers, and the Prince gave her his, but she said it was not a good one, and exchanged it with someone else. The Empress seemed very lively, more so than Princess Victoria who had Admiral Keppel on one side and Lord Stanmore, who is staying here, on the other, and answered him in monosyllables. But after lunch she came and talked to me about Venice brightly enough. The Empress whirled round in walking through the drawing-room as if from sheer high spirits. The staff took every opportunity of the Royalties being out of sight to sit down. Then after smoking and coffee, more curtseys and handshakes and they left. The Queen and Empress are inseparable and the time the Empress is to leave is kept a secret, as there are said to be anarchists about looking for her."

To W.B.Y.: —

"I went to tea at Mme. Wiles and Lady O. was there,

and began to talk about George Meredith whose death is in
the papers and said, 'There had been an address given him
on his seventieth birthday signed by thirty; and I had gone
in to dinner with ten of them.'

"Good accounts of my little Richard, and a bit of paper
with scratches by his own hand. I hope the crosses on it are
for his grandmother and not for him, if come they must.

"Gresley, the American Ambassador, said the Duchess of
Aosta had made him write to Roosevelt before he left
America, saying she must see him when he came to Naples,
as she is such a sportswoman, and Roosevelt consented. But
when they set out for her villa he grew more and more
restless and said, 'Why should I go? They only look on me
as a sort of wild beast, and I can't keep up my character by
biting off the Duchess's nose.' However, they got on very
well after all.

"We went to the Montalbas. Clara showed me her pictures,
full of sunlight and colour, and she said she admired so
much what I am doing, and asked about you. She is the first
person I have met here who knows I have ever done anything
at all. Very good for me, and indeed a rest, no character
to keep up!

"The son of the man who is over the Exhibition wanted
to talk English to the Queen all the time she was there, and
Enid heard him telling her, 'that picture is by a died artist'.

"William O'Brien was laid up in the hospital and Enid
sat with him a couple of times, and liked him, but didn't
quite agree when he said, 'If you get five or six thousand
people together and speak to them you may be sure their
instinct will be a right one.'

"I think you would like Venice just now. It must be good
to live sometimes in a place where all is beauty. I think I
have never seen it so beautiful. I am getting quite well, at
least I think so, and expect soon to want to be at work . . .
And being here again, with old friends and surroundings,
it often seems as if the last ten years had been a dream, and
Cuchulain and the theatre had never existed. Ireland seems
extraordinarily far away—but when my courage comes back
I shall probably feel more ready for it. The Piazza is beautiful
and the bronze horses are shining—Why not put yourself
into the train? You would have a fortnight.

"That letter of poor Synge's is touching, coming now when
we thought we could have no word from him" (the letter
asking us to decide which of his MSS. should be published)

. . . "If they could let us have all the papers we could go
through them quietly at Coole and not have to judge in a
hurry.

"I meant to settle a plan of life here, but it is too warm
and sleepy. My mind is asleep."

1 June 1909. "I think I only want London as a tonic, a
month twice in the year would be enough, at a good time,
but not much chance of it.

"My mind is torpid and I talk small talk. Yesterday at
lunch we talked of wedding presents, and I said perhaps,
though fewer, there were better ones given long ago; the
people who gave spent something on a present. Now, one
sees in the papers, 'The Duke and Duchess of Draggletail—
a buttonhook'. Mrs. F. says, 'The Duke of what did you say?'
I said, 'I was only generalizing—I said Draggletail.' She says,
'And you say they gave a buttonhook?' and meditates. I had
said to her before that I looked on Bridge as a sort of
Esperanto, to give people some general means of communica-
tin, and she said, 'What is Esperanto?'

"There was a very pretty party in last evening at Lady
Helen Vincent's; a Roman courtyard and a wide stone staircase, lit by moonlight; a gallery or room 145 feet long, the
walls all hung with rose-coloured striped velvet. Lady Helen
looked lovely, with an emerald tiara. I talked for a while
with Lord Percy—but I only wanted to look.

"Lady Layard says the pictures here were saved from the
fire at the Pantechnicon, where they would have been but
that they had been lent to Ireland, Doyle having asked for
them.

"Two young Herberts came, one, Mervyn, to stay (from
Embassy at Rome), the other, Arthur, from Macedonia. He
is in Parliament and said, 'It is the most interesting time
since '48. A wave of Socialism now as there was of Revolution
then'."

I wrote just before leaving Venice: "The London life and
that abroad with my husband (but for the constant pain of
leaving Robert) went by swiftly and delightfully. Yet how
little remains from it. I should not care for it, I think, again.
I see it was the gradual absorption in Irish things, first
Cuchulain and then the Theatre and playwriting, that drew
my mind away from the everyday babbling, and probably
makes me dull in general society. And anyhow I couldn't
afford it; expenses greater, and the Dublin time all I can
afford. My Venice visit, ending to-morrow morning, has I

think restored me to health and strength, I sleep at last, and hope my mind may revive when I leave. Yet I could not bear much of it, it is too far from my world. And Ireland still seems far off and a place of disappointment. *Playboy* this time has gone off without opposition, except, Yeats writes, from the Nationalist papers. I am reading Burne Jones's *Life,* and that company of artists seems to me the happy life; they understand one another's aims . . ."

Then in June I wrote from day to day from 1 Old Burlington Street, where I was staying with Sir Arthur Birch and Una: —

"The plays last night . . . The Court looked rather empty, but they say it is the best house we have opened to. *Dervorgilla* went rather flat, just got its double curtain. Miss Allgood had lost her voice and said it like a recitation . . . Friends paid me compliments and Rothstein seems really to like it, 'beautiful and noble', and another man said the last sentence was so fine, and was much amused when I said I had written it under Augustus John's drawing of me!" (The swift unflinching terrible judgment of the young—.)

"*Playboy* went very well. *Cathleen ni Houlihan* went beautifully, and afterwards I went round to the Shaws' box, and G.B.S. said his wife had 'howled' all through, and he said, 'When I see that play I feel it might lead a man to do something foolish' (I was as much surprised as if I had seen one of the Nelson lions scratch himself). Then he went on to talk of Synge, 'a big man'.

"*Workhouse* went splendidly, and though I didn't think *Hyacinth* went as well as usual, Herbert Trench after seeing it asked for it for his Repertory Theatre, and asked, 'May I write to you about it?' I said, 'yes', and that I should like him to ask Fay to act, and he said he would.

"I told him, however, I thought *Workhouse* a better play, and that it could be done better with its small cast, and he came again to see that and he brought his manager to introduce to me. He thought Workhouse the freshest, *Hyacinth* the most amusing, wants both, wants *all* my comedies, and I still said, 'Yes'. And I was vexed at Yeats objecting, for I want to earn a little money.

"But now I have changed my mind. I see it would weaken our own theatre if my plays were taken from it, or even made common here. And it is better to keep it going with as much energy as possible to the end, and I have written to Mr. Trench I won't give them. *Workhouse* is the greatest success I think. Mrs. Patrick Campbell is 'raving' about it, and sent Lord Charles Beresford 'to cheer his sad heart'. But on the night he came there was only *Hyacinth* and he shook with laughter and said to Sir A. Birch going out, 'I came here for a laugh and I am going away crying'. On the Friday night the applause and cries of 'Author' went on till I had to come on the stage, and I was cheered just as at *Rising of the Moon* at Great Queen Street Theatre. But I was better pleased at Yeats's lecture on 'Sinn Fein' last night, to find the opposition to *Playboy* had died away, and that we got nothing but approval for having gone on with it. It is seeing how our Theatre has helped to educate these young men and women that makes one wish to hold on. We have helped towards the freeing of their intellect.

"We have done so well (though a very small profit I'm afraid) that the plays are to be brought back after the three days at Oxford for three more performances here. And then Mrs. Patrick Campbell offered to come if we could stay another week and play *Deirdre* with one of our people again and that will be a draw.

"I went to a big party for the Press representatives at Stafford House, enjoying the pomp and vanity of the world again, and the beautiful rooms and dresses, though I felt a 'revenant' and saw shades, Lady Reay, Meresia Nevill, Sir A. Lyall, I think I have had the best of it, not being here all the time. The Duchess wonderful, with the right word for everyone. To me—'What a splendid notice in the *Morning Post*!'.

"Last night I went to the Friday *salon* there, the ground floor rooms and a small party, but pleasant enough. Some of our audience had come on, and some talking of the plays and one doesn't feel 'astray' when one has a topic, and Yeats was happy with a folk-lore lady, a Campbell who told him of the angel of death appearing as a Peacock in Scotland, with a human head.

"I lunched at the Lionel Phillipses', millionaires, at ugly big Beit House. Mrs. Phillips is quite ready to start the Johannesburg gallery at Hugh's bidding. He has already got her to buy three Steers as a start. She is going to get money from other millionaires, £50,000 if she can. She says very sensibly, 'When there is a man like Mr. Lane to be had one should use him'.

"Mrs. Pat was delighted when we told her of our visit to

the Z. play. She said, 'Isn't it great rubbish?' and Yeats said, 'Oh, I don't mind it. As someone said about the Order of the Garter, there's no beastly brains about it.'"

To W.B.Y.: —

"The dinner at Old Burlington last night was very pleasant. I had on one side a Grant Duff, First Secretary at Madrid, and who liked talking of his father, and hearing family news. He is very proud of his wife and hoped to make her an Ambassadress. On the other side was a judge, Sir Charles Darling . . . It was my business to be pleasant, and I enlivened him repeating the old verse (I had read it the other day in my diary), 'Deptford is for Darlin, and not for Wilfrid Blunt', and that set him off on reminiscences of his election. He had thought it most unfair W. Blunt being in gaol, it got him so much sympathy, and had been much afraid of his winning, but having a large meeting of non-conformists he had taken out, 'A book of sonnets, did you ever hear of it?' and read a most improper one to some woman, and had said, 'That was written by the man who wants you to elect him. And who did he marry? The grand-daughter of Lord Byron, the man who wrote *Don Juan*.' He said he made a point of never speaking to any of the Irish members the whole time he was in Parliament.

"There was a great deal of money at the B. dinner party, and I had on my other side Mr. K., said to be the richest man in London, very big and fat. He told me Sargent has refused to paint any more portraits, so I suppose he has been refused. I am very glad we settled for you to be done. I don't like you to have only second best in anything.

"I went with Una Birch to meet Hugh Lane at his Chelsea house which is being panelled and floored and decorated. It will be beautiful. He is a wonder!

"Then on my last day in London I went down to Wheat-hampton to Wilts to see Bernard Shaw. He met me at the station and we went to his house, a rather uninteresting little villa (it is a rectory), in the sort of country I hate, all green hedges and red villages and parish churches and no horizon. We talked the theatre matter out. He is very sympathetic, says we have done wonders, and the players have come on very much, and agrees that Synge's plays could not be given by any English players, and it is unlikely they will want to give them. But he calculates we ought to have £5,000 to our back to apply for a new patent, and says

he can't take it on himself, for he had to pay £6,000 for the
Granville Barker Vedrenne experiment that failed. It would,
he thinks, have succeeded if only his plays had been done,
but he insisted on other plays by new men being put on,
and that knocked it over, and Barker had to pawn every
security he had. And he won't come as Director, for he never
will do that unless he can work at a thing, 'and the irony of
it is, I am engaged in trying to build up a theatre in
England'. But he will think it over, and help us if a means
should arise.

"He thought we would get help from the Corporation,
but I said we should lose our independence doing that, the
first thing they would do would be to forbid *Playboy*.

"He gave me *Blanco Posnet* and says the Censor objects
to the sentence, 'I accuse Feemy of immoral relations with
Strapper', not to the so-called blasphemy. He spoke of Dublin
and the dislike he had had to re-visiting it, and how at last
he had come in a motor, and hadn't minded coming in, as
it were, by the back door. It looked to him just as before,
the houses had never been painted since, and the little shops
had eggs in the windows, with mice and rats running over
them, and rubbish that looked as if on its way to the dust
heap. I said there were at least two new bright spots now,
our theatre and Hugh Lane's gallery, and he cordially
agreed, and said the gallery was wonderful. I said good-bye,
and got back in time to get my luggage from Burlington
Street, and off by train from Euston.

"It was rather a shock at Mullingar to meet Shawe-Taylor,
and find she had never heard of the plays . . . But R. and
Margaret are delighted, and Richard is splendid and all is
well.

"Not settled to work, but collecting mad dog scraps for a
possible comedy. Read Lord R. Churchill's *Life*. It is with
political parties as with our relations, they don't mind one's
opinions, only one's independence."

When Yeats came to Coole I asked if we couldn't put on
Blanco Posnet as the Censor has refused leave for it in
London, and he said, "Yes", and Shaw has agreed. That
should be a help to us and I don't know anything that would
show up British hypocrisy so clearly as the rejecting of this
play, when we look at the many that are passed.

As to our tragi-comic fight with Dublin Castle when we
put it on in August 1909, I have given the story of it in

Our Irish Theatre.

To W.B.Y.: —

1910. Saturday. "I had enclosed telegram telling of the King's death and asking if the theatre should be closed, and answered, 'Should close through courtesy'. Do you approve? It was very provoking, its being a Saturday, but I suppose the poor King would have put it off if he could."

In the June of the Coronation year, 1911, we took the plays again to London. I stayed with Hugh Lane at his Chelsea house, and wrote from there: —

"There has been a good deal of business about the proposed American tour. Then, in what I may call accidental work, on Tuesday night when I arrived at the theatre I found that Robinson had forgotten to send *Mixed Marriage,* announced and booked for the next night, to the Censor, and it was an awkward business, as besides our *Blanco* fight, we have been rather worrying the Censor about our *Nativity Play,* and this gave him a chance to get a knife into us. I remembered that Tree was on good terms with the Censor, having supported him at the enquiry, so I telephoned to ask if I might see him on urgent business and had an answer, yes, but that he was just going on to the stage. So I went off in a taxi to His Majesty's, and after a while Tree appeared as Malvolio, pompous at first but very amiable when he found what I wanted, and told his clerk to try and get Redford on the telephone, and began a sprightly conversation telling me how he dreaded the day when he would be called 'The Evergreen Tree', and that the sign of old age coming on was when everyone tells you how well you are looking, and when publishers begin to ask for your reminiscences. I said to him that I should not so much mind this Censor muddle if we were English but that if we had to put off the play everyone would say, 'These slovenly Irish!' and he smiled and said he had once taken a letter of great importance to the G.P.O. in Dublin to buy a stamp, and the clerk said, 'We are out of stamps here but you will get one at the public house opposite'. (I thought to myself, that couldn't have happened to him but to the O'Flynn.) Then his secretary came to say Redford was not in the telephone directory but Tree luckily remembered the address and sent to call him. Just as Redford was sent for to come to the telephone, Tree was called off to the stage, and I was left at the one end with Redford at the other! I had to explain what had happened and give my name, however he was very amiable and said if I would send round the play he would try and pass it in time, I guaranteeing it was all right, and we got the permission next day early.

"Thursday night when I got to the theatre, I had a message that Bernard Shaw could see me if I came round to the Little Theatre. I had been deputed by the agents to find out how much he would demand for *Blanco,* which he is giving us leave to take to America, and they were afraid he would ask a prohibitive price. So I went there, and found *Fanny's First Play* going on, and went into his box, and between the Acts did my business, and he did not name a price but said I might set my mind at rest, that it would be all right. I lunched with him and Mrs. Shaw yesterday. Delius the musician and his wife there. Music talked of. Delius said there was no English composer. Shaw said there was, there was Elgar. Delius didn't think much of him, said where would he have been but for Wagner and someone else. Shaw said no one could be the same after Wagner as before, but that Elgar had personality, that he had moulded it to express the feelings of the English country gentleman, but there it was. He said Elgar had been to see *Fanny's First Play* one night, a play which the average country gentleman would be shocked and pained by. When he was leaving at the end, Granville Barker said, 'Won't you stay and make the acquaintance of the author' and Elgar said, 'Certainly I shall not. I should particularly dislike doing so!' Delius said the English had no music in them and no emotional quality. Shaw said, 'they have a great deal of emotional quality but they are too cute to show it. They don't allow themselves to think. If they were to sit down and think before going into their wars of aggression for instance, they could never carry them out, but they don't think. Cromwell knew them when he said, "The man goes farthest who doesn't know where he is going". The English have so much emotional feeling that they are the dupes of Art. In France a man reads a novel with one eye on the author, knowing it is an invention, in England a man is taken in by it. Take the Bible for instance. It has wonderful style, is a wonderful piece of literature, and for that reason the Englishman believes it must be inspired and true.' He had been in the Isle of Wight at a little inn and had found there a copy of *Robinson Crusoe* and had read it through with delight. The landlady was pleased and said it was her husband's favourite

book. Shaw talked of it and said it was a wonderful invention.
The landlady was sad and said, 'Oh, sir, don't say that to
my husband, he would be miserable if he was told it was
not all true!' Delius attacked Strauss, said he was jerky and
irresponsible and ought to stick to comic themes and pantomime tricks. Shaw defended him, and said at the end, 'I can't
but feel that all you have said of him has been applied to
G. B. Shaw!' which was just what I had been thinking.
Shaw very full of the old Flemish music. He says all music
is careless now, just like painting. The old painters were
workmen. But if you come out of the Academy now having
looked at the work of these gentlemen painters you think,
as you look at the carriages waiting at the door, 'Those
carriages were painted by workmen, but not the pictures
inside'.

"After lunch he went through the proposed American
agreement with me and said that if we had to pay any share
of the royalties on *Blanco* he would give us back that share,
very good of him*."

On Monday evening I went to Miss MacNaughton's
(author of *Lame Dog's Diary*). She received in the hall, and
we sat there and then went in to supper. I was between
Maurice Hewlett and A. W. Mason . . . they were all
excited about our plays, and there was pleasant talk. Miss
MacNaughton herself is very bright and amusing.

"I went to a lecture by Ellen Terry, she looked very nice,
dressed all in pale [blank in typescript] and standing in a
mass of flowers and plants, and she spoke so well and had
her audience in hand. We went to the reception on the
stage afterwards, very crowded and badly managed. Ellen
Terry came tired and asking for something solid, and they
kept offering her little cakes, and at last one sandwich left
on a plate, and then two or three more left on another
plate, and she asked leave to sit on the table, she was so
tired, and they never got her a chair. I asked her to come
to our plays and she said, 'Oh, yes, and you must put on
that little hospital piece (*Workhouse Ward*) again'. (I remembered her having stood up and clapped when it was out once
before.)"

1910. "I went to lunch with Lady Tweeddale. It was like
old times hearing about Southwark, which she has never

* He was as good as his word, giving me a cheque for our theatre
on our return.

deserted. She got up a fund to help Mr. Dodge to retire, as he was breaking down from overwork, and he and his second wife live very happily at Norwood.

"Last night Granville Barker came and sat in my box. He is rather worn out with the production of the gala performance, (I have heard he and Tree had had words on Saturday and that he had walked off). He says he was rehearsing Tree in *Julius Caesar* as Mark Anthony and that Willard insisted on having that part, and then Tree took part of Barker business and put in some of his own and Willard ditto, and the crowd was played the mischief with, and anyhow wanted a fortnight or six weeks more rehearsing. He says at the command performance every star brought his own prompter and Tree two! They had had a committee meeting at which Mrs. Campbell had been so violent that no one but Trench had taken her part which he had done by saying she was known to be a hell-cat. They were to have done the *Man of Destiny* at Downing Street for the King, but for some reason not explained it was considered dangerous and taken off. Barker is very anxious to see the *Unicorn* acted, and Poel was in my box just then and said how much he had admired it when he saw it in public. Barker didn't like the audience laughing during *Well of the Saints*, but Poel said it was quite right, that where there was wit one should laugh.

"Hugh had told Mrs. Asquith I was staying with him, and she said she was so anxious to meet me, and he blew my trumpet and told her Mahaffy had said to him I was the cleverest woman in Europe and one of the most charming. Then he suddenly remembered himself and said, 'Of course he cannot have known you', but she said, 'Oh yes, it is the people who know me best, my most intimate friends, who speak like that of Lady Gregory.'

"Colonel Leslie said Shane would not condescend to stay for the Coronation but had gone to Ireland 'where perhaps he hopes to be crowned himself' . . .

"Yesterday Coronation Day. Lady Ardilaun had asked me to bring some of the players to see the procession from her house in Carlton House Terrace . . . I got there just as a heavy shower began, but we had an awning, not like the Admiralty people opposite who had to put up their umbrellas. But the rain soon cleared off and the Guards began to march past, and one had a fall just at our stand and a policeman caught the horse and was cheered, and a banjo player delighted Sinclair more than anything else, and he hoped the cinematograph working opposite would put us in, and means to go to all the shows till he finds if they did. The processions looked very fine with the background of trees, all preparing for the Cinderella coach with the right cream horses. The King looked quite imposing in his ermine cape. We watched the crowd for a little time, and then lunch was announced, and such a good one . . .

"At Lindsay House I was having tea at 5.00 o'clock, and a lady was announced, and it was Ellen Terry, to say young H. had asked her to his party at the Theatre, and she didn't like accepting without knowing if I would like it. She is very *Grande Dame.*

"Lady H. is getting up quite an enthusiasm for the King and Queen, 'they are so good'. Prince John intends to be King some day and was asked if he would behead his brothers to that end and said, 'I would'. The Prince of Wales says there are three things he will do away with when King; the cutting off of puppy's tails, the use of bearing reins, and *Sin.* On the Coronation Day the Prince of Wales used his precedence to get into the carriage first, and Princess Mary kicked his shins and put him aside and got in before him . . ."

To W.B.Y.: —

"I am sorry Mc's play[4] should have been so coldly greeted, but I think it is partly our own fault, it would have got a better welcome a year ago—We have been humouring our audience instead of educating it, which is work we ought to do. It is not only having so much X. and young authors, it's the want of good work pressed on, and I believe the want of verse, which they respect anyhow . . . I think the pressing on of Synge's two plays is the best thing we can do for this season. We have a great backing now in his reputation. In the last battle, when we cried up his genius, we were supposed to do it for our own interest."

[4] Probably *When the Dawn is Come* by Thomas McDonagh, first performed 15 October 1908. The first typed version has "M. Connell's play (1909)," so it is possible she was thinking of *Time* or *An Imaginary Conversation* both by Conal O'Riordan and first performed in 1909.

XXV

ROOSEVELT

"The Interpreter then called for a man-servant of his, one
Great Heart."
                                                Pilgrim's Progress

    Concerning brave Captains our age hath made known
    For all men to honour, one standeth alone
    Of whom o'er both oceans both peoples may say:—
    Our realm is diminished with Great Heart away . . .
                                                Rudyard Kipling

SHOULD EVER my memory come for judgment, I think that
against whatever faults and failings may be in the writ my
advocate may ask countenance for me through the worthiness
of my friends. I used to say of a sister, more gifted as I think
by nature than myself, but one who for conscience' sake surrounded herself with ministers and preachers without
intellectual force or training, not only of her Church but of
many Evangelical sects, that the main difference between
us was that she liked to live with her intellectual inferiors,
I with my superiors. And at home with husband, with chosen
guests, or abroad with many friends whose names are in
these pages, I have been fortune-favoured and have had
my desire.

I have told of kind words written by Mr. Roosevelt, at
that time President, about my first books of Irish legend. And
he wrote to me later from the White House when I had sent
him my *Poets and Dreamers* . . . "I did not know I had
spoken publicly of *Cuchulain*. By the way it started me in
reading various Erse epics, and I took two or three off with
me on my recent trip.

"One thing may amuse you. The children's nurse, who
was also my wife's nurse from the moment she was born,
and the two maids—who like the nurse are valued family
friends, are all Irish, and it appears that quite a number of
the stories you relate were already known to my children,
having been told them either by the nurse or one of the
maids; and Mrs. Roosevelt herself knew one or two.

"I was much interested in the Boer songs. The farmer's
song seemed to me in its simplicity to get much of the real

Boer spirit. The last you give, however, if I remember aright, which you have translated, ("The Curse of the Boers on England" by *An Craoibhin*) is the most impressive of all, and seems to me to be Celtic through and through. I often wonder what the literary future of my country will be. The average American has in his blood the strains of very many different race stocks, though of course all the newcomers are much more affected by the ways of life and habits of thought of those who gave the nation the shape in infancy than in return they affect the latter; still they do affect the latter often unconsciously to both parties, and the surroundings, mental and physical, and the mere sweep of events, also exert a very strong pressure and influence upon all our people, the newcomers as well as the descendants of those who came here two and three centuries ago. What the exact outcome will be I suppose no human being can forsee."

I did not meet Mr. Roosevelt until the summer of 1910, the Coronation year. He had written to me from Naples that he would be in London soon and hoped to see me; and he wrote again when he had arrived, and I was in London looking after the Irish plays at the Court Theatre, inviting me to lunch with him at Mr. Arthur Lee's house where he was staying, and to bring with me Mr. Yeats. Then came another note saying he had been "summoned to meet the King at lunch" on the day chosen, but asking us to come in the afternoon instead. So I wrote home: —

7 June 1910. "Yeats and I went to tea with Roosevelt yesterday at Mr. Arthur Lee's. He was not there when we arrived, and Mrs. Roosevelt received us with great charm of manner. She had been to see *The Image* and liked it very much and could follow the dialect quite well, from an Irish nurse having brought her up. Mr. Lee, who was with her, found some little difficulty and had liked *The Rising of the Moon* better.

"Then Roosevelt came in, spoke to various people, there were about eight or ten there, a daughter of Sir Samuel Baker who had brought him her father's books, and Sir Frank Lascelles among them. Then he came to me and looked puzzled, and Mrs. Lee told him who I was, and he shook hands twice over and said, 'O, Lady Gregory, I am indeed delighted to meet you. I have "read after you" as they say in Kansas, you have opened to me the ivory gates, not the gates of horn.' He was interrupted now and then, but at last got a cup of tea and dragged over a chair and sat down. He said, 'I liked very much that little *Kiltartan History Book* of yours. That is the way history was written in the time of Herodotus.' I said, 'Yes, and of Plutarch, he is full of folk-lore.' 'Yes,' he said, 'your book reminded me of one I had read about the folk-lore of the Russian peasant. It gives a traditional idea of Napoleon the Great. The peasants say that Napoleon could not have gone on winning victories after so many of his men had been killed, but he entered into a compact with the devil that when he said the word "Buonaparte" where the dead men lie, they would rise up and fight for him. But this power was only to last while he showed no sympathy for them. But one night was very cold, and he said, "Poor men, it is hard they should come back to this". And when he said then "Buonaparte" they did not rise.'

" 'I don't know if you are acquainted with the Irish members I lunched with the other day, Redmond and the others. I have had indignant remonstrances since then from William O'Brien and my old friend Tim Healy. But what else could I do? I could not leave the seventy to lunch with the seven. I have always been a Home Ruler, that is known, but I have always hoped Ireland would then become a contented portion of the Empire. We are too far off, or she might be taken as a State. We are able to do those things.' I said, 'I have always said I am not working for Home Rule; I am preparing for it by trying to raise the dignity of the country.' He said, 'That is just what you are doing and the best and most splendid thing to do. Nothing can be better than that.' He apologised again for having put us off for lunch, saying having been bidden to lunch with the King, 'I told the King that I had been obliged to put off you and Mr. Yeats, but he made no response. Do you think he has any interest in literature?'

"He was called away but rushed back in a minute, bringing Sidney Lee, whom he introduced. 'Do you know what this man has just said to me? That it is only in Ireland a real literature is being written in English. When he said that I had to bring him up and introduce him to you two. But in America we can produce short stories, and some novels that are very good.' He turned to Yeats and said, 'There is a book now in my room, a book of fairy tales. I opened it and began to read a poem at the beginning, and I said, "This is written by a man born in the purple" and I looked at the end and saw "Yeats", so I carried it up to my room for the sake of the poem.' Then he said, 'Will you ever be over on our side?' I said, 'No, but we may send our Theatre.' He said, 'Mrs. Roosevelt went to see your play on her own hook and told me all about it. If ever you send your Theatre over, write to me and I will do all I can for it, not perhaps as much as you think, for if some do like me there are others who do not.' I said, 'That is like the dog the nuns at Gort asked a friend to choose for them, it was to be very quiet at some hours of the day and equally ferocious at other hours.' 'Yes,' he said, 'just like that. But all I can do for the success of your Theatre I will do.' And so we said good-bye. Mrs. Roosevelt had told us of the doctor who attended him for loss of voice, saying he himself was so much better for the amount of energy his patient had put into him!

"I little thought at that time that I should ever go to America. In the next year, 1911, I talked of going at last to see Killarney, Loch Leinne of the Finn legends, for I had always planned to go there when travelling days in other lands were at an end. But that was put off yet again. I have told in *Our Irish Theatre* of the sudden call to me in that autumn to go with the Abbey Players to the United States, and of the opposition to Synge's *Playboy* and of the fight over it threatened in Boston and growing to riot in New York. I am glad I need not go over that story again, save where it touches on the 'benefit of friends and their help' (foretold for that very autumn by an astrologer who had worked out my horoscope years before)."

And to tell of one of those helpers I will give a letter written home, 26 November 1911, just after our arrival in New York. I wrote, "I am going off just now to Oyster Bay for the night, to Roosevelt's. He has written two or three times giving exact directions about train and station, etc., as if he had nothing else to do." When we arrived at Sagamore Hill, Roosevelt rushed out on the steps to welcome us, and Mrs. Roosevelt was in the hall, apparently none the worse for her accident. It is a quite unpretentious house, wooden, and they have built on a large room, with a large open fireplace with blazing logs. After some minutes I was aware of Mrs. R. who was talking to another guest, saying 'What are you and my husband talking about? I cannot make either of you hear when I offer you tea?' 'We were comparing grandchildren and the pride of having them!' He has only one, a girl, only three months and still in long clothes and he hasn't seen her yet but is none the less pleased." (But five years later he was able to write, "the grandchildren are at this moment screaming and romping outside, and as soon as there is a lull I will give them your book".) "I said I looked on the joy as one we had hardly a right to expect, a sort of bonus given at the end of life! We talked about the opposition to the plays. He says the Irish Societies here are 'used to have bouquets thrown to them'. He says though a strong Home Ruler he has never once in a speech said anything about it because he would not like to feel he had got one vote on any but an American question. Mr. Seale, of Appleby's Publishing House came to dinner, with his wife, and I talked to him a good deal and Roosevelt to Mrs. Seale till he suddenly banged the table and said, 'There is nothing in the world I would not give to have Lady Gregory here working for America!' He was delighted when I told him that in my lectures at colleges here I discourage even the learning of Gaelic by the students while there is so much to explore in their own country and I feel sure a whole literature to be gathered from the various races in it. 'Yes, look at me! When other men were taking moors and going abroad for sport I stayed at home shooting prairie chickens!' He has a quite simple vanity; I told him of an old Mrs. Field who had come to see me and had said, 'Washington was the Father of his country'. She had also said, 'I have one son, and every night when I kneel down I pray for him and for Theodore Roosevelt'. He was very excited and delighted over this, jumped up and rushed up and down the room saying, 'That is the sort of thing that frightens one! I don't mind being abused but when I hear of anyone trusting me like that it makes me terrified lest I should ever disappoint such hopes!' After dinner we showed his trophies, heads, etc., not many for he has given most to a museum. There was a lion's head in my room I kept tumbling over. There is a splendid pair of tusks given by Menelek of Abyssinia. The Kaiser had given him several books, all badly got up and in bad taste, and one on art with the most ridiculous inscription about the duty of kings to take its guidance in their hands. But he says his criticisms written in military books given by him are very good. The Kaiser had also given him a vase of immense size and hideousness, with two gilt handles representing nude figures, and the portrait of himself with moustache uptwisted on the side in colours. 'We bore with it for a short while and then lent it to a museum.' He has several photographs of himself and the Kaiser together at the Berlin review, with notes written by K. at back, 'the Colonel of the Rough Riders advises the Head of the Imperial army', etc. and on 'A Conference: Beware Carnegie' and another, 'Agreement of the Powers and bother Carnegie', or something of the sort. The Chancellor had come to try and recover these from him but he would not give them up. He says, 'I had at one time a fatal fascination for the Kaiser, he wrote me more letters than anyone except Senator Beverly. Once, when he was in a panic about invasion, I advised him to read Thackeray's *Book of Snobs,* there are some waiters in it who are in much the same panic. I like the Kings. I could talk to them as white men. Haakon is my favourite and I liked playing with little Olaf his son, and when he was being sent to bed one evening he said, 'but isn't Mr. Roosevelt going to play with me? I gave King George a good talking to about Home Rule. But I pity them, Lady Gregory, I pity Kings and Queens (a rush across the room). They are socially the superiors of everyone and intellectually the inferiors of most people. What chance is there for them?' He had got one fine book from the Emperor, a fine copy of the *Nibelungenlied.* He doesn't care for Morris's verse, says heroes didn't talk like that then and wouldn't talk like that if they were living now. Someone asked if I knew Z. and he said, 'She was, when I met her, in America practising a sort of sham socialism, getting the butler up to play the flute while the girls played the piano.' I said I liked Z. and he said, 'If I could afford a great aunt, I would like to have her sitting in a corner knitting stockings.' We talked of the police and he said, 'It is curious the German are a free nation, and trained by Frederick the Great, and the Irish have been serfs, and yet one Irish policeman can lick two German ones. When we get an American into the police we put him on a very hard beat, and generally it is too much for him and he goes to pieces, but if he gets through that he is the best of all.' I asked for the name of a good American novel, and he made all conversation stop till he had fixed on half-a-dozen, and I asked Mrs. Seale to write down the names. He disliked games, having become so professional and never goes to see any professional games except prize fighting, which he delights in. I think this is all I can remember of the volume of talk bursting out. But he is a good listener as well, and remembers all one says.

"I left at eight o'clock next morning to get back to New York here in time for rehearsal, and he and Ethel were down to breakfast. I said I agreed with him on everything so far as I knew except phonetic spelling and he said, 'Well, my family and my Cabinet turned on me about that'. Ethel began to laugh and said he had received a letter from a convert, in phonetic spelling, and he had not been able to read it—'Mother and I had to make it out for him'."

The half-dozen novels he recommended were sent to me next day by Mr. Seale; I still possess five of them, the other has disappeared and I cannot remember its name. They are *Coniston* by Winston Churchill; *The Iron Woman*, Margaret Deland; *The Gentleman from Indiana*, Booth Tarkington; *The Blazed Trail*, Stewart Edward White; *Mam' Linda*, by Will N. Harben; *Knights in Fustian*, Caroline Brown. I wrote in each, "Recommended by Theodore Roosevelt, given by T. H. Seale", and in the last (*Knights in Fustian*), "Mr. Seale says this one is rather out of date, but he didn't like to contradict Col. Roosevelt."

Mr. Roosevelt gave me his *Strenuous Life,* and later *America and the World War;* and sent me also later two books by James Connolly, *Sonnie Boy's People* and *Out of Gloucester.*

I wrote again . . . "He had promised to come and see the *Playboy* a few evenings later, and to dine with me before it. But meanwhile there had been a riot at its first performance and I was not sure if he would think it right to attend. But I wrote to Yeats, 29 November: "I was in such a rush last night, and mail going, I sent off my letters very untidily. I hadn't time even to change my dress for dinner. It went off very well, John Quinn, Colonel Emmet, great grand nephew of the patriot, and Flynn (a great compliment to him). I had asked Peter Dunne (Mr. Dooley) but he was engaged to dinner at eight, but came and sat through ours which was earlier. Roosevelt came full trot into the hall, where we were waiting, wrapped in a fur coat and looking much like one of his namesakes . . . 'Pitchforks would not have kept me away now you have been attacked!' He said two of his chief helpers in politics had come to him during the day and said it would be very injurious to him to come to *Playboy,* but he had said, 'Look here, if I deserted Lady Gregory I should be a yellow cur, just a yellow cur'. When we sat down to dinner he announced, 'Lady Gregory's son has two fine leaping horses, and he has called one after

Patrick Sarsfield and the other after me', and recited some
lines about Sarsfield. I said even a third generation appreciated him, as little grandson goes to sleep hugging his
Teddy Bear. It was in the restaurant, so he was fairly
discreet for him, and when Dunne came they chaffed each
other. We talked of all the races in America, the difficulty
of digesting them and he said, 'Well, that doesn't intimidate
me, I have Dutch blood and Irish and French and a little
German. Nine generations ago all my ancestors hated each
other, and I am the result! It will be the same with America.'
He said that on Sunday when I had told them there would
be trouble on Monday I had 'stiffened a little', and his
daughter, Ethel, had said afterwards, 'Isn't Lady Gregory
splendid, she is a valiant soul!' Isn't she a dear girl, wasn't
that a nice thing for her to say? A valiant soul. When we
got to the theatre and into the box, people saw him and
began to clap and at last he had to get up, but he took my
hand and dragged me on my feet too, and there was renewed
cheering. It was great fun, the Chief Magistrate McAdoo
was to have dined with me, but sent an apology, the Mayor
having deputed him to act as Censor in consequence of a
deputation he thought he ought to go independently. But
he could not resist sitting in our box, which must have
exasperated the enemy . . . Roosevelt when President had
made him Secretary of the Navy . . . Towards the end of
Gaol Gate there was a great outbreak of coughing and
sneezing, and then there was a scuffle in the gallery and a
man throwing red pepper was put out. Roosevelt said he
would never forget *Gaol Gate* and thought it wonderful.
There was a scuffle every now and then in *Playboy*, but
nothing violent, and always great clapping when the offender
was chucked out, and Roosevelt always clapped loudest of
all. We played with the lights up. After the first act I took
my party on to the stage, and introduced the players, and
R. spoke separately to them and then made a little speech
saying how much he admired them and that he felt they
were doing a great deal to increase the dignity of Ireland
(he has adopted my phrase) and lift it, and that he 'envies
them and Lady Gregory for America'. They were quite
delighted and Kerrigan had tears in his eyes. His daughter,
who was with another party, then appeared, and he introduced her to them, remembering all the names, 'This is
Mr. Morgan, this is Miss Nesbitt' . . . I brought him a cup
of tea, and it was hard to tear him away to let the curtain

go up. I stayed in my room beside the stage writing letters during the second act and when I came back a swarm of reporters was surrounding R. and he was declaiming from the box, 'I would as soon discuss the question as discuss a pipe dream with an out-patient of Bedlam'; this was about an accusation in some paper they had just showed him saying he had had a secret understanding with some trusts. He was shaking his fist and saying, 'I am giving you that straight, mind you take it down as I say it'. When the play was over he stayed in the box a few minutes discussing it, said he will write a note on an article he wants John Quinn to write about us. As to the play, he had been dubious at first, and then enthusiastic about the language and fantasy, and then when the father is killed a second time I saw him grow rather cold. He said at the end he was very glad to have seen it and thinks it a most extraordinary play but he hopes never to see it again or another like it, and would not bring Mrs. R. as it is morbid. But our whole work he is as enthusiastic about as ever. When we left the box we found the whole way to the door packed, just a narrow lane we could walk through, and everyone taking off their hats (evidently all gallery people) and looking at him with real reverence and affection, so unlike those Royal crowds in London. He was very much pleased and said, 'They always treat me like this'. Quinn and Emmet had been a little afraid his coming might injure him, but said at the end it was a most popular thing for him to do, showing real courage, and would do him good. He proposed coming back for a chat and we sat till about midnight. I told him Quinn was the hardest working man in New York and that it was a charity to make him idle, and he said, 'Come and spend next Saturday morning with me' and Quinn agreed, and I see they are going to be great friends, Quinn had only met him once before, with Hyde. Roosevelt and Col. Emmet began recalling their army time, and R., thinking I was neglected, suddenly seized my hand and said enthusiastically, 'Isn't she a dear!' It was an extraordinary kindness for him to have done."

Yeats wrote back from Dublin, (1911): "The Roosevelt episode has had a great effect here. There has, I believe, been a danger of a regular open clerical campaign against us but as things are we have too many friends. So far as I know we have not lost one of our 63 or 64 pupils because of it. Bye the bye, the pupils have the advantage of giving us a wide circle of friends who feel they are part of the Abbey.

"I admire both you and Roosevelt immensely. I could not have brought him. It is most lucky you, not I, were in charge, and your courage is all the finer because, unlike mine, it is not combative."

I wrote home . . . "I had tea at the Club with Mrs. Payne Whitney, very pretty and charming, and Mrs. Douglas Robinson, a sister of Roosevelt's, very nice and telling me about Theodore's boyhood. He wrote a book on natural history when he was seven, which contained a chapter on 'the Foregoing ant', a phrase he had picked up in a book and thought was a new species.

"The lunch at the *Outlook* office was great fun, the Editors, and an Admiral and some others, and after lunch Ethel Roosevelt called for silence that Lady Gregory might be questioned! So they asked questions from here and there, if the riots had affected our audience. I said, yes, more people had come to see us pelted than playing, and that I had met a few days before a General Green who told me that when driving through crowds cheering Roosevelt after a big speech he had made, he had said to him, 'Theodore, don't you feel elated by this?' and Mr. Roosevelt had said to him, 'Frank, I always keep in mind what the Duke of Wellington said on a similar occasion, "How many more would come to see me hanged?"' (great applause). I forget what question led me to say that my father and mother had, save for one honeymoon visit to Germany, lived their whole lives at home, only moving for fishing or shooting or sea bathing from one property to another in their own county. And I said I sometimes thought it may have been their conservation of energy that was now supplying fire to some of their descendants, among them John Shawe-Taylor and Hugh Lane. Ethel R. came up laughing afterwards to say she had never seen her father in such a state of delighted appreciation, that he could hardly sit on his chair when I was speaking, but seemed to vibrate with approval! "

26 December. "I went to tea on Tuesday with Mrs. Douglas Robinson. She had asked a large party to meet me, chiefly women, looking very rich in pearl necklaces and furs, Mrs. Andrew Carnegie among them. Then tea, and then Roosevelt telephoned that he was coming to see me. Luckily a good many had gone when he came, for everybody wanted to be introduced or have a word with him, except a few men who

said they had been asked to meet me. I told Mrs. Robinson it was like inviting people to meet Lodore, and letting in Niagara as an afterthought. At last, all but one or two went away and we that were left sat down. He said, 'I have had endless letters since my article has appeared, accusing me of encouraging parricide by going to see that play. They seem to think I am making parricide a plank in my platform. My wife said to me across the table, "Theodore, you have a very sweet disposition". I said, "So have you, my dear", and she said, "Yes, I suppose mine is the best, for you have only to live with me and I have to live with you".' Then he made me tell about the beginning of the Theatre and said, 'Lady Gregory is like Columbus, while we are all trying to make the egg stand, she has done it.' He talked again of national and local colour and material and his pleasure in the head on the coinage with the Indian feathers instead of the Phrygian cap. He said, 'sculptors have been the most helpful so far'. Mrs. Robinson went out with the last visitor and we were alone for a minute or two and he said, 'I want to thank you for what you have done for me. You have brought a new thing into my life. I cared for the epics but you have made me care for the drama and see what it means and may mean to this country. I thank you for it. And it is such a pleasure that my wife and I are now at one, for she did not care for spice, but it was she who discovered and first cared for the plays and now we both do, and Ethel thinks there is no one like you, you have our hearts.' I said good-bye, and he took me down to the taxi with some cheery words, the chauffeur evidently recognised him and him and grinning broadly. I should not like to see him again this time, I feel overpowered by his help and without words to say what I feel.

"In the evening I dined at the Guinnesses' and met Peter Dunne and talked with him all the evening. He admired Roosevelt tremendously, is sure he will be in office again. He says he is afraid of nothing except perhaps a little of ridicule, and he thinks he is sometimes uneasy about the Catholics, because of the episode with the Pope. But he does not think it possible for them to combine against him. He says Devoy and his group are 'forty-eight' men and live in a dream of the past. He is very fond of Devoy and thinks him quite unselfish, 'though John Quinn is angry with him'. He will write of *Playboy*, 'if you don't mind having a little fun poked at you'. I said that was the best thing he could do, give a humorous side to soften the enemy for next year."

I wrote later, in 1913, on arriving again in America: "Quinn came to meet us at New York. He had met Roosevelt just in the height of the election, and he had asked him to come and see him, but Quinn said better not as he was working for the Democrats, but Roosevelt said, 'But I want to come and talk to Lady Gregory'."

It happened that one day in 1912 I was at luncheon in a London house and one or two of the guests were finding fault with the violence of some of Roosevelt's speeches, for he was then fighting his "Progressive" campaign. But Sir Edward Grey, who was next me, said very quietly, "I don't think we ought to judge the violence of the words in such a case, but rather consider whether the cause in which they are used is the right one." And the cavillers were silent while he spoke, and agreed, and turned to some other theme. And when I went home I thought, "It would please Mr. Roosevelt to hear that"; for he had told me that he had never fallen into so close a sudden friendship with any man as with Sir Edward Grey. And so I wrote it to him, and he answered on July 2: "I very much appreciate your letter and am gratified with what Grey said. He expresses exactly my feelings. The important point is to fight on the right side; and yet we continually meet nice rather milk and water creatures, who are so shocked at fighting that they utterly forget to consider whether the battle *is* for the right . . . I am up to my ears in about as ugly a fight as I have ever been in; I think I should rather flatter myself if I spoke of the issue as doubtful; and yet in all my life I have never been in a fight where I was more certain as to my duty. I just could not have kept out . . ."

And again from the hospital in Chicago where he was recovering from the wound he had received, 19 October 1912: "Mrs. Roosevelt is knitting while sitting here in the room at the hospital, and I am feeling as good as possible and fit for a prize fight. Well, ever since you left last year, I have been having about as many different experiences as anyone could have. Seriously, my dear Lady Gregory, I want you to know that I have really been campaigning with all my heart for as good a cause as ever was fought for. The shooting was only the natural and inevitable result of the kind of way that for a good many years now I have been assaulted."

Theodore Roosevelt. A photograph taken during his presidency, 1901-1909. Courtesy the American Embassy.

Above left: Robert Gregory as a child. Above right: Robert Gregory in flyin
kit. Below left: Margaret Gregory with Richard. Below right: l. to r. Catherin
Anne and Richard.

I had written to W.B.Y. 14 February 1913: "In New York I went to the Bull Moose dinner on Wednesday, the first the party has held and an immense success, thirteen hundred there and great enthusiasm. I was a guest of Burke Cochrane and went with John Quinn and was put next Peter Dunne and another writer; quite pleasant and I enjoyed it. Mrs. Longworth was at my table, and young Theodore came to ask to be introduced, having heard so much of me from his father, and before the end of dinner Roosevelt, who was with the other speakers at a raised table, stood up and gesticulated wildly and at last it was understood that he wanted Lady Gregory up there, so I was led up and he made me sit next him for a while, and introduced me to the people near, and then I went back when the speaking began . . . There was no eloquence that can so be called except Cochrane's, who it interested me to hear, he must be so much of the O'Connell type. Roosevelt spoke last for over an hour . . . There was a great deal of cheering and waving of red bandana handkerchiefs . . . It was past midnight when it was over."

One day in 1915, when I was again in America, I found him listening to an American officer who had been sent to Europe on some official mission, and who was telling him as I came in that a German officer who was taking him round Antwerp had pointed to the German eagle flying over the city and had said, "Look at that flag. It will *never* be taken down." I had not seen him so angry, except once when the newspapers told that Kuno Meyer, brought to talk to him on Irish mythology, had declared at a meeting that Mr. Roosevelt had said he believed the Germans would win the war. "It is a lie, an absolute lie. You are going back to England, Lady Gregory, I charge you to deny it wherever you can."

Roosevelt wrote to me 11 September 1916. "It is very dreadful to have our boys go and not return, but it would be worse if they failed to go. It is my sincere conviction that if the President had acted as he had power to act during the last four years, this war would have been over long ago, and with an infinite saving of bloodshed. Our sons must pay with their blood for the sins of the pacifists and of the cold and selfish politicians."

I last saw him on my last day in America in 1915, for I, like his doctor, found the sound of his voice, the touch of his hand, seemed to give new strength and energy, and I wanted to take this back to Ireland, and so arranged to go and see him on the very way to the boat. He was saddened then by the war, and by the refusal of America to give help to what he felt certain was the right side. Yet I could see from a later letter that he was perhaps, yet sadder, and certainly sorely disappointed, when his country had joined, but he himself was not allowed to take a personal share of fighting and of danger.

SOME LETTERS

I HAD not thought when I met Mr. Roosevelt in the summer of 1911 that I should ever be in America . . . I had (and have) never seen Killarney and had said that now my days of foreign travel were over I should find opportunity for that short pilgrimage. But in that autumn, as I have told in *Our Irish Theatre,* I was obliged to go across the ocean to take charge of our Abbey Company which had been engaged to play in the United States, and I have told also of the fight over Synge's *Playboy.* I went again, more than once, first with the Company and then to give lectures, but I lived too much in trains and at work to send back much record of those much occupied months; months which were made much happier by the beautiful kindness of many who I met as strangers and have kept in memory ever since as friends.

I can but give scraps of letters written now and again, most often to Yeats.

S.S. Majestic. January 1913. "Such a week of rough weather, and yesterday a real storm, shutters down and no one allowed on deck if they wanted to go! . . . Today is quite fine and bright and we are all upstairs, but they say we won't get in till Saturday, we were due this morning; it will run us tight at Chicago. Miss Allgood has been really ill. Such a wasted week! I could not write a word or read much. And my instinct was right calling out for a few days of London, for home cares and anxieties have come with me, there has been nothing to get me off them. However, I have in my mind re-arranged *Damer* and am getting at a 'Conversation' lecture —'our conversation is in Heaven' a sort of text. We all have conversation with Heaven itself, but it is hard for us to talk to one another as on its plains, the wall is thicker between man and man, than between man and the skies. The earthly part will be easy enough.

"Friday. Calm but foggy. We had quite a nice little concert last night for a charity. Sinclair and Kerrigan acted *Workhouse* on two deckchairs. The concert made £2.18.0, we

did it all ourselves. I am almost sad leaving the peace of
the ship for the unknown perils."

To W.B.Y. New York. 15 March: "Such lovely weather
here—such air and sky! John Quinn says, 'we can boast of
our climate as we didn't make it', and I say, 'yes, but not
of your energy, for that is made by it'. It is we in damp
Ireland who deserve praise for doing any work at all.

"I met a man last night who spoke of *Countess Cathleen*.
He said the ideas reminded him of Moses wanting to give
his own soul for the people. I have looked at the text (Exodus
xxxii, 32), 'Oh, this people have sinned a great sin, and have
made them gods of gold, Yet now if thou wilt forgive their
sin—and if not, blot me, I pray thee, out of thy book which
thou hast written.' It might be useful in a controversy some
time."

On board S.S. *Orduna* (1915). "We hope to land
to-morrow after a bad voyage which had delayed us a day,
gales and blizzard and a heavy sea all the time, but today
very fine . . . I have been reading *Les Miserables*, a wonderful
book, an epic, I find a good many of your father's ideas
sketched out in it. I had to put by Henry James, one wants
stability under one to pursue those maze-like sentences . . .
I dreamed last night that you were reciting a poem that
ended 'and lakes and queens', and I asked but got no answer
what lakes and queens had to do with each other . . . Horrid
people are reading a comic paper aloud . . ."

Pittsburgh . . . "I think this place is over-Carnegie insti-
tuted, and they are afraid of anything that may turn into a
means of improvement or education; all tell me musical
comedies are the only success."

To Hugh Lane . . . "I have been telling everyone that if
I were a really good aunt I would have discouraged subscriptions and encouraged you to sell the pictures and live in
luxury. You have become quite a hero out here, and if you
ever want an heiress you will only have to show yourself . . .
I gave a lecture at Montreal to which Princess Patricia came.
She asked for you and was very nice. She and the Duke
came twice to the plays, and the second time the Duke sent
his A.D.C., Lord Francis Scott, to thank me for bringing
such delightful plays, and to invite me to the Royal box,
where I sat between him and the Princess through
Workhouse Ward."

To W.B.Y. Chicago. 18 February. "At Duluth where I
spoke on 'Worlds Unseen' the R.C. Bishop was in the

audience. I didn't know it till afterwards when he came to thank me, quite emotionally, for my help in revealing 'things invisible', both in my speaking and in my writings. I wish all my countrymen could have heard him!''

Liverpool, 1915, leaving for U.S.A. "I insured jewellery with Cook, £600, but he sent afterwards to say it was cancelled, they have orders from London to insure nothing over £100. It is calm but raining."

S.S. *California*. 10 October 1915. "We were kept tacking about after we had started on Saturday, and when I awoke on Sunday I thought we should be out of the channel. But when I wanted a bath they said the water was too dirty— we were still close to Liverpool! I felt like Harry Lorrequer on his way to France. And through Sunday we kept stopping and turning 'by Government orders' and there was a notice put up that saloon passengers were allotted to No. 1 lifeboat, and the lifeboats were kept ready swung. After we passed Cork we took a dip to the south, and by Monday we were said to be safe . . . I am at a little table with the Captain, who hardly ever appears, and Sir Frederick Donaldson, head of munitions at Woolwich; he is very official and afraid to speak on any subject but food . . . A cheerful young man, an O'Sullivan, had just brought up three nice young priests from the second class, and I have been reading them *Kiltartan History Book*. I have been going over my lectures a good deal, that has given me plenty of work; and I found some Swedenborg books in the library, and have been reading *Divine Love* and *Heaven and Hell*. Of course, it is extraordinarily interesting to me just now when my thoughts are so much on the other side . . . It is a bad summer to look back on, too many shocks—first Hugh—. Sir F. Donaldson says fourteen are killed out of every thirty aviators who go out . . . If I get through America well I shall have new courage, and I hope I may make enough money anyhow to put off cutting trees."

12 October 1915. "We are to land tomorrow morning. A wireless from Pond that they have put off Andover (today's lecture) till 18th, and that I must start from Haverill directly on arrival.

"Thinking about interviewers, etc., I think I must tell our intention of, when the war is over and Home Rule in force, giving over the Theatre 'into the hands of Trustees and a gift to the nation' or 'in trust for the nation'. This will do away with the fear of its ravelling into music halls.

So, as these things come back, you had perhaps better take first opportunity of making some such announcement . . . I often think of that very happy day on the lake, when Richard caught his big fish."

N.Y. December 1915.   "Your father says a friend of his used to lecture in Ireland and found his chief employers were the Quakers. They liked lectures because they had mentality without education. And that when Mr. C. R. criticised his wife's dream as they were going to a dinner she looked at him and said, 'I can never forget that I am married to an attorney'."

N.Y. Ocotber 1915.   "A clergyman at Seattle told me he had been with Stevenson in Samoa when news came of Matthew Arnold's death, and Stevenson said, 'poor Matthew Arnold! I hope he hasn't gone to Heaven, because he didn't like God'."

January 1916.   "My New Year's dinner at the Guinnesses was very pleasant. There were small tables about the room, at my table Mr. Guinness and John Quinn and Peter Dunne (Mr. Dooley), Mrs. Astor and Melba. We were each given a pencil as a new year's gift. I said, 'It's a pity we haven't an artist among us'. Someone said, 'Mme. Melba is an artist'. She said, 'only in music', and Peter Dunne said, 'We all know you *draw*', and I pinched him for his pun. Melba said she had been a very naughty child. I asked her what was the naughtiest thing she had ever done. She said, 'I cut the cane seats out of a set of chairs with a knife'. We asked what punishment she was given, she said, 'None'. Her mother had pretended to see nothing, and she and her brothers sat down as best they could on the bottomless chairs; and then her mother looked at them, and asked each one if they had done it, and they all said, 'No', till it came to her turn, and she said, 'It was I'. Mr. Guinness asked her to tell us of the naughtiness of her later life, and she shook her head, and I said, 'you wouldn't have her take the bread out of the mouth of her biographer'. Mrs. Z. coming in late, had made an attempt to monopolise Peter, but I told of the 'Union of Hearts' pocket handkerchief that had come out in London at one time, with 'a picture of the President shaking hands over the Atlantic, with a representative of Britannia and how proud an Imperialistic friend of mine (Lady Layard) had been of it until 'Mr. Dooley's article "Hands acrost the sea and into somewan's pockets" had come out, and then the handkerchief had been given to me, discarded, for my historical collection', and that made the conversation general again. Peter told us of a regiment of Jews in some war, and the report after the battle, 'None dead, none wounded, all missing'."

Coole. April 1916. "I arrived here unexpectedly on Sunday, and the door was opened by Richard, who shouted and jumped for joy! . . . I am happy in having done with catching trains and shaking hands and having no life of my own— no that is ungrateful, I was given many delightful days . . . I have (in the luxury of having time for reading again) attacked your big Blake book; and it seems to me that our Theatre has from the immeasurable become concrete, has fallen from imagination to reason, from Beulah to Orc-Ulro, or the Mundane, or Satan, of whatever A.B.C. and D. represent. I don't see how we can help it" . . . I am trying to get things into order, including my own scattered mind. I don't think I have sat down to do an honest day's writing since December, indeed except on board ship I never had leisure . . .

"Richard took notice of one of those books on you and asked if you had written it. I said, No, it was written about you, and he might be able to write a book about you some day. He said, 'I'd say I caught the biggest perch'. The egotism of the biographer begins at an early age.

"I have been sent a funny little poem from a Chicago paper called 'How Yeats shakes hands'. I showed it to my sister and said, 'Do you remember how Yeats shakes hands?' She said, 'Yes, like the Man in the Moon'.

"Cave has been fishing all the morning and I heard him and Harvey agreeing it is no use. No one can catch fish but Mr. Yeats or at all events he must be in the house."

Royal Hospital, Dublin. "Here is a nice compliment. Lady Littleton writing to ask John Morley to meet me said, 'She is a mixture of genius, gentleness and fire!'

"About the Abbey lectures, I do think something is needed to associate our Theatre with 'things invisible' after the reign of A. and Z. I don't know if we can ever expand again, but I think of the early days when all seemed possible, even a seventh day of creation. I don't wonder that you are looking for a new audience, one must find it somewhere or become barren. I thought with a pang of our days of poverty, of Synge being annoyed because the *White Cockade* week had taken more than the *Well of the Saints* week, and that only

£3 altogether. In fact, I was a revenant, disapproving of my heirs but helpless."

Dublin. "I lectured F. on speaking to the gallery, and said that before he and Miss O'Neill had gone to that deplorable and accursed England (from a stage point of view) they hadn't known what a gallery was.

"Yesterday I attended F.'s class. They did *Land of Heart's Desire* very well, perhaps slightly too static as the girl— the fairy child (Miss L.) doesn't dance at all. I suggested her coming in throwing up flowers or a cowslip ball, just something to give an impression of joy. All the speaking was good, I felt quite encouraged, I think we shall at last arrive at some fine performances of your plays. I feel we have begun building again.

"I had such a pleasant dinner in London with Wilfrid Blunt, only George Wyndham and Hudson of *The Purple Land*. We talked of birds and beasts and trees and folk-lore and ghosts and eternity—never once of the elections. I am sorry you didn't meet Balfour, he has an interesting mind, at least one would like to know why anyone whose mind has such a wide and happy range should take to the dryness of politics."

Coole. 1914. "Robert has come back today in good spirits about his exhibition, which all say is a great advance upon his last. An American collector bought one of the large ones, and Hugh another (is much impressed by them this time) and some stranger another. They will still be going on next week, though Whitsun week is not a very good one, I'm afraid. The *Pall Mall*, putting him with Lamb, says, 'In both there is the triumph of manner that is matter of a vital kind' and the *Observer* says he expresses the character of our scenery 'with a passionate intensity'.

"I came upon your poem that you had given me, 'Suddenly I saw the cold and rook-delighting Heaven' to-day. It is wonderfuly fine. I wish we were both at creative work." (And Yeats wrote back that he had lost his own manuscript of that poem, and had forgotten some of the lines, and I was so glad to have it to give to him, I have just noticed that my typist, as typists do, has tried to improve the sense of it and put "Suddenly I saw the cold and *took delight in* Heaven!")

13 December 1912. "I have really finished the book (*Our Irish Theatre*) and can send it off at any time. Such a mercy! It was crushing work and no joy in it, except for certain

swiftness of narrative now and then that pleased me. But it will save a great deal of trouble to us all in the future.

"Proofs of *New Comedies* have come, and I must re-arrange *Damer* before sending them back. I am getting on at a great rate by putting dinner off later and later every night, and think to-morrow I may get MS. of *Our Irish Theatre* off. What easy work writing poems must be! Nice clean sheets and so few of them and no facts or dates!

"The first, bad Mars day, was full enough of small worries to justify itself I thought. But at evening that beautiful filly across the lake, Sarsfield's sister—died of convulsions. I should be sadder still if I thought my Mars had done it.

"John Rurke has just been to see me. He is still a policeman at Belfast and all his sympathies are with it. He says they have built up a splendid city with their own work and don't want it to be pulled down."

The Theatre was never very far from my mind and when the Company was going to America in 1914 I wrote early in February to Yeats who was lecturing there: —

"Another idea for the Abbey. I don't like to think of it shut and the Pit people without it. Yesterday I was wondering if I could get Fay for three months to teach, and have performances with him in parts, 'Given by Abbey Dramatic School' or some such name. I should like to enlarge Pit, or lower prices. Something to go in the direction of a 'People's Theatre'."

13 February 1914. "I am going on Monday to Dublin. I have engaged a voice producer, Miss Sheddon . . . I have *Lord Mayor* and a short powerful tragedy from Cork (*Kinship*) and a little comedy of Ervine's[1] . . . I will start rehearsing these, but not try for too many productions . . . But these things must seem so far from you now! It is good to be far away sometimes and get a right perspective, as I suppose we shall of this world, after we have gone from it."

19 March 1914. "I am in great spirits . . . We had a splendid audience on Patrick's Day. At night we took two rows of stalls into the pit, which did away with that vacuum. It made me feel all my efforts and, I may say, sufferings were rewarded, for all these people would have been at some music hall probably but for us. The rehearsals are pleasant

---

[1] *The Orangemen* by St. John Ervine and *The Lord Mayor* by Edward McNulty were first performed at the Abbey Theatre on 13 March, and *Kinship*, by J. Bernard McCarthy on 2 April.

enough but the classes very tiring. I take them every evening and two afternoons, and just the people who want to put in parts—three weeks more of them.

"Now I must compose some charades for my pupils to act this afternoon. I have taken classes of those pupils who are not good enough to take parts, even small ones, all the parts we could give, even for a private performance, were already filled. I went through plays with them, but lay awake one night feeling that I wasn't doing enough for them and wondering what to do. Then I remembered Mr. Gilbert at Boston who trains pupils for the Opera, making them act in dumb show at first, to get gesture right. And as I meditated on that, I thought of the children's game, Dumb Crambo, that we sometimes played at Coole, and the next day at the class I proposed it and it was the greatest success, they had to express themselves through gesture, and understood and were interested at once. Now I have to go on to charades; they have to speak as well as act . . ." (They got on so well that before the few weeks classes came to an end they were able to give an invitation performance, to the delight of their relations and friends.)

16 April 1915. "The Shaws are here. They are very easy to entertain, he is so extraordinarily light in hand, a sort of kindly joyousness about him, and they have their motor so are independent. He says *Shanwalla* is the best ghost play he ever saw, and thinks Sinclair *very* fine in it . . . The children are greater darlings than ever, little Catherine developing great energy."

Wednesday 21st. "A wire has come saying we must decide at once about taking the plays to London, followed by a letter to-day. I read it to G.B.S. He said decidedly we ought to go, and if we must die, die gloriously, and I was glad to have his definite opinion, for of course I realise the risk.

. . ."I write in a hurry because little Anne is ill to-day, and I am anxious and have just had the doctor. It is a throat affection, laryngitis. G.B.S. has been so kind, followed the doctor up the mountain and got him here. I trust it won't be anything serious, but my bones melt when anything goes wrong with the chicks."

Thursday 29th. "G.B.S. came in to photograph me ten minutes ago at my writing table, and I said it was one of life's ironies that I who had done so much literary work should be photographed writing, as I was, to engage a kitchen maid! Just after I had begun this letter he took another and said we must offer a prize to whoever could guess by the expression whether I was writing to the kitchen-maid or to you! . . . Did I tell you of his being lost last Saturday in the woods, of which he declares there are seventy-seven. He didn't get home till 11.00 o'clock at night, having walked for five hours, when he got to Gort through Inchy, and took a car. The people all say already he was led 'astray'.

"I took Bailey to church in G.B.S.'s car—that was behaving well to the Archdeacon. Mrs. Shaw very pleasant and is always delightfuly happy and courteous."

Coole. July 1915. (After Hugh Lane's death.) "Ups and downs, very downhearted today . . . A day or two I awoke with a rule of life in my mind—'Law and Love; Law the serenity of order. Love the joy of self-sacrifice."

August. "I had some very dark days, and seemed to have lost all courage, and that lasted through my week in Galway. But suddenly I grew serene and went back to Jacob Boehme and his 'friends worth having' and have even begun to write a comedy, or notes for one." (*The Dragon*.)

Coole. 1915. "I return Stephens's book. I don't care much for the inset stories, but otherwise I think it a very fine book—infinitely better than Anatole France's (*Le Retour des Dieux*) which is thin and an echo—this is original and has a background . . . I have been typing my play (*The Dragon*), very tiring. I think I must have been a very useful secretary to you when you were going for your first American tour. I remember at Gower Street, re-writing *Hanrahan* with one hand and typing your lectures with the other. But I have to gather my own straw."

". . . A while ago I had written in a little book where I sometimes put down a stray thought, 'When we are born our mother bears the pain and travail. When we are re-born, re-made, the pain and travail must be borne by oneself'."

Wilfrid Blunt had written to me from time to time about old interests and new: 7 March 1901. Sheykh Obeyd. "I am delighted with your Irish book *Ideals in Ireland* and only wish I had a strain of Celtic blood in me to join in the work of de-Englishing Ireland. But I have looked through my pedigree in vain, from the time of Elizabeth downwards, and can find nothing in it which will pass muster as such unless it is my Scawen descent which is Cornish . . . I think there is a good deal in the idea of language getting used up, though I was surprised in reading the new *Oxford Verse*

Book to find how well XIX Century poetry stands compared with the XVIIIth or even XVIIth centuries (Shakespeare apart). I expect, however, that the XXth Century will be mostly barren, unless indeed the British Empire breaks up and we become an oppressed, instead of an oppressing, nationality. It is a misfortune to have been born an Englishman in these days of swagger and vulgarity."

Sheykh Obeyd. 30 October 1901. "I was already on the point of writing to you to tell you of a joyful little feast at which we entertained Arabi here on Saturday. You will be interested more than anyone else to hear it. He came with Ali Fehmi and an old Nationalist doctor, and I asked Mohammed Abdou to step over from his house, which is just outside our garden, to meet him. You may imagine that the occasion was almost an historic one and that we met not without an inclination to tears. He is looking wonderfully well and hearty, and now that his beard is white he is a really grand figure of a grand old fellah. His reception in Egypt has been of a rather mixed character, but on the whole a fairly satisfactory one."

Sheykh Obeyd. 5 February 1905. "I need not say that I am delighted to hear of *Fand* having been read, and especially that Yeats thinks well of it, for I have the highest opinion of his critical judgment. I quite agree with him that dramatists ought to have been men of action, as I believe they generally have been since all the interests of plays lies in the true display of character in action. Youth can hardly guess at this without experience. For myself I can only say that I could not have written any kind of drama at thirty or I think at forty, nor should I have attempted it at my mature sixty and odd but for your asking me to try. Now, I fear, it is too late for me to do anything much farther, though I feel that I could do much better than *Fand* if I had the physical power of work. But this infernal influenza (excuse the word) has taken at least a year out of my life, and what little energy I have left I must devote to my memoirs. I am at present getting into shape for putting in print when I get home my Egyptian memoirs . . . you may be sure you will be the first person to read them."

Sheykh Obeyd. 3 January 1896. "I read the papers however and am pleased and amused to notice the new union of hearts in Ireland. I feel sure that you are among the Landlord Nationalists, and if you are, my hopes for Ireland are higher than they have been any time for the last ten years."

Newbuildings. 1 September 1906. "I am glad to have your letter about Lovelace. He was a man of very mixed merits, moral and intellectual—original, almost to the point of genius, but without the smallest sense of proportion—as a companion, most pleasant, especially in his later years, but dangerous as friend. I am glad to have got through with my thirty-seven years connection with him without serious quarrel. His death will make a terrible gap in Anne's life; for she was entirely devoted to him and latterly more so than ever. I had seen very little of him for some time. In politics he generally went with me and at times did excellent service. But he was too much wrapped up in his family history to have time to work seriously at anything else. His Byron book was the result of fifty years of agitation and ten or twenty years of labour. Hence its great merit. I don't think he would ever have written another."

The New Generation.
9 March 1909. "I am so glad you have a grandson. It is, I think, a better relationship than with one's own children, for old age and childhood are nearer together in their tastes and amusement and views of life. I find it very difficult now to mix in general society, feeling shy and uncomfortable with the foolish pretty women of the day, and the funny little young men one meets if one goes out to luncheon anywhere. Their language is strange to me and their ways, and the strong scents they (the women) use. I don't know what to do or say.

A wasp without its sting.
Newbuildings. 28 November 1909. "I send you a copy of my new book, *India under Ripon*. It is a bowdlerised version of my diary which you read many years ago. I wanted to add some chapters about the India of today, but could not get a publisher to look at it, so it is a wasp without its sting. But as it is I think it will interest you. I am, however, getting very tired of these controversies and should like to die at peace with my enemies, though the fighting always does me good, and I am quite well again and enjoying my summer life."

The wild fallow deer.
Worth Manor House. 24 October 1912. "I am writing this from a little house I have just finished building in Worth Forest, and where I spend half my time now. In this autumn weather I prefer it to Newbuildings, and it lies 300 feet

higher, out of the fogs, and has the romance of containing wild fallow deer, which are vocal at this time of the year, besides other game."

He envies me my work in Ireland.

Newbuildings. 3 November 1912. "I am glad you are so busy and so successful. Apart from western things I am as you may imagine in a woeful despondency—all is going to ruin in the East and Egypt is lost past redemption. I feel that I have wasted thirty years of my life on it, and it is little consolation to think that the British Empire will go down with the rest, though that too I think will happen. You are lucky to live in an age of advance at home and not of decay."

His Collected Edition.

7 January 1914. "Now for the other part of your letter, about the re-publication of my poems. Of course, if Macmillan will really do it, nothing could be better. But from what you say I gather that his idea would be a selection, or at any rate not a quite complete collection. He would want to exclude *The Wind and the Whirlwind* and *Satan Absolved,* just as Henley did when he published his volume. But this would not fulfil my object which is, if it is done at all, to put *all* my verse within the reach of readers. Otherwise it seems to me that it is hardly worth doing. When I say *all* I mean all that is not technically bad verse. *The Wind and the Whirlwind* and *Satan Absolved* are quite as much part of myself and my view of things as *The Sonnets of Proteus* are, and to leave them out in a Collected Edition would be a recantation of feelings and opinions I am not prepared for. If my poetry has any value I feel it lies in its sincerity, for I have really never written any verse for writing's sake, only as a way of expressing myself, and I have felt as deeply and strongly about certain aspects of what are called world politics as I have about love. My poetry has been my justification in both fields of my active life, not the pursuit of an art for art's sake. Macmillan will very likely be shy of connecting himself with this. Still, if he will do it, nobody I am sure could do it better, and he would find me easy as to terms. I should like the issue to be a cheap one, so as to secure the largest number of readers possible. Perhaps you would show him this letter . . . I hope you are to be of the poets' party to give a countenance at it, I should feel it lacked reality without you."

As to the poets' visit, Yeats had written to me near the end of 1913: "Ezra Pound has a project which he wants me to ask you about. He and some of the younger writers would like to get up a dinner in honour of Wilfrid Blunt. Of course I approve of the scheme. He wants to know if you think Blunt would come and if he would care about it. It would be entirely a men's dinner . . ." Mr. Blunt could not come to London, but invited them instead to come and lunch at Newbuildings. He had at that time a large flock of peafowl, so large that some were killed and eaten from time to time. And in suggesting that one would be an appropriate dish at his lunch I had told him how Yeats had once been tempted to go to a reception at some London house by the rumour that a roast peacock was always a feature of the supper; and in his disappointment at not finding this he had quoted to some fellow guest a poem written about Coole by a country poet, who after many extravagant praises had written discontentedly in the margin, "did not see the wildcat".

Mr. Blunt wrote on 7 January 1914: "I sent a telegram to say that Sunday the 18th would suit me well for the poets' visit here. As a matter of fact, however, one day is the same as another to me for it, and whatever day they choose I shall be equally ready to receive them. As I never take a meal away from home, they will always find me here at lunch-time at 12.20, though I should like a word beforehand. Also don't let them worry themselves with presenting me with anything more than their good wishes—on paper if they like, with their names—but as simply as possible. I am past the age for caring for Christmas boxes and should not know what to do with one. There shall certainly be a peacock for luncheon. The idea is just to my fancy and one quite easy to realize at Newbuildings."

19 January 1914. "I write to report that all went off most successfully yesterday. I found all the young men charming and think they enjoyed their meal, most of them, Miss Lawrence tells me, eating two helpings of the peacock, which figured in full plumage on the table . . . The marble box was presented and Ezra Pound read an address in verse which the six poets had signed and I made a little speech in thanks, and Yeats made a speech in reply, and there was some good talk about literature, which they all seemed to know far better than I do, and then Belloc came in . . . Yeats did his part of cicerone admirably and I think all were pleased. I know I found all of them interesting and hope they

will come down again separately some day and spend a week-end with us, so that I may make their acquaintance better, for you know how difficult it is to talk to half-a-dozen people you do not know altogether. I only wish you had been with us." The six poets were Yeats, Sturge Moore, Aldington, Ezra Pound, Flint, Plarr—Masefield had joined but was unable to come! This was the address written by Ezra Pound and given in a white marble box designed by Brzeska: —

> Because you have gone your individual gait,
> Written fine verses, made mock of the world
> Swung the grand style, not made a trade of art,
> Upheld Mazzini and detested institutions.
>
> We, who are little given to respect,
> Respect you, and having no better way to show it,
> Bring you this stone to be some record of it.

A great pleasure.
9 February 1914. "The little episode of the poets' visit has been a great amusement and pleasure to me, and I am altogether in earnest in hoping to see more of them. I liked them *all*. But Newbuildings is a place for summer rather than for winter and I shall wait the coming of the flowers before I make any further move in the way of invitations, though they will be welcome here at any time."

And Yeats had written in February 1914: "I dined with Mrs. Fowler last night. She tells me that a man in the Foreign Office called X., whom I have met at her house, says, 'he will never speak to any of those poets again'. This because of your paying honour to Blunt. I promised to tell you about that day at Newbuildings. I think all went well. We had lunch at 12.30 and there was a peacock which tasted just like turkey I thought, though Ezra said a more divine turkey, and after lunch we presented our stone box. Ezra read out his poem, and Blunt spoke and proposed my health, to which I responded with a speech. Blunt asked us to stay for Belloc, who came about 3.30, and finding himself in a company who could not be shocked was, I think, a little bewildered. All the poets behaved modestly and said what they should say . . .

"Blunt asked all there to invite themselves down from a Saturday to Monday any time they chose . . . Sturge Moore is a little unhappy about Ezra's verses, as he says he respects

A photograph of a bronze of W. B. Yeats. Sculptor unknown, but a similar one by a sculptress called Jones, is in the possession of Miss Anne Yeats.

Above left: W. B. Yeats and George Moore outside Coole. Above right: Bernard Shaw outside Coole. Below left: a rapid self portrait of George Russell (A.E.) in Lady Gregory's scrapbook. Below right: a sketch of J. M. Synge by Robert Gregory.

a lot of things, and Ezra has made him say he doesn't. All were delighted with Blunt.

"Z.[2], one of the young poets who went down to Blunt's, went off to enlist (I hope with a book in his mind) but is home again and indignant, for owing to the wildness of his appearance, instead of being taken as a recruit he was arrested as a spy. His emotion made him incoherent and he was shut up in a barrack-room of some kind for a while. He is the poet who wears no hat because he has never found one to suit him."

Later letters from Mr. Blunt say: —

19 April 1915. "You tell me Bernard Shaw is with you. I have an admiration for him equalling his own, preferring his plays infinitely to Shakespeare's and his wit to Voltaire's. Indeed, I am inclined to think that wit began with Shaw, at least in the English tongue . . . I have been living all this winter on Belloc . . .

"Don't be deterred from coming to London next month. This place is at its best in May when oaks are in their first leaf and the birds are singing their best. We heard the first cuckoo on Friday and gathered the first bluebells yesterday."

6 July 1917. 'You will have seen Mary Wentworth's death in the papers. It was a long illness of four years, the last two having been spent almost entirely in bed, consumption of a very gradual kind. Hers was an uneventful but not, I think, unhappy life, for she had never had ambition, and so was not disappointed, enjoying small things and avoiding all the excitement of hope most girls indulge in. I think she never was in love or wished to be married. She was pleased in a quiet way with her little dignity of being a peeress of the realm, but without putting it forward except on the single occasion of her attending a coronation. I was fond of her, having been *in loco parentis* when we had care of her with Judith at Crabbet, and I think she was fond of me. She was very well looked after during her last year by a little West Indian girl she had made friends with at Trinidad, where she had been sent for her health, and who came back with her and devoted herself entirely to her, and she had a sufficient income to live comfortably in her little villa at Ascot with her dog and her parrot and a doctor whom she liked and a priest. Perhaps a negative life like this is the wisest.'

2 F. S. Flint, most probably.

7 November 1917. "A few friends have come to see me
this summer, including Madeline Wyndham, George's
mother, who stayed with me a fortnight. It was a great
pleasure to me, as it took me back to days fifty years and
more ago when I cared more for art than politics and she
was being painted by Watts. I took up a brush again and
we did some colouring together in the Jubilee Room which
makes a good studio (it was not painting) and I enjoyed it
like a return to youth . . . Anne is still kept in Egypt by the
submarines, but I hear from her pretty regularly, and have
some confidence that what is happening in Italy may hasten
the war. She has now succeeded to her Wentworth peerage
through the death of her niece, and will have, I suppose, to
come back as soon as the Mediterranean is free on business
connected with it, though there is no property concerned."
On the death of his wife. (Lady Anne Blunt, Lady Wentworth) died in Egypt, December 1917: —

8 January 1918. "If I have been long in answering your
letter you will understand how it has been with me and
how these short winter days leave little time. It has indeed
been a great blow to me, far more than it would have been
ten years ago, for I was counting as the chief joy of what
remained to me of life her return in the spring, when we
had plans of doing much together that needed doing. I
counted too on peace, or at least an armistice which should
make her journey possible, and now peace seems really
coming, but too late for her. I hope it may come in time
for you and bring Robert back to you . . . The winter has
been a sad one, passed by me most of it in bed, but I am
still able to write prose and so am getting through it. But
I shall write no more verse. That needs an overflow of vital
force which cannot be renewed."

These are some passages from Yeats's letters: —
London. January 1911. "Here is a little lyric written in
twenty minutes for a second act of *Countess Cathleen* and
it is much better than the lyrics I spent two weeks over.
The dancers are of the faery host: —

> Lift up the white knee;
> That's what they sing,
> Those young dancers
> That in a ring
> Raved but now
> Of the hearts that break

Long, long ago
For their sake;
But the dance changes,
So lift up the gown,
For all that sorrow
Is trodden down.

I made the little dance poem after seeing the Moscow dancers.

"I am enjoying my Chaucer reading very much and am beginning to get excited by the change of method that came when poets wrote to be read out, not to be sung. Chaucer is being read to me and I myself am reading a certain amount of his predecessors and contemporaries. I must say the Irish lyrics of that time seem to be finer than any except some parts of Chaucer.

"I have had a mass of letters to write (I don't quite know what about) but am comforted by the thought of that poem and by the peace of mind I get from my growing knowledge of Chaucer and his time."

23 January 1911. "Yesterday I was so tired with the strain of the lyric which was just finished that I went to Hampstead Heath where I saw an old man flying a kite in the mist. It was entirely out of sight and he was walking up and down in the most evident pride. One thought of some eastern magician as one watched the string vanish in the sky."

Dublin. 2 February 1911. "I was greatly disappointed to find you had only stayed one day. I had thought you would be here for some days and had even decided what book you would read out to me. I wanted to get a few hours of life free from business, a little of our old tranquil friendship.

"I cannot tell you what a joy *Canavans* has been to me. I told the audience in my speech before the curtain that of all our comedies it was my favourite.

"St. John Ervine (author of *Magnanimous Lover*) spoke of you the other day as the first "comic genius" who has been a woman."

15 May 1911. "The lyric is not finished yet, though I work at it every day. It is a metrical experiment and may not be very good. I am working very hard not wasting a moment and but for my wearisome dreadful evenings very happily. I seem to have conquered my indolence by often changing my work."

22 May. "I believe I have at last finished the lyric. For

more than two weeks I have worked at it for at least two hours every day. Nothing ever gave me so much trouble and it is certainly not among my best things. I am hoping that even playwriting will seem easy after it."

18 November 1911. "I was so much struck by the rehearsal of the *Shepherd's Play* that I went to see Edward Martyn yesterday and asked him, if our Second Company were to specialize in religious drama would the priests take it up as they are doing in Paris. The Second Company could quite well go about to Parish Halls and the like, especially a little way from Dublin. He said that he greatly approved of the idea but that he thought they were too suspicious of us, they thought our movement not only anti-Catholic, but anti-Christian. I said that it was none of these things, but that it was the interest of his Church to encourage a distinguished and intellectual life in Ireland for the alternative would be crude atheism in a few years. He agreed to my surprise very heartily in this, but said they were not clever enough to see it . . . however, he is to do his best . . ."

8 February 1912. "I think the refutation here of two or three of the fables has had a good effect. I think the respectable papers are beginning to see that the attack on Synge has been overdone. I was amused to read today in the *Independent* an attack not on Synge, but upon his followers, so Robinson may be the next public enemy, we shall see Synge accepted as a wicked immortal, an invulnerable devil who cannot be shot even with a silver bullet. I don't think nationalist Catholic Dublin, of the easy-going kind, is particularly annoyed with us, but I do see that we will have the open opposition of the bigots."

7 December 1911. "We have just arranged a scheme to give after Christmas a cycle of religious plays, one an *Annunciation,* second *A Shepherd's Play,* third a *King's Play,* fourth *A Nativity* and possibly *A Flight into Egypt.* I am slightly nervous about the effect of the American row here. Two significant things happened; last week a priest denounced us from the altar, and Larkin the socialist, who is getting up all the strikes here, praised the *Playboy* in his speech—there one has the forecast and one would just as soon they didn't fight about us."

18 January 1912. "It will be ten or twenty years before the Academic Committee matters so far as one's public position is concerned, the one advantage of it is that one gets to know writers and to find out one's friends and enemies. I never

look at old X. for five minutes without a desire to cut his throat. We are getting up a Browning celebration; he will probably deliver the oration. In the middle of his last (it was Sir Alfred Lyall's memorial meeting), Maurice Hewlett said to Henry James, 'This is dull', to which Henry James sternly replied, 'Hewlett, we are not here to enjoy ourselves'."
Dublin. 11 January 1912. "(School of Acting.) At first we kept off the old repertory but I made up my mind a little while ago that it was more important to train the people and to know whose places they take if necessary, than to get audiences, especially as getting audiences in the present state of public opinion isn't easy. It will blow over soon enough. One of the curious things is the lying rumours that have been put in circulation everywhere, one of which seems to be believed as a matter of course, that Synge died of disease contracted by living an immoral life. I was told the other day that everyone knew that the story about cancer had been invented to hide this. The other slander is about the character of the players, it seems to have begun in the *Leader* but it has got among people who hardly know of the existence of that paper. Miss B. tells me that a Protestant woman said to her the other day, 'What I object to about the Abbey and the reason that a great many people will not go there, is that whenever a doubtful character such as the woman in *Blanco Posnet* is put on the stage they bring in a character from the streets to play the part'."
London. December 1912. "I was at Masefield's the other night and some woman who had one of the Synge books open at his portrait began telling me it was such a tragic face, so sad. I said, 'he didn't make that impression on people when they met him. He used to seem in good enough spirits'. She said, 'Did you know Synge?' 'Yes,' I said. 'But know him well I mean?' she said. I saw that I was interfering with the most modern popular conception of a genius as a drunken Calvinist. Strindberg is the type—the literature of a bad conscience."
1 December 1915. "Last Saturday evening I dined with Lady Cunard to meet Balfour . . . he is a most charming and sympathetic listener, so charming and sympathetic that he lures one on into more and more vehemence of speech."
7 February 1913. "I am thoroughly with you in not pressing *Playboy* unduly. Above all I think it scandalous of the management to put it on for the first night in Catholic towns, especially when you are going for a very short visit.

It would be as bad taste for us to flourish it in Catholic faces as for us to withdraw it to please them. We must go on our way without petulance or yielding. It must be there for its own public to find, but it would be sheer bad manners for us to thrust it without need in any man's face. I suppose Tyler wants the advertising of another row, but all wise governments know that one of the privileges of victory is to make concession without seeming weak."

London. "I spent Saturday to Monday at Oxford and with Robert Bridges, and had a very pleasant talkative visit. Bridges is a delightful person, both to look at and to listen to.

"Craig came here on Sunday and at once discovered Robert's designs. He was enthusiastic and began considering how one could get on the stage the cold light. He thought a few candles could get it ... I am anxious to get into my new book (or edition) some of Robert's designs."

March 1913. "Ricketts brought me to the Russian ballet last night. This time I was well in front and could see the whole picture, (do you remember our box high up at one side?), and thought it most exquisite, most simple and strangely profound. The one beautiful thing I have seen on the stage of recent years. I saw *The Pretenders* a week ago. I was disappointed. When I read it I thought it a great play but on the stage all seemed to vanish but melodrama. There is a curious triteness in the emotional elements which is increased by the acting."

8 February 1913. "If we get a good American engagement for next autumn and winter I think it would be well to make no music hall engagements. They do not help our work which is after all to educate Ireland ... I feel that the Dublin public will have a real cause of complaint if we neglect them for music halls where we have no educative or artistic mission. As far as I know, everybody is agreed as to the evil effect of large halls and music hall audiences on any fine and sincere dramatic art. It would be a poor thing if Home Rule should find us not able to take advantage of the new life in the country but with our own art made cheap and our players with what sense of Ireland remains to them gone."

9 May 1912. (With a rejected play.) "You might tell him that the play was rejected because it was spoilt as a play by the substitution of propagandist conceptions for the disinterested curiosity about human life out of which good plays are made."

May 1912. "I have been reading James Stephens' poems and Starkie's. I think that Stephens has very fine lines and verses, but is a good deal spoiled by his schoolboy theology of defiance, but at his best he really is very fine. Starkie, on the other hand, has surprised me with his really delicate technical skill, he has gradually shaped himself into real force and beauty. He is a good deal better than Stephens as at present, but Stephens is younger."

14 May 1912. "I hear that Masefield's poem 'Biography', in which Woburn Buildings and St. Pancras Church give him about his best passage, is in the *English Review*. He mourns over the disappearance of the house at the corner, 'the sweet house, he calls it, and the old blind beggar.

"Today I return to the revision of the long blank verse poem. I have not yet breakfasted. I have adopted the French breakfast I spoke of; a doctor has told me to take coffee, which I prefer, as I have a fine old coffee and tea caddy which I got in Dublin. The mischief is that the milkman does not come before 9.30 and cannot come earlier he says. This morning, in order to go to bed earlier tonight and so shorten the long hours when my eyes smart, I got up at 8.30. It is now after 9.30. Xmas letters I suppose. The milk has not come. I will keep the custom however. It seems better for me, and my cooking at lunch-time is better than for breakfast . . .

"The milkman came as I wrote these words and I have had my breakfast. The postman has come too, and brought me a leather-bound book from Florence, in which I shall start a new 'Diary', and a bottle of Chartreuse from Oldmeadow, he sends this to all his customers at Christmas. It is in a little box with an imitation Watteau on the lid, just the box Oldmeadow, turned wine merchant, would choose . . . I am beginning to get my rooms very pretty and comfortable, for all this year I have been one by one taking away the ugly old Tottenham Road cheap furniture. My tea caddy, which takes the place of a ninepenny tin, is the latest. It was in such bad order when I came from Dublin that Mr. Old, who has put it to rights, is convinced that it was prised open by the railway guard in mistake for a jewel box, and not even prised open with care, but I think it has merely suffered from Dublin business habits."

22 December 1912. "I have been greatly distressed to hear that Mabel Beardsley is dying of cancer. She is receiving her friends in the hospital in seemingly very serene spirits. I

never saw her more than once or twice in the year, and very often not at all, but I have always found her sweet and gracious. A young musician met her here, and being very tongue-tied tried to express his emotion afterwards by saying 'She is like—like—O, she is like King Arthur!'."

8 January 1913. "Strange that just after writing those lines on the Rhymers who 'unrepenting faced their ends' I should be at the bedside of the dying sister of Beardsley, who was practically one of us. She had had a week of great pain but on Sunday was I think free from it. She was propped up on pillows, with her cheeks I think a little rouged and looking very beautiful. Beside here was a Christmas tree with little toys containing sweets, which she gave us. Mrs. Davis had brought it, I daresay it was Rickett's idea. I will keep the little toy she gave me and I daresay she knew that. On a table near were four dolls dressed like people out of her brother's drawings; women with lose trousers and boys that looked like women. Ricketts had made them, modelling the faces and sewing the clothes. They must have taken him days. She had all her great lady airs and asked after my work and my health as if they were the most important things in the world to her. 'A palmist told me,' she said, 'that when I was forty-two my life would take a turn for the better, and now I shall spend my forty-second year in heaven.' And then emphatically, pretending that we were incredulous, 'Oh yes, I shall go to heaven, Papists do'. When I told her what Mrs. Emery was doing in Ceylon she said, 'How fine of her —but a girls' school! Why she used to make even me blush.' Then she began telling wicked stories and inciting us (there were two men beside myself) to do the like. At moments she shook with laughter. Just as I was going, her mother came in and saw me to the door. As we were standing at it, she said, 'I do not think she wishes to live—how could she after such agony. She is all I have left now' . . . I lay awake most of the night with a poem in my head. I cannot overstate her strange charm—the pathetic gaiety. It was her brother, but her brother was not I think lovable, only astonishing and intrepid. She has been ill since June last.

"Mabel Beardsley has given me a most charming Chinese quilt. She is as merry as ever, and has taken of late to having conjuring performances, in addition to two concerts a week, to keep her from gloom. A professional conjurer will come and put a little table close up to the bed, and do the three card trick and the pea under the three cups and so on for her solitary enjoyment. She says the only defect is the badness of the jokes that tires her out, as she has to do her stage laugh constantly for an hour or the conjurer would be discouraged.

"I have written three little lyrics about Mabel Beardsley dying, but I will not send you them till I have done a fourth to link them together. I think they are really quaint and touching; I describe the dolls, the drawings people gave her. I was there on Sunday, she had had a bad three or four days but was seemingly in good spirits; made me tell the visitors my last George story . . ."

11 February 1913. "Mabel Beardsley said to me on Sunday, 'I wonder who will introduce me in heaven. It should be my brother but then they might not appreciate the introduction. They may not have very good taste.' She said of her brother, 'He hated the people who denied the existence of evil. He had a passion for reality.' She has the same passion, and puts aside any attempt to suggest recovery, yet I have never seen her in low spirits. She talked of a play she wanted to see: 'If I could only send my head and my legs,' she said, 'for they are quite well'. Till one questions her, she tries to make one forget that she is ill. I always see her alone now, she keeps Sunday afternoon for me. I will send you the little series of poems when they are finished. One or two are I think very good."

London. 7 February 1913. "I am deep in my seventh lyric about Mabel Beardsley. I must give it the morning hours if I wake up in good health. I find that one has to be at one's best for lyrics."

28 February 1913. "I send you a copy of my verses about Mabel Beardsley. I like the last two. Ezra Pound and Bullen (who turned up yesterday full of projects) admire them, but I think M. was a little troubled—possibly even a little shocked. He lives amid earnest women and the sort of men they collect.

"She has asked me to go oftener to see her, so I am going twice a week. Last time I was there she showed me how thin her hair had become (it had been very abundant—one of the things that made her beautiful) and talked of it seemingly quite cheerful, without self pity. She has much pain because she will not take any drug which stupefies the mind. She says she never enjoyed so much intimate friendship, and that she has happy memories. I found her last time I went reading old letters, chiefly from Captain Scott, a friend of many years. One day she talked to me about the other world.

Her confessor has told her he could not help her, he had
no strong conviction, and he suggested that she should get
a new confessor. And her comment was, 'No, I would not
exchange that man and his doubt for a man who would insult
me with his certainty.'

"It is this life in which she is passionately interested as
ever.

"It was some kind of clairvoyant prevision that set me
writing that poem I made at Coole (the Kings) about Death
and its irremediableness. I did not know she was ill then.
I shall remember her always as one who attained to a perfectly distinguished personality, in an old aristocratic way."

These are the two last lyrics of the seven: —

Her Courage

When her soul flies to the predestined dancing-place
(I have no speech but symbol, the pagan speech I made
Amid the dreams of youth) let her come face to face,
While wondering still to be a shade, with Grania's shade,
All but the perils of the woodland flight forgot
That made her Diarmuid dear, and some old cardinal
Pacing with half-closed eyelids in a sunny spot
Who had murmured of Giorgione at his latest breath—
Aye, and Achilles, Timor, Babar, Barhaim, all
Who have lived in joy and laughed into the face of Death.

Her Friends Bring Her A Christmas Tree

Pardon, great enemy,
Without an angry thought
We've carried in our tree,
And here and there have bought
Till all the boughs are gay
And she may look from the bed
On pretty things that may
Please a fantastic head.
Give her a little grace
What if a laughing eye
Have looked into your face—
It is about to die.

I liked very much one that is called *Her Race*

She has not grown uncivil
As narrow natures would
And called the pleasures evil
Happier days thought good;
She knows herself a woman

No red and white of a face,
Or rank, raised from a common
Unreckonable race;
And how should her heart fail her
Or sickness break her will
With her dead brother's valour
For an example still?

Stone Cottage, Colman's Hatch. 23 January 1915. "We have just had a call from the Vicar. (Ezra says I have brought this upon myself by reading Wordsworth.) I hope all is well with you. I dreamt about a week ago that I was to take the chair at a lecture of yours and that I waited half-an-hour and you didn't come, upon which I said to the audience, 'Something must have happened to her because she has never missed an appointment or even been five minutes late in her life'. Evidently my subconscious being is anxious lest you fatigue yourself."

14 January 1915. "I saw Robert's picture at the New English and thought it very beautiful. It was the only thing there that I cared for. The picture is hung very well, given the central place of a wall."

12 February 1915. "I saw Pope Hennessy and Mrs. Pope Hennessy at Mrs. Huth Jackson's on Thursday evening. He was in good spirits about the war. I praised Robert's pictures to him, and Mrs. Pope Hennessy said, 'He is developing late like his mother'. Then somebody joined in who knew you years ago and said if he had been told in those days that you were going to do all that you have done since, he would not have believed it. He thought you were 'very quiet'. I don't know whether you will take this as a compliment or not."

5 March 1915. "I am sorry my time in the country is over. I did much work and read nearly the whole of Wordsworth and had Doughty's *Arabia Deserta* read out to me, 2 vols.; *Grettir the Strong; Burnt Njal;* and some small sagas, and Browning's *Sordello*. I never feel at home in town after the country.

"I opened at the Club yesterday Bodkin's *Recollections of a County Court Judge* or some such title, and I found a very enthusiastic account of Shaw-Taylor put into the mouth of Judge Adams. He describes him as settling the land question. I was glad to see it as one does not want the professional politicians to get all credit in the eye of history. He himself talks with admiration of Hugh Lane.

"I had a curious dream, which was I hope, prophetic. I and you and some others were in the kitchen of some old Irish castle (Tillyra I thought), a strange romantic place. A queer sort of juggler came in. He took out a mutton bone and told us to cut meat from it and then, according as where and how we cut, foretold our future. All, as I woke, faded except one sentence spoken to you, 'you will never lack goods'."

March 1916. "I went out to Dulac's on Tuesday evening and saw the mask that he has made for Cuchulain, in my *Hawk's Well*, a Greek head and helmet with the look of something older, perhaps Egyptian. Cuchulain will be a wonderful figure, magnificent in face and dress, and it is quite easy to speak in a mask. I put it on and recited in it. He had begun on an old man's mask for the other speaking character. I have added several lyrics to the play and will try and send you a copy. I have a fancy that if we ever do up the Mechanics' Institute, the big room in it might do for plays of this kind. The aim would be to get those who cared for poetry and nobody else. The invention of the masks gets rid of all kinds of difficulties of age and appearance, doubling of parts, etc.

"I have a dream that such plays, especially, perhaps, if in Irish, might be taken into country districts. They need no stage, or at the utmost, if the audience has grown beyond let us say fifty, a square platform. It would be the old waggon theatre again. However, that will not be my work but it might be the Gaelic League's. I feel that all one can do is to make an art form and let others apply it."

25 August 1916. "I had a gloomy night of it, thinking that for the first time for nearly twenty years I am not at Coole at the end of August . . . I have a cold this morning, perhaps one reason for my gloom. I think it will be impossible to be quite the same after finishing the memoirs—the futility of all but all of the personal life—a general impression of turbulence. I have now got to about 1899."

Dublin. 13 November 1916. "Here is a queer story. Last night a rather drunken man got into my carriage coming from Greystones. I was in a first to escape the crowd. Just after we left the station a drunken man came lurching along the corridor and into my carriage. 'First class carriage, third class ticket—do it on principle,' he said, and then, 'Why are the third class carriages so bad? Can you answer me that now?' Then after asking me if I had known Tom Kettle he

said, 'Why are so many men dead that should be alive, and
so many men alive that should be dead? Can you answer
me that now?' He then said something had happened to him
once that he could not understand. He was in Tipperary
during the Rising and he heard a lot of plainly false news.
The guard of the train brought it and the police sergeant
spread it. He thought it would be a good joke to spread his
own false news, so he said to the sergeant, 'Sheehy Skeffington
has been shot', and he saw the sergeant spreading it and the
people coming out of the shops to listen. 'And he was shot
that very morning and not a soul knew it. Now is not that
a queer thing? Did you ever hear a queerer story? Can you
answer me that now?' When I got back to the Stephen's
Green Club where I am staying I found the smoking-room
empty but for one man who was sitting over the fire. I told
him the story and he said that he himself had just the same
experience. When at school he had invented as he thought
a story of Lord Frederick Cavendish being killed, and when
later in the day news arrived of the assassination, he thought
it but his own story come back again and would not believe
it. Probably that is how news spread in India. People get the
thought by telepathy and think they are inventing, or
repeating what someone had told them'."
13 May 1914. "On Monday we went, Maud Gonne coming
too, five hours into the country (where we stayed the night)
to investigate an amazing 'religious miracle'. We found an
old priest, charming and seeming holy, who had been a
private tutor and chaplain but had lived for twenty years in
his little country town, looking after his garden, full of
flowers and pigeons, and embroidering vestments, and copying on to his ceiling and his walls religious pictures which
he copies fairly well. He has a chapel in his house, twenty
feet by eight or so, where he says Mass, and in this chapel
hung a common oleograph, the Sacred Heart. This oleograph
about two years ago began to bleed. It was sent to Rome
and the one that took its place began to bleed, and the
oleographs given by the priests to various pious people, it
seems, have bled also. The oleograph was moved from the
chapel to a farm building on a hill where the priest is to
build a great church, and when we saw it there it had drops
of fresh blood, some of which Fielding took away for analysis.
The priest prays at 3.00 a.m. in the morning; after our first
visit God spoke to him and said Maud Gonne would some
day live in the house the priest lives in now, and I am it

seems intended for the mystic apostolate, and the voice used
this strange sentence, 'If he does not give his intelligence to
me, I will take his intelligence away and leave him at the
mercy of the heart.' The whole thing puzzled Fielding and
myself greatly for of course the orthodox explanation is
impossible, and a sceptical explanation difficult. Maud Gonne
fell on her knees early in the day and remained on them as
far as possible. She delighted Fielding, who burst out when
he had left us at the Paris railway station, 'dear, good,
charming creature'."

17 May. "I doubt if the miracle working priest meant what
you think. He is on bad terms with his bishop and says,
'France is sick because of the evil of the priests', but the
whole thing is a puzzle. When you see my account you will
find some strange light on our folk-lore. He says, 'All places
like this require victims'. His victim is a stigmatized woman
in Germany who visits his chapel in the spirit. She is
paralyzed."

London. 20 May 1913. "Yesterday I brought a page of
automatic script to the British Museum; it contained various
languages. I went from department to department and had
them read. Perfectly correct Hebrew, perfectly correct Greek,
perfectly correct Latin, perfectly correct Welsh, perfectly
correct Chinese, and apparently correct ancient Egyptian,
(600 B.C.), but in this case my tracing was not sufficiently
good, so only part of the inscription could be read. The
contents of the inscription were as remarkable as the form.
They were evidently carefully arranged so as to make
impossible every scientific theory which accounts for things
of the kind by the emergence of submerged memories,
memories that is of things perceived by the unconscious,
though not necessarily by the conscious mind. These sentences throw light on one another, and in one case contained
a statement about a Hebrew writer of the 2nd century,
which puzzled the British Museum authority. He only got
it right on second reading. The whole page was evidently
arranged to prove the presence of a learned intelligence
working through a comparatively ignorant girl. She had
taken no trouble to have it interpreted, except in a very
superficial way; it is probably the most sensational page in
psychical research. While I was with her last week the script
was interrupted by a spirit who wanted to find out if a book
which he wrote was still read. He gave us facts to identify
him by and the name of the book. He was a German

traveller who travelled in the Caucasus early in the 18th century. I promised to find out for him. I found him yesterday in a French biographical dictionary. I found also another spirit who told us as a help to his identification that he had known Marie Antoinette and Monsieur Carrick. I have found him, and Carrick was evidently his French mispronunciation of Garrick. I excited myself to such an extent that I slept for twelve hours last night and am fit for very little today; so far I have investigated not a hundredth part of the whole script. The girl has taken it home with her, but Mrs. Fowler has promised to make copies of the Greek as a beginning. As a beginning I want to find out whether it is Greek of a different period, and then I want to make a study of the errors in the script. I want to find out if they are visual or auditory, as is apparently the case with Monsieur *Carrick*. Unfortunately, the controls themselves forbid publication . . . It is what I have been waiting for before finishing the essay."

These are from letters written to me by J. B. Yeats, who died in New York last year (1922): —
London. 29 July 1898. "I have finished the sketch of Mr. Horace Plunkett. I enjoyed my time drawing him very much. He told me several very interesting things about the M.Ps., but we had not much conversation. I find such good sittings as he gives tend to silence. When the 'sitting' or posing is lax one's attention flags, then the tongues begin to wag. His sitting earned my gratitude every minute."
28 August. (W.B.Y. criticised the portrait, said it made Mr. Plunkett look like a member of the Young Men's Christian Association.) "He is a perfectly fresh and individual personality. The young man of the Christian Association is a manufactured article. I had not much conversation with him but everything he said was good. He said Chamberlain had never known repose. Even his orchids were business, to get the first in the market his great interest.
"Healy he said was himself a loveable and tender-hearted man. In politics his spirit was impish, almost Satanic, his great defect being that he had no policy. Lately he was working with some consistency, his personal *animus* impelling him to oppose everything that came from John Dillon. He spoke with a sort of bright-eyed incisiveness. Redmond, he said, he greatly liked and a born orator—he would never come to anything because of indolence. He spoke with an emphasis, half laughter and half disgust, of

the great Ashmead Bartlett. I never met a man who was so little the made-up plated article. I fancy he has a very strong brain and though the meekest of men, has swallowed the formulas as completely as the turbulent Mirabeau . . . It seems to me that Healy's intellect resembles very closely Irish cultivated intellect, at any rate as we have it in Dublin inside and outside of T.C.D., that is to say it is purely destructive and critical.

"I am very busy on a portrait of my daughter Lilly and mean it to be the corner stone of my fortune. Lilly being a natural honest person like Horace Plunkett and unlike Christian Society's young men sits with great patience and alacrity, jealously watching the whole performance . . ."

Bedford Park. 18 September 1898. "I should like to know why Dublin people are the most prosaic in the world and are so in *direct proportion* to the amount of education amassed. I suppose it is because it is altogether *critical*, which pulverizes the desires, and desire is the life of imagination.

"Desire is a sort of furious mason—and out of the materials supplied him by observation, argument, knowledge, he builds himself a habitation. Given the desire in full strength, the rest follows by a law of mind as inevitable as that of gravitation. I don't think you know F.X. In her you have the curious conflict always in progress between active impetuous desire and this same highly critical milieu in all Dublin in which she lives. That is why she is so interesting and so alive and so unhappy. Paris taught her to treat desire with respect."

May. "I am so glad you like Jack, and I am so glad you asked him and his wife to stay with you. I expect to see them greatly improved and *expanded* by the liberating influence of your house and presence. There are so many people we like because we think well of them, but from the first moment one likes Jack and thinks well of him because we like him, which is the only basis of lasting friendship. When his wife, with wifely glee, told how Jack did everything you wanted him to do, my brother said, 'there is no resisting those courageous eyes'."

2 August 1898. "Elton, who is brother-in-law to McColl (Willie will know these names), said to me that the latter said he did not know whether Jack was a great humorist or a great poet. Willie will tell you McColl is most given to chastening his friends."

London. 16 June 1899. "S. and L. went away on Monday leaving the house a desert. Every house needs a woman, a professed woman. In this house just now there is no unoccupied person into whose sympathetic ear I can drop a confidential remark."

New York. 1907. "I hope Willie succeeded with his fishing —how well I understand the joy of unpacking a new rod . . . happiness goes with the angler, behind him a lone black care never stands. Years ago a wild imaginative man, L. C. Heron, had an ideal death, he had just hooked a salmon when he was struck down with death (paralysis or apoplexy). The boy with him took the rod and played the fish, and Heron's dying eyes up to the last were intent on that line and fish. What a comfort to his friends if they knew it and had the sense to appreciate. He is fishing now in the river of Paradise."

28 November 1911. (After the *Playboy* disturbance, and congratulating me on what I was reported as having said to the interviews). "It was so clever, witty, with the good nature of what the Americans call 'perfect poise'—it was at once so winning and so disconcerting. You gave the giant Stupidity a mortal thrust with a courteous smile. Where now are the Omodawns? . . . I am more grateful to you than I can express."

25 November 1911. (During *Playboy* trouble). "I am watching your career with the greatest anxiety, I think the people have 'caught on' to a great interest in your personality. You have only to show yourself as much as possible. *Personality* fascinates the American mind, it is the result of their boss system of politics. Your look breathes courage and honesty. It is honesty against dishonesty, and life against death and courage against vicious and venomous poltroonery and free men against slaves."

11 October 1912. "For months past I have been suffering terribly from indigestion—only the indigestion is strictly mental. To cure it I have 'taken' two big lives of Goethe, one of these in three immense volumes, I have also read for the first time Eckermann's *Conversations,* one of the most inspiring books I have ever read. Out of Goethe came Carlyle and Matthew Arnold and all art and literary criticism, at least I think so. The whole cause of my indigestion is an attempt to write two articles which simply won't consent to

become finished articles, one of these on art and the other
on how to develop *personality*, big subjects you will say.
I have also been busy painting a self-portrait for John Quinn
who is *to pay me any price* I like to ask. Under these
circumstances a self-portrait becomes a collossal business, a
wild labyrinth of infinite effort. Sometimes I say I will satisfy
myself with a mere impression like Sargent, and then I feel
I must have emotion, and again I 'go' for clear outline and
profuse details, after the antique. The age is critical rather
than creative, hence this constant preoccupation with
varieties of technique. I think I shall come home next year.
I am getting tired of the homelessness of my life here. Here
I can have no country life, mosquitoes make that impossible,
and in America are no tall trees, and the birds don't sing,
only give a sort of nervous note. Every summer I have had
invitations to spend the whole summer away by the margin
of big lakes. They are noble people, primitive in the sense
we shall all become in the future; their likings and dislikes
not spoiled by any refracting medium. One is ashamed of
one's own sophistication. I often feel myself to be vulgar
among them. They are often ridiculous but never vulgar.
Englishmen are never ridiculous, but they are incessantly
vulgar, both middle and upper class, only the poor escape,
and they are brutal.

"Do you read Walt Whitman? Here is something out of
him which will interest you and Willie—'The Democracy
ought to be supreme but should never control . . .' (Written
in later) I have looked it up and the words are, 'I put my faith
in the rise, the supremacy (note this rule) of the superb
masses.' The men who do things, the workers; they are our
hope. This is not the sort of letter I meant to write."

9 October 1914. "I think Willie is staying with you, but
if not would you please forward the enclosed letter, only
I would ask you first to read it yourself, perhaps it may
interest and perhaps it may please you, which will greatly
please me. You are yourself so rich in the finite which you
convert by your creative gift into reconciling humour, that
combination of laughter and pity which is your form of the
artistic and the beautiful, that perhaps you will be interested
in my little theory on the relation between the finite and
the infinite, the infinite being my name for that region in
which human desire can range unimpeded . . . I often see
Quinn, he is again and again my good Samaritan unwearied
in well doing."

25 February 1916. "I met Masefield at luncheon, a small party, small and select, but one had not much chance of talking with the poet who was kept very busy after lunch writing his name in Mrs. Z.'s books. You will recognise this kind of entertainment provided for the distinguished stranger. Masefield was patient in his un-smiling way (sketch). Colum says Pittsburgh is pervaded by the spirit of the North of Ireland and Chicago by the South of Ireland. Some day, when the history is being written of these days, Irish people will recognise how Synge and you and Willie have rescued and saved the Irish element from absorbtion and made it conscious of itself."

20 November 1916. "I am very much obliged to you for rescuing those critiques from Willie's basket and sending them to me, it was characteristic of your unsleeping vigilance in thinking about other people. I can see by these critiques that Willie is now a classic, a sort of sovereign poet and anointed king. This is new to me in criticism of his work . . . I wish you could live here among my friends for a few weeks. I would like to lead you about on a personally conducted tour. We in Europe live in the past, these in the future. It is not that they despise the past—they have not heard of its existence. It is, I assure you, startling. How it would have surprised Matt Arnold! After a few struggles to maintain his equilibrium, he would have grown ashamed of his small and acidulated personality. I know, of course, that he travelled here, but that was years ago, and the people he met were scared of him and of England."

22 November 1916. "So Willie owns landed property . . . I think land love is as native to the heart as mother love, leasehold is only a stepmother's love. The philosophers with their claws of iron, rusty or newly polished, are everywhere, but they can't scratch out certain things written from time immemorial, a mother's love for her children or a man's for his plot of earth, and this last is patriotism in germ. Tagore has just given a lecture against Nationalism; if Nationalism means Imperialism—away with it—but patriotism that is affection for the land of our earliest association will survive; if not where would be the poets?—and Socialism will never drive out man's longing affection for his belongings. But reformers care nothing for psychology, and the poets are all gone in a body over to the Reformers—we must make a new Thermopylae against the Persian hordes."

June 1917. "I saw Quinn on Sunday, he is himself an

epitome of American life, worn out by things that don't matter, which at least to a man of his personality don't matter. Why should the racehorse harness itself to the heavy cart, within whose shafts should be the slow Flemish horse?" 23 July 1917. "Many thanks indeed for that paper with the extracts from E.S.'s letters. E. always had a great name and authority among his T.C.D. contemporaries and the book would impress them, among whom I had no kind of esteem, but I suppose they are all dead and gone. The Bishop, of the two, had the more poetic mind, because of his misfortunes, a crazy wife and an arctic religion, and he loyal to both, notwithstanding a freely working intelligence. He was brimful of reality—life with him like a boiling spring. Sometimes he would read out to me something from *The Golden Treasury* and when I read any of these poems his voice and look and manner are all before me, part of that poem. That shows that was the right man to read it, a true poet. I used to compare him to a burning mountain not allowed to erupt."

20 October 1917. "I saw Quinn yesterday and lunched with him. He is much wrought up over a book by a light-headed bad-hearted Scot, M.H., who has written a book called 'T.O.E.' on the strength of which the cowardly slanderer is about to give a round course of lectures. Quinn's activity, vigilant and ceaseless, is phenomenal, it keeps away from me the slimy waters of stagnation, though you will ask how could anyone sink into such conditions at the present moment. Well! if I am not stagnant I am stunned and deafened and horror-stricken; most of us vegetate and grow old because the Supreme has never cared enough about us to take us. Quinn is different, the Supreme keeps him alive because he is useful; therefore, though he looks so frail and white and drawn and over-worked he will live till some day he is thrown aside. I have never believed in any religion except the one doctrine of Predestination—we are here for us. Some are on the reserve, they are parents and grandparents—ancestors, from whom may come a remote descendant that will enter the fighting line. I am doubtful as whether I ought to inflict on you the trouble of reading this letter, I write so illegibly, and I do try to make it legible. Quinn never attempts it, he just hands any letters from me to the stenographer whose business it is to read the illegible and she makes a typewritten copy. Quinn's stenographer is a wonder, extraordinarily efficient, very silent, very very tall, fair-haired and

light-eyed. We have never been introduced, but when she sees me she smiles—and she chills me." (Sketch.)

June 1917. "It is strange and interesting watching America 'getting up' the war fever. I think that there has always been latent in the unconscious mind of the people a hatred for the German, kept down by fear. The fear is passing. In a tobacco shop, a man behind the counter, said to me, 'I don't want to see them licked, I want to see them wiped out'. I demurred and he went on to a tirade against their insufferable insolence and brutish ways, manifested every time they entered his shop. I think the Germans are themselves a little frightened and ashamed in this country of the Free. (Sketch —The Tobacco Man.) Exactly like him, a sober-minded intelligent man, a good specimen of the average American."

23 June 1917. "By this post I have sent to Willie a letter on listeners and talkers, making distinctions. Thackeray, I think, was a listener, and G. Moore a talker who would not listen at all. If you are not too busy, which I can well believe, I should like you to read what I have written. For you are yourself the best of listeners, as well as a good talker. Willie is a good talker but he has undoubtedly the disinterestedness of the good listener and can be quite genially sympathetic to people whether they are his friends or foes."

21 October 1917. "Mrs. X. told me she was present at a meeting at —— house presided over by the judge himself, in which an effort was being made to get money for bombs, etc., to be used in English towns, and that she herself made protests—he replied that she was 'overwrought' . . . In my list of hatreds I forgot one grand hatred, the combative kind. It is not a real hatred for it has no malignity. When old Simon de Montfort was in his last battle and knew that death was certain he had leisure to admire the skill of his enemy, merely claiming that they had learned it from him, and then he fought using his sword with both hands till he was killed with a stroke delivered from behind. Garibaldi, when he fought at Rome a losing fight, was in the thick of it all, killing and killing, sword in hand, and as he fought he sang. In this kind of hatred there is no malignity, the joy of the combat makes malignity impossible. Garibaldi hated his enemies when he was plotting and combining, not when the lists were set. The soldiers at the front probably don't hate the Germans as we do, perfect love casts out fear and joy casts out hatred. 'Fear the enemy when at a distance,' said ——, 'but don't hate him when he is close at hand'."

New York. 10 November 1917.   "Many thanks for the book
and more thanks still for your extremely interesting letter.
I like the book very much but am not surprised that you
and probably Willie do not care for it. You see I used to be
just like that, we were all like that; it was the temper of our
generation and besides, behind the words I find, so receptive
and inquisitive and so affectionate.

"It was T.C.D. and Unionism and Anglo-Irishmen (very
different from the real English) that weakened him. From
these influences I escaped as he never did, because I went
to London and met Nettleship and through him the
influence of Rossetti, though alas, through my own fault,
not the direct influence of Rossetti—I mean that I did not
meet his bodily presence. All through his life E. was insincere,
and why? because he, like the rest of us at that time, did not
trust his imagination. A man discovers himself by trusting
his imagination. The saving grace of the sinner, whether he
does his sinning in stealth or riotously, is that he trusts his
imagination and so acquires the virtue of sincerity—the
phrase is Burne Jones's—and so, as Jones confesses, made
him. All his years E. was haunted by his imagination and
often he listened but always when too late. He had a glimpse
of her as it were, but only as she vanished through his study
door, so that at times he was the saddest of men, a lover
who had thrown away his happiness, and who he knew, would
go on throwing it away for ever. For that reason he avoided,
as I think he did, myself among others, and clung to people
who knew nothing of imagination. I think his second wife,
a noble courageous woman, perfectly understood this 'situation', but what can a wife do? So together consoling
themselves with their (or this) friendship they trod the path
of insincerity—really to them a path rough and stony but
to the outside world all smoothness and honour and dignity,
and now left alone she looks round wistfully for a kind word
on her behalf from the men of imagination whom he and
she avoided while they longed for them. I always talked with
him and her as with a pair of Roman Catholic priests—
people who have given up so much and whom one must not
remind of their sacrifice. E. tried hard to fence himself all
round with irony, but his irony also lacked conviction, he
went through life a half-hearted man—sick bodily and
mentally.

"I am reading a book on Swinburne that interests me by
a man called Drinkwater. Here in New York one rains

blessings on the old Scotsman Carnegie, for to him we owe that this city is full of libraries where charming young ladies polite and efficient wait on starving intellects (by them well fed)."

1 April 1918. "It is interesting to watch America catching fire, and it is amusing to watch the Petitpas fury with their slowness. 'They do not know how to treat a soldier, they say how nice he looks in his uniform—but we—we where there is a soldier give him the wine and take the water—we give him the meat and ourselves take the bread.' So the pretty Celestine said to me—and she grimaced and tried to look ugly." (Sketch.)

"The President has inaugurated a new kind of statesman-ship—he says to everyone that he is the servant not the leader of his party, and he told an acquaintance of mine that he himself thought it would be better for the Americans not to go to France, but what, he asked, could he do 'with Roosevelt yelling at me—this he said to Mr. X. of one of the big Reviews. If he was in a Parliament like Lloyd George he could be heckled and interrogated, what would happen? But thanks to the naked and unashamed abominableness of Germany, America itself is springing to her feet—no—not springing—but she is wiping the sleep out of her eyes— thanks very much to Roosevelt whose influence is growing. He has not a great or original mind but he can 'yell' as the President said and no one doubts his rectitude. In England a man like Roosevelt would strive to carry with him the men of intellect and knowledge *with all manner of alluring and subtle touches*—here it is not so—no one attempts to speak *our* language, it would only put to sleep an audience that wants to shout, hallo, and stamp their feet. I once went to a political meeting; it was like Bedlam let loose—and I remembered our Irish audiences, some of the peasants who hardly cheer at all. I remember being present at a workman's gathering in England with John Stuart Mill speaking. No one cheered but kept up a quiet accompaniment of pleased and comfortable laughter as he made his points.

". . . I lectured the other day at Princeton—a large audience of ladies . . . I was not very well at the time, my complaint which I think the ancients would have called lethargy, very bad for a lecturer. The nobleman of whom Shakespeare wrote his sonnets, died of lethargy at thirty-seven and he the handsomest and most accomplished and most popular man of his time. I think lethargy is a sick self-love,

natural to a young and handsome nobleman but disgraceful
in a man of my age, so that on second thoughts I don't think
it was my illness, and that I had influenza and a cold in the
head, only it has lasted for weeks so that I fancied myself
like a very old man—which of course is nonsense."

29 July 1918. (To the *Sun,* refuting something said of
Synge.) "I never met a man of greater personal dignity. I
think I was present on the only occasion on which he met
Moore and he was so taciturn and difficult that I don't
wonder at Moore's afterwards describing him as 'morose'.
Of course he was not morose except to Moore, whom I know
he disliked. His affection for the Irish peasant made him
hostile to George Moore."

29 August 1918. "There is a letter on this war in today's
paper from G. B. Shaw. Shaw sees in a man nothing but
economics, hence his triumphs, hence his failures. Love of
success, that is of fame or money, is an always abiding force
in the poet. The poet is born a poet, but for some external
necessity, such as that of making a living, human nature
would sink into somnolence, yet once started an *inner*
necessity which has little to do with the external good, rules
the issue. I should like to be present at G. B. Shaw's death-
bed. So much patience would be an edifying spectacle for
arrogant man. A benevolent pawnbroker in an embarrassed
community is, I suppose, a possible conception; watching
with sly wisdom and testing everyone's solvency, he sees
nothing but money. G.B.S. is such a man and for all his
reading and his opportunities is resolved out of a kind of
cussedness not to change his attitude for anybody. When at
the end this cussedness is gone like a clap of thunder, this
spirit is broken, he will say, 'My friends I was wrong about
Shakespeare, I have been wrong about human nature. There
are more things in Heaven and Earth than I dreamed.'
Perhaps the only people present will be his own followers
and they will refuse to give poor G.B.S. his absolution.
——, in appearance a dandy, asked me what I thought of
Tennyson's being made a peer, and when I murmured some
banality, said impatiently would it not have been better
if he had written some good useful book. V. is now a middle-
aged shopkeeper somewhere in Dublin. I have not seen him
since that day."

New York. 29 September 1919. "As to America. It is a
nation of men and women who are not 'grown-ups' all
schoolboys and schoolgirls being educated together, there

is the charm of schoolboys—the usher if he is anaemic, thinks them devils incarnate—if he is healthy, with quiet nerves, he thinks them amusing, though devils. The headmaster loves them because he is a little remote from them in his headmastership and because he is full of his own conceit and believes that they are inchoate angels only waiting for his guidance and wisdom to emerge from devilry.

"Did you ever read an American novel? It is to me tiresome. I cannot get interested either in the author or his 'characters', not a 'grown-up' among them—all crazy about some theory—the theory only the suppression of some instinct or appetite or passion; though I adore intellect, I abhor theory, that is to say sentimentalism masquerading as intellect.

"Intellect is the truth that comes out of the well, and the well is reality—not this or that fragment of truth—but the whole thing. The reason I prefer my wife's people so much to their social 'betters' is that in them I find that kind of reality which I call the whole truth. Mentally, socially, they were nothing, socially the most disagreeable, that is the crossest people I ever met, but all the time with an all pervading sincerity—a vulgar Pollexfen to me as unthinkable as a dishonest one—among them I was not happy, but I was a pupil at a good school and had the sense to know it. This kind of reality does not exist in America—like schoolboys they are good-natured and charmingly naive but tiresome, except at first. My daughter's letters are the joy of my heart, they are so real. With the Pollexfen blood and tradition it could not be otherwise. It was Coleridge who said the substance of poetry is good sense, he means an abiding sense of multiplied and complete reality, the deep well, transparent and yet from its depth dark that no eye can penetrate to find its bottom nor can anyone find its scource. There intellect, the faculty of truth, dwells, whereas theoretical intelligence ranges over the whole earth, busy spinning out theories of love and hatred and of the appetites and passions.

"Meantime I don't forget that there are 900,000 of these people and that I have only seen and read about a small section, yet this section is dominant.

"I like America very much, only I think the literature rather raw, and besides they don't have the critical mind, and I have nothing else."

New York. 24 October 1919. "Today by registered post I sent you some MS. about Hugh. I said that light-mindedness is characteristic of the superior mind—and light-mindedness is a vile phrase. Yet what can I use? A young wife waiting for the arrival of her first-born and busy with her preparations—in spite of all her serious thoughts—and who so serious?—she will sing joyously.

She is light-minded.

"And so it runs through all animated natures when people are harmonious with themselves, and then they are most serious, there is it seems to me light-mindedness—a sort of triumphant singing together of all the parts that make the unity of bird or beast or man.

"Out of this light-mindedness come all the forms of art—discord brings the heavy mind. I mean discord within oneself; but harmony within oneself means light-mindedness—the mind like a bird on the wing for open spaces and flying with such ease and naturalness.

"I would rehabilitate that word light-mindedness."

8 July 1920. "I thought that what I wrote about Mrs. C. would amuse you by a picture of Hugh Lane's dexterity in dealing with that grotesque little person, really formidable because so grotesque, in face a monster who yet had the placetia(?), and besides Hugh Lane *enjoyed* her. I don't think humour derives its satisfaction from a sense of superiority so much as from a sense of difference—a sense of difference with a practical result, a sense *not* of superiority (your true humorist will deprecate the idea) but of *giving protection* (it must be one of the attributes of God the Father). When the helpless Mancini was in Dublin, Hugh Lane went about with him everywhere, spending every evening with him and obviously enjoyed every moment of his time; was that because he wanted to enjoy the sense of superiority—or was it from some mysterious enjoyment in the sense of giving a constant protection because Mancini by his queer ways and crazy notions was a constant shock? I think a shock, a sudden surprise always makes us laugh unless one is frightened or angry—and it was not easy to frighten Lane."

8 July 1920. "As to America, their trouble here is that there are no great men, or perhaps it is only that the country needs a stage manager, someone skilful in backgrounds and scenery and in managing the limelight. Here men spring into prominence and for a while are before the audience and then disappear and no one knows anything about them—and that is democracy, and the mob which loves itself too well to acknowledge any authority.

"Queen Elizabeth had her favourites whom she enriched
and who flattered her, but she had also her great men . . .
However, this is not what I mean by the absence of a good
stage manager from American life. In England the stage is
set, there is long preparation. Lloyd George is but a man
of yesterday and now look at him and how he is surrounded.
Every time I think of him I see him with a retinue, my
historic sense comes to my aid; I see him in long succession;
I see the House of Lords and the King and Westminster
Abbey.

"Here they don't like great men, for every American is
himself a great man and therefore he will have no rivals,
and if a man 'pops up' into momentary glory he shows
himself a true American by immediately ducking if only
he gets the hint.

"They like Walt Whitman because he flattered their kind
of conceit. Other poets have thought pathetically, tragically,
for the poor individual man in his forlorn isolation. Walt
is for the triumphant collective man. Walt is a traitor among
poets."

New York. 14 August 1920. "Some time ago you wrote a
letter to me that never was Ireland as interesting; that the
Sinn Fein was gaining respect and that you believed cranky
Ulster would come in. Your words have come true if today's
papers are to be trusted. In time of crisis and national peril
there is no counsellor like courage—courage with you is a
gift of nature—timidity is like the dust and dimness that
gathers on the glass on one's spectacles (mine for instance
when I paint); courage keeps the glass clean.

"My dear friends the Petitpas go to France on the 28th
and I feel lost. The new people have a great deal more of
the French politeness in which these Breton women were
rather deficient. Have they the French honesty and veracity?
Because of these qualities, I always found the Petitpas the
most stimulating of my friends.

"Surely veracity is the French quality. From France have
come all the great movements towards fact and reality. It
is England and not France who cultivates falseness and
humbug—that awful fiction written by Joyce has this quality.
I dislike it, yet have for him and it a profound respect. His
portrait published in this month's *Little Review* reminds me
of Synge. I wonder has he Synge's sweet and gentle temper . . .

"The Petitpas have taken a house near Paris 'with a
beautiful garden' where they will stay a year. Enjoyment is

a French art; but for France it would be lost to the world; doubtless they will enjoy themselves.

"Joyce's writing is a revelation of that obscenity, the mind of the Dublin 'cad'. In the old days I knew there were such people, but never met them and never thought about them and it was so with us all, we ignored these creatures. Now Joyce has dragged them into the light and it had to be done for they are powerful and making themselves felt. It was, of course, they that denounced the theatre and Synge, perhaps they will read Joyce and be cured by horror and self-disgust.

"I think contrary to the general idea that most of us would rise in our opinion if we saw ourselves as we really are. I don't mean as others see us. Oh! No! No!—My God! No. That I am a better man than I 'think for' (a Yorkshire expression) is my one hope of salvation."

XXVII

THE FOLK-LORE OF THE WAR

12 AUGUST 1914. The war has been going on ten days.

The day before yesterday an old woman from Gort told me there would soon not be a man left in Gort; they were being tracked for the reserve and as out-soldiers. She said the war had begun in Mayo. "There were guns in a house, and information was given and they were brought away, and those they were brought from began burning and scalding. That is the way the fight began, and now there are five nations in it."

A.W. writes from Galway, "Three of O'Flaherty's best tram horses have been taken and he finds it hard to manage with five. A tram accident was caused by an untrained horse which ran off the line. Mary the cook found it hard to get change for a note on Thursday, the shopkeepers seem to have taken fright, and two near this charged 1/- and 1/6d. for changing a note.

"P. is putting her servants on a lower diet, eggs only twice a week. A. is giving her servants potatoes only on alternate days for fear of famine, and thinks of lessening their weekly $\frac{1}{4}$lb. of tea. I have only ordered the pullets to be kept for laying, and blackcurrants to be bottled so far."

15 August. Lady Gough writes that Hugo left for "an unknown destination" on Wednesday with the Guards. The secret is wonderfuly well kept, not a word as to where the English force is. Mona Gough writes also that Guy has gone with his regiment. He telephoned good-bye to them at dinner. Hugo was splendid, making out little things for his mother to do, making her search the London shops for a revolver he thought was not to be had, being obsolete, but which unluckily she found,. She writes, "If he does not come back I shall love to remember all this and if he comes back its memory will increase the joy." Very brave, as he is her only son!

A.W. writes from Galway, "The Graces showed me a typewritten letter from the wholesale place which supplies his sugar, saying they could not execute his order as they hadn't an ounce of sugar on hand. One of the maids returned last night from the Bog of Allen where her home is near. Two men had been seen taking soundings and prowling about the bog for days saying they were going to make the peat into petrol and cloth. They were in treaty for a field with Mrs. Butler. When arrested, plans, maps, etc., were found on them." But I don't think the Bog of Allen would be of much use as an entrenchment!

16 August. Slight Belgian victories reported at the Post Office and we had a special service and collection ("by request of the Prince of Wales"). The Gort Volunteers are said to have scattered for the most part on hearing of the war, but the Kiltartan ones are drilling well.

20 August. An old man mending the sea wall at Burren says this was was prophesied hundreds of years ago by Columcille, and it will not leave a man living in Ireland.

Marian has been to Gort to pay the books, and says only postal orders are given now to the old age pensioners, and when they went to do their shopping a publican refused to take them in exchange. So they went back to the Post Office, and Mrs. Mitchell sent for the constable, and he sent for the publican and told him that if he did not take postal orders when offered his licence would be opposed at the next sessions.

To-day's news is that Brussels has been occupied by the Germans.

Namur taken, that is the great blow. Old Niland tells me that we shall be saved by the Russians. His cousin had been in the Crimean war and said, "Three nations against them and they were the best of all. He'd frighten your heart talking of it. Where he was they had dykes dug, and to be waiting till the day came, and as many as sheep in a field you'd see the Russians firing."

An aeroplane is said to have flown over Kinvara and turned its searchlight down on the streets.

The Abbey re-opened last night, we must try and make enough for wages.

29 October 1914. A woman from Slieve Echtge says, "Priests we have giving a mission, we are going there every night. They have great talk of the war. It is the English they say will be defeated and put down. They bade the boys to keep silent for a while, where a whole fleet of them, seventy or eighty, were out drilling in the fields every night. Guns they were expecting, and they had clothes down. But there is no drilling since the war, and they are not in it, for they are

in dread they will be brought away by the Press. And the priest said to keep silent, that they would not be brought away, and to see what way it would turn out. He talked of the Boer War too, and he said that at the end of it there used to be but two men fighting one another in a field; and it will be the same in this war he said, for they are cutting down men the same as a field of corn. I heard the old people saying Buonaparte was coming to land in Ireland one time, and when he was half way he turned back. And I pray to the Lord it will be the same with these, for they are very wicked and are killing all before them."

Another poor woman says: "Isn't the war terrible! The oldest people in the country are saying it is the worst thing that was ever in the world.

"It was in the prophecies long ago. And there was a priest prophesied it would come as far as Kilchriest, and the cross would be lifted up there and it would stop.

"They are fighting out in some place where St. John used to be, and there is a monument to him. And the Germans were firing night and day at that monument but they could not hit it, and no shot anchored in it at all.

"I wonder will the Lord put out his hand to stop it? And it would be a pity for it to come to Ireland, for we had fighting enough here, and what will we do if they come into Ireland? It would kill the whole of us with the fright. And the army itself wouldn't be the worst, but the scamps and schemers they send on ahead of them."

20 August. The Basket Maker says: "There are volunteers drilling in Gort the same as in Grattan's time in 1792. The English were at war with America at that time, and if the Volunteers held to their arms Ireland would be free. But the English made them disarm, being so witty and so keen; and what could they do then? Look at Carson, the other day they wanted him to do the same thing, but he said, 'No', he'd hold to his arms.

"The King—no one knows is he for it or against it—but he is but one man, and what can he do? A King has no leave to get his own way. Look at Charles the Second (sic), how they whipped the head off him. Look at the reverses Napoleon had and he got the better of them, he having a heart of marble."

29 August. The doctor was here yesterday, says a good many Volunteers at Cahir Feakle have enlisted in the army. They are having regular drill at Ardrahan. The sergeant at

Ardrahan told him the 'Belgian' cook A. had lately employed at Castle Taylor was a German spy. O. has on hand 7,000 rounds of ammunition, and ten miniature rifles intended for instruction of the local Volunteers, but as she refused to have any who will not join under the War Office no one has come forward. K. spoke of her German governess but is quite sure she is all right, "as she is always abusing the Kaiser!".

There was a collection at Kiltartan chapel door yesterday for the Volunteers, but the priest did not speak of it or mention if they were under any central authority.

August 1914. Yeats writes from London. "I have just left Stephen Gwynn, we lunched together and I send you his gloomy prophecy as much in his own words as I can. 'Churchill and Grey have won Asquith over to a postponement of the Home Rule question. There will be a series of adjournments and growing suspicion in Ireland. The Liberals are so angry that the Government may be turned out and a coalition Government formed, possibly with Churchill as Premier. A Coalition Government will hang up till after the war all Bills under the Parliament Act. The position will become very difficult but if there is a cataclysm of some kind and a Conservative Government elected it will become desperate. The Conservatives are pledged against Home Rule. Should that happen, Ireland will have been betrayed by the Liberals; and the Irish party' (and this he adds, 'is Redmond's position') 'will cease to exist. It will leave all political power to the Volunteers and let them make what terms they can. The Ulster Volunteers will then be formed into Yeomanry by the Unionists, and as they are better drilled and armed, they will be more than a match for the National Volunteers. It will be a very serious business, especially in Galway—very serious round about Lady Gregory.' He himself is going to Galway on the first possible moment to join the Volunteers in Galway town." I wrote in return, "Can the Home Rule Bill be thrown over in spite of all the promises of the Government? They were quite as much pledged to that as to France."

30 August 1914. Yeats writes again: "I have just come from Mabel Beardsley's. Just before I came, a great friend of hers and attaché in the Rumanian Embassy, had left and he had brought with him a friend from the French Embassy. The Rumanian said the German Ambassador to England is possibly to be tried for high treason. He became great friends with Morley and Haldane, and took their politeness about

Germany for an assurance that England would not fight her, and also mistook the Ulster situation . . . London is full of rumours and the Rumanian or his friend contradicted one that is all over the place, that 70,000 Russians were landed in Aberdeen a day ago. While I was there Henry Arthur Jones came in and said he had met a man who has seen the Cossacks in Edinburgh, so one does not know what to say. . . . Outside our little world which is busy much as usual, people do nothing but read newspapers and talk each other into a fright! Henry Arthur Jones said he had not done any work for weeks, and I hear much the same perpetually. I now understand Gwynn's frame of mind better. I can imagine the nervous strain of the House of Commons. One remembers Wolfe as he rode to the battle, reading Gray's *Elegy*, the need of his nature, one imagines, for tranquillity that his mind might be freed for rapid decisions."

31 August. Old Mrs. Glynn says: "I often heard Maurteen's mother telling of the war of Buonaparte; and she said if you were hid down in the deepest hole of Ireland you should put your head up to see that war, that was the greatest the world ever knew."

A Kerry piper says: "My father remembered the great war that was at the time of Waterloo. £2 they would give a recruit that time in Loughrea, and he had to go through his right-hand turn and his left-hand turn. Old men the recruiting sergeant would take, and them that are upon one arm and one leg."

J.Q. says: "I remember the war of the Crimea; it was the French gained that for the English. It was a great war and lasted two and a half years but if it did there was only a field day once a week, but now they are fighting day and night.

"If I was the English I wouldn't be bringing German prisoners into England, or as they're going in Tipperary. I'd put a bullet through the head of every damn one of them.

"Sure to be reading about them in the papers and the way they are killing nuns and priests would rise the hair on your head."

12 September. An old woman at the workhouse says: "Sure the Germans have the whole world killed!"

Edward Martyn came over, says there is a strong feeling for the Germans among the people. And I see the *Coiste Gnota* at its meeting makes a rule that at Gaelic Meetings members are not to take the side of either of the belligerents!

"One must try and digest the war, not let it digest us.

"The Kerry piper at the door says, 'There is a great deal of talk about the war but I say better the ruler you know than the ruler you don't know'."

5 October. "I saw our Kiltartan Volunteers drilling yesterday as I drove by the schoolhouse going to Burren, and I watched them and gave them apples, but with much doubt as to what will come of it."

8 October. "Sarah who has come back from Limerick says the reservists there are going to America, deserting there. 'They don't want to go to the war, fearing it would drive them mad. The missioners are preaching of the horrors of the war to put them in mind of what there will be in hell!'

"Mrs. O.'s niece writes to Mrs. O. at the South of England town where she is staying, and in the house where she is a Belgian child has been brought as a refugee, with both its hands cut off. It never smiled for days, but at last when a dog was doing some tricks it laughed and tried to clap its hands! She says also that an English friend there had sent her little girl to Germany, taking a German child in return according to some educational custom. When the war broke out they sent the German child back, second class, and well provided. Their own child arrived after some time almost naked, starved, and with its toes cut off. I am asking R. to try and find out the truth of this, if not true it ought not to be told, if true it ought to be put on the list against the Kaiser."

26 September. A.P. writes from Galway, "Someone told me they saw a motor with a placard, 'You King and Country want you. If you wish to join, hold up your finger and the motor will take you to the recruiting office.' Payne Seddon is bringing *Charley's Aunt* to Galway for one night and has posters up saying how wrong it is to train up people to cater for your amusement and then leave them to starve because you will not go to the theatre on account of the war, and ending by saying that Gladstone the night he heard of Gordon's death went to the theatre."

5 October. The long battle of the Seven Rivers still going on. L.W. who had written that Russians had passed through Cheltenham, now writes: "People say that they were Finns not Russians that passed through, anyway any member in Adrian's club who mentions the word 'Russian' is fined sixpence as they have been so annoying bringing in reports of what their friends have seen."

We think of putting down red carpets and playing the National Anthem at the Abbey now Home Rule has been officially passed*. Stephen Gwynn says Redmond wishes it to be accepted and W. F. Bailey writes: "I think your idea is a good one. The Nationalist party is now all for closing up the chapter of the past and commencing a new one. At the meeting (Asquith's) in the Mansion House on Friday, the immense audience sang, 'God save the King' as I never heard it sung before. John Dillon, who was next to me, said to me, 'This is the first time in my life that I have sung it'."

But Yeats wrote to me in November 1915 when I was in America: —

London. "I am now trying to find out how opinion in Dublin would be affected by the Viceroy coming to Theatre, and have asked Bailey and Ervine to make soundings.

"I think people are fairly content with the war. There is a general belief that Germany is near exhausted and I hear Asquith told somebody the other day that they expected peace terms favourable to England.

"Now I am in correspondence with Bailey on another point. It will probably surprise you, but with every month that has passed I have got more anxious about the proposal to have the Viceroy present. When I suggested this a year ago the Home Rule Bill had just become law, and Redmond had made his speech. There was a new fact which everyone recognised. I am afraid it is now too late unless we can get another new fact. What I am afraid of is that our Pit, in which all the ancient suspicions are alive again, will in all probability either desert the theatre or boo the Viceroy. I do not know which would be worse. But what I have done is this. I have asked Bailey to see Redmond and try if he can to get him to write one of those letters to 'a correspondent' (which politicians are fond of) defining the reasons for abandoning Parnell's declaration of 1885. Redmond has himself been to the Viceregal Lodge but I don't think that is sufficient, especially as it has passed without notice. Even with this declaration we shall lose some support in the Pit, but our action will be intelligible in the same way as it would have been intelligible twelve months ago. We shall not seem to drift along some channel of least resistance in the way Nationalists rightly resent. I have too to think of my own consistency in the matter."

18 October. Last Saturday W. F. Bailey motored here to

*On 19 September 1914 the Home Rule Bill became law, but with its operations indefinitely put off.

lunch. He says Dillon told him he knows as a fact that a great deal of German money comes to Ireland, through the American Irish. I asked what they expect of the Germans. He says they seem to have the idea that if they support them and the Germans win, they will make Ireland an independent state.

19 October. Old Niland says: "Johnny Quinn of Duras was telling me that the English will not be put down till the time the sea will get dry. And it's as well, for without their law in the country the Irish would have one another ate and killed. But the Germans are like starlings going through the air; and the prophecy of Columcille is coming true, that the time would come when an old man would be turned three times in his bed to know could he show garrison duties in the barracks, and to know could he go to the war when the best soldiers would be gone.

"In the Crimea it was in a song that the Russians were coming on ahead, and in no dread, but that the English would put them to fear in no time."

3 November. Luke said on Sunday there had been firing heard as if at sea, "and all the pheasants in the wood roaring at the sound". Then Margaret wrote from Burren that she had heard the firing and had been told "men were killed in Galway", but nothing more has been heard of it here in Galway.

5 November. The papers say the firing was target practice of British ships.

6 November. Luke says the Germans seemed to be making great headway, but he hears the Austrians "are making great complaints now, with the scarcity of food, the bread so stale that they cannot stand with it. And indeed it is time to give them a check with their spies all over the world in every port and place."

9 November. But he says it is looking better now "the Japs are after giving them a sweep and it's likely all the other nations will give them a sweep."

10 December. Old Martin Glynn says, "They say the Germans will be coming here. If they do break in I suppose we must go on their side or it'll be worse for us." But the old wife says from the bed, "Ah, what about them? We have but the one death—we have not two deaths to die."

13 November. F. writes from Galway, "They say the Archbishop does not wish Belgians to come here, as he considers

they are lax, not good Catholics, and would be a bad example
to his flock."

14 December. Niland says: "As to why they brought about
the war, there was too much of a population in it, and they
wanted to gain more ground and they drew the war. Diving
boats they have, and flyboats in the air. A man of the name
of Hartigan was telling me the Germans have near enough
of it, and it's time for them to be put down, destroying all
in the streets and in the deep sea. Things they have the size
of turnips, and they burst up and blow them through the
elements. But all that is drowned or killed or is a corpse
laid down in the ground will come before God at the last
day in his own uniform. Every man will be a scholar that
time and will be able to read all we did in our life, that will
be written in our forehead. But it is not in the purpose of
God that anyone he made would be destroyed, as it is well
he earned them. And it is often, I said, after going to the
chapel, 'If it wasn't for the priests beckoning hell to us,
what way would they get their living? There's no one
would give them a ha'penny."

A piper says: "What nature now have they for us over
the Belgians? It is a very threatening thing to go to the front
of the war. In the Crimea they were not liable but to an
odd day or two, but now they are fighting every day. There
is a man in Ardrahan came back wounded. It grieved me
beyond measure to see him dragging the foot after him."

13 December. R. back from London yesterday, likes it in
the darkness and says people seem pretty cheerful, as they
may well be with Russians and Servians doing well and
Admiral Sturdee's victory.

I asked what the "naval mystery" the papers keep hinting
at was. He says it was the old rumour of the loss of the
Dreadnought in Lough Swilly. He had heard it definitely in
Whitney and Moore's office, and then he met some people
living on Lough Swilly who absolutely denied it. But the
other day in London he met at dinner some man who is
Winston Churchill's right hand man, and they had been
looking through the German papers together to see if this
loss had leaked out yet. The true story is, according to him,
that the *Audacious* struck a mine off the North of Ireland
and was taken in tow by the *Olympic* which was bringing
home passengers from America. But before they got to land
the *Audacious* sank. All the crew were saved except two
stokers. The mine had been laid from a fishing boat from

Arklow where there is a cordite factory, and a good many Germans have been working. The boat was taken and the fishermen were court-martialled and shot. The passengers on the *Olympic* were bound over to say nothing.

15 December 1914. Yeats writes: "I saw F. on Thursday night. *Audacious* story all a fable. He says the censors get all sorts of detailed stories all over the country, naval battles, shelling of Yarmouth and the like, and all most detailed and all lies. He knows Sir Roger Casement and says he is a charming person, a selfless enthusiast, a Don Quixote, who gives away his money and has spent his life in righting wrongs."

14 December 1914. M.G. came over yesterday, just from London. Staff officers say the war will be over in May, they judge by the exhaustion of German soldiers, all the best have been used up, and all possible called out and there are none to replace them. The German line could now be broken in at least three places in France and Belgium, but Joffre won't do it yet, though Sir John French is anxious to. And Kitchener doesn't want the invasion begun till February or March, when his new army will be ready. O. was with her and says her brother (killed soon after) has been at the front and came back for four days leave. He is safe, though twice blown off his feet by a shell, but he *hates* it, the butchery and horror. O. says he has a strange look in his eyes, and she has noticed the same in all who have come from the front, as if they had seen some terrible thing. She asked him if he had killed anyone and he said, "Yes", but would speak no more about it. They hate the bayonet charges. He had been left in charge (all but three of the officers of his battalion killed or wounded) and was ordered to go to the help of two other regiments but refused, as he saw nothing could be done. It turned out his regiment would have been swept away with them, and he was commended. M. says Sir John Gough, in examining men for commissions, asked a sergeant if he would absolutely promise to obey orders, and he said, "No, sir, not if my judgment is against it", and General Gough at once gave him his commission.

17 December. Robert and I at dinner last night, and a wire came from M. in London, "Scarborough, Whitby, Hartlepool shelled. Flotillas engaged at various points." Next day a letter from Yeats, he said, "M. came to see me on Monday night. He is now head of a Government Department for influencing

neutrals, and a friend of Admiral Fisher's. He told me that the English fleet has been bombarding Heligoland for the last week, as part of a plan of Fisher's to entice the German fleet out. Fisher says, 'I count on their pride!' Fisher has ships full of concrete ready to be sunk in the mouth of the Elbe so that they may never get back. He says Fisher is a Eurasian and used to be called 'The Yellow Peril'." (But they did get back!)

20 December. F. coming from Galway says she heard a man asking what the Austrians would do with Ireland if they got it, as they are supposed to have planned out. He was asking the woman of the shop, and she said, "Look out the door. Do you see that street and that tram line? Well, the Austrians would leave Ireland as bare as that, and little you'd ever get out of it."

"Sturge Moore is much afraid of being put to milk a cow as he is afraid of cattle. His next-door neighbour is already milking."

26 December. The Wrenboys today instead of bringing a dead wren brought one of their number dressed as a German soldier and drove him off in triumph, firing imaginary shots at him with a holly bough. But afterwards they sang a song about the Volunteers, and how we'll fight Carson's men and turn them upside down.

Nora, back from seeing her naval brother in Galway, says his news is that the admiral where he has been is dismissed because he had laid mines all round their own ships so that they could not get out till they sent minesweepers.

Niland. 8 August 1915. "That thunder yesterday, it was from the war that came, the clouds being moved out of their places with the fighting and aeroplanes."

My nephew, Dudley Persse, wrote from the *Archer*—North Sea, Sunday, 20 August: "Dear Aunt Augusta, Thanks so much for your nice letter. I am afraid I cannot put an address on account of the censorship. We have a fairly good time and so far we have only seen one German. There was some doubt as to which kind of cruiser she was, so we didn't do more than exchange a few shots. They made very good shooting, as the splashes of their projectiles drenched some of our people, but nobody was hit. It afterwards appeared that she was a light cruiser, so we again chased her but could not find her—it was rather disgraceful as there were twenty of us destroyers against one German. This was the 'certain liveliness' of the newspapers.

"We were quite close when the *Königin Louise* was sunk. The Germans were very plucky in their fight and afterwards were very surprised at being picked up when she sank, as the rule in their navy is to shoot anybody struggling in the water from a sinking ship. The country seems to be alive with spies who send information by carrier pigeons to Germany. I keep my gun always ready on the bridge, in case one comes along. Some of the pigeons came on board one night but could not be caught. Our submarines have had some lively times as they are the closest to the Germans. It was rather a bad show about the *Amphion* which hit a mine, as they came back over the same water where they had seen and sunk the minelayer the day before.

"One German was blown overboard from the minelayer by an explosion. He was picked up unhurt by the *Amphion*. Next day the same thing happened to him and he was picked up unhurt by a destroyer—the *Lance;* he was drying his clothes by the fire there when the magazine and shell room of the *Amphion* blew up some distance away, and a stray shell came along and killed him—very hard luck I call it!

"We intercept press messages from both Germany and France, they are generally entirely contradictory, but the French view is always passed on to places like the U.S.A.!"

Being vexed one evening by what I thought unjust anger against the individual soldier of the enemy, I made these verses during a sleepless night, calling them "Pat and Fritz". They were published later in the *Nation*. And it was a few weeks later a poor woman from the seaside, grieving because her son thought of enlisting, said, "he that never saw fighting unless it was in a fair—"

> "Who are these soldiers from the war
> That dare not knock upon the door?"
>
> "Oh shining angel, in the fight
> It was for Germany he died
> And I for England, wrong or right,
> On God or on the Devil's side,
> How would we know? A Mayo lad
> That took the shilling, being poor,
> And he that did as he was bade
> And no leave asked, but 'Join the war!'
> So one of us must be in dread
> Of no right welcome overhead.

"I'd seen no fighting but in fairs
And at the roaring of the guns
I thought the Day of Judgment near
It's little would have made me run;
But when I saw this lad take aim
(He says he shook but made no sign)
The heart-drops of a dragon came
I took his life and he took mine;
And had our pleasure in the fight
Yet cannot both be in the right."

"Give over Fritz and Pat your fear
We got report the way you died;
We want good soldiers here as there
From this day out you'll know your side;
Solomon's wisdom could say
'These all are wrong, all these are right'
Down where your body's making clay;
But we upon this airy height,
The King of Friday giving laws,
Are well contented with our cause.

"Here the recruiting sergeants come,
Here are the ribbons and the drum
So right about and through the door,
It's now you'll have your fill of war!"

18 February 1915. I am very sorry indeed about Rudolph
Persse. I wonder if history will ever know at what man's
door to lay the crime of this inexplicable war. I suppose,
like most wars it is at root a bagman's war, a sacrifice of the
best for the worst. I feel strangely enough most for the young
Germans who are now being killed. These spectacled,
dreamy faces, or so I picture them, remind me more of men
that I have known than the strong-bodied young English
football players who pass my door at Woburn Buildings
daily, marching in their khaki or the positive-minded young
Frenchmen. *The Times* has begun to prepare us for a
changed England, victorious and stupid and has been abusing
Fanny's First Play in a mood of Philistinism whose like has
not been for thirty years. However, if Germany wins she
will be more intolerable still.

Yeats writes, 11 March 1915, from Dublin: "As the boat
came in, the steward pointed to boats which he said were
sweeping for mines. Submarines had been seen off Dalkey
the night before. There were fairly numerous passengers and

nobody seemed nervous. Hyde, however, said last night in his simple honest way that he would be afraid to go from Ireland now."

Coole. April 1915. A.G. to W.B.Y.: "G.B.S. is laid up with one of his bad headaches. He had been very well up to this and so kind and cheery . . . Mrs. Shaw was lamenting about not having him painted by a good artist and I suggested having John over, and she jumped at it, and Robert is to bring him over on Monday . . .

"Augustus John wired from Dublin yesterday that he would come on today. G.B.S. had his hair cut in Galway yesterday as a preliminary, but too much was taken off while Hayes McCoy was telling him that a German warship had sailed into Galway Bay, but when the admiral put up his spy-glass and saw the ruins, he said, 'We must have been here already', and sailed away!"

Tim says: "As to France, that's a country that is done away with in the heat of the war."

N. says: "How could you cross to America with mines and disturbances in the sea?"

The Basket-Maker says: "Sure the Germans marched through Paris victorious in Bismarck's time, and they demanded all before them, and the best of the ladies of Paris had to throw them out their gold bracelets. For the Germans are a terribly numerous race. McMahon said of them they were coming up every day like a swarm of flies. Whatever number of them were killed they would be coming next day as if out of the ground, the same as a second Resurrection."

2 May 1915. J.Q. says: "The Germans are showing some slacking, but they are strong enough yet. Sure they were educated to the army, not like Kitchener's million men that if you would put a gun in their hand wouldn't hit a haycock. A lad that went out from Gort and that came back was telling me if you put an egg on your head and let it fall it would frighten them. Devilment in the air and devilment on the earth and under the sea. It is the greatest war the world ever saw."

An old woman by the sea in Galway says: "Isn't the Kaiser terrible to send his son out fighting till he got his death? A fine young man, it would be better have sent him on a pleasure trip to London."

21 October. Yesterday M. wrote from Burren that three German ships have been seen off the coast, and the police have been told of them by wire. To-day she writes that they are said to be motor boats, painted white and numbered and that the Galway lights have been put out at nights. The *Irish Times* says today there are to be no weather forecasts published. It is a stormy day, and if they are off the coast they will have a rough time.

A.S. has arrived today from Galway. She says there were crowds at the stations going to Queenstown, the Archdeacon was there and said they were Sinn Feiners going to escape the Ballot Act which it is rumoured is coming in. She heard a woman say to one of the men going off, "Take care would they stop you at Queenstown", but another said the Act had not come into force yet. The A.D. thinks it a good thing, that it will get rid of a good many corner-boys. She was told by the N. the Irish Guards twice mutinied before starting and it was with great difficulty they were got out of England, but once at the Front, as we know, they fought splendidly. The Basket-Maker says, 'They would go (the Volunteers) if they got Home Rule, but it is not real Home Rule, it was only put on the statute book."

22 October. The German vessels turn out to have been Queenstown trawlers!

T. heard two women talking of the war in a Galway shop. One said it was a terrible thing bringing the Indians into it, but the other said, "Ah, the Germans are worse. The Indians would kill you before they ate you!"

Yeats wrote from London, 13 October 1915: "I have a great deal to write and so I shall divide my letter into three chapters; the Municipal Gallery, the Lane pictures and the Theatre. About the pictures . . . I wrote to McColl and said I wanted to see him, and last night I met at his house Witt and Tonks . . . This time our chief trouble is going to be not in Dublin but here in London. I find that Tonks, Witt and I imagine, McColl, though he said nothing, are furious with the National Gallery for proposing to give up the pictures. They think it merely a symptom of the general incompetence of the Trustees who are going to give up the pictures because they are too stupid to know their value. They choose to believe that the codicil was written in momentary irritation with the English National Gallery; they threaten a press campaign which will "create such a public opinion against the Trustees that they won't dare to give up the pictures."

Witt was particularly decided. I told him that he might do as he liked, that he had a chance, that we could make quite as good a fight, and that the moment they took that line it will be an international question between England and Ireland—and that the next time the English Government refused something that all Ireland wanted, they would give Ireland the pictures on the Dickens principle.

"Owing to threats—

"An exciting event has just happened which has put completely out of my head what I was going to say when I dictated the appropriate words 'Owing to threats'. There has been a Zeppelin raid. In the middle of that sentence there came a tremendous noise—series of them. We went down to the door (I am dictating in Miss Jacob's office opposite the British Museum)—it sounded as if the Museum was bombed. We saw a group of people running past and I shouted, 'Where is it?' And they said right overhead, so I thought it better that we should keep inside the house. However, as nothing happened we went across and stood under the Museum railings, where we found four or five other people. We then saw the Zeppelin at a comfortable distance—somewhere over the city I should think—shrapnel bursting round it with tremendous detonations. Then about five minutes ago it disappeared and the detonations ceased, but a number of taxi-cabs keep passing the window—soldiers I suppose and police going to the points of danger. Unless it begins again it will not have lasted more than about ten minutes. It has the terrifying effect of thunder—I mean an emotional effect quite distinct from any consciousness of danger. I feel inclined to say what Professor James said in the middle of the Chicago earthquake, 'I have always understood that an earthquake produces a sensation of nausea, I have no such sensation.' The sentence infuriated Professor James' wife. I have just said to Miss Jacobs, 'Twenty minutes is enough for the day of judgment so I will take up my letter.' I am so puzzled by those words, 'owing to threats' that I am half inclined to think that they were written automatically by Miss Jacobs . . . "

17 October 1915. "The Zeppelin was much nearer than I thought the other night. It smashed a house or two in Gray's Inn and in Kingsway and in Chancery Lane. A friend's housekeeper has written to him from somewhere in that neighbourhood, 'Providence has preserved us but we are very shook'."

(I must have been a long way off when I received this letter, for I see a note written on the back of it by me in pencil—I must have been lending it to someone—"This will tell you how the Gallery, etc., goes on. Please keep it for me. I am at Denver, and going up the Rockies this morning, and speaking afternoon, and going on to California tonight. Tired but getting on all right.")

6 November. Yeats came yesterday. He had seen on Monday Mr. C. of the Foreign Office who thinks the war will last a long time; says the Russians (?) are digging themselves in and will stay dug in for six months till they have their communications right, and the Allies will stay dug in in France, but that all this time Germany will be feeling the economic pressure more and more and weakening, and France and England growing stronger and better prepared. Mr. Fowler says the last of his heavy guns (engines) is to be delivered next July, and these are intended for the Rhine fortifications.

M.M. says (after the battle of Verdun), "the French are standing well and fired well and hit them that they went up into the air."

Power says, "the Kaiser thought he'd walk the world, like Napoleon at Waterloo. He drew a lot of trouble, he drew all that."

6 November. Yeats came yesterday. He heard a conversation in the third class carriage as he came from Euston to Holyhead between an Italian sea cook, an English working man and a non-commissioned officer.

The working man said, "What I want to know is, what's the cause of this war? When I was a boy I went all over the world with my father so I never learned to read or write. So I said to my father, 'What is the cause of this war?' 'Well, I'll tell you,' said he. 'There is a German family and we have one of them on the throne, and in Germany they've got another; and being cousins, as is the way with cousins, they have fallen out, and that's the reason why we're at war.' And what I want to know is, if it's all a dispute as to who's to be in the chair, what difference would it make to us?" The Italian sea cook said, "That's not the cause of the war. The Kaiser said to France ten years ago, 'I've got a lot of people and I've got no land to put them on, and you have land in the North of Africa and nobody to put on it. Give me some of that land.' If the French had done what he wanted, there'd have been no war." The English working

man then said that anybody that wanted to stop the war
before the German Emperor was shot should be shot himself.
He then asked Yeats how long he thought the war would
last. Yeats said that he heard somebody in London say that
it might be over in February. Up to this time the non-
commissioned officer had been leaning back in the carriage
with his arms folded. Once the British working man had
quoted something said to him, "by a man with two stripes,
like that man there in the corner", and this he said with
reverence. But now the non-commissioned officer joined in,
"No, then it won't, for it'll begin again in February, they'll
begin fighting to know who is to win Germany." The British
workman said, "No, they won't do any fighting, they'll all
have the bellyaches." Then they discussed the food in the
steerage and the British working man gave an account of
the bad cooking of potatoes seventeen years ago. The sea cook
said it was all changed now and though he himself cooked
for the first class he knew all about it. On his last voyage
from Valparaiso there were 250 reservists and they started
treating the cook. Presently someone came to him and said,
"the cook in the third class is drunk so you have to do for
them". He went dish by dish through all the meals, and said
that most of the great steamers now had three cooks in the
steerage, one for the Germans, one for the French and
Italians, one for the English and the Jews. Yeats asked why
the Jews and the English were put together, and he said,
"Because they are the only people in the world who eat
three meals a day". Yeats said, "Is your country going to
join the war?" and he answered, "No, for the country that
does not fight has victory. France had one million on our
borders; we said, 'you may take them away and fight the
Germans', but they'll have to give us something for that. We
will get something out of everybody."

Yeats's housekeeper had said to him, "It's all very well
for the Belgians, they had somewhere to run to, but where
are we to run?"

26 December.   Yeats says a voluble lawyer at the Club said:
"The Irish are cowards, it is because the priests are always
teaching them that it is hard enough for them to get to
heaven even if they die at home with prayers and all to
help them; and what can they expect if they die on the
battlefield, without anything of the kind and the people
swearing around them. So it is only the sinful men from

the towns that will enlist, because they have to give up their theology for the sake of their comfort!"

But the chair-mender says that everyone that dies in the war will go to Heaven. He says it is the Indians that brought in that doctrine.

Old Niland says: "It would be a good job the Germans to be beat. Sure, the Almighty God wouldn't be above without he'd have revenge on them."

Mr. Blunt had written in October 1914: —

"Here is an advance copy of Macmillan's book. I consider it extremely well turned out but am annoyed at its having been priced at fifteen shillings instead of ten or twelve shillings, as it will prove I fear a prohibitive price for anyone not a millionaire and I particularly wanted the edition to be a cheap one. However, with the war going on, it could not be other than a failure and I have ceased to interest myself about it . . .

"What are you doing in Ireland about the Volunteers? I hope not sending them abroad. They will be wanted at home and have no business in an English battle line . . .

"I have just refused to join Hall Caine in signing an address to the King of the Belgians as a distinguished literary character, approving the nonsense talked by Asquith . . . Neville was here yesterday in a hideous khaki suit, having just been gazetted captain of a 'Southdown' regiment. For the first time in his life I found him a bore with his military talk."

And in December: "How are you taking it all in Ireland? I hope less hysterically than we are here. Here we do nothing but boast and swagger and call upon God and denounce the bombardment of Scarborough as though we had never bombarded Alexandria . . .

"The Press has been on the whole very friendly to my book, and though I never expect to be popular I think I have now an acquired position of some sort in the poetic world and there I must rest. All of us, however, who have been artists in any branch of art will have three parts of their credit with the public by the war, and I doubt if any great attention will be paid to literature, painting, music or the drama for a generation to come . . ."

And again, "I have washed my hands finally of Irish politics since I read Redmond's speech declaring that 'for an Irishman to die for England in this war was the same thing as his dying for Ireland'. I prefer to be the last Fenian living in exile in Sussex, the only one that has remained true to the tradition of Fontenoy. What a topsy-turvey [situation (?)] it is!" Again (21 November 1915), "It is a desperate game now of doubles or quits. Indeed, the nations of Europe remind me of nothing so much as of the gamblers I used to watch in old days at Homberg sitting at the *trente et quarante* tables, winning here and losing there, but all of them threatened with bankruptcy and increasing their stakes the more money they lost."

In October I had written, "A poor man at the door says: "This is a terrible war—a great war. A great shame any crowned head to have leave to bring such trouble into the world. There are a good many going away because they are fearing to be taken in spite of themselves. At the time of Buonaparte's wars there were good bounties given to the recruits at one time, £21 and a bottle of whisky and a leg of mutton, and a silver watch, all given into the hand before ever they'd take the oath. But one day a sergeant that was recruiting said, 'If you won't take it today you won't get it after 12.00 o'clock tomorrow'. And sure enough the next day they were taken by the Press, and put in tenders one on top of the other.

"The Kaiser was preparing for it this long time. He must be a terrible man, his five sons out with the army, and himself out with it; and look at all they did in Belgium.

"That was the way in ancient Rome with an Emperor called Diocletian. Killing men all the day he was, and his valet catching flies for him to kill at night."

A travelling man showing the notice from the War Office of his son's death says, "This is not a natural war, but shooting from the air and from the depths of the sea. The Zulu war was a decent war, that I was in. Six hundred of the blacks we killed one time, and took eight hundred of their cattle. They were let go back after, if they would pay seven pound for each head of cattle, and that was divided among the soldiers. After the fight was over Lord Roberts gave us a week to enjoy ourselves, and there was a house, and all ready for us. Wasn't he a great man to do that?"

An old woman called by her neighbours "Mary the Dancer", and said to be "a little wrong in the head", came to see me from time to time and gave her account of the war in balanced sentences: "The war is terrible; there is a whole lot of nations carrying on there that they didn't know at all. Indians there are in it, and the men from that island near America that is called Canada. But the English are very headstrong and they'll put them down yet.

"There is a priest going out there, a great man out and out. He says he'll go through them, and he'll lose his life or he'll change them. He'll take the flag before them and the colours.

"That priest will hold up the Cross before them, and they'll all die like chickens. They cannot break in on Ireland, there's a great victory turning against them.

"The Gipsies (Germans) is terrible, they are worse than the blacks, going up in the air and firing down and knocking. Worse than the blacks they are, its of the Gipsies they got no good at all.

"I'm afraid it will do away with a great deal of people; the war is very bad and very strong.

"The Gipsies would not kill you out, they would only wound you. It's short God Almighty will be doing away with it, if some nation will come in and cut them down.

"There never since the world came a world was such a great war as this war. They are fighting night and day; all the men in Ireland will be brought out. They'll be pressed in the houses. Where there's three, two will be taken and when there's two, one will be taken.

"There is not a horse in the world but they're going out; sure, I saw them going yesterday through Gort, knotted with bows and bits of paper upon their neck, and knots that is on their tails. It is the officers and the big heads and the gentlemen the Gipsies do be knocking. Lord Gough's son is in the hospital; it was the Gipsies that came at him.

"Knocking officers the way they'll break in on Ireland, that's the reason the war began. It's the biggest war that ever God created, knocking them down like chickens. Guns they have and balls filled with fire, they can shoot them as far as Loughrea.

"We'll be destroyed if they come to Ireland. There is nothing to save us unless that Ireland is blessed. The Pope even is blessing it. Sure, out in foreign there is snakes and dirty things going about in it. I hope they will not destroy us, if the Lord gets settlement at all."

And again, "The Gipsies are terrible; didn't they burn the three best towns of England; they to break with Ireland they'll burn it the same as England, and put it up into the air.

"That building was the best out in the blessed land;

three hundred years it was building and I don't know was it four or five; the best building out in France it was. They blew it and broke it down. There is many a sore heart through them; they are the terriblest swarm that ever came in the world."

Again in July, 1915: "Halloran that went to the war yesterday, it's not likely he'll come back; he was frightened going; he is a weighty man. A handy man he was, he'd slate the house for you, shearing people and cutting the hair; he'd wash the dogs for the curates or turn down their bed, and shave the dead without charge. Down the lane they're lonesome after Halloran.

"Terrible they are, there's not a ship going over or hither but they'll drown; it's on the paper the witness of it, they'll be drowned and swallowed down.

"There's no settlement or nothing, but always, always, slaughtering.

"To die natural, and the priest and the doctor beside the bed, and a beautiful coffin after; what is that beside being thrown and murdered and killed and dead without shriving or a coffin, or to be drowned and swallowed down.

"It was prophesied women would reap the harvest, but God help the harvest women'll reap! What way could I myself take a hook in my hand?

"Sooner than to die by drowning I would face a bullet and ten guns. If ever I heard I was to get my death in that way I would pray to the Almighty to shoot me.

"They are going up in the air knocking down ships. It is the war that you never heard such a war in your life."

12 November 1918.   We think the armistice must be signed and the war over, but we haven't had the papers yet. But yesterday, on the way from Cregclare, John Diviney bethought himself of telling me that a soldier at Stephenson's had mentioned that a telegram had come saying that there had been peace since four o'clock in the morning. And today Mike says he hears it is so. I said something about the Kaiser's fall and that he deserved it, but Mike says, "Sure, it was King George they say that got up the war. The Kaiser said that himself, that it was all settled at the daughter's wedding."

13 November 1918.   Last night Marian came to say there were guns firing. I was playing draughts with the children and we went out, and heard them, I was startled for the moment, thinking of the report of troops (including blacks)

pouring into Limerick, and Catherine was frightened and began to whimper, thought it was the Germans, but said afterwards, "they might only be firing at wicked people in cages". And then we heard drums and music and knew it was the soldiers at Gort Barracks celebrating the peace.

14 November. Mike John this morning is aggrieved, because in the scarcity of cartridges he had just made a few bullets, and found some black powder, and was stalking a flock of wild duck out on Inchy splash, when the guns began, and they made off to the lake.

XXVIII

THE RISING

COOLE. 26 APRIL 1916. Yesterday morning the postman brought news that Dublin Castle and the General Post Office had been blown up by Sinn Feiners. We sometimes hear exaggerated rumours, and sent in early for the second post that we might know what had happened, but no letters or newspapers came. They have often been late in these last weeks, they say because of submarines, the mail boats are uncertain in crossing but this does not interfere with the Dublin papers. Meanwhile, we had had a troublesome interview with M. Quinn, who wants to buy Ballinamantane, and Margaret had decided to go to Dublin and see Whitney & Moore and Sir H. Doran of the Congested Districts Board. She set out to drive to Athenry in the victoria at 2.00 o'clock.

An hour later I was in the garden with the children, when Amy Shawe-Taylor came in her motor. She had been to Lough Cutra to leave Lady Gough at home. She said Lady Gough had set out for London the day before, Easter Monday but when she got to Mullingar the train was stopped, and she was told she couldn't get on to Dublin. She said she would sleep there if she could get on next day, but they said there was no chance of that. She thought it was on account of some accident and got back by a slow train to Athenry, slept there, drove on to Castle Taylor in the morning, when Amy motored her home.

It is impossible to know what has happened or which of the rumours are true. It is said that the Sinn Feiners took possession of the General Post Office and Bank and other buildings, that the military were called out and that the Sinn Feiners turned machine guns on them and killed over a hundred. It is said that the railway bridges have been broken, that both Dublin and Cork are isolated, that Renmore Barracks in Galway have been blown up. Late in the evening Margaret returned. She had got to Athenry unsuspectingly, had there been told all this, and that there is no railway communication with Dublin and no telegraphic communication with any place at all. On the way home she noticed that telegraph posts had been cut down with hatchets even on the bridge at Athenry station, which is always guarded by policemen. She called at the Martins' and they confirmed all this. Jim Martin is High Sheriff this year and had warned the Judges at the Assizes of the state of the country. One had thanked him but the other had pooh-poohed it and said it was all nonsense, that the disturbers couldn't do anything. Another thing said is that the Government have purposely allowed it to come to a head that they may get at them. Some say it has been arranged for at this time to draw soldiers from England, and that a German invasion will come at the same time.

Amy had said there was a landing of arms at Kinvara on Monday and that the police had got hold of a man from Kilbecanty, who had gone with a motor to distribute them. The basket-maker came later and said he had seen three prisoners being brought from Kinvara by the police. We were a little anxious but tired and I slept well.

Margaret had met Amy as she came home motoring to Gort in search of police as there had been a fight at Kilcolgan and a policeman had been beaten.

This morning there was no post, and we have only heard that the Gort police expected an attack last night and sent their children out of the barracks, but nothing happened. A man at Ballycahel has been taken, sixteen police went in search of him on the mountain. J., who drove Margaret yesterday, says he saw, what she could not see because the hood was up, a party of men marching, near Craughwell, about twenty, armed with rifles.

Margaret went to Gort to see the Archdeacon and has just come back, 6.00 o'clock. It was true about the Kinvara landing of arms. A schoolmaster near Gort was taken by the police helping this. There were two men with him who ran away; F. fired five shots at the policeman but only shot him through the arm. The police had information that three roads to Gort were barricaded with carts of seaweed, but brought him by another road, and at midnight a car arrived from Dublin and took him away, it was sent by the authorities. This car brought official news; there was terrible slaughter in Dublin, fourteen hundred killed at Kingsbridge, six hundred at Broadstone. (*Not true.*) A great part of the line between Mullingar and Dublin is up. Ten thousand English troops have arrived in Dublin, they shelled Liberty Hall from the Liffey. They know all the Sinn Feiners quite well, and will arrest them later and try by Court Martial.

The line between Galway and Athenry is also up. The
telegraph wires were cut by the Government to prevent
news spreading. We begin to understand better what the
Rising meant, for the official news from the Government
car was that on Monday a German cruiser disguised as a
neutral had come to the Kerry coast escorted by two submarines. The Government had information and it was
followed, and when it came near the coast it was fired at
and sunk. Then they went to rescue some of the men
struggling in the water and got among them . . . Margaret
said, "Who do you guess? . . . It was Sir Roger Casement.
And he has offered to turn informer and tell all the German
and Irish plans if his life is spared." (*Not true.*) At Kinvara
Johnson's shop was entered and the guns taken and the
police barracks fired into. Three policemen were overpowered and carried off, and are hidden, being kept as
hostages. Marian came in here to say that Mike John, who
had been over the lake to Cranagh looking for hatching hens
for me, had seen Burke who had just come from Kinvara
and said the Sinn Feiners are marching up and down, armed,
the police have withdrawn, not being strong enough to
resist, but they are doing no harm, and had gone into the
convent and demanded food. We are still without telegraphic
messages or posts. Tim's theory is that there was to be a
meeting in Parliament (the Secret Session) on the Tuesday,
and that conscription was to be decided on for Ireland, and
that this rising was to prevent it, and not have them taken
away from their homes. A Kilcolgan priest (Father
O'Meehan) is said to have left a meeting in Gort on Sunday
evening saying he had an appointment; and was seen at
4.00 o'clock next morning at the landing of arms at Kinvara.

J.F., the herd's son who enlisted, wrote the other day from
the barracks in Dublin that they were less afraid of the
Germans than of the Sinn Feiners, "They are awful".

27th. No post or news, except that a young fellow, Coen,
has been arrested at Ballymacquiff. He is only twenty-two
and has young brothers and sisters, his parents both dead.
He is said to have fired into Castle Taylor, but that may
be a guess. (*Not true.*) Fahy, the schoolmaster, was a teacher
of Irish only. They say he had 200 men under him, and had
distributed £200 among them. The post boy, who brought
a letter from Gort only, says an attack is expected on the
police barracks today, and more police are expected.

Mr. Bagot here, has been to Gort. He says martial law

has been proclaimed and special constables are being sworn in. At Clarenbridge five policemen are besieged in the barracks. The priest came and begged them to surrender for the sake of peace and quiet, but they would not. There are 1,200 or 1,500 Sinn Feiners encamped and entrenched between Athenry and Galway (*only 400*). They have requisitioned all the motor cars in the neighbourhood, and have taken cattle from the Department model farm for provisions. Clare is peaceful, which used to be the worst in Land League times. Mr. Bagot was lodging his guns in Gort, that he may not tempt a raid for arms. At Kilcolgan, Stanton's public house was ransacked and all the wines and spirits taken, the Sinn Feiners sitting by the road side and drinking them. Lady Gough has written to ask us all to Lough Cutra for safety, but I refused.

Amy Shawe-Taylor called to say there is a chance of posting letters if we send them to Gort tonight. There is a motor going to Limerick in the morning. Her house was not fired into; she hears F. Shawe-Taylor's motor was requisitioned with others. A woman she knows bicycled into Galway being anxious about her children there, and came back saying there were barricades across the roads in two places but the Sinn Feiners had been quite polite and lifted her bicycle over. Galway was in a state of panic, though there did not seem to have been fighting, and all the provisions in the shops were being bought up for fear of shortage. One or two priests, besides Father ——, seem to be leaders. I have written to Yeats and John Quinn to tell of our safety so far.

28th. Mike John heard in Gort that warships are in Galway Bay, and have shelled the racecourse, where the Sinn Feiners are encamped. He came back to ask that Robert's gun and his own should be sent away in case they come looking for arms. We have put them upstairs. John Diveney says three priests set out in a motor for Galway, where the Bishop is very ill, but had to come back, trees had been cut down by the roadside and barricades made across. Mike hears a thousand blue-jackets have landed in Galway. John hears that all the people of Oranmore have cleared out by orders. Amy has taken the children for safety to Lough Cutra. Mike has been out warning our grass tenants to clear off their cattle before May Day, and is relieved to find them against the disturbers, a sign that they are not believed to be winning. I asked what the disturbers have in mind, and he says, "They heard conscription is coming in, and they say the Irish regiments are always sent to the front to save the English". This is what the Burren priests said in a sermon last summer.

I am beginning to find what a stimulant it is to conversation, getting all one's news from word of mouth and none by letters or telegrams or newspapers.

Mr. Bagot here, says the Kilcolgan police have been relieved.

Mike hears a girl and boy at Peterswell were shot by the disturbers because they would not join them, and are in the infirmary. Amy Shawe-Taylor motored from Lough Cutra. She had had three warnings after she left this last evening that the enemy were tired of Moyode, which they had seized and encamped in (it is empty) and had said they would come and spend the night at Castle Taylor, would allow Mrs. Shawe-Taylor to leave, and keep the girls in the house to cook for them, so she went off with the children to Lough Cutra. However, she had been home to-day and found no one had come. The line between Craughwell and Athenry has been injured and some workmen were brought to repair it but were afraid to get out of the train. The police patrol came in a motor to take our guns in charge, said it was not safe to leave them here. Our messenger came back from Gort with short supplies, train service with Limerick is broken and there is no butter or flour to be had. The police think it will be some days before we get any. Martial law is in force, Amy was stopped by the police both in Gort and Ardrahan. They let her go on as they knew her but say their orders are to search everyone.

29 April. Mike hears Fahy, the Irish teacher, has been shot. (*Not true.*) Raftery hears that Coen's traveller came from Dublin, by foot and getting a lift now and then, and says fifteen men were brought out and shot in the Dublin street. He hears the Redmond Volunteers from Loughrea are marching out to fight the others, who are moving from Athenry towards Ardrahan. Mr. Bagot came by Gort, only saw the Head Constable, who says there are a thousand military at Loughrea. He also said the Bishop of Galway (*no, it was not the Bishop but his secretary*) had motored out to Gort and was very indignant at being stopped by the police, as was necessary, no motor being allowed to move now without a permit. He had lamented the state of things and said, "and our beautiful city was shelled", so it may be true

about Galway. Gort can now wire to Ardrahan but no farther. There is a proclamation signed by John Redmond put up at the Post Office by Government orders. One of the changes that follow time. Kerin's shop at Labane has been closed by order of the police; he has been ordered to keep all provisions for the use of the military. There was not enough money at the Post Office to pay the old age pensioners yesterday and there was anxiety about food till some flour arrived from Ennis. James, who came with a note, said, "England was being shelled and America had joined with the Sinn Feiners". The military seem to be going about in motors with the police, and Lawrence at night said the three Howley brothers from Eserkelly had been arrested.

30 April. Marian, when she called me this morning, had heard that Roxborough had been taken and Castleboy, (*not true*) and the disturbers were killing sheep for food. Last night Lawrence had brought us a paper, the *Clare Champion*, with yesterday's date, giving us our first certain news, the official statement of the sinking of the German cruiser and Casement's capture, and Asquith's statement about the General Post Office having been seized and eleven lives lost, and Birrell's saying that outside Dublin there are but "one or two slight disturbances". We feel rather aggrieved at our week's siege and anxiety being made so little of. Sarah came from Gort chapel and says the Monsignor read a proclamation from the Commander-in-Chief that the rising has been put down in Dublin, and added that they ought to be ashamed of themselves. We are still without post. Simon, not a Sinn Feiner, refused his motor to the police, but they took it, but both he and another refused to drive it; there has been real fear of their, the disturbers, success. Taylor at Kilchriest is said to have been arrested, James and Peter ran out on the road to see a motor with police passing, and were all but fired at, supposed to be vanguards of an attack.

3.00 o'clock. A knock at the door, and V.[1] appeared (a cousin of my husband's), he is a District Inspector now, and was sent from Lisburn to help here. He had two friends with him, Northerners who had lent their motor, and a Constable. I gave them lunch and got some authentic news. The rebels had been camped at Moyode, some hundreds, and he had wanted to go out and attack them, but the military arrived and took command and were very slow in their

[1] Vere Gregory, author of *The House of Gregory*, Dublin, 1943.

methods, as if they were preparing for a winter campaign in Flanders, and thought so much of strategy and taking a distant castle which might be a vantage point, that by the time they arrived at Mayode all the rebels had vanished, it was said to Roxborough, but they had gone to Lime Park and then dispersed. A great deal of bloodshed saved thereby, one can't be sorry for that. They know all the leaders and have arrested most of them. They had a great deal of money, evidently for organising. He told of Lord Dunraven being shot in the streets of Dublin (*not true*), a terrible thing, he had been so good an Irishman. He showed me Pearse's submission and promise to lay down arms in Dublin; poor Pearse, whose interests had seemed to be in literature. He says they took the Post Office and a great many Dublin houses, and kept firing from the windows and they had to be bombed out room by room, and it will be impossible to tell who are killed and who may have escaped. Someone told him he had seen the sentry at Dublin Castle shot as the preliminary of battle. The Lord Lieutenant was besieged for some hours in the Viceregal Lodge. On the very day that Asquith said eleven lives had been lost, an officer of the Sherwood Foresters told him they had lost between dead and wounded eighteen officers and 250 men. Ulster and Redmond Volunteers had helped each other in some place, I forget where, one of the Northern men said, that it may help towards real unity. There are rumours, he says, that seventeen German battleships with twenty to thirty soldiers on board tried to get in, but were attacked and sunk, six British ships being lost. (*Not true.*)

V. was motoring on to Galway, the road being reported clear, and at last I was able to send a note to A. telling her we were safe. There were two priests with the Moyode party, but he doesn't think they will be arrested, but given the benefit of the doubt. The disturbers believe there has been an informer among them and are making for the mountains.

Margaret came back from Lough Cutra where she had lunched. They said there that though Monsignor Fahey had read Pearse's submission, which had been sent to all priests, Father C. in another chapel had said after giving out some parish notices, "I have another paper here, but it does not concern you or me, and I have had no orders about it from the Bishop", and he crumpled it up and flung it behind the altar. Mrs. Mitchell told them this, and Margaret said, "that was brave of him", but she said, "Not at all brave when he

knew his congregation were all in sympathy with him".
This, though there were police among the congregation!
News had just come of Townshend's surrender at Kut.
1 May. Mike says, "People slept quiet in their beds last
night, what they didn't for the last week", and "they had
sense to give in where they were smashed". The disturbers
are said to have left nine tons of flour, two carts of potatoes
and a cart of beef at Lime Park, and to have abandoned all
the motors, ass-cars, etc., they had stopped on the roads and
made barricades of. The three policemen who were carried
off have all made their escape, through different groups of
sentries. Pat D. says it is all the fault of the Government,
"things went wild since those petty magistrates were put on
the bench". The postboy says, "Peace is talked of"—peace
with Germany that we had almost forgotten! Mr. Bagot
says a schoolmaster has been shot at Lough George, that he
was searched, then let go and shot at ten yards, that's the
country story. He brought copies of the *Daily Sketch* of 28th
and 29th, a column headed "Silence in Ireland" but others
say the disturbance is spreading in the West, so our friends
may give us a thought.

Another visit from V. and his friends on their way back
from Galway. They found only the remains of barricades
on the road, but the Sinn Feiners have made off with several
of the motors they commandeered and are supposed to have
taken them to the Derrybrian mountain. He says it was the
same party all through, about 400 . . . They marched on
Galway and the police had warning and entrenched, or
rather hid themselves in the graveyard outside the town, but
the Sinn Feiners had scouts out and saw them and they came
by another road, and entrenched themselves. They were
shelled out by the gun-boat, though no lives lost, and then
they left, went to Athenry, had a brush with the police on
the way, and shot a big policeman, Whelan, dead. They
went on to Athenry, took the Agricultural Department yard
there and stayed a day or two, then to Moyode, and so on to
Lime Park. They could easily have been overpowered by
the military, but the Dublin authorities were so terrified by
the work in Dublin that they would not let them attack
Moyode without so many preparations that they were too
late; then would not allow them to follow the disturbers to
Lime Park, orders came from Dublin they were on no
account to attack unless fired on, or to run any risk. It was
the police who had to follow them and they have made off

to the mountains, leaving their provisions. The police have now been reinforced in Kilcolgan and Clarenbridge and Kinvara. V. heard a rumour that there had been another rising in Dublin yesterday in which they shot Pearse for having surrendered, but I don't know how they could have got at him. Connolly has been killed, the other leader in the fighting. (*Not true, he was executed afterwards.*) Some say Madame Markievicz has been killed, some that she is in prison. They say most of the Sackville Street buildings were bombed to get the rebels out.

2 May. No letter or papers. The postboy who brought a note from the Archdeacon says there is a message that Sackville Street has all been burned. The A.D. had hoped to get to Dublin to-day and M. was going with him to this C.D.B. business, but he writes that the trains to Dublin are not running yet, and that no motors are allowed to travel except by order, both to save petrol and lest they should fall into Sinn Fein hands. I have so much extra time without papers or letter-writing that I am reading Shelley straight through and am going through Hugh Lane's letters and all the Gallery correspondence.

1.30 o'clock. Margaret went to Gort to find if she could get to Dublin, and has set out to get there though the line is not open nearer Dublin than Sallins. They say there was another disturbance in Dublin last night, and 700 arrested. (*Not true.*)

3.00 o'clock. J. back from Gort, the guard of the train told him there had been thirty six arrests this morning in Athenry and eight in Ardrahan. They were taken to Galway Gaol and there is a warship to take others. Fourteen motors arrived in Gort while he was there, with police, they don't know if for arrests. Clare is quiet, but the people are drinking so little that it is suspicious, and the police have gone back there.

3 May. Marian comes to call me this morning with stories of arrests in Ballinderreen, Athenry, and many more in Ardrahan. They say women have been out helping the disturbers, cooking for them, and that one who waved flags was shot at by the police. More police motors have arrived in Gort and there seems uneasiness as to what arrests may be made there. Marian says, quoting from Columcille's prophecies, "The daughter will be saying, 'Mother! I seen a man!'", so many men will be taken away.

V. says most of the prisoners taken were young fellows

and some boys of fifteen had been taken but these were let go. Some of them were very downcast, but at Kinvara they kept up their spirits and were cheered by the people as they drove off. A young fellow who was with the Moyode contingent told them that he had not wanted to join, but they called for him at night and said that they would shoot him if he didn't go, and he took his master's gun and went. He said they were expecting orders that didn't come, and expecting risings in Athenry and other parts that they could join on to. When they arrived at Lime Park a strange priest, he thinks from Loughrea, came and told them their chance was gone and that the Irish Guards were in Galway with Maxims, and then they dispersed. He said they had thrown their arms over hedges and walls, but hardly any arms have been found, they must have been hidden. Vere says no arms were landed at Kinvara, but a boat was expected there, it was for that Father M. and others were watching at the pier. It may have been Casement's boat. He laments the inaction of the soldiers at Loughrea, and says one aeroplane would have easily got them all the information they wanted as to the whereabouts of the enemy. The heads of police at Galway and some other places had done very well indeed. Heard of Galway had faced them with ten men, but some Inspectors raised from the ranks had been stupid and sent on rumours of wire entrenchments at Moyode.

He says the orders given the police since the war have been vacillating and confusing in the extreme. At one time he received orders in the morning to seize the *Volunteer* and carried out the order. Two hours later there was an order to restore to Eason (the newsagent) any of his copies they had taken. A couple of hours later still, an order to restore *all* the copies they had taken from anyone. After the Hartlepool scare orders were sent to the police in Ireland that in case of a German invasion they were to lay down or destroy their arms and do nothing but civil work! In a little time this was followed by an order that in case of an invasion other than German but officered by Germans they were still to take the breech from their rifles, but at the same time strenuously to resist the enemy (probably American Invincibles), presumably with the butt of the rifles. This may have touched someone's sense of humour as after a while it was suspended. The police have had their confidence shaken, never knowing if what they do in the morning will be undone in the evening.

Yeats wired yesterday to ask if all was well with us, our first message from outside our own parish, but the messenger who brought it said no answer may be sent, none are allowed except on police business. Mike says a quantity of arms and ammunition have been found under the floor of L.'s house.

Telegrams are to be allowed through to England to-day and I am sending one to Yeats, and a couple of belated *Times* have arrived. Poor Lee, the Killaloe carpenter, came to me weeping, having heard conscription is certain, and begs me to get him off. "What would my little weak family do without me?"

There is still a little sniping going on in one part of Dublin. Mr. Gardner has been there through it. He says that as the first English regiment was coming into Dublin from Kingstown, a man tried to stop them, told them there were Sinn Feiners in ambush to attack them, but the Commanding Officer was angry and ordered him away. They went on and within a quarter of an hour many were shot down.

Margaret came back from Dublin with account of the devastation there. She says Pearse and the others died splendidly. One begins to distinguish between the leaders who had some ideal, and the village tyrants. They say there was an order to shell Craughwell if necessary, and the officer said they need not be particular as to how the shells fell, as it would be impossible to hit a house that did not contain a murderer! Marian was in Gort and came back agitated, all the shopkeepers talking of the plans found for blowing up barracks and post offices, and there were plans of the country houses found for the same purpose.

Margaret was told in Dublin that the authorities had expected the rising a Sunday earlier, though it was put off later by the priests because of its being Easter Sunday and that they wrote to Birrell in London that it was expected; but he wrote, "How very interesting" on the paper and sent it back.

They say the plan for attack on Gort Barracks was very well thought out; 670 men were to be stationed at different points of attack, and a hole had been made in the wall of the Mill that commands the barracks for a gun to be placed in.

The police had been sent off on a wild goose chase to look for a cave at Kilcolgan where the rebels were supposed to be hiding, but could find neither cave nor anything else.

The police have gone back to the North to-day, and we may
settle down to everyday life. But they seem to have shot
those best worth keeping in Dublin.

Miss M'Conaghy wrote from the Abbey yesterday that
Sean Connolly who acted with us in the second Company,
"was a Volunteer and was shot while on the roof of the
City Hall, and was buried in the Castle grounds.

14 May. Tim had said yesterday that V. had the name of
not being harsh and had let some off, and that this was a
good place for him to have been because "Your ladyship has
always a kind word".

The police have been looking for civil witnesses at Kinvara
for the trials as police witness alone would not be accepted.

15 May. M. back from Gort says military have arrived there
and are to put up at the Barracks. They are said to have
come to take up arms. G. back from Kiltartan chapel says
Father C. preached congratulating the parish on having got
off so well. He also said that theology required three things
to justify a revolution, one of them being success, but he is
not one who calls them murderers or would refuse them
absolution. I told her what G.B.S. had said in his letter to
the *Daily News,* and she said that was just the priests' view.

They say the military were in a pitiful way in Gort, going
about knocking at doors asking that a kettle of water might
be boiled for them, no preparations made, and they had to
sleep on the Courthouse floor, "not much encouragement
to anyone to recruit"; and that they were starved at Kinvara
where they only took their day's food. M. hears all the
people speak well of V. and of me for having put in a good
word for them, as indeed I did.

I have just been to the sheep-washing at the Natural
Bridge, with the children, and seeing so many young men,
farmers' sons and helpers so happy in the work. I thought
sadly of those in the neighbourhood who have been taken to
gaol. Not one from our own parish, yet if Limerick had risen
and there had been any seccess, they might have joined. A.
told Margaret at Limerick that the Sinn Feiners there had
marched out, having been given absolution by a priest who
marched with them but a message met them a little way
from the city that Casement had been taken, and they
dispersed.

22 May. M. says Tillyra was searched, a maid there told
his daughter so. She had refused the keys and they broke

the door open and took away arms and guns, and what she thinks worse of, a leg of mutton. For he says those soldiers are great schemers, and have a woman near Tulla robbed; they went into her public house and took what they wanted, and paid for nothing though they had just been given their two months pay. The military would let no one into Gort last night after 8.00 o'clock. A little chap had been to play with his children, and the father came to get him in time for fear he would be stopped, as there were soldiers at the entrance to Crow Lane and others a couple of hundred yards higher up. Some man who has been to Dublin says he saw the Gort prisoners "learning drill" (exercising in gaol?) "and S. was being checked, because he did not keep right step with the others".

Michael said yesterday the soldiers had ordered all lights out in Gort at 8.00 o'clock Saturday evening. He still trembled at the thought of what would have happened if Gort had been seized by the disturbers, and says, "It is time for them to learn that Ireland is the same as a bird's nest in England's hands when it comes to fighting. And as to the German's promising to land and help them, can't they remember two hundred years ago when the French did the same thing, and what good did it do them?"

25 May. Tim says the military are considered very rude in Gort. They broke into an unoccupied labourer's cottage and lighted a fire and "did all sorts of things". And on Sunday evening they would not let people leave Gort after eight o'clock by new time, and the Monsignor had given vespers by old time, and the congregation or any of them who came from outside had to get a pass.

I wrote to Yeats. May 1916. "My mind is filled with sorrow at the Dublin Tragedy, the death of Pearse and McDonough who ought to have been on our side, the side of intellectual freedom, and I keep considering whether we could not have brought them into the intellectual movement. Perhaps those Abbey lectures we often spoke of might have helped. I have a more personal grief for Sean Connolly, whom I had not only admiration but affection for. He was shot on the roof of the City Hall—there is no one to blame—but one grieves all the same. It seems as if those leaders were what is wanted in Ireland and will be even more wanted in the future, a fearsome and imaginative opposition to the conventional and opportunist Parliamentarians who have never helped our work even by intelligent opposition[2]. Dillon just denounces us about *Playboy* in his dull popular way.

". . . I knew it would all stir you very much, and you got your news in a more stirring way than we did here, with the foreground of a local and ineffectual rising."

7 May 1916. "What a smoothing away from your friend's life of confusion, which I have come to think is the worst thing that can come into anybody's life. Perhaps I think it because now that the railways are mended and the barricades on the Galway road have been thrown down, papers and letters of the last fortnight come rushing in, and we had learned to do so well without them. I had such a quiet time with Shelley and Meredith, now small annoyances come in, a stupid title page for one . . . And one feels sick at coming back to the war with Germany and its slaughter and 'as you were' and the recriminations that seem like petty and spiteful gossip between nations . . . I don't know how far the censorship goes. I am sorry for Pearse and McDonagh, they were enthusiasts. The looting and brutality were by the rank and file, I fancy. The bricks of fallen buildings had actually fallen upon the steps of the Abbey.

"To-day we have just got papers and letters of the last fortnight by a mail-car guarded by National troops in lorries from Galway, to remove barricades and guard it. And this also has been a quiet time, alone, so with less anxiety, except for the children's home, but that has been untouched, thank God. And this is a far sadder war, being brother against brother, friend against friend."

14 May 1916. "I have read the newspapers you sent, but they are hardly worth considering; in questions like this one must go to one's own roots. I think Shelley right and that he goes to the roots when he says we know so little about death that we have no business 'to compel a person to know all that can be known by the dead . . . to punish or reward him in a degree incalculable and incomprehensible by us'. And he says, what is very applicable to this moment, 'persons of energetic character, in whom as in men who suffer for political crimes, there is a large measure of enterprise and fortitude and disinterestedness, and the elements, though misguided and disarranged, by which the strength and holiness of a nation might have been cemented, die in such

[2] See her and W. B. Yeats's play *Heads or Harps* (Collected Plays of Lady Gregory IV, Colin Smythe, 1971, pp. 343-350) where this feeling is carried further.

a manner as to make death appear not evil but good. The death of what is called a traitor, that is, a person who, from whatever motive would abolish the government of the day, is as often a triumphant exhibition of suffering virtue as the warning of a culprit.' The government gave over their own business to soldiers, and they will suffer for that stupidity. I don't think so far they have been harsh in the country, at least in the places I know. They carried off a great many prisoners for trial, but I was told that police evidence is not to count against them without the evidence of civilians, or evidence found in their own possession. Yet I must not forget that there have been brutal murders and woundings in these last years, when no one was brought to book, and it is right to break the power of terrorizing gangs while it can be done.

". . . We have been calling out against those armed bullies who have been terrorizing the district for the last couple of years. Mackein, at the gate when he got notice, threatened us with 'the boys from Kilbecanty and Ballindereen'; and these boys marched down in force a while ago to frighten one of our tenants who was having a quarrel with another. They were just village tyrants drifting about in search of trouble. We had fretted against them and welcomed their dispersal. But as a matter of fact I would not even mention the names to V. of some Gort and other ruffians who were arrested afterwards, some with evidence in their houses, and some not. He told me he did not think there would be heavy punishment for any of those from our district (there were none arrested on the estate).

"There was no killing, except of one policeman near Galway, and I don't anticipate any hard sentences. So I don't think you need be disturbed by the *Westminster Gazette*.

"On the other hand, what I am rather upset by to-day, is the putting on of *Playboy* at this moment. Our managers have shirked it for years and now it seems as if we were snatching a rather mean triumph by putting it forward just as those who might have attacked it are dead or in prison*. I don't know if this is folly, but I don't like it. And I wish we could have won that 'enterprise and fortitude and disinterestness' to our side. I believe we should have done so but for the Rising."

---

*I was glad to hear later that it had been published in *Young Ireland* that Pearse had said he was sorry he had ever attacked the *Playboy*.

4 June 1916. Yesterday I came up to Dublin, because of the dismissal of the Company (by Ervine), to meet Yeats about reconstruction. We dined at W. E. Bailey's, and there was a good deal of talk about the Rising.

Ervine said some of the actors were gathered for the matinee when they heard shots and realised by degrees what was going on. Kerrigan turned very white. Sinclair, when he came in, threw up his hat for the Sinn Feiners and said, "I never thought they'd do it! I thought they'd turn out like the Players who reneged me on the Halls." Shields, when he went to what he thought was an ordinary parade and found what was going on, felt in honour bound to join, but hesitated for a moment as he said he was to act in the Abbey matinee, and the Commander said he might go and act, and come back and join them after it.

He pointed out a house in Stephen's Green where the rebels had been shooting from the roof. The lady it belongs to said she did not like this, and they said it was all right, if the soldiers came she could go down to the cellar and be safe. But she said she didn't like the noise, and so then they moved off to another roof.

As to looting, a woman carried out a load and laid it on the pavement and while she was getting another load someone carried off the first, and when she came back she flew into a rage and cursed and said wasn't it a terrible country, where you couldn't lay a thing down but it would be taken!

Yeats spoke against the executions, said England was stupid as usual and ought not, in her own interest, to have "allowed them to make their own ballads", Joseph Plunkett's marriage for instance. He hears Sir John Maxwell was sent back from Egypt because of severity. He had threatened to turn machine guns on the Australians, who deserved it, having burned two streets inhabited by natives.

They had all died very bravely. Plunkett had whistled *The Soldier's Song*. He was beginning the second verse when he was shot.

McDonagh had asked for a drink of water, but when he found it had to be sent for he said, "No, don't delay, it doesn't matter". I had last met him in a tram, one Saturday. He had a gun and was going to Limerick for the Sunday, to drill with the Volunteers. In his play that we put on at the Abbey, *When the Dawn is Come,* he makes the protagonist, Turlough, say "To save my life? To lengthen out this part of life I know? What if our lives are here but just begun, here but begun—elsewhere accomplished . . . Life but a fragment here, beyond may be achieved. Men see not in their own day the truth of their own day. So is still revered the martyr-blood that once was traitor blood." Pearse I had seen in the little office of the *Claidheamh Soluis*. He had asked me to write when I could for it, and had written in 1905 in a kind letter, "I have been trying in it to promote a closer comradeship between the Gaelic League and the Irish National Theatre and Anglo-Irish writers. After all, we are all allies."

Yeats had heard that he once said to his school, "I dreamed last night that I saw one of my boys going to be hanged. He looked very happy." He himself would make no defence. He said before his execution that he knew the Rising could not succeed, but "a sacrifice was necessary". This is a translation I have made of one of his poems, "Mise Eire": —

> I am Ireland:
> Older than the Hag of Beara.
>
> Great my pride:
> I gave birth to brave Cuchulain.
>
> Great my shame:
> My own children killed their mother.
>
> I am Ireland:
> Lonelier than the Hag of Beara.

I wrote to Yeats, who was in France in August: "I had been a little puzzled by your apparent indifference to Ireland after your excitement about the Rising.

"I believe there is a great deal you can do, all is unrest and is discontent, there is nowhere for the imagination to rest; but there must be some spiritual building possible just as after Parnell's fall, but perhaps more intense, and you have a big name among the young men. I daresay your being away and having time for thought, and your thinking over the '98 time may all be a help in the end. I don't exactly know what I want, except that Debating Society; and that I want the Theatre to at least interest the restless minds rather than amuse the dull ones."

And again in September: "I cannot but be glad all this trouble turns you back to Ireland. I have something of the same feeling, my thoughts turning to the Gaelic League if the Theatre should slip away."

Yeats said when he had heard this chapter, "You have given us the most important part of history, its lies. Nature notes a fact and gets rid of it as quickly as possible, that is how she lures us. I don't believe that events have been shaped so much by the facts as by the lies that people believed about them. When I had my political year I noticed that every prominent man was hated by somebody because of some anecdote told of him in a whisper by somebody else. It is those whispers that shape events. I was in London during the Rising, I had not foreseen it, though I remember saying, 'Pearse is a dangerous man; he has the vertigo of self-sacrifice'. We had little more news than you. One tale said that the Viceroy and all his Council had been captured.

"My first emotion was one of deep depression. I thought now everybody in Ireland will turn against idealist politics and even our theatre and our literature. They will think of nothing but the burned houses; and it wasn't till the executions that my mood changed.

"I was in Dublin a little later and I found everyone talking of the last moments of the executed men. Some of the fine things had been said and done but many were legends. Dublin cynicism had passed away and was inventing beautiful, instead of derisive, fables. They told me that Madame Markiewicz had kissed her revolver when she surrendered, that the officer who witnessed Pearse's execution said that he died like a great prince, and perhaps the finest of all was the death of that turbulent toper, MacBride, saying kindly to the soldier whose hands were trembling, "Don't take to heart anything that it is your duty to do as a soldier, I have looked down the barrels of English rifles all my life." I said that my real grief was for Sean Connolly. "Yes," Yeats said, "and all the more because very few know how much was lost there, our Theatre has produced comedians and actors of objective tragedy, but he was our only actor of subjective genius."

XXIX

MY GRIEF

THAT[1] WAS how news came to Coole that the war was ended,
But to me, as to many others, it had brought such heavy
sorrow that its general course had already become indistinct,
while there could never be any forgetting of its grief and
pain.

Four of my nephews had fallen, fighting in France, each
leaving a gallant record; Rudolph Persse, Dudley Persse,
Henry and Aubrey Persse, all these my brother's sons.
Another of these, another Dudley Persse, a sailor to whom
his Admiral had written, after a brave deed in the Mediterranean: "I don't know how you felt when you were bringing
that burning ship to land, but I know that I should have
felt very much frightened", was wounded and weakened and
came home to die. His elder brother, Geoffrey, having come
back with the Australians, was killed at Gallipoli. A young
great-nephew, Percy Trench, the next generation not spared,
died in a battle beside the Tigris. Hugh Lane, my sister's
son, his frail health not allowing him to go into the war,
his last public act the splendid promise of £10,000 for the
Red Cross, was lost with the *Lusitania;* he also a victim of
the war.

I had written to Yeats from time to time: —

July 1916. "Robert is with the flying scouts at Gosport
and may be sent out any day. His C.O. said in his confidential
report, 'Everything good . . . flying very good. Exceptionally
able pilot; should make a good "pusher" scout pilot.'

"Margaret has gone back to Portsmouth, where Robert
has been employed in taking over new aeroplanes, said to
be the best yet made, to France. But then his squadron was
ordered to the front, and he came back to join it. He was
to go out with it yesterday. The machines are single-seated,
he will be alone, with a machine gun. He has splendid
nerve and likes his work and is evidently thought a great
deal of. I have always that background of anxiety, but try

[1] At the end of Chapter XXVII.

to go on as usual, and have done the best I can for him by leaving Margaret free to be with him when possible."

26 December 1916. "I had the great joy of a sudden visit from Robert. He has a fortnight's leave and looks so well, and is in such good spirits. And it so wonderful awaking this morning, knowing him to be safe after the long, long anxiety."

2 June 1917. "Robert came home on Wednesday and leaves on Monday. He is to be kept in England for about three months, but at hard work all the time, so I may not see much more of him, but he seems much nearer and it will be a relief for a while. The day after he arrived he had a telegram from his squadron in France congratulating him on having had the Legion of Honour conferred on him, his first intimation. He is of course pleased and all the people here are much impressed. It is nice to think his getting it fighting for France. He had a splendid send-off from the squadron, who evidently think a great deal of him. Even the men (against rules) presented him with a gold watch."

And a little later: "He is at Salisbury now, trying some new machines and then is to have a home squadron for a bit."

15 November 1916. "Robert wrote to M. after the air battle on Friday, 'just had a very bad day, a lot of very heavy fighting. Captain Mappleoch killed and Evans brought down in enemy lines. I think I saved him from being altogether done in. I had a very tough fight and a long flight back to our lines. I am very tired and lucky to be back.'"

And in writing to Yeats on his marriage in the autumn of 1917, I said, "It is really an ease to my mind your going into good hands. I had often felt remorseful at having been able to do so little for you now, with the increasing claims here, looking after this place for Robert, and teaching and playing with the children, and trying to keep the wheels working; and probably with some ebbing of strength all the time, though I try not to give in to that. And there is only half of me here while Robert is in danger. He is in France this week, inspecting aerodromes, and will I think get a short leave afterwards, so there is less anxiety for the moment."

And on 22 November. "Robert has gone—probably to Italy. He wrote from some point (probably Marseilles), very much pleased at having brought his squadron there in six hours under time, and said he was looking forward to the journey."

3 December. (Margaret) had a cheery letter from Robert yesterday from Milan. He had brought his squadron there safely, and had a very pleasant journey, a train for themselves. They stopped for the nights, took six days, and had lovely scenery west of Avignon to the Riviera, through Cannes and Nice; they bathed in the tanks in the mornings. And in Italy, all along the line, the people cheered them and brought fruit and flowers. The letter was written ten days ago, so I suppose he is now at the front, but I am glad he had such a good time after being so long at one place in France. There is danger in both countries, but Italy seems more worth fighting for, and has beauty everywhere."

I wrote to Yeats in August 1918: —

"Often I had wondered, or there had been speculation in the background of my mind, for I tried to put away the thought, as to how one would hear, would bear the news that had become possible from the day Robert joined the Flying Corps. Every evening I had been thankful that no such news had come, every morning I had prayed for the safety of my child. Twice on my last visit to London I had received a telegram—and telegrams, however frequent, always gave one a throb of the heart—beginning 'Deeply regret", and my heart had seemed to stop before I could take in the other words, regret—from friends at the breaking of some engagement."

I had come home from Dublin on Thursday, the 31st January. I had been there for the Mansion House meeting about Hugh's pictures, and had been cheered by the enthusiasm and the crowded room. I had spoken. Kind words had been said. It seemed as if we might really bring back the pictures.

I wrote to Robert from Dublin, 27 January: "It will be wonderful if we get them back—I shall feel 'Now lettest Thou thy servant depart in peace' if they come. I had gone off my sleep, there had been so many happy possibilities to think of, the pictures here for one. And at home the new bit of planting, when the little formal rows of silver and larch were done, opened visions where the imagination might work, with inlets of elm and sycamore, and the' égayement of what Mike calls 'the brink' with silver birch and broom . . . The Convention is very exciting too, or rather its probable breakdown. The Government are evidently going to try and make some settlement, and one's hopes come up again that at last there may be political peace, and that responsibility may bring a conscience into the country . . . My last excitement, which almost quite drove sleep away, was the prospect of seeing the darlings in Galway on my way here yesterday! I went in by an early train and found them very lively— Richard quite a schoolboy with a catapult . . . Oh, what a happy world it might be with you back and the war at an end! God bless you, my child."

When I came home from Dublin two days later I went to the wood where I was planting. I was vexed because in my absence timber had been given away, and there were men cutting the young ash that had come into sight with the cutting of the spruce and that with the blue hills showing through them I had thought Robert would enjoy seeing on his next leave. I had been planting broom and flowering trees also, and they would have pleased him. Next morning I determined to spend the whole day at the wood. I had a sandwich put up and the donkey carriage made ready, and went to the drawing-room to write some necessary letter. I was at my writing table when I heard Marian come in, very slowly. I looked up and saw she was crying. She had a telegram in her hand and gave it to me. It was addressed to Mrs. Gregory, and I thought, "This is telling of Robert's death, it is to Margaret they would send it." The first words I saw were "killed in action" and then at the top, "Deeply regret". It was on the 23rd he had died. I said, "How can I tell her? Who will tell her?" For Margaret was in Galway with her children. I tried to stand up but could not. I said to Marian, "Who is there to go and tell Mrs. Gregory?" I felt that I must not cry or think, I must fix my mind on that one thing. I said, "I cannot go. Who is there? You may have to go." I asked about the train. There was time to get it, and I told her to order some vehicle to meet it. I sat there, as if frozen. She came back and said, "There is no one to go but yourself, Mrs. Mitchell sent me a note from the Post Office saying you would know how to break it to Mrs. Gregory." I got up and went upstairs and put up my things for the journey, even changing my dress. Then I came down and got into the carriage and drove to Gort. As I went up to dress I had seen John, his head hanging, leading the donkey back to the yard, and I knew he had heard it. I stayed in the brougham till the train came in, I forget how I got my ticket, I think the porter got it. When the train came and I went on the platform, Frank (my brother) called to me from a carriage and asked me to get in. I could not, I could not speak, I went to another carriage where there was some lady, a stranger. The terrible thought was still, "How shall I tell her?" At Craughwell, Frank came to the window, and I tried to tell him but could not speak and held out the telegram, but he said, "I know all about it". He had guessed from my face that some dreadful thing had happened, and had sent young Daly to the carriage to ask John D. As the train went on, a few tears came. The stranger, an Englishwoman, made tea for herself and got out her lunch-basket and offered me some. I could but shake my head. I wondered she did not know she was near so much grief. I changed into the Galway train. Daly, the porter we knew, was not there, or he would have known. I was glad there was no one who guessed. In the train I felt it was cruel to be going so quickly to break Margaret's heart, I wished the train could go slower. I took a car at Galway and drove to the house, giving the man his fare. A maid opened the door. It was agony knowing the journey was at an end. I asked if Mrs. Gregory was in, she said, "Yes, in the study with the mistress". I went to A.'s room and told the maid to send her to me there. I stood there, and Margaret came in. She cried at once, "Is he dead?" . . . Then I sat down on the floor and cried . . .

That was six months ago.

I must leave it to others to say how he was esteemed. This is a summary from one of the papers: —

"Major Robert Gregory, R.F.C., of Coole Park, Co. Galway, killed in action on January 23rd. The only son of the late Rt. Hon. Sir William Gregory, he was educated at Harrow, where he took the first classical scholarship of the year, and at New College, Oxford. He afterwards studied painting in Paris, under Blanche, whose opinion of his work was that it 'had reached the highest level of artistic and intellectual merit'. He exhibited at the New English Art Club and other galleries, where his paintings of the West Irish landscape were found to express its sadness 'with a passionate intensity' and with a new sensitiveness towards shapes and towards designs. The Abbey Theatre, in its earlier days, owed much to the beautiful scenes painted and designed by him, especially for Synge's *Deirdre of the Sorrows,* Mr. Yeats's *Shadowy Waters,* and his mother's (Lady Gregory), *The Image.* He was a fine boxer, and was well known as a cricketer in the Phoenix and his county club, and was a fearless rider in the hunting field and in point to point races.

He joined the Connaught Rangers in the autumn of 1915, and in January 1916 began his R.F.C. training. He went to France in August, returning to England in the following July, after eleven months continuous active service in a Scout Squadron, and after having been awarded the Military Cross for acts of bravery in the air, and for 'having invariably displayed the highest courage and skill', and the Legion of Honour for 'many acts of conspicuous bravery'. Last autumn he was given command of a Scout Squadron in France, and in November took it to Italy, where our airmen have done such brilliant work . . ."

Colonel Robert Loraine, his Colonel, wrote to me on hearing of his death—"As you probably know he came to me at Gosport in 1916 and became a Flight Commander and a Squadron Commander whilst serving under my command . . . His work was from the first invariably magnificent . . . He always did more than was asked of him if possible . . . A recently published book, *An Airman's Life,* has some allusions to him under the name of Romney, and one bit of description hits him off unmistakably. It says, 'He is the dearest fellow in the world; and absolutely the stoutest hearted I have ever met'." Colonel Loraine enclosed a letter he had received from him a week or two before, written from Italy: "I was suddenly given 66 Squadron . . . and as soon as we had got our full establishment of machines— Camels—we were sent off to Italy . . . It has been very pleasant and interesting coming out here. We had a pleasant time in Milan and have had short stays in other Italian towns. We have started regular work; I got leave to lead some O.P.s to begin with but now that has been stopped. The Huns had been very offensive until the English squadrons arrived, but now they have their tails very much down and stay far over their own lines. It has been pretty cold out here but a pleasant dry cold and we have not had all the trouble of engines [seizing?] up that we used to get in France.

"It's a fine sight working over the mountains. Arch[1] springs surprises on one sometimes, firing down at one from a big peak. I am very pleased at getting out here. The work is quite interesting and the people and surroundings pleasant."

Captain Ffrench of his squadron wrote: ". . . Only the

[1] As typescript, but it could be mistyped and be 'Archie', W.W.I. slang for A.A. fire.

Italians saw him fall. He had gone out to watch our patrols work across the lines, he was not supposed to go across the lines at all, but he was so thorough in his work that no order would keep him this side *and that is the sort of C.O. that we want.*"[2]

Mr. Keymes, Chaplain to the Forces, 1st Brigade R.F.C., wrote from France, 13 February 1918: —

"I do not know of anyone who has done more for a squadron than he did for '40' . . . I can't tell you how much he helped me and encouraged me in my rather difficult 'job', and he has done very much to help me to a wider outlook and broader sympathy. He was just one of the 'biggest' men I have ever met and I do owe such a lot to him. He was an immense influence with the men as well as with the officers, and '40' owes more to him than I think to any other one man . . . I am sending you the enclosed because he helped me a good deal. It is he whom I have quoted on page 8."

In the pamphlet he enclosed *An Open Letter to the Clergy at Home,* he says in suggesting "some of the possible reasons for our failure": "I was discussing this matter the other day with an officer who is a keen thinker (before the war he was an artist), and he laid great stress upon the importance of taking into our calculations one great fact. Even before the war changed everything, the spirit of development, change and even chaos, seemed to be moving in all departments of life, and therefore anything in the nature of too 'nice' definition or of a religion too concisely organised seemed almost impossible. He pointed out that there are certain great 'principles' which are eternal and will abide, but that we must beware of the danger of cramping or obscuring them by impatience or a natural desire for definiteness. Have we been impatient with the spirit of this age and been anxious (as he put it) to 'answer' questions which have not been asked?"

Captain Langton Douglas, Director of our National Gallery, whose son was in the air service, wrote to me . . . "A man is always judged best by his peers. I know more about your son than many do who knew him in the flesh, because I have heard airmen talk freely and intimately of him, both

[2] According to the official records of the Royal Flying Corps, he was shot down in error by an Italian pilot. Neither his mother nor Yeats knew this.

as a pilot and as a man, and a friend. To them his splendid
courage seemed all the more splendid because he had passed
the usual age for flying, and had great responsibilities at
home. But it was never necessary to make any excuses for
him; he was a great airman and a fine soldier."

Another friend wrote: "I met a man here the other day
in the R.F.C. who knew Robert very well and went to his
funeral. He says he was absolutely *adored* by his men."

The letters of sympathy that came to me seemed to sum-
mon before me his whole life, coming as they did from the
old nurse of his childhood, Alice Crews, from the Kiltartan
National Schoolmaster who had taught him arithmetic, from
Mr. W. F. Rawnsley, Headmaster at his first school, Park
Hill. ("He had, as a boy, an affectionate nature and a penetrating mind, and seemed to me to be one of the ablest boys
I ever had under me") from Mr. A. J. Richardson, one of
his masters at Elstree; from Dr. Welldon, his Headmaster
at Harrow; from the Warden of New College, Oxford. And
nearer home from the Sister-in-Charge of the Gort Workhouse ("It must be a great consolation to you to know your
dear son was so good"); from the players of the Abbey
Theatre, old and new; even from its charwoman; from the
lawyer who had helped him through difficult land business
("He was so open, cheerful, simple-minded, straightforward
and brave"); from a mason who had worked under his
direction; from a garden boy of long ago.

And among his artist friends, from Mr. Charles Shannon
who had painted his portrait; Mr. Charles Ricketts; Mr.
Sturge Moore; Mr. Augustus John.

Mr. Henry Tonks wrote: "He was the finest type of a
gallant man, combined with the sensitiveness of a real
artist . . . I should like to know something about him as a
horseman, as it is so interesting in his case to know of the
combination of this sensitiveness and courage."

I think I sent in reply as well as that account of the
steeplechase, a letter that had just come from a member of
the Galway Hunt. "A gallant fellow, one of the very best.
I don't suppose he had an enemy in the world or that he
knew what fear was. A more fearless horseman never rode
over this country."

Yeats wrote also of that sensitiveness and that courage
. . . "Robert had more gallantry and genius combined than
any man I have ever known or shall know. He must have
faced the end always in thought, for a man so sensitive does

nothing in ignorance, and skill and courage showed how calmly he faced it. The courage of most men is but a blockish living in the moment, and even great danger brings them no conscious sacrifice. Side by side with your loss I felt the loss of what he might have been for Ireland and for us all. Some of his landscapes have moved me more than the work of any contemporary landscape painters . . ."

And after Yeats's noble poem, "In Memory of Major Robert Gregory", had been printed, a paragraph in some paper pleased me: "All who remember Gregory, a man so much the artist that he was never at pains to seem one, so much a man that the unobservant might never guess he was an artist, will love the epitaph his friend has written."

I must give but one more letter, it is from Bernard Shaw: "I have just met Tonks at the Burlington Fine Arts Club; he told me the news.

"These things made me rage and swear once; now I have come to taking them quietly. When I met Robert at the flying station on the west point, in abominably cold weather, with a frostbite on his face hardly healed, he told me that the six months he had been there had been the happiest of his life. An amazing thing to say considering his exceptionally fortunate circumstances at home; but he evidently meant it. To a man with his power of standing up to danger—which must mean enjoying it—war must have intensified his life as nothing else could; he got a grip of it that he could not through art or love. I suppose that is what makes the soldier . . ."

At home on the Sunday after that news had come, I was told "there was a crowd of men at Kiltartan in the chapel yard waiting for the mass to begin, and they were talking of him and of the good time he used to give them, leading them out at cricket, that was years ago, but you would think it was last Saturday the game was played, every stroke remembered, and there wasn't one of the whole of them but was sobbing."

Our people would come and talk to me about him. "It was never the courage failed him. There was a great run across Moneen and they came to a gate, and not one would face it, but Mr. Robert. And when he did they all shut their eyes. But he got over safe and sound.

"When he went down hunting in Clare he beat the record and left the whole of a hunt and went over five feet eight of a gate and at another time he beat the record and left the whole of the hunt and came out with himself by the old racecourse of ——.

"He was a whole gentleman through the whole of his lifetime. I travelled through counties with him up and down, and there never was a gentleman better liked or thought more of, going into a yard."

One of his old cricketers, bringing a dog he prized to my little grandson, said: "If it was worth the whole cost of the war I would give it to his father's son. If he was a gold dog I would not hold him back. Mr. Robert is in heaven if anyone is in heaven."

And the poor coming to the door had their memories; "Whenever he would see me he would give me a whole hand, and it never was an empty one. If I was a gentleman he could make no more of me. There was no pride at all in that man for all his riches." "He never knew how to insult anyone. A simple man that would shake hands with me at the door." "You got your own scourge, it is always the favourite that is taken." "Let you rise the trouble off your mind. He loved his wife and he loved his children and he loved his mother, and may God love him for that." "I'm thinking he wouldn't swap with us now. He is surely in some happy place." "I hope he is a prince in Heaven now." They were glad to hear of the place of his burial. "Why wouldn't he be happy, being laid in the Holy Ground of Padua where Saint Anthony was a great Saint, and the only one that got leave to help in the nursing of our Lord."

A. Gregory.

Coole. April 1923.

INITIALS USED IN THE TEXT

Relationships to the author are shown in brackets

W.S.B.—Wilfrid Scawen Blunt
Sir F.B.—Sir Frederic Burton
De B.—Count de Basterot
Sir M.E.G.D., M.G.D., M.E.—Sir Mountstuart Elphinstone
    Grant Duff
G.O.M.—The Grand Old Man, W. E. Gladstone.
G.—W. E. Gladstone
A.G.—Augusta Gregory, Lady Gregory
M.G., M.—Margaret Gregory (daughter-in-law)
R.G., R., W.R.G.—Robert Gregory (son)
R.G.G.—Richard Gregory (grandson)
W.H.G., W.—Sir William Gregory (husband)
V.—Vere Gregory (cousin of Sir William Gregory)
H.P.H.—Paul Harvey
H.P.L.—Sir Hugh Lane (nephew)
E.L.—Enid (Lady) Layard
A.H.L.—Sir Henry Layard
G.M.—George Moore
G.—Geraldine Persse (niece)
A.E.—George W. Russell
G.R.—G. W. E. Russell (not A.E.)
G.B.S.—George Bernard Shaw
A.W., A.—Arabella Waithman (sister)
Jack B. Y.—Jack B. Yeats
J.B.Y.—John Butler Yeats, the elder
W.B.Y.—W. B. Yeats

St. G.'s Place—3 St. George's Place, London, W.1

A SELECTED LIST OF LADY GREGORY'S PUBLICATIONS

1882   *Arabi & His Household.* London.
1888   *Over the River.* London.
1893   *Over the River.* St. Stephen's, Southwark.
        A Phantom's Pilgrimage or *Home Rule* (anon). London.
1894   *Sir William Gregory: An Autobiography* (editor). London.
1896   *Gort Industries.*
1898   *Mr. Gregory's Letter Box 1813-30* (editor). London.
c.1898 *A Short Catechism on the Financial Claims of Ireland* (anon) London Irish Financial Relations (London) Committee.
1901   *Ideals in Ireland* (editor) London and New York.
1902   *Cuchulain of Muirthemne.* London and New York.
1903   *Poets & Dreamers.* Dublin, London and New York.
1904   *Gods & Fighting Men.* London and New York.
        Irish Literature (associate editor), Philadelphia and Chicago.
1905   *Spreading the News.* New York.
        The White Cockade and *The Travelling Man.* New York.
        Kincora. New York and Dublin (different editions).
1906   *Hyacinth Halvey.* New York.
        Spreading the News, The Rising of the Moon and *The Poorhouse* (with Douglas Hyde). Dublin.
1906   *A Book of Saints and Wonders.* Dublin.
1907   *A Book of Saints and Wonders.* London and New York.
1909   *Seven Short Plays.* Dublin and New York (1911).
1909   *The Kiltartan History Book.* Dublin and New York.
1910   *The Image.* Dublin.
1910   *The Kiltartan Wonder Book.* Dublin.
        The Kiltartan Molière. Dublin.
1911   *The Full Moon.* Dublin.
1912   *Why the Irish Love Ireland.* New York.
        Irish Folk History Plays, first and second series. London and New York.

1913   *New Comedies.* New York and London.
        Our Irish Theatre. London and New York.
1916   *The Golden Apple.* London and New York.
1917   *Sir Hugh Lane's French Pictures.* London.
1918   *Sir Hugh Lane's French Pictures.* Report on Mansion
        House Meeting. Dublin.
        The Kiltartan Poetry Book. Dublin, and London
        and New York (1920).
1920   *Visions and Beliefs in the West of Ireland.* London
        and New York.
        The Dragon. London, Dublin and New York.
1921   *Hugh Lane's Life and Achievement.* London.
1922   *The Image and Other Plays.* London and New York.
1923   *Three Wonder Plays.* London and New York.
        New Irish Comedies. London and New York.
1924   *The Story Brought by Brigit.* London and New York.
        Mirandolina. London and New York.
1926   *On the Racecourse.* London and New York.
        The Kiltartan History Book (enlarged edition).
        London.
        *Case for the Return of Hugh Lane's Pictures to
        Dublin.* Dublin.
1928   *Three Last Plays.* London and New York.
1930   *My First Play.* London.
1931   *Coole.* Dublin.
1946   *Lady Gregory's Journals* (edited by Lennox Robin-
        son). London and New York.
1962   *Selected Plays* (selected by Elizabeth Coxhead). Lon-
        don and New York.

Different theatre editions appeared of Lady Gregory's plays
but they have not been included in the above list.

The Coole Edition of Lady Gregory's Writings
Colin Smythe Ltd. and Oxford University Press, New York.

So far published from 1970 to 1973.

I   *Visions & Beliefs in the West of Ireland*
II   *Cuchulain of Muirthemne*
III   *Gods & Fighting Men*
IV   *Our Irish Theatre*

V	*Collected Plays 1*	The Comedies: *Twenty Five, Spreading the News, The Rising of the Moon, The Jackdaw, The Workhouse Ward, The Bogie Men, Coats, Damer's Gold, Hanrahan's Oath, The Wrens, On the Racecourse, Michelin, The Meadow Gate, The Dispensary, The Shoelace, The Lighted Window, A Losing Game.*
VI	*Collected Plays 2*	The Tragedies: *The Gaol Gate, Grania, Kincora, Dervorgilla, McDonough's Wife.* The Tragic-Comedies: *The Image, The Canavans, The White Cockade, The Deliverer.* Also in this volume:— *The Old Woman Remembers.*
VII	*Collected Plays 3*	Wonder & Supernatural: *Colman & Guaire, The Travelling Man, The Full Moon, Shanwalla, The Golden Apple, The Jester, The Dragon, Aristotle's Bellows, The Story Brought by Brigit, Dave.*
VIII	*Collected Plays 4*	Translations & Adaptations: *Teja, The Doctor in Spite of Himself, The Rogueries of Scapin, The Miser, The Would-be Gentleman, Mirandolina, Sancho's Master.* Collaborations: *The Poorhouse, The Unicorn from the Stars, Heads or Harps.*
IX		*The Kiltartan Books,* containing *The Kiltartan Poetry Book, The History Book* and *The Kiltartan Wonder Book.*
X		*Sir Hugh Lane: His Life and Legacy,* containing *Sir Hugh Lane's Life and Achievement, Case for the Return of Sir Hugh Lane's Pictures to Dublin, Sir Hugh Lane's French Pictures,* etc.
XI		*Poets & Dreamers: Studies and Translations from the Irish.*

XII   *A Book of Saints and Wonders.*
XIII   *Seventy Years.*
   Future volumes of the Coole Edition are
            Lady Gregory's Lectures.
            Lady Gregory's Journals, Vol. I.
            Lady Gregory's Journals, Vol. II.
            Shorter Writings, Vol. I.
            Shorter Writings, Vol. II.
            Sir William Gregory: An Autobiography.
            Mr. Gregory's Letter-Box 1813-1830.
            General Index, bibliography, and catalogue of Coole Library.

INDEX

by Maurice Prior

Abbey Theatre, 315-16, 343n., 376, 386, 389, 411, 415, 473, 547, 554.
Abbot, 4; *Astronomy*, 4.
Abdullah, Colonel, 34, 42.
Abel, Dr., 120.
Abercorn, 3rd Duke of, 77.
Aberdeen, George Hamilton, 4th Earl of, 22, 294.
Abraham, Mr., 108.
Acton, John, 1st Baron, 190, 287, 298, 305.
A.E. *see* G. W. Russell.
Albert, Prince Consort, 148-9.
Alcester, Frederick Beaumont, Baron, 242.
Alcock, Sir Rutherford, 115.
Aldington, Richard, 480.
Alexandra, Queen, 120.
Alford, Lady Marion, 48, 62, 109.
Algoin, Frances, 5.
Ali Fehmi, Colonel, *see* Fehmi, Col. Ali.
Allgood, Sara, 388.
Ampthill, Odo William, 1st Baron, 286.
Anglesey, Henry William, 1st Marquess of, 300.
Arabi Bey, 34-55, 70, 114, 131-2, 207, 218, 223, 251, 252, 253, 256, 258: revolt of, 34-55; his wife, 39, 42.
Arch, J., 108.
Ardagh, Sir John, 342.
Ardilaun, Lady, 451.
Argyll, George Douglas, 8th Duke of, 228.
Arnold, Sir Edwin, 233, 236-7, 291.
Arnold, Matthew, 193, 197, 296, 297, 470, 497, 499; Tristam and Iseult (1852), 193.
Arnott, Lady, 359.
Arundel Society, 30, 178.
Ashbourne, Edward, 1st Baron, 248, 361, 372.
Ashburton, Lady, 135.

Ashley, Evelyn, 107-8, 341.
Asquith, Herbert, 1st Earl of Oxford and Asquith, 190, 512, 515, 527, 537-8.
Asquith, Mrs., 189, 451.
Astor, Mrs., 470.
Athenaeum, later the *Nation and Athenaeum*, 273, 304, 435.
Athenaeum Club, 126, 129-31, 134, 139, 144, 145, 146-7, 166, 188, 294.
Atkinson, Dr. R., 391, 406.
Augher, Father, 325.
Austin, Alfred, 200.
Austin, Mrs., 178, 269.
Ayrton, Mr., 158.

Bagot, Mr., 534-6, 539.
Bailey, W. F., 515, 547.
Baily's Magazine, 275.
Baker, Sir Samuel, 454.
Balfour, Arthur James, 1st Earl of, 60, 233, 235-6, 237, 238, 241, 256, 260, 298, 301, 472, 485.
Balfour, Lady Betty, 340, 342, 424.
Balfour, Gerald, 340, 367.
Ball, A., 273, 290.
Banbury, Sir Edward, 85.
Bancroft, Mrs., 110.
Barine, Madame Armede, 290; *Bourgeois et de Peu*, 290.
Baring, Sir Evelyn, 256, 259-60.
Barody, 36-7.
Bartlett, Ashmead, 496.
Basterot, Comte de, 308, 315, 350, 368, 370.
Bateman, Mr., 11.
Baxter, Richard, 130n.
Bean, Ainslie, 173.
Beardsley, Aubrey, 336, 488.
Beardsley, Mabel, 487-90, 512.
Beauchamp, Geraldine, 342, 356, 399.
Beaumont, Lady Margaret, 44, 99, 234.

Beaumont, Mr., 48, 67, 74.
Beaumont, Wentworth, 234, 298.
Bedford, Duke of, 103, 246.
Bedford (Adeline), Duchess of, 281.
Bell, Moberly, 54, 278.
Belloc, Hilaire, 479-81.
Belmondo, 286.
Bennett, Mr., editor of *Times of India*, 290.
Benson, Sir Francis, 386, 399.
Bentinck, Lord George, 22.
Beresford, Lord Charles, 445.
Beresford, Lord William, 222.
Berners, John Bouchier, 2nd Baron 26; edition of *Froissart's Chronicles*, 25.
Bernhardt, Sarah, 100.
Bessborough, Lady, 380.
Bijapur, 216-17.
Birch, Sir Arthur, 290, 338, 355, 357, 372, 444.
Birch, Lady, 444, 446.
Birch, Tony, 264-5.
Birch, Wyndham, 264-5, 320.
Birmingham Post, 68.
Birrell, A., 297, 537, 542.
Bismarck, Prince von, 74, 99-100, 121, 167, 173, 175, 238, 241, 286, 522.
Black and White, 289.
Blackwood's Magazine, 126, 130, 294n.
Blackwood, William, 132.
Blake, Mrs., 74.
Blake, Sir Henry, 290.
Blake, Lady, 290, 293.
Blake, Mrs. Jex, 217.
Blakeney, John, 27.
Blavatsky, Mme. H. P., 335.
Blumenthal, 170.
Blunt, Wilfrid Scawen, 33, 35-7, 39, 43-4, 47, 48, 50, 51-5, 57-8, 70-1, 77, 81, 132, 138, 203, 208, 210, 213, 225, 284, 290, 310, 337, 339-40, 363, 373, 381, 397, 446, 472, 475, 480-1, 527 : his denouncement of injustice, 203-4; arrest, 230; letters to Lady Gregory, 250-61, 481-2; illness of in Ceylon, 252-3; *My Diaries* (1919-1920), 203; *Fand* (1904), 476; *Ideas about India* (1885), 214; *Gordon at Khartoum* (1912), 47, 54; *In-dia under Ripon* (1909), 477; *Secret History of the Occupation of Egypt* (1907), 35.
    Poetry, *In Vinculis* (1889), 203, 237, 258; *Love Sonnets of Proteus* (1881 and 1892), 261. *The Wind and the Whirlwind* (1883), 54, 251, 252, 253.
Blunt, Lady Anne, 35-7, 39, 41, 207, 236³, 246, 248, 482.
Boehm, Sir Joseph, 103-4.
Boehme, Jacob, 475.
Boer War, outbreak of, 352, 363, 397, 511.
Boland, Davy, 266.
Bonn, Dr., 424.
Booth, General William, 79.
Borthwick, Miss Norma, 319-21, 332, 360.
Bossuet, Jacques, 123-4; *Histoire de la foi*, 123.
Boulanger, General George, 237, 258.
Bourget, Paul, 308.
Bowen, Lord Justice, 66, 119, 294.
Bowen, Lady, 88-9.
Boxall, Henry, 145, 149-50, 165.
Bradford, Sir Edward, 342.
Bradley, Dean, 291.
Bradley, Mrs., 291.
Brassey, Sir Thomas, 45, 51-2.
Bridges, Robert, 486.
Bright, John, 43, 63, 272.
Broderick, Mr., 72.
Broglie, Duc de, 46.
Bronson, Mrs., 200.
Bronte, E., *Remembrance*, 336.
Brown, Miss I. A., godmother, 1.
Browning, Miss, 201.
Browning, Oscar, 73.
Browning, Robert, 116, 148, 166, 173, 192, 198-202, 272, 297, 410, 491; *Sordello*, 491.
Browning, Mrs. Elizabeth Barrett, 297.
Brownlow, 3rd Earl, 77.
Bruce, 47.
Bryce, James, Viscount, 298.
Buckle, George, 133, 227, 239, 338.
Bullen, Frank, 346-7, 432, 489.
Buller, Sir Redvers, 112, 233, 295, 353, 355.

INDEX

569

Buller, Lady Audrey, 112.
Burdett-Coutts, Mr., 92-3.
Burdett-Coutts, Angela, Baroness, 92.
Burke, John, 321.
Burke, Tom, 72.
Burnand, Sir Francis, 103-4.
Burne-Jones, Sir Edward, 122-3, 502.
Burrows, Mr., 73.
Burton, Sir Frederic, 139-51, 165-6, 168, 178, 269, 276, 277, 278, 290, 292, 303, 333, 372 : paintings of, 142; becomes Director of National Gallery, 142-51.
Bushe, Chief Justice, 304.
Butt, Mr. Justice, 228n.
Byron, George, 6th Baron, of Rochdale, 109, 127, 168, 446; *Don Juan*, 446.

Cadogan, George Henry, 5th Earl, 77.
Cambridge, George William, Duke of, 105, 368.
Lord Colin Campbell, 345n.
Campbell, Lady Colin, 140, 345n.
Campbell, Mrs. Patrick, 345, 348, 436, 445, 451.
Camperdown, Lord, 76.
Canning, Sir Stratford, 155.
Canning, Lady, 155.
Carlingford, Chichester Samuel, Baron, 106n, 273, 276, 277.
Carlisle, George, 9th Earl of, 201, 243, 290.
Carlyle, Thomas, 105-6, 135, 148, 497.
Carlyle, Mrs. T., 135, 251.
Carnarvon, 4th Earl of, 64, 75, 239.
Carnegie, Andrew, 503.
Carnegie, Mrs. Andrew, 462.
Carr, Archbishop, 409-10.
Carr, Philip Comyns, 335, 366.
Cartwright, Mr., 70.
Casement, Sir Roger, 204, 305, 518, 534, 541; capture of, 537, 543.
Castleboy, 8, 11.
Castle Taylor estate, 7, 25, 27, 28, 381, 512, 532, 534, 536.
Castletown, 2nd Baron, 330-1, 337n.
Cavendish, Lord Frederick, 493.

Cavendish, Spencer Compton, 8th Duke, *see* Devonshire, Spencer Compton Cavendish, 8th Duke of.
Cawdor, Lord, 40.
Cecil, Arthur, 116.
Cecil, Lord Eustace, 338.
Cecil, Lord Robert, 339, 357.
Cecil, Robert Arthur, 3rd Marquess of Salisbury, 75-6, 113, 163, 168, 227, 229, 235, 255, 257, 297, 298, 332, 339, 341, 366, 372.
Chamberlain, Joseph, 67-9, 71, 77, 229, 353-5, 395.
Chamberlain ,Sir Neville, 276.
Chatham, William Pitt, 1st Earl of 156.
Chenery, Thomas, 44, 46, 49-50, 51, 55, 127-8, 130, 132, 239.
Chevy Chase, 7, 8.
Childe, E. Lee, 209, 290, 369.
Childe, Mrs. Lee, 121, 370.
Childers, Robert Erskine, 238, 245, 276, 290, 333.
Chronicle, 303-4, 371.
Churchill, Lord Randolph, 47, 50, 70-2, 75-7, 118-19, 207, 210, 227-8, 233, 237, 253, 257, 270, 447; resignation of, 75-6, 227.
Churchill, Lady Dorothy, 75, 83, 110, 114, 227, 274, 298, 338.
Churchill, Sir Winston, 357, 512, 517.
Life of Lord Randolph Churchill (1906), 447.
Churchill, Winston (American novelist), 459.
Clanmorris, Lord, 9.
Clanricarde, Marquess of, 9, 94, 99, 213, 231.
Clark, Sir Mansfield, 357.
Clay, Sir Arthur, 78, 289-90, 336, 341.
Clay, Lady, 78, 290.
Clemenceau, Georges, 189.
Clemens, Samuel (Mark Twain), 122, 362-4, 400-1, 415; *Joan of Arc*, 122.
Clemens, Mrs. S., 362, 401, 415.
Clonbrock, Lord, 8, 74, 360-2, 372.
Cochrane, Burke, 465.
Cockerell, Mr., 204.
Cockeville, 355.

Cockerell, Sydney, 435.
Cole, Alfred, 289, 291, 336.
Cole, Professor, 415.
Collins, Michael, 306, 321.
Colonels, revolt of the, 34.
Colvin, Sir Auckland, 34-5, 38, 40, 43, 54, 210, 273, 290.
Colvin, Sidney, 289, 292, 305, 357-8, 396.
Connacht, 1, 2.
Conolly, Sean, 393-4, 395, 396, 543, 544.
Conyngham, Lady, 209.
Cook, Lady, 66.
Coole Park, 1, 23, 24-5, 27, 28, 32, 38, 44, 77, 80, 141, 178, 186, 192, 211-12, 230, 256, 263, 266, 267, 283, 300, 304, 323, 329, 338, 342, 376, 378, 387, 389, 393, 400, 404, 417, 443, 479, 490, 532, 550.
Cordery, Mr., 213, 215, 217-19, 229, 241, 381.
Cork, Lord, 45, 358.
Cork, Lady, 358.
Cornhill Magazine, The, 370.
Cortelazzo, 169, 174.
Cortelazzo, Madame, 169.
Costa, Giovanni, 78.
Costi, 254.
Courtney, Leonard, 342.
Courtney, Mrs., 365.
Craufurd, Oswald, 289.
Craven, Mrs. Dacre, 80-2, 367.
Creighton, Mandell, 168; History of the Papacy during the Reformation, 168n.
Crewe, Robert Offley, 1st Marquess of, 234.
Crews, Alice, 557.
Crofton, Lord, 27.
Cromer, Evelyn Baring, 1st Earl of, 436.
Cumming, Dr., 13.
Cunard, Lady, 485.
Cunningham, Sir Henry, 303, 340.
Currie, Bertram, 259.
Currie, Francis, 258.
Currie, Lady, 368.
Curtis, Mr., 199-200.
Daily News, 271, 304, 543.
Daily Sketch, 539.
Daily Telegraph, The, 270, 271, 304.

Dalhousie, Lady, 103, 129.
Daly, Lady Anne, 231.
Dampier, William, 387.
Dante, Alighieri, 19, 49, 57, 177.
Darcy, Matt, 273.
Darling, Sir Charles, 446.
Darnley, Lady, 86.
Dartrey, Lady, 63, 228.
Darwinism, 128.
D'Aumale, Duc, 38.
Delane, 200, 239.
Delius, Frederick, 449-50.
Denbigh, 1st Earl of, 305.
Denby, Lady, 70.
Derby, Edward Henry, 15th Earl, 52, 54-5.
De Valera, Eamon, 321.
De Vere, Aubrey, 181.
Devonshire, Spencer Compton Cavdish, 8th Duke of, 45, 68, 103, 339.
Dicey, Edmund, 41, 43, 45, 46, 50, 292.
Dickens, Charles, 168, 331, 393, 524; Bleak House, 393q.
Dickson, Sir Collingwood, 156, 167.
Dilke, Sir Charles, 49, 51, 67, 73, 75, 116, 134.
Dillon, Gerald, 27.
Dillon, John, M.P., 70, 75, 226, 235, 241, 242, 244, 248, 292, 296, 495, 515-16, 545.
Disestablishment of the Church of Ireland, 11, 14, 33, 283.
Disraeli, Benjamin, 1st Earl of Beaconsfield, 23, 30, 33, 107, 150-1, 157, 269, 340.
Diveney, John, 390, 530, 535.
Dobson, Austin, 437.
Dome, The, 398.
Donaldson, Sir Frederick, 469.
Doughty, Charles Montagu, 260; Arabia Deserta, 491.
Douglas, Captain Langton, 556-7; tribute to Robert Gregory, 556-7.
Dowden, Edward, 18.
Doyle, Henry, 140, 144, 381.
Drake, Sir William, 115, 171.
Drayfus, Captain, 173.
Drinkwater, John, 502.
Drummond, Henry, 98.
Dublin Daily Express, 338.

Duff, Sir Mountstuart Elphinstone Grant, 65, 67, 69, 73, 108-9, 182, 189, 195, 224, 234, 238, 242, 269, 272, 274, 275, 289, 340-1, 355, 446; *Indian Diaries*, 340.
Duff, Lady Clara Grant, 222, 234, 238, 242, 269, 289, 341, 355.
Dufferin and Ava, Frederick Temple, 1st Marquess of, 50, 55, 64, 65, 67, 109, 190, 194, 195, 210, 215, 225-6, 229, 235, 238, 240, 247, 249, 254, 259, 272, 273, 276, 278, 294-5, 297.
Dugdale, Mrs., 336-7.
Dulier, Colonel, 39-40.
Du Maurier, George, 298; Works, *Trilby* (1894), 298, *Peter Ibbetson* (1891), 298.
Duncannon, Lord, 284, 354, 358.
Duncannon, Lady, 342, 358.
Dunkellin, Lord, 9, 9n, 157.
Dunne, Peter (Mr. Dooley), 459, 463, 465, 470.
Dunraven, Lord, 538.
Dunsandle, Lord, 275.
Du Quaire, Mme., 120.
Dynamite, 64.

East, Alfred, 437.
Eastern Question, 33.
Eastlake, Sir Charles, 144-5, 165.
Eastlake, Sir Charles, 144-5, 165.
Eastlake, Lady, 144.
Eckermann, Johann, 497; *Conversations*, 497.
Edgeworth, Maria, 141; Works, *Absentee*, 141; *Castle Rackrent*, 141.
Edinburgh Review, The, 117.
Edward VII, King, 118, 120, 397; death of, 448.
"Eglinton, John", 343, 380, 403.
Elcho, Lord, 45, 48, 49, 109.
Elder, Smith, 302, 339.
Eliot, George, 147-8, 290; *The Mill on the Floss*, 147.
Elliot, Sir George, 45.
Elliot, Miss, 94.
Ellis, Tristran, 113.
Emery, Mrs., 336-7, 353, 488.
Emmaus, Bishop of, 110.

Emmet, Colonel, 459, 461.
Enfield, Lord, 70.
English Review, 487.
Ervine, St. John, 473n, 483, 515, 547.
Evelyn, John, 25; *Silva*, 25.
Evening Standard, 271, 304.

Fahey, Dr., 317, 320-1, 398, 536, 538.
Farrer, Canon.
Fawcett, Mrs., 62n.
Fay brothers, 380, 389.
Fay, F., 418.
Fay, W., 413-14, 418, 420, 430, 431, 444.
Fehmi, Colonel Ali, 34, 476.
Fehmy, Hassan, 52.
Fenianism, 64, 75.
Ferguson, Sir Samuel, 142-3.
Ffrench, Captain, 555-6; tribute to Robert Gregory, 555-6.
Ffrench, Robert Percy, 98-9, 167.
Field, Cyprus, 106.
Fingall, Lady, 307, 359, 367.
Fisher, Admiral, 519.
Fitzgerald, Dr., 359.
Fitzgerald, Lord Edward, 213, 300.
Fitzgerald, Sir Gerald, 38.
Fitzgerald, Mrs., 37-8.
Flint, F. S., 480-1.
Flynn, 459.
Forbes, Archibald, 115.
Ford, Sir Clare, 93-4.
Ford, Mrs., 77, 118, 198.
Forster, W. E., 46, 118, 206, 340.
Fortnightly Review, The, 117, 206, 208, 267.
Fowler, Sir John, 118.
France, Anatole, 475; *Le Retour des Dieux*, 475.
Frederick William, Crown Prince, 174-6.
Freeman, Edward, 195; *History of England*, 195q.
Freeman's Journal, 284, 297, 359-61.
French, Sir John, 518.
Froude, James, 249, 272, 331; Works, *Erasmus*, 272.

G.O.M. *see* Gladstone, W. E.

Gaelic League, 306, 318, 320, 377, 402, 417, 424.

Geary, Neville, 290, 335.

George V, H.M. King, 530.

Gerothwohl, 415, 417.

Gibbon, Edward, 211; *Decline and Fall of the Roman Empire*, 211.

Gibson, Mr., 41.

Gill, T. P., 338, 374.

Gladstone, Sir Thomas, 101.

Gladstone, W. E., 22, 33, 43, 46, 47, 49, 51-4, 56-8, 63, 65-75, 79, 100-1, 103, 104, 106, 109, 112, 115, 117, 118, 129-30, 131, 133-4, 136-7, 150, 156, 158, 160, 161, 64, 190, 191, 205, 207, 210, 214, 229, 230, 233, 234, 236, 238, 244, 245, 249, 253, 254, 256, 259, 295, 297, 310, 330, 335, 337, 340, 366, 386, 514; personality, 57-8; oratory of, 59-61; prevalence of folk-lore concerning, 61-2; expropriation scheme, 65.

Gladstone, Mrs., 47, 48, 58, 59, 60, 61-2, 66, 69-71, 231, 237, 295.

Glyn, George Grenfell, 2nd Baron Wolverton, 72.

Glyn, Mary, 374.

Glynn, Martin, 516.

Goethe, Johan Wolfgang von, 335, 336, 497.

Goldsmid, Sir Frederic, 38-40, 43.

Goldsmith, Oliver, 101.

Gonne, Miss Maud, 309-10, 344n, 352-3, 493-4.

Gordon, Sir Arthur, 65, 195, 244.

Gordon, Lady, 195.

Gordon, Arthur, 1st Baron Stanmore, 294, 441.

Gordon, General Charles, 50, 52, 53, 133-4, 210, 259-60; *Journals*, 210.

Gore, Mr., 272.

Gort, Lord, 340.

Gort, 212, 307-8.

Goschen, George, 1st Viscount, 46, 59, 61, 68, 76-7, 112, 146, 161, 228, 229.

Gosse, Edmund, 334, 355, 436.

Gough, Lord, 213, 374, 383.

Gough, George, 311.

Gough, Sir John, 518.

Gough, Lady, 205, 206, 509, 536.

Gower, George Leveson, 73, 75.

Gowing, Mrs. Aylmer, 365.

Graham, Sir James, 22.

Granville, Lord, *see* Leveson-Gower, Granville George, 2nd Earl Granville.

Granville-Barker, Harley, 139, 447, 449, 451.

Graves, A. P., 304.

Gray, John, 273, 289.

Gregory, Anne, 3n, 26.

Gregory, Lady Augusta: birth, 1; love of reading, 5-7, 14; gaieties, 8, 17; teaching of religion to, 10-11; early childhood, 11-14; discrimination in book selection, 15; devotes considerable time to charitable purposes, 16; no formal "coming out", 17; forbidding of hunting, 17; study of dramatists, 18; visits Riviera, 19-20; marriage proposal from Sir William Gregory, 28; marriage to Sir William Gregory, 29; her visits abroad, 29-30; first society dinner party, 31; first ball, 31; attends Pope's reception at Vatican, 31 in Egypt, 34-44; her many visits to hospitals and slums, 80-95; attends places of interest, 85-7; at "Happy Evening", 88; visits to churches and poor people, 91; leaves for Spain, 93; first dinner party at Lough Cutra, 96; stays at Cannes, 96-7; further visit to Italy, 201; her friendship with Wilfrid Blunt, 204-61; views on Home Rule, 207; in India, 213; journeyings in India, 219-23 to Ceylon, 223-5; her work on husband's memoirs, 267-8; growing friendship with W. B. Yeats, 310; reviews of *Cuchulain*, 400-4; playwriting aspirations, 411-12; grief at death of son Robert, 554-9; *Autobiography* of Sir William Gregory (1894), 270, 273, 279, 284, 390; *Book of Saints and Wonders* (1906), 407, 408; *Cuchulain of Muirthemne* (1902), 285, 380, 399, 400, 401, 402, 429, 442, 443,

453; *Gods and Fighting Men* (1904), 380, 393, 405, 406; *Ideals in Ireland* (1901), 394, 395, 475; *Kiltartan History Book* (1909), 56, 455, 469; *Mr. Gregory's Letter Box* (1898), 304, 310, 390, 393; *Poets and Dreamers* (1903), 381, 409, 410, 414, 453; *Visions and Beliefs in the West of Ireland* (1920), 407; *Our Irish Theatre* (1913), 411n; *Hugh Lane's Life and Achievement* (1921), 411n.

Plays, *Dervorgilla*, 411, 444; *Hyacinth Halvey* (1905), 415, 420, 444, 445; *Kincora* (1905), 411, 432; *New Comedies* (1913), 473; *Rising of the Moon* (1907), 415, 411, 420, 445, 454; *The Rogueries of Scapin*, (1908), 420; *Seven Short Plays* (1909), 411; *Spreading the News* (1904), 56, 412, 415, 419; *The Canavans* (1906), 411, 483; *The Dragon* (1919), 475; *The Gaol Gate* (1906), 203, 251, 252, 460; *The Image* (1911), 411, 423, 454, 554; *The Miser* (1909), 418; The White Cockade (1905), 411, 415, 419; *The Workhouse Ward* (1908), 416, 420, 444, 450, 467, 468.

Poems, *Pat and Fritz*, 520-1.

Gregory, Catherine, 3n, 26.

Gregory, Margaret, wife of Robert, 411, 419, 428, 442, 447, 532-4, 538, 540, 542, 550, 551-2.

Gregory, Richard, 106.

Gregory, Richard, son of Robert and Margaret, 3n, 430, 438, 442, 447, 470.

Gregory, Robert, 29, 85-6, 103, 111, 208, 209, 210, 211, 213, 231, 232, 242, 248, 250, 264-9, 271, 274, 278, 281-5, 293, 300, 301, 305, 318, 329, 341, 355, 365, 367, 382, 385, 393, 399, 400, 418, 422, 426-7, 429, 447, 472, 486, 491, 518, 522, 535, 550-2; attends school at Elstree, 264; passes examination for Harrow, 281-2; leaves Harrow, 343; to Oxford University, 343; marriage to Margaret,

411; joins Flying Corps, 550; death, 553 tributes to, 553-9.

Gregory, Vere, 537-41, 543, 546.

Gregory, Rt. Hon. William (Under Secretary for Ireland 1813-30), 300.

Gregory, Rt. Hon. Sir William, 2, 22, 23, 26, 27, 28, 31, 33-4, 35-6, 46, 47, 55, 57, 66, 70, 71, 74, 76, 78, 84, 85, 91, 93, 94, 100, 102, 103, 105, 106, 109, 111, 115, 119, 140, 144-5, 146, 157, 162, 183, 206-8, 211, 213, 216, 222, 232, 239, 242, 248, 258, 262, 284, 300, 301, 329; husband of Lady Gregory, 8, 21; statesmanlike qualities, 21-2; personality, 21-2; intimate friendship with notabilities, 21-2 active connection with the Turf, 22; appointments, 22; his interest in future Lady Gregory, 27; proposes marriage, 28; marriage, 29; requested to stand as M.P., 33-4; meets Arabi Bey, 35; his support of Egyptian Nationalists, 35-6; writes to Mr. Gladstone regarding views on Egyptian Nationalism, 43; ordered to Ems, 45; supports Egyptian Exiles, 54-5; Gladstone's opinion of, 100; support of natives of Ceylon, 208; in India, 213-23; in Ceylon, 223-5; illness, 262; death, 263; *Autobiography*, Lady Gregory works on, 267-8; 270, 273, 279, 284, 390.

Grenfell, Mr., 273, 276.

Greville Memoirs, The, 276, 277.

Grey, Albert, 49, 272, 276.

Gribell, Miss, 88, 90, 94.

Griffin, Sir Lepel, 233.

Griffith, A., 417.

Grimwood, Mrs. 112.

Grossmith, George, 116-17.

Grosvenor, Hugh Lupus, 1st Duke of Westminster, 77, 171.

Groves, Archibald, 342.

Guillamore, Lord, 11.

Guinness, family, of New York, 463, 470.

Gwynn, Stephen, 197, 334, 370-1, 512, 513, 515.

Gyles, Althea, 345n.

H.P.H. see Harvey, Paul.
Haggard, Sir Henry Rider, 342.
Haldane, Richard Burdon, 1st Viscount, 77, 237, 512.
Haliburton, Sir A., Later 1st Baron, 295, 296, 342, 354, 358, 366-7.
Haliburton, Lady, 283, 295, 338, 342, 358, 396.
Halsbury, Hardinge, 1st Earl of, 358.
Halsbury, Lady, 358.
Hamilton, Ian, 388.
Hamley, Sir Edward, 132, 133-4.
Hankey, Thomson, 52-3, 58, 112, 118, 242.
Hankey, Mrs., 53, 58.
Harcourt, Sir William, 61, 116, 270-1, 272, 339.
Hardinge, 2nd Viscount, 151.
Hardy, Thomas, 139.
Harper's Magazine, 139.
Harris, Mr., 111.
Harris, George Robert, 4th Baron, 342.
Harrison, Sir Frederic, 50, 113, 188, 190, 245, 274, 275, 279, 297, 339.
Harrison, Lady Frederic, 355.
Hart, Solomon, 149.
Harte, Bret, 273, 275, 308, 366.
Hartington, see Devonshire, Spencer Compton Cavendish, 8th Duke of.
Harvey, Paul, 61, 68, 71, 73, 74, 77, 78, 93, 110, 112, 114, 120, 174, 175, 212, 216, 269, 274, 276, 281, 294, 383, 395, 399, 426, 471.
Hassan, Mehdi, 214, 219, 235.
Hatzfelt, the German Ambassador, 155.
Haweis, The Rev., 83.
Hayes, Mrs., 86, 87, 88.
Hayter, Lady, 48.
Hayward, Abraham, 45-6, 126-9, 131; character, 127-8; Art of Dining, 129.
Healy, Tim, 233, 245, 335, 357, 394, 455, 495.
Henley, William E., 326, 478; "Invictus", 326.
Hennessy, Pope, 491.
Hennessy, Mrs. Pope, 491.
Henniker, Lady, 93.
Henry, Mitchell, 67-8.

Herbert, Arthur, 443.
Herbert, George, 15.
Herbert, Mervyn, 443.
Herbert, Sidney, 294; Works, Life, 294.
Heron, L. C., 497.
Herschell, Farrer, 1st Baron, 112-13.
Hewlett, Maurice, 450, 485.
Hobhouse, Lord, 114.
Holland, Mr., 82.
Holland, Bernard, 192, 333, 397.
Home Rule Bill, 54, 56, 65, 66-7, 74, 77, 112, 136, 205, 232, 244, 515; opposition to, 56-7.
Homestead, The Irish, 327, 328.
Hope, Anthony, 437.
Hortensa, Queen, 8, "Partant pour la Syrie", 7.
Houghton, see Milnes, Richard Monckton, 1st Baron Houghton.
Houghton, Lady, 38.
Howard, George, 72, 74, 78.
Howth, Lord, 119-20.
Hozier, William, 94.
Hueffer, Ford Madox, 315.
Hull, Miss Eleanor, 391; Cuchullin Saga, 391.
Humphreys, Major, 221.
Hurburt, Mrs., 114.
Huxley, Thomas, 67-8.
Hyde, Dr. Douglas (Ar Craoibhin Aoibkin), 306, 317, 319-20, 321, 343, 358, 359, 362-3, 365, 372n, 377-9, 381, 382, 383, 394, 399, 400, 402, 403, 413, 417, 423-4, 431, 439, 520; proposes Beal Direach (Straight-Mouth) League, 383; Nativity, 317; Love Songs of Connacht, 379, 400; Religious Songs of Connacht, 400; The Lost Saint, 379; Twisting of the Rope, 381, 399.
Hyde, Mrs. Douglas, 382.
Hyderabad, 217.
Hyderabad, Nizam of, 214-15, 217-18, 229.
Hynes, Mary, 363, 398.
Hynes, Tommy, 321, 422.

Iddlesleigh, Stafford Henry, 1st Earl of, 76, 229.

Illerton, 16.
Independent, 345, 484.
Ingelow, Jean, 297.
Irish Church Disestablishment Bill, 107.
Irish Literary Theatre, 343, 352, 368, 386, 399, 413; establishment of, 352.
Irish Homestead, The, 327, 328.
Irish Literary Society, 318, 333-4, 358, 360, 421, 424.
Irish National Theatre, 419, 548.
Irish Theosophist, 311n.
Irish Texts Society, 382.
Irish Times, 360, 399, 523.
Irving, Sir Henry, 104.

Jackson, Mrs. Huth, 491.
James, Henry, 146, 181-5, 188-9, 250, 272, 274, 289, 342, 468, 485; character, 181-2; *Letters,* 181; *Roderick Hudson,* 181; *The Outcry,* 148, 184; *The Portrait of a Lady,* 185; *The Princess Casamassima,* 185.
James, Professor, 524.
Jameson Raid, 353n.
Jarvis, Charles, 24.
Jeune, Sir F., 342.
Jeune, Lady, 342.
Jeune, Mr., 110, 113.
Jeune, Mrs., 229-30.
John, Augustus, 522, 557.
John, Michael, 422, 530-1, 534-6, 539, 542, 544, 552.
Johnson, Sir Alan, 335.
Johnson, Samuel, 14, 25, 249; *Dictionary,* 25.
Johnston, Sir Harry, 274, 279, 293, 299, 336.
Jones, Henry Arthur, 513.
Jonson, Ben, 423, 434; *Silent Woman,* 434.
Joyce, James, 425-6, 507-8.
Jung, Salar, 214-15, 218.
Jusserand, Jean, 190.

Kaye, Mrs., 98, 280, 289, 292, 297.
Kegan Paul, 232-3, 237, 258, 261, 289.
Kelmscott Press, 260, 261.
Kirkoff, Madame, 72.

Keymes, Mr., 556; tribute to Robert Gregory, 556.
Kilchreest, 12, 26-7, 44.
Kildare, Lady, 209.
King-Harman, Sir Cecil, 59-60.
Kinglake, Alexander W., 7, 46, 48, 50, 62, 67, 69, 75, 81, 92, 126-7, 129, 131-8, 206, 226, 228, 229, 233-4, 246, 298; *Eothen,* 126, 131, 132; *History of the War in the Crimea,* 132, 135.
Kingsley, Charles, 199.
Kipling, Rudyard, 361, 366.
Kitchener, Horatio, Earl of Khartoum, 518.
Klein, Dr., 292.
Knowles, Sir James, 115, 117, 245, 278, 367.
Knox, Sir Ralph, 274.
Kruger, Stephanus, 285.
Kugler, Franz, 167.

E.L. *see* Layard, Lady Enid.
H.P.L. *see* Lane, Sir Hugh.
Labouchere, Henry, 68, 71, 74, 75, 78-9, 207, 240, 247, 339.
Ladysmith, Relief of, 362.
Land Bill, 284.
Land League, 45, 203, 208, 212, 225, 233, 246, 385.
Landlord Nationalists, 476.
Landseer, Sir Edwin, 110.
Landseer, Thomas, 148.
Lansdowne, Henry Charles, 5th Marquess of, 298, 353.
Lane, Adelaide (*neé* Persse, Lady Gregory's sister), 15.
Lane, Sir Hugh (Lady Gregory's nephew), 143, 159, 179-80, 183-4, 343, 356, 363, 411, 415, 435, 445, 446, 447, 448, 451, 462, 468, 472, 475, 492, 505-6, 540, 550, 552.
Lanyon, Owen, 358.
Lara, Isadore de, 114.
Lascelles, Sir Frank, 454.
Lawless, Emily, 181, 289, 343, 385; Works, *Grania,* 385; *Hurrish,* 385; *With Essex in Ireland,* 386.
Lawley, Hon. Frank, 21, 70, 75, 262, 270, 271, 275, 276, 277, 298, 304; *Racing Life of Lord George Bentinck,*

Lawson, Sir Wilfrid, 341.

Layard, Sir Henry, 32, 46-7, 57, 59, 62-3, 67, 70, 72, 76, 81, 102, 111, 140, 143-6, 149, 152-80, 200, 212, 254, 268, 277, 288, 289; his courage and plain speaking, 157-8; attacks British management of Army, 157; appointment, 158; unsettled years in Madrid, 159-60; independence of, 161-2; declines offer of Directorship of National Gallery, 165; friendship with Emperor and Empress Frederick, 175; death, 268.

Layard, Lady Enid, 25, 32, 60, 67, 111, 140, 144, 154, 156, 164, 168, 176, 177, 178, 200, 212, 264, 269, 281, 285-8, 289, 292-3, 295, 298, 300, 303, 307, 319, 341, 353, 362, 366, 372, 440, 441, 442, 443, 470.

Leader, The, 394, 485.

Lecky, W. E. H., 77, 114, 122, 271, 275, 277, 278, 279, 293, 294-5, 297, 299, 303, 304, 305, 319, 333, 337, 361, 362, 367, 368, 371, 396; History of European Morals from Augustine to Charlemagne, 299; History of Ireland in the 18th Century, 361, 367; History of Rationalism, 293; Leaders of Public Opinion, 299.

Lecky, Mrs., 77, 122, 275, 278, 293, 294, 296, 297, 299, 303, 319, 362, 371.

Lee, Arthur, 454.

Lee, Mrs., 454.

Lee, Sidney, 455.

Lefevre, George, 236, 241, 245, 279, 280.

Lefevre, Madeline, 296.

Lefevre, Miss Shaw, 65, 85.

Leighton, Sir Frederic, later Lord, 94, 140, 149, 335.

Lever, Charles, 9, 243.

Leveson-Gower, Freddy, 247, 295, 341.

Leveson-Gower, George Granville 3rd Duke of Sutherland, 105.

Leveson-Gower, George Granville, 3rd Earl Granville, 43, 51, 54, 61-2, 161, 164, 229.

Leveson-Gower, George, 73, 75.

Lewes, George, 148, 237.

Lindsey, Lady, 192, 269, 272, 291, 338.

Lingen, Lord, 297.

Little Review, 507.

Lloyd George, David, 1st Earl, 503, 507.

Loch, Henry, 1st Baron, 298, 299.

Loch, Lady, 298.

Londonderry, Lady, 338, 355.

Longden, Sir James, 54.

Loraine, Colonel Robert, 555; tribute to Robert Gregory, 555.

Lough Corrib, 14.

Louis Napoleon, Emperor of France, 2, 8, 13, 93, 135, 303, 331, 354, 455, 511, 525, 528.

Lovelace, 337, 342, 477.

Lowell, James, 70, 108, 109.

Lucy, Mr., 342.

Lyall, Sir Alfred, 59, 146, 186-97, 200, 228, 233, 240, 241, 273, 276, 289-90, 294, 333, 341, 356, 366, 381, 397, 445, 485; his deep interest in religion, 188; Asiatic Studies, 191, 197; Verses written in India, 186, 187.

Lyall, Lady Sophie, 336, 366, 397.

Lynton, Mrs. Lynn, 113, 247, 276.

Lyons, Richard, 1st Earl, 253.

Lyster, T. W., 359.

Lyttleton, Alfred, 331.

Lyttleton, Lady, 337, 471.

Lytton, Edward Robert, 1st Earl of, 114, 248, 250, 251, 259.

Lytton, Lady, 290.

M.E., M.E.G.D., M.G.D., see Duff, Sir Mountstuart Grant.

Macaulay, Thomas, 1st Baron, 98, 101.

Mackenzie, Dr. Morell, 176.

Mackinnon, Sir J., 231.

Macmanus, Miss, 399.

MacNaughton, Miss, 450; Lame Dog's Diary, 450.

MacNeill, Professor Eoin, 402, 404.

Madras, 222, 224.

Magrath, 359-60, 419.

Mahaffy, Dr., J.P., 119-20, 295, 337, 359, 369, 372, 391, 451; Art of Conversation, 119.

Malet, Sir E., 36-8, 43, 54, 101, 167, 241, 254, 260, 286.
Mallet, Sir L., 72.
Mallock, William, 115; *Is Life Worth Living?*, 115.
Malory, Sir Thomas, 16, 391-2; *Morte D'Arthur*, 16.
Manchester, Bishop of, 108.
Mangan, James Clarence, 143, 333-4.
Mangnall, Richmal, 4-5; *Historical and Miscellaneous Questions*, 4-5
Manning, Cardinal, 72, 123-4.
Manning, "Big", 345-6.
Markiewicz, Constance, Countess, 415, 540, 549.
Martin, Sir Theodore, 147.
Martin, Lady (Helen Faucit), 147.
Martin, Mrs. 365, 399.
Martin, Violet (Martin Ross), 388.
Martyn, Edward, 28, 264, 282, 290, 297, 308, 311, 314-15, 336, 353-4, 359, 360-1, 367, 368, 372, 374, 377, 383, 396, 413, 431, 439, 484, 513; Works, *Maeve*, 315q, 356q, 359q.
Martyn, Mrs., 309.
Masefield, John, 386-7, 406, 408-9, 436, 480, 485, 487, 499; *Dampier's Voyages*, 387.
Mason, A.E.W., 450.
Mathers, MacGregor, 345n, 346.
Matthews, Mr., 228.
Maxwell, Sir John, 547.
May, Sir Erskine, 43-4.
Mayo, Richard, 6th Earl of, 253.
McBride, Mr., 290.
McCarthy, Justin, 116.
McClintock, Leopold, 292.
McColl, Mr., 496, 523.
McDermot, 333.
McDonnell, Sir Anthony, 414.
McDonough, 8.
McDonagh, T., 545, 547.
McNeill, Swift, 369.
Meade, Sir R., 293.
Melba, Dame Nellie, 470.
Melbourne, William, 2nd Viscount, 300.
Meredith, George, 50, 442, 545.
Meyer, Kuno, 392-3, 465.
Middleton, Mrs., 289.
Mill, John Stuart, 503.

Millais, Sir John, 102-3, 115, 134, 209.
Millais, Miss, 339.
Milligan, Miss Alice, 353, 359; *The Last Feast of the Fianna*, 353n.
Milnes, Richard Monckton, 1st Baron Houghton, 35-9, 46, 47, 105-7; *Strangers Yet*, 106.
Milton, John, 24; *Prose*, 24.
Mitchel, John, 334.
Moffett, Sir Thomas, 301, 303.
Molesworth, Lady, 106.
Molière, 418, 434.
Monckton, Lady, 116.
"Monday books", 12.
Monkswell, 2nd Baron, 269.
Montague, C. E., 315.
Montalba, Hilda, 173-4.
Moonlighters, 236, 240.
Moore, George, 118, 335-6, 347, 353-4, 356, 358-9, 361-3, 365-6, 368, 370, 372n, 380, 386, 396, 412, 432, 501, 504; *A Drama in Muslin*, 118; *Esther Waters*, 336; *Hial and Farewell*, 386; Plays *The Bending of the Bough*, 352, 354, 358, 359, (with W. B. Yeats), *Diarmuid and Grania*, 386, 399, 412.
Moore, T. Sturge, 480-1, 519, 557.
Moran, D. P., 372n, 394-5, 413.
Morelli, 144.
Moretto, de Brescia, 144.
Morgan, Lady, 106.
Morley, John, 60, 68, 77, 113, 189, 190, 191, 213, 243, 245, 248, 249, 280, 284, 296, 297, 298, 339, 471, 512.
Morning Post, The, 271, 357, 445.
Morosini, Countess, 288.
Morpeth, Lord, 21.
Moroni, Giambattista, 144.
Morris, Edward Patrick, 1st Baron, 69-70, 77, 118-19, 213, 246, 248, 273, 274, 291, 298, 305, 319, 342, 353, 355, 372.
Morris, Lady, 273, 274, 275, 291, 305, 319, 342, 353, 359.
Morris, George, 301, 359.
Morris, Lewis, 297.
Morris, Martin, 297, 359.
Morris, Redmond, 359.
Mould, Henry, 52.

Mulkere, 394, 398.
Muniment, Paul, 185.
Muller, Max, 173, 206; Works, India, 206.
Murray, Hallam, 275, 290, 365.
Murray, John, 109, 167, 268, 271, 277, 278, 301, 338, 339, 401.

Napier, Mr., 49.
Nation, 520.
National Literary Society, 337n, 359.
Nelidorf, Aleksandr, 254.
Nevill, Lady Dorothy, 116, 226-7, 288.
Nevill, Meresia, 445.
New Ireland Review, 363.
Nietjens, Mme., 167.
Nietz_he, Friedrich, 432.
Ninet, 45.
Nineteenth Century, The, 115, 117, 337.
Noailles, Mme. de., 254.
Norbury, Lord, 3.
Normanby, 2nd Marquess, 278.
North, Colonel, 105, 237.
North American Review, 343, 352.
Northbrook, Lord, 44-5, 66, 70, 77, 213, 218, 233, 235, 277.
Northcote, J., 229.
Northumberland, 4th Duke of, 300.
Norton, C. E., 184.
Norton, Mrs., 273, 275, 276.
Nutt, Alfred, 357.

O'Brien, Barry, 63n, 65, 190, 196-7, 297-8, 329-30, 335-6, 339, 341, 353-4, 357; Fifty Years of Concessions to Ireland, 329; History of Ireland, 331; Life of Parnell, 63n, 65, 191, 329, 339, 341.
O'Brien, Edward, 23.
O'Brien, Mrs. Vere, 340.
O'Brien, William, 235, 238, 241, 242, 244, 245, 248, 272, 394, 423, 442, 455.
Observer, The, 50, 472.
O'Connell, Daniel, 21, 56, 62-3, 111, 143, 299, 301, 341, 396, 465.
O'Connor, T. P., 111, 290.
O'Flaherty, Edmund, 274-5, 278.

O'Grady, Archdeacon, 11.
O'Grady, Standish Hayes, 195-6, 314, 318, 332, 372n, 391, 392, 400, 403, 414, 439; History of Ireland, 195; Play, The Coming of Finn, 439.
O'Growney, Eugene, 318.
O'Hagan, Lady, 292.
O'Leary, John, 287, 359, 365.
Oldham, Mr., 359.
Oliphant, Laurence, 67-8, 101, 110, 111, 132, 155, 234, 238-9, 242; Altiora Peto, 111; Piccadilly, 111; Traits and Travesties, 111.
Oliphant, Mrs., 111.
O'Loughlin, Sir C., 64.
Onslow, Lord, 338.
Oodeypore, 216, 220-1, 225.
Orangemen, 69.
Oranmore and Browne, Baron, 10n.
Orchardson, Sir William, 299.
O'Reilly, Miss, 360.
Ormond, Lord, 66.
Ormond, Lady, 209.
Orpen, Sir William, 438.
Osborne, Lady, 71, 92.
Osborne, Walter, 361.
O'Shea v. Parnell, trial, 138, 160n.
Ossianic Society, 404.
Otway, Sir Arthur, 78.
Ouida (Marie Louise de la Ramée), 113, 230.
Outlook, The, 376, 462.
Owl, The, 9.

Paget, Sir Augustus, 31.
Paget, Lady, 31.
Paget, Sir James, 134.
Pall Mall Gazette, The, 117, 238, 244, 297, 472.
Palmer, Lady Sophia, 168, 269, 336.
Palmerston, Henry John Temple, 3rd Viscount, 22, 129, 156, 157.
Parker, Mr., 302.
Parnell, Charles Stewart, 57, 62-4, 67, 71, 75, 77, 118, 128, 138, 205, 229, 233, 239, 244, 245, 248, 257, 306, 308, 329-31, 335, 341, 366, 515; trial of, 232, 234, 236.
Parnellism, 64, 239.
Passini, 286.
Patmore, Coventry, 291.

Paul, Kegan, *see* Kegan Paul.
Pauncefote, Sir Julian, 55.
Pearse, P. H., 538, 540, 542, 545, 548, 549; execution of, 549.
Peel, Julia, 272.
Peel, Lord, 301-2, 305.
Peel, Sir Robert, 21-2, 109, 300, 301, 304, 393.
Peel, William, 315, 335.
Pender, Sir John, 136, 284.
Perpignan, Mlle. de, 175.
Persse, Algernon, 26-8, 44.
Persse, Aubrey, 550.
Persse, Augusta, *later* Lady Gregory, *see* Gregory, Lady Augusta.
Persse, Dudley, 5n, 8, 9, 20, 26, 28, 29, 519, 550.
Persse, Ed. Martin, 11n.
Persse, Frances, (the Mistress), 4-5, 10, 17, 20.
Persse, Gerald, 8.
Persse, Gertrude, 15, 19.
Persse, H., 1n.
Persse, Henry, 550.
Persse, Richard, 19, 23, 29.
Persse, Rudolph, 529, 550.
Persse, William, 13.
Phayre, Sir Robert, 220.
Phillips, Lionel, 445.
Pigott episode, 239-40.
Pim, 322.
Pinnock, William, 4.
Plarr, Victor, 480.
Plowden, Sir William, 88.
Plunket, Lord, 301.
Plunkett, Rt. Hon. Horace, 307, 314, 318, 322-3, 327, 329-32, 336-8, 349, 356, 367, 371, 412, 495, 496.
Plunkett, Joseph, 547.
Plunkett, Lady Victoria, 295.
Plutarch, 195-6, 204.
Pollock, Sir F., 192.
Ponsonby, Edward, 8th Earl of Bessborough, 78-9, 249.
Ponsonby, Lady, 104.
Ponsonby, Spencer, 109.
Pope, Alexander, 24; Work, *The Iliad*, 24.
Potter, Mrs. Brown, 338.
Pottimore, Lord, 342.
Pound, Ezzra, 479, 481, 489, 491.
Powell, Professor York, 401.

Power, O'Connor, 48.
Powerscourt, Lord, 359.
Poynter, Lady, 365.
Praed, Herbert, 90.
Praed, Mrs. Campbell, 88, 90, 113.
Princess Royal, The (Crown Princess of Prussia), 31, 174-7.
Punch, 118, 342.
Purser, Miss, 348, 365.
Pusani, Countess, 286-7.

Quarterly, The, 117, 128, 167, 276.
Quinn, John, 181, 376, 459, 461, 463-5, 468, 470, 498, 499-500.
Quinn, Johnny, 513, 516, 522.

Radowitz, Mme. de, 254.
Raffalovich, A., 111, 114, 116, 245, 274, 336.
Raftery, Anthony, 338, 343, 363, 377-8, 382, 394, 398-9, 409-10, 413, 536.
Rancour, 178.
Rawnsley, W. F., 557.
Reay, 210, 214, 222, 278.
Reay, Lady, 222, 445.
Redmond, John, 330-2, 362, 402, 428, 455, 495, 515, 527, 537.
Reeve, Henry, 114, 276.
Reeve, Mrs. H., 341.
Reform Association, 429.
Reid, Wemyss, 279.
Reinach, Solomon, 121, 369.
Renan, Ernest, 97.
Rendal, Lord, 298.
Rendal, Lady, 298.
Rendall, Bishop, 355.
Rhodes, Cecil, 78, 271, 298, 342, 355.
Rhys, Sir John, 402, 406.
Richardson, A. J., 557.
Ricketts, Charles, 557.
Ridgeway, Sir West, 298.
Ripon, George Frederick, Marquess of, 66, 241, 253.
Ritchie, Thackeray, 291.
Roberts, Frederick, 1st Earl, 366, 372, 528.
Roberts, Canon Page, 339.
Robinson, Mrs. Douglas, 462-3.
Robinson, Sir Hercules, 95, 116, 271, 276, 290, 294, 354.
Robinson, J. C., 93, 149.

Robinson, Lady, 82, 271, 276, 294.
Robsart, Amy, 102.
Rochester, Bishop of, 91-2.
Rolleston, T. W., 333, 358, 421.
Romilly, Colonel, 114.
Roosevelt, President Theodore, 285, 315, 376, 402-3, 442, 453-66, 467, 503; *America and the World War*, 459; *Strenuous Life*, 459.
Roosevelt, Mrs., 453-4, 456, 459, 461-4.
Rosebery, Archibald, 5th Earl of, 67, 100, 103, 115-16, 208, 213, 262, 270, 272, 273, 280, 304, 354; *Pitt* (1891), 262, 280.
Rosebery, Lady, 115.
Ross, Martin, *see* Martin, Violet.
Rossetti, Dante Gabriel, 201, 309, 502.
Rossetti, William, 152-3.
Rothenstein, Sir William, 435-6.
Rourke, John, 320.
Rousseau, Jean Jacques, 403; *Confessions*, 403.
Rowsell, Mr., 42-3.
Rowan, Hamilton, 3.
Roxborough, 1, 5, 7, 17, 20, 23, 25, 26-8, 44, 105, 130, 154, 211, 537-8.
Royle, Mr., 281.
Rumbold, Sir Horace, 23.
Rurke, John, 473.
Ruskin, John, 172, 337.
Russell, Lord Arthur, 72, 120, 165, 196-7, 237.
Russell, Lady Arthur, 87, 120, 237, 278, 293.
Russell of Killowen, Charles, 1st Baron, 334.
Russell, Sir Charles, 77.
Russell, Lady E., 241.
Russell, Sir G., 232, 247, 249.
Russell, George (A.E.), 311-14, 318, 322-4, 328, 337, 340, 343-4, 360, 372n, 374, 380, 383-6, 395, 399, 403, 413, 417, 424, 425; *Homeward Songs by the Way*, 312q.
Russell, G. W. E., 79, 197, 322.
Russell, Sir William ("Billy"), The *Times* correspondent, 104-5, 233, 283-4; character and reputation, 104-5.
Russell, Mrs., 113-14.

Russell, (Tony) Watts, 358, 389, 426.

Sala, George, 104, 291.
Salisbury, Lord, *see* Cecil, Robert Arthur, 3rd Marquess of Salisbury.
Salisbury, Lady, 227, 336.
Sarsfield, Patrick, 460, 473.
Savage Club, 116.
Schliemann, Dr., 32.
Schrieber, Lady Charlotte, 156.
Scott, Captain, 489.
Scott, Sir Walter, 16, 109, 272.
Scott, Mrs. Ware, 105.
Seale, Mr., 457, 459.
Seale, Mrs. 457-8.
Seckendorf, Count, 285-6.
Seddon, Payne, 514.
Selborne, Roundell Palmer, 1st Earl of, 70, 162-3, 269.
Selkirk, Lady, 354.
Seymour, Sir Barrington, 290.
Seymour, Sir Beauchamp, 45, 48.
Shaftesbury, Anthony Ashley Cooper, 7th Earl of, 107.
Shakespeare, William, 7, 15, 18, 52, 131, 248, 423, 476, 481, 503.
Shannon, Charles, 557.
Shaw, George Bernard, 313, 317, 380, 388, 444, 446-7, 449-50, 474-5, 481, 504, 522, 543, 558; *Fanny's First Play*, 449, 521; *The Shewing up of Blanco Posnet*, 420, 437, 447, 448, 449, 450, 485.
Shaw, Mrs. 444, 449, 474-5, 522.
Shawe-Taylor, Amy, 532-3, 535-6.
Shawe-Taylor, F., 535.
Shawe-Taylor, John, 402, 429, 462.
Shawe-Taylor, Vera, 24.
Shawe-Taylor, Walter T. N., 75, 311, 491.
Shelley, Percy Bysshe, 129, 312, 334, 349, 410, 540, 545; *The Water of the Wondrous Isles*, 313.
Sheridan, Mary, 2, 3, 19, 312.
Sherif Pasha, 34, 36, 48.
Sherwood, Mrs., 12.
Shrewsbury, Lady, 338, 355.
Sidhe, The, 8.
Sigerson, Dr., 359.

Sinn Fein, 417, 429, 507; rising by, 532-49.
Slieve Echtge, 1, 7, 8, 16, 121, 510.
Smalley, G. W., 100.
Smith, Arthur, 269-70.
Smith, Cecil, 82, 88, 290, 293.
Smith, Sir C. Euan, 286.
Smith, Lady Euan, 287.
Smith, Sir Montague, 114.
Smith, Parker, 243.
Smith, Reginald, 196, 302-3, 339. 356.
Smith, Sydney, 98.
Smith, Dr. William, 167.
Smyth, Dr. Ethel, 388.
Smythe, George, 107.
Soopyalat, Queen (Mrs. Theebaw), 222.
South Africa Company, 78.
Speaker, The, 365
Spectator, The, 198, 273, 304, 337, 390.
Spencer, Herbert, 297, 339.
Spencer, John, 5th Earl, 66, 72, 73, 77, 116, 190.
St. Albans, Duchess of, 269, 284.
Stanley, Lyulph, 66-7, 72.
Stanley, Lady, 66-7, 77, 172, 233, 236, 276, 290.
Starkie, Dr. Walter, 487.
Stead, W. T., 238.
Stephen, Sir James, 65, 76.
Stephens, Sir Fitzjames, 227.
Stephens, James, 487.
Stillmann, Lisa, 289.
St. John, *later* Lord Bolingbroke, 342.
Stanmore, *see* Gordon, Arthur, 1st Baron Stanmore.
Stokes, Margaret, 147, 337, 359, 372.
Stone, General, 39.
Strachey, John St. Loe, 337, 341.
Sullivan, Sir Arthur, 81, 105.
Sunday Books, 13.
Sutherland, Duke of, *see* Leveson-Gower, George Granville, 1st Duke of Sutherland.
Swift, Jonathan, 334-5.
Swinburne, Algernon, 191, 192-3, 198, 313, 435, 437, 502; *Poems and Ballads* (1878), 193; *Tristam of Lyonesse* (1882), 193.

Symons, Arthur, 139, 308, 344, 357-8, 397.
Synge, John Millington, 138, 316, 317, 321, 370, 379, 380, 388-9, 403, 414-15, 418, 420, 426, 431, 439, 442, 446, 452, 456, 467, 471, 484, 485, 499, 504, 507, 554; *Deirdre of the Sorrows,* 316, 554; *Playboy of the Western World,* 418n, 419, 421, 431, 444, 445, 447, 456, 460, 463, 467, 484, 485, 497, 545, 546; *Well of the Saints,* 415, 451, 471.

Tadema, Sir L. Alma, 369.
Tagore, Rabindranath, 499.
Tain bo Cuailgne, 398, 399.
Talbot, Colonel, 291.
Talbot, Henry John, 3rd Earl, 300, 301, 304, 338, 393.
Talbot, Lady, 338.
Taylor, J. F., 287, 333-4, 336.
Telegraph, The, 236.
Tennant, Sir Charles, 100, 233, 236, 276.
Tennant, Lady, *see* Stanley, Lady.
Tennyson, Alfred, 1st Baron, 16, 106, 110, 117, 137, 148, 188, 193-4, 197, 201, 504; *Maud,* 201.
Tennyson, Lady, 117.
Terry, Dame Ellen, 433, 450, 452.
Thackeray, William Makepeace, 331, 458, 501; *Book of Snobs,* 458.
Theosophist, The, 311.
Thistlewaite, Mrs., 129-30.
Thompson, Sir Edward, 397.
Thompson, Sir Henry, 163, 246, 268, 269.
Thompson, Yates, 238.
Thoreau, Henry, 324.
Tillyra Castle, 360, 381, 390, 395, 396, 492, 543.
Times, The, 6, 33, 35, 44, 45, 46, 47, 49, 50, 51, 59, 72, 104, 112, 127, 130, 131, 132, 133, 149, 157, 200, 207, 227, 230, 233, 239, 240, 271, 273, 278, 303, 338, 366, 368, 399, 433, 521, 542.
Tolstoy, Leo, 325, 327, 354; *What to Do,* 325.

Tonks, Henry, 523, 557-8; tribute to Robert Gregory, 557-8.
Toole, John, 114.
Traill, Henry Duff, 273, 274, 413.
Tree, Sir Herbert, 448, 451.
Trench, Herbert, 397, 444, 451.
Trench, Percy, 550.
Trevelyan, Sir Charles, 101, 229.
Trevelyan, Sir George, 77.
Truth, 238.
Tucker, Marwood, 340.
Turguenieff, Ivan, 316.
Tweeddale, Julia, Marchioness of, 94-5, 450-451.

United Irish League, 398, 423.
United Irishman, The, 370, 374.
United Service Club, 129.

Van der Nest, Mr., 37.
Vandyck, Sir Anthony, 113.
Vasari, Georgio, 195.
Vaughan, Dr., 293.
Victoria, Princess, 441.
Victoria, Queen, 148-51, 163-4, 167, 171, 183, 227, 228, 275, 287-8, 292-3, 302, 310, 311, 335, 347, 352, 365, 374; visit to Ireland, 352, 364, 367-8, 370, 372; death of, 395.
Vigar, 173.
Vincens, Mme. *see* Barine, Mme. A.
Vincent, Lady Helen, 443.

W. W.H.G., *see* Gregory, Sir William.
Wade, Sir Thomas, 272.
Waithman, Mrs. A. (Lady Gregory's sister), 417.
Walden, Roger, 324.
Waldegrave, 6th and 7th Earls of, Waldegrave, Lady, 106, 273, 277.
Wallace, Sir D. Mackenzie, 278.
Walpole, Sir S., 193, 273, 276, 298.
Ward, Humphry, 139, 339.
Ward, Mrs. Humphry, 118, 167, 237, 279, 296, 298.
Ward, Wilfrid, 367.
Wardle, Mr., 290.

Warner, Lee, 217-18.
Washington, George, 109.
Waterford, Lady, 44.
Watts, Theodore, 193.
Watts - Russell, Arthur Egerton (Tony), *see* Russell, Watts (Tony).
Webster, Sir R., 232.
Weekly Sun, 290.
Welby, Sir R. (Later Lord), 146, 337.
Welldon, Dr., 282-3, 291-2, 557.
Wellesley, Richard, Marquess, 300, 304, 393.
Wellington, Arthur Wellesley, 1st Duke of, 134.
Wemyss, Francis, Earl of, 50n, 52, 67, 73, 111, 251, 269, 310n.
Wentworth, Lord, afterwards Lord Lovelace, 61n, 227, 235-6, 246, 249, 337, 342, 477.
Wentworth, Lady Mary, 481.
West, Sir Algernon, 63.
Westminster, Duke of, *see* Grosvenor, Hugh Lupus, 1st Duke of.
Westminster Gazette, 546.
White, Montague, 354.
White Rose League, 229.
Whitman, Walt, 316, 498, 507.
Whitney, Mrs. Payne, 462.
Whitworth, Charles, Earl, 300, 301, 303.
Wilde, Oscar, 350.
Wilde, Sir William, 102.
William II, Kaiser, 457-8, 512, 522, 525, 528, 530.
Williams, Fischer, 275, 281, 289.
Willoughby, General, 113.
Wimborne, Lord, 168, 171.
Witt, 523.
Wolseley, Garnet, 1st Viscount, 47-8, 52-3, 68-9, 105, 353-4, 358.
Wolverton, *see* Glyn, George Grenfell, 2nd Baron.
Wood, Evelyn, 354.
Woodall, Mr., 58.
Woods, Mr., 297.
Wordsworth, William, 7, 272, 297, 313, 491.
World War 1, outbreak of, 509.
Wyndham, Charles, 116.
Wyndham, George, 472, 482.
Wyndham, Hugh, 254.

Wyndham, Mrs. Percy, 205.

Yeats, Jack, 141, 338, 342, 358-9,
363-4, 370, 376-7, 383-5, 388, 496.
Yeats, J. B., the elder, 382, 403,
495, 508.
Yeats, W. B., 97, 125, 128, 129-30,
138, 152, 178, 184, 186, 194, 195,
196, 197, 201-2, 250, 301, 307-19,
322-3, 326-7, 329, 331-7, 340-3,
349-53, 357-60, 362-3, 365-6, 368-
71, 372n, 377-9, 380, 381, 382,
384, 386, 388, 389, 390, 395, 396,
397, 398, 399, 400, 403, 404, 407,
411, 412, 413, 415, 416, 419, 422-
3, 425-6, 427, 431, 440, 441, 444,
446, 447-8, 452, 454-5, 461-2,
465, 467, 468, 471, 472, 476, 479,
480, 482-3, 495, 497, 498-9, 501-2,
512, 515, 518, 519, 525-6, 542,
544, 547, 548, 549, 550, 551, 552,
554, 557-8; forms Literary Society,
307; interest in folk-lore, 308-9,
313;
Works, The Celtic Twilight, 308,
432; Rosa Alchemica, 311; The

Secret Rose, 346.
Plays, Deirdre, 421, 445; Kath-
leen ni Houlihan, 415, 444;
The Land of Heart's Desire,
316; The Countess Cathleen,
315, 346, 347, 352, 468, 482;
The Hawk's Well, 429; The
Hour Glass, 415, 426; The
King's Threshold, 317, 427n,
Mosada, 432; The Shadowy
Waters, 343, 346, 352, 356, 357,
363, 413, 554; (with Lady Gre-
gory) Heads or Harps, 545n;
(with G. Moore) Diarmuid and
Grania, 386, 399, 412.
Poems, "The Withering of the
Boughs", 384; "The Seven
Words", 379; "A Friend's Ill-
ness", 438; "Her Courage",
490; "Her Friends bring Her
a Christmas Tree", 490; "Her
Race", 490-1; "In Memory of
Major Robert Gregory", 558.

Zetland, Lord, 77.